HISTORY OF THE
WAR IN SOUTH AFRICA
1899-1902

HISTORY

OF THE

WAR IN SOUTH AFRICA

1899–1902

COMPILED BY DIRECTION OF
HIS MAJESTY'S GOVERNMENT

BY

MAJOR-GENERAL SIR FREDERICK MAURICE, K.C.B.

WITH A STAFF OF OFFICERS

VOLUME I

The Naval & Military Press Ltd

Published by
The Naval & Military Press Ltd
5 Riverside, Brambleside, Bellbrook
Industrial Estate, Uckfield, East Sussex,
TN22 1QQ England
Tel: +44 (0) 1825 749494
Fax: +44 (0) 1825 765701
www.naval-military-press.com

In reprinting in facsimile from the original, any imperfections are inevitably reproduced and the quality may fall short of modern type and cartographic standards.

PREFACE.

THE decision of His Majesty's late Government, mentioned on the first page of this history, was not finally given till November, 1905. It was, therefore, not till December 12th, 1905, that I was able to obtain approval for the form in which the political facts connected with the war are mentioned in the first chapter. Since then the whole volume has necessarily been recast, and it was not possible to go to page proof till the first chapter had been approved. Hence the delay in the appearance of the volume. I took over the work from Colonel Henderson in July, 1903. He had not then written either narrative of, or comments on, the military operations.

F. MAURICE.

May 22nd, 1906, *London.*

CONTENTS.

VOLUME I.

CHAP.		PAGE
I.—Preparation for War		1
II.—The Outbreak of the War		35
III.—The Theatre of War		54
IV.—The Boer Army		68
V.—The British Army		87
VI.—The Navy in the Boer War		96
VII.—Talana Hill		123
VIII.—The Retreat from Dundee, and the action of Rietfontein		142
IX.—Elandslaagte		157
X.—Lombards Kop		172
XI.—The Arrival of Sir Redvers Buller		196
XII.—Advance from the Orange River		211
XIII.—Belmont		218
XIV.—Graspan		229
XV.—The Battle of the Modder River		243
XVI.—The Raid on Southern Natal		261
XVII.—Operations round Colesberg up to the 16th December		275
XVIII.—Stormberg		285
XIX.—Halt on the Modder River before Magersfontein		304
XX.—The Battle of Magersfontein		316
XXI.—Sir Redvers Buller in Face of Colenso		332
XXII.—Colenso, December 15th, 1899		351
XXIII.—Lord Roberts' Appointment to the Command in South Africa		376
XXIV.—Operations Round Colesberg—December 16th, 1899, to February 6th, 1900		389
XXV.—Lord Roberts at Capetown; reorganises		408
XXVI.—The Army Moves Forward		428

APPENDICES.

NO.		PAGE
1.	REINFORCEMENTS SANCTIONED ON 8TH SEPTEMBER, 1899	453
2.	DISTRIBUTION OF BRITISH FORCES ON 11TH OCTOBER, 1899, IN CAPE COLONY	455
3.	DISTRIBUTION OF BRITISH FORCES ON 11TH OCTOBER, 1899, IN NATAL	456
4.	STRENGTHS OF THE FORCES OF THE TRANSVAAL AND ORANGE FREE STATE	457
5.	LIST OF H.M. SHIPS AND VESSELS SERVING ON THE CAPE STATION, OCTOBER 11TH, 1899, TO JUNE 1ST, 1902	460
6.	APPROXIMATE STRENGTH AND CASUALTIES AT VARIOUS ENGAGEMENTS DESCRIBED IN VOLUME I.	462
7.	THE EXPEDITIONARY FORCE AS ORIGINALLY ORGANISED AND SENT TO SOUTH AFRICA	471
8.	THE COMPOSITION AND DISTRIBUTION OF BRITISH TROOPS IN SOUTHERN NATAL, 23RD NOVEMBER, 1899	477
9.	REINFORCEMENTS LANDED IN SOUTH AFRICA UP TO THE 13TH FEBRUARY, 1900, OTHER THAN THOSE GIVEN IN APPENDICES 1 AND 7	478
10.	DISTRIBUTION OF TROOPS IN SOUTH AFRICA ON 11TH FEBRUARY, 1900, WHEN THE MARCH FROM RAMDAM BEGAN	485
GLOSSARY		492
INDEX		497

LIST OF MAPS AND FREEHAND SKETCHES.
(In separate case.)

MAPS.

GENERAL MAP :—SOUTH AFRICA.
SPECIAL MAPS :—
- No. 1. INDEX MAP.
- No. 2. RELIEF MAP OF SOUTH AFRICA, to show Topographical Features and Theatre of War.
- No. 3. NORTHERN NATAL.
- No. 4. SOUTHERN NATAL.
- No. 5. TALANA. October 20th, 1899.
- No. 6. ELANDSLAAGTE. October 21st, 1899.
- No. 7. RIETFONTEIN. October 24th, 1899.
- No. 8. LOMBARDS KOP. October 30th, 1899. *Situation before 7 a.m.*
- No. 8 (A). LOMBARDS KOP. October 30th, 1899. *Situation from 7 a.m. to Close of Action.*
- No. 9. NORTH CAPE COLONY and PART of the ORANGE FREE STATE.
- No. 10. BELMONT. November 23rd, 1899. *Situation prior to Capture of Gun Hill.*
- No. 10 (A). BELMONT. November 23rd, 1899. *Situation prior to Capture of Mont Blanc.*
- No. 11. GRASPAN. November 25th, 1899. *Situation at 9 a.m.*
- No. 12. MODDER RIVER. November 28th, 1899. *Situation at about 3.30 p.m.*

MAPS—*continued.*

No. 13.   MAGERSFONTEIN. December 11th, 1899. *Situation at 4.30 a.m.*
No. 13 (A). MAGERSFONTEIN. December 11th, 1899. *Situation at 8 a.m.*
No. 13 (B). MAGERSFONTEIN. December 11th, 1899. *Situation at 3.30 p.m.*
No. 14.   STORMBERG. December 10th, 1899.
No. 15.   COLENSO. December 15th, 1899. *Situation at 8 a.m.*
No. 15 (A). COLENSO. December 15th, 1899. *Situation at 11 a.m.*
No. 16.   OPERATIONS AROUND COLESBERG.
No. 17.   SOUTH AFRICA. Map showing the approximate situation on the 31st December, 1899.

FREEHAND SKETCHES.

TALANA.	MAGERSFONTEIN.
RIETFONTEIN.	STORMBERG.
MODDER RIVER.	COLENSO.

LIST OF ABBREVIATIONS USED ON THE MAPS.

A. & S. Highrs.	Argyll and Sutherland Highlanders.
Art.	Artillery.
Art. Pos.	Artillery position.
B. M. I.	Bethune's Mounted Infantry.
Bn.	Battalion.
Border.	Border Regiment.
Br.	Brigade.
Car.	Carabineers.
Cav.	Cavalry.
Cold. Gds.	Coldstream Guards.
Co.	Company.
Devon.	Devonshire Regiment.
D. G.	Dragoon Guards.
Dns.	Dragoons.
Durh. L. I.	Durham Light Infantry.
E. Surr.	East Surrey Regiment.
Fus.	Fusiliers.
Glouc.	Gloucester Regiment.
Gordon., or Gordon Highrs.	Gordon Highlanders.
Gren. Gds.	Grenadier Guards.
Gds.	Guards.
Highrs.	Highlanders.
Hosp.	Hospital.
How.	Howitzers.
Hrs.	Hussars.
I. L. H.	Imperial Light Horse.
King's	King's Liverpool Regiment.
K. O. Y. L. I.	King's Own Yorkshire Light Infantry.

LIST OF ABBREVIATIONS USED ON THE MAPS—*continued*

K. R. Rif.	King's Royal Rifle Corps.
Lrs.	Lancers.
L. I.	Light Infantry.
Liv'rp'ls	King's Liverpool Regiment.
Manch.	Manchester Regiment.
M. B.	Mountain Battery.
M. I.	Mounted Infantry.
N. Car.	Natal Carabineers.
N. F. A.	Natal Field Artillery.
N. M. R.	Natal Mounted Rifles.
North'd Fus.	Northumberland Fusiliers.
North'n.	Northamptonshire Regiment.
N. Lan.	Loyal North Lancashire Regiment.
Prs.	Pounders (*e.g.*, Naval 12-prs.).
Queen's	Queen's Royal West Surrey Regiment.
R. E.	Royal Engineers.
R. F. A.	Royal Field Artillery.
R. H. A.	Royal Horse Artillery.
Rif. Brig.	Rifle Brigade.
R. I. Rif.	Royal Irish Rifles.
R. Irish Fus.	Royal Irish Fusiliers.
R. Innis. Fus.	Royal Inniskilling Fusiliers.
R. Fus.	Royal Fusiliers.
R. Muns. Fus.	Royal Munster Fusiliers.
R. Sc. Fus.	Royal Scots Fusiliers.
R. Welsh Fus.	Royal Welsh Fusiliers.
S. A. L. H.	South African Light Horse.
S. Gds.	Scots Guards.
Sco. Rif.	Scottish Rifles.
T. M. I.	Thorneycroft's Mounted Infantry.
W. Yorks	Prince of Wales's Own West Yorkshire Regiment.

MAPS TO VOLUME I.

PAINS have been taken to embody in the maps all topographical information existing up to date. A very considerable amount of valuable triangulation has been executed over portions of South Africa, but no systematic detailed survey has ever been made by any of the South African colonies or states. Maps have, however, been compiled by both Cape Colony and Natal. The former has prepared and published a map extending north as far as Lat. 26° 30′; this includes the Bechuanaland Protectorate and the Orange River Colony, but the topographical detail shown over these two areas is exceedingly scanty. The scale of the map is one inch to 12·62 miles.

The Natal Government have a map similarly prepared and drawn in the office of the Inspector of Schools, and published on a scale of one inch to five miles. Both these maps are very fair general maps, and show with rough accuracy the railways, main roads and large rivers, but the delineation of hills is little more than suggestive.

Of the Orange Free State and Transvaal the only general maps published are based on the farm surveys. As these surveys show only those topographical features which serve to fix the farm boundary, omitting all other features, the map resulting from their compilation is not of much use, especially for military purposes.

Of the north of Natal there exists a series of one inch reconnaissance surveys of the communications from Ladysmith to the Orange Free State and Transvaal frontiers, with sketches of the whole of the Biggarsberg and Laing's Nek positions, made in 1896 by Major S. C. N. Grant, Royal Engineers, assisted by Captain W. S. Melville, Leicestershire regiment, and Captain H. R. Gale, Royal Engineers.

It is from these sources, as modified here and there by special surveys made during or since the war, that the general maps 1, 3, 4, and 9 have been compiled.

Of the site of the battle of Talana no special survey has been made since the war, and map 5 is a reproduction of a portion of Major Grant's reconnaissance sketch before referred to.

Maps 6, 7, and 8, of the battles of Elandslaagte, Rietfontein and Lombards Kop, are prepared from surveys made since the events occurred, by No. 4 Survey section, Royal Engineers, working under Captain H. W. Gordon, R.E., and maps 14 and 16, of Stormberg and Colesberg, have been prepared also from sketches made by the same section.

Maps 10, 11, 12 and 13, of Belmont, Graspan, Modder River and Magersfontein, are from sketches made by Nos. 2 and 3 Survey sections, under Captain P. H. Casgrain, R.E. The two sections on map 12 are from drawings by Lieut. J. Cuthbert, Scots Guards.

Map No. 15, of Colenso, is from a sketch made immediately after the relief of Ladysmith by Major S. C. N. Grant, R.E., assisted by Captain P. McClear, Royal Dublin Fusiliers, and Lieut. S. A. Wilkinson, The King's (Liverpool) regiment, and the sections from a sketch by Lieut. M. G. Pollock, R.E.

In most instances the special survey of the site of the battle has had to be extended by enlarging portions of the general maps on smaller scales. This sometimes causes a difference in the amount of detail shown in different areas of the same map, but this is unavoidable if the map be made to illustrate, not only the action itself, but also the preceding and subsequent movements.

The six panoramic sketches embodied in this Volume are facsimile reproductions of a selection made from a number executed by the late Captain W. C. C. Erskine, Bethune's Mounted Infantry.

LIST OF ABBREVIATIONS IN THE TEXT

A. A. G.	Assistant Adjutant-General.
A. D. C.	Aide-de-Camp.
A. S. C.	Army Service Corps.
B. L.	Breech-loading.
Battn.	Battalion.
Brig. divn.	Brigade division = 2 batteries of horse, or 3 of field artillery, commanded by a Lieut.-Colonel. (The term has since been changed to "brigade.")
Captn.	Captain.
C. B.	Companion of the Order of the Bath.
C. I. F.	Cost, Insurance, Freight: *i.e.*, under the contract so designated the price paid included the cost of the article, its insurance while on the voyage, and freight.
C. M. G.	Companion of the Order of St. Michael and St. George.
Col.	Colonel.
C. O.	Commanding Officer.
Comder.	Commander.
Cos.	Companies.
Coy.	Company.
C. R. A.	Commanding Royal Artillery.
C. R. E.	Commanding Royal Engineers.
C. S. O.	Chief Staff Officer.
Cwt.	Hundred-weight.
D. A. A. G.	Deputy Assistant Adjutant-General.
D. A. A. G. I.	Deputy Assistant Adjutant-General for Intelligence.
Det.	Detachment.

LIST OF ABBREVIATIONS—*continued*.

D. C. L. I.	Duke of Cornwall's Light Infantry.
D. G. O.	Director General of Ordnance.
G. O. C.	General Officer Commanding.
Govt.	Government.
H. L. I.	Highland Light Infantry.
H. M. S.	His (or Her) Majesty's Ship.
I. L. H.	Imperial Light Horse.
in.	inch.
I. S. C.	Indian Staff Corps.
K. C. B.	Knight Commander of the Order of the Bath.
K. C. M. G.	Knight Commander of the Order of St. Michael and St. George.
K. O. Y. L. I.	King's Own Yorkshire Light Infantry.
K. R. R.	King's Royal Rifle Corps.
Lieut. or Lt.	Lieutenant.
Lt.-Col.	Lieutenant-Colonel.
L. of C.	Lines of communication.
L. I.	Light Infantry.
Maritzburg	Pietermaritzburg.
M. B.	Mountain battery.
m/m	millimetre.
M. I.	Mounted Infantry.
M. L.	Muzzle-loading.
N. N. V.	Natal Naval Volunteers.
N. S. W.	New South Wales.
N. S. W. L.	New South Wales Lancers.
N. Z.	New Zealand.
N. C. O.	Non-commissioned officer.
O. F. S.	Orange Free State.
pr.	pounder.
P. T. O.	Principal Transport Officer.
Q. F.	Quick-firing.
Q. M. G.	Quartermaster-general.
Regt.	Regiment.
R. M. L.	Rifle-muzzle-loading.
R. A. M. C.	Royal Army Medical Corps.
R. A.	,, Artillery.
R. B.	Rifle Brigade.

LIST OF ABBREVIATIONS IN THE TEXT.

Royal Commission.	Royal Commission on the War in South Africa (1903).
R. E.	Royal Engineers.
R. F. A.	,, Field Artillery.
R. G. A.	,, Garrison ,,
R. H. A.	,, Horse ,,
R. M. A.	,, Marine ,,
R. M. L. I.	,, ,, Light Infantry.
R. N.	,, Navy.
R. S. Fusiliers	Royal Scots Fusiliers.
Sec.	Section.
S. A.	South Africa.
S. A. R.	South African Republic.
Scots Greys	2nd Dragoons.
Sqdn. or Squadn.	Squadron.
Tel.	Telegram.
T. B.	Telegraph battalion.
V. C.	Victoria Cross.
W. O.	War Office.

LIST OF ERRATA.

Page 2, line 13 from top, omit "(Arabic)".

,, 14, ,, 2 ,, bottom, for "Sir H. Escombe" read "the Right Hon. H. Escombe."

,, 78, first marginal note, for "of" read "in."

,, 128, second marginal note, for "comma" read "full stop."

,, 144, line 3 from top, for "The troops a Ladysmith" read "The troops at Ladysmith."

,, 144, last marginal note, omit "full stop" and read on.

,, 160, bottom marginal note, for "full stop" read "comma."

,, 256, line 6 from bottom, for "Major T. Irvine" read "Captain T. Irvine."

,, 337, line 12 from bottom, for "semi-colon" read "comma."

THE WAR IN SOUTH AFRICA.

CHAPTER I.

PREPARATION FOR WAR.

THE war in South Africa which began on October 9th, 1899, ended so far happily on the 31st May, 1902, that, chiefly in consequence of the tactful management of the negotiations with the leaders who then guided them, those who had till then fought gallantly against the British Empire agreed to enter it as subjects of King Edward. Under the circumstances, His Majesty's late Government considered it undesirable to discuss here any questions that had been at issue between them and the rulers of the two republics, or any points that had been in dispute at home, and to confine this history to the military contest. The earlier period is mentioned only so far as it concerns those incidents which affected the preparation for war on the part of Great Britain, and the necessary modifications in the plan of campaign which were influenced by the unwillingness of Her Majesty's Government to believe in the necessity for war. *Scope of history.*

When, on October 9th, 1899, Mr. Kruger's ultimatum was placed in the hands of the British Agent at Pretoria the military situation was as follows. It was known that the Boer Governments could summon to arms over 50,000 burghers. British reinforcements of 2,000 men had been sanctioned on the 2nd of August for a garrison, at that date not exceeding 9,940 men; and on the 8th September the Viceroy of India had been *Situation Oct. 9th /99.*

THE WAR IN SOUTH AFRICA.

instructed by telegram to embark with the least possible delay for Durban a cavalry brigade, an infantry brigade, and a brigade division of field artillery. Another brigade division and the 1st Northumberland Fusiliers were also ordered out from home. The 1st battn. Border regiment was despatched from Malta, the 1st battn. Royal Irish Fusiliers from Egypt, the 2nd battn. Rifle Brigade from Crete, and a half-battn. 2nd King's Own Yorkshire Light Infantry from Mauritius. The total strength of these reinforcements, ordered on September 8th, amounted to 10,662 men of all ranks. On the same day, the 8th September, the General Officer Commanding in South Africa, Sir F. Forestier-Walker, was directed by telegram to provide land transport for these troops. For details see Appendix (Arabic) I.

Total forces.
The whole of these reinforcements, with the exceptions of the 9th Lancers and two squadrons of the 5th Dragoon Guards, whose departure from India was somewhat delayed by an attack of anthrax, a brigade division of artillery, the 1st Border regiment and the 2nd battalion Rifle Brigade, were landed in South Africa before the actual outbreak of war. Including 2,781 local troops, the British force in Natal was thus raised to 15,811 men of all ranks. In Cape Colony there were, either under arms or immediately available at the outbreak of war, 5,221 regular and 4,574 colonial troops. In southern Rhodesia 1,448 men, raised locally, had been organised under Colonel Baden-Powell, who had been sent out on the 3rd July to provide for the defence of that region. Thus the British total in South Africa, 27,054, was at least 20,000 smaller than the number of the burghers whom the two republics could place in the field, irrespective of any contingent that they might obtain from the disaffected in the two colonies. Early in June Sir Redvers Buller had been privately informed that, in the event of its becoming necessary to despatch an army corps to South Africa, he would be the officer to command it. On June 8th, the Commander-in-Chief had recommended that as a precautionary measure an army corps and cavalry division should be organised and concentrated on Salisbury Plain. He had proposed that one complete army corps, one cavalry division, one battalion of mounted

PREPARATION FOR WAR.

infantry, and four infantry battalions to guard the lines of communication, should be sent out to South Africa, and he was most anxious that the expeditionary force should be assembled beforehand, so as to render it more effective for war purposes. The course of the negotiations which were then being carried on convinced Her Majesty's Government that any such step would tend to precipitate war, and, the weakness of our troops at the time in South Africa being such as it was, that it would be impossible to reinforce them before serious attack might be made upon them. Moreover, there was this further difficulty, that adequate attention had not been directed publicly to the circumstances in South Africa which caused anxiety to the Government.

It was always possible to think that the preparations for war on a large scale, which were undoubtedly being made both by the Transvaal and by the Orange Free State, were the result of the anxiety which had been caused to the rulers of those republics by the circumstances of the Jameson raid. Every attempt by any statesman at home to bring the facts, as they presented themselves to those behind the scenes, before the world, was open to the imputation of being deliberately designed to lead up to a war which it was intended to bring about. Thus it was the very weakness of our position at that time in South Africa which made it difficult to relieve the military danger. Any premature effort to place our power there in a condition of adequate security tended to suggest to foreign states that the movements made were directed against the independence of the two republics; tended to shake public confidence at home, and even to excite jealousy in our own colonies. All through the long negotiations which were carried on during the summer and autumn months of 1899 it seemed better, therefore, to incur even some serious risk of military disadvantage rather than to lose that general support of the nation, whether at home or in the colonies, which would be secured by a more cautious policy, and to hope against hope that a peaceful solution might be reached.

Causes of delay.

In one respect there would appear to have been a misunder-

"Adequate strength."

standing between the Government and their military advisers as to the sense in which the reinforcements sent to South Africa were sufficient for the temporary protection of our interests on the sub-continent. It is remarkable that in the evidence subsequently given by the soldiers, not only do they admit that they anticipated beforehand that for this purpose the strength would be adequate, but that they assume, at the end of the war, that it had as a matter of fact proved so. This can obviously only be understood in the sense that the numbers then in South Africa were able to retard the Boer operations until a large army was thrown into the country. On the other hand, Lord Lansdowne, describing what was evidently the meaning in which this language was understood by himself and his colleagues, says : "I am not a soldier, but I never heard of sending out reinforcements to a country which might become the theatre of war merely in order that the reinforcements might successfully defend themselves against attack ; they are sent there, I imagine, for the purpose of securing something or somebody." And again : "I should say not sufficient to prevent raids and incursions, but sufficient to prevent the colonies from being overrun." It appears necessary, under its historical aspect, to draw attention to this discrepancy of view, because it is one that may be liable to repeat itself.

Plans delayed.

Another point influenced by the unwillingness of Her Majesty's Government to believe in the possibility of the Orange Free State, with which we had had for many years relations of the greatest friendliness, appearing in arms against us, was this : that it delayed for a very considerable time the determination of the general plan of campaign on which the war was to be carried on. Practically, supposing it became necessary to conduct an offensive war against the Transvaal, the choice of operations lay between a movement by way of Natal and one by way of the Orange Free State. Any advance by Natal had these serious disadvantages. In the first place, the mountain region through which it would be necessary to penetrate was one that gave very great advantages to the Boer riflemen. In the second place, it lay exposed, as soon as Northern Natal was entered, to attack throughout its entire length from the Orange Free State. On the other hand, the march by Bloemfontein opened up a country much more favourable for the operations of a regular army, whether that march, as was originally proposed, followed the direct line of railway through Bloemfontein, or, as it did ultimately, the railway to Kimberley and thence struck for Bloemfontein.* There remained, indeed, a third alternative, which had at one time been proposed by Lord Roberts, of a movement outside the Orange Free State through the north-western portion of Cape Colony, but this had ceased to be applicable at the time when war was declared. As a consequence of the uncertainties as to the ultimate attitude of the Orange Free State, and the extreme hope that that State would not prove hostile, it was not till the 3rd October that Lord Lansdowne was in a position to say: "We have now definitely decided to adopt the Cape Colony—Orange Free State route. It is intended that a force of 10,000 men should remain in Natal, on which side it will make a valuable diversion; that about 3,000 should be detailed for service on the west side (Kimberley, etc.), and that the main force should enter the Orange Free State from the south."

In all schemes for possible offensive war by Great Britain, subsequent to a memorandum by Mr. Stanhope, of 1st June, 1888,† it had been contemplated that the utmost strength

Limit of force.

---

* See Chapters II. and III. for full discussion on the Theatre of War.

† "Her Majesty's Government have carefully considered the question of the general objects for which our army is maintained. It has been considered in connection with the programme of the Admiralty, and with knowledge of the assistance which the navy is capable of rendering in the various contingencies which appear to be reasonably probable; and they decide that the general basis of the requirements from our army may be correctly laid down by stating that the objects of our military organisation are:—

(a) The effective support of the civil power in all parts of the United Kingdom.

(b) To find the number of men for India, which has been fixed by arrangement with the Government of India.

(c) To find the garrisons for all our fortresses and coaling stations, at home and abroad, according to a scale now laid down, and to maintain these garrisons at all times at the strength fixed for a peace or war footing.

(d) After providing for these requirements, to be able to mobilise rapidly for

which it would be necessary for us to embark from our shores would be that of two army corps with a cavalry division. Those army corps and the cavalry division were, however, neither actually, nor were they supposed to be, immediately ready to be sent out. To begin with, for their despatch shipping must be available, and this, as will be shown more in detail in a subsequent chapter, was a matter which would involve considerable delay and much preparation. During the time that the ships were being provided it would be essential that the successive portions of the army for which shipping could be obtained should be prepared for war by the return to the depôts of those soldiers who were not immediately fit for service, and by their replacement by men called in from the reserve to complete the ranks. None of these preparations could be made without attracting public attention to what was done. The reserves could not be summoned to the colours without an announcement in Parliament, nor, therefore, without debates, which must necessarily involve discussions which might be irritating to Boer susceptibilities at the very time when it was most hoped that a peaceful solution would be reached. It was not, therefore, till the 20th September that the details of the expeditionary force were communicated to the Admiralty by the War Office, nor till the 30th that the Admiralty was authorised to take up shipping. Meantime on September 22nd, a grant of £645,000 was made for immediate emergencies. On the 7th October the order for the mobilisation of the cavalry division, one army corps, and eight battalions of lines of communication troops was issued, and a Royal proclamation calling out the army reserve was

home defence two army corps of regular troops, and one partly composed of regulars and partly of militia; and to organise the auxiliary forces, not allotted to army corps or garrisons, for the defence of London and for the defensible positions in advance, and for the defence of mercantile ports.

(e) Subject to the foregoing considerations, and to their financial obligations, to aim at being able, in case of necessity, to send abroad two complete army corps, with cavalry division and line of communication. But it will be distinctly understood that the probability of the employment of an army corps in the field in any European war is sufficiently improbable to make it the primary duty of the military authorities to organise our forces efficiently for the defence of this country."—(*Report of Royal Commission on the War in South Africa*, p. 225.)

PREPARATION FOR WAR.

published. Of the excellent arrangements made by the Admiralty a full account will be found hereafter.

The scheme for mobilisation had been gradually developed during many years. The earliest stage was the appearance in the Army List of an organisation of the army in various army corps. This was chiefly useful in showing the deficiencies which existed. It had been drawn up by the late Colonel Home, R.E. In August, 1881, it was removed from the Army List.

The scheme of mobilisation.

Practically no mobilisation scheme really took shape until 1886, when Major-General H. Brackenbury,* on assuming office as head of the Intelligence branch, turned his attention to the question. The unorganised condition of our army and the deficiency of any system for either home defence or action abroad formed the subjects of three papers,† in which he showed that, at the time they were written, not even one army corps with its proper proportion of the different departmental branches, could have been placed in the field, either at home or abroad, while for a second army corps there would have been large deficiencies of artillery and engineers, and no departments. For horses there was no approach to an adequate provision. The urgent representations contained in these papers were strongly taken up by Lord Wolseley, then Adjutant-General, and pressed by him on the Secretary of State for War,‡ with the result that a committee of two, Sir Ralph Thompson§ and Major-General H. Brackenbury, was appointed to investigate the matter.

Various stages of scheme.

Their enquiry was entirely confined to the question of obtaining the maximum development from the existing cadres. Their report was divided under three headings, the first of which dealt with the "Field Army," and laid down that two army corps and lines of communication troops was the field army which the regular troops, as they then stood, were capable of producing. The subjects of "Garrisons" and "Mobilisation for Foreign

Sub-division to carry out.

---

* Now General the Right Honourable Sir Henry Brackenbury, G.C.B.
† Mobilisation reports, Numbers I., II. and III.
‡ The Right Honourable W. H. Smith.
§ Then Permanent Under-Secretary of State.

Service" were dealt with under the other two headings. Ultimately a Mobilisation sub-division, which was transferred from the Intelligence department to the Adjutant-General's department in 1889 and to the Commander-in-Chief's office, in 1897, was created.

<small>1890 to 1898.</small>

Working on the lines laid down, the mobilisation section first produced a complete scheme in 1890. Mobilisation regulations were issued in 1892. Further revised editions followed in 1894, and again in 1898. All were worked out on the basis of using what was available, and not what was needed.

<small>Scheme in 1899.</small>

In the spring of 1899, in anticipation of possible events, the mobilisation section turned their attention to the requirements of a force for South Africa. Seeing that the regulations of 1898 dealt principally with the mobilisation of the field army for service at home or in a temperate climate, considerable modifications, relating to such points as regimental transport, clothing, equipment, and regimental supplies, were necessary to meet the case of operations carried on in South Africa. Special "Regulations for the Mobilisation of a Field Force for Service in South Africa" were accordingly drawn up, with the object, not of superseding the Mobilisation regulations of 1898, but "in order to bring together, in a convenient form, the modifications necessary in those regulations." These regulations were completed, printed, and ready for issue in June, 1899. In their general application they provided for the preparation in time of peace of all that machinery which, on the advent of war, would be set in motion by the issue of the one word—"Mobilise."

<small>Success in practice.</small>

The mobilisation, thus carefully prepared in all its details beforehand, proved a complete success. Ninety-nine per cent. of the reservists when called out presented themselves for service, and 91 per cent. were found physically fit. The first units, twenty companies of the Army Service Corps, were embarked on the 6th of October. The embarkation of the remainder of the expeditionary force was begun on the 20th of October, and, with the exception of one cavalry regiment, delayed by horse-sickness, completed on the 17th November.

At an early stage in the war it became very plain that mere

PREPARATION FOR WAR.

drafts of details to replenish units would not suffice, but that organised reinforcements would have to be sent. Even before the embarkation of the field force was completed, orders were given for reinforcements to be despatched; and within three months from that time the mobilisation of four more divisions, fifteen extra batteries of artillery and a fourth cavalry brigade, was ordered.* {Fresh units needed.}

---

* The following extract from the Statement of the Mobilisation division gives the details and dates :—

"21. While the embarkation of the field force was proceeding, news of the loss of the greater part of two battalions of infantry and a mountain battery at Nicholson's Nek reached England. Orders were accordingly given on 31st October for the despatch of one mountain battery and three battalions of infantry, to make good this loss. All this reinforcement went from England, except one battalion. The embarkation from England was finished on 16th November.

22. On 3rd November it was decided to organise and send out a siege train. It embarked on 9th December.

23. Orders for the mobilisation of a 5th infantry division (the troops under Sir G. White, in Ladysmith, being counted as the 4th division) were issued on 11th November. An extra brigade division of artillery (three batteries horse artillery) was added on 20th November.

The embarkation of this 5th division began on 24th November, and was completed on 13th December. That of the three batteries horse artillery took place between 19th and 21st December.

24. Orders were given for the mobilisation of a 6th infantry division on 2nd December, *i.e.*, as soon as the embarkation of the 5th division was well under way. Mobilisation began on 4th December, and was completed by 11th December. All combatant units were embarked between 16th December and 1st January, 1900.

25. The order to mobilise the 7th infantry division was issued on 16th December. Mobilisation began on the 18th, and was completed on 27th December.

Embarkation began on 3rd January, and was completed on 18th January.

26. Meanwhile, on 16th and 22nd December, it had been decided to mobilise and prepare for embarkation four additional brigade divisions (twelve batteries) of field artillery, one brigade division being armed with howitzers. These were all embarked between 21st January and 27th January, 1900.

28. The order to mobilise an additional brigade of cavalry (the 4th cavalry brigade) was issued on 26th December. Mobilisation began on 28th December, and was completed on 2nd January, 1900.

The embarkation of this brigade was held back pending the arrival of Lord Roberts in South Africa, and the receipt of a communication from him.

Embarkation began on 8th February, and was completed on 17th February.

29. Orders were issued for the mobilisation of the 8th infantry division

Smooth working.

The machinery of the Mobilisation sub-division was equal to the task and continued to work smoothly, while the Adjutant-General's department was enabled, with little difficulty, to find men to complete units on mobilisation.† All these units were brought up to their establishment from their own regimental reserves. In order to keep them up to their strength it was estimated that it would be necessary to send out a series of drafts, calculated on a basis of 10 per cent. for every three months.‡ This was the system which was put into operation from the first, and subsequently adhered to as far as possible, drafts being detailed from regimental reserves. It was, however, soon found necessary to introduce modifications in accordance with the wastage which varied in the different arms, as well as in the different units.§ In addition to the regular stream of drafts, special drafts had occasionally to be sent out to make good instances of abnormal loss. Especially was this the case with infantry battalions.‖ Consequently, the regimental reserves of some units were exhausted before those of others, and it became necessary to draw on the reserves of other corps which had more than they required, their militia reserves being selected

on 19th January, 1900. Mobilisation began on 20th January. Embarkation began on 12th March, and the last unit embarked on 18th April, 1900.

30. With the despatch of the 8th division, the last organised and mobilised regular formation left this country, and the work of the Mobilisation sub-division, in connection with the despatch of reinforcements to South Africa, came to an end."

The executive work of organising, equipping, and despatching drafts of Militia, Volunteers, and Imperial Yeomanry was carried out entirely by the Adjutant-General, Quartermaster-General, and Director-General of Ordnance.

† Some difficulty was experienced in finding certain specialists, such as farriers, &c.

‡ Of this original force from England, all cavalry and artillery units and eleven infantry battalions went out with a "war establishment, plus excess numbers," which were calculated at 10 per cent. to make good casualties for the first three months. It was decided to adopt this standard in all cases.

§ The reserve of the artillery fell short almost at once, whereas the entire reserves of the cavalry were not called out until the end of February, 1901.

‖ For one battalion alone, the 2nd battalion Royal Irish Rifles, 1,831 duly qualified soldiers left England in six months, without having to draw on any reserves outside its own corps.

PREPARATION FOR WAR.

for the purpose. By the time the war had lasted a year the equivalents of five drafts on the 10 per cent. basis had left England. But a limit had been reached. "By the end of a year's campaigning our infantry reserves proper, including the now non-existent militia reserve, were exhausted, a point which was emphasised by Lord Lansdowne in the following words in his minute of 2nd June, 1900. . . . . :

<small>Inadequate reserve.</small>

" 'Two points stand out clearly : (1) That in future campaigns we must expect demands on a vast scale for infantry drafts ; (2) that our reserve is not large enough and must be increased.' "*

Short service had made it possible to build up a reserve substantial enough to minister to the unprecedented requirements of the regular army for a year. Without it, the end of our resources in trained men would have been reached at a very early stage.

One difficulty arose. Staffs of many formations, such as those of mounted infantry, ammunition columns and medical field units, did not exist. The completion of these new creations for the original field force necessitated the borrowing of officers and men from other bodies, which, as was supposed at that time, would not be mobilised. As the strain continually grew more severe it was found necessary to mobilise successive divisions and additional batteries. Then, not only had the loans to be made good to those depleted, but nearly the whole of the personnel had to be found for the further number of fresh organisms which were called into existence. This could only be done by yet more borrowing. The difficulty, therefore, progressively increased. More particularly was this the case with the ammunition columns, the creation of which, together with the additional batteries of artillery, caused a drain on artillery reservists, which resulted in their being absorbed more quickly than those of the other branches of the service.† All these

<small>Borrowing, with results.</small>

---

* Memorandum on Drafts prepared in the Adjutant-General's department, 30th September, 1902. See Appendix volume, Royal Commission, p. 86.

† The experiences of a particular battery, Royal Field artillery, afford an illustration of the consequences detailed above. From this battery, by the end of November, 1899, there had been drafted off to staff, service batteries,

special bodies, though essential for war, were outside the peace establishment of the army. It became, therefore, necessary to call out " the whole of the remainder of the Army Reserve, in order to be able to utilise the services of reservists belonging to Section D., none of whom could, by law, be called out until all the reservists of all arms, in Sections A. B. and C. had been called up."† This was done by special Army Order on December 20th, 1899.‡

<small>Mr. Stanhope's two corps exceeded.</small>

There was little breathing time between the successive embarkations of the mobilised divisions from the commencement on 20th October, 1899, to the completion on 18th April, 1900, with the result that in the space of six months more than the equivalent of the two army corps and the cavalry division, laid down in Mr. Stanhope's memorandum as that which we should be prepared to send abroad in case of necessity, had left our shores. By the despatch of these troops, followed by later demands for reinforcements, our organised field army was practically exhausted, and home defence, " the primary duty " of the whole army, was enfeebled to a dangerous degree. In place of the army corps, " partly composed of regulars and partly of Militia," required by the memorandum, there remained for home service a few regular troops, some hastily formed " Reserve Battalions," and such of the embodied Militia, the Yeomanry, and the Volunteers, as had not already gone abroad —all being for the most part unorganised, partially trained, and not fully equipped.

<small>ammunition columns, or excess numbers, the captain, the senior subaltern (the only one who had had four months' service in field artillery), five sergeants, one corporal, one bombardier, four shoeing smiths, two trumpeters, the wheeler, six gunners and five drivers. In December, 1899, the battery commander, with the whole of one sub-division, was taken away as the nucleus of a new battery to be formed. Ten days after this the mobilisation of the battery was ordered. Rather more than 50 per cent. of the battery when mobilised were men of Section D. of the Reserve, of whom about half had seen the gun which they were to work, while none had seen it fired.</small>

<small>† Statement of the Mobilisation sub-division.</small>

<small>‡ The effect of this, as regards the cavalry, was that some 2,000 reservists, over and above immediate requirements, were prematurely placed at the disposal of the department.</small>

PREPARATION FOR WAR. 13

Mr. Stanhope's view of the "improbable probability" * of the employment of "an army corps in the field in any European war"—and if not in Europe, then where else?—certainly not in South Africa—had had its effect. In respect of numbers, it imposed a limit on the powers of preparation; and the condition of affairs was precisely expressed by the following sentence: "The war conclusively proved, therefore, that Mr. Stanhope's memorandum did not make sufficient allowance for the general needs of the Empire." †

<small>Demand exceeds supply of units.</small>

Intelligence and Maps.

Whatever interpretation might be placed as between the Governments on the accumulation of warlike stores in the Transvaal and Free State, it had been obviously the duty of the Intelligence department of the War Office to watch these as closely as the prevailing conditions permitted. This had been done ever since 1896, when the Commander-in-Chief had directed the department to undertake the investigation. The material thus obtained was collated in June, 1898, in the form of a handbook, entitled, " Military Notes on the Dutch Republics of South Africa," which set forth in a concise form the military strength, armament, organisation and tactics of the Boer army. A revised edition of this book was issued in June, 1899. Other handbooks, containing special reconnaissances executed in the more important strategical localities of South Africa, and summaries of information as to the various states and colonies, were also prepared with a view to the possibility of active operations. The Royal Commission on the South African War was able to pronounce in its Report (paragraph 257) that the information contained in these handbooks, as well as in a "valuable" series

---

* " . . . But it will be distinctly understood that the probability of employment of an army corps in the field in any European war is sufficiently improbable to make it the primary duty of the military authorities to organise our forces efficiently for the defence of their country."—Mr. Stanhope's memorandum. See pp. 5, 6.

† Extract from note placed before the Royal Commission by Lieutenant-General Sir William Nicholson. A. 18,245.

of memoranda extending over several years, was in many respects remarkably accurate.

Maps—Transvaal and Free State. Adequate military maps of the vast theatre over which the operations of the 1899–1902 war subsequently spread could only have been produced by the employment for many years of a large survey staff. The production of correct maps of the Transvaal and Free State on a scale of four miles to the inch would alone have taken five years to complete, and would have cost £100,000. The state of tension existing between Great Britain and the two republics in the years immediately preceding the war rendered it impossible to undertake any serious work of this description within those States.

Maps—Cape and Natal. As regards the Cape Colony and Natal, the survey of all self-governing colonies has been, and still is, regarded by the Imperial Government as a matter for the Colonial Governments. The survey of Cape Colony alone on a scale large enough for tactical purposes would have cost £150,000, and it would have been perfectly useless to ask the Treasury to sanction the provision of any such sum. A map, on a scale of twelve and a half miles to an inch, had been produced by the Survey department of the Cape Government, covering Cape Colony, Natal, Orange Free State, and part of the Transvaal, and arrangements were made with the Colonial Government for supplies of this for issue to the troops on the outbreak of war. Of the northern parts of Natal two military maps, produced during the previous wars on a scale of four miles and one mile to an inch were available. But, though copies of one of these maps were subsequently reproduced by the Boers and used by them in their operations on the Tugela, it was well known that they were not accurate and had not been corrected up to date. By arrangement, therefore, with the Natal Government and at their expense, the Director of Military Intelligence sent Major S. C. N. Grant, R.E., from England, in 1896, to execute a more careful reconnaissance of the portion of Natal north of Ladysmith. Recognising that the map thus produced might prove insufficient, Sir J. Ardagh, in 1897, urged personally on Sir H. Escombe, the Prime Minister of Natal, the importance of continuing this survey, and the latter promised to endeavour to make such arrangements as he could, although he stated that political considerations rendered it difficult for him to ask the Natal Parliament to provide funds for a survey of the colony avowedly for military purposes. Sir H. Escombe's Ministry subsequently went out of office, and the only map of Natal existing at the outbreak of war, besides those above referred to, was one on a scale of five miles to an inch prepared locally for educational purposes.

For the Transvaal and Orange Free State the compilation, from all the material available, of a map on a scale 1–250,000 was commenced in January, 1899, by the Intelligence division; twelve sheets were completed and issued before October, 1899, and the remainder shortly afterwards. In the same year a map of the Transvaal, compiled by C. Jeppe from farm surveys, was produced under the auspices of the Government of that State. A limited number of copies of this map were obtained by the Intelligence division and issued on the outbreak of war to the higher staffs. Subsequently in January, 1900, Colonel G. F. R. Henderson, Lord Roberts' Director of Military Intelligence, was fortunate enough to seize at Capetown a thousand copies of this survey, and maps were compiled from them by the Field Intelligence department. These proved of great service in the advance northward. {Intelligence map and Jeppe's.}

The provision of maps for the many possible theatres of war in which British troops may be employed is a difficult question. In the present case the above statement will account for the fact that the maps provided by the War Office at the outbreak of the South African war were pronounced by the Royal Commission on that war to have been, "with perhaps one exception, very incomplete und unreliable" (paragraph 261). {A large question.}

These matters preparatory to the war were not, in the ordinary work of the departments, separated by any distinct break from the routine necessary after hostilities had begun.

The Distribution of responsibility between the several offices in regard to the despatch of an army to the field was as follows.

16   THE WAR IN SOUTH AFRICA.

The Adjutant-General's department was charged with all that affected the actual personnel—the flesh and blood—in such matters as the necessary qualifications of age or service, the completion of cadres with specialists, and the maintenance of recruiting. It was the province of the Military Secretary's department of the Commander-in-Chief's office to select the staffs and allot the commands. The provision of equipment, clothing, and ordnance supplies was the duty of the Director-General of Ordnance; with the Quartermaster-General rested the provision of animals to complete the war establishment, supplies of food, and, in conjunction with the Admiralty, arrangements for sea transport. The two departments of the Director-General and Quartermaster-General, long before the final sanction was given, had worked out on paper the details of future requirements.

<small>Personal action at War Office.</small> Apart from those proposals of the Commander-in-Chief to which it had not been possible for Her Majesty's Government to accede, for the reason already given, the several officers at Headquarters had done what they could to make for possible future events such preparation as did not involve expenditure. Sir Evelyn Wood, both as Quartermaster-General and as Adjutant-General, carried on a vigorous private correspondence with the several General Officers Commanding at the Cape, and it was at his instance that as early as the autumn of 1896 contracts were made with Messrs. Weil, who had complete command of the Cape market, for the supply of horses, mules, and wagons at short notice when called for. He sent for one of the firm to come to England, but a decision was given in the spring of 1897 against immediate action. In April, 1898, he again asked that the whole subject, both of transport and of the despatch of cavalry and artillery to South Africa, should be taken up. Moreover, in 1897, he had pressed for horse-fittings for shipping, fearing the trouble in this matter, which subsequently actually occurred. On taking over the duties of Adjutant-General on October 1st, 1897, he, in view of the extensive territory lately acquired in Rhodesia, proposed the addition of 9,000 infantry to the army. The Commander-in-Chief, in forwarding this

PREPARATION FOR WAR.

memorandum, added to his request an additional 4,000 men beyond what Sir E. Wood had recommended. As late as February, 1898, the transport, necessary to make the troops in South Africa fit to take the field, was refused, though pressed for by the Commander-in-Chief, in consequence of a private letter to Sir E. Wood, which showed Sir A. Milner's anxiety on the subject. To suppress a small rebel Basuto chief it would have required a month to get transport ready. At a time when a man so intimate with South African affairs as Mr. Rhodes was deriding all fears of Boer power, war was not believed to be imminent, and the long habit of saving the public purse during peace time was operative against expenditure, which would not be needed if there were no war and no need for suppressing Basuto rebels. The same cause had delayed till April, 1897, the necessary supply of horses to infantry regiments, at which date £36,000 was granted for this purpose. Both these horses and the training of mounted infantry at home had been repeatedly asked for by Sir Evelyn Wood as Quartermaster-General, by Sir Redvers Buller as Adjutant-General, and by Lord Wolseley as Commander-in-Chief.

Equipment and Transport.

From the great variety of countries and climates, in which it has been the fate of the British army to be engaged for the last hundred years or more, it has always been impossible to foresee what the particular equipment required for any given expedition would be.* To keep up permanently all the transport animals and the large reserves of food supplies needed for both animals and men would have been wasteful extravagance. In one campaign, only human porterage had been possible; in another, only transport by river boats; in another, it had been necessary to rely chiefly on camels; in another, on the development of canal and railway communication. Therefore, much time is always needed before it is possible so to prepare a British army that it is ready to wage war. An army is as little able to

* See also Chapter V.

THE WAR IN SOUTH AFRICA.

march till it is supplied with the necessary transport as a man would be without proper shoes, or a cavalryman without his horse. For such a war as was in prospect in South Africa, ranging possibly over tens of thousands of square miles, immense quantities, both of animals and vehicles, would be needed. A considerable proportion of these could no doubt be procured in the country itself, but from the numbers required it was necessary to extend our purchases over almost all the civilised world. This was another of the cases in which the necessity not to provoke war tended to prevent preparations for war.

Land transport S.A.

The question of land transport, on which so much of the conduct of a campaign must depend, was one of the highest importance. The nature of the South African country, and the absence of roads, rendered it necessary that transport vehicles, intended for horse-draught, should be adapted for draught by animals suitable to the country and likely to be obtainable—namely, oxen and mules. The form of the wagons in use had been settled twenty years before on South African experience, by a committee consisting of Sir Redvers Buller and Colonel H. S. E. Reeves, but the South African brake, not being convenient for home service, was no longer used, so that this had to be supplied. Moreover, it was necessary to convert the carriages to pole draught for mule traction. The Director-General of Ordnance* asked, on July 26th, 1899, for authority to carry out this change, involving an outlay of £17,650, but at this time, for reasons already given, sanction was refused to any expenditure on preparations for despatching an army to South Africa.

"On the 1st September the Director-General of Ordnance again asked for authority. On the 5th September, in putting forward a schedule of requirements, he pointed out that this service would take ten weeks, and said the sanction of those items should be given at once, on account of the time required to manufacture and obtain them, and that if put off till the force

---

* General Sir H. Brackenbury.

PREPARATION FOR WAR.

is ordered to mobilise it would be impossible to guarantee their being ready in time." *

In the still existing circumstances, neither the importance of the demand, nor the smallness of the sum asked, saved the requisition from sharing the fate of others, and authority for the expenditure was not received until the partial grant of September 22nd.† Once begun, the work was actually carried out in sixteen days less than the estimated time, but the delay was sufficient to prevent sixteen or more units from being accompanied by the vehicles of their regimental transport.‡ Delay.

Early in September an arrangement had been come to between the Director-General of Ordnance (who, under normal conditions, was responsible for the provision of all transport vehicles and harness) and the Quartermaster-General, whereby the latter undertook the furnishing of transport wagons and harness for supply trains and parks. This in fact was carried out in South Africa. Q.M.G. provides vehicles.

The Quartermaster-General, in response to demands from the General Officer Commanding in South Africa, had sent two months' reserve supplies from time to time since the beginning of June for the troops already there. On receipt of the authority of September 22nd, one month's reserves for 50,000 men, 12,000 horses and 15,000 mules were ordered, and these were shipped by October 30th. Further expenditure was sanctioned on September 29th. Another month's supplies for the same numbers were therefore ordered to be despatched about November 18th. The provision of such quantities took time and, in consequence of the delay in obtaining sanction for expenditure, the Quartermaster-General was hard pressed in furnishing the supplies early enough, but succeeded in doing so. Q.M.G. and supplies.

Remount Department.

The provision of horses and mules to complete the war establishment for mounted units was one function of the

---

* Extract from Minute by the Director-General of Ordnance to the Commander-in-Chief, dated October 10th. See Vol. I. Minutes of Evidence, Royal Commission, p. 76.

† See p. 6.   ‡ Water carts and ammunition carts.

Quartermaster-General. The Inspector-General of Remounts was charged, under him, with the detail work connected therewith. As far back as 1887 a system of registration of horses had been established in order to form a reserve to meet a national emergency. With the aid of this reserve, it was calculated that horses could be provided in sufficient numbers to complete the mobilisation of the force laid down in Mr. Stanhope's memorandum and to make good the wastage of the first six months. The number estimated for these purposes was 25,000.* No difficulty, it was thought, would be experienced in obtaining this number and, with the supply for six months' wastage in hand, time would be available to arrange for meeting further demands if they arose.

<small>Purchase of mules and horses.</small>

Transport mules would in any case have to be purchased abroad and records were preserved of the resources of different mule-producing countries; but there had been no expectation of having to supplement, to any extent, the home supply of horses. The Inspector-General of Remounts had personal experience of horse purchase in Argentina, and the success which had attended his transactions there, coupled with his knowledge of the market, led him to believe that there would be no difficulty in obtaining from that country a supply of good and suitable horses, sufficient to meet any demand that might be reasonably expected.† Information regarding the horse markets of other countries did not go beyond such personal knowledge as a few individuals in the department happened to possess. So enormous did demands eventually become, that it is open to question whether, had all possible information been at command,

---

* "On mobilisation being ordered, horses to the number of 3,682 were bought from the registered reserve, the remainder required being obtained in the open market, and all units received their full complement with 10 per cent. of spare horses. No units were delayed for want of horses." (Court of Inquiry, Remount department, 5,344–5).

The number of horses actually purchased from the registered reserve, and in the open market at home, amounted to 73,000 by the end of 1901.

† A proposal to send 700 Argentine horses and mules " to acclimatise, anticipating next year's casualties," was sent to the General Officer Commanding S. Africa, in April, 1899.—Tel. Q.M.G. to G.O.C., S.A., 28th April. (S.A. Series No. 3.)

PREPARATION FOR WAR.

there existed for sale anywhere a sufficient number of horses of the right age and stamp, trained to saddle and in condition, to furnish the numbers required.* Purchases of horses were, indeed, made in South Africa before the war, under the orders of the General Officer Commanding in that country. This was done as a mere matter of local convenience, not as a preparation for war. Furthermore, in the middle of September financial approval was given for the purchase " of 260 Australian horses to replace the next year's casualties." † Illusions as to the sufficiency of the home supply were speedily dispelled by the unforeseen conditions accompanying the transition from peace to war. Not only was the Remount department required to provide horses and mules for a far larger British army than had ever before taken the field, but that army was operating at an immense distance from its base over a larger extent of country than any over which a British army had ever before been called upon to act. Besides this, no force previously sent into the field by any nation has included in its composition such a large proportion of mounted men. Consequently, the demands on the Remount department were of unprecedented magnitude.‡

What contributed not a little to these demands was the absence of preparation in South Africa in establishing beforehand depôts from which a regular supply could be maintained, and in which imported animals could rest after the voyage and become to a certain extent acclimatised before they were used in the field.

Absence of depôts.

---

* The total number of animals furnished by the Remount department up to August, 1902, was as follows :—

Horses.		Mules and Donkeys.	Total.
With units.	Remounts.		
20,251	450,223	149,648	620,122

† Court of Enquiry on Army Remounts. Q. 8, Minutes of Evidence.
‡ Court of Enquiry on Army Remounts. Report, Para. 234.

THE WAR IN SOUTH AFRICA.

Partial provision of depôts.

In June, 1899, the Inspector-General had represented the necessity of sending out a proper remount establishment to receive animals, and a supervising staff. This proposal was only adopted to the extent that, on June 22nd, sanction was given for an Assistant-Inspector of Remounts, accompanied by a small staff, to go to South Africa. In August, 1899, approval was given for the retention of the existing depôt at Stellenbosch as a temporary measure, while on the Natal side "the present depôt" was reported by the Officer Commanding troops as being "sufficient for all that the War Office had sanctioned."*

Mules and oxen.

Estimates of the number of mules which would be required to be purchased abroad for regimental transport had been worked out in June. A limited number had already been obtained in South Africa, and before the war broke out the General Officer Commanding there had entered into contracts for the supply of 1,470 additional animals. This met the immediate necessity, and the subsequent purchases from all parts of the world enabled every unit landing in Cape Colony to be completely equipped with regimental transport when it reached its concentration station.† In Natal ox-transport was principally used as being more suitable for the country.

Animals from abroad.

In order to supplement this supply and "with a view to possible contingencies, about the middle of July, 1899, commissions of officers, to make preliminary enquiries, were sent to the United States of America, to Spain and to Italy." ‡ In order that these preparations, indispensable if war was declared, should not tend to excite war, the Secretary of State had given instructions that these officers should not attract attention to their mission. They were not allowed to make any purchases until they received instructions. These were telegraphed on 23rd September, 1899, authorising the buying of 1,000 in Spain, 3,000 in Italy, and 4,000 at New Orleans.

---

* Telegram General Officer Commanding South Africa, to Secretary of State, 3rd September. (South African Series, No. 200.)

† There were three concentration stations in the Cape Colony, viz. : De Aar, Naauwpoort and Queenstown.

‡ Report, Court of Inquiry, Remount department, p. 3, para. 12.

PREPARATION FOR WAR. 23

The conveyance of mules (but not horses) from ports abroad was carried out by the Admiralty, and some difficulty was experienced at first in chartering ships suitable for the purpose. The first ship-load did not arrive in South Africa until 8th November. Mules for troops from India were shipped under arrangements made by the Indian Government in conjunction with the Admiralty Transport Officer. *[Ships for mules.]*

The department succeeded in furnishing, and even in exceeding, the numbers demanded from time to time. It had undertaken the transport of horses purchased abroad, an arrangement which, while relieving the Admiralty, caused no competition, as a different class of ship was required. Horses and mules purchased in various countries were poured into South Africa. They were used up almost as soon as they arrived. *[Demands fully met.]*

There was no arrangement made for easy and rapid expansion. "The Inspector-General of Remounts could do no more with the organisation with which he was furnished; his functions were strictly limited, and his staff even more so. It was inevitable that when a department so equipped, and with no provision for expansion, was called upon to extend its operations largely, there must be some lack of system."* In addition to these difficulties, the department had to face others. It was from the first made the object of attacks in the Press and in Parliament. It was scarcely possible that the circumstances as here recorded should be understood. To the labours of the officials, already worked to breaking strain, was added the duty of preparing constant written explanations of their actions, and this to an extent that seriously interfered with the despatch of their current business. *[Difficulties of Remount department.]*

Army Service Corps.

There was no difficulty in bringing the personnel of the transport companies and supply detachments of the Army Service Corps up to the war establishment laid down for them. Yet the total strength of the corps, with its reserves called up, was far below what was required to meet the calls which were eventually

---
* Report of Royal Commission, Para. 187.

made on it. "After withdrawing nearly every officer of the corps from England and stations abroad it was necessary to employ in South Africa 126 additional officers of other corps up to June, 1900, which number was increased to nearly 250 later on in the war. To replace officers in England and stations abroad, 98 retired and reserve officers were employed. The transport personnel (non-commissioned officers and artificers) of the companies in South Africa, when they were subsequently divided into two, was hardly sufficient to carry on the work, but a large number of promotions were made to fill up the deficiencies. With the supply branch in South Africa, 364 civilians were engaged as clerks, bakers, and issuers, and civilians were employed at every station at home to take the place of Army Service Corps clerks." *

Local Drivers relieve A.S.C.

On the other hand, the nature of the transport in South Africa rendered the employment of native mule and ox drivers almost imperative. A surplus of Army Service Corps drivers was thus created sufficient to enable 600 to be lent to the Royal artillery, leaving enough to be retained for duty at home and abroad. The duties of four remount depôts in Cape Colony and one in Natal were also carried out by the Army Service Corps during the first part of the war until relieved by remount depôts from England and India.

Early despatch of A.S.C.

A notable feature in connection with the Army Service Corps was its employment, before the outbreak of hostilities, in a rôle that was essentially preparatory. For the first time in the history of the corps, transport companies and supply detachments were sent in advance of the troops whom they were to serve, and prepared the way for them. With the despatch of two companies in July to make good the transport of the existing force in South Africa, five officers also proceeded to South Africa to assist in organising the supply and transport duties in the event of a large force being sent out.† Further embarkations took place in September and October, and the remainder of the

* Statement of Quartermaster-General, 23rd September, 1902.

† The General Officer Commanding South Africa had applied for special service officers acquainted with "B." duties.

Army Service Corps units, detailed for duty with the army corps, embarked before war had actually been declared, and before any of the troops of the army corps had sailed. The advantages attending these measures were that not only did all units on arriving at their concentration stations in South Africa find their transport ready for them, but the transport and supply services generally were organised and in working order for their share of the operations.

Royal Army Medical Corps.

In respect of preparations, even up to the two army corps standard, the Royal Army Medical Corps was weak in numbers. Barely sufficient in its personnel even for peace requirements, it possessed no organisation for expansion in war. The establishment of officers was designed to provide for the bearer companies and field hospitals of two army corps and a cavalry division, with seven stationary and three general hospitals on the lines of communication. This only allowed for under 3 per cent. of the troops having beds in general and stationary hospitals. Without withdrawing officers from the colonies,* the aid of 99 civil surgeons would be required. These gentlemen were to be selected when their services were needed, but as there was no registered list, no claim on the service of anyone could be exacted. When the field army was provided for, the home hospitals were entirely denuded of personnel. The work was carried on by retired officers and civil surgeons. The establishment of non-commissioned officers and men was designed only for peace purposes, and beyond the reserve there was no estimate for additions in case of war. A state of war was to be met by civilian assistance, increased employment of women nurses, and active recruiting. An increase of establishment which had been proposed for the estimates of 1893-4 and successive years had gradually obtained complete sanction by 1898.† The increase of the army as a whole and the known

---

* The establishment for India is distinct.

† An increase of 212 was asked for, and was obtained by successive grants of 54, 53, 52 and 55—total, 214.

weakness in South Africa caused demands for yet larger numbers in the estimates of 1899-1900. The Army Board were not disposed to recommend more than a portion of these additions.* The difficulty of obtaining sanction for expenditure on measures of greater urgency required that that which was considered of less importance should be dispensed with, so the hospital orderly had to be rejected in favour of the soldier to fill the ranks. To provide the general and stationary hospitals that accompanied the First Army Corps with complete personnel, it became necessary to denude the bearer companies and field hospitals of the Second Army Corps. It is not surprising, therefore, that " war having been declared, and practically the whole available personnel having been swept off to South Africa with the first demands, it became necessary to seek for other means of supply." † Hospital equipment was dealt with by the Director-General of Ordnance, but with surgical and medical stores the Army Medical Department was itself concerned. Funds to replace the old-fashioned instruments then in use were asked for in 1896, and between that date and the outbreak of war great improvements had been made. The change, however, had not been universally completed, and on the outbreak of war a few instruments of comparatively antiquated type were still to be found in South Africa. A similar argument to that which prevailed against the increase of personnel met the several requests for storage room. It was represented that the indifferent storage available deteriorated the instruments and made the drugs worthless. On the other hand, the perishable nature of drugs renders it inadvisable to keep a large amount in store, besides which, ample supplies can always be purchased in the market. The subsequent experience went to prove that there was no difficulty in this matter. Throughout the war the department was wonderfully well equipped as regards drugs and instruments, and no branch was more successful than that concerned with medical supplies.

* The estimate was for 400 of all ranks, and 150 were granted. The balance was granted in November, 1899, and the men were of course untrained.

† Statement by Surgeon-General Jameson, Royal Commission on South African Hospitals.

Army Veterinary Department.

On the outbreak of war the Director-General of the Army Veterinary department was responsible to the Adjutant-General for the efficiency of his department and the maintenance of veterinary supplies. The superior control was subsequently transferred to the Quartermaster-General. The proportion of the veterinary service which should accompany a force on active service was not laid down. Not only was there no organisation to admit of expansion but, owing to the unattractive conditions attaching to service in the department, the number of officers was actually below the authorised establishment. In addition to the discharge of ordinary duty, heavy demands were made by the Remount department for veterinary officers to assist in the purchase and transport of horses and mules. It was necessary, therefore, almost from the first, to engage civilian veterinary surgeons.* The personnel of the department did not include any subordinate staff. The Director-General† of the department was in process of adopting, with improvements, the Indian system of equipment, for which he had himself been responsible. The amount of this equipment which it had been possible to prepare before the outbreak of war was insufficient, but the deficiency was remedied by indenting on India for four field veterinary hospitals and 100 field chests, which enabled the supply to be kept up to the subsequent demands.

Inspector-General of Fortifications.

This officer was responsible for engineer stores. The nature of those required depends largely on the country in which the campaign is to be carried on; therefore, practically no reserve was maintained of such ordinary items as can easily be bought in the market. Of manufactured goods, such as railway plant, telegraph material and pontoons, which require time for produc-

---

* The home establishment of the department was 63; 121 civilian veterinary surgeons were employed in South Africa, besides those engaged by local Volunteers.

† Veterinary Colonel F. Duck, C.B., F.R.C.V.S.

tion, there was an insufficient reserve, notably of the last named. In order to send out a number sufficient to meet the probable requirements in South Africa, all reserve pontoons, including some of questionable value, were collected, and the country was denuded. This deficiency had been represented on different occasions, but for want of funds nothing could be done towards the provision of new pontoons until October, 1899.

Ordnance.

Of all the departments, this was subjected to the greatest strain and was the least prepared to meet it. The reasons were as follows. For some years previous to 1897 the system in force was that, although the Director-General of Ordnance was charged with the supply of stores to the army, the financial control and the entire direction of the ordnance factories rested with the Financial Secretary to the War Office, who belonged to the Ministry of the day. No supplies could be obtained by the former unless with the permission and by the order of the latter. The system conduced to a lack of sympathy of motive, which caused a disinclination on the one part to ask for what on the other there would be more than a disinclination to give. This tended to crystallise the national proneness to defer until the emergency arose the measures necessary to meet it. It followed, then, that while attention was given to the needs of the moment, practically all provision for the requirements of the future was relegated to the background. A further defect in the system was that it resulted in there being no proper understanding between those who had intimate knowledge of what was required by the army and those who were responsible for manufacture.

<small>Sir Henry Brackenbury's appointment.</small> During the three years that Lieutenant-General Sir Henry Brackenbury had been President of the Ordnance Committee at Woolwich he had been impressed by the unsatisfactory working of the system and, on being offered the appointment of Director-General of Ordnance, in November, 1898, he urged that the direction of the ordnance factories should be transferred to the holder of that appointment. The matter was dis-

PREPARATION FOR WAR.

cussed by the Cabinet and, on its being decided to make the transfer, Sir H. Brackenbury took up the appointment in February, 1899. The transfer was effected by the Order in Council of March 7th, 1899, which enumerated the duties with which the Director-General of Ordnance was charged,* and included in them that of the direction of the manufacturing departments of the army. The financial control of the factories still remained with the Financial Secretary.

The Secretary of State himself had felt some concern as to the condition of affairs in the Ordnance department and it was on his initiative that Sir Henry Brackenbury was selected to set matters right. On taking up the duties of Director-General of Ordnance, the new chief commenced an enquiry into the condition of the armament and the state of reserves of all ordnance stores. In the early months of the year the greater part of his time and attention was taken up by the important question of replacing the obsolete armament of our sea defences. From June onwards the whole energies of the department were directed towards meeting the requirements of the force which might possibly have to take the field. It was not until the despatch of this force that the true barrenness of the land came to be revealed, and melancholy was the outlook it presented. *State of ordnance stores.*

Early in 1899 the Director-General of Ordnance issued confidential instructions to General Officers Commanding districts regarding special scales of clothing and equipment for the field force contemplated for service in South Africa. These instructions enabled demands to be prepared, so that they could be put forward without delay on the order to mobilise. *Warning to G.Os.C.*

Wherever storage buildings were available the war equipment of units was kept on their charge. In other cases it was apportioned to units but held in store for them by the Ordnance department. When mobilisation was ordered, there was war equipment practically complete to enable two army corps, a cavalry division, and lines of communication troops to take the field. *Method of keeping equipment.*

* The duties are detailed in Sir Henry Brackenbury's reply to the Royal Commission, A. 1,555.

Clothing.

The special clothing prescribed for South Africa entailed an entire change of dress—helmet, body-clothing, and boots. Sanction had been given in April, 1899, for the storage of a reserve of khaki drill suits,* of which the amount authorised would have been insufficient, but fortunately the Clothing department had a surplus which enabled a complete issue to be made on mobilisation. It had been represented from South Africa, with the support of the Director-General of the Army Medical Service at home, that serge was more appropriate to the climate than cotton drill, and the substitution had been approved by the Commander-in-Chief on August 18th. No steps towards effecting the change could be taken until the grant of September 22nd, and the first three divisions embarked with cotton drill clothing.† It is probable, however, that even had the money been forthcoming when the change was first approved, not more than half the amount required could have been obtained in the time. One difficulty experienced in connection with the issue of clothing was that of providing each unit with the right number of suits of particular sizes. Many of the reservists who presented themselves on mobilisation were found to have increased considerably in figure, and consequently much fitting and alteration was necessary. This caused delay. At that time the boot for foreign service differed in pattern from that for home service, and an issue of the former was made. The supply on hand was only sufficient to allow a complete issue to men of the mounted services, while dismounted soldiers had one pair of each pattern, reservists having home service pattern entirely. The sudden demand on the market for the materials necessary for these articles of clothing entailed a considerable increase of cost, without, at the outset at least, ensuring provision of the best quality.

War equipment.

At the outbreak of war the authorised war equipment was prac-

* This reserve consisted of 40,000 suits; the number actually issued was sufficient to equip the force completely.

† At the time of year this was suitable, and serge clothing was eventually sent out. Troops subsequently, up to May, 1900, took one suit of drill and one suit of serge. Later each man took two suits of serge.

PREPARATION FOR WAR.

tically complete, and there remained the equipment for a third army corps, but suitable only for service at home. Beyond this, there was no provision of special reserves to meet the continual drain by service in the field abroad. Such reserve material as there was for batteries of both horse and field artillery was speedily exhausted; while to provide heavier ordnance it was necessary to draw upon the movable armament for home defence. More speedy still was the exhaustion of gun ammunition, and not even the suspension of Naval orders in the factories, with loans from the Navy and from India, could enable demands to be complied with quickly enough. Similarly, the deficiencies in other stores, such as camp equipment, vehicles, harness, saddlery and horse-shoes, made themselves apparent at a very early date in the war.*

Any idea that may have existed that the ordnance factories and the trade would be able to meet all demands from week to week was quickly dispelled. The supply could not keep pace with the need, and in some cases the exhaustion of the home market necessitated large purchases in Europe, Canada, and the United States. Of rifles and other weapons at this time the store was ample, except in the case of sabres, of which, owing to a contemplated change in pattern, the reserve had been allowed to fall very low. There was a complete reserve of ball ammunition of the kinds approved for use in the earlier part of 1899, viz.: Mark II. and Mark IV., the latter having an expanding bullet. During the summer of 1899 it was found that under certain conditions the Mark IV. ammunition developed such serious defects that, apart from the inexpediency of using a bullet which the signatories to the Hague Convention† had condemned, it was deemed advisable to withdraw this particular kind of ammunition as unsuitable for war purposes. This meant that two-fifths of the reserve was unserviceable.

Purchases abroad.

Mark IV

* In the matter of hospital equipment previous to mobilisation there had been stores for field hospitals of three army corps; but there was no reserve of equipment for stationary hospitals or general hospitals, except for one general hospital and two stationary hospitals, which were not included in the army corps organisation.

† The British Government was not a party to this clause.

On 15th December, 1899, as the result of his enquiry, Sir Henry Brackenbury put forward his report to the Commander-in-Chief, in which he enumerated in detail the various deficiencies of stores brought to light by the war in South Africa. The condition of affairs was such as to cause grave apprehension. To use his own words : " That war has now disclosed a situation as regards armaments, and reserves of guns, ammunition, stores and clothing, and as regards the power of output of material of war in emergency which is, in my opinion, full of peril to the Empire ; and I, therefore, think it my duty, without waiting to elaborate details, to lay before you at once the state of affairs, and to make proposals, to which I invite, through you, the earnest and immediate attention of the Secretary of State." These proposals dealt with the provision of armaments, reserves of ammunition, stores and clothing, and the improvement of factories and storage-buildings, with the object of putting the country in a condition of safety and preventing the possibility of the recurrence of the state of affairs disclosed.*

Alarming minute from D.G.O.

In his minute Sir Henry Brackenbury also insisted on the necessity of a free hand being given in time of war to the Inspector-General of Fortifications as regards works and buildings, and to the Director-General of Ordnance as regards armaments, stores and clothing. He had, through the Army Board, on the 22nd September, brought to the notice of the Secretary of State the difficulties and delays inseparable from the financial system which obtained in peace time, and had been granted practically what he asked in his expenditure for the supply of the army during the war. On this point Sir Henry Brackenbury remarked in his report :—

A free hand.

"It is only by such a free hand having been given to us since the outbreak of war in October that it has been possible to supply the army in the field, and even so, owing to the want of reserves, we have been too late with many of the most important articles."

---

* Sir H. Brackenbury's representation was laid before the Cabinet and resulted, on the recommendations of the Mowatt and Grant Committees, in a grant of £10,500,900 to be distributed over a period of three years.

PREPARATION FOR WAR.

The tale of deficiencies was thus summed up by the Secretary of State :—

"It is, I think, abundantly clear from Sir H. Brackenbury's Report, that we were not sufficiently prepared even for the equipment of the comparatively small force which we had always contemplated might be employed beyond the limits of this country in the initial stages of a campaign. For the much larger force which we have actually found it necessary to employ our resources were absolutely and miserably inadequate. The result has been that the department, even by working under conditions which have nearly led to a breakdown, has been barely able to keep pace with the requirements of the army." *

<small>Lord Lansdowne's note.</small>

Colonies.

Offers of assistance had poured in from Greater Britain from the moment that the imminence of war in South Africa was realised. It was not the first time that our kinsmen had sent their sons for the general service of the Empire. In 1881, within twenty-four hours of the receipt of the news of the action at Laing's Nek, two thousand men of the Australian local forces had volunteered for employment in South Africa, but were not accepted. Four years later, eight hundred colonists from New South Wales were welcomed for service at Suakim, while a special corps of Canadian voyageurs was enlisted for the advance up the Nile. But on neither of these occasions was the tender of patriotic help so welcome to the Mother Country as in the present instance, for it was felt that the whole Empire was concerned in the contest for the establishment in South Africa of equal rights for all white men independent of race, and that it was, therefore, peculiarly fitting that the younger States of the great Imperial Commonwealth should make the quarrel their own. As early as July, 1899, Queensland, Victoria, New South Wales, the Malay States and Lagos, had tendered their services, and Her Majesty's Government, though not then able to accept

* Extract from memorandum of May 21st, 1900, by the Marquess of Lansdowne.

the offers made, had gratefully acknowledged them. In September, Queensland and Victoria renewed their proposals, and further offers of assistance were received from Canada, New Zealand, Western Australia, South Australia, Tasmania, and Hong Kong. The majority of a squadron of the New South Wales Lancers, which had been sent to England to undergo a special course of training at Aldershot, also volunteered for South Africa. As regards Natal and Cape Colony, it was assumed as a matter of course, both by the Colonial troops themselves and by the Imperial and Colonial Governments, that they would cheerfully do their duty if called out for local defence. The whole of the Natal local forces were mobilised for active service on 29th September,* the day after President Kruger commandeered his burghers. A portion of the Cape Volunteers were called out on 5th October, and the remainder during the first month of the war.† On the 3rd October the Secretary of State for the Colonies telegraphed to various Colonial Governments a grateful acceptance by Her Majesty's Government of the services of their contingents, indicating in each case the units considered desirable. It was not found possible to take advantage of the offers of some of the Crown Colonies, but from the self-governing Colonies, troops numbernig about 2,500 of all ranks were accepted.‡ These proved but the advance guard to the total force of nearly 30,000 men from Canada, Australia, New Zealand, India and Ceylon, who at various times represented Greater Britain in the army of South Africa.

* The corps mobilised were Natal Naval Volunteers, Natal Field Artillery, Natal Royal Rifles, Durban Light Infantry, Natal Mounted Rifles, Natal Carbineers, Umvoti Mounted Rifles, Border Mounted Rifles.

† For the local forces called out in Cape Colony, see Chapter II., p. 53.

‡ For arrivals of "Oversea Colonials," see Appendix 9. The whole subject is treated more fully in Vol. II. in a chapter on the Colonial Corps.

CHAPTER II.

THE OUTBREAK OF THE WAR.*

It has been convenient to carry the statement of the measures adopted for preparation at home in certain matters beyond the actual date of the declaration of war. It is now necessary to view the state of affairs in South Africa at that time. Although British preparations for war had been retarded by the hope of the Queen's Government that the grave issues with the Dutch Republics might be determined by diplomatic action, yet the weakness of our military position in South Africa had long been felt as keenly by the local military authorities as it had been by the Headquarter staff at the War Office. In schemes for the defence of the British colonies, submitted in 1896 and 1897 by Lieut.-General Sir W. H. Goodenough, who was then commanding in South Africa, the extraordinary extent of the frontiers to be defended, the disadvantages entailed by their shape, and the overwhelming numerical superiority of the Boers over the handful of British troops then in South Africa, made it necessary to base the protection even of the most important strategical points on sheer audacity. Defence plans of local authorities. Genl. Goodenough.

A letter addressed by the War Office to General Goodenough's successor, Lieut.-General Sir W. Butler, on 21st December, 1898, had requested him to reconsider his predecessor's proposals, and to report at an early date the distribution of troops he would make in the event of war with the two Dutch Republics. In a review of the strategical situation, that despatch drew attention to the fact that the troops then stationed in the command " would be inadequate for any other than a defensive attitude, War Office to Gen. Butler Dec. /98.

---

* See general map of South Africa, Relief map No. 2, and map No. 3.

pending the arrival of reinforcements from England." In the same paper the effect of the frontiers on the questions, both of defence in the earlier stages of the war, and of the ultimate form of offence, is so fully treated that it will be convenient to quote here the official statement of the case. It must be premised that it is assumed in it, as in fact proved to be the case, that both sides would tacitly agree, for the sake of not raising the native difficulty, to treat Basuto territory as neutral. That mountain region was therefore throughout considered as an impassable obstacle :—

"The frontiers of the Transvaal and the Free State are conterminous with English territory for over 1,000 miles, but the defence of this enormous frontier by Her Majesty's troops is impossible to contemplate. Southern Rhodesia, although a possible objective for a Boer raid, must rely entirely for its defence upon its own local forces, and, although the line from Kimberley to Buluwayo is of some strategic importance, yet its protection north of the Vaal river would be altogether out of our power during the earlier stages of the war. Basutoland may also be eliminated from defensive calculations, as its invasion by the Boers would be improbable; moreover, the Basutos, if invaded, would be able for some time to maintain an effective resistance.

"The frontier, therefore, the observation and defence of which appears to need definite consideration, may be held to extend in Cape Colony from Fourteen Streams bridge in the north to the south-west corner of Basutoland, and to include in Natal the triangle, of which Charlestown is the apex, and a line drawn from Mont Aux Sources to the Intonganeni* district of Zululand the base.

"The mountains and broken country of Basutoland and Griqualand East, which lie between Natal and the Cape Colony, are unpierced by railways and ill-supplied by roads. It must be accepted, therefore, that a force acting on the defensive in Natal will be out of touch with a force in Cape Colony, and the two can only operate from separate bases.

* Now spelt Emtonjaneni on the general map.

THE OUTBREAK OF THE WAR. 37

Dec. /98, from W.O.

"As regards the Cape frontier, for the portion lying between Basutoland and Hopetown railway bridge,* the Orange river forms a military obstacle of some importance, impassable, as a rule, during the first three months of the year, except at the bridges, and even at other times difficult to cross, owing to its quicksands, and liability to sudden flood. Between Hopetown railway bridge and the Vaal the frontier is, however, protected by no physical features and lies open to invasion.

"As regards the Natal frontier its salient confers on the enemy facilities for cutting our line of communications, and for outflanking at pleasure the positions of Laing's Nek and the Biggarsberg. This facility is accentuated by the influence of the Drakensberg, which forms a screen, behind which an enemy can assemble unobserved and debouch on our flanks through its numerous passes. These passes, however, have been recently examined and found to be for the most part but rough mountain tracks available for raids, but unsuitable for the advance of any large force accompanied by transport. To this Van Reenen's Pass, through which the railway and main road issue from Natal into the Free State, and Laing's Nek (across and under which the main road and railway pass into the Transvaal) are notable exceptions, and the possession of these two passes necessarily carry with them great strategical advantages.

"An appreciation of the relative importance of the defence of the two frontiers of Cape Colony and Natal would, no doubt, be assisted if the line by which the main advance on the Transvaal will ultimately be undertaken were determined; but I am to say that in the Commander-in-Chief's opinion the plan for offensive operations must depend upon the political and military situation of the moment, and cannot now be definitely fixed. The fact, however, that an offensive advance will ultimately be undertaken, as soon as sufficient forces have arrived, must be especially borne in mind in considering arrangements for the first or defensive stage of the campaign."

The despatch then stated that the following should be taken as the basis of Sir William Butler's arrangements for frontier

* The railway bridge at Orange River station.

defence: "The latest information in the possession of the War Office as to the military strength of the two States will be found in the recent pamphlet entitled 'Military Notes on the Dutch Republics of South Africa,' copies of which are in your possession. You will observe that in that publication it is estimated that the total forces of the two republics amount to over 40,000 men, and that of these some 27,000* would be available for offensive operations beyond their frontiers. It is known that projects for such offensive operations have actually been under the consideration of the War department of Pretoria, but although an attempt may be made on Kimberley and the northern strip of Natal may be occupied by the Boers, yet it is considered to be unlikely that any further serious advance into the heart of either colony would be undertaken. Raids, however, of 2,000 to 3,000 men may be expected, and it is against such raids that careful preparation on your part is necessary."

June /99. Sir W. Butler's reply.

Sir W. Butler, being occupied by other duties, did not reply to this despatch until pressed by telegrams at the beginning of June of the following year. He then reported by telegraph and in a letter to the War Office, dated 12th June, 1899, that he intended, in the event of war, to divide the troops in Natal into two; one part at Dundee-Glencoe with orders to patrol to the Buffalo river on the east, Ingagane on the north, and the Drakensberg Passes on the west, and the other at Ladysmith, with instructions "to support Glencoe and maintain the line of the Biggarsberg, or to operate against Van Reenen's Pass should circumstances necessitate." In Cape Colony he proposed, with the small number of troops then available (*i.e.*, three battalions, six guns and a R.E. company), to hold the important railway

---

* A later edition of the Military Notes (June, 1899) estimated the total strength of the burgher and permanent levies to be 53,743, and further that these would be joined at the outbreak of war by 4,000 Colonial rebels. It was calculated that of this total, and exclusive of those detached for frontier defence and to hold in check Kimberley and Mafeking, 27,000 effectives would be available as a field army for offensive operations. When these estimates were made, the large number of Uitlanders in Johannesburg made it probable that a considerable Boer force would be detained to watch that city.

THE OUTBREAK OF THE WAR. 39

stations of De Aar, Naauwpoort and Molteno (or Stormberg), with strong detachments at Orange River station, and possibly Kimberley, and outposts at Colesberg, Burghersdorp, and Philipstown. It will be seen, therefore, that, while deprecating the actual occupation of the Drakensberg Passes and of the Colesberg and Bethulie bridges over the Orange river, which had been proposed by his predecessor and approved by Lord Wolseley, Sir William Butler did not shrink from the forward policy of endeavouring to bluff the enemy with weak detachments stationed in close proximity to the frontier.

It was in conformity with this policy that, in July, 1899, the War Office despatched Col. R. S. S. Baden-Powell, with a staff of special service officers, to organise a force in southern Rhodesia. It was hoped that, in the event of war, his column might detain a portion of the Boer commandos in that quarter, since its position threatened the northern Transvaal. To his task was subsequently added the organisation of a mounted infantry corps which, based on Mafeking, might similarly hold back the burghers of the western districts of the South African Republic. *Baden-Powell sent out.*

The cloud of war rapidly spread over the whole of the South African horizon, and the strategical situation became sharply defined. As regards the determination of the plan of offence referred to in the above War Office despatch, the difficulty was due to the hope entertained by the Cabinet that, in the event of war between this country and the Transvaal, the Orange Free State would remain neutral. The choice in that case would have lain between an advance based on Warrenton, *i.e.*, on the Kimberley-to-Mafeking railway, or a movement parallel to the Natal-to-Johannesburg railway. By the middle of 1899, however, the Headquarter staff at the War Office were convinced that, if war should supervene, the two republics would make common cause. A memorandum, entitled, " The Direction of a Line of Advance Against the Transvaal," was prepared by the Intelligence division on that basis and submitted on 3rd June, 1899. It was contended in this memorandum that the lack of any railway between Fourteen Streams and the Transvaal *Choice of Routes.*

capital eliminated that route from consideration, and that the choice now lay between the line running up through the centre of the Free State and the Natal route.

The better line.

In comparing the relative merits of these two routes it was shown that strategically the Natal line would, owing to the shape of the frontier and the parallel screen of the Drakensberg, be constantly exposed to dangerous flank attacks, while the flanks of the Free State route would be comparatively safe. "The Basutos' sympathies will be entirely with us, while on the west the garrison of Kimberley will hold the approaches."

Reasons.

Tactically, it was pointed out, the Natal route traversed " an ideal terrain for the Boers," and crossed the " immensely strong " position of Laing's Nek. On the other hand, a force advancing by the Free State route, once over the Orange river, would have only to deal with the Bethulie position, and would then reach open plains, which " afford the freest scope for the manœuvres of all three arms."

Conclusion.

Furthermore, the Free State route could be fed by three distinct lines of railway from three ports, while the Natal route would be dependent on a single line and one port. The memorandum, therefore, submitted the conclusion that " the main line of advance against the Transvaal should be based on the Cape Colony, and should follow generally the line of railway through the Orange Free State to Johannesburg and Pretoria."

Natal threatened.

In June it became evident that the vague designs of the Boer Governments against Natal, of which the British Intelligence department had had cognizance in the previous year, were taking definite shape, and that, at any rate, so far as the Transvaal forces were concerned, the eastern colony would probably become the main object of their attack. The only British reinforcements immediately available were therefore assigned to that colony. On the Cape side it was manifest that the determining factor was the attitude of restless elements within the colony itself. It was known that secret agents from the Transvaal had, during the past two years, visited many parts of the colony, and that arms had been distributed by those agents. The investigations of the Intelli-

THE OUTBREAK OF THE WAR. 41

gence department had, however, failed to discover proofs of the establishment of such organisations as would enable any formidable rising in the colony to coincide with a declaration of war by the republics. It was fully realised that it could not but be the case that there would be among many of the Dutch colonial farmers some natural sympathy with their kinsmen, and that a certain number of the younger and wilder would possibly slip across the border to join the enemy's forces; but it was believed that, provided this class of the community was not encouraged by any sign of weakness to enter into relations with the republics, they would be, as a whole, loath to throw off their allegiance to a State to which they and their forefathers had for many generations been loyal, and under whose rule they had enjoyed equal liberties, self-government and much prosperity.

If these conclusions were sound—and the course of events during the first month of the war was to prove their general correctness—it was highly desirable that detachments of British troops should remain in the northern districts of the colony, and thus carry out the double function of encouraging the loyal while checking lawless spirits, and of retaining possession of those lines of railways, the use of which would be a matter of vital importance to the field army in its subsequent advance from the coast. It was obvious that these isolated posts of a few hundred men would run serious risks. Thrust forward in close proximity to the enemy's frontier, they were separated from their base on the coast by some four to five hundred miles of country, throughout which there might be possible enemies; thus their communications might at any moment be cut. Furthermore, until troops arrived from England or India, no reinforcements would be available for their assistance. But the alternative of abandoning the whole of the northern districts of Cape Colony to the enemy, and thus allowing them to enforce recruitments from colonists who might otherwise live in peaceful security under the British flag, involved dangers far graver, and was, in fact, never contemplated by the military authorities either in London or at the Cape, except in the remote contingency

Protective Posts.

of war with some maritime Power coinciding with the outbreak of hostilities with the Boer Republics. Moreover, by the middle of September, 1899, the organisation and training of Colonel Baden-Powell's two newly-raised corps, the one at Tuli and the other near Mafeking, were already sufficiently advanced to afford good hope of their being able to sustain effectively the rôle which had been assigned to them, while arrangements were being taken in hand to secure Kimberley from being captured by any *coup de main*.*

Forestier-Walker adopts Butler's plan.

Although, therefore, at that moment the only regular troops in Cape Colony were three and a half battalions of infantry, two companies Royal engineers, and two companies of Royal Garrison artillery, General Sir F. Forestier-Walker, who, on September 6th, 1899, arrived at Cape Town, replacing Sir William Butler, decided to adhere to his forward defence policy, and to carry out unchanged the arrangements contemplated by him. Thus, by the end of September, a series of military posts had been formed encircling the western and southern frontiers of the Free State at Kimberley, Orange River station, De Aar, Naauwpoort, and Stormberg, each post including a half-battalion of regular infantry, and a section of engineers. To Kimberley were also sent six 7-pr. R.M.L. screw guns, and to Orange River station, Naauwpoort and Stormberg, two 9-pr. R.M.L. guns each. Each of these three-named had also a company of mounted infantry. The guns were manned by garrison artillerymen from the naval base at Cape Town. By arrangement with the Colonial authorities the Cape Police furnished various posts of observation in advanced positions. Behind the weak line thus boldly pushed out in the face of the enemy there were no regular troops whatever in the Colony, except half a battalion and a handful of garrison gunners in the Cape peninsula.

Sir Redvers approves.

Sir F. Forestier-Walker had, however, the satisfaction to find that these dispositions, which he had carried out on his own initiative after consulting the High Commissioner, fitted in well with the plans of Sir Redvers Buller, and were acceptable to that

* See Vol. II.

THE OUTBREAK OF THE WAR. 43

officer. A telegram from Sir Redvers, dated London, 29th September, 1899, informed Forestier-Walker that an expedition made up of an army corps, a cavalry division, and seven battalions for the lines of communication would be sent out to South Africa and would advance on Pretoria through the Free State. That general was therefore directed to make, so far as was compatible with secrecy, preliminary arrangements for the disembarkation of this army at the three ports, Cape Town, Port Elizabeth and East London. In acknowledging these orders on the following day, Sir F. Forestier-Walker accordingly reported by telegram that he would arrange for the disembarkation bases and that he was establishing advanced depôts at De Aar, Naauwpoort, and Stormberg;* Sir Redvers Buller, in a message despatched from London on 2nd October, replied:—

"Your proposals are just what I wish, but I feared suggesting depôts at Naauwpoort and Stormberg, as I did not then know if you had sufficient troops to guard them. It will not do to risk loss. I leave this to your local knowledge."

On the 7th of October, 1899, the 1st Northumberland Fusiliers landed at Cape Town from England and were sent on the 10th to De Aar; a wing of the 1st Royal Munster Fusiliers left Stellenbosch by train for the same destination on the 9th. Stores were already accumulating at De Aar but, having regard to Dutch restlessness in the vicinity of Naauwpoort and Stormberg, Sir F. Forestier-Walker, after personal inspection, considered it inadvisable to risk any large amount of material at either until more troops could be spared to hold them. For the moment it appeared to him desirable to concentrate all available mobile troops at the Orange River station, where he retained command of both banks of the river, and thus, as soon as adequate strength was organised, could operate thence towards Kimberley or on some point in the

Further Steps of Defence.

---

* These places had been suggested as suitable for advanced depôts in "Notes on the Lines of Communication in Cape Colony," issued by the Intelligence Division, W. O., in June, 1899.

Free State. The energy of Lieut.-Colonel R. G. Kekewich, Loyal North Lancashire regiment, who had been despatched to Kimberley to take command, assisted by Mr. Cecil Rhodes and the officials of the De Beers Company, had placed that town in a fair state of defence. At Mafeking it was realised that Colonel Baden-Powell's troops would be unable to do more than protect the large quantities of stores accumulated by merchants at that station against the formidable Boer force which was concentrating for attack upon it. Nevertheless, by so doing, Baden-Powell would fulfil the rôle assigned to him, since he would prevent large numbers of the enemy from engaging in the serious invasion of the exposed frontier territories of Cape Colony. The actual distribution of troops in the Colony at the outbreak of war is shown in Appendix 2.

Natal defence— Generals Cox and Goodenough, 96,/97.

Reports on the frontier defence of Natal had been submitted during the years 1896–7, by Major-General G. Cox, who was then holding the sub-command of that colony, and by Lieut.-General Goodenough. After a careful examination of the question whether the tunnel under Laing's Nek, the Dundee coalfields to the south, and Van Reenen's Pass could be protected with the troops available, General Goodenough decided that none of these could be guarded. Having then only one regiment of cavalry, one mountain battery, and one infantry battalion, he thought it better to concentrate nearly all of them at Ladysmith, the point of junction of the branch railway to Harrismith with the main line to the Transvaal, sending only small detachments to Colenso and Estcourt. On the despatch to Natal, in the second quarter of 1897, of reinforcements, consisting of another cavalry regiment, a second battalion of infantry, and a brigade division of artillery, temporary quarters were erected at Ladysmith for this increase to the garrison of the colony, and Sir William Goodenough informed the War Office that in case of emergency he proposed to watch the whole frontier with the Natal Police, to hold Newcastle with colonial troops and to despatch most of the cavalry, one field battery, and half a battalion of infantry to Glencoe to cover the Dundee coalfields. The remainder of the regular troops,

THE OUTBREAK OF THE WAR. 45

consisting of a battalion and a half, a few cavalry, and two batteries, would be placed at Ladysmith, where a detachment of a battalion and the mountain battery would be kept ready to occupy and entrench itself at Van Reenen's Pass. These proposals were approved for execution on an emergency "so far as the exigencies of the occasion may admit."*

Sir W. Butler's report of 12th June, 1899, adopted practically the same plan of defence. To a suggestion as to a possible occupation of Laing's Nek,† General Butler had replied that he did not think the immediate possession of that place of great importance and that its occupation by a weak force would be a dangerous operation. The regular troops in Natal had at this date been only reinforced by one more battalion, and consisted of but two cavalry regiments, one brigade division field artillery, one mountain battery, and three infantry battalions. To these must be added the Natal Police, a corps about 400 strong, admirably trained as mounted infantry, and nearly 2,000 Colonial Volunteers of the best type.

<small>Natal defence— Sir W. Butler, /99.</small>

The communication of this scheme of defence to the Natal Ministry in July, 1899, led them to prefer an urgent request that sufficient reinforcements should be sent out to defend the whole colony. In the long telegraphic despatch addressed on 6th September, 1899, by the Governor, Sir Walter Hely-Hutchinson, to the Colonial Office, it was urged that: "In the opinion of the Ministers, such a catastrophe as the seizure of Laing's Nek, and the destruction of the northern portion of the railway . . . . . would have a most demoralising effect on the natives and the loyal Europeans in the colony, and would afford great encouragement to the Boers and their sympathisers." The announcement from home of the early despatch of reinforcements from India which was received by Sir W. Hely-Hutchinson in reply to this telegram, did not, in the opinion of Sir F. Forestier-Walker, or of Major-General Sir W. Penn Symons, who had succeeded General Cox in the local command of Natal, justify a deviation from the scheme

<small>Protest of Natal Government, July /99.</small>

---

* W. O. letter, September 3rd, 1897.
† W. O. letter, February 23rd, 1899.

of defence put forward by their predecessors. Apart from the difficulty of a water supply for a force occupying Laing's Nek, it was felt that such a forward position would be strategically unsafe, and would impose on the troops in Natal a task beyond their powers. On the other hand, the decision to give the coalfields at Dundee the protection contemplated by Sir W. Butler was adopted.

<small>Sept. 25th, /99. Glencoe held.</small>

By the 24th September the Governor told General Symons that the gravity of the political situation was such that the dispositions of the troops previously agreed on for the defence of the colony must at once be carried out. The necessary permission to act having been obtained by telegram from the General Officer Commanding South Africa, the 1st Leicester and 2nd Royal Dublin Fusiliers, with a squadron of the 18th Hussars were entrained at Ladysmith for Glencoe on the morning of the 25th September, the remainder of the 18th Hussars, with a mounted infantry company and two field batteries reaching Glencoe by march route on the 26th. The gaps these changes made in the Ladysmith garrison were filled up, the 5th Lancers, 1st King's Royal Rifles, and 1st Manchester being ordered to move to that place from Maritzburg.

<small>Sir George White, Oct. 7th, wishes to withdraw from Glencoe.</small>

Sir George White had been despatched early in September from England to command the troops in Natal. When, on October 7th, he arrived and assumed command, he found that the forces at his disposal were divided into two bodies, the one at Glencoe and the other at Ladysmith. On leaving England he had been given no instructions on the subject, nor had the previous correspondence with the local military authorities as to the defence of Natal been seen by him, but he held that from a military point of view the only sound policy was to concentrate the whole of the British troops in such a position that he would be able to strike with his full strength at the enemy the moment an opportunity offered. He determined, therefore, to withdraw the Glencoe detachment and assemble the whole at Ladysmith, the importance of which was increased by the preliminary dispositions of the Boer commandos, to be described later. The Governor, on being informed of this

THE OUTBREAK OF THE WAR. 47

intention, remonstrated against the withdrawal from Glencoe in terms which are thus recorded in his subsequent report of the interview to the Secretary of State for the Colonies :—

"Now that we were there, withdrawal would, in my opinion, involve grave political results, loyalists would be disgusted and discouraged; the results as regards the Dutch would be grave, many, if not most, would very likely rise, believing us to be afraid, and the evil might very likely spread to the Dutch in Cape Colony; and the effect on our natives, of whom there were 750,000 in Natal and Zululand, might be disastrous. They as yet believe in our power—they look to us—but if we withdraw from Glencoe they will look on it in the light of a defeat, and I could not answer for what they, or at all events a large proportion of them, might do." Protest by Governor.

Influenced by these strong representations and especially by the suggestion that the evacuation of Glencoe might lead to a general rising of the natives—a very grave consideration in the eyes of an officer with long Indian experience—the British commander decided to acquiesce for the moment in the separation of his troops which had been arranged by Major-General Symons. Sir George conceived, however, from the Intelligence reports before him that the bulk of the Boer commandos were assembling behind the screen of the Drakensberg, and that the northern portion of Natal would be their primary and principal object. He retained his own belief that the safety of the colony could only be fully secured by decisive strokes at the enemy's columns as they emerged from the mountain passes and, in pursuance of this policy, General White impressed on his staff the necessity for making such preparations as would set free the maximum number of troops for active operations in the field. Under these circumstances Sir W. Penn Symons started for Dundee on October 10th and on October 11th Sir George White went by train from Maritzburg to Ladysmith. The distribution of the forces in Natal on the outbreak of war will be found in Appendix 3. Sir G. White yields and retains Glencoe.

The exertions of ten special service officers despatched Boer plans.

to South Africa three months earlier had ensured the acquisition of accurate information as to the enemy's mobilisation, strength, and points of concentration. Sir George White's appreciation of the situation was, therefore, in conformity with the actual facts. The main strength of the enemy had been concentrated for an invasion of Natal. The President hoped that it would sweep that colony clear of British troops down to the sea, and would hoist the Vierkleur over the port of Durban. Small detachments had been told off to guard the Colesberg, Bethulie, and Aliwal North bridges and to watch Basutoland. On the western frontiers of the Transvaal and the Free State strong commandos were assembling for the destruction of Baden-Powell's retaining force at Mafeking and for the capture of Kimberley. Both Kruger and Steyn aimed at results other than those achieved by the initiatory victories of 1880-1. They cherished the hope that the time had come for the establishment of a Boer Republic reaching from the Zambesi to Table Mountain; but, for the accomplishment of so great an enterprise, external assistance was necessary, the aid of their kinsmen in the south, and ultimately, as they hoped, an alliance with other Powers across the seas. The authorities at Pretoria and Bloemfontein realised fully that, though they might expect to have sympathisers in the colonies, active co-operation on any large scale was not to be counted on until successes in the field should persuade the waverers that, in casting in their lot definitely with the republican forces, they would be supporting the winning side. The conquest of Natal and the capture of Kimberley would, it was thought, suffice to convince the most doubtful and timid. As soon, therefore, as the British troops in Natal had been overwhelmed and Kimberley occupied, the Boer commandos in the western theatre of war were to move south across the Cape frontier to excite a rising in that colony. A situation would thus be created which, as they calculated, would lead to the intervention of one or more European Powers, and terminate in the permanent expulsion of all British authority from South Africa.

It was with these designs and based on this far-reaching plan

THE OUTBREAK OF THE WAR. 49

of campaign that the mobilisation of the burghers in both the republics was ordered during the last week of September, and by the 11th of October the following was approximately the constitution, strength and distribution of the field forces.* The army for the invasion of Natal was made up of three distinct bodies; the principal and most important of these remained under the personal orders of General P. Joubert, the Commandant-General of the Boer forces, and was concentrated at Zandspruit and Wakkerstroom Nek, in immediate proximity to the northern apex of Natal. It included the Krugersdorp, Bethel, Heidelberg, Johannesburg, Boksburg and Germiston, Standerton, Pretoria, Middelburg, and Ermelo commandos, the Transvaal Staats Artillerie, and small Irish, Hollander and German corps of adventurers; the total strength of this force was about 11,300 men. Its armament included 16 field guns and three 6-inch Creusots. On the eastern border of Natal, facing the British force at Dundee, lay the Utrecht, Vryheid, Piet Retief and Wakkerstroom commandos, under the leadership of General Lukas Meyer; this detachment numbered about 2,870 men. Westward, a Free State contingent, amounting to some 9,500 burghers, and consisting of the Vrede, Heilbron, Kroonstad, Winburg, Bethlehem and Harrismith commandos, occupied Botha's, Bezuidenhout, Tintwa, Van Reenen's, and Olivier's Hoek passes. The republican forces, to whom the task of conquering Natal had been assigned, amounted therefore at the outset of war to about 23,500 men.†

For the attack on Colonel Baden-Powell's small garrison at Mafeking, a body, in strength about 7,000, consisting of the Potchefstroom, Lichtenburg, Marico, Wolmaranstad and Rus-

Distribution Oct. 11th, /99.

For Natal.

For Mafeking.

---

* This statement is based on information obtained from Boer sources during and since the war, but the numbers must only be taken as approximately accurate.

† Reinforcements, amounting in all to about 3,240 men, joined the Boer Natal army during the months November-December; these were made up of 1,300 Johannesburg police and burghers, 290 Swaziland police and burghers and the Lydenburg and Carolina commandos. These reinforcements were, however, counterbalanced by the transfer of detachments of the Free State commandos to the western theatre of war.

50   THE WAR IN SOUTH AFRICA.

tenburg commandos, with a company of Scandinavian adventurers, had been concentrated close to the western border. General Piet Cronje was in supreme command on this side, his two principal subordinates being Generals Snyman and J. H. De la Rey.

<small>For Kimberley.</small>
The capture of Kimberley and the duty of holding in check the British troops at the Orange River station were assigned to Free State levies composed of the Fauresmith, Jacobsdal, Bloemfontein, Ladybrand, Boshof and Hoopstad commandos, the first two of these corps being assembled at Boshof and the remainder at Jacobsdal. Their total strength was probably about 7,500; a Transvaal detachment, about 1,700 strong, composed of the Fordsburg and Bloemhof commandos, was concentrated at Fourteen Streams, ready to join hands with the Free Staters.

<small>For other points.</small>
The Philippolis, Bethulie, Rouxville, and Caledon commandos, under the orders of Commandants Grobelaar, Olivier and Swanepoel, were assembling at Donkerpoort, Bethulie, and a little to the north of Aliwal North for the protection, or possibly destruction, of the Norval's Pont, Bethulie, and Aliwal bridges. These four commandos had an approximate strength of 2,500 burghers. Detachments, amounting in all to about 1,000 men, were watching the Basuto border; on the extreme north of the Transvaal about 2,000 Waterberg and Zoutpansberg burghers were piqueting the drifts across the Limpopo river. A small guard had been placed at Komati Poort to protect the vulnerable portion of the railway to Delagoa Bay, while the Lydenburg and Carolina commandos, about 1,600 strong, under Schalk Burger, watched the native population of Swaziland. Thus, including the police and a few other detachments left to guard Johannesburg, about 48,000 burghers were under arms at the outbreak of war.

<small>Large influence of Baden-Powell on them.</small>
The most remarkable feature of the Boer dispositions is the influence on them of Baden-Powell's contingent. His two little corps, each numbering barely 500 men, had drawn away nearly 8,000 of the best burghers. Mafeking was in itself a place of no strategic value, and, had the enemy been content to watch,

THE OUTBREAK OF THE WAR. 51

and hold with equal numbers, Lt.-Cols. H. C. O. Plumer's and C. O. Hore's regiments and the police and volunteers assisting them, a contingent of 5,000 Transvaalers might have been added to the army invading Natal, thus adding greatly to the difficulties of Sir George White's defence. Alternatively it might have ensured the capture of Kimberley, or might have marched as a recruiting column from the Orange river through the disaffected districts and have gradually occupied the whole of the British lines of communication down to the coast.

The general distribution, therefore, of the Queen's troops in South Africa at the outbreak of war appears, with the exception of the division of the field force in Natal, to have been the best that could have been devised, having due regard to the advantage of the initiative possessed by the enemy, and to the supreme importance of preventing, or at any rate retarding, any rising of the disloyal in Cape Colony. Nevertheless, the situation was one of grave anxiety. The reinforcements which would form the field army were not due for some weeks. Meanwhile, in the eastern theatre of operations, the Boers would have made their supreme effort with all the advantages of superior numbers, greater mobility, and a *terrain* admirably suited to their methods of fighting. A considerable portion of the British troops under Sir G. White were, moreover, mere units, lacking war organisation except on paper, unknown to their leaders and staff, unacquainted with the country, and with both horses and men out of condition after their sea voyage. In the western theatre, the safety of Kimberley and Mafeking mainly depended on the untried fighting qualities of recently enlisted colonial corps, volunteers, and hastily organised town-guards; detachments of regular troops dotted along the northern frontier of Cape Colony were without hope of support either from the coast or each other, and would be cut off and crushed in detail in the case of serious attack or of a rising in their rear. Thus, the initiative lay absolutely with the enemy, and, so far as could be foreseen, must remain in his hands until the British army corps and cavalry division should be ready to take the field about the middle of December.

<small>Anxiety of British situation.</small>

Actual movement of Boers begins.

According to the terms of the ultimatum of October 9th, a state of war ensued at 5 p.m. on the 11th. The advance of the Boer forces destined for the attack of Mafeking and Kimberley began on the following day, and by the 14th both places were cut off from Cape Colony. On the 17th the enemy occupied Belmont railway station. To meet these movements the 9th Lancers, the squadrons of which disembarked at Cape Town from India on the 14th, 15th, and 18th, were sent up to Orange River station immediately on their arrival. The 1st battalion Northumberland Fusiliers were also moved by train on the 15th from De Aar to Orange River, being replaced at the former station by a half-battalion of the 2nd battalion King's Own Yorkshire Light Infantry, which reached Cape Town on the 14th, having been brought with extraordinary swiftness from Mauritius by H.M.S. *Powerful*. The Orange River bridge garrison was further strengthened by two 12-pr. B.L. guns manned by Prince Alfred's Own Cape artillery. The first field artillery to land in Cape Colony, the 62nd and half 75th batteries, were, on the evening of their disembarkation, the 25th, entrained at once for Orange River. The 1st Border regiment, which arrived from Malta on the 22nd, was despatched immediately to De Aar, but subsequently, at the urgent request of Sir George White, was sent by train to East London and re-embarked for Natal. Steps were taken to make the Orange River railway bridge passable by artillery and cavalry, by planking the space between the rails. Meanwhile, on the advice of the local magistrate, Colonel Money, who was in command at Orange River, destroyed Hopetown road bridge, eleven miles to the westward, as it was feared the enemy's guns might cross the river at that point. Raiding parties of the Boers had overrun Bechuanaland and Griqualand West and spread proclamations annexing the former district to the Transvaal and the latter to the Free State. On the eastern side of the colony the enemy made no move, but still hung back on the north bank of the Orange River. The British garrison of Stormberg was reinforced by two naval 12-pr. 8-cwt. guns, accompanied by 357 officers and men of the Royal Navy and Marines, lent from Simon's

THE OUTBREAK OF THE WAR.   53

Town by the Naval commander-in-chief. In the opinion of General Forestier-Walker, this reinforcement made this important railway junction, for the moment, reasonably secure. Three months' supplies had been stored at all the advanced posts.

Two thousand of the Cape volunteer forces* were called out by the Governor on the 16th October and placed at the disposal of the General Officer Commanding the regular troops, on the understanding that they were to be paid and rationed from Imperial funds. These corps were at first employed as garrisons for Cape Town, Port Elizabeth, East London, Queenstown, and King William's Town ; detachments of the Kaffrarian Rifles being also stationed at Barkly East, Cathcart, Molteno, and Indwe ; but by the end of October the Colonial volunteers were drawn upon to furnish military posts on the three lines of railway from the coast, viz. : Touw's River, Fraserburg Road, and Beaufort West, on the western system ; at Cookhouse and Witmoss on the central, and at Molteno and Sterkstroom, on the eastern. Arrangements were made for patrolling the line between these posts by railway employés. Having regard, however, to the great length of these lines, it was obvious that protection of this description, although useful in checking individual attempts to obstruct trains, or destroy bridges and culverts, would be of no value against any armed bodies of the enemy or of rebels.

<small>Cape Volunteers called out.</small>

Thus, in the western theatre of war, although the investment of Kimberley, and, in a lesser degree, the attack on Mafeking, were causes of grave alarm to the loyalists of Cape Colony, yet, from a larger point of view, the forward policy of frontier defence successfully tided over the dangerous weeks previous to the arrival of the first units of the army corps from home.

<small>General success of policy of bluff.</small>

* The corps mobilised were Prince Alfred's Own Cape Field artillery, the Cape Garrison Artillery, the Kaffrarian Mounted Rifles, Prince Alfred's Volunteer Guard, the Duke of Edinburgh's Volunteer Rifles, and the Cape Town Highlanders. The Kimberley and Mafeking corps had been called out before the commencement of the war. Subsequently the Uitenhage Rifles and the Komgha Mounted Rifles were called out on the 10th of November, the Cape Medical Staff Corps was mobilised on the 16th of November, and the Frontier Mounted Rifles on the 24th of November, 1899.

CHAPTER III.

THE THEATRE OF WAR.*

<small>Three chapters dealing with the ground and the two armies engaged.</small>

WHEN the challenge to war, recorded in the first chapter, startled the British people, it met with an immediate response alike in the home islands, and in the Colonies, in India, or elsewhere, wherever they happened to be. In order to understand the problems of no small complexity confronting the statesmen at home and the generals who in the field had to carry out the will of the nation by taking up the gauntlet so thrown down, it is necessary, first, that the characteristics of the vast area which was about to become the scene of operations should be realised; secondly, that the strength of the forces on which the challenger relied for making good his words should be estimated; and, thirdly, that certain peculiarities in the constitution of our own army, which materially affected the nature of the task which lay before both Ministers and soldiers, whether in London or in South Africa, should be recognised. The next three chapters will deal in succession with each of these subjects. The attempt which is here made to portray in a few pages the mountains, the rolling prairies, and the rivers of the sub-continent must be aided by an examination of the map which has been specially prepared in order to make the description intelligible.

<small>General aspect of area.</small>

The tableland of South Africa is some 1,360,000 square miles in extent, and of a mean altitude of 3,000 to 5,000 feet above sea level. To the Indian Ocean on the east it shows a face of scarped mountains. Following the coast-line at a distance inland of

---

* See general map of South Africa, Relief map, No. 2, and map, No. 3.

THE THEATRE OF WAR.

from 70 to 100 miles, these sweep round from north to south: then stretch straight across the extreme south-west of the continent through Cape Colony, dwindling as they once more turn northward into the sand-hills of Namaqualand, and rising again to the eminences above Mossamedes in Portuguese territory. The rampart, however, though continuous for a distance of more than 1,200 miles, scarcely anywhere presents an abrupt wall to the seaboard, but on the contrary descends to it in some parts in one gigantic step, in others in a series of steps, or terraces.

Of the States within it, Cape Colony first claims considera- *Cape Colony: the Karroos.* tion. In the central section the step or terrace formation is so marked, and the flats, which intervene between the rises, are of such extent, and of a nature so curious, that they form one of the most remarkable features of South Africa. They are known as "the Karroos," vast plains stretching northward, firstly as the Little Karroo from the lower coast ranges to the more elevated Zwarte Bergen, thence as the Great Karroo to the still loftier Nieuwveld Mountains. In the rainless season they present an aspect indescribably desolate, and at the same time a formidable military obstacle to any invasion of Cape Colony on a large scale from the north. They are then mere wastes of sand and dead scrub, lifeless and waterless. The first fall of rain produces a transformation as rapid as any effected by nature. The vegetable life of the Karroos, which has only been suspended, not extinguished, is then released; the arid watercourses are filled in a few hours, and the great desert tract becomes within that brief time a garden of flowers. Even then, from the scarcity of buildings and inhabitants, and hence of supplies, the Karroos still form a barrier not to be lightly attempted, unless by an army fully equipped, and carrying its own magazines; or, on the other hand, by a band of partisans so insignificant as to be able to subsist on the scanty resources available, and to disappear when these are exhausted, or the enemy approaches in strength.

The first noticeable feature of the hill systems which bind *Hills above Karroos.* these steppes is their regularity of disposition, and the second, their steadily increasing altitude northwards to that mountain group which, running roughly along the 32nd parallel of latitude, culminates in the Sneeuw Bergen, where the Compass Peak (8,500 feet) stands above the plains of Graaf Reinet. North of these heights, only the low Karree Bergen, about 150 miles distant, and the slightly higher Hartzogsrand, occur to break the monotonous fall of the ground towards the bed of the Orange. All the geographical and strategical interest lies to the north and east of the Compass Peak, where with the Zuurbergen commences the great range, known to the natives as Quathlamba,* but to the Voortrekkers, peopling its mysterious fastnesses with monsters of their imagination, as the Drakensberg.† Throwing out spurs over the length and breadth of Basutoland, this granite series, here rising to lofty mountains, there dwindling to rounded downs, runs northward to the Limpopo river, still clinging to the coast, that is to say, for a distance of over 1,250 miles. The Zuurbergen, the western extremity, are of no great elevation. They form a downward step from the Compass and the Great Winterberg to the Orange river, whose waters they part from those of the Great Fish and Great Kei rivers. The Stormbergen, on the other hand, which sweep in a bold curve round to the north-east until, on the borders of Basutoland, they merge into the central mass, are high, rugged, and pierced by exceedingly few roads, forming a strong line of defence.

Passes. It may be said generally of the Cape highlands that the only passes really practicable for armies are those through which, in 1899, the railways wound upwards to the greater altitudes. These lines of approach to the Free State frontier were as follows :—

1.—THE CAPE COLONY—DE AAR line.
2.—THE PORT ELIZABETH—NORVAL'S PONT line.
3.—THE EAST LONDON—BETHULIE AND ALIWAL NORTH lines.

These were connected by two transverse branches; elsewhere throughout their length they were not only almost completely isolated, but divided by great tracts of pathless

---

* "Piled up and rugged." † "Mountains of the Dragons."

THE THEATRE OF WAR. 57

mountains and barren plains, rendering, except at the points mentioned, or by way of the sea, the transfer of troops from one to the other a difficult process. Therefore the branch lines (1. De Aar—Naauwpoort; 2. Stormberg—Rosmead) had a significance hardly inferior to that of the three ports, Cape Town, Port Elizabeth, and East London. These varied greatly in the facilities they afforded. Table Bay, with its docks, wharves and store-houses, took rank among the great commercial harbours of the world. Port Elizabeth, 430 miles eastward, had no true harbour. Its open roadstead, although frequented by the mercantile marine, was exposed to the dangerous south-east gales prevalent on that coast. At East London, 140 miles yet further eastwards, there was a small although excellent harbour. Its deep basin allowed ocean steamers to moor alongside the railway wharf, but the water area was limited and a sandbank at the mouth of the river Buffalo, which flows in here, barred the approach of vessels exceeding 4,000 tons in burden. On the east coast, Durban, at a distance of 300 miles from East London and 830 miles from Cape Town, formed a satisfactory base. The difficulties of a bar at the entrance to the harbour, similar to that at East London, had been overcome by the energy and enterprise of the colonial authorities. There was no direct communication by land between these four ports, but this was of little consequence to a power holding command at sea.

North of the Stormbergen the Drakensberg range maintains its north-easterly trend continuously until it breaks up in the valley of the Limpopo. Along the eastern Basuto border, from the Natal to the Free State frontiers, its characteristics, which have been always grand, become magnificent. Here it is joined by the Maluti Mountains, a range which, bisecting the domains of the Basuto, and traversing them with its great spurs, has earned for the little state the title of the South African Switzerland. At the junction of the Basutoland, Free State, and Natal frontiers stands Potong, an imposing table-shaped mass, called by the French missionaries Mont Aux Sources, from the fact that it forms the chief water parting between the numerous streams flowing west and east. Further south tower

The northern Drakensberg.

Cathkin (or Champagne Castle), Giants Castle, and Mount Hamilton, the latter within the Basuto border. All these and many lesser peaks are joined by ridge after ridge of rugged grandeur.

<small>Drakensberg passes.</small>

Between the Basuto border and Laing's Nek lies the chief strategic interest of the Drakensberg. Of less elevation than the lofty giants which lie behind it to the southward, this portion still preserves, with a mean altitude of 8,000 feet, the peculiar scenic beauty of the system. From the Basuto border northwards the mountains formed the frontier between Natal and the Orange Free State. They are pierced by a number of passes of which none are easy, with the exception of Laing's Nek, leading into the Transvaal. The best known, starting from the southern extremity of this frontier section, are Olivier's Hoek, Bezuidenhout, and Tintwa Passes at the head-stream of the Tugela river; Van Reenen's, a steep tortuous gap over which the railway from Ladysmith to Harrismith, and a broad highway, wind upwards through a strange profusion of sudden peaks and flat-topped heights; De Beers, Cundycleugh, and Sunday's River Passes giving access by rough bridle paths from the Free State into Natal, abreast of the Dundee coalfields; Müller's and Botha's Passes debouching on Newcastle and Ingogo; and finally Laing's Nek, the widest and most important of all, by which a fair road over a rounded saddle crosses the Drakensberg, the Transvaal frontier lying four miles to the north of its summit. Some of the eastern spurs thrown off from this section of the Drakensberg completely traverse, and form formidable barriers across, Natal. Such are the Biggarsberg, a range of lofty downs running from Cundycleugh Pass across the apex of Natal to Dundee, and pierced by the railway from Waschbank to Glencoe. Further to the south, Mount Tintwa throws south-eastward down to the river Tugela a long, irregular spur, of which the chief features are the eminences of Tabanyama and Spion Kop. This spur, indeed, after a brief subsidence below the last-named Kop, continues to flank the whole of the northern bank of the Tugela as far as the railway, culminating there in the heights of Pieters, and the lofty

THE THEATRE OF WAR. 59

downs of Grobelaars Kloof, both of which overhang the river. East of the railway another series of heights prolongs the barrier, and joins hands with the lower slopes of the Biggarsberg, which descends to the Tugela between Sunday's and Buffalo rivers. Further south still, broad spurs from Cathkin and Giants Castle strike out through Estcourt and Highlands, and connect the Drakensberg with Zululand.

North of Basutoland, the western spurs of the Drakensberg, jutting out on to the Orange Free State uplands, are far less numerous and pronounced than those in Natal, where the mountains dip steeply down towards the sea; but the Versamelberg, the Witteberg, and the Koranaberg further south, although of no great height, are strategical features of importance. *Spurs of Drakensberg.*

Beyond Laing's Nek, the Drakensberg, no longer a watershed, and losing much both of its continuity and splendour, still preserves its north-easterly trend, dropping still further to a mean altitude of between 5,000 and 6,000 feet, and passing under many local appellations, through the eastern Transvaal, until near Lydenburg, it again rises in the Mauch Berg. Along its eastern edge the Drakensberg here descends in the ruggedest slopes and precipices to the plains which divide it from the Lobombo Mountains, a range which, commencing at the Pongola river opposite Lake St. Lucia, runs parallel to the Drakensberg, the two systems inclining inward to coalesce at the Limpopo. South of that river the Lobombo formed throughout its length the eastern frontier of the Transvaal State. *Drakensberg and Lobombo ranges.*

North of the Oliphant river, which pierces both the Drakensberg and Lobombo, the character of the Drakensberg becomes still more fragmentary. Here its most important features are the transverse ridges, or *rands*, thrown off from it in a direction generally south-westerly. Chief amongst these are the Murchison and Zoutpansberg Mountains, which, covering more than 350 miles of the country, unite in the Witfontein Berg in the Rustenburg district. These ridges, though of an elevation of over 4,000 feet above the sea level, rise nowhere more than, and seldom as much as, 1,500 feet above the terrain, and do little to relieve the monotony of the great prairies they *The rands.*

traverse and surround. The same type is preserved by the various low ridges running parallel to and south of them towards the Orange Free State border. One of these is the famous Witwaters Rand, extending from Krugersdorp to Springs, and another the Magaliesberg, a chain of more imposing character, connecting Pretoria and Rustenburg to the north-east, and disappearing in the fertile Marico valley. North of the Limpopo the Drakensberg, though becoming more broken and complicated, still presents a bold front where the great sub-continental plateau descends suddenly northwards to the Zambesi, and eastwards to Portuguese territory, *i.e.*, on the northern and eastern frontiers of Mashonaland. Almost at the junction of these boundaries it is joined by the Matoppo Hills, which rise from the north-eastern limits of Khama's Country, bisect obliquely the region between the Zambesi and the Limpopo, and culminate in Mount Hampden (5,000 feet), near Salisbury.

Rivers Limpopo and Orange.

Passing from the mountains to the great plateau they enclose, the first point to be noted is that its surface is set at two opposite " tilts," the portion north of the Witwaters Rand inclining downward to the east, the other, south of that ridge, to the west. The drainage, therefore, runs respectively east and west, and it is effected by the two great streams of the **Limpopo** and the **Orange**, with their many affluents. The general river system of the central plains is thus of the simplest; the Indian Ocean receives their northern waters, the Atlantic their southern;

The water-parting.

the remarkable factor of the arrangement being that a physical feature so insignificant as the Witwaters Rand should perform the function of water-parting for a region so gigantic.*

Course of Limpopo.

The Limpopo, or Crocodile river, rises as a paltry stream in the Witwaters Rand between Johannesburg and Pretoria, and flows into the Indian Ocean, 80 miles north of Delagoa Bay, covering in its course fully 1,350 miles.

Course of Orange.

The Orange has three distinct sets of headstreams from

* There are, of course, in South Africa numerous minor and local watersheds (*e.g.*, the Drakensberg, where they initiate the drainage of Natal in an easterly direction, and the mountains of southern Cape Colony, which send some of her rivers southward to the Indian Ocean). These have been necessarily almost disregarded in so general a survey of the sub-continent as that aimed at in the present chapter.

the western flank of the Drakensberg, and a total length of 1,300 miles. From the Basuto border to Ramah, on the Kimberley railway, about 220 miles, it divided the Orange Free State from Cape Colony. The Orange receives on its right bank its greatest affluent, the Vaal, which is between 500 and 600 miles in length. Commercially, both the Orange and the Vaal are as useless as their smallest tributary, being entirely unnavigable at all times of the year. Raging floods in the wet season, and mere driblets in the dry, they are at present denied to the most powerful or shallowest of river steamboats. The prospects of the Orange river as a potential waterway are in any case practically destroyed by a great bar which blocks approach to the estuary from the sea.

The streams of the South African plateau, whether river, spruit, sluit, or donga, have, in addition to their extreme variability, another marked and almost universal peculiarity. Running in deep beds, of which the banks are usually level with the surrounding country, and the sides terraced from the highest to the lowest water-mark, they constitute natural entrenchments which are generally invisible, except where rarely defined by a line of bushes, and, owing to the dead uniformity of the surrounding country, are almost impossible to reconnoitre. Nor, in 1899, were their defensive capabilities lessened by the dearth of bridges, by the dangers of the drifts, and by the absence of defined approaches to all crossing-places away from the main roads. The "drifts," or fords, especially rendered the laying out of a line of operations in South Africa a complex problem. Their depth varied with the weather of the day; they were known by many names even to local residents, and were of many types; but all alike were so liable to sudden change or even destruction, that any information concerning them, except the most recent, was practically useless. *Military character of streams of S. A.*

To comprehend broadly the salient physiological features of a region so enormous as South Africa, the causes of the climatic influences which affect them must be understood. These causes are simplicity itself. The warm winds blow from the east, and the cold from the west; the former, from the warm Mozambique *Effect of winds on climate.*

current, skirting the eastern seaboard, the latter, from the frigid Antarctic stream, setting from south to north, and striking the western coast about Cape St. Martin. It follows, therefore, that the climate and country become more genial and fertile the further they are removed from the desiccating influence emanating from the western seaboard. The dreariness of the solitudes between Little Namaqualand and Griqualand West, the latter slightly more smiling than the former, attests this fact. But the comparative inhospitality of the Boer States—comparative, that is, to what might be expected from their proximity to the warm Indian Ocean—demands further explanation. From the Atlantic to the eastern frontiers of these States no mountain ranges of any elevation intervene to break the progress of the dry, cold breezes; from the mouth of the Orange river to the Drakensberg the country is subject almost uninterruptedly to their influence. But it is not so with the milder winds from the east. The great screen of the Drakensberg meets and turns them from end to end of South Africa; no country west of this range profits by their moisture, whereas the regions east of it receive it to the full. Hence the almost tropical fertility of Natal and eastern Cape Colony, with their high rainfall, their luxuriance of vegetation, indigo, figs, and coffee, and the jungles of cactus and mimosa which choke their torrid kloofs. Hence, equally, the more austere veld of the central tableland, the great grass wildernesses, which are as characteristic of South Africa as the prairies and the pampas of America, and, like them, became the home and hunting-ground of a race of martial horsemen. Agriculture, following nature, divides the veld into three parts, the "High," "Bush," and "Low" Velds; but it is the first and greatest of these which stamps the central tableland with its peculiar military characteristics. Almost the whole of the Orange Free State, and the Transvaal east of the Natal railway, are High Veld, which may be taken to mean any grassland lying at an elevation of about 4,000 feet, upon which all vegetation withers in the dry season, while in spring and summer it is covered with nutritious herbage. The Low Veld lies properly between longitude 31° and the tropical eastern

The velds.

THE THEATRE OF WAR.

coast; while the Bush Veld is usually understood to mean the country lying between the Pretoria-Delagoa railway and the Limpopo river. The terms, however, are very loosely used. The Low Veld differs widely from the High Veld. Upon the former is rich—almost rank—vegetation and pasture flourishing throughout the year. But the climate is hot, moist, and unhealthy; and the Boer farmers, forced by the course of the seasons to drive their flocks from the sparkling, invigorating air of the uplands to the steamy lowlands, were wont to take the task in turn amongst themselves, as an unpleasant one to be performed as seldom as possible.

The High Veld of the Transvaal differs slightly from that of the Free State in appearance. It is more broken and undulating; the range of vision, at times apparently boundless in the southern state, is rarely extensive, except from the summit of a kopje, being usually bounded by the low ridge-lines of one of those great, gentle, almost imperceptible, rolls of the ground which are a feature of the Transvaal veld, and with its hidden watercourses, its peculiar tactical danger. A mountain range is seldom out of sight; and, speaking generally, the Transvaal may be said to be less sombre than the southern or western districts of the great plateau. *Transvaal High Veld.*

If the veld can only be compared with the sea, the kopjes which accentuate, rather than relieve, its monotony resemble in quite as marked a degree the isolated islands which rise abruptly from the waters of some tropic archipelago. Sometimes, indeed, the kopjes form a rough series of broken knolls, extending over a space of several miles, as, for instance, the ridges of Magersfontein and Spytfontein, between Kimberley and the Modder; sometimes a group of three or four, disposed irregularly in all directions, become a conspicuous landmark, as at the positions of Belmont and Graspan; and it is not uncommon to find larger masses, not less irregular, enclosing the river reaches which their drainage has created, among which may be enumerated the heights south-east of Jacobsdal, and by the river Riet, and those about Koffyfontein and Jagersfontein on the same stream. *The kopjes.*

But, as a rule, the kopje of the veld is a lonely hill, a mass of igneous rock—flat-topped or sharp-pointed. From 200 to 800 feet in height, without spur or under-feature, accessible only by winding paths among gigantic boulders, sheer of face and narrow of crest, it is more useful as a post of observation than as a natural fortress; for it can almost always be surrounded, and the line of retreat, as a general rule, is naked to view and fire.

So far as tactical positions are concerned, any force on the defensive upon the veld of the Boer States must be mainly dependent on the rivers. Yet the spurs of the Drakensberg, blending in a range of ridges, form a mountain stronghold admirably adapted for guerilla warfare; and all along the Basuto border, at a distance of from 10 to 20 miles west of the Caledon, stands out a series of high, detached hills, which form a covered way along the eastern boundary of the Free State, crossing the Orange, and leading into the recesses of the Stormberg Mountains.

For every wavelet of land upon the surface of the Boer States, a hundred great billows stand up in Natal. Kopje succeeds kopje, all steep, and many precipitous, yet not the bare, stony cairns of the transmontane regions, but moist green masses of verdure, seldom parched even in the dry season, and in the wet, glistening with a thousand cascades; not severely conical or rectangular, like the bizarre eminences which cover Cape Colony with the models of a school of geometry, but nobly outlined. Many of the foothills, it is true, are mere heaps of rock and stone; but even these are rarely such naked and uncompromising piles as are found on the higher levels. Even where northern Natal occasionally widens and subsides to a savannah, as it does below the Biggarsberg, and again south of Colenso, the expanse, compared with the tremendous stretches of the Boer veld, is but a meadow.

As a theatre of war South Africa had one advantage, that it was for the most part eminently healthy. Enteric fever, the scourge of armies, was bound to be prevalent amongst thousands exposed to hardships in a country where the water supply was indifferent, where sanitation was usually primitive amongst the inhabitants, and impossible to improvise hurriedly. But

THE THEATRE OF WAR.

the purity of the air, the geniality of the temperature, the cool nights, the brilliant sunshine, and the hard dry soil were palliatives of evils inseparable from all campaigning. Otherwise, for regular armies of invasion, South Africa was unfavourable. The railways were so few that the business of supply and movement was always arduous; spaces so vast that large forces were swallowed up; the enormous distances from one strategical point to another, intensified, in difficulty by the almost entire absence of good roads, the scarcity of substantial bridges, of well-built towns, of commodious harbours, and of even such ordinary necessaries as flour or fuel, all these complicated every military problem to a degree not readily intelligible to the student of European warfare alone.

It is not easy to sum up briefly the typical qualities as a fighting area of a region so vast and diversified as South Africa; but its dominant feature is undoubtedly the great central plateau comprising southern Rhodesia, all the Transvaal, except a narrow fringe on the eastward, the Bechuanaland Protectorate, the Orange Free State, and the northern and central portions of Cape Colony. Westward this tableland slopes gradually and imperceptibly to sea level; to the south it reaches the Atlantic in the series of terraces and escarpments already described. Eastward it is shut in by the Drakensberg, whose spurs, projecting to the Indian Ocean, traverse at right angles Natal, Zululand, Swaziland, and Portuguese East Africa. *The central plateau.*

Upon the central South African plateau tactical and strategical success is dependent upon rapid manœuvring. Positions are so readily turned that they can seldom be resolutely held. It is difficult, therefore, to bring an evasive enemy to decisive action, and the fruits of victory must chiefly be plucked by pursuit. The horse is as important as the man, and the infantry arm is reduced to the position of a first reserve, or to the rôle of piquets on the lines of communication, which remain always open to attack. Superior numbers and, above all, superior speed, are irresistible. There are no first-class physical obstacles; the rivers, excepting only the Orange and the Vaal, are, as a rule, fordable; the hill features for the most *Effect on operations of plateau,* part insignificant or easy to mask. Mobility is thus at once the chief enemy and aid to military success.

and of lower spurs.

But on the stairway descending from the south of this plateau, and on the spurs reaching up from the coast on the east, all this is reversed. The approach of an army acting on the offensive, uphill or across the series of ridges, is commanded by so many points, that a small number of defenders can readily arrest its advance. Position leads but to position, and these, prolonged almost indefinitely on either flank, are not readily turned, or, if turned, still offer locally a strong frontal defence, should the enemy be sufficiently mobile to reach them in time. Streamlets, which would be negligible on the plateau, become formidable obstacles in their deep beds. The horseman's occupation is greatly limited, for he can neither reconnoitre nor gallop. Marches must, therefore, be made painfully in battle formation, for every advance may entail an action. Thus strategy is grievously cramped by the constant necessity for caution, and still more by the tedious movements of the mass of transport, without which no army can continue to operate in a country sparsely inhabited, and as sparsely cultivated.

Variety of rainfall.

In South Africa even the rainfall militates against concurrent operations on a wide scale, for, at the same season of the year, the conditions prevalent upon one side of the sub-continent are exactly the opposite to those obtaining on the other. In the western provinces, the rainy season occurs in the winter months (May—October), in the eastern, including the Boer States, the rain falls chiefly in the summer (October—March). Yet so capricious are these phenomena that a commander, who counted absolutely upon them for his schemes, might easily find them in abeyance, or even for a period reversed.

Variety of S.A. climate.

Beyond the broad facts stated above, the extent of South Africa renders it as impossible to specify any typical climatic or scenic peculiarities common to the whole of it, as to fix upon any strategical or tactical character that is universal. Cape Colony alone exhibits such antitheses of landscape as the moist verdure of the Stormberg and the parched dreariness of Bushman and Little Namaqua Lands, and a rainfall ranging from

THE THEATRE OF WAR.

two to seventy-two inches per annum. The variations in other parts are little less striking. The temperature of the High Veld, for instance, is wont to rise or fall no less than sixty degrees in twelve hours, or less. Thus, whilst one portion of an army on a wide front might be operating in the tropics, another might be in the snows, whilst a third was sheltering from the sun by day, from the frost by night, conditions which actually obtained during the contest about to be described. What effect such divergencies must exercise on plans of campaign, on supplies of clothing, shelter, food, forage, and on military animals themselves, may be readily imagined.

CHAPTER IV.

THE BOER ARMY.

<small>Many previous cases compare with Boer resistance.</small>

ANY force of irregulars which offers a prolonged resistance, not unmarked by tactical successes, to a regular army of superior strength is apt to be regarded as a phenomenon. Yet, from the earliest times, history has shown how seasoned troops may be checked by an enemy who is inferior in numbers, discipline and armament, but possessed of certain counterbalancing resources, due either to the nature of his country, to his own natural characteristics, or to a combination of both.* Of such resources the Boers at the close of the nineteenth century possessed, largely by inheritance, a full share. With their forefathers, the early Afrikanders, loneliness had been a passion to which their very presence north of the Orange river was due. Flying from society, from burdens and responsibilities which they considered

<small>Inherited faculties.</small>

intolerable, from pleasures which seemed to them godless, from a stir which bewildered them, and from regularity which wearied them, they had penetrated the wilds northward in bands as small as possible, each man of which was wrapped in a dream of solitude, careless whither he went so long as he went unseen. It troubled these pioneers little that they were plunging into a sea of enemies. Society, with its conventions and trammels, and most of all, perhaps, with its taxes, was the only enemy whom they feared, the only one they could never escape. But before it caught them up, their combats with corporeal foes

---

* *E.G.*, the revolt of La Vendée, the resistance of the Maories, the Red Indians, the Achinese, the Montenegrins, of the Trans-Indus Highlanders, of Andreas Hofer's Tyrolese, of Shamyl's Caucasians.

THE BOER ARMY. 69

were incessant and deadly. Wild beasts prowled round their herds; savages swooped upon their homesteads; all animated nature was in arms against them; every farmhouse was a fortress, usually in a state of siege. In the great spaces of the wilderness the cry for help was but seldom heard, or if heard, only by one who had his own safety to look to. The Boer farmer of the forties, therefore, had to work out his rescue, as he worked out every other problem of his existence, for himself, acquiring thereby, a supreme individuality and self-reliance in the presence of danger. He acquired also other characteristics. The fighting men of his nation were few in number; every mature life was little less valuable to the State than it was to the homestead whose existence depended upon it. The burgher's hope of injuring his enemy was therefore subordinated to solicitude for his own preservation, and he studied only safe methods of being dangerous. Even when in later days the Boer expeditionary bands, reclaiming to the full from the blacks the toll of blood and cruelty which had been levied on themselves, were more often the attackers than the attacked, their aggression was always tempered by the caution of the individual Boers, who would still forego a chance of striking a blow should it contain an undue element of hazard. The republican warriors relied, indeed, less on attack than on defence. They trusted yet more to that weapon, perfected by many small races which have been compelled to work out their own methods of warfare, the weapon of evasion. Nearly always outnumbered, never sure of victory, the burghers always provided, then kept their eyes continually upon, a loophole of escape, for if that were closed they felt themselves to be lost. These characteristics, with many more which will be noted, the early Boer bequeathed to his sons and grandsons; a legacy so strangely composed that many of the very qualities which brought temporary victory to the campaigners of 1899 foredoomed them to ultimate defeat.

Self-reliance and individuality are factors of extraordinary military importance under any conditions, but especially under circumstances involving such dispersion of combatants, such distances between commanders and commanded, as were brought *Value of these in present warfare.*

about by the conjunction of long-range arms, an open terrain and the clearest atmosphere in the world. South Africa was a country which gave the freest play to the deadly properties of small-bore rifles. The new weapons fitted into the Boer's inherited conceptions of warfare as if they were a part for which his military organisers had long been hoping and waiting. He had an antipathy to fighting at close quarters, but he knew the value and necessity of striking; the Mauser enabled him to strike at the extreme limit of vision, multiplying tenfold the losses and difficulties of the enemy who attempted to close with him. The portability of the ammunition, the accuracy of the sighting, the absence of betraying smoke, all these increased the Boer's already great trust in himself, and he took the field against the British regular infantryman with more confidence than his sires had felt when they held their laagers against the Zulu and the Matabele. The modern rifle, moreover, still further increased his self-reliance by rendering avoidance of close combat, which alone he feared, a much simpler matter than hitherto. His father had escaped the bayonets of the British at Boomplaats; he himself was no more willing or likely to be caught by the steel fifty years later, when he could kill at two thousand yards instead of two hundred, or failing to kill, had hours instead of minutes in which to gain his pony and disappear. Yet the long-range rifle had improved his weapon of retreat until it had become a danger instead of an aid to his cause. Failing so completely to understand the military value of self-sacrifice, that he actually pitied, and slightly despised it, when he saw it resorted to by his enemies, his refusal to risk his life often proved disastrous to his side at times when more resolution might have turned the scale of battle in his favour.

There was much to be admired in the Boer defensive; up to a certain point it was stubborn and dangerous. The musketry from a position, poured upon zones of ground over which the British troops must pass rather than upon the troops themselves, was heavy and effective, and not easily quelled by bombardment. In battle, artillery may do its work without causing a casualty; but so long as he had cover for his body, the soul of the Boer rifleman was little shaken by the bursting of projectiles; fierce firing came often from portions of a position which appeared to be smothered by shrapnel, and invisible in the reek of exploding lyddite.

Nor did the Boer armies, as regular armies have done, cling to strong positions simply because they were strong. They considered a position as a means to an end, and if it ceased to be the best, they discarded it without hesitation, no matter with what toil it had been prepared. Nevertheless, on ground of their own choosing, the abandonment without a shot of strong, laboriously entrenched, positions by no means always meant retirement. Much as they dreaded being enveloped, their flanks, or what would have been the flanks of an European army, might be threatened again and again only to be converted each time into new and formidable fronts. The nature of the country, and the comparative mobility of the opposing forces rendered these rapid changes of front easy of execution, but they demanded promptness, and a genius for the appreciation of the value of ground, not only on the part of the Boer leaders, but also on that of the rank and file. In the ranks of the commandos persuasion had to take the place of word of command; the Boer soldier, before he quitted one position for another, had to be convinced of the necessity for a repetition of the severe toil of entrenching which had apparently been wasted. But his eye was as quick, his tactical and topographical instinct as keen as those of his commander, and if the new dispositions were not selected for him, he often selected them himself. *Special habits of fighting.*

Once on the ground the burghers' first care was to conceal themselves quickly and cunningly, cutting deep and narrow entrenchments, if possible upon the rearward crest, leaving the forward crest, of which they carefully took the range, to the outposts. Upon the naked slope between, which was often obstructed with barbed wire, they relied to deny approach to their schanzes. A not uncommon device was the placing of the main trench, not at the top, but along the base of the position. Here the riflemen, secure and invisible, lay while the hostile artillery bombarded the untenanted ridge lines behind *Their defences: strong points.*

them. Such traps presented an enhanced danger from the fact that the Boers would rarely open fire from them until the front of the attack was well committed, though, on the other hand, they seldom had nerve or patience to withhold their musketry until the moment when it might be completely decisive. As regards the Boer artillery, its concealment was usually perfect, its location original and independent, its service accurate and intelligent. Dotted thinly over a wide front, the few guns were nevertheless often turned upon a common target, and were as difficult to detect from their invisibility, as to silence from the strength of the defences, in the case of the heavy ordnance, and in the case of the lighter pieces, from their instant change of position when discovered.

A weakness in defence.

Nevertheless, with all these virtues, the Boer defensive, by reason of the above-mentioned characteristics of the individual soldiers, was no insurmountable barrier, but only an obstacle to a determined attack. Many of the positions occupied by the Republicans during the campaigns seemed impregnable. Prepared as skilfully as they had been selected, in them some troops would have been unconquerable. But at the moment when they must be lost without a serried front, the reverse slopes would be covered with flying horsemen, whilst but a handful of the defenders remained in the trenches. Nor, except on the feeblest and most local scale, would the defenders at any time venture anything in the nature of a counter stroke, though the attack staggered, or even recoiled, upon the bullet-swept glacis, and victory trembled in the balance.

A weakness in attack.

If the Boer defensive was force passive, their general attack became force dissipated as soon as it entered the medium rifle zone. Excessive individuality marked its every stage, the thought of victory seldom held the first place. In the old days, when an assault had to be attempted, as at Thaba Bosigo and Amajuba, it had been the custom to call for volunteers. But when President Kruger pitted his burghers against large armies, this expedient was no longer available; instead of a few score such affairs required thousands, and they were not forthcoming. The desire to close, the only spirit which can compel decisive

THE BOER ARMY.

victory, entered into the Boer fighting philosophy even less than the desire to be closed with; the non-provision of bayonets was no careless omission on the part of their War department. During an assault the Commandants might set, as they often did, a splendid example of courage, but they could never rely on being followed to the end by more than a fraction of their men. The attack, therefore, of the Boers differed from that of a force of regulars in that it was never made in full strength, and was never pushed home; and from that of the Afghans, Afridis or Soudanese in that there was no strong body of spectators to rush forward and assure the victory half won by the bolder spirits in front. Their attack was, in consequence, little to be feared, so long as the defence was well covered from the incessant rifle fire which supported and accompanied it; for none but a few gallant individuals would ever venture to close upon a trench or sangar whose defenders yet remained alive behind it. Both in attack and defence, therefore, the Boer army lacked the last essentials to victory.

It was in the warfare of the partisan that the Boer excelled, As partisans. in the raid on a post or convoy, the surprise and surrounding of a detachment, the harassing of the flanks and the rear of a column, and the dash upon a railway. Their scouting has not often been excelled; their adversaries seldom pitched or struck a camp unwatched, or marched undogged by distant horsemen. How little the Boer generals and Intelligence department knew how to utilise the fruits of this constant watchfulness will be fully shown elsewhere, but the lack of deductive power on the part of the leaders detracts nothing from the unwearied cunning of their men.

The combinations of scattered bands at a given rendezvous Use of for a common purpose were not seldom marvellous, effected ground. as they often were by rides of extraordinary speed and directness by night, when the men had to feel with their hands for the goat and Kaffir tracks if astray, but rarely astray, even in the most tangled maze of kopjes, or, still more wonderful, on the broadest savannah of featureless grass. With the Boer, direction had become a sense; not only were topographical features, once seen, engraved indelibly on his memory, but many which would be utterly invisible to untrained eyes were often detected at once by inference so unconscious as to verge on instinct. He knew "ground" and its secrets as intimately as the seaman knows the sea, and his memory for locality was that of the Red Indian scout.

Mixed qualities.

Thus the Boer riflemen possessed many of the characteristics of the same formidable type of irregular soldier as the backwoodsmen of America or the picked warriors of the Hindustan border. Yet an exact prototype of qualities so contradictory as those which composed this military temperament is not to be recalled. No fighting men have been more ready for war, yet so indifferent to military glory, more imbued with patriotism, yet so prone to fight for themselves alone, more courageous, yet so careful of their lives, more lethargic, or even languid by nature, and yet so capable of the most strenuous activity. Such were the Boers of the veld. In one particular they had never been surpassed by any troops. No Boer but was a bold horseman and a skilled horsemaster, who kept his mount ready at any moment for the longest march or the swiftest gallop, in darkness, or over the roughest ground. In camp the ponies grazed each one within reach of its master; in action every burgher took care that his perfectly trained animal stood, saddled and bridled, under cover within a short run to the rear. In remote valleys great herds of ponies, some fresh, some recouping their strength after the fatigues of a campaign, roamed at pasture until they should be driven to the front as remounts.

Mobility.

The unrivalled mobility of the Boer armies, therefore, and the vastness of its theatre of action, gave to them strength out of all proportion to their numbers. A muster roll is little indication of the fighting power of a force which can march three or four times as fast as its opponent, can anticipate him at every point, dictating the hour and place of the conflict, can keep him under constant surveillance, can leave its communications without misgivings, and finally, which can dispense with reserves in action, so quickly can it reinforce from the furthest portions

THE BOER ARMY.

of its line of battle. Yet in this particular again, the Boers' constitutional antipathy to the offensive robbed them of half their power. They employed their mobility, their peculiar strength, chiefly on the defensive and on tactics of evasion, often, indeed, resigning it altogether, to undertake a prolonged and half-hearted investment of some place of arms. Amongst their leaders there appeared some who did all that was possible, and much more than had seemed possible, with a few hundreds of devoted followers. But the Republics possessed no Sheridan. Men who foresaw that in this mobility might lie the making of a successful campaign, that the feats of the raider might be achieved tenfold by large well-mounted armies, were missing from their councils.

Organisation. The Boer forces which took the field in 1899 were composed of two divisions :—

       (I.) The Burgher Commandos.
       (II.) The Regular Forces.

Of the former the whole male population, black and white, between the ages of sixteen and sixty, formed the material,* the "Wyk" or Ward, the lowest electoral unit, the recruiting basis. Upon the Field Cornet, the chief officer of a Ward, elected by its votes for a term of three years, devolved many responsibilities besides the civil duties of collecting the taxes, administering the law, and maintaining order in his small satrapy. He was also the sole representative of Army Headquarters. One of the most important of his functions was that of compiling the registers of burghers liable to war service.†

Field cornet. It was his business, moreover, to see that each man of his levy took the field with clothing, rifle, horse and ammunition in

---

* Exemptions similar to those which obtain in European schemes of universal service were sanctioned by the military law of the Boer Republics.

† These lists were of three kinds, comprising :—
       (I.) Youths under 18 and men over 50.
       (II.) Men between 18 and 34.
       (III.) Men between 34 and 50.
In the event of war, Class II. was first liable to service, then Class III., and, as a last resort, Class I.

76   THE WAR IN SOUTH AFRICA.

good and serviceable order; and if, as was rarely the case, means of transport were insufficiently contributed by the burghers themselves, to provide them by commandeering from the most convenient source. The whole military responsibility, in short, of his Ward fell on him; and though the men he inspected annually were rather his neighbours than his subordinates, their habitual readiness for emergencies smoothed what, in most other communities, would have been the thorniest of official paths, and rendered seldom necessary even the mild law he could invoke.

Ward levy.

The first acts of the Ward levy at the rendezvous were to elect an Assistant Field Cornet and two or more Corporals, the former to serve their commander during the campaign, the latter to serve themselves by distributing rations and ammunition, and supervising generally their comfort in laager, by performing, in fact, all the duties performed by a section commander in the British infantry except that of command.

The commando and commandant.

The Field Cornet then rode with his burghers to the meeting-place of the commando, usually the market town of the District. There a Commandant, elected by the votes of the District, as the Field Cornet had been by those of the Ward, assumed command of the levies of all the Wards, and forthwith led them out to war, a Boer commando.

A nation in arms.

Thus, at the order to mobilised, the manhoo of the Boer Republics sprang to arms as quickly, as well prepared, and with incomparably more zeal than the best trained conscripts of Europe. Not urged to the front like slaves by the whips of innumerable penalties, their needs not considered to the provision of a button, or a ration of salt, shabby even to squalor in their appointments, they gathered in response to a call which it was easy for the laggard to disobey, and almost uncared for by the forethought of anyone but themselves.

Defects of system.

In so far, therefore, as it applied to the actual enrolment and mobilisation of the commandos, the military system of the Boer Republics appeared well-nigh perfect. Yet it had radical and grievous defects, and these, being in its most vital parts, robbed it of half its efficiency. The election of military officers

THE BOER ARMY. 77

by the votes of the men they were destined to command would be a hazardous expedient in the most Utopian of communities; it was doubly dangerous with a people trained in habits formed by the accustomed life of the Boers in the nineteenth century. Its evil effects were felt throughout their armies. Officers of all grades had been selected for any other qualities than those purely military. Property, family interest, and politics had often weighed more heavily in the balance than aptitude for command. In the field the results were disastrous. Few of the officers had sufficient strength of character to let it be seen that they did not intend to remain subject to the favour which had created them. The burghers were not slow to profit by the humility of their superiors. Jealous of their democratic rights, conscious of their own individual value in a community so small, the rank and file were too ignorant of war to perceive the necessity of subordination. Especially were these failings of leaders and led harmful in the Krijgsraads, or Councils of War, which, attended by every officer from corporal upwards, preceded any military movement of importance. Since most of the members owed their presence to social and civic popularity, sound military decisions were in any case not to be expected. Moreover, as the majority of the officers truckled to the electorate which had conferred upon them their rank, it followed that the decisions of a Krijgsraad were often purely those of the Boer soldiers, who hung on its outskirts, and did not scruple, when their predilections were in danger of being disregarded, to buttonhole their representatives and dictate their votes. Finally, there were not wanting instances of unauthorised Krijgsraads being assembled at critical junctures, avowedly in mutinous opposition to a lawful assembly, and actually overriding the latter's decision.

In Boer army doubly dangerous.

There was, however, discipline of a theoretical kind in the commandos. Two authorised forms of Courts-Martial existed to deal with offences committed on active service. But Courts-Martial were an empty terror to evil-doers. They were rarely convened, and when they were, the burgher of the close of the nineteenth century knew as many methods of evading the

Forms of discipline.

stroke of justice as did his father of escaping the stalk of a lion or the rush of a Zulu spearman.

<small>Uncertain number of units.</small>

A serious defect inherent in this military system was the inequality of the strength of the units created by it. A commando was a commando, of whatever numbers it consisted ; and these, contributed by districts greatly varying in population, ranged from 300 to 3,000 men. Thus the generals, placed in command of forces composed of many commandos of which they knew nothing but the names, were ever in doubt as to the numbers of men at their disposal, a difficulty increased tenfold by the constantly shifting strength of the commandos themselves. Straggling and absenteeism are evils incident to all irregular or hastily enrolled armies, however drastic their codes of discipline, or however fervent their enthusiasm ; with the Boers these maladies were prevalent to an incredible degree. Many and stringent circulars were promulgated by the Boer Presidents to cope with this disastrous source of weakness. But one and all failed in their object, from the impotence of the officers whose duty it was to enforce them, and at every stage of the campaign many more than the authorised 10 per cent. of the fighting line were absent from their posts.

<small>Untrained staff.</small>

If such were the faults of the machine, those of the motive power were not less glaring. No provision had been made in peace for the training of men for the duties of the Staff. At Pretoria, the Commandant-General, forced to reign alone over the twin kingdoms of administration and command, had not unnaturally failed to govern either. The chain of authority between Commander-in-Chief and private soldier, a chain whose every link must be tempered and tested in time of peace, was with the Boers not forged until war was upon them, and then so hurriedly that it could not bear the strain. When prompt orders were most needed, there was often no one to issue them, no one to carry then, or, even if issued and delivered, no one present who could enforce them. Nor were the ramifications of departmental duty, which, like arteries, should carry vitality to every portion of the army, of any more tried material. In

THE BOER ARMY. 79

most existing departments there was chaos; many that are indispensable did not exist at all.

The service arms of the burgher forces were the Mauser ·276 rifle and carbine. Arms.

The exact number of Mauser rifles brought into the Boer States is, and will probably be always, uncertain. At least 53,375 can be accounted for, of which 43,000 were imported by the Transvaal and the remainder by the Orange Free State, the latter drawing a further 5,000 from the stores of the sister Republic. These, with approximately 50,000 Martini-Henry and other rifles known to have been in the arsenals and in possession of the burghers before the commencement of hostilities, made up over 100,000 serviceable weapons at the disposal of the two countries.* Ammunition was ample, though, again, it is idle to discuss actual figures. Neither the stock in the magazines, nor that in the possession of the farmers, was for certain known to any man. The most moderate of the Republican officials in a position to form a credible estimate placed it at seventy millions of rounds; it was more probably nearer one hundred millions. The Boer farmer, still uncertain of security in the outlying solitudes of the veld, still unaccustomed to it in the more frequented districts, never wasted ammunition even though a use for it seemed remote. He hoarded it as other men hoard gold; for deeply rooted in him was the thought, sown in the perilous days of the past, that cartridges, with which to preserve the lives of himself and his family, might at any moment become of more value than gold pieces, which could only give to life the comfort he somewhat despised. Thus

---

* The following is a fairly accurate estimate in detail :—

Mausers	53,375
Martini-Henry	35,875
Westley-Richards	9,780
Guedes	6,049
Lee-Metfords	2,850
Krag-Jörgensen	200
	108,129

Besides the above, there were about 6,000 Webley pistols in store.

the arsenals of the larger towns were not the only, or even the chief, repositories of small-arm ammunition. Every farm was a magazine; lonely caves hid packets and boxes of cartridges; they lay covered beneath the roots of many a solitary tree, beneath conspicuous stones, often beneath the surface of the bare veld itself. Whatever were the actual amounts of arms and ammunition at the disposal of the Republican riflemen, it was plain they were not only adequate but extravagant. There was significance in the excess. The Boers possessed sufficient munitions of war to arm and equip 30,000 or 40,000 men over and above their own greatest available strength. It will be seen in due course for whose hands this over-plus was designed.

Rifle practice.

The Republican Governments had not been satisfied with the mere issue of arms. As early as 1892 in the Transvaal, and 1895 in the Orange Free State, rifle practice, at the periodical inspections of arms and equipment, called Wapenschouws, had been made compulsory for the burghers. For these exercises ammunition was provided free, and money appropriated from the State funds for prizes. Every effort, in short, was made to preserve the old skill and interest in rifle-shooting, which it was feared would vanish with the vanishing elands and gemsbok. If the skill had diminished, the interest had not. A rifle had at all times an irresistible fascination for a Boer. The Bedouin Arab did not expend more care upon his steed of pure Kehailan blood, nor the mediæval British archer upon his bow, than did the veld farmer upon his weapon. Even he who kept clean no other possession, allowed no speck of dirt on barrel or stock. On the introduction of the new rifles, not only had shooting clubs sprung up in all quarters, but, in aiding them with funds, ammunition, and prizes, the Republican authorities, before they disappeared, had given at least one lesson to Governments, that of fostering to the utmost any national predilection which may be of service to the State.

THE REGULAR FORCE.

Regular forces of similar, it not identical, composition were authorised by the constitutions of both Republics, consisting in

THE BOER ARMY.

the Transvaal of artillery and police, and in the Free State of artillery only. These differed in no respects from similar units of any European organisation, being raised, equipped, officered, instructed, and paid in the ordinary manner, and quartered in barracks or forts.

The regular forces of the Transvaal consisted of :— Regulars.

    (a) The State Artillery.
    (b) The South African Republic Police.
    (c) The Swaziland Police.

The State Artillery of the South African Republic was as Artillery. complete and efficient a unit as any of its kind in existence. Originally incorporated with the Police at the inception of both in 1881, it was re-organised on a separate footing in 1894, in which year it also first saw active service against Malaboch in the Blue Mountains. At this time the strength of the Corps was but 100 gunners, 12 non-commissioned officers and 7 officers. After the Jameson Raid, however, the force was quadrupled and reorganised; the field and fortress departments were differentiated, larger barracks built, and steps taken generally to ensure the greatest possible efficiency and readiness for instant service, the avowed object of the Government being to make the Corps " the nucleus of the military forces of the Republic."* The only qualifications necessary for the 300 additional men required by the scheme were citizenship, either by birth or naturalisation, age not to be less than 16, and the possession of a certificate of good conduct from the Field Cornet. Service was for three years, with the option of prolongation to six years, after which followed a period of service in the reserve until the age of 35 was reached.†

---

* Law of Reorganisation, 1896.

† Pay of Officers of the State Artillery :—

Commandant	£700 per annum.
Major	600 ,,
Captain	500 ,,
First Lieutenant	350 ,,
Second Lieutenant	275 ,,

All ranks received a horse from the Government, a special board supervising the purchase.

Military courts.

For the maintenance of discipline the Corps had three Military Courts of its own, whose powers extended from detention to death. They differed in no way from similar tribunals in the British army save in one respect, that convicted prisoners had a right of appeal from a lower Court to that above it. Drill was on the German model, but the language was Dutch. The Boer gunners were ready pupils, having much the same natural aptitude for the handling of ordnance as is observable in British recruits. Only 20 rounds per gun were allowed for the yearly target practice.

Artillery divisions.

The State Artillery was divided into the following principal departments :—†

    (a) Field Artillery.
    (b) Fortress Artillery.
    (c) Field Telegraph.

Artillery weapons.

At the date of the outbreak of hostilities the modern armament of the field artillery was as follows :—

6 Creusot Q.F. 75 m/m (about 3 inches), supplied with 11,009‡ rounds.
4 Krupp Howitzers 120 m/m (4·7-in.), supplied with 3,978 rounds.
8 Krupp Guns Q.F. 75 m/m, supplied with 5,600 rounds.
21 Vickers-Maxim (pom-pom) 37·5 m/m (about 1½ inches),

and issue of remounts. Rations and uniforms were also free issues, and on a most generous scale to officers and men alike.

The pay of non-commissioned officers and men was as follows :—

Warrant Officers	£180 and £150 per annum.
Farriers and Sergeants	6s. 6d. a day.
Corporals	5s. 6d. ,,
Gunners	5s. 0d. ,,

† There were in addition an Intendance Service, Medical, Educational, Farriery, and Artificer staffs, and a band of 20 performers; all maintained in a high state of efficiency.

‡ During the war about 26,000 projectiles of various patterns were manufactured in Johannesburg. Both at that place and at Pretoria an immense amount of manufacturing and repairing of war material was effected, including the making of a new 120 m/m Howitzer and the shortening of a 6-in. Creusot.

THE BOER ARMY.

supplied with 72,000 rounds (14,000 pointed steel, 58,000 common).

4 Vickers Mountain Guns 75 m/m. Ammunition not known.
4 Nordenfeldts 75 m/m, supplied with 2,483 rounds.
1 Armstrong 15-pr. Ammunition not known.
1 Armstrong 12-pr. Ammunition not known.

In addition to this the field artillery possessed 12 Maxims for ·303 rifle ammunition, and 10 for the ·450 Martini-Henry. For the latter 1,871,176 rounds of nickel-covered ammunition were in store. The total modern armament of the field artillery, therefore, capable of service in the field, was—excluding the 22 Maxims—49 pieces. The following more or less obsolete weapons were also in charge of the Corps:—

4 Krupp Mountain Guns, 65 m/m.
6 7-pr. Mountain Guns.
3 5-pr. Armstrong Guns.

The personnel of the field artillery was, on a peace footing, 12 officers and 394 N.C.O.s and men, but in the field this was found to be very inadequate, and was eked out by the incorporation of volunteers from the commandos.* {Manning of artillery.}

The fortress artillery had 9 officers and 151 N.C.O.s and men, but, like the field artillery, drew many willing helpers from the burgher ranks. Its armament consisted of:—

4 Creusot 155 m/m (about 6 inches),† supplied with 8,745 rounds.
6 Hotchkiss 37 m/m on parapet mounting, supplied with 3,663 rounds.
1 Mortar 150 m/m. Ammunition not known.
1 Howitzer 64-pr. Ammunition not known.

Besides these, a few guns of odd and mostly obsolete patterns,

---

* As many as thirty-nine ordinary burghers were noticed doing duty with a battery in action.

† The 6-in. Creusots were of somewhat peculiar construction, having narrow iron wheels, not at all promising the mobility which the Boers attained from them. The shell weighed 94 lbs., charge 20 lbs. black powder, bursting charge for shrapnel 5 lbs. melinite. Recoil was absorbed pneumatically.

including three Krupp, were on the books of the Fortress department.

The third division of the State Artillery, the field telegraph section, comprised 2 officers and 65 N.C.O.s and men.

The State Artillery of the Transvaal, to sum up, was (excluding Maxims) armed with 61 effective and about 20 semi-effective weapons, manned by a personnel of about 800 men (including reservists).

THE POLICE.

The Police, Transvaal.

The Transvaal Police consisted of two bodies :—

(a) The South African Republic Police.
(b) The Swaziland Police.

The former, whose *sobriquet* of "Zarps" war made more famous with the British than peace had rendered it infamous, numbered some 1,200 whites and 200 blacks under 13 officers and 64 non-commissioned officers. In peace time they were stationed chiefly in Johannesburg, with detachments at Pretoria, Krugersdorp, and a few outlying stations. Qualifications for service were an age of 21 years, with burgher rights by birth, and the term for three years, with subsequent yearly renewals.

The S.A.R. Police, who were a purely regular force, were divided into foot and mounted organisations of about 800 and 500 respectively. They were thoroughly drilled, their fire discipline being on the most approved German model. Their rigid training, however, had apparently robbed them of much of the individual initiative which safeguarded the persons and lost the battles of their less educated compatriots in the ranks of the commandos.

Police, Swaziland.

The Swaziland Police were a small body of some 300 white and black men, commanded by eight officers and 27 of non-commissioned rank. Their formation was much more that of an ordinary commando than that of the Europeanised "Zarps," and, in fact, from the commencement of the war, they operated as a wing of the local commando.

THE BOER ARMY.

REGULAR FORCES OF THE FREE STATE.

These consisted of artillery only, numbering some 375 men (including 200 reservists), and possessed of the following armament :—* *Free State Regulars.*

- 14 Krupp Guns 75 m/m, with 9,008 rounds.
- 5 Armstrong Guns 9-pr., with 1,300 rounds.
- 1 Krupp Q.F. 37 m/m. Ammunition not known.
- 3 Armstrong Mountain Guns 3-pr., with 786 rounds.
- 3 Maxim Guns.

With all furniture and wagons complete.

The Corps was by no means so thoroughly organised as the artillery of the Transvaal. There was no division into batteries, the guns being entrusted to the care of any commando which "liked to have a gun with it."† Yet there was considerable *esprit de corps* amongst the gunners, who maintained their material, as well as their discipline, in surprisingly good order considering the lack of officers, and the general slovenliness of their surroundings. The conditions of service for the men were the same as those which obtained in the Transvaal Corps. *Inferior organisation.*

The Corps also possessed a small but efficient telegraph section. The barracks, at Bloemfontein, compared most unfavourably with the fine buildings which housed the Transvaal artillery at Pretoria.

NUMBERS OF THE BOER FORCES.

Figures of exact accuracy are, and must be for ever, unobtainable, for none of the data from which they could be compiled were either precisely recorded, or can be remembered. The Field Cornets' books, and consequently the State lists, of those liable to service were all alike full of errors and discrepancies. The statistical machinery of the Republics, too primitively, and it may be added too loosely, managed to be equal to the work of even a complete census in time of peace, made no attempt to cope with the levy which crowded around the Field Cornets *Uncertainty of Boer figures.*

---

* Three Krupp and three Maxims were on order in Europe, but were not delivered in time to reach the Free State capital.

† Boer Account.

in every market place at the issue of the Ultimatum in October, 1899. Muster rolls of even those actually and officially present in the field do not exist. Only one leader in either Republican army ventured to call a roll of his command, and the loud discontent of the burghers, scandalised at the militarism of the proceeding, did not encourage other officers to follow his example.

Total engaged.

The estimate, however, of 87,365, has been arrived at after the collation of so much independent testimony, that it may be taken as fairly accurate.*

The grand total does not, of course, represent the number of men in the field at any one time. It is an estimate of the numbers of all who bore arms against the British troops at any time whatever during the campaign. The Boer army numerically was the most unstable known to history,† varying in strength as it varied in fortune in the field, varying even with the weather, or with that mercurial mental condition of which, in irregular forces, the numbers present at the front best mark the barometer. Those numbers, even in the heroic stages of the campaign, ranged from about 55,000 men to 15,000, with every intermediate graduation. It is impossible to trace the vicissitudes of an army which lost, regained, then lost again fifty per cent. of its strength within a week. Nor is a periodic enumeration of vital military interest. With the Boers the numbers actually present in the fighting line were not, as with European troops, the measure of their effective force. For the Boer, whether as absentee at his farm, or wandering demoralised over the veld, was often little less a portion of the strength of his side than his comrade who happened to be lying alert in a shelter trench at the same moment. He intended to fight again ; and instances were not wanting of parties of burghers, thus deserting their proper front, being attracted by the sound or the news of fighting in a totally different direction, and riding thither to form a reinforcement, as little expected upon the new battle ground by their friends as by their enemies.

* See Appendix 4.

† The armies during the war between North and South in America ran it close in this respect.

CHAPTER V.

THE BRITISH ARMY.

EVERY army necessarily grows up according to the traditions of its past history. Those of the Continent having only to cross a frontier, marked by Royal, Imperial or Republican stones, have, in their rare but terrible campaigns, to pursue definite objects that can be anticipated in nearly all their details years beforehand. The British army, on the contrary, throughout the nineteenth century, since the great war came to an end in 1815, has had to carry out a series of expeditions in every variety of climate, in all quarters of the globe, amidst the deserts of North Africa, the hills, plains and tropical forests of South Africa, the mountains of India, the swamps of Burma, or the vast regions of Canada. Such expeditions have been more numerous than the years of the century; each of them has differed from the other in almost all its conditions. Amongst its employments this army has had to face, also, the forces of a great Empire and troops armed and trained by Britain herself. Accordingly, it has happened that the experience of one campaign has almost invariably been reversed in the next. To take only recent illustrations, the fighting which was suitable for dealing with Zulu warriors, moving in compact formations, heroic savages armed with spears or assegais, was not the best for meeting a great body of skilled riflemen, mounted on well-managed horses. Moreover, the necessary accessories of an army, without which it cannot make war, such as its transport and its equipment, have had to be changed with the circumstances of each incident. Just as it has been impossible to

Various employments of British Army.

preserve throughout all its parts one uniform pattern, such as is established everywhere by the nations of the Continent, so it has not been possible to have ready either the suitable clothing, the most convenient equipment, or the transport best adapted for the particular campaign which it happened to be at the moment necessary to undertake. More serious than this, and more vital in its effect on the contest about to be described, was the fact that the services thus required continually of British troops prevented the formation of larger bodies of definite organisation in which the whole staff, needed to give vitality and unity to anything more than a battalion or a brigade, was trained together. For such wars as those in Egypt, or for the earlier wars in South Africa, in Canada, or in many other countries, it was much more practical to select for each enterprise the men whose experience suited them for the particular circumstances, and form staffs as well as corps of the kind that were needed, both in strength and composition, for that especial work. This was a very serious disadvantage, when it came to be necessary to make up a great host, in which not a certain number of battalions, batteries, and cavalry regiments had to be employed, but in which ultimately a vast organisation of 300,000 men, many of whom were entirely new to army life, had to be brought into the field. It is one thing for the army corps of a great Continental State, in which everyone has been practising his own special part precisely as he will be engaged in war, to march straight upon its enemy in its then existing formation, and it is quite another to draw together a staff formed of men, each of them experienced both in war and peace, none of whom have worked together, while few have fulfilled the identical functions which they have to discharge for the first time when bullets are flying and shells are bursting. It will so often appear in the course of this history that the operations seriously suffered, because the necessary links between a general in command and the units which he has to direct were inadequate, that it is only fair to the many officers of excellent quality who were employed on the staff that the nature of this comparison should be clearly appreciated. It was no fault of theirs, but a

THE BRITISH ARMY. 89

consequence of that past history which had built up the British Empire, that they had neither previously worked together, nor practised in peace time their special part in an organisation which had, in fact, to be created anew for the immediate task in hand.

When the war began, and when there were in South Africa, as already narrated, 27,054 troops,* there nominally stood behind them, if all those who were armed and equipped throughout the British Empire be included, more than a million men. These were of every religion, of many colours, types and classes. On the 28th July, 1899, the Prime Minister had made for the kingdom a self-denying declaration by which one vast body of these forces was eliminated from the campaign. He announced that none but white soldiers would be employed by us. Of white men, 67,921 were in India, 3,699 in Egypt, 7,496 in Malta, 5,104 in Gibraltar, 738 in Barbados, 570 in Jamaica, 1,599 in Canada, 1,896 in Bermuda, 962 in Mauritius, 1,689 in China and Hong Kong, and 1,407 in the Straits Settlements. Even these are only examples of the nature of the duties on which the great mass of the British army was employed. They are chiefly interesting, because the proportion between the 67,921 men and the millions of the subject races of India, between the 3,699 men and the vast regions throughout which they maintained order under the sway of the Khedive, suggests to how fine a point had been carried the doing of much with mere representatives bearing the flag and little more. The extent of territory, the numbers of possible enemies, the vastness of the interests which the 1,689 men in China and the 1,407 men in the Straits Settlements had to watch, are perhaps, to those who realise the geography, almost as significant. Always it had been assumed that, if at any time some addition was necessary to reinforce these far extended outposts of Empire, it was to be provided from the regular army stationed at home. Up to the year 1888 no official declaration had ever been made of the purposes for which the home army was to be used. In that year Mr. Stanhope issued the necessarily often mentioned

The total forces of Empire.

* See Chap. I., p. 2.

memorandum, which declared that, though it was highly improbable that so large a force would ever be required, yet two army corps, with a cavalry division, or a total of 81,952 men, were to be available for the purposes of action beyond the seas. As will be seen from the chapter on the work of the Navy, it was only in the year 1899 that the Admiralty, who necessarily would have to transport whatever strength was thus employed, became aware for the first time that the War Office would need shipping for more than one army corps. The British army has had more, and more varied, service during the nineteenth century than any other in the world. It undoubtedly included more officers and men, who had experienced what it meant to be under fire, than any other. But these experiences had all been gained in comparatively small detachments, and each was so unlike that of any other, that it was practically impossible that those trainings by service, which are much more efficient in their influence on the practical action of an army than any prescriptions, should be uniform throughout it. At the same time, this had given both to officers and men a habit of adapting themselves to unexpected incidents which may perhaps, without national immodesty, be said to be unique. In the year 1870 what is known as the short service system had been introduced. Under that system there were, in 1899, in the British Islands, 81,134 reservists available to be called up when required for war, retained only by a small fee. The principle on which the scheme was worked at the time was this : that as soon as the army was ordered to be mobilised all those men who had not completed their training in the ranks, or had not yet reached the age for service abroad, were relegated to depôts ; their places were taken by the trained men from the reserve, and out of the excess numbers of the reservists and the men who gradually each month in succession completed their training, a supplementary reserve to maintain the cadres of the army in the field was created. Inevitably, as the numbers ultimately employed in this case far exceeded the two army corps for which alone provision had been made, these supplies of men only lasted for the first twelve months ; but as long as they did so, the waste of

Short service.

THE BRITISH ARMY.

war was compensated to an extent such as never has been known in our campaigns before, and hardly in those of any other Power except Japan, who appears to have borrowed our methods exactly for her great struggle with Russia.

At the time of Kruger's ultimatum of October 9, 1899, the British regular army was composed as follows :—

	Officers.	Warrant, Non-Commissioned Officers, and men.	
Cavalry	780	18,853	Regulars.
Royal Horse and Royal Field Artillery	660	18,855	White troops.
Royal Garrison Artillery*	775	20,103	
Royal Engineers	962	7,323	
Infantry	4,362	144,103	
Army Service Corps	240	3,858	
Army Ordnance Department and Corps	227	1,433	
Royal Army Medical Corps	831	2,876	
Army Pay Department and Corps	205	582	
Army Veterinary Department	131	—	
	9,173	217,986	

TOTAL, all ranks 227,159.

These were all white troops; but it is essential that their distribution over the surface of the globe should be realised. The remarks which have been made as to the special cases quoted could easily, with slight modification, be shown to apply in practically every instance. *Their dispersion.*

There were, including troops on the seas, on 1st October, 1899 :—

Aden (Naval base)	1,092
South Africa (Naval base at Simon's Bay)	22,179
West Africa (Naval base at Sierra Leone)	138
Barbados	738
Bermuda (Naval base)	1,896
Canada (Naval bases at Esquimault and Halifax)	1,599
Ceylon (Naval base at Trincomalee)	1,402
China (Naval base at Hong Kong)	1,689
Crete	1,628
Cyprus	116

* Not including Royal Malta Artillery, 833 of all ranks.

Egypt	3,699
Gibraltar (Naval base)	5,104
Jamaica	570
Malta* (Naval base)	7,496
Mauritius (Naval base)	962
St. Helena (Coaling station)	211
Straits Settlements (Naval base at Singapore)	1,407
Particular Service	47
India (less garrison of Aden)	67,921
United Kingdom (exclusive of Reserves)	108,098
	227,992

White Officers with natives. This total does not include the white officers employed with native troops, who numbered in all 1,814. The functions of these, however, will be best understood when the figures which follow have been considered, and the yet greater area of the earth's surface covered by those who served under the British flag has been taken into account. They are not matters for an appendix, but for the close study with a map of every adult and every child in the realm.

Total strength and dispersion. The effective strength of the armed land forces of the British Empire (exclusive of the Royal Marines, but inclusive of local colonial naval contingents for harbour defence), in September–October, 1899, was :—

	Officers.	Other ranks.	All ranks.	
Regular Army (European) on Oct. 1st, 1899.				
With Colours	9,173	217,986	227,159	
Reserves	1,803	81,134	82,937	
Royal Malta Artillery	31	802	833	
Regular Army (Colonial Corps, European Officers, Native Troops)	233	7,798	8,031	
				318,960
Regular Army of India.				
With Colours (European Officers, Native Troops)	1,460	171,216	172,676	
Reserves	—	18,644	18,644	
				191,320
Hyderabad Contingent.				
(Officered by Europeans)	121	7,386	7,507	7,507
Imperial Service Troops.				
(A few European Officers)	—	18,289	18,289	18,289

* Includes Royal Malta Artillery.

THE BRITISH ARMY.

	Officers.	Other ranks.	All ranks.	
Auxiliary Troops of the United Kingdom.				
Militia	3,036	106,515	109,551	
Yeomanry	654	9,460	10,114	
Volunteers	8,020	215,901	223,921	
Honourable Artillery Company	39	497	536	
				344,122
Indian Volunteers	—	—	29,219	29,219
Indian Military Police	—	—	30,284	30,284
Channel Isles Militia	150	3,278	3,428	3,428
Malta Militia	60	1,755	1,815	1,815
Cyprus Police	26	731	757	757
Canada :				
Local regular troops	91	936	1,027	
Militia	2,398	28,463	30,861	
Police (including 92 Newfoundland)	105	1,191	1,296	
Naval Forces	50	472	522	
				33,706
Australasia :				
New South Wales.				
Local regular troops	49	876	925	
Militia	228	3,815	4,043	
Volunteers	97	2,724	2,821	
Reserves	111	1,535	1,646	
Police	—	—	1,977	
Naval Forces	39	576	615	
				12,027
Queensland.				
Local regular troops	22	265	287	
Militia	198	2,801	2,999	
Volunteers	50	758	808	
Cadets	—	—	875	
Police	—	—	869	
Rifle Clubs	—	—	2,520	
Naval Forces	—	—	584	
				8,942
South Australia.				
Local regular troops	3	31	34	
Militia	72	625	697	
Reserves	40	529	569	
Police	—	—	349	
Rifle Clubs	—	—	1,003	
Naval Forces	—	—	120	
				2,772

THE WAR IN SOUTH AFRICA.

	Officers.	Other ranks.	All ranks.	
Tasmania.				
Local regular troops	2	20	22	
Volunteers	88	1,696	1,784	
Cadets	8	250	258	
Police	—	—	60	
				2,124
Victoria.				
Local regular troops	24	349	373	
Militia	158	2,867	3,025	
Volunteers	110	1,598	1,708	
Naval Forces	—	—	286	
				5,392
West Australia.				
Local regular troops	15	261	276	
Volunteers	46	883	929	
				1,205
New Zealand.				
Local regular troops	11	277	288	
Volunteers	330	6,368	6,698	
Naval Forces	30	682	712	
				7,698
Fiji.				
Volunteers	19	189	208	
Police	16	143	159	
				367
Cape Colony.				
Local regular troops	38	1,028	1,066	
Volunteers	186	3,486	3,672	
Cadets	—	—	2,000	
Police	—	—	1,401	
Mounted Rifle Clubs	64	997	1,061	
				9,200
Natal.				
Volunteers	112	1,489	1,601	
Cadets	—	—	1,062	
Police	—	—	659	
Naval Forces	6	116	122	
				3,444
Rhodesia.				
Protectorate Regt. (raised by Col. Baden-Powell) / Rhodesian Regt. / British South Africa Police	92	2,387	2,479	2,479
Zululand.				
Police	—	—	500	500
Basutoland.				
Police	—	—	260	260

THE BRITISH ARMY. 95

	Officers.	Other ranks.	All ranks.	
Bechuanaland Protectorate.				
Police	14	190	204	204
West Indies.				
Militia	23	574	597	
Volunteers	122	1,845	1,967	
Police	54	2,924	2,978	
				5,542
Falkland Isles.				
Volunteers	3	78	81	81
Colonies in Asia.				
Local regular troops (Malay State Guides)	9	623	632	
Volunteers	93	1,556	1,649	
Police	47	2,881	2,928	
				5,209
St. Helena.				
Volunteers	4	51	55	55
West Africa.				
Local regular troops	219	4,196	4,415	
Volunteers	11	187	198	
Police	40	2,202	2,242	
Naval Forces	15	87	102	
				6,957
GRAND TOTAL		..	..	1,053,865

EAST AND CENTRAL AFRICA.

The local troops serving in Uganda, British East Africa, British Central Africa, and Somaliland, are not given. The aggregate area of these Protectorates is nearly four times that of Great Britain. The majority of their inhabitants were, and still are, but semi-civilised or wholly savage, and internal order has often to be maintained by serious fighting. In 1899 the force included three and a half battalions, but as it was then in process of reorganisation into one corps, the "King's African Rifles," its precise strength at that time cannot now be ascertained.

CHAPTER VI.

THE NAVY IN THE BOER WAR.*

SECTION I. THE GENERAL WORK OF THE NAVY.

THE duty of the Navy in this, as in all war was :—

(1) To acquire and keep the command of the sea.

(2) To undertake, by full use of our great mercantile marine, all sea transport.

(3) To carry out the instructions of Government for stopping the enemy's supplies by sea.

(4) To render any local or temporary assistance to the Army that circumstances might require.

<small>Command of sea.</small>

<small>Transport.</small>

<small>Stopping supplies.</small>

During the Boer War the command of the sea was never disputed, so that it gave rise to no anxiety after the first few months. The second duty, that of transport, at once assumed extreme importance owing to the 6,000 miles distance of the base of operations (Cape Town) from England, the large number of men and animals, and the great quantity of stores to be dealt with. The third duty, involving the much disputed matter of contraband, etc., was, and is always likely to be, a difficult one, owing to the rather nebulous state of International Law on questions which were likely to, and did arise, and to the many interests, belligerent and neutral, which might be involved. It was further complicated by the fact that the enemy possessed no seaport and no carrying trade of his own, so that all goods for him from over sea had to be landed either at a neutral port or in a British colonial port. The fourth duty, that of local

* For vessels serving on the Cape station during the war, see Appendix 5.

THE NAVY IN THE BOER WAR.

assistance, was a simpler matter. Owing to causes recorded elsewhere, the armed forces of Great Britain in South Africa were not anything like adequate for the task before them when the war broke out on October 9th, 1899. The grave differences that existed between England and the Dutch Republics, and the absolutely vital British interests involved, had, as the year 1899 wore on, been realised not only by the Government, but by all the world. It was inevitable that the delay in strengthening the garrison, due to extreme unwillingness to present even the appearance of forcing on the quarrel, should throw an exceptional responsibility on the Navy. It became necessary to develop to the utmost limit the strength that could be spared for work on shore in order to gain time for the arrival of reinforcements. Happily our public services, both civil and military, have grown up in the traditions that each branch and department, while it has special grooves in which its own particular duty runs, is at all times on the look-out to help any other department. The Navy and Army are no strangers to this practice of mutual aid. Their special duties have in times past so often led to each helping the other in some way, that perhaps there exists between them in a rather special degree that feeling of comradeship which is engendered by sharing the same duties and the same perils and hardships; just as boys who have gone through the same mill at school, and got into and out of the same scrapes together, are undoubtedly imbued with an *esprit de corps* which is often a valuable possession in after-life.

SECTION II. SEA TRANSPORT.

The Army Sea Transport work was carried out by the Admiralty through its Transport department, with the following exceptions. Arrangements for the Indian contingent, the Remounts, and all else sent from India, were made by the Director of Indian Marine, for the outward voyage; by the Admiralty for the return voyage. For the Colonial contingents, passage was provided partly in freight ships locally engaged by the Colonial Governments and partly in Admiralty transports sent from the

Cape. The return voyage in all cases was regulated by the Admiralty. Remounts (horses) from ports abroad were conveyed in freight ships hired by the Remount department up to February, 1901; after that date they were conveyed by the Admiralty. Stores from ports abroad were delivered in South Africa by the contractors, from whom the War Office obtained them at "C.I.F." rates; that is to say, that the price which was paid for the stores included delivery. All other sea transport for men, animals, and stores was organised by the Admiralty. The services of the Admiralty shipping agents (Messrs. Hogg and Robinson) were utilised as regards stores, but these agents worked under the supervision of the Admiralty Transport department.

"Freight" and "transport" ships.

As the terms used above, " freight ships " and " transports," will frequently recur in this chapter, it is necessary to give an explanation of their meaning and of the distinction between them. Troops are carried either in a transport or a freight ship. A transport is a vessel wholly taken up by the Government on a time charter. A freight ship is one in which the whole or a portion of the accommodation is engaged at a rate per head, or for a lump sum for a definite voyage. For a single voyage, freight, when obtainable, is generally cheaper. But owners will not always divert their ships under other than a time charter, and it is necessary that the bulk of the engagements for the conveyance of troops should be on time charter in order to secure control over the ships. Transports, when continuously employed and utilised both ways, are cheaper than freight ships. Under the transport charter the vessel, though engaged for a named period certain, is at the disposal of the Admiralty so long as the Government choose to retain her, except when it is expressly stipulated otherwise.

Govt. sea transport.

The method by which the Government carries out the sea transport of the Army is as follows :

The Board of Admiralty, as agents for, and on the requisition of, the Secretary of State for War, undertakes all this work, except coastwise conveyance in the United Kingdom.

Office method.

Since 1st April, 1888, Army Sea Transport has been always

THE NAVY IN THE BOER WAR.

charged to Army instead of to Navy Votes; but the control of the Admiralty over the Transport service remains unimpaired. The Admiralty has always held that the work can be efficiently and satisfactorily carried out only by an Admiralty department, in connection with similar work for the Navy. For convenience sake the Director of Transports is placed in direct communication with the War Office as to all ordinary matters. An officer of the Quartermaster-General's department visits the Transport department frequently in peace time, and in war time he is placed at the Admiralty to assist the Director of Transports in military questions. All claims chargeable to Army Votes, after examination in the Transport department, receive, before they are passed to the War Office for payment, the concurrence of Army examiners, who visit the Admiralty daily. The Director of Transports is responsible for the whole work; administration, claims and accounts, custody of Army Transport stores, such as troop-bedding, horse-gear, etc., etc. The system by which one department does the work, while another provides for the cost, seems somewhat anomalous. But the experience of the Boer War, in which it was put to a test of some magnitude, has conclusively proved that it works well. That experience has, moreover, fully shown the necessity of the Sea Transport service remaining as it always has been, under the control of the Admiralty.

Ever since 1876 the Transport department has been organised in such a manner as to be ready to ship a considerable force oversea at short notice. The office establishment, both clerical and professional, was intended to be a sufficient nucleus to admit of rapid expansion in time of war. Full particulars of all ships suitable for the conveyance of men and animals were kept recorded in special books. A stock of troop-bedding, horse fittings, etc., etc., was kept in the Government depôts, and standing contracts for putting these fittings in place, etc., were in existence. Arrangements had been made with the Director of Victualling and the War Office respectively for the food supply of the troops to be embarked, and for the forage of the horses. Stocks of printed forms ready for issue to the transports

Transport department at work.

were also kept in hand. All calculations were based on the understanding that the Admiralty would not be called upon to convey much more than an army corps without due warning. Bedding and horse fittings (of the old kind) for 55,000 men and 10,000 horses were immediately available. Moreover, a committee had recently met to provide for an increase of the stocks in hand in consequence of information from the War Office that two army corps could be ready to go abroad if required.

<small>Time needed</small>

In August, 1899, the Director of Transports was asked how long it would take to despatch 49,000 men and 8,000 horses. His reply was that in the then state of the labour market, four to five weeks would be required. Tentative enquiries of this kind, and the evidently critical state of affairs in South Africa, had led the Transport department, as early as July, to make for eventualities every preparation that was possible within the department—such as conferring with contractors, marine shipping superintendents, etc., and having all troop-bedding and hammocks washed and overhauled, so that on receipt of any definite instructions work might be commenced within an hour.

<small>23rd Sept./99 First grant.</small>

On the 23rd September, 1899, the Secretary of State for War authorised the expenditure of £25,000. This included money for a new pattern of horse fittings which had been approved. On the same date came a requisition for the conveyance of 7,000 mules from various foreign ports. On 20th September the Quartermaster-General had sent to the department a list giving details of the force proposed to be embarked if it should become necessary. This list showed ports of embarkation, and on receipt of it the Admiralty, without waiting for formal requisition, and on their own responsibility, decided to engage two large vessels of the Union-Castle Steamship Company, and to hold them in readiness, and this was done.* Also on their own initiative the Admiralty issued that same evening confidential circulars to thirty-five leading shipowners, asking what ships now ready, or to be ready shortly, they were prepared to place at Government disposal for use as troop-trans-

* It is impossible, of course, to engage a ship beforehand without incurring expenditure.

THE NAVY IN THE BOER WAR.

ports, etc., for two months certain, asking for a reply the following day.

On 30th September there was a conference at the War Office, at which the Admiralty was represented, and verbal authority was then given to the Director of Transports to engage vessels for the conveyance of the force. It was there stated by the Commander-in-Chief (Lord Wolseley) that the troops would not be ready to begin embarking before the 21st October. That same night, 30th September, twenty vessels were engaged from those of which particulars were given in the replies already received; and from that time the work of engaging and preparing the vessels proceeded continuously. Immediately, additions were made to the professional and clerical staff, and more office accommodation was provided at the Admiralty. On the 9th October, 1899, an official requisition was received for the conveyance of 46,000 men and 8,600 horses, and a notice that 24,000 of the men and 4,000 horses would be ready to embark between the 21st October and the 25th October. By the middle of November this whole force was embarked.

Ships engaged Sept. 30/99.

A certain amount of time (ten to twelve days) and money (£2,000 to £5,000, according to the kind of ship) is required to fit a vessel for carrying either troops or animals after she is empty of cargo. The vessel having been selected (sometimes even while she is still at sea), has to be surveyed in order to decide details of the work necessary, and also in order to obtain the Board of Trade's passenger certificate if she is to carry men. Troops and horses cannot be carried in ready-fitted accommodation. The space ordinarily devoted to cargo or cattle is appropriated, and the requisite accommodation built up. In the best cavalry ships, which are generally cattle ships adapted, saloon and cabin accommodation has to be increased. This is done at the owner's expense as part of the bargain. Height between decks is an important factor. Even more height is required for horses than for men. Ships otherwise good often have to be rejected for failure in this respect. Mounted troops always travel men and horses together. The men are for sanitary reasons placed on a deck below the horses. In such cases the

Time for fitting up.

horses are not, as a rule, carried on exposed decks. This is both for the sake of the horses and because the deck space is required for exercising the men. For remount and mule freight-ships the exposed decks are utilised, unless the nature of the voyage renders it undesirable.

<small>Provision for horses.</small>

Horses must be carried either on wooden or wood-sheathed decks, or on cemented decks, or on platforms over metal decks with the gangways cemented. For men, in all cases, the decks must be wood or wood-sheathed. As modern vessels, other than passenger ships, usually have steel decks, this becomes a considerable item in the time and cost of fitting. It is also frequently necessary to cut such extra side-lights as are essential for carrying men or horses. Extra lighting, ventilation and distilling apparatus, mess tables, stools, and provision for men's hammocks must all be obtained. Latrines have to be built, as well as a prison, a hospital, and the numerous store-rooms and issue-rooms that are required. Horse stalls have to be fitted, and sometimes even an extra deck has to be laid. A considerable number of horse stalls are kept at the Government depôts, and the contractors who work for the Government are bound to be ready to fit up a certain number of transports at short notice. For this war the stock of horse fittings in hand was only utilised to a small extent, as it had been decided, a short time before the war broke out, to adopt a longer stall (eight feet) without horse hammocks, instead of the existing six feet six inches stall with hammock. There is no doubt that the new fitting was a great improvement.

<small>"Transports." Mode of fitting up.

"Freight" ships. Different method.</small>

Transports are always fitted at the expense of Government. The work is done either by (a) contractors who hold a standing contract, (b) special supplementary contractors, or (c) the owners on behalf of the Government. Freight ships, on the contrary, are fitted by the shipowners, the cost being covered by the rate per head, whether they take troops or animals. Horses in freight ships were provided with the long stall under a modified specification. The fittings on these ships were often required for one voyage only, whereas in the transports they were used again and again. Mules were in all cases placed in pens. These held, as a rule, five mules, and no detailed specifications were necessary. Trade fittings were accepted if satisfactory to the shipping officer. In all ships carrying animals, whether transports or freight ships, spare stalls to the extent of five per cent. were allowed to provide for sick animals and for shifting the animals for cleaning purposes.

Hospital Ships.—Eight transports in all were fitted up as hospital ships. Two, the *Spartan* and *Trojan*, each of about 3,500 tons gross, were prepared in England for local service at the Cape. The other six, ranging from 4,000 to 6,000 tons gross, were infantry transports converted at Durban, as they were required, for bringing sick and wounded from the Cape to England. All were equipped in concert with the Army Medical Officers, in accordance with plans which had been found suitable on previous expeditions. All ordinary fittings were cleared out, and the ship was arranged in "wards," with special cots; operating rooms, laundries, ice room, special cooking appliances, radiators for warming, punkahs and electric fans, cot lifts, and everything else that medical science suggested, were added.

These ships were not officially declared under the Geneva Convention and did not fly the Red Cross flag, as they were occasionally employed during the return voyage for the conveyance of combatants. Besides these eight vessels there were available the *Maine*, lent by the Atlantic Transport Company, and most generously and at great cost fitted out and maintained by the American Ladies' Committee, who spared no time, trouble, or expense in making her most efficient and comfortable. Their kindly action will not soon be forgotten by the officers and men who benefited by her, by their immediate friends, or by the British nation. There was also the *Princess of Wales*, similarly sent out by the Central Red Cross Society, to whom much gratitude was naturally felt. H.M. Queen Alexandra, then H.R.H. the Princess of Wales, took special interest in the equipment of this vessel.

It will be seen, therefore, that no ships exist which can be

Not a ship available at once.

utilised for sea transport without extensive adaptation and alteration. It is perhaps hardly realised generally how much work has to be done both by Government and the shipowner before a transport can be ready for sea. In addition to all that has been described the ship must be docked and her bottom coated with anti-fouling composition, and she must be ballasted as needed. Boats, awnings and crews, efficient services of fresh and salt water, and provision against fire, have to be secured, and before any of the work can be started the ship herself must be definitely engaged.

Animals.—The units to be employed in the war were not carried by sea complete with their transport animals. The cavalry and artillery were accompanied by their horses, but nearly all the transport animals were taken direct to South Africa from ports abroad. Remounts and mules from abroad were conveyed by freight ships at rates per animal, which included forage, attendance, horse-gear and fittings, and all expenses.

Stores.—It was decided from the first not to utilise the spare space in the transports for conveying stores, because on arrival it might well be that the stores were urgently required at the first port, while the troops were wanted elsewhere with equal urgency. This would have led to delay and confusion. Moreover, if the cargo could not be at once received, the transport would be hampered in her movements and inconvenience and expense would follow. Stores from England were therefore carried in freight ships, either in full cargo ships engaged at a lump sum, with special terms for varying ports and demurrage, or in the regular liners at rates per ton.

Infantry and mounted troops.

For infantry, passenger ships or large fast cargo boats are selected. The latter are preferred as the former require more extensive alterations. Mounted troops are usually carried in ships specially designed for the conveyance of live stock; remounts and mules in similar vessels, or in specially roomy cargo ships. The vessels employed for infantry and mounted troops

THE NAVY IN THE BOER WAR.

were, in fact, running ships belonging to good lines, and they had to possess, or take out, a Board of Trade passenger certificate. The owners naturally do not keep such ships waiting on the off-chance of Government employment. They are in full work and have to sacrifice their own lucrative business to accept an Admiralty contract.

Coaling Arrangements.—Whenever possible, space was appropriated in the holds of the transports for additional coal bunkers, so that the quantity of coal taken from England might be as great as possible. The contractors at St. Vincent, Las Palmas and Teneriffe were also given special instructions, and a constant stream of colliers was kept going to the Cape. The transports were made to call at the three first-named places in such rotation as should ensure there being no block at any of them. A man-of-war was stationed at St. Vincent, one at Las Palmas, and one at Teneriffe to supervise the arrangements and to make such preparation and give such help as should preclude delay in dealing with each of the ships as they arrived. This system proved to be a good one. There was plenty of coal and no delay, but it was found that the high-speed vessels, owing to their enormous coal consumption, were not so suitable as others of more moderate speed. Eminently suited as they were for the short run across the Atlantic, it was really hardly worth while using them for the long voyage to the Cape.

Victualling.—The first batch of troops sent out was victualled from the Navy Yards, and this practice was partially continued till early in 1900. But, owing to considerations of the reserve of stores, and to the fact that the Navy salt meat ration was new to the troops and not liked by them, this was then changed. The owners contracted to victual the men at a rate per head per day, and this, though more expensive, worked well. Moreover, it gave greater satisfaction to the men, as it was more like what they were accustomed to on shore; and it was an important point to land them in the best possible condition. Volunteers and yeomanry when carried separate from the regulars were fed on a slightly better scale than the latter. If carried in the same ship all were fed alike on the better scale.

Forage in transports was in all cases supplied from the Government stores. In freight ships it was supplied by the owners, and was included in the rate per animal.

Troop-bedding and horse-gear are supplied by Government in all transports. Though a large stock is always kept on hand, special purchases of both had also to be made from time to time as the war went on to meet unexpectedly great demands.

Staff of the Transport Department.—To meet the requirements of this sudden expansion of work, Naval staffs were sent out to Cape Town, Durban, Port Elizabeth and East London, under Captain Sir Edward Chichester, R.N., and at home—to assist the normal peace establishment (which consisted of the Director of Transports, Rear-Admiral Bouverie F. Clark, Captain F. J. Pitt, R.N., the Naval Assistant, and Mr. Stephen J. Graff, the Civil Assistant, with their respective staffs)—the clerical establishment was enlarged and two captains, four lieutenants, engineers, and paymasters, and the requisite staff were appointed —some to each of the three districts, the Thames, Liverpool, and Southampton. These three places are, by reason of local considerations such as dock and repair accommodation, railway service and tidal conditions, the most suitable for such work, and with few exceptions the embarking was done in those districts.

General Remarks and Statistics.—Tables are given on pages 108-9, showing the number of vessels employed and of the troops, etc., carried. The total number of voyages out and home with troops, animals or stores was about 1,500, representing over 9,000,000 miles steaming, exclusive of coast movements at the Cape, and in addition to about 1,000,000 miles of cross voyages by the transports to India, Australia, Bermuda, etc. The ships selected for the conveyance of troops were chosen as the best adapted for the special work they had to perform, viz. : to deliver

THE NAVY IN THE BOER WAR. 107

them at their destination with the least risk and in healthy condition, fit to take the field at once. That the choice was not unsuccessful is evidenced by the fact that throughout these vast operations not a single life was lost at sea from causes due to the ship, and the only serious casualties were the loss of one cavalry transport, the *Ismore*, with guns and 315 horses; one mule freight ship, the *Carinthea*, with 400 mules; and two store freight ships, the *Denton Grange* and the *Madura*, the latter by fire. Looking to the mileage run, this is a wonderful record, and one which reflects the highest credit on the mercantile marine in general, and on the management of the shipping lines concerned in particular.

There was no delay in getting the troops off. From 20th October, 1899, when the first units of the army corps were ready to embark, to the 30th November, 1899, no less than 58,000 men and 9,000 horses left England, and a steady stream continued month after month, the largest shipment in one month being February, 1900, when 33,500 men and 5,500 horses left this country. The removal from South Africa was even more speedy. From 1st June, 1902, to 31st July, 53,800 men embarked. By the end of August the number was 94,000 men, and by the end of September, 133,000 men had left South Africa. The homeward move was simplified by there being no horses, and by the Government being able to utilise to their full extent the resources of the Union-Castle Company, whose large fleet of vessels, specially suitable for carrying troops, had an important share in the work. *The voyage to and fro.*

The shipowners, as a body, showed every desire throughout the war to meet the wishes of the Admiralty, often (in the early days) placing their ships at the disposal of the Government at great inconvenience to their own trade, and making great personal exertions to expedite the despatch of the troops and to ensure their comfort. In no case was any vessel engaged, either for troops, animals, or stores, which was not a registered British ship, and as far as possible the crews were British subjects; practically the crews of all troop transports were then exclusively so. *Patriotism of shipowners.*

Numbers conveyed.

The following figures will convey an idea of the extent of the Sea Transport work in connection with the war, from its commencement up to the 31st December, 1902.

The numbers conveyed were :

To South Africa.	Personnel.	Horses.	Mules.
From Home and Mediterranean:			
Troops, &c.	338,547	84,213	249
South African Constabulary	8,482	—	—
British South Africa Police	353	—	—
Imperial Military Railways	320	—	—
Colonial Office Details	59	—	—
Various	89	—	—
From India:			
Troops, &c.	19,438	8,611	1,117
Natives	10,528	—	—
From Ceylon, Mauritius, &c.:			
Troops, &c.	690	—	—
Natives	26	—	—
Various	8	—	—
From Colonies:			
Contingents	29,793	27,465	19
South African Constabulary	1,249	—	—
Remounts	—	36,660	—
From other countries:			
Remounts, &c.	—	195,915	102,627
Prisoners of War and Escorts	22,790	—	—
Totals	432,372	352,864	104,012
From South Africa:			
To United Kingdom, Colonies, India, &c., including Boer prisoners	372,320	2,460	—
Grand Total	804,692 persons.	459,336 animals.	

The tonnage of stores carried to South Africa was as follows, exclusive of wagons, guns, baggage, and equipment accompanying the troops, and of the vast quantities of supplies delivered by contractors from abroad at rates inclusive of freight :

In the Transports	4,990 tons.
Otherwise	1,369,080 tons.
Total	1,374,070 tons.

THE NAVY IN THE BOER WAR.

The number of specially engaged ships employed on the work was as follows :

	No.	
Transports engaged by the Admiralty	117	
Transports engaged in India	41	
		158

Troop freight ships :

		No.	
Outwards.	Engaged by Admiralty	115	
	Engaged by Colonial Governments	13	
Homewards.	Engaged by Admiralty	104	
	Engaged by P.T.O., South Africa	21	
			253

Remount freight ships :

	No.	
Engaged by Remount Department	107	
Engaged by Admiralty	201	
		308
Mule Freight Ships engaged by Admiralty	98	
Full Cargo Freight Ships engaged by Admiralty	210	
		1,027

Numbers of ships.

Nearly all the transports made several voyages, and some of them were in continuous employment for over three years, and went to the Cape and back as many as ten times besides coastal and colonial voyages.

The 210 full cargo ships carried 974,000 tons of the stores, besides 3,745 oxen. The remainder was conveyed in running ships at current rates. The transports engaged by the Admiralty were the property of thirty-six owners, mostly Liverpool or London firms; their average size was 6,400 tons gross, ranging from 12,600 to 3,500 tons, the range of speed from nineteen to eleven knots. The proportion of tonnage per man and per horse turns out, over the whole, four tons per man, twelve and a half tons per horse. This estimate is made by calculating the tonnage per man on the infantry ships alone, and allowing for the men at that rate by casting out the tonnage per horse over the transports which conveyed both men and horses. The

Tonnage, transports and owners.

Report of Royal Commission.

following is an extract from the report of His Majesty's Commissioners appointed to enquire into matters in connection with the war in South Africa, dated 9th July, 1903, pp. 125, 126.

"TRANSPORT BY SEA.

"The transport by sea to South Africa from the United Kingdom and the Colonies of a force much larger than any which had ever crossed the seas before in the service of this or any other country affords a remarkable illustration not only of the greatness of British maritime resources, but also of what can be done when careful forethought and preparation is applied to the object of utilising rapidly in war instruments which are in peace solely engaged in the purposes of civil life. If the same forethought had been applied throughout, there would have been little criticism to make with regard to the South African War. A full account of the Sea Transport organisation will be found in the evidence of Mr. Stephen Graff, Assistant Director of Transports at the Admiralty, and of Captain F. J. Pitt, R.N., Naval Assistant Director of Transports.

* * * * * * *

"It had been represented by the Admiralty in a letter of the 4th April, 1898 (in continuation of earlier representations), that the stock of horse fittings and water tanks was inadequate even for one Army Corps, inasmuch as one Army Corps, with a Cavalry Brigade and Line of Communication troops, requires over 15,000 horses, and it was represented that an expenditure of £25,000 to provide complete fittings would be necessary. In April, 1899, there was a conference between the Admiralty and War Office officials, who came to the conclusion that 'the present stock of fittings, horse-gear, etc., is dangerously insufficient and inadequate to ensure the rapid despatch of even one Army Corps, one Cavalry Brigade and Line of Communication troops.' At this time it had been intimated by the War Office that transport for two Army Corps might be needed. On the 19th July, 1899, the Committee recommended the purchase of 6,000 new pattern stalls, and on the 23rd September the Secretary of State for War authorised the expenditure of £25,000. The engage-

THE NAVY IN THE BOER WAR.

ment and preparation of ships began on the 30th September. It does not appear that the absence of a sufficient stock of horse fittings caused any appreciable delay. To a large extent the difficulty was met by fitting up with lighter fittings the Liverpool cattle ships, which are in many ways so constructed as to be admirable conveyances for horses. The plan of using these ships, and the kind of fittings to be used on them, had been worked out some time before the war by Captain Pitt, R.N.

* * * * * * *

"The adjustment of ships to transport purposes involves much labour, but the ships appear to have been ready as soon, or almost as soon, as the troops were ready to start. The arrangements between the War Office and the Admiralty for the embarkation of troops worked with great success. Sir Charles M. Clarke, then Quartermaster-General, stated that the demands of the War Office were 'most admirably met.' The accommodation on the ships appears to have been well calculated. The timing of the departures and arrivals, so as to regulate the pressure on intermediate coaling stations and terminal ports, also seems to have been satisfactory. The delays in disembarkation of men and stores were slight, and, when they occurred, were due to insufficient berthing accommodation at Cape Town. The accidents on voyage were few, and only one ship, the *Ismore*, was entirely lost, together with a battery of artillery."

NOTE BY THE OFFICIAL HISTORIAN.

The record above given of the splendid triumph of the Admiralty administration of Sea Transport during the war has been compiled by Capt. A. H. Limpus, R.N., with the cordial assistance of the Transport department of the Admiralty. The conclusion that the work of carrying the Army by sea could not have been in more competent hands is one which admits of no doubt in the mind of any reader who studies it. There are, nevertheless, certain deductions to be made in regard to the passengers carried—the greatest army ever delivered by any country over 6,000 miles of sea-way—which closely concern

Effect on Army.

Questions of above record.

the efficiency of the instrument with which the blow of Britain has to be struck, at points so distant from her shores. It is essential that the management of railways shall be in the hands of the officials of the particular company which conveys an excursion; but in order that the undertaking may be a great success many things are needed besides the perfect management of the trains. No one who has seen the amount of labour and the kind of organisation required by those who yearly send to the country the holiday-children, for instance, will fail to know that the passengers also need to be prepared beforehand for their part in the day. Moreover, some knowledge on the part of the most admirable railway officials of the special needs of those they carry is required; and, further, if any sudden change is made in the carriages themselves, in the sequence of trains, or in other matters strictly belonging to the functions of the company, this, if not communicated to the managers of the excursion, may introduce dire confusion.

<small>A new experience needs special training.</small>

An army has over the holiday travellers the advantage of its long-established unity, its discipline, and its training, but embarkation and disembarkation are entirely outside its ordinary experience. It needs, therefore, being much accustomed to work by habit, to be prepared both for getting on board ship, and, still more, for getting off it, in the manner that will best enable it to fulfil its duties, and, as time is very precious, to do this with the least possible delay, both in order to play completely into the hands of the officers in charge of the ships and in order to be itself at its best when it lands. This is the more easily accomplished because a ship in dock is virtually a part of the mainland. Everything that has to be done by troops in embarking can be imitated perfectly on shore, if the ordinary fittings of a ship are placed in a hut or other building outside which such a gangway is erected as that over which men and horses have to be passed in entering a ship. Now, by the willing assistance of the Admiralty in furnishing the exact fittings used in transports, this practice had been carried out by all arms—cavalry, horse and field artillery, army service corps and infantry—at least in some instances. Practical adaptations

THE NAVY IN THE BOER WAR. 113

in the training of each corps had been made by the experiments conducted on shore by each. Printed regulations embodying these had been framed.

Unfortunately, the sudden improvement in the ship fittings mentioned above, coming as it did at the very moment of war, completely, for the Army, upset the conditions on which the drill had been framed. It had been devised to make the passage of horses on board as rapid as it could be when the horses had to be placed in slings. Men, specially trained in slinging, were in each corps detailed to do the work. To find, when the embarkation began, that there were no slings, naturally involved at the last moment a change in method. Moreover, horses always obey more kindly, especially in strange circumstances, the men to whom they are accustomed, those by whom they are groomed and fed. It was, nevertheless, not surprising that the shipping authorities, unaware that the soldiers were dealing with conditions already familiar to them, should have detailed men of the ship to place the horses in their stalls. The horses did not like the unfamiliar hands; the soldiers were puzzled by their horses being taken from them. In some cases much delay and confusion occurred, and, indeed, it needed all the tact and good-fellowship of the navy and army officers to adjust things satisfactorily. Relatively to other matters the incident was a small one, but it illustrates the importance of a thorough understanding between the two services such as can only be gained by continued practice during peace-time for war. *Necessity for mutual understanding shown by incident.*

In the matter of stores a difficulty, which had been very strongly commented upon in the case of the Egyptian expedition of 1882, again presented itself. In 1882, in the disembarkation at Ismailia in the Suez Canal, where the facilities were much less than they were in the several harbours of South Africa, it became a very serious point that the stores required by the Army at once on landing were at the bottom of the holds. The ample landing capacities of Cape Town, of Durban, and almost, relatively to Ismailia, of East London and Port Elizabeth, made this in the present war less serious; but even in this case it drew a strongly-worded telegram of remonstrance. It would *Importance of the right stores being on top.*

be impossible to reckon upon our having always at our disposal conveniences so great as these for disembarking an army. It becomes, therefore, for future expeditions, important to note that the trouble which became so grave in 1882 was not removed at the ports of embarkation when this war began. To say the least, it was not the universally established practice to give to the naval officer in charge or to any one else a list showing the order in which the material embarked would be required on landing; and to ask that those things which would be first needed should be put in last, so that they might be on the top.

<small>Co-operation in forcing a landing.</small>

The army in South Africa had not to land against an opposing enemy. It is obviously important that in conjoint practice of the two services the possibility of an opposed landing should be taken into account. It was unfortunate, therefore, that as a consequence of the limited time at disposal, the other duties of the fleet, and the cost of demurrage, it became necessary for the Admiralty, when it was wisely decided to have combined manœuvres of navy and army in the autumn of 1904, in order to practise embarkation and disembarkation, to direct that the landing should be carried out under peace conditions. As a consequence of this the first party landed on a shore, supposed to be hostile, was one of unarmed sailors; and orders, at least in one instance, filled the foremost boats with the clerks and clerkly paraphernalia of a divisional Headquarters. That may have been the routine rightly followed in many cases at Cape Town, but the true application of the lessons of history does not consist in blind imitation of precedent from the past in those respects in which the conditions have changed. Joint action in manœuvre will be valueless unless it is used to familiarise each service with the work of the other as it will be in the actual fighting of the time. During the great war at the end of the eighteenth and beginning of the nineteenth century failure followed failure because the services had not practised together. At last they did so and the result was a brilliant success. The Japanese have undoubtedly owed many of their triumphs to their having profited by *our* historical records. Their disembarkations have been models of combined action.

THE NAVY IN THE BOER WAR. 115

On one other point the Naval triumph is of great importance to the Army. The passage quoted above (page 111) from the report of the Commission on the War marks well the facts. "The ships appear to have been ready as soon, or almost as soon, as the troops were ready to start." It follows that the shipping was just ready and no more for the Army, after mobilisation, when the reserves had been called in and incorporated. Moreover, it is to be noticed (page 100) that this result was only secured by a splendid audacity in expenditure by the Naval authorities, supplementing an admirable organisation. Now, as in every war we carry out abroad, the earliest time at which any armed force can move towards its object is the hour when the ships are ready to convey it, it follows that no delay whatever was caused by the necessity for summoning to the colours trained men retained for service by a small fee. On the other hand very great delay was caused by the impossibility of preparing for the particular campaign without threatening those whom we desired to conciliate. It, therefore, further follows that if there were ready at all times a force which did not need to be ostentatiously prepared, we should avoid the crux of not being able to make war without preparing for it and of not being able to prepare lest we should provoke war. On the other hand, this instance admirably illustrates the invariable law that the strength that can be so used is strictly limited by the number of properly fitted ships that the Admiralty can have ready at any given moment. An examination of Captain Limpus' careful statement will show how very small this inevitably is, and how much time is needed to fit those that are not available. Moreover, there is, on the Army side, as has been shown in Chapter V., this further restriction, that the equipment and transport, without which a campaign cannot be carried on, must be of the kind suited to the particular case.

_{Causes of delay, real and imaginary.}

_{Limit of striking force.}

SECTION III. THE WORK OF THE NAVY.
THE STOPPAGE OF CONTRABAND.

The task of the Navy in this matter lay so entirely outside the sphere of the military operations on land that it will be sufficient to say here that, despite the extreme delicacy of the situation created by the fact that it was only through neutral ports that the Boers could obtain supplies after the war had begun, the vigilance exercised was remarkably effective. The amount of contraband which reached the enemy was insignificant, yet very few claims for compensation were successfully sustained by neutrals. Ordinary trade, through Lourenço Marques, including, unfortunately, British trade, was uninterrupted till, towards the end of 1900, in consequence of the progress of the war, it died a natural death. In their careful watching of the coast and river-mouths the sailors, under Captain W. B. Fisher, of the *Magicienne*, had some trying experiences. Lieut. Massy Dawson, of the *Forte*, and Lieut. H. S. Leckie, of H.M.S. *Widgeon*, who received the Albert medal, did most gallant service.

SECTION IV. THE ASSISTANCE OF THE NAVY ON SHORE.

<small>The Navy on shore.</small>

This is incorporated in the accounts of the several campaigns and battles, but there were certain preparations made beforehand on board-ship which must here be recorded. During a cruise up the east coast in the month of July, 1899, Admiral Harris, the Naval Commander-in-Chief, was convinced that there would be war and that the Boers were only waiting till the grass was in fit condition for their cattle, to invade the colonies. He therefore took steps to have all the ships ready for service. He concentrated the fleet within easy reach of call. Early in October he sent to the G.O.C. at the Cape a list of small guns, etc., which he could furnish if needful. He was then told that it was not anticipated that such assistance would be necessary. Nevertheless, a Naval brigade of 500 men was exercised and prepared for landing. When the ultimatum was delivered it was clear enough that the troops were not in adequate strength to resist the forces the Boers could place against them, and that the enemy were bringing into the field guns of unusual calibre and range. The utmost numbers which it was possible to land were about 2,500, but heavy guns were the very weapons with which the sailors were most familiar. It seemed likely that these might prove to be of great value. On September 19th, the Admiral was informed that the *Terrible*, which was to have relieved the *Powerful*, viâ the Canal, would, instead, meet her on her voyage home at the Cape. On the 14th October the *Terrible* reached Simon's Bay. By October 21st, Captain Scott, her commanding officer, had devised a field mounting for a long-range 12-pr. and, having put it through a satisfactory firing trial, was authorised by the Commander-in-Chief to make several more. When, on October 24th, the Admiralty telegraphed that the War Office would be glad of all the assistance that the Navy could render, and that all was to be given that would not cripple the ships, the order had been so far anticipated that the upper decks of the *Terrible, Powerful, Monarch* and *Doris*, as well as the dockyard itself, had already assumed the appearance of a gun-carriage factory.

On October 24th, the day when this message was received from home, the Admiral arranged with Sir A. Milner that the *Powerful* should go to Durban on the 26th. On October 25th the Governor of Natal telegraphed to the Admiral that " Sir George White suggests that, in view of the heavy guns with Joubert, the Navy should be consulted with the view of sending a detachment of bluejackets with long-range guns firing heavy projectiles." He also revealed to the Admiral the gravity of the situation, and the scanty means available for defending Maritzburg and even Durban itself. The Admiral replied at once, saying, " *Powerful* arrives Durban 29th. She can on emergency land four 12-prs. and 9 Maxims." He then saw Captain Scott of the *Terrible*, and enquired if he could design a mounting to take a 4·7-in. and have two ready for the following afternoon, 26th. This Captain Scott did. By the next evening two such mountings had been put on board the *Powerful*, and before midnight she sailed for Durban. These 4·7-in. mountings were meant for use as guns of position, and not as field guns. They consisted—briefly described—of four 12-in. baulks of timber 14 feet long, bolted together in the form of a double cross. This made a rough platform to which was secured the plate and spindle which was used to carry the ordinary ship mounting of the 4·7-in. guns. They were intended to

Preparation of heavy guns for landing.

be placed in a hole in the ground 15 feet square and 2 feet deep, and the ends of the timber baulks were to be secured with chains to weights sunk in the ground. But this securing of the timbers was found to be quite unnecessary when a mounting of this kind was put through a firing trial near Simon's Town, and so it was not subsequently employed with these "platform" mountings, as they came to be called. Sir George White, in Ladysmith, to which place the first two "platform" mountings had been promptly taken by the *Powerful's* Naval brigade, was, on October 30th, informed by telegram of the result of the firing trial, also that no moorings had been found necessary.

Scott's travelling carriage. Captain Scott now obtained permission to make a travelling carriage for a 4·7-in. gun. It consisted of a double trail of 14-inch timber fitted with plates and bearings to carry the cradle of the ordinary ship mounting. A pair of steel wheels and a heavy axle were required, and all the work was done in the dockyard under Captain Scott's supervision. This mounting was satisfactorily tried and embarked on the *Terrible* for Durban on November 3rd.

In giving this brief description of the mountings which enabled long-range guns to be put at the disposal of the General Officer Commanding-in-Chief, the events which led to their use have been anticipated. The foregoing explanation is necessary, because, though the warships were already supplied with field mountings for the 12-pr. 8-cwt. and some smaller guns, and these were therefore available, and to a certain extent were used during the war, yet when more powerful guns were required it became necessary to extemporise a carriage for them.

Numbers employed. The first long 12-pr. was tried on October 21st, and by November 3rd there were already prepared for use, or actually in use :—

    21 field mountings for 12-pr. 12-cwt. guns.
    3 platform mountings for 4·7-in.
    1 travelling carriage for 4·7-in.

Later developments. This number was, soon afterwards, largely increased, and a 6-in. Q.F. 7-ton gun was also mounted on a travelling carriage

THE NAVY IN THE BOER WAR. 119

at the Durban Locomotive Works under Captain Scott's supervision. As more mountings were made and other people's ideas were enlisted, modifications were introduced; some mountings, entirely of steel, were indeed used for 4.7-in. guns; but in the main these mountings resembled those which were so hurriedly prepared in the last ten days of October.

To resume the sequence of Naval events at the Cape.

The Commander-in-Chief found himself, when war broke out, with his small squadron of ships ready for any service, and a Naval brigade of 500 of their crews ready whenever called for. He had informed the military Commander-in-Chief to what extent he could give help on shore, and his squadron was shortly increased as told above. He was none too strong for the purely Naval duties which war would involve, though a sufficient staff of officers was sent out to relieve him to a large extent of the Sea Transport duty. Still he found himself with the considerable responsibility of keeping the seaports—Table Bay, Simon's Bay, Port Elizabeth, East London and Durban, secure and available for our troops, and in the case of Durban, as the situation developed, this promised to be no light matter. The timely distribution of the coal supply, both for his own reinforced squadron and for the transports, had to be arranged. At one time the unfortunate grounding of a transport, the *Ismore*, caused extra work and anxiety. The enemy's supplies by sea had also to be stopped. There were precautions to be taken for the safety of H.M. ships while lying in harbour, for the arriving transports, and the Naval establishments. Later on there was the care of a considerable number of Boer prisoners until regular camps could be formed for them. Altogether, therefore, if the squadron was to be kept always fit for sea, some circumspection was required when determining to land men and guns for service on shore.

Difficulties of Naval C.-in-C.

Although in detail the record of the services of the men actually landed falls into its place in the course of the campaigns, it should here be noticed that these contingents resolved themselves eventually into three Naval brigades.

The Naval brigades.

First, the Western brigade, a force of 357 of all ranks and

Western brigade.

two short 12-pounders under Commander Ethelston of the *Powerful*. This was originally employed to garrison Stormberg, was then withdrawn to Queenstown, and finally recalled to Simon's Bay viâ East London, to be reorganised, strengthened, and sent up under Captain Prothero with four long 12-prs, and about 400 men, to join Lord Methuen's force for the relief of Kimberley. It left behind two short 12-pr. field guns at Queenstown for the use of the Army. After Graspan, where it suffered considerably, Captain J. E. Bearcroft was sent to replace Captain Prothero, who was wounded, and the brigade was much augmented. It then accompanied Lord Roberts' main advance; parties with guns being sent on various detached services—until by 17th October, 1900, the men of this brigade had all been recalled to their ships.

Ladysmith brigade.

Second, the Ladysmith brigade. The *Powerful* having been sent to Durban to comply with Sir George White's request for guns, there were landed on arrival on October 29th, and taken at once to Ladysmith, two 4·7-in. guns on platform mountings, three long 12-pounders, one short 12-pounder, and four Maxims, with 283 of all ranks under Captain the Hon. Hedworth Lambton. They arrived on the 30th October, 9.30 a.m., in time to take part in the action of Lombards Kop, and remained in Ladysmith during the siege.

Natal brigade.

The third, or Natal brigade, had its origin in the *Terrible* being sent to Durban, where she arrived on November 6th. Her Captain, Percy Scott, at once became Commandant and organised—from the *Terrible, Thetis, Forte, Philomel,* and *Tartar,* the defence of that town. Over thirty guns were placed in position and put under the command of Commander Limpus, of the *Terrible*, while a pair of 12-pounders, drawn from the *Powerful*, had been pushed on to Maritzburg and placed under Lieutenant James, of the *Tartar*, with the men of that ship already up there. It was from this force that, as troops arrived, Sir Redvers Buller drew the Naval brigade which accompanied the Ladysmith relief column. Captain E. P. Jones, of the *Forte*, commanded this brigade, with Commander A. H. Limpus, of the *Terrible*, second in command. After the relief of Lady-

THE NAVY IN THE BOER WAR. 121

smith, Captain Jones re-organised the Naval brigade with ranks and ratings from the *Forte, Philomel,* and *Tartar.* The *Terribles* and *Powerfuls* rejoined their ships by March 13th. So reconstituted, the brigade served on with the Natal Field Force until June 24th, 1900, when all but the *Philomel's* and *Tartar's* men, under Lieutenant Halsey, were recalled to their ships. Lieutenant Halsey, with four officers and thirty-eight men of the *Philomel,* one officer and eighteen men of the *Tartar,* remained until October, 1900, when they also returned.

Essential as were the services rendered on shore* it was always arranged that, if it had become advisable at any time to recall officers and men to their ships, they should be able to rejoin them long before their presence was needed on board. Also as soon as any article, including guns and ammunition, was landed from the fleet it was replaced from England. When it became clear that the safety of Durban was assured, its naval defence force was re-embarked; but Captain Percy Scott remained on shore with his staff as Commandant until 14th March, 1900. His work there, in preparing and sending additional guns to General Buller—among them a 6-in. gun on a wheeled carriage— and also as an able Commandant of Durban under martial law, was highly appreciated.† {All Naval brigades within recall.}

A welcome addition was made to the strength of the Natal brigade by a party of Natal Naval Volunteers, under Lieutenants T. Anderton and Nicholas Chiazzari, who with forty-eight men of all ratings, joined Captain Jones' force at Frere on 10th December, and reinforced the crews of the 4·7-in. guns. Lieut. Barrett, N.N.V., also joined the Naval brigade with the Natal Field Force after the relief of Ladysmith. The Natal Naval Volunteers proved to be a most valuable addition to the brigade, composed as they were of intelligent, resourceful men, who were familiar with the ways of the country, and many of whom spoke both the Taal and native languages. They were part of a {Natal Naval Volunteers.}

---

* See despatches giving the views of Sir Redvers Buller, etc., on these.

† See despatch from the Governor of Natal to Admiral Harris, dated 9.3.00, and letter from the Colonial Office to the Admiralty, dated 7.5.00.

corps which had its origin in the previous scheme for the defence of Durban, and possessed muzzle-loading 9-prs.

<small>Why they joined.</small>
They had been stationed at Colenso when the southward advance of the Boers compelled the evacuation of that position on 3rd November, 1899. Although told to abandon their guns they had carried them bodily away with them in the retirement. Forced to recognise that such guns were quite useless in the field, and unable to obtain better weapons locally, they had eagerly volunteered to join the Naval brigade under Captain Jones. Fortunately they obtained their wish, and the Naval brigade gained the services of a body of men who soon proved their sterling worth, and whose traditions will henceforth always be closely associated with those of the Royal Navy.

CHAPTER VII.

TALANA HILL.*

THE last four chapters have dealt with subjects affecting the whole course of the war, the theatre of operations, the two opposed armies, and the British navy. The present one, which describes the first action in the campaign, connects immediately with the second, that on the outbreak of the war, taking up the narrative from the time when, as a consequence of the conference at Maritzburg between the Governor (Sir W. Hely-Hutchinson), Sir George White, Sir A. Hunter and Maj.-Genl. Sir W. Penn Symons, the latter officer had been despatched to take over the command at Dundee while Sir George White had gone to Ladysmith. Connection with Chap. II.

On October 12th, the day when the British agent quitted Pretoria, Major-General Sir W. Penn Symons arrived at Dundee, and took over command of 3,280 infantry, 497 cavalry and eighteen guns from Brigadier-General J. H. Yule.† He had gained his point. Dundee was to be held, and held by him. As early as the 13th news came that a strong commando was concentrating at the Doornberg east of De Jager's Drift, and that small parties of the enemy had been sighted four miles north of Newcastle, whilst to his left rear the Free Staters were reported so close to Ladysmith, and in such strength, as to cause Sir George White to recall one of Symons' own battalions, the 2nd Royal Dublin Fusiliers, to strengthen a column which was pushed out on October 13th towards Tintwa Pass to get touch with the Arrival, Oct. 12th/99, of Symons at Dundee.

---

* See maps Nos. 3, 5, and the panoramic sketch.
† For composition of this force see Appendix 3.

124   THE WAR IN SOUTH AFRICA.

enemy. This column* failed, however, to observe even patrols of the enemy, and the Dublin Fusiliers returned to Dundee by train the same night. On this day the enemy fell upon a piquet of Natal Policemen posted at De Jager's Drift, and made them prisoners. A patrol of the 18th Hussars proceeding to reconnoitre the spot next day, the 14th, came upon a scouting party of forty of the enemy a mile on the British side of the Buffalo. On the 16th a fugitive from Newcastle announced the arrival of a commando, 3,000 strong, before Newcastle, another in Botha's Pass, whilst across Wools Drift, on the Buffalo, six miles of wagons had been seen trekking slowly southwards. If the left, then, was for the moment clear, it was plain that strong bodies were coming down on Symons' front and right, a front whose key was Impati, a right whose only bulwark was the hill of Talana.

Oct. 12th Joubert also starts. Joubert quitted Zandspruit on the 12th October, and was at Volksrust in the evening, with the forces of Generals Kock and Lukas Meyer thrown widely forward on his right and left flanks respectively. Kock, coming through Botha's Pass with his motley foreign levies,† halted for the night at the mouth of the defile, whilst the units of the left horn of the invading crescent, reinforced this day by the commandos of Middelburg and Wakkerstroom, lay under Meyer some forty miles eastward, some in Utrecht, some in Vryheid, and some already at the concentration point, the Doornberg. On the 13th, whilst the wings remained quiescent, Joubert, with the main column, occupied Laing's Nek, having first, either by an excess of precaution, or from a fear lest the gap between him and Meyer were too great, made good that formidable obstacle by a turning movement around the left and over the Buffalo at Wools Drift; this was executed by his advance guard (Pretoria, Boksburg, part of Heidelberg, Standerton, Ermelo) under Erasmus. But though a coal-truck drawn by cables through the long tunnel,

---

* Composition: 5th Lancers, detachment of 19th Hussars, Natal Mounted Rifles, three batteries Royal Field artillery, 1st Liverpool, 1st Devonshire, 2nd Gordon Highlanders.

† See Appendix 4.

TALANA HILL.

which penetrated the Nek, proved it to be neither blocked nor mined, this stroke of fortune rather increased than allayed the caution of the Boer General, to whom, grown old in Native wars, nothing appeared more suspicious than an unimpeded advance against an enemy. On the 14th he was still on the Nek, whilst Erasmus moved timidly on Newcastle, and Kock, who remained on the Ingagane, despatched a reconnoitring party of the German Corps along the Drakensberg, to gain touch with Trüter's Free Staters at Müller's Pass. This patrol, riding back next day, found Newcastle occupied by the commandos of Erasmus. The little town was almost empty of inhabitants, and the burghers wrought havoc amongst the deserted shops and houses. Not all the remonstrances of their officers, nor the general order from Headquarters, nor even the heavy wrath of their Commandant-General, who arrived in the town on the 18th, could stop their ruthless plundering, and by nightfall the township was a scene of sordid devastation.

On the afternoon of the 16th Joubert called a council of war. So far he had been without any settled scheme, and, owing to the straggling and indiscipline of his burghers, the march was rapidly becoming unmanageable. The commander, whose plans and army require consolidation after but four days, may well look with foreboding upon the campaign he has taken in hand, and Joubert was as little hopeful as any invader in history. Nevertheless, at Newcastle he devised a net which, had it been cast as he designed, might by entangling one British force beyond salvation, have weakened another beyond repair and perhaps have laid Natal at his feet. Whilst Erasmus with his 5,000 men moved straight down upon Dundee, Kock with 800 riflemen, composed of Schiel's Germans, Lombard's Hollanders, and 200 men of Johannesburg under Viljoen, with two guns, was to reconnoitre towards Ladysmith, gaining touch with the Free Staters at Van Reenen's and the other passes of the Drakensberg. He was then to take up a position in the Biggarsberg range, cutting the railway between Dundee and Ladysmith. Thus isolated, the garrison of Dundee appeared to

Joubert's net.

Slow movement of Boers.

be at the mercy of a combined attack by Erasmus from the north, and Lukas Meyer from the east.

Kock and Erasmus had left the neighbourhood of Newcastle on the 17th, and on the afternoon of the 18th the latter's advance guard came into collision with a squadron of the 18th Hussars, from Dundee, north of Hatting Spruit. Meanwhile Meyer, who was much behindhand with his concentration, lay so close in his camp at the Doornberg, that the British patrols scouted up to De Jager's Drift again without opposition. Meyer still lacked two commandos (Krugersdorp and Bethel) and four guns, and as his transport animals were in a deplorable condition, it was with relief rather than with impatience that he watched the tardiness of his coadjutors. His missing units arrived in the evening, however; Erasmus' advanced guard was close behind Impati on the morning of the 19th, and Meyer then issued orders for a march.

Sir George White recalls Dundee detachment.

Meanwhile, on the 15th October, an officer of the Headquarter staff visited Dundee, and on his return to Ladysmith was questioned by Sir G. White as to the state of the defences existing at the post. To his surprise he learnt that, properly speaking, no defences existed at all—no position, no entrenchments, and, most important of all, no assured and defended supply of water. His instructions, in short, conditional upon which alone he had consented to the retention of Dundee, had not been carried out. Not until three days had elapsed, however, did he telegraph to Sir W. Penn Symons that, failing an assurance of compliance, Dundee must be evacuated at once. In answer, Symons admitted that he could not give the required assurance, and must therefore carry out the order to retire. At the same time he stated his requirements in the matter of rolling-stock for the withdrawal of military stores and the non-combatant inhabitants of Dundee. This reply raised a new point. To send the whole of the rolling-stock—and nothing less would suffice—would be to expose it to the gravest danger, for the railway line was in hourly insecurity. Two hours after the despatch of his first telegram, therefore, Sir George White sent a second, which became the determining factor of subsequent events.

TALANA HILL.

"With regard to water, are you confident you can supply your camp for an indefinite period ? The difficulties and risk of withdrawing of civil population and military stores are great. The railway may be cut any day. Do you yourself, after considering these difficulties, think it better to remain at Dundee, and prefer it ? "

Sir W. Penn Symons replied as follows : " We can and must stay here. I have no doubt whatever that this is the proper course. I have cancelled all orders for moving." Cancels recall.

The question thus finally decided for good or ill, Sir George White sent a third telegram :

" I fully support you. Make particulars referred to by me as safe as possible. Difficulties and disadvantages of other course have decided me to support your views."

Sir W. Penn Symons, his only fear about Dundee—that of being withdrawn from it—thus finally removed, turned to the front again to face the converging enemy with equanimity. His information continued to be full and accurate. Erasmus' advance, Meyer's concentration at the Doornberg, Kock's circuitous passage over the Biggarsberg, were all known to him. On October 19th he received detailed warning that an attack was to be made on him that very night by Erasmus from the north, Meyer from the east, and Viljoen from the west. By midday, communication by rail with Ladysmith was cut off—not, however, until a party of fifty of the 1st King's Royal Rifles had returned in safety from a visit to Waschbank, where they had rescued some derelict trucks left by a train, which, having been fired on at Elandslaagte, had dropped them for greater speed. Three companies 2nd Royal Dublin Fusiliers, which had been railed to the Navigation Collieries, north-east of Hatting Spruit, at 3 a.m., to bring back eight tons of mealies which the General was unwilling to leave for the enemy, also returned in safety. Symons faces a known situation.

At sundown on October 19th, Lukas Meyer left his bivouac with about 3,500 men and seven guns. De Jager's Drift was crossed about 9 p.m. ; then, pressing through the Sunday's* Meyer Oct. 19th moves forward,

* See map No. 5.

river south-west of Maybole farm, Meyer's force emerged on to the bleak expanse of veld stretching east of Dundee. The Boer scouts, moving parallel to and north of the Landman's Drift road, drew with great caution towards Talana. At 2.30 a.m. a party of burghers came upon a British piquet of the Dublin Fusiliers mounted infantry, commanded by Lieut. C. T. W. Grimshaw, at the junction of the road with the track to Vant's Drift. Shots were exchanged, the piquet disappeared, and the Boer advance guard was upon the flat summit of Talana an hour before dawn, with Dundee sleeping five hundred feet below. Close on the heels of the scouts pressed the Utrecht and Wakkerstroom commandos, under Commandants Hatting and Joshua Joubert, of about 900 and 600 men respectively, with some 300 Krugersdorpers under Potgieter in addition, and a few men of the Ermelo commando. The rest of the main body, consisting of the Vryheid commando (600 men, under Van Staaden), the Middelburg commando (some 900 men, under Trichardt), portion of the Swazi Police, portion of the Piet Retief commando (170 men, under Englebrecht), and odd men of the Bethel and other absent commandos, made their way rapidly across the Dundee road, and took up position on the heights south of it. Of the artillery, two field-pieces (Creusot 75 m/m) were hauled into a depression nearly at the rear edge of the top of Talana, a "pom-pom" (37·5 m/m Vickers-Maxim) pushed forward to the advanced crest of the same eminence, and the remainder, consisting of two Krupps (75 m/m) and two more pom-poms, sent across under charge of the Vryheid men to their position to the south.

Talana Hill, situated about 5,000 yards east of the British camp, from which it was separated by the wire-intersected environs of Dundee and by the sunken bed of the Sand Spruit, was peculiarly adapted for defence. From the summit a precipitous rocky face dropped on the Dundee side to a nearly flat terrace, 160 feet below it, whose fifty to eighty yards of width were commanded throughout by the boulder-strewn brow of the mountain. A low stone wall bounded this terrace at its outer edge, immediately below which the hillside again fell suddenly,

TALANA HILL.

affording from ten to fifteen yards of ground dead to the crest directly above it, but vulnerable to fire, both from Lennox Hill, a slightly higher eminence on the other side of a Nek to the south-east, and from a salient protruding from the northern extremity of the hill. From the wall bounding the upper terrace, however, other walls, running down-hill, intersected this face of the mountain at right angles, and served as low traverses affording some protection from flanking fire. These formed the enclosures of Smith's farm, a group of tree-encircled buildings around an open space at the base of the mountain, near its centre, and some 400 feet below its summit. Below, and on either side of the homestead stood copses of eucalyptus trees, which, roughly in all some 500 yards square, occupied the top of the glacis whose base was the Sand Spruit, which 800 yards of bare and open grass-land separated from the edge of the wood.*

Such was the position crowned by the Boer commandos in the first light of October 20th. Swift as had been its captors, news of their success was at once in the hands of the British commander. At 3 a.m. a sergeant from Grimshaw's piquet, which had been surprised at the cross roads, hurried into camp and reported the approach of the enemy in force across the veld. Sir W. Penn Symons thereupon ordered two companies of the Dublin Fusiliers to turn out in support. The rest of the camp slept undisturbed, and the two companies, stumbling through the dark and obstructed suburbs of Dundee, gained the shelter of the Sand Spruit, where they found Grimshaw already arrived. The first shots had stampeded his horses, which had galloped back to Smith's Nek, the col between Talana and Lennox Hills. Retiring on foot, the piquet had gained the Nek, recovered its horses, and making its way first to Smith's farm, and thence to the cover of the Sand Spruit, had turned and faced the enemy as he appeared over the crest of Talana Hill. *Symons receives the news.*

At 5 a.m. the British troops stood to arms as usual. It was a wet and misty morning. As the men, few of whom knew of *The morning parade dismissed.*

---

* A sketch of the position, as seen from the side of the British advance from Dundee, will be found in the case of maps accompanying this volume.

the occurrences of the night, waited in quarter-column, to a few keen ears came the fitful sound of musketry from the east. It was the fire of Grimshaw's piquet just then at bay below Talana. The parade having been dismissed, at 5.20 a message from Headquarters assured commanding officers that all was clear. A few companies moved directly from their lines for skirmishing drill around the camp, the men of others hung about in groups expecting the word to fall in for a similar purpose; the horses of two of the three batteries, and all the transport animals, filed out to water a mile and a half away. Suddenly at 5.30 a.m., the mist upon Talana, wasting before the rising sun, lifted and revealed the summit alive with figures.

<small>The Boers make their presence known.</small>

Ten minutes later the report of a gun sounded from the top, and a projectile fell into the western enclosures of the town. Others, better aimed, followed in quick succession; the camp came under a rapid bombardment, accurate but harmless, for the small common shell from the enemy's field-pieces failed to explode on impact with the sodden ground. The cavalry and the mounted infantry, whose horses had remained in camp, moved out of sight behind a stony kopje in front of it; the infantry, already equipped, fell rapidly into their places, each company before its own line of tents, and were immediately marched at the "double" into the shelter of a ravine some 200 yards to the south of the camp, where fighting formations were organised.

<small>Symons prepares to clear Talana.</small>

The General had already decided upon an assault. Before the infantry were clear of camp he called out the artillery. Whilst the 67th battery, whose horses were now hurrying back from water, replied to the Boer shells from the gun-park itself, the 69th battery, already horsed, waiting neither for its wagons nor an escort, galloped out along the road to the railway station, swept through the town, and swinging sharply to the right at the south-eastern extremity, came into action on a roll of the veld immediately west of the colliery extension railway line. As it advanced the Boers turned their guns upon it, but within twenty minutes of the falling of the first shell in camp, the 69th commenced a rapid and effective fire at 3,750 yards upon the crest. Ten minutes later the 13th battery wheeled into line alongside the 69th. In five minutes more the practice of the Boer ordnance dropped to spasmodic bursts; in five more it was temporarily silenced. Meanwhile the General, who had ridden out soon after the batteries, had set his infantry in motion, and so fast did they go forward that before the 69th had ended its first round they were already almost beyond Dundee.

To the 67th battery and the 1st Leicestershire regiment, with one company from each of the other battalions, was now entrusted the defence of the camp from the expected attack of Erasmus from Impati. An officer of the King's Royal Rifles carried the orders to the cavalry from the General: "Colonel Möller is to wait under cover, it may be for one or two hours, and I will send him word when to advance. But he may advance if he sees a good opportunity. The M.I. are to go with the 18th Hussars." The Royal Dublin Fusiliers were first in the bed of the spruit at about 6.30 a.m., picking up the two companies which had lain there since 4.30 a.m. in support of Grimshaw's piquet. By 7 a.m. the whole of the infantry were in security in the same shelter, 1,600 to 2,000 yards from the crest of the position. General Penn Symons himself then rode down thither, and sending for commanding officers, detailed orders for the assault. The Dublin Fusiliers were to form the first line, with the King's Royal Rifles in support, the Royal Irish Fusiliers in reserve. Brigadier-General Yule would command the attack. *He guards against Erasmus and gives orders for attack.*

At 7.20 a.m. the right-hand company of the Dublin emerged from the Sand Spruit, the men extended to ten paces interval, and steadily in quick-time moved towards the boundary of the wood. The other companies, advancing in order from the right, soon followed. Before the last of them was fairly clear, the King's Royal Rifles were released and pressed forward. On the appearance of the first lines, a hot fire, direct from Talana itself and crosswise from Lennox Hill on the right, quickly caused casualties. Eager to be at closer quarters, the men increased their pace, breaking from quick-time into the double, and from that to a swift run upon the edge of the wood. A low stone wall, topped by a broken-down fence of wire which ringed the *Infantry push up the hill.*

copse on this side, was tumbled flat, and the foremost soldiers of the Dublin, pouring through the thicket, penetrated to the wall and hedge on the farther side. Here their line was prolonged by the King's Royal Rifles, who had come through the wood on the right. In front of this line the crest of Talana was 550 yards distant. With the Dublin Fusiliers, the general trend had been towards the left; now after a short pause at the edge of the plantation they attempted to push on in that direction. Enticed by a donga, which, quitting the wood at its northern angle, looked like a covered way towards the crest of the hill, the three leading companies ("A." "F." and "G.") worked steadily along it in hopes of arriving within striking distance of the enemy under comparative shelter. But the watercourse not only faded to nothing before it reached the terrace wall, but was open to the enemy's view and enfiladed by his musketry throughout its length. A storm of bullets descending into it when it teemed with men, brought down many and checked further progress.

A treacherous donga.

Of the King's Royal Rifles, four companies, under Colonel R. H. Gunning, advancing through the right-hand half of the plantation, found themselves amongst the Dublin Fusiliers at its forward edge, and became in part intermingled with them. The three remaining companies moved upon the buildings of Smith's farm, and gained the front and right edges. Somewhat ahead of the general line, this portion of the force was enfiladed from the crest of Talana on its left, and from Lennox Hill on its right, and received so hot a cross-fire that it was ordered to fall back to the cover of the farm walls. This it did with the loss of three officers and many men; but from their more secure location the Rifles here began a telling reply, both upon the crest in front and upon the clouds of sharpshooters which hung upon the summit and slopes of Lennox Hill.

K.R.R. and Dublin reach edge of wood.

K.R.R. hold Smith's farm.

Lieut.-Colonel F. R. C. Carleton, 1st Royal Irish Fusiliers, immediately on entering the plantation, had detached two of his companies ("B." and "H.") to line the left face of the wood, whence they could watch the open ground beyond that flank. These sent volleys against the enemy's right upon Talana.

"B." and "H." of R.I.F. on left of wood.

TALANA HILL.

The remainder were held in reserve, as ordered, amongst the small dongas and depressions in the wood. The Maxim guns of all three battalions moved to the south-eastern angle of the wood, and opened at 1,700 yards upon Smith's Nek and Lennox Hill to their right front and right, doing much to alleviate the musketry which came incessantly from these flanking and partially invisible eminences. *Maxims at S.E. angle.*

Such was the situation at eight o'clock. At that hour the 69th and 13th batteries, quitting the position from which they had silenced the Boer artillery, moved through the town, and unlimbered on rising ground between the eastern boundary of Dundee and the Sand Spruit. Thence they opened again, the 69th upon Talana at 2,300 yards, the 13th upon Lennox Hill at 2,500. Though they and their escort of King's Royal Riflemen were targets for both hills, their practice was admirable, and had it been more rapid, must speedily have smothered the enemy's fire. But the artillery commander, fearing to run short, and knowing his inability to replenish, was obliged continually to check expenditure.* For a time the fight remained stationary. The momentum of the attack had died away, and Yule found it impossible to get it in motion again at once, in spite of numerous messages he received from Sir W. Penn Symons urging immediate advance. At 9 a.m. the infantry being still inert, the patience of the General was exhausted. Despite the remonstrances of his staff, he, with three staff officers and orderlies, rode into the wood, and, dismounting, hurried into the foremost lines of the Royal Irish Fusiliers, at its northern angle. Calling to these to "push on!" he then pressed along inside the boundary, animating by word and gesture all the troops he passed, and halted for a moment to face the hill a little beyond where the afore-mentioned donga disappeared into the wood. Here Major F. Hammersley, of his staff, was wounded, and, immediately after, the General himself was shot in the stomach. Directing Brigadier-General Yule to proceed with the attack, he turned and walked calmly to the rear. Then, meeting his horse, he mounted, and not until he had passed entirely through *69th and 13th batteries change their ground. Reduced fire. Symons gives impulse. He receives his mortal wound.*

* There were for each gun 154 rounds, including 60 reserve.

the troops was any sign of suffering allowed to escape him. At the station of the Bearer company he dismounted, and was carried to the dressing station in a dhoolie. Five minutes later, at 9.35 a.m., the surgeon pronounced his wound to be fatal, and the news was telegraphed to Ladysmith.

<small>His impulse tells.</small>

The life of the General was not thrown away; his action had immediate effect. Before he had quitted the wood a dying man, parties of soldiers were already pushing forward from its front wall across the 100 yards of bullet-swept flat intervening between them and the first slopes of Talana proper. On the right, the first to break cover, four and a half companies of the King's Royal Rifles emerged in small parties from Smith's farm.

<small>K.R.R. seize wall of upper terrace.</small>

Leaving there two companies in support, they pushed up along the right side of the transverse wall, in full view of Lennox Hill, and suffering from its fire. So rapid were their movements that the Boer shooting was hasty and ill-aimed, and the losses were but few. Some distance forward they leapt across to the left of the transverse wall, and reconnoitring that bounding the upper terrace, found it, to their surprise, unoccupied by the enemy.* Other groups, in response to signals, then worked their way upward, until soon a considerable number of Riflemen were under the wall. On their left the Royal Irish Fusiliers sup-

<small>R.I.F. join and also threaten Boer right.</small>

ported the attack. Two and a half companies (" E.," " F." and half of " C.") of this battalion had, when General Symons came to the front, been sent to the edge of the wood, and these, seeing what the Rifles had done, streamed straight up to the wall. " A." and half of " D." companies, which had been boldly and independently handled wide on the left, avoiding the dongas, pushed on gradually to well within five hundred yards of the enemy's extreme right, on which they brought their rifles to bear. The other half of " C." company, with men of other battalions, amounting to about one hundred in all, had lain with the three

---

* The omission of the Boers to man this breastwork, situated as it was within 400 yards of the edge of the wood, and commanding every inch of the ground in front, was not owing to any fears on the part of Lukas Meyer as to its not being tenable. The orders of that general had been plainly that the wall was to be held, but as he did not remain to see them carried out, the burghers, fearing to hold what appeared to them isolated and inadequate cover, neglected it entirely.

TALANA HILL.

companies of King's Royal Rifles in the enclosure of Smith's farm, and advanced with them. One company ("B.") Royal Irish Fusiliers had been ordered forward on the left by General Symons himself immediately he arrived in the wood. This company, perceiving the fallacious donga winding apparently to the front, had dropped into it, and following it up with the same expectations as had encouraged the Dublin Fusiliers, was speedily in the same predicament at its open extremity. Another company ("H."), taking this route with many losses, was similarly blocked at the same point. But with the exception of these two companies, which could not move for a time, the advance of the King's Royal Rifles to the wall was strongly backed by the Royal Irish Fusiliers, whose men appeared from all the near parts of the hill to join in with the rest. With them ran many of the Dublin Fusiliers. This regiment, much entangled in the watercourse already mentioned and in others equally exposed and useless more to the right, could not progress, and, though a few men managed to reach the upper wall direct, it was only possible to do so by first going back to the edge of the wood, an attempt of great hazard.

The battle came to a standstill once more. The upper wall was won, but the heavy and incessant fusilade directed upon it and upon the ground below it, rendered its occupation precarious, and reinforcement a matter of extreme difficulty. Not until two hours had passed were sufficient men collected under it to render the last stage possible, and the long delay cost many casualties. At 11 a.m. the officer commanding the artillery received a request by flag-signal to cease firing, as the assault was about to be delivered. He did so; but time to acquire strength was still needed, and the artillery, itself harassed by musketry, re-opened. At 11.30 a.m. the order was repeated, and once more Colonel E. H. Pickwoad stopped his guns. Immediately after, the batteries galloped forward, awaking against themselves the full energy of all parts of the Boer line. They crossed a wide donga and came into action again on the flat plain between the Sand Spruit and Talana, sending their shells clear over and past the left edge of the wood

_{Two hours check.}

_{Guns gallop forward.}

136   THE WAR IN SOUTH AFRICA.

at a range of 1,400 yards from the crest of the enemy's stronghold. Under the rapid bombardment the Mausers slackened and at last were silent. For the third time the order was signalled to cease firing. It was duly obeyed. Colonel Gunning, of the King's Royal Rifles, who had called up his two supporting companies from Smith's farm, passed the word, "Get ready to go over!" The men rose to their knees; then, at the command "Advance!" scrambled and fell over the obstacle. A blaze burst from the crest as the first figures wavered on the wall, and many fell backward dead or wounded. Some could not surmount the obstruction, which in parts was over-high for vaulting; some, falling on the far side, picked themselves up and were struck down in the first leap of their charge. A few, more fortunate, held on. But the onset had not much weight, and losses quickly lightened it still further. Many of the Boers had fled at the first sight of the soldiers rushing forward, but of those who remained, not a few actually came towards them, and shot rapidly point-blank at the assailants, who were clawing their way up the last precipitous rampart of the natural fortress. The artillery, therefore, knowing only that the onslaught had been checked, about 12.30 p.m. re-opened with quick and devastating rounds. But during the charge the light had been bad, and the gunners had not all observed the foremost groups of their comrades lying amongst the rocks close to the crest. Soon shell after shell burst amongst the latter.

A signaller of the Royal Irish Fusiliers, standing up near the top of the hill, attracted the attention of the artillerymen, but was unable to make them understand his message. Another of the same regiment failed similarly from the wall. As the discharges, destroying both combatants alike, became more overwhelming, both drew back. On the extreme right a few of the Rifles still clung on. At first the Boers melted from the front alone, but the shrapnel beat all over the hill, and the retreat became a run before the rear edge was reached.

Behind the wall the regimental commanders, taking the cessation of Boer fire as signal for a last successful attack, met in hasty conference, and agreed to lead their men forward simul-

The Infantry dash in.

The onslaught having weakened, the Artillery opens fire again.

It checks both sides.

The final charge.

taneously. Soon after 1 p.m. the whole British line surged over the wall, and clambering up the hill, flooded its flat summit from end to end.

From Lennox Hill this final charge was marked, and in a few moments it, too, was empty of Boers. Before 2 p.m. the entire position was won, and Brigadier-General Yule, to whom the loss of General Symons had given the command, at once ordered the artillery to the summit of Smith's Nek, from whence they might shell the now flying foe. The cavalry, looked for amongst the defeated Boers, who covered the plain for miles in the direction of the Buffalo river, were nowhere to be seen. On the guns then rested the last hope of confirming the victory, but they, having gained the Nek, were, to the wonderment of all, pointed silently at the receding commandos. Doubt had at this critical moment assailed the artillery commander. Just before the final stroke, about 1.30 p.m., a message, purporting to come from Lukas Meyer, proposing an armistice to look for the wounded, had passed through his hands on its way to the General. No authoritative information as to its having been accorded or not having reached him, he, with other officers, became uncertain as to the propriety of continuing the battle. At this time a bystander exclaimed that the Boer hospital was retreating before him, and believing that he himself saw red-crossed flags waving over the Boer column moving slowly away within shrapnel range, his hesitation deepened. He refrained from opening fire, and the Boer army, defeated, but not crushed, made despondently, but without further losses, for the laager under the Doornberg, from which it had marched the night before. *The Boers abandon Lennox Hill.* *Cavalry and guns both fail to make defeat crushing.* *A fatal error.*

Brigadier-General Yule, beset with anxiety concerning the Boer army, which had menaced his flank all day from Impati, had no thought but to secure his men in quarters before night and the still expected attack fell upon them together. The infantry, therefore, after searching the hill for wounded, were sent from the field. By 6 p.m., as evening fell amid a storm of rain, all were back in camp. The mounted troops alone, unseen since the early morning, did not return to their lines, nor was *The return to camp.*

138   THE WAR IN SOUTH AFRICA.

there any sign of them until, at 7 p.m., two squadrons of the 18th Hussars, under Major Knox, reported themselves. No more came in that night, nor next morning, nor at any time.

Möller's disastrous day.

The brief orders given to Colonel Möller at the commencement of the action have already been detailed, and even before the enemy's guns were silenced that officer began to put them into execution with promise of brilliant results. As early as 5.45 a.m. he despatched a squadron of the 18th Hussars, with instructions to move round the northern extremity of Talana, and report if it were possible to take ground on the flank from which the enemy's retreat or, at least, his loose ponies might be threatened. The reconnaissance was perfectly successful. Moving northwards a mile down an arm of the Sand Spruit, under the harmless fire of two guns, Major E. C. Knox guided his squadron across the watercourse, and hidden, by the mist from Impati, by a spur from Talana, turned north-east. Then crossing the main spruit, above the point where its northerly trend is deflected by the spurs of the two mountains, he swung boldly south-east and, unperceived by the enemy, seized a kopje from which he could actually look into the right rear of their position upon Talana, only 1,200 yards distant to the south-west. Behind the mountain stood herds of saddled ponies, whose masters lay out of sight in action along the western crest. A message despatched to Colonel Möller informing him of this achievement, and asking for reinforcements, brought to the spot another squadron of the 18th and the regimental machine gun, with the section of the King's Royal Rifles mounted infantry. These made their way at first through a sharp fire from the pom-pom near the northern end of Talana, but, like their predecessors, were neglected as soon as they moved out of sight around the spur swelling up from the Sand Spruit to the right flank of the Boer fastness. Shortly afterwards, in response to a message from the General, who thought that the enemy's guns, now suddenly silent, were being withdrawn, and that a general retreat would shortly follow, Colonel Möller himself hurried after with the remaining squadron of the 18th and the mounted infantry

TALANA HILL. 139

company of the Dublin Fusiliers. The cavalry were now in rear of the flank of an enemy already wavering, and certain to fly shortly, whose lines of retreat would be at their mercy, whose means of retreat, the ponies, they could already partially destroy. But here, Möller, refusing the requests of his subordinates to be allowed to open fire on the closely-packed ponies on Talana, first despatched a squadron under Major Knox towards the rear of Talana, then himself quitted his vantage ground and lined up his force in some plough land towards Schultz' farm, and later in the open veld astride of the Landman's Drift road, two and a half miles in rear of the centre of the Boer position. Whilst moving in accordance with these dispositions, a section of the Dublin Fusiliers mounted infantry, turning aside to assail a party of Boers in a small farmhouse on the flank, captured seven of them.

Meanwhile the squadron under Knox, reconnoitring towards the rear of Smith's Nek, had been harassed by hostile patrols on its left flank. These were speedily dispersed with a loss of ten prisoners by the charge of a troop. But other and stronger patrols coming up from the direction of Landman's Drift hung so persistently on the flank that a charge by the whole squadron was necessary. It was completely successful, two of the enemy being killed and about twenty-five captured. The other patrols then drew off, and the squadron, finding nothing more to do, returned to hand over the prisoners. But Möller, seeing the enemy swarming about the rear of Lennox Hill, at once ordered Knox out again in that direction, this time with two squadrons and a troop, directing him to get behind the hill, which, in prolongation of Lennox Hill to the south, overlooks the coalfields on one side and on the other abuts on the heights of Halifax. *Knox's happy charge.*

He himself remained out in the open with his diminished force of mounted infantry and two troops of cavalry. Now the enemy were quitting Talana and Lennox Hills in numbers which increased momentarily, and when the mounted infantry opened fire upon them, they began to converge on the insignificant party which barred the road to safety. Möller at length perceived his danger, and commencing a series of rapid retirements *Möller's surrender.*

towards the northern spur of Impati, fixed his only hope on the possibility of riding completely around that mountain, outwork though it was of the main Boer army in its descent from the frontier. In a spruit, a branch of the Sand river, which runs through Schultz' farm, the Maxim, outpaced and overdriven, stuck fast, and it was promptly attacked and captured by a party of twenty-five of the enemy who had descried its plight from Talana, its detachment holding out until all were killed or wounded. In this affair nine Boer prisoners were also released. About 1.15 p.m., a party of two hundred Boers was seen descending Impati through the collieries at its northern extremity. The mountain already held the enemy's van; Möller's retreat was cut off. Adelaide farm lay close ahead, and here for the first time he faced about for a stand. The men of the 18th Hussars, with the section of the King's Royal Rifles mounted infantry, and one of the Dublin mounted infantry, lined the farm walls; the remaining two sections of the mounted infantry of the Dublin Fusiliers held a small kopje, two hundred yards from the building. The Boers closed around in force and poured a bitter fusilade upon the troopers. A gun, which had opened ineffectively from the colliery, was then brought forward to 1,400 yards, and its projectiles shattered the buildings, and scattered the horses. In a few moments another gun opened more to the left and 1,100 yards distant. At 4 p.m. the white flag was by Möller's order waved in the farmyard, and he capitulated to Commandant Trichardt. Nine officers and 205 men laid down their arms after a loss of 8 men killed, 3 officers and 20 men wounded. This affair all but doubled the day's casualties, which now numbered 500.*

Knox wins his way home.

Meanwhile Knox's two squadrons were in little less danger in the opposite direction. Attempting to intercept with dismounted fire parties of the enemy, who were retiring towards Halifax, the little force became the focus of every wandering party of the enemy, not only of those evacuating the positions of Talana and Lennox Hill, but also of many riding in from the Buffalo. For the hills and plain were full of Boers who had taken no part

* For detailed casualties, see Appendix 6.

in the battle. But Knox was not to be trapped. Moving swiftly towards Malungeni, and favoured by a slight mist, he slipped away, though nearly surrounded, and halted for half an hour under cover. Then, whilst the Boers were puzzled by his circuitous track, he dashed westwards through their intervals and escaped.

CHAPTER VIII.

THE RETREAT FROM DUNDEE, AND THE ACTION OF RIETFONTEIN.*

Yule decides not to retreat, but shifts his ground.

At 5, on the morning of October 21st, the troops again stood to arms. There was no sign of life upon Talana; the cavalry scouted out unmolested on that side. The mounted patrols, however, supported by "F." company of the Royal Irish Fusiliers, reconnoitring northward, discovered the enemy on the Dannhauser road, and the foremost scouts were driven in. At the same time information came of a hostile movement to the westward. Whatever illusions may have existed previously about the strategical situation, none now remained. General Yule himself had at no time shared them; yet he was disinclined to retreat. He re-created a staff,† examined a fresh defensive position, and determined to stand his ground. Sending for his commanding officers shortly after midday, he pointed out the new site he had selected below the sloping shoulder of one of the foremost spurs of Indumeni, about a mile south of their present camp, and desired them to rendezvous upon it with their commands at 2.30 p.m., less, however, with any intention of occupying it definitely than of seeing how the troops "fitted into the ground." In view of the expected bombardment from Impati, the whole of the tents except those of the hospital had previously been lowered, and in them the men's

---

* See maps Nos. 3, 5 and 7.

† Appointing Major A. J. Murray, Royal Inniskilling Fusiliers, (late D.A.A.G.I.) as A.A.G., Lieut. G. E. R. Kenrick, the Queen's Regiment, as acting D.A.A.G., Captain C. K. Burnett, 18th Hussars, as Brigade Major to the 8th infantry brigade, and Lieut. F. D. Murray, the Black Watch, as A.D.C.

THE RETREAT FROM DUNDEE.

kits had been left ready packed for a move. The cavalry and artillery started at once. Before the hour appointed for the march of the rest of the troops the enemy made his presence on Impati felt. At 1.35 p.m. a squadron of the 18th Hussars, reconnoitring near the Dannhauser road, came suddenly under the fire of four guns and many rifles from the north-western slopes of the mountain.

The Royal Irish Fusiliers led off towards the rendezvous at 2 p.m. By 3 p.m. all were in their places, Royal Irish Fusiliers, Royal Dublin Fusiliers, Leicestershire regiment and King's Royal Rifles, in the order named from right to left. It was cold and dull, and the slight rain turned to a heavy downpour, which filled the shallow trenches as soon as they were made. At 3.30 p.m. Yule, receiving reports from his patrols that the enemy was mounting guns upon Impati, and realising more fully his peril, despatched a telegram to Ladysmith reporting his arrangements, declaring his expectation of being attacked from both sides, and asking for reinforcements. Before the message had reached its destination, a shell from a heavy piece upon the western shoulder of Impati burst in front of the new line. Others followed quickly, some into the deserted camp where the hospital tents stood up as a target, some into the entrenchments, others into the cavalry, who had taken ground in the rear of the line of defence, and further up the slopes of Indumeni. One falling into a tin house, which lay behind the left, killed Lieut. W. M. J. Hannah, of the Leicestershire M.I., who was sheltering from the storm, and wounded two of his men; elsewhere a gunner was killed and another wounded. Another and a smaller gun then opened from a point below the western crest of Impati. The accuracy of the piece and the smallness of its calibre challenged the British batteries to reply. But the first shrapnel burst at the foot of the mountain, far below the Boer artillery, and when sinking the trails failed to give the necessary elevation by some two thousand yards, the gunners desisted.

Yule asks for reinforcements.

Shortly before 4 p.m. Brigadier-General Yule received the compliments of Sir George White upon his appointment to the rank of Major-General. An hour later, a second telegram

Reinforcements cannot be sent.

from Ladysmith informed him that the reinforcements, which at this juncture he desired more than promotion, could not be sent. The troops a Ladysmith,—telegraphed the Chief Staff Officer,—were engaged at Elandslaagte and the Commander-in-Chief was in the field with them. General Yule's request would be submitted to him on his return, but little hopes could be held out of its being complied with.

Yule will wait.

Still the General was unwilling to retreat. Accompanied by his staff officer, he was on his way to find new ground, out of range of Impati, before that mountain had become indistinct in the twilight. He was long in the saddle, examining the northern slopes of Indumeni for a suitable spot. Night drew on, the rain increasing with the dying light; the regular fire of the enemy's guns became intermittent, then ceased, and darkness closed round the British force on the spur.

He moves again.

At midnight Yule gave instructions for a move at 3 a.m. to the spot he had selected, a flat-topped foothill of Indumeni, on its northern side, and some two miles south of the bivouac. Before that hour the transport, escorted by the cavalry and mounted infantry, was quietly withdrawn, and made its way safely to the place appointed, where it found cover behind the reverse slopes. The remainder, marching punctually, covered by a rear-guard of the Royal Irish Fusiliers, reached the new position at 5 a.m., and took up an open line along the crest, facing generally north in the following order of units from left to right: Royal Dublin Fusiliers, Leicestershire regiment, Royal Irish Fusiliers and King's Royal Rifles.

Receives news of Elandslaagte.

At 8 a.m., October 22nd, two despatch riders arriving from Helpmakaar delivered a message from the Prime Minister of Natal, announcing a victory on the previous day at Elandslaagte. "The British force from Ladysmith,"—telegraphed Sir Albert Hime,—"completely defeated Boer force over a thousand strong at Elandslaagte, capturing guns, tents and equipment. Cavalry in full pursuit."

Yule marches to intercept.

It was at once apparent to General Yule that he was directly on the line of retreat of the Boers flying from Sir George White's cavalry, and he determined to attempt to intercept them.

THE RETREAT FROM DUNDEE. 145

Glencoe Junction, at the mouth of the Biggarsberg, appeared to be the point most likely to promise success; he immediately issued orders for a general march in that direction.

fugitives.

At 10 a.m. an advance guard of the 69th battery, the mounted infantry, and the 18th Hussars moved off at the trot for Glencoe. A wounded Boer, who had been pushed up along the railway from Elandslaagte on a trolly, was their only capture, and less than a dozen rounds of shrapnel at 3,800 yards dispersed the few scattered parties of the enemy visible along the kopjes. The remainder of the column wended their way across the lower spurs of Indumeni. Soon a portion of the baggage, seeking an easier road too near the camp, was descried from Impati by the Boer gunners, who turned their pieces on both camp and troops, and opened a rapid fire. The 67th battery, which had previously been directed upon the Glencoe kopjes, now endeavoured in vain to silence the Impati battery from near the left of the Dublin Fusiliers. The enemy's shooting was as accurate as it was impartial, though it was singularly ineffective. Shells of 96 lbs. weight burst between the guns of the 67th battery, amongst the troops and baggage, and all over the camp, doing no other damage than to add to the sufferings of the wounded lying, with the apprehension of helpless men, in the field hospital.* The descent of mist, however, soon put an end to the bombardment, and the mounted arms, pushing forward towards Glencoe, endeavoured to carry out the original intention. But instead of fugitives, they found the Boers showing a firm front on the high land north and west of the station, and some slight interchange of shots took place, during which a troop of the 18th Hussars, reconnoitring too boldly, was cut off, and was seen no more that day.† With the enemy in this attitude upon strong ground, General Yule saw the inutility of further efforts of this kind, and gave the order for retirement. At 1 p.m. the force was again below Indumeni, as it had been in the morning,

Catches a Tartar and returns.

---

* The Red Cross flag was so placed, and so small, as to be invisible to the Boers.

† This patrol, finding its retreat impossible, made straight for Ladysmith, where it arrived safely next day.

VOL. I. 10

having effected nothing. As the men climbed the last few yards of the precipitous ascent, the fog, rolling for a short time from the summit of Impati, once more gave the Boer artillerymen on their lofty platform a view of the plain below, and again the sufferers in the hospital endured the explosion of the heavy projectiles of the Creusot cannon close outside their shelter.

<small>Yule ordered to attempt retreat, prepares for it.</small>

Yule, whose health, previously bad, had given way under the toil, anxiety and exposure, now unwillingly decided to retire on Ladysmith whilst the road still remained open, and at 5.45 p.m. he dictated a message acquainting Sir G. White with his determination. Before it could be despatched, at 6.30 p.m. a telegram from Ladysmith was placed in his hands. It was Sir G. White's reply to his request for reinforcements, and it banished the last cause for hesitation. "I cannot reinforce you without sacrificing Ladysmith and the Colony behind. You must try and fall back on Ladysmith. I will do what I may to help you when nearer." Acknowledging its contents, Yule prepared for retreat.

<small>Retreat begins.</small>

No sooner had darkness fallen than Major Wickham, of the Indian Commissariat, taking with him thirty-three wagons guarded by two companies of the Leicestershire regiment, left the hill and moved with great precaution into the deserted camp. The convoy performed its short but dangerous journey without attracting the attention of the enemy, and the wagons, after being quickly loaded with as many stores as the darkness, the confusion of the levelled tents, and limited time made possible, were drawn up on the outskirts to await the passing of the column. At 9 p.m. the whole force fell in. The night was fine but intensely dark, and the units had some difficulty in reaching their stations in the carefully arranged order of march. At 9.30 p.m. all being ready, the column, guided by Colonel Dartnell, went quietly down the mountain side towards Dundee, the southern boundary of which it was necessary to skirt to gain the Helpmakaar road. By 11.15 p.m. the last company was clear of the mountain, and, striking the track to Dundee at the foot of Indumeni, the troops passed close to the bivouac ground of the 21st October. Outside the town Major Wickham's convoy

THE RETREAT FROM DUNDEE.

stood waiting, and when, at the right moment, the signal was given, the above-mentioned wagons fell into their place in the line of march. The pace was rapid, despite the impenetrable gloom. Skirting Dundee, the route turned sharply south-east around the corner of the Helpmakaar road. On the edge of the town the precaution was taken to cut the telegraph wire to Greytown.* By 4.30 a.m. October 23rd, the leading files having traversed safely the defile of Blesboklaagte†, had made good twelve miles of the road to Helpmakaar, fourteen miles from the starting-point. Near Dewaas, Yule, sending a message to Ladysmith to announce his progress, halted on open ground, over which piquets were at once thrown out on every side, and the batteries formed up for action. Ten a.m. was the hour of starting again, the Royal Irish Fusiliers relieving the King's Royal Rifles as advance guard. A blazing sun beating upon the treeless downs, and a rumour of the enemy having been seen ahead, now made marching toilsome and slow. By 12.30 p.m., less than five miles having been covered, Yule decided to halt again, until darkness should arrive to lessen both the fatigue and the risk of discovery by the enemy. His situation was hazardous in the extreme. Behind him the Boers would be soon on his heels, if they were not so already; before him lay a defile known as Van Tonders Pass, deep and difficult, some six miles in length. But at the slow rate of movement, necessitated by the nature of the route through it, the passage of this dangerous ground would take so much time and cause such disorder, that, balancing the evils, Yule, after reconnoitring the obstacle, bivouacked at 2 p.m. on a high and open spur of the Biggarsberg, overlooking the valley of the Waschbank river, two miles east-south-east of Beith, and one mile west of the junction of the Helpmakaar and Ladysmith roads. Here he waited anxiously for the night.

Late on the morning of the 23rd the Boers, after reconnoitring the camp and its vicinity as closely as they dared, opened once more from Impati with their heavy gun. The first shell burst in the hospital lines, and Major J. F. Donegan, the chief medical officer, who, fearing to prejudice General Yule's

The Boers occupy Dundee.

---

* See map No. 4.   † See map No. 3.

148   THE WAR IN SOUTH AFRICA.

operations, had done nothing to inform the enemy that his marquees were the only inhabited tents, now determined to spare the wounded the horrors of further bombardment. Captain A. E. Milner was therefore sent with a white flag to ask that the fire should be stopped. Thereupon Erasmus' men, to whom news of Yule's evacuation was a complete surprise, filed down the mountain, and approached, not without caution. There was soon no room for doubt; Dundee had fallen, and Erasmus' prize was large in inverse proportion to the share he had taken in capturing it. No sooner was the absence of the British soldiers established beyond a doubt, than the burghers made haste to sack the camp and town. In a short time every tent, except those of the hospitals, which were scrupulously respected, was ransacked, and every shop turned inside out. Commandant-General Joubert now sent orders to Lukas Meyer to pursue Yule with a thousand men. Meyer did so, but marching late and slowly, failed to come up with the British.

Night march Oct. 23rd Oct. 24th.

At 11 p.m. Yule roused his men for a fresh effort. A hot day had given place to a bleak and bitter night. But though the road was steep and obstructed, and Van Tonders Pass plunged in profound gloom, the column, headed by the Dublin Fusiliers, marched punctually and well. By dawn the dangerous defile was safely threaded and the force debouched on to the broad veld which rolls about the southern buttresses of the Biggarsberg. At 6 a.m., October 24th, the vanguard was at the Waschbank river, some thirteen miles from Beith, and on its southern bank the troops were allowed to bivouac, the rearguard closing up at 10 a.m., after ten weary hours' marching.

Yule, Oct. 24th, moves to sound of guns.

As they halted, heavy and prolonged reports of artillery sounded from the westward. It was evident that Sir G. White was fighting an action upon the flank near Elandslaagte or Modder Spruit, and, in response to the urgent request of his senior officers, Yule determined to despatch at once a portion of his command to co-operate. Yule himself, though now almost prostrate with illness and fatigue, rode out westward at the head of the 67th and 69th field batteries, two squadrons 18th Hussars, and two companies M.I. The remainder of the troops were

THE RETREAT FROM DUNDEE. 149

left by the Waschbank under command of Lieut.-Col. Carleton, Royal Irish Fusiliers, who took up a defensive position on the northern bank.

Yule moved rapidly westwards over the shadeless tract lying between the Sunday's and Waschbank rivers. Nine miles his mounted men pressed towards the sound of the guns, but still the most advanced scouts saw nothing, and when, about 2 p.m., the noise of the firing, still far ahead, began to die away, he gave the order to retire to the Waschbank. His men were back in bivouac at 4 p.m. No sooner had the infantry from the height above filed over the muddy pools than a storm, which had been gathering all day in the terrible heat, burst, and cooled the sun-baked ground with a waterspout of rain. The Waschbank, which had all but perished in the drought, in less than an hour rose from three inches to a height of twelve feet of roaring water, thirty-five yards in breadth. The rearmost infantry plunged hurriedly across before it had attained its strength. A piquet of the Royal Dublin Fusiliers, and a patrol of the 18th Hussars, who had covered the passage, found themselves cut off, and remained long on the enemy's side of the river.   *Yule recrosses Waschbank Oct. 24th.*

At 4 a.m. on the 25th the march was resumed along the southern and least direct* of the two routes, which bifurcate at the Waschbank. At 8.30 a.m. the advance guard was at and over Sunday's river, seven miles further on, the rearguard crossing by the steep drift at noon, and here the column rested. At 1 p.m. it was on the move again, breasting the gentler ascent which swells upwards from the southern bank of the stream, and after covering some four and a half miles, was again halted at 3.45 p.m. upon the summit of a high ridge due north of Kankana Mountain. Here preparations were made to pass the night; the piquets went out, rations were distributed and cooked. At 5 p.m., however, a patrol of the 5th Lancers from Ladysmith rode up with orders from Sir G. White. Behind them a column under Lt.-Col. J. A. Coxhead, R.A., was on the way from Ladysmith to assist the Dundee detachment over the last stage. There were reports that the enemy was about to close in from   *Oct. 25 Yule gets touch with White.*

* The northern road had been reconnoitred and found to be without water.

every side. General Yule was to effect a junction with Coxhead at once, and to proceed without another check into Ladysmith.

Night march Oct. 25th-26th.

At 6 p.m. began a night march of great distress and trouble. Soon after the advance guard moved off, a heavy downpour converted the road into a sea of semi-liquid mire, which the transport ploughed into waves and furrows. These, invisible in the black darkness, almost held down the soldiers plunging knee-deep into them. The teams of mules, exhausted by prolonged labour and insufficient food, impatient by nature of wet and darkness, strove with much suffering to drag the rocking wagons through the mud, and, as is their habit when overmastered by their load, threw themselves often in confusion athwart the track and enforced a halt. At 9 p.m. the whole of the transport stuck fast for more than two hours. The rearguard closed up, but the troops in front of the baggage, knowing nothing of its misfortunes, and travelling on a road not destroyed by its struggles, pushed on and left it. With great efforts it was set in motion again, but some half-dozen of the wagons, being imbedded hopelessly, had to be abandoned.* Half a mile further the convoy was again in difficulties. From this point all cohesion was lost. Some of the wagons passed on, some remained; it was impossible for their escorts to tell which were derelict and which they must still consider as in their charge.

Coxhead's relief column.

Throughout the night Lieut.-Col. Coxhead, R.A., who had left Ladysmith at 9 a.m. on October 25th, lay waiting about a mile east of the Nek between Bulwana† and Lombards Kop for the Dundee column to join hands with his own. With him were the 5th Lancers, half a battalion 2nd Gordon Highlanders, half a battalion 1st Manchester regiment, the 21st battery R.F.A., and a convoy containing two days' supplies, which General Yule had asked for, in a message despatched from the bivouac at the Waschbank river on the 24th. Coxhead immediately gained touch with Yule by means of his mounted troops, and learning that the food would not be required, sent the wagons back. All day the troops from Ladysmith remained on the Helpmakaar road. But night and torrents of rain fell together, and Cox-

---

* They were recovered next day.   † Or Umbulwana.

THE RETREAT FROM DUNDEE. 151

head's men bivouacked in discomfort only less than that of their comrades toiling towards them, still nine miles distant.

At 3.30 a.m. on the 26th, just as the Ladysmith garrison was getting under arms, in case a sally to bring in Yule might after all be necessary, the foremost of the mounted men from Dundee rode up to Modder Spruit. An hour later the Leicestershire regiment and the King's Royal Rifles arrived, much exhausted, but in good order. After a brief halt they went on into the town, which they entered at 6 a.m. The other regiments, with the transport which had delayed them, coming up to Coxhead between 7 a.m. and 8 a.m., halted for two hours, and had breakfast before pushing on. *The retreat ends Oct 26th.*

It is necessary now to revert to the action which had, on October 24th, been heard in the bivouac by the Waschbank, that action of which a ride of nine miles westward had failed to disclose either the purport or the scene. The arrival on the 23rd of Free State commandos upon the heights north and west of the railway had redoubled Sir G. White's already great anxiety for the safety of the retreat from Dundee. In reality, the presence of the Free State forces on the commanding ranges to the west of Elandslaagte was less dangerous than it appeared, for Yule was marching in greater obscurity than either he, or Sir G. White, imagined. When, indeed, on the morning of the 24th, the Free Staters saw troops issuing from Ladysmith, they believed them to be the combined forces of Generals White and Yule,* though the latter was at the moment still actually upon the wrong side of the Waschbank. At still greater cross-purposes was Erasmus, who set off on the morning of the 24th, with so little hope of overtaking the retreat that he chose the only route by which it was impossible for him to do so, the main road west of the railway. Nevertheless, on the evening of the 25th, Erasmus' bivouac was near Elandslaagte, and the wisdom of Sir G. White's order for the instant continuance of the march of the column on that afternoon was manifested. Had that march not been executed, Yule, the action of Rietfontein notwithstanding, would have had the vanguard of Joubert's army upon his flank next day, when *Cause of Rietfontein action, Oct. 24th.*

* C. de Wet, " Three Years' War."

only operations from Ladysmith on the largest scale could have extricated him.

<small>The Rietfontein position.</small>
Some seven miles north-east of Ladysmith, Rietfontein* farmhouse lay by a branch of the Modder Spruit, south-west of a long, low ridge, which descended to the railway line in smooth and easy slopes dotted with ant-heaps, with on its forehead a sparse eyebrow of stones. Beyond the crest line, to the northward, the ground sank with a gentle sweep, broken only by two rough under-features jutting from the western extremity of the ridge, to rear itself again eight hundred yards beyond into a line of abrupt heights. The southernmost of these, called Intintanyoni,† leaped up steeply from the hollow, and beyond and behind it stretched many leagues of rolling ground, with scarce a subsidence until they merged in the tumultuous billows of the Drakensberg. Two grassy pinnacles, nearly equal in height, flanked Intintanyoni. Of these the western looked across a deep and narrow gorge over to Nodashwana or Swaatbouys Kop, of a somewhat greater elevation, whilst below the eastern, deep re-entrants, both on the north and south, divided Intintanyoni from the magnificent curve of highlands, which terminated west of Elandslaagte in the wooded mass of Jonono's Kop. ‡

<small>The Boer occupation of it.</small>
East of the twin peaks of Intintanyoni various lesser eminences and hollow Neks completed the tempestuous irregularity of this singular feature, along whose crest six Free State commandos lay waiting for their first battle on the morning of October 24th. To the east, with patrols upon Jonono's Kop, lay the men of Bethlehem, Vrede, and Heilbron; about the eastern peak of Intintanyoni the Winburg commando held the ground, in charge of two pieces of artillery; on their right, occupying the rest of the mountain, the burghers of Kroonstad made ready; whilst those of Harrismith disposed themselves partly upon a supporting position in rear, and partly as piquets

---

* See map No. 7.
† Also called Tintwa Inyoni.
‡ A free hand sketch of the position from Nodashwana to Jonono's Kop will be found in the case of maps accompanying this volume. Jonono's Kop is not shown in the plan of Rietfontein, no part of the battle having been near it.

and observation posts on outlying kopjes, amongst others the lofty Nodashwana. Some 6,000 riflemen in all filled the six-mile line of heights. They were commanded by General A. P. Cronje, who had arrived only on this morning, the 24th, to replace de Villiers, who had been in temporary charge.

Sir G. White moved out from Ladysmith at 5 a.m. with the 5th Lancers, 19th Hussars, Imperial Light Horse, Natal Mounted Rifles, 42nd and 53rd batteries R.F.A., No. 10 Mountain battery R.G.A., 1st Liverpool, 1st Devon, 1st Gloucestershire regiments, and 2nd King's Royal Rifle Corps, in all, some 5,300 officers and men, assuming himself the direction of an operation certain to be delicate, likely to be extremely dangerous. Moving up the Newcastle road from its rendezvous near the junction of the Free State railway, the force had proceeded six miles when the advanced screen of cavalry came under a dropping rifle fire at 7 a.m. from the heights on their left. Their action was prompt. Pushing rapidly across the Modder Spruit, a squadron of 5th Lancers, supported by two others, drove back at the gallop the small parties of Boers hovering in that neighbourhood, and themselves seized and held this advanced position. The remainder of the cavalry, stringing out along high ground dominating the western bank of the spruit, and facing more to the eastward, formed a strong flank guard towards Jonono's Kop. At 8 a.m., whilst fitful discharges of musketry rose and fell along the widely-extended line of troopers, the infantry had come up to Rietfontein. No sooner had they arrived at a point on the road some five hundred yards east of the Modder Spruit, than a loud report broke from the eastern peak of Intintanyoni, and a shell, bursting on impact, fell into the head of the column. Thereupon the British artillery wheeled out from the route, and in line of batteries trotted towards a level crossing over the railway, some six hundred yards west of the road. Arrived at this defile, and forming column inwards to traverse it, the first gun had scarcely passed the rails, when both the Boer guns on the high green rampart ahead opened upon the point, which had been taken as one of their range marks. Five hundred yards beyond it the artillery deployed behind a rise. The second round from

Sir George marches out, Oct. 24th.

the 53rd battery, fused at 3,600 yards, burst full upon one of the Boer pieces, and the gunners of both weapons fled. After a few more rounds the 53rd limbered up and prepared to advance.

The infantry seize ridge facing hill.

The infantry were already over the railway, and moving forward—Gloucester regiment on the left, Liverpool regiment on the right—up the gentle but protected slope, swelling to the summit of the low ridge of Rietfontein. The 1st Devonshire regiment, in support, lay at the base, whilst the 2nd King's Royal Rifles remained in rear in charge of the baggage. On the appearance of the leading companies upon the crest, firing broke out from the whole length of the crest of Intintanyoni, to which the British infantry, lying prone, soon replied as vigorously. Of the artillery, the 42nd battery was quickly in action near the centre of the front, whilst the 53rd unlimbered some six hundred yards to the left, and began shelling a rocky underfeature of Intintanyoni, at a range of 1,500 yards. Sharp musketry assailed them. Then the 42nd battery, being ordered further to the left, passed behind the 53rd and the 10th Mountain battery, which had come into line on the left of the 53rd, and opened 1,900 yards from the summit of Intintanyoni. Thus began a severe fire fight at ranges varying from one to two thousand yards. Especially was it hotly contested where the Gloucester on the left of the British opposed the 1,400 Kroonstad men, who, under Nel, maintained the Boer right. Heavy exchanges of rifle fire swept across the valley in this part, and in spite of the steady practice of the artillery, it became necessary to reinforce the attackers. For this purpose the Devonshire regiment was pushed up on the left of the Gloucester, half the King's Royal Rifles coming from the baggage train to fill its place in support.

An untoward incident.

Sir G. White had all but accomplished his purpose, that of intervening between the Free State commandos and Yule's line of march, when one of those accidents of war, inexplicable because of the death of those who alone could explain them, largely increased his hitherto insignificant losses. Shortly before midday Colonel E. P. Wilford, commanding the 1st Gloucestershire, taking a company of his battalion and the regimental Maxim gun, dashed out of cover down the open slope as if to assault. An-

THE RETREAT FROM DUNDEE.

other half company of the battalion moved on ahead to cut a wire fence which obstructed the front. The Boers, who for a time had lain quiet under the shrapnel, which searched their position from end to end, at once opened a fierce fusilade. Colonel Wilford was shot dead, and his men fell rapidly, the detachment finally halting upon a low ridge beneath Intintanyoni. Further advance was impossible. Only with difficulty could both the Gloucestershire and "D." squadron I.L.H., which had joined in the attack, be withdrawn. Fortunately, as the attempt was promptly ordered to cease, though many had been wounded, only six were killed in the adventure. Meanwhile the shooting over their heads had been continuous. The enemy, encouraged by this event, and by the immobility of Sir G. White's line of battle, which they imagined to be awed from its purpose by their resistance, still clung to their fastness, and maintained a heavy though spasmodic fire. More than once the gunners of the still uninjured piece beneath the eastern peak made efforts to drag it forward into action, but the British artillerymen watched the spot narrowly, and each attempt was blown back by shrapnel, under which Intintanyoni burst into flames. Many of the Boer ponies herded in rear, terrified by the blaze, stampeded. Then, up on Nodashwana, amongst the Harrismith men, a stir was descried which seemed to threaten an outflanking manœuvre against the British left. Sir G. White, anxious for his communications with Ladysmith, promptly countered the movement by calling the Natal Mounted Rifles across from his right, and sending them on in front of his left flank.* The Colonial riflemen went with such skill into the maze of broken ground below the mountain, that they not only succeeded in outflanking the outflankers, but actually drove by enfilade fire all of the Kroonstad commando, who were upon the right of Intintanyoni, far back across the hill to where the Winburgers lay at the eastern extremity. All danger ceased definitely on this side when two guns of the 42nd battery, turning towards the ridges of Nodashwana, in a few moments cleared it of the enemy, and converted it also into a huge bonfire

* The situation at this time is depicted on map No. 7.

of blazing grass. At 1.30 p.m. the Boer fire had dwindled all along the main ridge, and an hour later it ceased altogether. Only from the far right came the sound of musketry from the cavalry still fencing with scattered detachments of the Heilbron, Vrede and Bethlehem burghers, who clung to them pertinaciously.

<small>Return to Ladysmith.</small> At 3 p.m. Sir G. White gave the order for a general retirement. His object was accomplished, with the not undue loss of 114 casualties. Yule was now safe for that day, and he believed the Free State army to have suffered severely enough to keep it inactive on the next, when he intended to assist the Dundee column by other means. But the Boers watched the withdrawal of the British troops with very little despondency. Unaware of the true situation of the Dundee column, they misunderstood operations designed to keep them from it. The demonstration against Intintanyoni seemed to them nothing less than a serious attempt to drive them from their hold, and the retreat of the British to be that of a baffled army. Thus, ignorant of their strategical defeat, they rejoiced at what seemed a tactical victory. Moreover, their losses* had been small. The cavalry alone, now called upon to protect the rear—as all day they had covered the right—had difficulty in returning. For some distance they had to maintain a running fire fight, and it was nearly 7 p.m. before the rearmost troopers entered Ladysmith, which the head of the infantry column had reached two hours and a half earlier.†

* 13 killed, 31 wounded. † For detailed casualties, see Appendix 6.

CHAPTER IX.

ELANDSLAAGTE.*

DURING the time (Oct. 12th-Oct. 26th, 1899) occupied by the episode of the Dundee detachment, including the action of Rietfontein fought to assist it in retreat, much had happened elsewhere.

Early days in Ladysmith, Oct. 11th to 19th.

Sir G. White arrived in Ladysmith on the 11th October. On the 12th telegraphic communication by Harrismith entirely ceased, and the mail train from that town failed to arrive. Early on the 12th a telegram from a post of observation of Natal Carbineers at Acton Homes gave information that a strong column of Boers, with four miles of train, was on the march through Tintwa Pass, the head of it being already across the border; furthermore, that there seemed to be an advance guard concealed in Van Reenen's Pass. Sir G. White prepared to strike instantly; but a British detachment which reached Dewdrop next day saw the Boer vanguard, halted in the mouth of Tintwa Pass, and as previously described (p. 123) returned to Ladysmith. A cavalry reconnaissance† in the same direction on the 16th found that the commandos had not stirred and, though Olivier's Hoek, Bezuidenhout's, Tintwa and Van Reenen's Passes were all occupied,‡ the country east of them was as clear of the enemy as heretofore. There appeared an unaccountable

Oct. 16th.

---

* See maps Nos. 3 and 6.

† 5th Lancers, 19th Hussars, M.I., 1st King's (Liverpool) regiment.

‡ On the 15th the Intelligence estimate of the Free State forces in the Drakensberg was as follows:—Olivier's Hoek, 3,000; Tintwa, 1,000; Van Reenen's, 1,200, with 15 guns; Nelson's Kop, 3,500, with detachments in the passes to the north. Total, 11,000 men.

hesitation amongst the Free Staters. Rumours of disagreement, and even of actual hostilities between the commandos, reached the British camp. They were not altogether groundless, and Sir G. White, utilising the respite, set himself to consider how his field force might be turned into a garrison, and his place of rest into a fortress, should it be necessary, as now seemed likely, to stand a siege in Ladysmith. A complete scheme of defence was drawn up on the 16th, and a mobile column organised for instant service in any quarter. But, whilst the real enemy lay idle on the west, rumour, working in his favour far to the southward, troubled the British general and robbed him of troops he could ill spare. On the 17th a telegram from the Governor of Natal announced that there was evidence of a contemplated Boer raid viâ Zululand upon Pietermaritzburg and Durban,* and asked for reinforcements for the defenceless capital. They were promptly sent,† and quitted Ladysmith just as the Free Staters in the mountains received with much discussion the order to cross the frontier. Before dawn of the 18th all the commandos were on the move down the defiles, the men of Bethlehem in Olivier's Hoek Pass, of Heilbron in Bezuidenhout's, of Kroonstad in Tintwa, of Winburg in Van Reenen's, of Harrismith in De Beer's, of Vrede in Müller's. By 8 a.m. Acton Homes was in the hands of 3,000 Boers, and shortly after, west of Bester's station, a piquet of the Natal Carbineers was sharply attacked by the Harrismith commando, and forced to retire with loss. The Boers then occupied Bester's station, where they halted for the night. The news of this rapid development caused a great stir in Ladysmith. As early as the 15th Sir George White had decided upon the evacuation of the camp, which lay outside the town, but hitherto no orders had been issued to this effect. All the 18th the work of removing the

Oct. 17th.

Oct. 18th.

---

* Telegram No. 30 of 18th October, 1899, Ladysmith. Sir G. White to Secretary of State.

† Strength: 19th Hussars, one field battery, five squadrons Imperial Light Horse (raised at Maritzburg in Sept. 1899), seven companies Liverpool regiment, half-battalion 2nd King's Royal Rifles, under Brigadier-General C. B. H. Wolseley-Jenkins. The other half of the latter battalion was already in Maritzburg.

ELANDSLAAGTE.

troops and stores from the camp to the town defences previously selected was pushed on with such despatch, that by 10 p.m. these were well manned. The Pietermaritzburg column, which had reached Colenso, was ordered back to Onderbrook. Next day the General rode around Ladysmith, re-adjusting with great care the line of defence selected on the 16th. Instructions were then sent to Wolseley-Jenkins to resume his march to Pietermaritzburg, the Imperial Light Horse alone being taken from the column and brought back into Ladysmith.* *Oct. 19th.*

Meanwhile, the Boer General, Kock, having arrived on the summit of the Biggarsberg on the 19th, promptly pushed patrols down the southern slopes. Field Cornet Potgieter, the leader of one of these, pressing on in company with a party of Viljoen's men, under Field Cornet Pienaar, dashed into Elandslaagte station, some twenty miles southward, and attacked and captured a supply train which was steaming through the station on its way to Glencoe. Potgieter at once sent back word to Kock, who, replying with the order: "Hold on to the trains at any cost, I am following with the whole detachment," marched all night, and joined his lieutenant near the looted train at break of day on the 20th. *Kock Oct. 19th and night of Oct. 19th-20th seizes Elandslaagte station.*

News of the event was quickly received at Headquarters. At 11 a.m. on the 20th Major-General J. D. P. French, who had only arrived at 5 a.m. that morning, left Ladysmith with the 5th Lancers, the Natal Mounted Rifles and Natal Carbineers, and a battery Royal Field artillery, to ascertain the situation at Elandslaagte. An infantry brigade, under Colonel Ian Hamilton, moved out in support. But whilst they were on the march, the Free Staters at Bester's became so active that Sir George White, fearing an attack whilst part of his force was absent, sent orders to check the reconnaissance before it was half completed, and by sunset French was back in Ladysmith, having seen nothing but the German commando, Kock's screen. *French moves out Oct. 20th, but is recalled.*

By this time news of the victory at Talana† had come in. *Encouraged by news of Talana,*

---
* The whole of Wolseley-Jenkins' column eventually returned to Ladysmith during the night of 22nd-23rd October.

† Telegraphic communication by Greytown was still intact.

160   THE WAR IN SOUTH AFRICA.

White, Oct. 21st, sends French out again to Elandslaagte.

Its partial extent not fully understood at first, it not only lifted a load from the General's mind, but showed him where he too could strike a blow. The commandos at Elandslaagte, yesterday dangerous from their position on Symons' line of retreat, were to-day in peril themselves, and he determined to give them no time to remove into safety. At 4 a.m. on the 21st French was again on the move towards Elandslaagte* with five squadrons (338 men) Imperial Light Horse and the Natal Field artillery. At 6 a.m. a half battalion (330 men) of the 1st Manchester regiment, with Railway and Royal engineer detachments, followed by rail, preceded by the armoured train manned by one company of the same battalion. Moving along the Newcastle road, French made straight for the high ground south-west of Elandslaagte station, and at 7 a.m. his advance and right flank guards (Imperial Light Horse) came in touch with the enemy, the former south of the collieries, the latter on the open veld some four miles south of the railway. As the mist lifted, parties of Boers were seen all about the station and colliery buildings, and over the undulating veld, and it was observed that most of these, on sighting the British scouts, drew back upon a group of kopjes situated about a mile south-east of the station. French immediately ordered up the Natal battery on to a flat hillock which rose between the railway and the Newcastle road, south-east of Woodcote farm, and at 8 a.m. a shot from the 7-pounders, sighted at 1,900 yards, crashed into the tin out-buildings of the station.

French retakes station.

A crowd of Boers swarmed out at the explosion and with them some of the British captured in the train the day before, the former galloping for the kopjes, the latter making for the protection of their countrymen at the battery. At the same time a squadron of the Imperial Light Horse galloped for the station in extended files, captured the Boer guard, and released the station and colliery officials who were there in durance. But in a few moments shells from the group of kopjes beyond the station began to fall into the battery, one smashing an ammunition wagon. The gunners attempted in vain to reply;

---

* See map No. 3. Orders were to " clear the neighbourhood of Elandslaagte of the enemy and cover the re-construction of the railway and telegraphic lines."

their pieces were outranged by over 500 yards, and at 8.15, on the arrival of the infantry near at hand, they fell back leaving the wagon derelict. At 8.30 a.m. French withdrew to a point four miles south of Woodcote farm, and from here sent a report to Sir George White, informing him that about 400 Boers with three guns were before him on a prepared position, and asking for support. The enemy's artillery continued to shell the troops, and French, after questioning the prisoners and the released Britons, and examining more closely, came to the conclusion that there were from 800 to 1,000 Boers in front of him. When parties of the enemy began to appear also upon Jonono's Kop to the north-west he judged it prudent to withdraw his weak detachment still further, and by 11.30 a.m. was back nearly at the Modder Spruit. On the way he fell in with a reinforcement from Ladysmith consisting of one squadron 5th Lancers,* one squadron 5th Dragoon Guards, and the 42nd battery Field artillery, all under Colonel Coxhead, R.A., and with these he retraced his steps to the Modder Spruit siding, where a halt was called. *[margin: but falls back.]*

It was now evident to General French that an action of great importance could be fought or avoided before nightfall. At noon, therefore, he communicated with Sir George White, and, after informing him of his own and the enemy's situations, and the best line of attack, stated that in his opinion the numbers required would be three battalions of infantry, two batteries, and more cavalry than he had at the moment. He would await instructions. They came with promptitude; for Sir G. White had determined to ruin this commando, and sweep it from Yule's communications, before it could separate. "The enemy must be beaten, and driven off," he wrote to French. "Time of great importance." Within a quarter of an hour of the receipt of the above message, French had promulgated his orders; within half an hour, at 1.30 p.m., before the arrival of the reinforcements, the advance upon the kopjes had begun. *[margin: He asks for reinforcements and orders.]*

---

* Another squadron, 5th Lancers, supported from Pepworth Hill by a company of the 1st Devonshire regiment, turned aside when four miles out to watch the Free Staters towards Bester's.

162   THE WAR IN SOUTH AFRICA.

The ground held by Boers.   Running south-east, with its northern extremity about a mile from the station, the ground held by the enemy covered some 4,000 yards from flank to flank, and consisted of four boulder-strewn kopjes. That nearest the station was steep and rocky, its top 200 yards broad and sloping rearwards ; next and somewhat retired from the general line, 700 yards distant, on the far side of a deep cup scored with dongas, arose one of those singular isosceles triangular eminences of which South Africa almost alone possesses the mould. A Nek, carrying the roadway to a farm behind, separated this from the main feature 500 yards away. This was a bluff and precipitous hill, thatched here and there with long grasses on its northern face, on its eastern sloping easily down to the veld which rolled in rounded waves towards Ladysmith. Its summit was almost flat, a bouldered plateau, 400 yards long by 200 wide, falling in rocky spurs to the river a mile and a half in rear, and slanting at its southern extremity into a broad and broken Nek. This climbed again 2,000 yards away up to the last kopje of the position, whose top, also flat, swung first south, then sharply west, to merge finally into the grassy rises which approached almost to Modder Spruit. Though the general elevation was no more than some 300 feet from the ground level, so bare was the terrain about its base, that the insignificant hills presented a formidable face to the south-west. Across the railway, some six miles to the north-west, Jonono's Kop looked over these low ridges, and threw great spurs, dotted with Kaffir villages, down into the undulating prairie which rolled between them. On one of these spurs, which came down to the Newcastle road, 100 men of the German commando, under Schiel, had, on the retirement of the British, taken post, supported on an under-feature close to the eastward by Field Cornet Joubert's Johannesburgers, and Vrede men (100) under De Jager. The rest of the commandos occupied the main feature above described, the remainder of the Germans the kopje nearest the station, strong skirmishing parties being thrown out, under Field Cornet Pienaar, along the uplands which ran out southward in front of their left flank. Slightly retired from the forward crest of the

ELANDSLAAGTE.

main hill were posted the two guns, below and behind the right of which, beside the roadway creeping between the bluff and the tall triangular kopje, the laager had been pitched on a flat of sun-baked mud.

Major-General French moved forward quickly without waiting for the reinforcements from Ladysmith. A squadron 5th Dragoon Guards under Major St. J. C. Gore on the west of the railway, and one of the 5th Lancers on the east, each covering two miles, scouted in front of the batteries and Imperial Light Horse, the 1st Manchester following slowly in the train. The Lancers were first in touch with the enemy, their progress being checked at 2 p.m. by Pienaar's piquets posted, as already described, on the low ridge running parallel to the railway, the ridge, indeed, which General French had selected as the springboard for his attack. A gun, opening from the hills behind, supported the skirmishers: the Lancer squadron had to retire. But Colonel Scott Chisholme quickly brought up four squadrons Imperial Light Horse, which, pressing forward in squadron-column with extended files, with the 5th Lancer squadron on the right, stormed the ridge and cleared it. The crest thus secured, the Manchester detrained under its cover at 2.30 p.m. about three miles south-west of Elandslaagte. Ten minutes later they were joined by a half-battalion 2nd Gordon Highlanders and seven companies of the 1st Devonshire regiment, who formed up on the veld in brigade-line of quarter-columns, facing north-east, Devonshire on the right, Manchester on the left. Before starting, the 7th brigade was addressed in inspiriting terms by its commander, Colonel Ian Hamilton. The Manchester led the way, heading for the ridge occupied by the Imperial Light Horse, with two companies covering 500 yards in front line; the Devonshire supported, and the Highlanders marched in reserve. As the brigade began to move, a burst of musketry from across the railway to the north told that the squadron of the 5th Dragoon Guards had run into the enemy on the lower spurs of Jonono's Kop. So strong did the opposition there appear that the 42nd and 21st batteries, with a squadron 5th Lancers which had just escorted the guns from

French attacks at once.

The infantry reinforcements arrive.

Ladysmith, were despatched to the spot in support. A few shrapnel from the 42nd battery sufficed to silence the Mausers, and the artillery recrossed the railway, the 5th Dragoon Guards also receiving an order to come in. The artillery were then ordered to go on at once and open against the main position. On their way to the front they passed the marching infantry, whose directions were now somewhat altered; for whilst the Manchester in the van still pushed eastwards for Scott Chisholme's captured ridge, the Devonshire, diverging half left from this line, now led upon the enemy's right flank, and behind, in the ever increasing interval thus created between the two battalions, the Gordon Highlanders were extending in reserve.

Sir George arrives and approves. The Boer guns are silenced.

Whilst the advance was in progress Sir G. White, who had ridden fast from Ladysmith, arrived upon the field, escorted by a troop of Natal Mounted Rifles. Recognising the excellence of General French's plans and arrangements, he remained only as a spectator, leaving to his subordinate complete control of the battle. A few moments later, at 4 p.m., the British guns came into action in front of the infantry at a range of 4,400 yards. The enemy replied, shells bursting in the 21st battery. So rapid a bombardment was at once delivered against the hill that, after firing twenty rounds, all of which fell among the guns, the Boer gunners fled from their pieces. Then the artillery, changing their target continually, searched all the top with shrapnel. The 1st Devonshire regiment, pushing west of the rise to a point 800 yards north of the batteries, lay down on a front of 500 yards. At 3.30 p.m. this battalion had received an order to move, when the artillery preparation should cease, right across the open grass plain which separated them from the enemy, and to hold him to his defences.

Manchester with Gordons assail left.

A thousand yards south-east of the Devonshire, beyond the batteries, the Manchester had halted near the crest at the point of its curve northward, and this curve they were ordered to follow until it brought them upon the opposed left flank. A mile in rear, still, therefore, in the plain below, the Gordon Highlanders halted, and orders came to them to support the Manchester at the next stage. At 4.30 p.m. the infantry rose and moved forward. On the left the Devonshire, with three companies covering some 600 yards in front, and four companies in reserve, in column, with 50 paces distance between the single ranks, steered upon the tall cone which marked the right-centre of the Boers. Their march led them at first downhill into the broad bowl which lay below the foot of the kopjes, a hollow as smooth as a meadow but for the infrequent ant-hills. Shrapnel began from the first to burst over the battalion, but the soldiers pressed steadily onward until, at a point some 1,200 yards from the enemy, severe rifle-fire began to play upon them, and they were halted to reply to it. Their section volleys soon beat heavily about the Boer right, and pinned the burghers to their sangars. A little later, the Devonshire firing line, now stiffened by the supports, advanced again down the bullet-swept slope and gained a shallow donga about 850 yards from the crest. Here Major C. W. Park disposed his battalion for a musketry fight. He had carried out the first part of his orders, and it was necessary now to await the development of the attack in progress against the other flank. With some loss, therefore, the Devonshire lay within close range of the hostile lines. So briskly, however, did they engage them, that the attention of a great part of the Boer force was drawn to that direction, and for a time the simultaneous movement against the other flank proceeded almost unnoticed. The Manchester, indeed, during the early portion of their advance, were not easily to be seen from the Boers' left. Skilfully led, they made their way with two companies extended in the firing line, over broken ground under the crest of the ridge, and only some shells, aimed at the artillery, dropped amongst them. Out of sight on the right the Imperial Light Horse and the squadron 5th Lancers worked ahead on a parallel route, having drawn towards the outer flank on the infantry coming up to them. In rear the Gordon Highlanders, inclining to the right, followed in support of the Manchester, in echelon of companies at 60 paces interval, the companies marching in column of sections. A brisk shell fire assailed this battalion as it crossed the rear of the batteries, but, like the Manchester, the Highlanders for a time escaped the

Devonshire pin right.

notice of the Boer riflemen, and they pushed on with trifling loss.

Guns silence Boer artillery.

Thus by 4.30 p.m. the whole British force, 3,500 men in all, was in motion, and Coxhead, during the temporary silence of the enemy's artillery, ordered his command to support more closely. As the batteries limbered up, the Boers re-opened and followed them with shells. Only one horse fell, however, and the British guns, moving swiftly between the Devonshire and Manchester regiments, were shortly in action again three quarters of a mile nearer to the front. Under their rapid rounds at 3,200 yards the hostile gunners relapsed immediately and finally into silence.

Difficulties of approach to Boer left.

In approaching the occupied zone the cavalry on the right were first closely engaged. A screen of skirmishers still lay out before the Boer left, and these, as they fell back slowly, had an easy target in the mounted men, who were working over ground of great difficulty. Then the Manchester, emerging from their covered way, found themselves upon the crest of a smooth and open plateau, which, sloping downwards for 200 yards from them almost imperceptibly, was traversed by a wire fence, beyond which stony outcrops again gave promise of shelter. As the foremost soldiers showed above the fringe of stones at the crest line, a sudden rush of bullets drummed upon the sun-dried level in front of them, and the men, in obedience to an order, dropped again behind the protecting stones to reply. As they did so, some of the officers of the Manchester, leaving their men in the security of the rocks, ran through the storm of lead and severed the wires obstructing advance. But the line was as yet too weak for a forward dash.

The attack on Boer left.

For a quarter of an hour the Manchester lay where they were, with frequent casualties, but using their weapons so vigorously that soon the Boers on their front, an advanced party of Lombard's commando, gave back in spite of their leader's efforts to hold them, and at 5.20 p.m. the Manchester poured from the stones after them. They were closely followed by the Gordon, who, though under cover below them, had suffered somewhat from the shots grazing the edge of the plateau. At their appearance heavy musketry burst from the kopjes 1,200 yards ahead. The soldiers were in a moment at the wire fence. This obstacle, only partially destroyed, had been taken as a known range by the Boer marksmen, and so accurate therefore was their shooting that soon there was scarce a strand unrent by the bullets. In the crowding which ensued many men fell amongst the now dangling wires, some pushed through, and some could find no gap. Though the front of the brigade thus became broken and confused, the advance continued uninterruptedly. Now Lieut.-Colonel W. H. Dick-Cunyngham sent the Gordon Highlanders forward into the gaps opening in the lines of the Manchester, some to the left, some to the right, some wherever they could find room. The Imperial Light Horse, who had been contending every foot of their progress with the cloud of skirmishers retiring slowly before them, here joined on to the right of the Gordon. Once at the edge of the ridge, from which, as the troops rushed forward, a detached party of Boers fell back, still shooting bitterly, the brigade found itself facing due north, and the Boer left flank lay exposed.

Meanwhile Gore, reinforced by a squadron 5th Lancers, had moved out yet further to the left, cutting in between the Boer main body and Schiel's Germans, so that the latter only saved themselves by a circuitous gallop behind Woodcote farm, not drawing rein until they arrived in rear of the left of the main position. Gore then gained a secure foothold near the colliery 1,700 yards from the enemy's right rear. Here he concealed his squadrons, and awaiting the development of the infantry attack, watched the rear face of the enemy's kopjes for signs of a break away. *[Gore, dashing in, halts on Boer right rear.]*

Strengthened by the arrival of Schiel, the Boer left poured their bullets chiefly upon that portion of the line occupied by the right companies of the Gordon Highlanders and the Imperial Light Horse. Below the fence the ground sloped gently downward to the foot of the kopjes, where it again rose more steeply to the summit, some 350 yards distant. Down the incline the firing line went rapidly, for the most part by rushes of sections, carried out independently, yet with great dash and unanimity. *[The position is captured.]*

But the slope was exposed throughout, and there were many casualties. About 5.30 p.m. the line of battle had arrived at the foot of the kopjes; then, swinging slightly towards the left, so as to envelop still more the flank of the enemy above, all supports and reserves being now absorbed, it began to make head upwards, still by short rushes. It was now nearly dark; rain burst down on them in a torrent: the men, breathless from their eager pace, began to slacken somewhat in their difficult progress up the hill-sides. At this moment Colonel Hamilton, who had previously ridden to where the Devonshire still held fast the Boer right with their volleys, hurried back to the main attack. He at once ordered the "charge" to be sounded, and running to the front, himself led the last onset. The Devonshire simultaneously leaped from the donga where they had lain more than an hour, and, advancing by companies from the right, reached the base of the final kopje. For an instant they halted to gain breath and fix bayonets, then, coming to the charge, assaulted the portion before them, and carried it without a check, four companies swinging to the left against the northernmost kopje, and three moving straight upon the main hill whereon stood the enemy's artillery. Here, as occurred all along the Boer line, though many fled at the sound of the charge, many stood and continued shooting at the troops until the latter were within twenty yards of them. Below the main crest a bitter contest was also maintained, for as at Talana, many Boers, seeing the soldiers determined to win the summit, pressed forward to oppose them, and lay firing behind the rocks until their assailants were almost upon them. Some acting thus were made prisoners; some escaped to the rear at the last moment; many were shot down as they ran. The assault poured on unchecked, the two guns falling to the converging Devonshire. At 5.55 p.m. the infantry held all the upper part of the hill.

Gore attacks the flying Boers.

By that time the cavalry, lying in wait at Elandslaagte, had already dealt their blow. A quarter of an hour before the infantry gained the crest the majority of the defenders had begun to vacate the summit, and, descending to the open ground behind, streamed raggedly across the front, many within five

ELANDSLAAGTE. 169

hundred yards, of the concealed troopers. The light was failing rapidly, and with it the chance of action. Though the crowd in the loose disorder of retreat seemed to offer an indefinite object for a charge, there was no likelihood of a better whilst sufficient light remained. At 5.30 p.m. Gore gave the word and pushed out eastwards with a squadron of the 5th Lancers on the right of his line, and one of the 5th Dragoon Guards on the left, both in extended files. The ground was difficult, boulders strewed the surface, and a series of dongas, intersecting it at all angles, seriously impeded progress. These obstacles once cleared, the cavalry moved on rapidly and, topping a slight rise, came suddenly into full view of the foremost Boers, some 300 in number, who were riding slowly northward away from the ridges all but captured behind them. The charge was instantly delivered, and the Boer retirement was dashed to pieces in all directions. Then, having traversed completely the zone of retreat, the cavalry were rallied and reformed into line. The gallop had carried the squadrons more than a mile and a half from their starting-place, and the intervening space was again covered by the enemy, now in full flight from the kopjes. Once more, therefore, the troopers charged, and, scouring in loose order back over the same ground, cleared it of the enemy, and drew rein with many prisoners near Elandslaagte, just as the last gleam of light died and gave place to darkness.

Meanwhile there had occurred an anxious moment for the infantry, victorious along the summit of the kopjes. Pressing forward from the captured crest in pursuit, and firing fast, the soldiers were some distance down the gentle reverse slope when a white flag was seen to be waving from the conical kopje above the laager, and Colonel Hamilton, believing it to signify a general capitulation, ordered the " cease fire " to be sounded. Suddenly a body of some fifty Boers charged boldly up-hill against that section in which were the right company of the Gordon Highlanders and the Imperial Light Horse, and, seizing a small spur within twenty yards of the crest, turned their rifles upon the surprised troops. For a moment there was some confusion. The soldiers were scattered; some were continuing the pursuit,

A Boer rally after "cease fire."

some were seeking their units; many were resting; the cross fire which thus assailed them was severe and accurate.

The enemy is swept off.

But the effect of this counter-attack was but momentary. Once more the "advance" was sounded, and that part of the line, rallied by the voice and example of Colonel Hamilton himself, surged forward again,* and tumbled the last remnant of the enemy down the reverse slopes. During this incident some of the Imperial Light Horse on the extreme right, swinging round the enemy's left, surrounded a farmhouse which had been the rallying point of the above counter-attack, and, after a sharp encounter, stormed it, capturing twenty-one prisoners.

Effect of the action

Thus terminated an action of which there can be no greater praise than that it was swiftly planned, carried out with determination, and that its complete success was gained exactly as designed. That success, moreover, was of more than local importance. Kock's hold upon the communications of Dundee had been of the briefest. He himself was a prisoner, mortally wounded, in British hands, and his force, rushing headlong back to Newcastle from the battlefield, upon which it had left over two hundred killed and wounded, nearly two hundred prisoners, two guns and a complete laager, carried despondency into the Boer Headquarters, so recently alarmed at the rebuff of Talana. Moreover, the battle did more than clear Yule's rear; it also safeguarded his front, by persuading Erasmus, already timorous upon Impati, to cling to his mountain, at a time when Yule's exhausted battalions were in no condition to resist the attack of 5,000 fresh enemies.

French is recalled to Ladysmith.

It formed no part of Sir G. White's plan to keep the ground that had been won. The position of Elandslaagte was useless alike for observation, defence, or offence. Even had it been of value, the presence of the Free State army upon its flank rendered the occupation of it too hazardous in the view of a

---

* For conspicuous gallantry in rallying their men for this advance the following officers received the Victoria Cross :—Captain M. F. M. Meiklejohn, Gordon Highlanders, whose wound on the occasion deprived him of an arm, and Captains C. H. Mullins and R. Johnstone, of the Imperial Light Horse. Sergt.-Major W. Robertson, Gordon Highlanders, was also awarded the Victoria Cross.

General already impressed by the dangers of detachments. Throughout the day, indeed, the Free Staters themselves had been reminding him of these dangers. As early as 11 a.m. the piquets to the west of Ladysmith had reported significant developments about Van Reenen's Pass, and these, as the day wore on, became so threatening that at 5.30 p.m. General Hunter despatched a message to Sir G. White, who was at that time still at Elandslaagte, informing him that there was a hostile advance upon Ladysmith from Bester's station. It was necessary, therefore, to recall French at once, and at 9 p.m. he was so instructed by telephone.

At 11 p.m. General French issued orders for the return to Ladysmith on the morrow, and the troops bivouacked on the field, the infantry upon the kopjes, the cavalry about the station. The day's losses amounted to 263 officers and men killed and wounded.* Bivouacks on ground night 21st-22nd.

At 3 a.m. on the 22nd the three batteries, the 5th Lancers and the Natal Mounted Rifles† left by road for Ladysmith, the loaded ambulance train quitting the station at the same time. From that hour onwards the trains, bearing the soldiers, steamed away from the battlefield, the last to leave by rail being a portion of the Manchester escorting forty prisoners. They were detained until 3.20 p.m. The 5th Dragoon Guards, who had reconnoitred northward, followed last of all by road, and by evening the position was empty. All back in Ladysmith, Oct. 22/99.

* For detailed casualties, etc., see Appendix 6.

† This corps had remained as escort to the Natal Field artillery, and as support to Gore's cavalry, throughout the action.

CHAPTER X.

LOMBARDS KOP.*

<small>Boer forces unite Oct. 26th. French reconnoitres, Oct. 27th.</small>

ON the very day of Yule's junction with Coxhead†, Erasmus was in touch with A. P. Cronje, next day with Lukas Meyer, who, still feeling the blow of Talana, had moved timidly, wide on the left. At 4 a.m. on the morning of the 27th a brigade of cavalry left Ladysmith under Major-General French, and, proceeding to scout along the Newcastle and Helpmakaar roads, was sighted at dawn by Meyer, who was then in laager about seven miles south of Elandslaagte. The Boer leader, anticipating a general attack, at once signalled to Erasmus, upon which a strong contingent of the Ermelo burghers, accompanied by guns, made their way across to him from their camp. French reconnoitred boldly, and at 10.35 a.m. he was able to send in to Sir George White his estimate of the numbers confronting him. On Intintanyoni were 4,000–5,000 men. Other strong bodies hovered between Rietfontein and Pepworth Hill, whilst the enemy to his immediate front appeared to separate themselves into two laagers, whose sites could be clearly distinguished. One, sheltering about 2,000 men, lay at the junction of the Beith and Glencoe roads, some five miles south-east of Modder Spruit station, whilst the other, a much larger encampment, was situated four miles nearer to the railway, that is to say, one mile south-east of it.

<small>Hamilton with Infantry and</small>

Meanwhile Colonel Ian Hamilton had at 10 a.m. marched out of Ladysmith to the Neks between Gun Hill, Lombards Kop and Umbulwana, with a brigade consisting of the 1st Devonshire

---

* See maps Nos. 3, 8 and 8 (a). † See page 150.

and 1st Manchester regiments, the 1st Royal Irish Fusiliers and the 2nd Gordon Highlanders, with a brigade division of the 21st, 42nd and 53rd batteries R.F.A., joined later by the 1st Liverpool regiment and the 13th battery R.F.A. This brigade, lying out all day in support of the cavalry reconnaissance, caused continual apprehension to the enemy, who covered all his positions with men and cannon in momentary expectation of an attack. Altogether some 10,000 men with fifteen guns were observed, and for the purpose intended by Sir George White, who was only anxious to gain information, the object of the reconnaissance was accomplished. The attack of the laagers was considered by Sir George White, who rode out beyond Lombards Nek in the afternoon to confer with General French and Colonel Hamilton; but after careful examination it was ultimately decided to await a more suitable opportunity, and the troops were withdrawn. *[Artillery supports him. Troops return to camp.]*

On October 28th Lukas Meyer with 2,000 men and three guns pushed forward to Modder Spruit, where he went into laager behind a long flat kopje, now called Long Hill, situated some four thousand yards south-east of Pepworth Hill, the summit of which the Ermelo commando had already piqueted. The Free Staters, coming down from Intintanyoni, rode westward and lay in the evening upon the farm Kleinfontein, joining hands with their allies of the Transvaal across Surprise Hill and the heights above the Bell Spruit. Through their main laager on Kleinfontein ran the railway line to Van Reenen's Pass. *[Both Transvaalers and Free Staters approach Ladysmith, Oct. 28th.]*

On the 29th the cavalry made a reconnaissance eastwards, and reported as follows. The laager which had been close to the Modder Spruit station on the 27th had disappeared, but there were now two encampments to the east and south-east of Lombards Kop, of which the lower appeared to command the road to Pieters, thus threatening the line of communication. Pepworth Hill was strongly occupied, and artillery were now upon it; a large camp lay close to the north-west of the height. The enemy was numerous upon Long Hill. Upon its flat top two or three guns were already emplaced, and an *[Cavalry reports Boer dispositions, Oct. 29th.]*

epaulment for another was in course of construction. Behind the hill was a laager.

<small>White decides on attack.</small>

This reconnaissance seemed to Sir G. White to furnish the reasons he desired for assuming the offensive. The capture of Long Hill would at least throw back the investing line of Transvaalers. It might do more—break through it altogether, when a sweep north against Pepworth would bid fair to drive together the Transvaal commandos in upon their centre, and roll up the whole. The Free Staters, strung out as they now are, thinly north-west and west, would then be cut off from the rest.

<small>Plan arranged, Oct. 29th.</small>

At 4 p.m. on the afternoon of the 29th his plans were formulated. Long Hill was to be the primary, Pepworth Hill the secondary object, and to secure them the whole of the troops were to be employed. His main army he divided into two bodies, with separate missions. One, consisting of No. 10 Mountain battery, the 1st Royal Irish Fusiliers and the 1st Gloucester regiment, all commanded by Lieutenant-Colonel F. R. C. Carleton, of the first-named battalion, was to move at 10 p.m. that night northward along the Bell Spruit. The duties of this force were twofold: first, to cover the left flank of the main operation; secondly, to gain and hold such a position towards Nicholson's Nek (if possible, the Nek itself) as would enable the cavalry to debouch safely upon the open ground beyond, should opportunity arise for a pursuit, or, better still, an interception of the Transvaalers as they fell back on the Drakensberg passes. The left flank thus provided for, a cavalry brigade, consisting of the 5th Lancers, 19th Hussars, and Colonel Royston's regiment of Colonials, under Major-General French, were to reach the ridges north-east of Gun Hill before dawn, from which, by demonstrating against the enemy's left, they would cover the British right. Between these wings, the main infantry attack was to be carried out by the 8th brigade, which, in the absence of its proper commander, Colonel F. Howard, was under Colonel G. G. Grimwood, 2nd King's Royal Rifles, whose five battalions would include the 1st and 2nd King's Royal Rifles, the 1st Leicestershire, and 1st King's (Liverpool) regiments and the 2nd Royal Dublin Fusiliers. The 1st brigade

<small>Carleton to approach Nicholson's Nek that night.</small>

<small>Cavalry by dawn of 30th to be on ridges n.e. of Gun Hill.</small>

<small>Grimwood to seize Long Hill.</small>

division Royal Field artillery and the Natal Field battery were to be attached to Grimwood's command. A general reserve of the 7th brigade, consisting of the 2nd Gordon Highlanders, 1st Manchester and 1st Devonshire regiments, and, should it arrive from Maritzburg in time, the 2nd Rifle Brigade, were to be under the command of Colonel Ian Hamilton, who, besides his infantry, would have with him the 5th Dragoon Guards, the 18th Hussars, the Imperial Light Horse, two companies mounted infantry, and the 2nd brigade division of artillery. Grimwood was to take Long Hill, and his path thereto was to be cleared by the shrapnel of both brigade divisions. That position carried, he was to hold it, whilst Colonel Hamilton, supported in turn by the fire of the united artillery, was to throw his fresh infantry against Pepworth Hill, and complete the victory. *Hamilton then to capture Pepworth.*

At 10 p.m. Carleton left his parade ground with six companies (16 officers, 518 other ranks) and 46 mules, and at 11 p.m. arrived at the rendezvous, the level crossing of the Newcastle road close to the Orange Free State railway junction, where the rest of his command had been awaiting him for an hour. It consisted of five and a half companies (some 450 men) of the Gloucester regiment, with 57 mules and a Maxim gun; the 10th Mountain battery, comprising 137 N.C.O.s and men, 6 guns, with 100 rounds for each, 133 mules, with 52 Cape Boys as muleteers, and 10 horses. The total strength of the column was thus about 1,140 men and 250 animals. *Carleton's column parades 11 p.m. Oct. 29th.*

Half an hour after midnight Grimwood's brigade (8th) set out eastward in the following order: 1st and 2nd battalions King's Royal Rifles, 1st Leicestershire regiment, 1st brigade division R.F.A., 1st King's (Liverpool) regiment, and the Natal Field battery, with a rearguard of the 2nd Royal Dublin Fusiliers.* Another brigade division, the 2nd, joining the line of march soon after it was put in motion, marched in front of the 1st Liverpool regiment. The whole pressed on for a time quietly and in order. Soon, however, the last arrival, the 2nd brigade division of *Grimwood starts same night at 12.30.*

---

* These battalions were not complete. The King's Royal Rifles had left two companies in Ladysmith, the Dublin Fusiliers three, the Leicester regiment two, the King's (Liverpool) regiment two.

artillery, in pursuance of orders, when between Flag and Limit hills, drew away from out of the column to the left and passed under the shelter of Flag Hill. The two battalions behind, not being aware of any special instructions given to the artillery, followed it, whilst those in front still pursued their proper route, so that Grimwood's force was cut in two and separated whilst yet but half his march was over. An hour before dawn, Grimwood, unconscious of the mishap to his rear, gained some low kopjes 1,800 yards from the south-eastern flank of Long Hill, and extended his troops across them, the two battalions King's Royal Rifles in firing line, Leicester in support, facing north-west. Here he waited for light. One company, "F." of the 1st King's Royal Rifles, moved cautiously forward to a small kopje, slightly in advance, to cover the front.

<small>Grimwood's column broken by error.</small>

At 3 a.m. Major-General French rode out of Ladysmith with his two regiments and pushed for Lombards Kop, dismounting his command in a hollow basin between Gun Hill and Lombards Kop, some 4,000 yards in rear, and out of sight, of Grimwood's infantry. The Natal Volunteers, who had been on the ground since the previous night, went on, and, dividing right and left, secured the summits of Lombards Kop and Umbulwana Mountain. Colonel Hamilton, quitting his rendezvous between Tunnel and Junction Hills at 4 a.m., moved, as directed, on Limit Hill, which had been piqueted throughout the night by "G." and "H." companies Gordon Highlanders. As Hamilton rode at the head of his brigade, a man was brought to him who proved to be a muleteer of the 10th Mountain battery. He reported that a sudden disturbance had occurred in the midst of Carleton's night march; all the mules of the battery had broken away, and, so far as he knew, had never been seen again. A little further on an officer of the Scottish Rifles, who had been attached to the Gloucester regiment a few hours previously, appeared amongst the Gordon Highlanders. He, too, told of a stampede amongst the battery mules, and, in addition, of resulting disturbance of some of the infantry companies, amongst others that which he accompanied. Yet a third warning of misadventure on the left was received before dawn. In the

<small>French starting 3 a.m. dismounts 4,000 yards in rear of Grimwood.</small>

<small>Hamilton at 4 a.m. moves on Limit Hill.</small>

<small>First news of disaster to Carleton.</small>

early morning the sentries of the piquet of the Leicester regiment at Cove Redoubt, one of the northerly outposts of Ladysmith, became aware of the sound of hoofs and the rattle of harness coming towards them from the north, and the soldiers, running down, captured several mules bearing the equipment of mountain guns. A patrol of the 5th Dragoon Guards,* which had been despatched by Sir G. White to try to get news of Carleton's column, was checked at the Bell Spruit, but met on the road a gunner of the 10th Mountain battery, who related the same tale as had already reached that General. This man said that the battery had been suddenly fired on at 2 a.m.; the mules had stampeded and disappeared. Both its ammunition and portions of most of its guns had been carried off. Finally, a brief note from Carleton himself to the Commander-in-Chief announced what had then happened.

At dawn Pickwoad's brigade division, which was now deployed 1½ miles south-eastward of Limit Hill, opened at Long Hill at 3,700 yards. But Long Hill was silent. The three gun emplacements visible upon the crest were empty. Instead, at 5.15 a.m., a heavy piece fired from Pepworth Hill, and a 96-pound shell fell near the town, its explosion greeting the 2nd Rifle Brigade, which, having detrained at 2.30 a.m., was marching out to join Hamilton's force at Limit Hill. The next, following quickly, burst in Pickwoad's line of guns, and Coxhead's artillery, which attempted to reply, found itself far outranged, whilst Pickwoad's three batteries maintained for a time their bombardment of Long Hill. In a few moments four long-range Creusots of smaller calibre (75 m/m) joined in from either side of the 96-pounder, two others from lower ground about the railway below the height. Both Coxhead's and Pickwoad's batteries were covered with missiles. Colonel C. M. H. Downing, commanding all the artillery, quickly assumed the offensive. Dissatisfied with his position, the left of which, lying to the east of Limit Hill, was so encumbered with rocks that of the 53rd battery only two guns could fire at all, and those of the other batteries of the 2nd brigade

Pickwoad shells Long Hill.

Pepworth replies.

Downing moves the two Brigade Divs. against Pepworth,

* For gallantry on this occasion Second-Lieut. J. Norwood, 5th Dragoon Guards, was awarded the Victoria Cross.

division only by indirect laying, he drew that part of his line clear, and moved Coxhead's three batteries, the 21st, 42nd, and 53rd, out into the open, facing north-west, to within 4,000 yards of Pepworth.* Troubled, while the change was in course of taking place, by the accurate shooting from that hill, Downing then ordered Pickwoad to change front to the left and come into action against Pepworth on the right of, but some distance from, the 2nd brigade division. The guns on the low ground under the shadow of Pepworth were soon mastered. The battery upon its summit, at distant range for shrapnel, withstood yet awhile; but ere long the gunners there, too, temporarily abandoned their weapons, and only returned when a slackening of Pickwoad's fire gave opportunity for a hasty round. At 6.30 a.m., therefore, and for some half hour more, the trend of battle seemed to the artillery to be in favour of the British. After that, however, fresh hostile guns opened, and the rattle of rifles arose in ever-increasing volume, not only from the broken ground to the right, where Grimwood's infantry lay lost to view amongst the low, rolling kopjes by the Modder Spruit, but also far to the rear, towards Lombards Kop. Yet no British were seen advancing. It was evident that the infantry and cavalry were not delivering but withstanding an onslaught.

The attack which Grimwood found to be developing rapidly against him was less surprising from its suddenness than from the direction from which it assailed him. Those with him, as described above, lay in the precise position designed for them. He had taken the precaution of covering his right rear, until it should be protected by the cavalry, at first with a half company ("A.") of the Leicestershire regiment, then with two more ("F." and "H.") of the same battalion and the Maxim gun. Furthermore, a kopje to the right front, seen in the growing light to command from the eastward that already occupied by "F." company 1st King's Royal Rifles, was now crowned by "H." company of the same battalion, and all had seemed safe on that side. But now a raking fire from the right assailed all his lines, and Grimwood, instead of outflanking, was outflanked.

* This is shown on map 8 as the first artillery position.

Every moment this fire grew more severe; beyond the Modder, Boer reinforcements were streaming in full view up to the line of riflemen shooting along the Modder Spruit. Two guns, which began to shoot from a well-concealed spot near the Elandslaagte road, now took the British line in enfilade, and partially in reverse. The Boer gunners upon Pepworth and the low ground east of it again fired, the smaller pieces into the batteries and infantry, the great Creusot frequently into the town.

Instead of the anticipated change of front to the left for the destruction of the enemy Grimwood had now, therefore, to prepare a new frontage most speedily, almost to his present rear, for the safety of his brigade. "H." company 1st King's Royal Rifles, on the advanced kopje, first turned towards the east, and coming under heavy fire from three directions, was later reinforced by "A." company of the same battalion. "B." company, which had lain in support of "F.," moved to the new right of "H." and "A.," and, with "E." company, lined up along the rocks facing the Modder Spruit. Meanwhile the officer commanding "F.," the other advanced company, who had turned east, now found his left assailed, and threw back half his command in that direction. The tripod Maxim gun of the 2nd King's Royal Rifles was placed in the centre of this company.* Grimwood fronts the new danger.

The 2nd King's Royal Rifles, which had lain in support whilst the front circled round, were now sent to reinforce. Leaving two companies still in support, the battalion changed front to the right, and, extending from right to left, filled the gap between the right of the 1st King's Royal Rifles and the detached 2½ companies of the Leicester regiment. These, with a Maxim, somewhat isolated on the kopje on what was now the right flank, were beginning to be hotly engaged. 2nd K.R.R. fills gap between 1st K.R.R. and Leicester detachment.

Thus under incessant and increasing fire the 8th brigade swung round, pivoting on the left company 1st King's Royal Rifles, with the detachment of the Leicester as "marker," so to speak, to its outer flank. Two companies of the missing Royal The arrival of two companies R.D.F. connects Grimwood with Cavalry.

* It was found to be impossible to get the wheeled gun of the 1st King's Royal Rifles over the boulders of the kopje.

Dublin Fusiliers* now arrived to assist the Leicester, and were immediately assailed by some sharpshooters who had worked around the right flank. They therefore prolonged the line to the right, towards the northern spurs of Lombards Kop, and here about 7 a.m. they joined hands with the cavalry, whose movements must now be related.

French's operations. Waiting until the artillery duel seemed to be going in favour of Downing's batteries, French gave the word for advance about 5.30 a.m. The 5th Lancers and 19th Hussars, who had been lying in mass in the hollow, quickly extended in a north-easterly direction, with orders to work round the Boer left. The route taken by the brigade lay for some distance within rifle range of the western flank of a line of low kopjes, which, running down north-east as an irregular spur of Lombards Kop, and parallel to the Modder Spruit, pointed in the direction of Long Hill. At the termination of this ridge, the high ground, dropping sharply to the plain, offered an outlet to the eastward. For this gateway French's two regiments were making. They had all but reached it when a sharp blaze of rifles broke from the kopjes to their right. The squadrons thereupon wheeled to the right, the troopers dismounted, and running a short way to the new front, they soon reinforced a ridge, already thinly held by the right of Grimwood's infantry, from whence they replied to the sharpshooters on the kopjes beyond. It was soon evident that the Mausers were becoming the masters of the carbines, and French, seeing the impossibility of breaking through, at any rate at this period, ordered his brigade to retire. As the men took to their horses, a gun, opening from the enemy's left, threw shell rapidly amongst them, and made the inequality of the combat yet more apparent. The two squadrons of the 5th Lancers, who were on the left, drew back over the plain, whilst the 19th Hussars retraced their path under the ridges, both rejoining General French under the lee of Lombards Kop, north of Gun Hill and of their original point of departure. French immediately threw his command forward again, and his two regiments, with some of the Natal Carbineers, all dismounted,

* See p. 176.

LOMBARDS KOP.

crowned the high ridges running northward and downward from the summit of Lombards Kop, and were soon deep in action with superior numbers all along the line. About 8 a.m. Major-General J. F. Brocklehurst, who had only reached Ladysmith at 3 a.m., arrived at Lombards Kop with two squadrons ("B." and "D.") of the 5th Dragoon Guards, followed by the 18th Hussars; and Downing, withdrawing the 69th battery from the line of guns still shelling Pepworth, despatched it with all haste in the same direction. Of Brocklehurst's reinforcement, the two squadrons 5th Dragoon Guards came up on the right of the 19th Hussars on the crest, and found themselves at once under fire from the front and right flank. Of the three weak squadrons of the 18th Hussars—all that remained after the catastrophe of Adelaide Farm*—one was directed to reinforce the 19th Hussars on the eastern slope of Lombards, the other two climbed to the right of the 5th Dragoon Guards to the south. Sharp fire from a pom-pom and many rifles met them on the shoulder of the ridge, and it seemed as if the British right was to be overmatched. But the 69th battery, which had moved up the Helpmakaar road, escorted by a squadron of the 5th Lancers, now arrived, and, boldly handled, quickly relieved the pressure in this portion of the field by drawing the enemy's attention to itself. Pushing on through the Nek which joins Lombards Kop to Umbulwana this battery came into action on an under-feature south of the road one mile beyond it, and enfiladed the Boer left. Soon, however, it found itself the focus of an increasing fusilade, and its commander, Major F. D. V. Wing, saw that to continue to work the guns would entail a grave loss of men. He therefore determined to withdraw from his dangerously advanced position. It was impossible to bring up the teams, but the gunners ran the guns back by hand. The battery withdrew almost intact, and, coming into action again, kept the balance level by steady practice carried on from the Nek itself.†

Meanwhile, Grimwood was being hard pressed on the low kopjes to the northward, and his line became thinner every

Grimwood receives Artillery support.

* Following Talana, see p. 140.
† This is the position shown on map 8 (a).

moment as he endeavoured to meet the continual attempts upon his flanks. Two Boer guns shelled steadily the much exposed 8th brigade from various points, and when about 8 a.m. a pom-pom, joining in the bombardment, killed with its first discharges some of the ammunition mules and scattered the rest far and wide, Grimwood sent urgent messages to the artillery for support. Sir G. White was at that moment himself with the batteries, which were being enfiladed again, this time by some guns on the low ground below and south of Pepworth. He promptly despatched the 21st and 53rd batteries to positions from which, facing eastwards, they could support both the cavalry and Grimwood. The 21st moved far southward, and from a gap in the hills between the infantry and cavalry soon rendered for the left of the latter the same service as the 69th was performing for the right. The 53rd battery, coming into action near the Elandslaagte road, engaged the Boer guns on Grimwood's front, and though kept at extreme range by Sir G. White's orders, succeeded in much reducing their effect. At the same time the 13th battery also left the line facing Pepworth, and, wheeling eastward, shelled the hostile artillery on the left front of the infantry with good results.

9 to 11 a.m., a stationary battle.

For two hours, from about 9 a.m. to 11 a.m., the engagement continued with little movement of either army. The Boers, being now within 800 yards of the British, could advance no further, but sent a steady stream of bullets against the ridges, pinning the cavalry to Lombards Kop and the infantry to their line of hillocks along the Modder. By 9.30 a.m. Grimwood's last available reserve was put into the firing line, and he could prolong his front no more, though the enemy still threatened his flanks. The artillery was strangely dispersed. Far on the right the 69th battery stood in action upon Umbulwana Nek; the 21st battery on the northern side of Lombards Kop covered French's left and Grimwood's right; out in the open to their left rear the 53rd battery shot above the heads of the right wing of the infantry, whilst farther northward the 13th sent shrapnel over the left wing. Only the 42nd and 67th batteries remained on the site first held by the artillery facing north-west, where the former suffered considerable losses from the heavy enfilade and frontal fire which recommenced. For the Boer artillerymen, encouraged by the diminution of the British gun-power at this point, had not only returned to the pieces upon Pepworth, but placed fresh ones upon the northernmost spurs of Long Hill itself.

The reserve on Limit Hill, under Colonel Ian Hamilton's command, had been reduced considerably by the successive demands of the battle. He had been early deprived of most of his cavalry and all his artillery, and shortly after 8 a.m., on a report coming of a hostile advance against the left flank, two squadrons ("E." and "F.") of his remaining mounted troops, the Imperial Light Horse, had left him to occupy some kopjes on either side of the railway close to Aller Park, from which they could see the enemy moving in strength about the heights of Bell Spruit. At 10 a.m. the 1st Manchester regiment was also withdrawn from Hamilton's brigade, the right half-battalion proceeding towards Lombards Kop, the left half passing into the open as escort to the artillery. The former portion eventually became incorporated with French's firing line, whilst the latter lay out upon the shelterless ground between the original artillery position and the new one taken up by the 13th battery, where they suffered somewhat severely from the intermittent shells. *Reserve absorbed by action.*

Meanwhile Colonel W. G. Knox, who, in the absence of the army, had been placed in charge of the defences of Ladysmith, was by no means secure. Left with a garrison of a few companies of infantry, he detailed two of these, with the 23rd of the Royal engineers, and the two Boer guns captured at Elandslaagte, to cover the north of the town, posting them upon a ridge north-west of Observation Hill. Here he found himself confronted immediately by strong bodies and two guns of the enemy, who manœuvred about Bell's and the adjacent kopjes. He was soon strengthened by two guns and 88 men of the 10th Mountain battery, hastily collected and re-organised after their stampede from Carleton's party. But at no time could Knox do more than hold his own, and the strength and boldness of the Boers, who at one time *Ladysmith threatened.*

threatened the town, seemed the last confirmation of Carleton's fate.

Sir George withdraws the troops.

About 11 a.m. Sir G. White, having first despatched his Chief of the Staff, Major-General A. Hunter, to investigate the situation, decided to withdraw. To cover the movement he sent out three squadrons (" B.," " C." and " D.") of the Imperial Light Horse which remained in reserve at Limit Hill. The 13th battery, receiving an order to support them as closely as possible, galloped in and unlimbered 800 yards behind Grimwood's line. So screened, the infantry began to retreat at 11.30 a.m. As the men rose from their shelters, a storm of fire broke from the enemy's ridges. But the gunners of the 13th battery,

13th battery covers retreat.

turning the hail of bullets from the infantry, faced it themselves. Almost the whole volume of the enemy's fire soon centred on this battery. From the right, four Boer guns concealed in the scrub raked the line ; those upon Long Hill bombarded from the left, whilst from the left rear the heavy shells from Pepworth also struck in, hitting direct four of the six guns. When twenty minutes had passed thus, and Grimwood's brigade had almost removed itself into safety, the battery which had shielded it looked as if it must itself be lost.

53rd battery relieves 13th.

From their rear Major A. J. Abdy, commanding the 53rd battery, had marked the perilous situation of the 13th and, obtaining permission from Colonel Coxhead, advanced to succour it. Galloping to the front, across a deep donga, the 53rd wheeled to the right of the 13th and ranged upon some Boer artillery 2,350 yards to the eastward. By the orders of Major-General Hunter, who was on the spot, the 13th retired first, some 800 yards. But before it could come into action again, the 53rd, left alone on the plain, drew in its turn the fire of all the Boer guns. A shell exploded beneath a limber, blowing the wheels to fragments, so that the gun could not be removed, and had to be temporarily abandoned. As soon as the 13th re-opened the 53rd was able to draw back. In re-crossing the donga a gun upset, and the enemy's shells burst over it, but whilst the battery fell back to a new site to support the 13th, Lieutenant J. F. A. Higgins, having been left with the team in the donga, succeeded in righting the gun, and restored it to its place in the line. A few minutes previously, Captain W. Thwaites, with six men, had ridden forward, and now returned, bringing with him on a new limber the gun which had been disabled in the open. Only the old limber and a wagon of stores remained derelict.

So covered, the infantry had been getting away with unimpaired discipline, but in great confusion, owing to the intermixture of units and the extreme exhaustion of the men. Two Maxims were abandoned, but useless, on the kopjes—those of the Leicestershire regiment and 2nd King's Royal Rifles—the mules of both having been shot or stampeded by the last outburst from the Boer lines. The enemy made no serious attempt to follow up the retirement. Some Boers did indeed speed forward to the now empty kopjes, and began shooting rapidly from thence, but under the fine practice of the 13th battery the musketry soon dwindled. The Creusot on Pepworth Hill sounded on the right, and every part of the route to be traversed by the troops lay within range of its projectiles. About noon, a report, as loud as that of the great French cannon itself, came from the direction of the town, and the batteries on Pepworth sank immediately to silence under the repeated strokes of shells from British Naval guns. Captain the Honourable Hedworth Lambton, R.N., had detrained his command of two 4.7-in., three 12-pr. 12-cwt. quick-firing guns, with some smaller pieces, 16 officers and 267 men at 10 a.m., the very time when the enemy's 6-in. shells were bursting over the railway station.* After conferring with Colonel Knox, he was in two hours on his way towards the fight with the 12-pounders, reaching the place held by Hamilton's brigade. But in view of the imminent retirement, this was too far forward, and Lambton was ordered back. Whilst he was in the act of

sidenote: The Infantry, under the protection of the guns, get away.

sidenote: The Naval guns appear and silence the Boers.

---

* Rear-Admiral Sir R. Harris, K.C.M.G., in Naval command at the Cape, had been requested (October 24th) by Sir G. White to send a heavy gun detachment to Ladysmith " in view of heavy guns being brought by General Joubert from the north." It will be seen with what promptitude the request was acceded to and acted upon by the Naval commander. In ninety-six hours the guns were disembarked from H.M.S. *Powerful* at Durban; seventeen hours later they were in action.

186   THE WAR IN SOUTH AFRICA.

withdrawing, the gunners on Pepworth, descrying the strings of moving bullocks, launched a shell which pitched exactly upon one of the guns, and tumbled it over. Lambton, however, coming into action nearer the town, opened heavily and accurately on his antagonist, and reduced him to immediate silence.

The garrison reaches Ladysmith by 2.30 p.m.
At 1 p.m. the cavalry on the right gave up the crests which they had maintained so long, covered up to the last by the 21st battery on the left, and on the right by the 69th battery, whose escort had been strengthened by "C" squadron 5th Dragoon Guards taken from Limit Hill. At 2.30 p.m. French's command was in Ladysmith, following the 1st Manchester regiment, which had retired on the right of the cavalry. With the exception of four companies of the 1st Devonshire regiment, left upon Limit Hill, the rest of the troops engaged had reached their camps a short time previously. Only the tents of Carleton's two battalions were seen to be empty when evening fell.

Carleton's night march begins 11.15 p.m. 29th Oct./99.
Carleton's detachment had moved from the rendezvous at 11.15 p.m. in the following order: first, under Major C. S. Kincaid, a small party of 1st Royal Irish Fusiliers, who marched with fixed bayonets; then Colonel Carleton himself, with Major W. Adye, D.A.A.G. for Intelligence, and the guides; behind them the 1st Royal Irish Fusiliers, followed by their 46 mules; then the 10th Mountain battery, with 133 mules; then the 57 mules of the 1st Gloucester regiment; next five and a half companies of that battalion, and finally a small rearguard, under Captain B. O. Fyffe, of the Gloucester. The valley of the Bell Spruit was wrapped in profound darkness, yet the force pushed on at a rapid pace, and, in spite of the noise of its progress, was undetected by the Boer piquets on the hills on either side. Shortly after 1 a.m. the van was opposite the southern spur of the height called Kainguba, at the other extremity of which, some two miles due north, lay the object of the expedition, Nicholson's Nek. The column was here in perfect order, the road to the Nek was good, and there was promise of about two hours of darkness to conceal the remainder of the march. But Colonel Carle-

ton, thinking more of the lateness of his start than of the excellence of his progress, and remembering that his orders had not bound him absolutely to Nicholson's Nek, came to the conclusion at this point that, if, as seemed possible, he could not reach the Nek before dawn, it would be extremely rash to be surprised by daylight in a narrow defile. He decided, therefore, at least to make good the dangerous high ground on his left by occupying the nearest crest of Kainguba above him, intending, if time allowed, to continue his march to the Nek from this vantage ground. He therefore wheeled the leading files to the left, and at their head began the boulder-obstructed and finally almost precipitous ascent of the mountain, ordering guides to be left to indicate the point of the change of direction to the units following the Royal Irish Fusiliers. When the head of that *The disaster.* battalion had climbed two-thirds of the steep a mysterious and fatal incident occurred. Suddenly from the darkness encircling the clambering soldiers broke out a roar " like that of an approaching train,"* there was a rush of hoofs and the clatter of scattering stones. In a moment a group of loose animals, whether horses, mules or cattle, it was impossible to discern, bounding down the rocky precipice, tore past the last companies of the Royal Irish Fusiliers and disappeared as quickly as they had come into the gloom of the valley. The rear of the Irish Fusiliers checked and staggered back upon the long line of ammunition mules. The natural timidity of these animals, many of them almost untrained, had been increased by their long wait at the rendezvous, and by the fact that they were led by strange and unskilled men. Now it became an uncontrollable panic. Leaping round, dragging their muleteers with them, they plunged backwards in terror, wrenched themselves loose, and thundered over the steep slope upon all below them. The battery mules and those of the Gloucester regiment were dashed downwards and joined the riot, and the whole mass poured upon the Gloucester regiment, which had just begun to breast the hill. A shout arose; the men of the front companies were buffeted and swept from the track in every direction. A few shots rang sharply

* The simile of an officer present.

from behind, and a few more faintly from a startled Boer piquet on Surprise Hill. Then the uproar died away in the valley of the Bell Spruit, leaving the column disordered and amazed at its own wreck. It was a disaster complete, sudden, and incurred by no fault of officers or men. Up to this point the night march, conducted in deep darkness and between the enemy's piquets, had been a conspicuous success, and now in one swift moment the hand of fate had changed order into chaos, and success into destruction. But the troops quickly recovered, and indeed but few had yielded to the shock. Many had gathered about their officers with fixed bayonets; many, hurled to the ground, had nevertheless gripped their weapons and looked not for safety, but the enemy. Only fifty of the infantry, and these included many who had been actually stunned by the onset of the frenzied mules, failed to fall into the ranks at the summons of the officers, who, even before the tumult had ceased, were strenuously working to re-organise their commands.

2 a.m. the column reaches summit without guns or reserve ammunition;

About 2 a.m. the leading files pressed over the crest on to the top of the mountain. An hour of uncertainty and, had the enemy been near, of extreme danger followed. Most of the Irish Fusiliers were now upon the summit, disposed, as best could be, for defence. But the Gloucester at the bottom were not yet formed, and when, about 3 a.m., they came up in such order as they had been able to contrive, they brought only nine of their fifty-nine mules with them. The Irish Fusiliers had recovered but eight. The reserve of ammunition was thus practically swept away. The Mountain battery did not appear at all. Only two of the gun mules eventually arrived, carrying portions of two pieces. Eighty-eight gunners and one hundred and thirty mules had dropped out, and not a complete gun of all the six was available.

bivouacks on southern edge and awaits dawn.

When at last both regiments reached the top they were formed in line of quarter-columns—Gloucester on the right. Guided by Adye, they moved towards the southern extremity of the ridge, where they halted, lay down around the crest, and waited for light. Dawn revealed the nature of the position which the diminished detachment occupied. Behind, the southern end of the mountain dropped almost sheer to the valley. In front, to the northward, the hill-top first sloped downward somewhat to a point, where, like Talana, it was narrowed by a deep reentrant on one side, then rose to a new sky line, which hid from the British troops the remainder of the ridge some 1,200 or more yards from the southern crest. Over it the hill-top narrowed, and ran on for a mile and a half towards Nicholson's Nek. A jungle of tall grass, hiding innumerable boulders, clothed the mountain up to and a little beyond the sky line, ceasing some 700 yards from the southern crest, and between this thicket and the British line were dotted a few ruined stone kraals, of a circular shape and some two feet high. Across the valley of the Bell Spruit, to the east, a group of kopjes stood within long rifle range of, but lower than, Kainguba. In the midst of the British position itself, a small knoll, crowned by two trees, and nearly as high as the grass-grown sky line in front, arose at the end of the mountain before it plunged into the depth behind. Carleton, now decided to stand on the defensive where he was, despatched a message at 3.55 a.m. by a native, acquainting Sir G. White with his mishap, his position, and his plan, and issued orders for the disposition and entrenchment of the troops. The left or western crest of the hill was assigned to the Gloucester regiment, the right to the Irish Fusiliers, a reserve, consisting of two companies ("G." and "H.") of the latter battalion, taking post in front of the knoll at the southern extremity of the summit. The men began at once to build sangars. The position of the Gloucester, which it is necessary to describe in detail, was as follows: Along half of the southern and south-western crest lay "A." company, its right being prolonged by "B." company, and at first by "C." This last-named unit, however, was soon extended across the north of the hill, at right angles to the crest and "B." company, and had half completed a defensive wall when it was again pushed forward about 100 yards to the front, "B." company increasing its extension along the crest to maintain junction with the left of "C." The right flank of "C." company was marked by a round kraal, behind which stood up a small tree, and beyond this the line across the mountain-top was taken up by

The ground.

Carleton chooses a defensive position.

Distribution of companies.

a company ("E.") of the Royal Irish Fusiliers, which, in its turn, linked on to the defenders ("A.," "B.," "F." companies Royal Irish Fusiliers) of the eastern crest. The formation thus took the shape of a semicircle, behind a diameter, composed of one company Gloucester and one Royal Irish Fusiliers, facing the rise to the northward. Some 700 yards back from these the arc followed the contour of the mountain in rear. Thus back from the fighting line the ground sloped upwards, hiding from it the reserves, and exposing reinforcements from them, or men retreating back to them, to the full view and fire of anyone upon the shoulder which arose in front. Over the brow of this rise " D." company Gloucester entrenched itself in a position to support both "C." company Gloucester and "E." company Royal Irish Fusiliers. Though less than 150 yards in rear, " D." company was, owing to the bulging ground, invisible to " C." company, and the officers of the latter knew nothing of the proximity of its support. The movements necessary to these dispositions had scarcely begun when a slow rifle-fire, commencing from Surprise Hill to the south-west, showed that the presence of the British on the mountain was discovered, and from the very first the toiling soldiers thus found themselves taken in flank and reverse. Stones of manageable size were scarce, tools were lacking with which to move the large ones, and, with the smaller, defences of but the most paltry dimensions could be erected. At this time the danger of the dead ground ahead, and below the left front, became apparent to Carleton, and "E." company of the Gloucester, moving out beyond the front line, took post upon the densely-grown summit of the rise, 400 yards in front of "C." turning its left section to face west. Here it was shortly joined by the half of " H." company, some twenty men in all, sent forward by the O. C. Gloucester in response to Carleton's order (which did not name any precise strength) to reinforce.

7 a.m. Boers appear. At 7 a.m. bands of mounted men came down from Intintanyoni to the heights east of Bell Spruit, whence they opened fire upon the right rear of the British position. An hour later a hostile battery of apparently four guns suddenly appeared upon

LOMBARDS KOP.

the northern end of these heights, and, unlimbering for action, threatened Kainguba in silence for some time, only to disappear northwards without firing a shot. A number of horsemen were seen to ride away with it, and these, bearing to the left, vanished behind Nicholson's Nek.

At 9 a.m. a movement still more threatening was descried from the lines of the Royal Irish Fusiliers. Groups of horsemen, breaking away from the main laager visible at Pepworth, came riding up the valleys and behind the crests towards the northern end of Kainguba. On the right, amongst the Irish Fusiliers, the Maxim of the Gloucester regiment stood ready for action, and the officer in charge commenced a slow fire upon the stream of Boers. Opening at 1,200 yards, he gradually increased the range to 2,000 yards, and the trotting horsemen had just broken into a gallop as the bullets began to lash amongst them, when an order was received not to fire unless the enemy showed in masses at closer distances, ammunition being scarce.

9 a.m. they threaten rear.

At 2 a.m. Commandant Van Dam, lying in bivouac with his Johannesburg Police* beneath Pepworth, received orders from Joubert in person to proceed at once to the northern summit of Kainguba and hold the ridge above Nicholson's Nek. The Boer officer thereupon galloped for that spot with 400 men, being warned of the proximity of British troops by a Field Cornet of the Pretoria commando, who lay with thirty men on the northern slope of the high ground east of Bell Spruit. Gaining the Nek, the Police found it occupied by 150 Free Staters, who moved away further west on their approach. Van Dam's plan was quickly made. Sending a message to the Free Staters that if they would ride round to the flank and rear of the British, he would attack straight over the top of the mountain, he left fifty burghers in the Nek in charge of the horses, and led the remainder on foot in straggling order up the hill. The crest was gained and half the summit traversed before shots rang out from the shelters of the advanced companies of the Gloucester. But the Boers fired no round until, at 800 yards, the foremost British sangar was visible

Boer movements.

* Or South African Republic Police (the "Zarps").

through the long grass. Meanwhile the Free Staters, under Christian De Wet and Steenkamp, crept around the foot of the steep ground under Van Dam's right, swinging northward. Then they, too, began to climb, and by 10 a.m. Carleton's column was entrapped.

<small>Development of attack.</small>

The weak company and a half in front of the Gloucester, badly sheltered from the converging fire, could do little more than check the foremost burghers. This, however, they did so effectually for a time that Van Dam, fearing for the issue of a merely frontal attack, and hearing nothing of the Free Staters, who had not yet reached their goal, ordered one of his officers, Lieutenant Pohlmann, to take fifty men out of sight under the hill to the right, and not to fire a shot until he arrived within decisive range of the British. Pohlmann moved boldly and skilfully, and, appearing suddenly upon the left of " E." company Gloucester, poured a destructive shower over the defences. The captain of " E." company perceived at once the hopelessness of his situation, asked and received permission to retire, and took his men and those of " H." company back under a heavy fusilade and with severe loss, passing the left flank of " C." company, into whose sangars many dropped for shelter. The section detached to the left, not receiving the order—unable to retire, if it had received it—was shot down to a man. The commander was taken prisoner. Carleton, who had not authorised this retirement, and placed as he was, knew nothing of the necessity for it, then ordered Major S. Humphery to reinforce the diminished companies, and send them back to the abandoned sangars. This Humphery found to be impossible, and thus the front of the position receded to the line of " C." company Gloucester and of " E." company Royal Irish Fusiliers, slightly to their right rear. Nor was this to remain long unbroken ; for most of the men of this company of Royal Irish Fusiliers, finding their feeble defences crumbling to nothing under the tremendous fire, drew off gradually towards their comrades on the right, and soon the officers of " C." company Gloucester saw that the prolongation of their line had vanished, and that their right was now completely exposed.

LOMBARDS KOP.

About this time (11.30 a.m.) a heliograph from Sir G. White's main body was seen. Carleton called for signallers to read the message; but so deadly was the fire that three men were wounded in succession, and one man thrice, as they stood by Carleton spelling out the signal. This ran :—" Retire on Ladysmith as opportunity offers." The only heliograph with the column had vanished in the stampede, and Carleton, encircled by musketry, knew that he was as powerless to obey the order as to acknowledge it.

11.30 a.m. A heliograph cannot be answered.

The Boers, who had turned " E." company, Gloucester, crawled on to within forty yards of the right of " B." company, threatening to roll it up, and Lieutenant C. S. Knox, its commander, surrounded by dead, found it necessary to go back to fetch up more men. Near him, in the sangar of " C." company, lay Captain S. Willcock of " H." company, and Knox, before starting back, waved his arms to attract his attention, shouting to him that the Boers were coming up from behind, that he, Knox, had to go back, and that Willcock must look to his left. But Knox, with a gesture of his arms, had unwittingly imitated the military signal to retire, and the musketry, which was now one sustained roar upon the mountain, drowned all of his shouting, except the words "from behind." Willcock, therefore, imagining that he was receiving an order to retire, which might have been sent forward from the commanding officer, passed it on to Captain Fyffe, who, in turn, communicated it to Captain Duncan, the senior officer in the sangar. In the short retirement which followed nearly forty-five per cent. fell.

A fatal misunderstanding.

Following their retreating companies, Captains Duncan and Fyffe (the latter wounded) halted by a small ruined kraal some fifty yards back, leaped into it with six or eight men, and determined to make a stand. Behind the kraal, the ground sloping upwards, hid the rest of the British lines entirely from a man lying prone in the sorry shelter. So close now were the Boers that the uproar of their rapid and incessant shots overwhelmed all else. To the occupants of the kraal it seemed as though silence had fallen over the British part of the position,

Duncan occupies a kraal, and then surrenders.

and this, though "D." company was shooting steadily, unshaken in the sangar not fifty yards to their right rear. They thought that Colonel Carleton had taken his column from the hill, and that they were alone. For a few moments they lay, the helpless focus of hundreds of rifles, and then, after a brief conversation with his wounded junior, Duncan decided to surrender. Two handkerchiefs tied to the muzzle of an uplifted rifle were apparently invisible to the Boers, whose fire continued unabated. But the white rags, fluttering just clear of the brow of the rise, were marked in an instant from the sangar of "D." company, of whose proximity Duncan and his party were absolutely unaware, and Captain R. Conner, who lay there with the commanding officer of the Gloucester, rushed out towards them over some fifty yards of bullet-swept ground shouting an enquiry. Meanwhile, as the storm of lead still beat upon the shelter, Duncan, taking a towel from a soldier near him, tied it to his sword and held it aloft. For a minute or two the enemy did not desist, and in this interval Conner, running by order of his commanding officer, across to Colonel Carleton, acquainted him with the fact that the flag had been upraised in Duncan's sangar. At the same time a bugle, whether British or Boer will never be known, sounded the "cease fire" somewhere on the British left. There was a hasty consultation between Carleton and Adye as to the possibility of repudiating the surrender altogether, or of applying it solely to the small party which had yielded. But the former officer, raising his eyes towards the spot, saw that the enemy had practically decided the question for him. Having passed by Duncan's kraal they were close in front of his main line, moving quickly forward with shouts and waving of hats, with rifles held confidently at the "trail." Many were already on the flank of the right portion of the British line, which, surrender or not as it would, was thus placed in an utterly untenable position. This right, consisting of the Royal Irish Fusiliers, absorbed in action to the front, knew nothing of the events on the left.

Carleton submits for all.

There was yet time to disown the flag. The Boers had so far possessed themselves only of Duncan's sangar; but Carleton

LOMBARDS KOP.

shrank from doing what he knew would be construed into the blackest treachery by his opponents, which he knew, moreover, could but prolong the resistance of his trapped and exhausted battalions some half an hour or less. Calling a bugler to him he bade him sound the "cease fire," set a match to his maps and papers, and, with Adye, walked out towards the enemy. Some of the Irish Fusiliers still fought on whilst Carleton, meeting Commandant Steenkamp, handed over to him his sword and revolver; it was some time before the bursts of firing ceased altogether on the right. At about 1.30 p.m. 37 officers and 917 men became prisoners of war.*

* For detailed casualties, etc., see Appendix 6.

CHAPTER XI.

THE ARRIVAL OF SIR REDVERS BULLER.

<small>Hopes of Sir George White's strength felt at home.</small>

REPORTS of the concentration of large commandos of Transvaal and Free State burghers on the Natal border had been telegraphed home by the High Commissioner and the Governor of Natal on the 28th of September, and reached the Colonial Office during the night of the 28th-29th. The plan, therefore, of an advance through the Orange Free State, which was adopted by the Cabinet on the following day, by implication assumed that the force assigned to Sir George White for the defence of Natal would be sufficient to check the threatened invasion until a forward movement of the army corps in the western theatre of war should draw away from the republican host the Free State men for the protection of their own territory.

<small>Situation when Sir R. Buller arrived.</small>

The events of the first three weeks of the war showed that Sir George White, without assistance, would not be able to protect Natal, and the situation which met General Buller on his disembarkation in South Africa on the morning of the 31st October could not but cause him grave anxiety. The Natal Field Force, after three strenuous efforts at Talana, Elandslaagte and Lombards Kop to repel the enemy's columns of invasion, lay concentrated at Ladysmith, and to the north, east, and west was already closely watched by the enemy in superior strength. General Buller was convinced that the troops needed rest, and could for a time only act on the defensive. He therefore telegraphed to General White, on 1st November, suggesting that he should entrench and await events either at Ladysmith

THE ARRIVAL OF SIR REDVERS BULLER.

or at Colenso. Sir George's reply showed that he had already entrenched himself at Ladysmith, and could not now withdraw. South of Ladysmith there were only very weak posts at Colenso and Estcourt, and one regular battalion at Maritzburg. For the moment, the safety of the capital of Natal appeared to be precarious, and Sir Redvers even deemed it necessary to request the Naval Commander-in-Chief to take steps for the protection of Durban from land attack. In Cape Colony the Boer forces close to the Orange river had been strengthened by reinforcements from the commandos originally assigned to watch the Basuto border. Moreover, there was some reason to believe that another commando from the north was moving down upon Kimberley, and this report, coupled with the lack of news from Mafeking, rendered it for the moment doubtful whether Baden-Powell might not have been overwhelmed.* The first units of the expeditionary force were not due at Cape Town for some ten days. The complete disembarkation at Cape Town, Port Elizabeth, and East London would not be finished until early in December.† The British Commander-in-Chief could not hope, therefore, for at least a month, that his field army would be complete in organisation, equipment, and transport, and ready to commence an advance into the Free State. Notwithstanding these anxieties, General Buller was at first inclined to adhere to the scheme originally designed, and to wait until he could remove the pressure on Ladysmith and Kimberley by striking straight at Bloemfontein. He so informed Lord Wolseley in a telegram despatched from Cape Town on 1st November. Yet a few hours later it became evident that the whole case was graver than Sir Redvers had at first conceived. Both from the telegrams of Sir George White and from those of Sir Archibald Hunter, from whom, as his own chief-of-staff, Buller had called

* See Sir R. Buller's despatch to Secretary of State for War, dated 1st November, 1899.

† Before leaving England Sir R. Buller had informed the War Office that he proposed to disembark the 1st (Methuen's) division at Cape Town, the 2nd (Clery's) at Port Elizabeth, and the 3rd (Gatacre's) at East London; but, having regard to possible changes in the strategic situation, he requested that every ship should call at Cape Town for orders.

for a personal report on affairs in Natal, it was manifest that Ladysmith was certain to be cut off from the outer world. General White telegraphed : " I have the greatest confidence in holding the Boers for as long as necessary," but he added that " reinforcements should be sent to Natal at once. Ladysmith strongly entrenched, but lines not continuous and perimeter so large that Boers can exercise their usual tactics." General Hunter reported that " Ladysmith lies in a hollow, commanded by heights too distant for us to hold, and now possessed by the enemy " ; and that " the Boers are superior in numbers, mobility, and long-range artillery." In Cape Colony the Intelligence officers at Naauwpoort and Stormberg telegraphed that a commando, 800 strong, had crossed the Orange river at Norval's Pont, and that another Boer force, stated to be 3,000 strong, with two guns and a Maxim, was crossing the Bethulie bridge. The enemy's successes in Natal were, in fact, encouraging the Free State commandos to establish connection with the disaffected in the eastern and midland districts of Cape Colony. As regards the general attitude of those in the Colonies who sympathised with the Boers, General Buller was aware that for the most part they possessed arms and ammunition, and that if their districts were invaded the young men would join the enemy. The information in his possession led to a belief that the greater number were for the moment still very undecided, wondering which side would win, and that their whole attention was fixed on Ladysmith and Kimberley. If the relief of those places could be effected, the hostile elements, it was held, would not stir ; but if the two towns should fall, a dangerous rising was thought probable. Meanwhile at Kimberley, although the reports of the officer in command of the garrison did not appear to Sir Redvers to show any immediate anxiety, yet the successful defence of that place depended on other than the regular troops,* and there were indications that the strain of the situation was being already felt. Urgent appeals were addressed by the civil community to the High Commissioner, drawing his attention to the large number of

* See Vol. II.

THE ARRIVAL OF SIR REDVERS BULLER.

women and children within the town, the possibility of the cattle, on which the meat supplies of the invested population mainly depended, being captured by the enemy, and the difficulty of maintaining order amongst the 10,000 "raw savages" employed in the mine compounds.

The consideration of these reports and representations made it evident that the whole situation had changed from that contemplated when the original plan of campaign had been drawn up. For an aggressive advance on Bloemfontein there was as yet no adequate army. The component parts of it were on the high seas. Even after they should have arrived, much time and labour would be required, before they could be welded together, and supplied with all that was needed for an offensive march into a country so distant from the coast. On the other hand, if Ladysmith should meanwhile fall, the Boer commandos at present surrounding that town would be set free to seize not only Maritzburg but probably also the seaport of Durban, the possession of which would give to the republics direct access to the outer world, and would, as was believed by both Boer and British, be a signal to all the disaffected in Cape Colony to take up arms. In the western theatre of war, the early relief of Kimberley was an object dear to the hearts of all loyalists, and its loss would undoubtedly give an immediate impetus to the wave of rebellion. The necessity for immediate action was urgent, both in Natal and Cape Colony, but the former appeared for the moment to present the more critical situation. Sir Redvers, therefore, on the 2nd November, telegraphed to the War Office: *[Difficulties to be dealt with.]*

"I consider that I must reinforce Natal, hang on to Orange River bridge, and give myself to organise troops expected from England. I am, therefore, withdrawing the garrisons at Naauwpoort and Stormberg. I shall send Gatacre's division on arrival to Natal, and with Methuen's and Clery's try to keep the main line open, and to relieve Kimberley. I do not wish to be pessimistic, but it seems to me I shall have to wait until March to commence active operations."

On receipt of this report Lord Lansdowne telegraphed an enquiry whether the division sent to Natal should be replaced by a fresh division from England. On the 3rd November, in *[Messages from and to home. "Extreme gravity."]*

consequence of further reports from Natal, Sir Redvers telegraphed to the Secretary of State:

> "Telegraphic connection with Ladysmith was interrupted yesterday, and White's force is isolated. He is well supplied with everything, except ammunition for his naval 12-pounders, which are the only guns that can compete with hostile artillery. I regard the situation as one of extreme gravity. Colenso bridge and Maritzburg are held by one battalion each; we are protecting Durban from the fleet. I shall despatch the first reinforcements I receive to Durban, but I cannot conceal from myself that if the enemy previously occupy, even with a small force, the country south of Mooi River, the relief of White by troops just landed will be an almost impossible operation, unless he can hold out six weeks at least from now."

Nov. 4/99. Sir Redvers decides to go to Natal.

By the following day, 4th November, General Buller had been able to work out his plans more in detail. It had become more and more apparent that Natal, where now the bulk of the enemy's strength lay, was for the moment the scene of most difficulty and danger, and that the relief of Ladysmith was all-important. For these reasons Sir Redvers decided to proceed himself to Natal for a time to supervise personally that critical operation. He telegraphed, therefore, to the Secretary of State:

> "My intentions are as follows: I propose to send Clery and Headquarters 2nd division to Natal to command. With him will go the first three brigade Headquarters except Guards that arrive. These three brigades will be composed of the first line battalions that arrive. Headquarters 1st division will land at Cape Town, and Lord Methuen will command advance on Kimberley with Guards' brigade and one other. Headquarters 3rd division will land at Cape Town or East London, as circumstances require, and will be completed with a new brigade, under Fetherstonhaugh, formed of three extra regiments and one from line of communications, or else colonial regiment.
>
> "I propose to take charge of advance on Ladysmith. If under Providence we are successful there and at Kimberley, I think collapse of opposition possible. These proposals are subject to High Commissioner's views of state of Cape Colony, and to what may happen meantime anywhere else.
>
> "Preparation of extra division seems desirable, but I do not yet see need for its despatch from England. I shall speak with more confidence when I see French, who is, I hope, en route here from Ladysmith."

More hopeful views.

On the 5th November Sir Redvers telegraphed further to the War Office that 40 days' supplies for the force under orders for Natal should be shipped direct from England to Durban. The more hopeful view the General Commanding-in-Chief

THE ARRIVAL OF SIR REDVERS BULLER.

was already taking may be judged from the fact that on the following day, the 6th of November, he requested the War Office to read "January" instead of "March" in the last sentence of his above quoted cypher of November 2nd. Five days later, in reply to a telegram from Lord Lansdowne, stating that another infantry division was being mobilised, and asking by what date it would be required, General Buller reported:

> "The defence of Ladysmith seems to have so thoroughly checked advance of enemy, that I have some grounds for hoping the successful relief of Kimberley and Ladysmith may end opposition. On the other hand, reliable Dutch here predict guerilla warfare as a certainty. I think, therefore, that I ought to have another division as soon as possible. My great want at present is mounted men. I am raising as many as I can, and should like, as soon as possible, a few good special service officers."

To this despatch the War Office answered on 14th November that a fifth infantry division would be sent out at an early date, under command of Sir C. Warren.

In arriving at the decisions recorded in the above official telegrams, Sir Redvers Buller had not abandoned the intention of carrying out ultimately the original plan of campaign. On the contrary, with a view to its resumption, after the relief of Ladysmith had been effected, he determined to instruct the General Officer Commanding the 1st division, Lieut.-General Lord Methuen, as soon as he had thrust aside the Boer commandos between the Orange river and Kimberley, to throw into that town supplies and a reinforcement of one and a half battalions of infantry and some naval long-range guns, and then move back to the Orange river, withdrawing with him the women and children and natives. Meantime, while the cavalry division, as its units arrived from England, was being prepared for the front at a camp near Cape Town, its commander, Lieut.-General French, who had been recalled from Ladysmith, was to form a flying column at Naauwpoort, with instructions to risk no engagement, but to manœuvre and worry the enemy, and thus check any invasion of the central districts of the Cape. On the eastern side of that colony,

The original scheme of march through Free State to be carried out after relief of Ladysmith.

the Commander-in-Chief decided to assemble at Queenstown a force, under Lieut.-General Sir W. Gatacre, the commander of the 3rd infantry division, whose duty it would be to operate northwards, and endeavour to stop recruiting by the enemy and protect the loyal. On Lord Methuen's return to Orange River, it was Sir Redvers' intention that he should march eastwards in conjunction with French, occupy the bridges of Colesberg, Norval's Pont and Bethulie, and thus prepare for the advance on Bloemfontein, which would be undertaken as soon as the relief of Ladysmith set him (Sir Redvers) free from Natal.

Dissolution of Army organisation. The decision to despatch to Natal the bulk of the earliest reinforcements arriving from home has been often referred to as "the break-up of the army corps." In a sense it was much more than that. From the point of view of organisation, the transfer of one or more intact divisions of the original army corps to Natal would have been immaterial, since they would have remained still under the supreme control of the General himself. But the urgency of the situation compelled the British Commander not only to detach portions of the army corps, but to improvise hastily, from the general officers and regimental units as they arrived in transports at Cape Town, special forces with hardly any regard to the composition of the divisions as originally fixed by the War Office. Thus to the commander of the 2nd division, Lieut.-General Sir C. F. Clery, who was selected by Sir Redvers Buller to make preparation for the relief of Ladysmith, and to act as his second in command in that enterprise, two cavalry regiments, four brigades of infantry,* two brigade divisions of field artillery, a company of Royal engineers, and a pontoon troop were assigned. But of these units, only the 4th brigade, commanded by Major-General the Hon. N. G. Lyttelton, and Lt.-Colonel L. W. Parsons' brigade division, R.F.A. (63rd, 64th, and 73rd batteries), belonged to Clery's division. The 2nd infantry brigade, under Major-General H. J. T. Hildyard, and Lt.-Colonel

* The decision to despatch a fourth brigade to Natal was made about 22nd November, after the development of Joubert's raid south of the Tugela.

THE ARRIVAL OF SIR REDVERS BULLER.

H. V. Hunt's brigade division (7th, 14th, and 66th batteries), being the first units of infantry and artillery to arrive from England, were removed from Methuen's division, and sent on at once to Natal. To these were subsequently added both the infantry brigades of the 3rd division (the 5th, under command of Major-General A. FitzRoy Hart, and the 6th, under Major-General G. Barton), the 13th Hussars, originally designated as corps troops, the Royal Dragoons, drawn from the 2nd cavalry brigade, and the pontoon troop of the army corps.

The 3rd, or Highland brigade, under Major-General A. G. Wauchope, was at first assigned by the Commander-in-Chief to Lord Methuen, to replace the 2nd brigade, transferred to Natal; but, as it was found later that Wauchope's battalions would at the outset be needed to guard the railway line in rear of Methuen's column, a 9th brigade, under Major-General R. S. R. Fetherstonhaugh, was formed out of the infantry units already at Orange River station, viz.: the half-battalion 1st Loyal North Lancashire, 2nd King's Own Yorkshire Light Infantry, 1st Northumberland Fusiliers, and 2nd Northamptonshire. Lt.-Colonel F. H. Hall's brigade division (18th, 62nd, and 75th batteries*) and the 9th Lancers were also allotted to the 1st division.

<small>Various new distributions.</small>

For Naauwpoort, General French, in addition to the original garrison of that place, was at first given the assistance of the 12th Lancers, a battery of R.H.A., and a half-battalion of the Black Watch, besides two companies of M.I. To these other units were to be gradually added, as soon as they became available.

<small>French's command.</small>

Sir W. Gatacre was instructed to develop a force on the eastern railway line from the original Stormberg garrison,† the 1st Royal Scots (originally allotted as corps troops), the 2nd Northumberland Fusiliers (a lines of communication battalion),

<small>Gatacre's.</small>

---

* The 62nd and half the 75th had been sent up to Orange River in October; the other half of the 75th and the 18th batteries were delayed on the voyage out by the breaking down of their transport, the *Zibenghla*, and did not land at Cape Town until 1st November.

† See Chapters II. and XVIII.

the 2nd Royal Irish Rifles (detached from the 5th brigade*), and the brigade division (74th, 77th and 79th batteries), of the 3rd division, supplemented by such colonial corps as he could gather together locally.

The dates of the arrival of the various expeditionary units at Cape Town and their disposal are shown in Appendix No. 7.

Less serious injury of the recasting of army because of ordinary British habit.

The dislocation of the infantry divisions, which was caused by the necessity for these sweeping changes, would have been even more seriously detrimental had those divisions actually existed prior to the embarkation of the troops from England; but, as has been shown in an earlier chapter, one of the weak points of the British army in 1899 was the imperfect development in peace time of the higher organisation of the troops. Except, therefore, in Major-General Hildyard's brigade, which came direct from Aldershot,† and had been trained there by its brigadier under the immediate eye of Sir R. Buller, that confidence, which is established between troops and their superior leaders by intimate mutual knowledge, did not exist, and could not be affected by that reorganisation, which the strategical situation necessitated.

Yet serious enough. Sir Redvers goes to Natal without a staff.

Nevertheless, as regards staff arrangements, serious inconvenience was for the moment inevitable. Sir F. Forestier-Walker, although appointed officially to the post of General Officer Commanding the lines of communication, had, through some oversight in London, not been given the full staff, as prescribed by the regulations, for an officer performing those onerous duties, and had been forced to improvise assistants from such special service officers as he could lay hands on. There was from the outset, therefore, a shortage of staff. Officers were, moreover, urgently required for the development of local troops and for censorship duties. The original Headquarter staff had been calculated on the hypothesis that the whole of the expeditionary corps would operate in the western theatre

---

* This battalion was replaced in Hart's brigade by the 1st Border regiment.

† Major-Generals Lyttelton and Hart no longer had under their command the whole of the battalions which had composed their brigades at Aldershot.

THE ARRIVAL OF SIR REDVERS BULLER.

of war, Sir George White being responsible for the Natal command. The rearrangement carried out by Sir R. Buller created in Natal a second field army. For this no Headquarter staff was available, without robbing the Cape of needed men. He therefore kept with him only his personal staff during his temporary absence in Natal, and issued orders there through the divisional staff of General Clery. He decided to leave the rest of the Headquarter staff at Cape Town to supervise the disembarkation of the reinforcements from England and their formation into a field army.

The reports of the fighting during the opening phases of the war had shown that our difficulties were mainly due to three causes—the superior numbers of the enemy, their greater mobility, and the longer range of their guns. In the operations he was now about to undertake, Sir Redvers hoped partially to make good these deficiencies by borrowing ships' guns from the Navy and by locally raising mounted men. The Naval Commander-in-Chief had already lent one contingent, under Commander A. P. Ethelston, R.N., to garrison Stormberg. Another such contingent, under Captain the Hon. H. Lambton, R.N., was in Ladysmith, and, at the request of Sir R. Buller, Captain Percy Scott, R.N., in H.M.S. *Terrible*, had been despatched to Durban to arrange the land defences of that port. Rear-Admiral Harris, with the approval of the Admiralty, now consented to the Stormberg party being brought back to Cape Town, with a view to its marching under the command of Capt. R. C. Prothero, R.N., with Lord Methuen's column, to Kimberley and there remaining as a reinforcement of the garrison. The Naval Commander-in-Chief further agreed to organise yet a third detachment to assist in the relief of Ladysmith. The cheerfulness with which the Naval authorities rendered assistance to the army in this time of stress and strain was only in conformity with the traditions of both services; yet the readiness shown by the officers and men of the Royal Navy and Marines in adapting themselves and their weapons to the circumstances of a land campaign won the profound admiration even of those who were best acquainted with the

[margin: Help from the fleet.]

practical nature of the normal training of the personnel of the fleet.

<small>Raising colonial corps, for Natal.</small>

The calling out of colonial mounted corps, both in Cape Colony and Natal, is mentioned in Chapter I. and Chapter II. Mounted men were urgently needed by all the columns in process of preparation, but, adhering to his opinion that success in the relief of Ladysmith was the most crucial matter, Sir Redvers decided to despatch to Natal the first unit enlisted at Cape Town—the South African Light Horse. The first party of "Light Horse" embarked at Cape Town for Natal on the 22nd November. In Natal itself two mounted corps, under the command of Major (local Lieut.-Colonel) A. W. Thorneycroft, Royal Scots Fusiliers, and Major (local Lieut.-Colonel) E. C. Bethune, 16th Lancers, were already being formed.

<small>Brabant in eastern districts.</small>

Mr. Schreiner, the Prime Minister of Cape Colony, had, at the suggestion of General Buller, endeavoured to raise in the districts of Middleburg, Cradock, and Somerset East, a burgher force to maintain internal order and repel invasion, but the local civil authorities were unanimous in advising that an application of the Cape Burgher law would furnish some recruits for the enemy. Captain Brabant (now Major-General Sir E. Brabant), an ex-Imperial officer, was, with the concurrence of the Cape Government, instructed to raise a mounted corps from the loyalists in the eastern districts.

<small>Work now done.</small>

It will readily be conceived from the brief summary of the facts which have been above recorded that the tasks which the Commander-in-Chief, assisted by the Headquarter and lines of communication staffs, had to carry out during the first three weeks of November were of an overwhelming nature. These included the reorganisation of the various bodies of troops which, from the 9th November onwards, arrived daily in Table Bay from England; the disembarkation of the units; their equipment for the field and despatch to the front; the issue of operation orders to the troops in Natal and Cape Colony already in touch with the enemy; the establishment of supply depôts for the field forces, the defence of Maritzburg and Durban from the Boer raid, which threatened those very important towns; the

THE ARRIVAL OF SIR REDVERS BULLER.

protection of the lines of railway through Cape Colony, with the mere handful of troops at first available; and the checking of the invasion of the Free Staters across the Orange river. To these must be added the anxious watching of the signs in disaffected districts of smouldering rebellion, which a single success of the enemy might fan into a burst of flame; these and other cares formed an accumulation of pressing duties and heavy responsibilities, which fully justify the frank statement of Sir R. Buller to Lt.-Gen. Forestier-Walker on 20th November that "Ever since I have been here we have been like the man who, with a long day's work before him, over-slept himself and so was late for everything all day."* The position of affairs in South Africa throughout these anxious weeks, in fact, forcibly proved the truth of Lord Wolseley's warning, addressed on 3rd September, 1899, to the Secretary of State that: "We have committed one of the greatest blunders in war, namely, we have given the enemy the initiative. He is in a position to take the offensive, and by striking the first blow to ensure the great advantage of winning the first round."

Yet by the 22nd November the labours of the Headquarter staff of the army in South Africa, assisted by the fullest co-operation of the two Governors, Sir Alfred Milner and Sir W. Hely-Hutchinson, and aided by the strenuous exertions of the lines of communication staff in Cape Colony and Natal, had sensibly improved the general situation in both the western and eastern theatres of war. In Cape Colony, no part of Bechuanaland and Griqualand West, it is true, except the areas defended by the garrisons of Mafeking, Kuruman and Kimberley, remained under British authority. But cheery reports from Colonel Baden-Powell gave promise of a prolonged stand at the little northern town, while Lord Methuen's column had on the previous day (the 21st November) crossed the Orange river and made good the first eleven miles of its march on Kimberley. Southward, Major-General Wauchope's brigade was holding the section of the railway line from Orange River station, viâ De Aar, to Naauwpoort, the latter station having been re-occupied, and the

Improved prospects.

* See the end of this chapter.

formation of a column, to harass and menace the enemy in the direction of Colesberg, had commenced under the direction of Lieut.-General French. On the eastern side of the Colony only had the Boers made any substantial advance; a strong Free State commando had seized Burghersdorp and detached parties to Aliwal North and Lady Grey. Sir W. Gatacre, on the other hand, had assumed command of colonial corps and one and a half battalions of regular troops at Queenstown, and was preparing to move northward, to check the commandeering of British subjects, which Commandant Olivier had instituted in the territory occupied by his burghers. The Basuto chiefs remained true to their allegiance to the "Great White Queen," and by tacit consent their territory was treated by both sides as neutral. In Griqualand East and the native territories east of Cape Colony, the Pondo, Tembu and Fingo tribes continued loyal, and arrangements for the defence of these great masses of native population against Boer raids were being made by Major Sir H. Elliott, who as Commandant-General, under the sanction of the Governor, was defending the passes leading from Barkly East with the Cape Mounted Rifles and some Volunteers.

Natal. Sir G. White detains bulk of Boers. Time thus gained.

In Natal Sir George White was holding his own at Ladysmith, and, as he had anticipated, detaining north of the Tugela the main strength of the enemy's army. After some hesitation on the part of the Boer leaders, a raid in force had been made to the south, and had for the moment caused much alarm. But the delay in the movement had greatly diminished its chances of reaching Maritzburg, although the local condition was still one of some anxiety. Reinforcements as they arrived at Durban had been pushed rapidly up by rail north of Maritzburg, and the British troops were now echeloned along the railway up to Estcourt. The vanguard of the enemy's raiding column had reached Mooi River, and his scouts had even penetrated as far as Nottingham Road, but a day's ride from Maritzburg. The Boers were, therefore, well in rear of the British advanced posts, and Lieut.-General Clery felt some doubt whether a temporary retirement from Estcourt might not prove necessary. The chief

THE ARRIVAL OF SIR REDVERS BULLER.

difficulty was the lack of mounted troops to bring the enemy to action and put a stop to his pillaging the outlying farms of the Natal colonists.

Sir Redvers, 22nd Nov./99, starts for Natal.

Such were throughout South Africa the facts known to him when Sir Redvers Buller, having issued instructions for the guidance of the senior officer in Cape Colony, Sir F. Forestier-Walker, and for the three commanders in the field, Lieut.-Generals Lord Methuen, French, and Sir W. Gatacre, embarked at 7 p.m., the 22nd November, in the S.S. *Mohawk* for Natal. His military secretary, Col. the Hon. F. Stopford, and aides-de-camp accompanied him. The rest of the Headquarter staff remained at Cape Town.

His views at that time.

The appreciation of the situation written by the General commanding-in-chief forty-eight hours earlier will place the reader in possession of his views on the eve of his embarkation for Durban. The memorandum ran as follows :—

Cape Town,
November 20th, 1899.

GENERAL WALKER,

Before starting for Natal I think I should leave you my appreciation of the situation.

1. Ever since I have been here we have been like the man, who, with a long day's work before him, overslept himself and so was late for everything all day.

2. In disposing the troops which arrived from England I have considered that it was of the first importance to keep Cape Colony from rebellion, even if by so doing I temporarily lost Maritzburg.

3. I consequently have formed a strong column under Lord Methuen which is in a position to take the field and I am forming a force of mounted men and horse artillery under General French, which will, I hope, be able to meet any commandos which may invade the Colony. I have also done all I can to safeguard the western and eastern lines of railway.

4. The state of Kimberley necessitated the first employment of Lord Methuen's force in that direction. He starts to-day. General French is at Naauwpoort, organising a column to attack Colesberg at the earliest possible date.

5. My hope is that the Boers at Colesberg will have been defeated before Lord Methuen returns from Kimberley.

On his return he should send a force to attack the Boers at Burghersdorp. There should then be 1,000,000 rations at Orange River and 1,000,000 at De Aar, and I have directed that supply should be accumulated at Port Elizabeth and East London. He can then open new lines of supply as he moves eastward.

6. As soon as they can be occupied General Gatacre's force should be advanced to Molteno or Stormberg, and any force at Burghersdorp should be attacked.

If the Burghersdorp force has meanwhile advanced south it would be attacked by Lord Methuen, aided by part of General French's force, the two being based on Naauwpoort or Middleburg.

7. The exact nature of this operation must depend on the actual circumstances at the time. The main point is, there will be rations at De Aar and near it to enable a force under Lord Methuen to move along the line eastward, repairing it as he goes, and strong enough to clear the northern districts.

8. As soon as ever circumstances admit the bridges at Norval's Pont and Bethulie will, of course, be seized; in short, the plan is, clear the northern districts by working from west to east, seize the bridges, and, as occasion admits, bring the shorter lines of supply into use. Then concentrate for an advance on Bloemfontein.

9. I think there are enough troops in the Colony to work this programme, except that:

(1) There should be a battalion at Port Elizabeth.
(2) General Gatacre wants another battalion and a battery of field artillery.
(3) General French should have the second battery Royal Horse artillery, and eventually three cavalry regiments, and, if possible, one more battalion.

10. With regard to Natal, I propose to send the 6th Dragoon Guards and 10th Hussars, the 63rd, 64th, and 73rd batteries Royal Field artillery, the remainder of General Hart's Brigade, *i.e.*, three battalions, as soon as they come in. We must do with them the best we can.

11. I think the Colonial contingents had better go to Natal.

12. In my opinion, so long as General White holds Ladysmith the force able to attack you from the Orange Free State is not likely to be serious, but if Natal goes you will have to concentrate for defence, and you should make up your mind what positions to hold. Probably the best military positions about Queenstown, Middleburg, and Beaufort West will be found most convenient.

REDVERS BULLER,
General.

CHAPTER XII.

ADVANCE FROM THE ORANGE RIVER.

ON the 10th of November Lord Methuen, with his staff, left Cape Town for Orange River station, where he arrived two days later. The orders which he had received from Sir Redvers Buller ran as follows :— *Lord Methuen's instructions. Nov. 10/99.*

November 10th, 1899.

1. You will take command of the troops at De Aar and Orange River stations,* with the object of marching on Kimberley as rapidly as possible.

2. In addition to the troops now at De Aar, the infantry of which are being formed into the 9th brigade under Colonel Fetherstonhaugh, you will have under your command :—

   i. The 1st Infantry Brigade.—Major-Gen. Colvile.
   ii. The Highland Brigade.—Major-Gen. Wauchope.
   iii. The 9th Lancers.
   iv. The Brigade Division, Royal Field Artillery, under Colonel Hall.
   v. The Divisional Troops except Cavalry of the Division.
   vi. Certain Royal Engineers, Army Service Corps and Medical Details which have been collected at the two stations.

I wish you to march from the Orange river to the Modder river, communicate with Kimberley, and to hold the line De

---
* See map No. 9.

Aar, Modder river, so that we shall be able to bring up stores and heavy guns and pass them into Kimberley.

3. The half-battalion Loyal North Lancashire regiment, which will form part of the 9th brigade, is to be left in Kimberley.

4. You will afford help to Kimberley to remove such of the natives as they wish to get rid of, and, generally, you will give such advice and assistance in perfecting the defences as you may be able to afford.

5. You will make the people of Kimberley understand that you have not come to remain charged with its defence, but to afford it better means of maintaining its defence, which will at the same time be assisted by an advance on Bloemfontein.

REDVERS BULLER, General.

Four days later, the Commander-in-Chief in South Africa addressed the following letter to General Methuen :—

Cape Town,
November 14th, 1899.

LORD METHUEN,—

Personal advice from Sir Redvers, Nov. 14th.

I do not want to tie your hands in any way, but I send this letter for such use as you choose to make of it.

1. I think that you will find that the Guards and the 9th Brigade and two batteries Royal Field Artillery will be as large a portion of your force as you can take with advantage.

2. As to mounted men, you will of course take what you require. I think it will be advisable to leave one-half of Rimington's Guides, the party at Hanover Road, and sufficient others to scout 20 to 25 miles on all sides of the line held by General Wauchope.

3. On your departure General Wauchope will have, including the two half-battalions of Berkshire and Munster, four battalions; and if you leave him one battery, six guns Royal Field Artillery, with them he should be able to hold the line to Belmont with perfect safety. Orange River bridge must of course be held at all costs. I hope you will not remain a day longer at Kimberley than you can help.

ADVANCE FROM THE ORANGE RIVER.

5. I have already told you that I am sending with you a Naval brigade with four 12-pr. 12-cwt. guns; these guns range 6,000 yards. You will not start without them, will leave them at Kimberley, and such reinforcements not exceeding one-and-a-half battalions as the commandant may require.

6. I have said in my instructions that you will proceed to Modder river. If you can from there get a clear road to Kimberley, so much the better, but you will act according to circumstances. The main object is to save time.*

* * * * * * *

R. BULLER.

Before Lord Methuen's arrival at Orange River station, the mounted troops had been engaged in reconnoitring and sketching the country in the neighbourhood of the railway bridge. On the 6th of November a party of the 9th Lancers and mounted infantry, accompanied by guns, had scouted up the railway to within five miles of Belmont. On the 9th another reconnaissance was made up the line, past Belmont, to Honey Nest Kloof, 37 miles from Orange River station. No Boers were seen about Belmont, though they had left traces of their presence in broken culverts and other damage to the railway. After falling back for the night to Witteputs, the patrol marched north-eastward on the morning of the 10th, and encountered several hundred Boers, with field guns, a few miles to the east of Belmont. A skirmish ensued in which Lt.-Col. C. E. Keith-Falconer was killed, Lt. C. C. Wood mortally wounded, and Lts. F. Bevan and H. C. Hall and four men wounded. To the westward of the railway line a detachment of thirty of Rimington's Guides successfully reconnoitred as far as Prieska. Though the information brought back by these reconnaissances was mainly negative, on the 18th November Major R. N. R. Reade, Lord Methuen's Intelligence officer, was able from various sources of information to report that a force, estimated at from 700 to 1,200 men, with four guns, was at or near Belmont; and that a small commando under

Information gathered before the march, up to Nov. 21st.

---

* The remainder of the letter contains suggestions on tactics and so forth, which are not directly relevant to the subject of this chapter, and are therefore omitted.

THE WAR IN SOUTH AFRICA.

Jourdaan had been successfully recruiting from the disloyal farmers in the districts of Barkly West, Campbell, Douglas, and Griquatown, which lay to the west and north-west of the line of advance to Kimberley.

Constitution of 1st Division. Thanks to the strenuous efforts of the staff and the departmental corps, the reconstituted first division* was by the 20th of November ready to take the field. Equipped with mule transport, and marching with a minimum of baggage, Lord Methuen's column consisted of about 7,726 infantry, 850 cavalry and mounted infantry, two batteries of Royal Field artillery, four companies of Royal engineers and a Naval brigade.

It was thus composed :—

Naval brigade—Captain R. C. Prothero, R.N. :—
> Four naval 12-pr. 12-cwt. guns, with 363 officers and men of the Royal Navy, sailors, Royal Marine artillery and Royal Marine Light Infantry.†

Mounted troops :—
> 9th Lancers.
> One company mounted infantry Northumberland Fusiliers.
> One company mounted infantry Loyal North Lancashire.
> Half company mounted infantry King's Own Yorkshire Light Infantry.
> New South Wales Lancers (30 of all ranks).
> Rimington's Guides.

Royal Field Artillery :—
> Brigade division R.F.A.—Lt.-Colonel F. H. Hall.
> 18th and 75th Field batteries (15-pr. guns).‡

---

* For the causes which led to the partial dispersion of the 1st division on its arrival in South Africa, see Chapter XI.

† Owing to difficulties with transport, the Naval brigade did not reach the 1st division until 1 a.m. on the 23rd.

‡ The 62nd Field battery, which formed part of Colonel Hall's brigade division of artillery, was left on the line of communication, and did not rejoin until the battle of Modder River.

ADVANCE FROM THE ORANGE RIVER.

Royal Engineers—Lt.-Colonel J. B. Sharpe :—
    7th Field company.
    8th Railway company.
    11th Field company.
    30th Fortress company.
    Telegraph section.

1st (Guards) brigade—Major-General Sir H. E. Colvile :—
    3rd battalion Grenadier Guards.
    1st battalion Coldstream Guards.*
    2nd battalion Coldstream Guards.
    1st battalion Scots Guards.

9th Infantry brigade—Maj.-Gen. R. S. R. Fetherstonhaugh :—†
    1st battalion Northumberland Fusiliers.
    Half-battalion 1st Loyal North Lancashire.‡
    2nd battalion Northamptonshire.
    2nd battalion King's Own Yorkshire Light Infantry.

The medical services for the 9th infantry brigade were furnished by the divisional Field Hospital of the 1st division, and the 3rd brigade Field Hospital formed the new divisional Field Hospital. Subsequently, when the 3rd (Highland) brigade joined Lord Methuen's force at Modder river, its Field Hospital was provided by the 2nd division Field Hospital and the Bearer company by " A." company Cape Medical Staff Corps, under Lieut.-Col. Hartley, V.C.

Behind the 1st division, the Highland brigade, under Maj.-Gen. A. G. Wauchope, guarded the railway up to the Orange river, and overawed the disaffected element among the inhabitants along the line of communication. In the neighbourhood of Colesberg, Lieut.-General French, with a mixed force of all arms,

Supporting forces. Wauchope. French.

---

* The 1st battalion Coldstream Guards landed from Gibraltar on 16th November, and was detained at Orange River, guarding the railway until the 22nd, when it was relieved by the 1st battalion Highland Light Infantry and at once pushed on to Belmont, where it arrived late on the night of the 22nd.

† Two companies of the Royal Munster Fusiliers also arrived at Belmont from Orange River on the 22nd November, and were attached to the 9th brigade.

‡ The remainder of this battalion formed part of the garrison of Kimberley.

was engaged in stemming the tide of invasion from the Free State, and by incessantly occupying the attention of the commandos opposed to him, prevented their massing against Lord Methuen's right flank as he advanced towards Kimberley.

<small>March fully known by Boers. They prepare to meet it.</small>

The Boers were not taken by surprise by Lord Methuen's preparations for an advance. Their spies and sympathisers kept them fully informed of all the steps taken. In anticipation of a dash upon Kimberley they had carefully prepared defensive positions along the railway at Belmont and at Rooilaagte, or, as we term it, Graspan. To some 2,500 burghers, under Commandant Jacobus Prinsloo, was entrusted the duty of thrusting the British back towards the Orange ; and, if the task should prove beyond their strength, De la Rey, who, with his commando was then investing the southern defences of Kimberley, could easily reinforce them. A large supply of stores had been collected at Jacobsdal, while subsidiary depôts had been formed at Graspan and in the neighbourhood of Koffyfontein.

<small>4 a.m., Nov. 21st., march begins.</small>

At 4 a.m., on the 21st of November, the 1st division marched from their bivouac on the northern bank of the Orange river. The General followed the course of the railway in order to facilitate the carriage of supplies, not only for his own column, but also for the inhabitants of the town into which he was to throw stores and reinforcements. The troops halted about 8 a.m. at Fincham's farm, near Witteputs, twelve miles north of the Orange River bridge. The 9th Lancers and mounted infantry were at once thrown forward with orders to reconnoitre northwards on a front of about twelve miles. They found the enemy in some strength among the hills which lie to the east of Belmont station, and drew fire, fortunately with very slight loss. Lieut.-Colonel Willoughby Verner, D.A.A.G., for topography to the army corps, sketched the Boer position from the low hills east of Thomas' farm, about a mile and a half south-east of Belmont station.* These sketches were subsequently reproduced and distributed among the officers of the column before the action of the 23rd. Later in the day Lord Methuen himself studied the ground from the hills near Thomas' farm, and then

* See map No. 10.

ADVANCE FROM THE ORANGE RIVER. 217

returned to Witteputs, followed by the mounted troops, many of whom had covered forty miles during the day.

In the grey of the morning of the 22nd of November, the mounted infantry swooped from Witteputs upon Thomas' farm, occupied it, and threw out a chain of posts facing the station of Belmont and the hills to the east. Lord Methuen, with his staff, the brigadiers commanding the infantry brigades, Lt.-Col. Hall, C.R.A., and Lt.-Col. Sharpe, C.R.E., arrived shortly afterwards, and again reconnoitred the Boer position from the high ground above Thomas' farm. When the General had completed his reconnaissance, he dictated the orders for the attack which he proposed to deliver on the morrow. Then, leaving the mounted infantry to hold the ground they occupied, and to protect the companies of Royal engineers who were on their way from Witteputs to repair the railway, Lord Methuen returned with his staff to the column, to prepare for a further advance that afternoon. During the morning there was intermittent firing between the mounted infantry outposts and parties of the enemy, who occasionally showed themselves for a short time, and then disappeared without affording any clue as to the strength of the force concealed among the kopjes. In the afternoon the Boers brought two guns into action, chiefly directed against the 7th Field company R.E., then employed in improving the supply of water at the site selected for that night's bivouac near Thomas' farm. To silence this artillery fire the 18th and 75th batteries were hurriedly despatched from Witteputs, and in order to save the troops at Belmont as quickly as possible from this annoyance, the Officer Commanding trotted nearly the whole distance. The horses, still weak from the effects of the long sea voyage, suffered severely from the strain. Five indeed actually died of exhaustion, and all were so weary that during the engagement of the 23rd, the artillery was unable to move with any degree of rapidity.

At 4.30 p.m. the remainder of the troops marched from Witteputs and reached their bivouac at Thomas' farm just before nightfall.

Approach to Belmont.

Division gathers before Belmont, Nov. 22nd.

CHAPTER XIII.

BELMONT.*

<small>The Boer position.
Nov. 23rd/99.</small> LORD METHUEN'S dispositions for attack were necessarily determined by the ground which the Boers had taken up to oppose his advance. Some two miles to the south-east of Belmont station a hill, in form like a sugar-loaf, rises abruptly about 280 feet above the veld. From it extends northwards a broken line of kopjes which for several miles runs parallel with the railway in its course from Orange River station to Kimberley. Twelve hundred yards to the north of the "Sugar Loaf" there is a precipitous hill of nearly equal height, which acquired the name of the "Razor Back." The northern side of it overhangs a steep ravine, some 600 yards wide. The most important feature of the range, termed "Mont Blanc" by Lord Methuen, stretches northward from beyond this ravine for three miles. It is irregular in outline and broadens on its northern face to a width of a mile. Its average height may be taken at 300 feet above the plain. To the south and west its slopes are very steep; on the east they present fewer difficulties; on the north they are comparatively easy. Between Mont Blanc and the railway is a secondary line of heights about a mile and a half long, of an average width of 1,200 yards. The northern portion of this western range is a steep-sided, flat-topped hill, called "Table Mountain" in the orders for the battle; it lies about a mile due west of the central portion of Mont Blanc. Its average height is perhaps

<small>* See maps Nos. 10 and 10 (a).</small>

BELMONT.

100 feet lower than Mont Blanc, but here and there its surface is broken by knolls which dominate not only the plateau itself, but the surrounding country in every direction. A well-defined depression, almost amounting to a valley, running from south-east to north-west, separates Table Mountain from the southern half of the western heights. To these the name of "Gun Hill" has been given. Gun Hill consists of a series of undulations, bounded on the west and south by kopjes, in places as precipitous as the sides of Table Mountain, and varying in height from 80 to 120 feet above the plain. After the engagement the most southerly of these knolls became known to Lord Methuen's force as "Grenadier Hill." The valley between Mont Blanc and the western range is open, but intersected by deep dongas running from the north and north-east. The hills in both lines of heights are covered with huge iron-stone boulders, in places so steeply piled that men have to climb them on hands and knees, and their indented outlines form many salients from which cross fire can be poured on troops advancing to the attack.

As seen from the railway, the direct line of advance on Kimberley, the Mont Blanc range stands out of the veld like a fortress. This, the main range, is surrounded on the south and east by a level plain which affords advancing troops no cover from fire. Its western face, fronting the railway, has as natural outworks the heights of Table Mountain and Gun Hill. Thus, when Lord Methuen at first designed to drive off the Boers who flanked and menaced his further progress, the nearest part of the enemy's position to him was Gun Hill, and beyond this, further north, was Table Mountain, while supporting these from the east was the main ridge of Mont Blanc. Therefore, in order to clear away the enemy thus threatening him on his right, it was necessary first to arrange the positions of rendezvous so that the division should be arrayed against the hills about to be assailed. Thus the 9th brigade on the left of the attack looked towards Table Mountain. The Guards on the right, that is, to the south of the 9th brigade, similarly faced Gun Hill. The Guards were both nearer to the part to

Position as presented to the assailants. Nov. 23rd.

be assailed by them, and more immediately opposite to it, than was the 9th brigade to the object of its attack.

<small>Mode of attack as designed.</small>

The 9th brigade was to assault the western face of Table Mountain, while the Guards' brigade attacked Gun Hill. As soon as the enemy had been driven off Table Mountain, the 9th brigade was to move eastwards, swinging its left round so as to attack Mont Blanc from the north, while supported by the fire of the Guards from the eastern side of Gun Hill. The 75th battery on the left, the Naval guns and the 18th battery on the right, were to co-operate with the infantry by searching the heights with shrapnel. The mounted troops were to guard the flanks, prevent the escape of the enemy to the east, and, if possible, capture the Boer laager. With this object, two squadrons of the 9th Lancers under Colonel B. Gough were to be on the left flank of the 9th brigade, with one and a half companies of mounted infantry; while the remaining squadron of the 9th Lancers, a company of M.I. and Rimington's Guides, the whole under Major M. F. Rimington, were to work on the outer flank of the brigade of Guards. The troops were to march off from their respective rendezvous at 3 a.m. By this attack on Mont Blanc from the north, after the outworks of Table Mountain and Gun Hill had been carried, the Boers would be driven, not back along the railway towards Kimberley, but eastwards, well off Lord Methuen's proposed line of advance.

<small>Strength and disposition of Boers.</small>

The enemy under Jacobus Prinsloo consisted of the Jacobsdal, Winburg, Fauresmith and Bloemfontein commandos, with detachments from Kroonstad, Hoopstad and Boshof. It is difficult to arrive at an exact conclusion as to their strength, for the Boers themselves do not agree as to the number of burghers who took part in the action. Their estimates vary from 2,100 to 2,500 men, with two field guns and a pom-pom. Their artillery, however, hardly fired at all, nor were the reinforcements which De la Rey brought from Kimberley actively engaged. The exact ground held by each commando cannot be accurately stated, but their approximate dispositions are shown upon the maps No. 10 and 10 (a). There is some reason to believe that the Boer general had intended

BELMONT.

to throw part of his right wing across the railway, as trenches were found west of the line, so constructed as to bring flanking fire against an attack on Table Mountain; but whether these works were occupied on the morning of the 23rd cannot be ascertained. That the enemy had posts along the line to the north of Belmont is proved by the fact that one of these parties was captured by Colonel Gough's detachment of mounted men.

The troops left their bivouacs about 2 a.m. on the 23rd, reached their respective rendezvous at the time appointed, and at about 3.15 moved off towards the various parts of the enemy's position, to the attack of which they had been assigned.

3.15 a.m. Nov. 23rd. Attack begins.

In the assault on Gun Hill by the brigade of Guards, the two battalions of the Coldstream Guards were in reserve; the 1st battalion Scots Guards and the 3rd battalion Grenadier Guards were detailed to deliver the attack. As the latter battalions, moving in line of quarter-column, reached the wire fences along the railway line, they demolished them or scrambled through them as best they could* and then deployed into fighting formation. Four half companies, extended to five paces, formed the firing line of each battalion, supported at 200 paces distance by the remainder of these four companies, also extended to five paces. The battalion reserve, which followed about 200 paces behind the supports, consisted of four companies, which moved in the same formation as the leading companies but with a smaller extension between the men. As soon as the deployment was completed the advance began, and the troops moved forward through the darkness, over ground fairly open, but here and there made difficult by rocks and ant-bear holes. The only sound to be heard was the steady tramp of feet, which in the stillness of the night could be distinguished many hundred yards away by the 9th brigade. In admirable order, with their intervals and distances well maintained, the long lines of men advanced, straining their eyes to catch a glimpse

Guards move against Gun Hill.

---

* In some cases it was found that the wires were too strong to be cut by the wire-cutters.

of the kopjes they were to attack, and wondering when the Boers would open fire upon them. They had not long to wait. Towards 4 a.m., when the outlines of the hills began dimly to appear against the first glimmer of dawn, a violent burst of musketry rang out. Each rifle as it flashed against the dark back-ground showed where it had been discharged. The enemy were thus seen to be dotted at irregular intervals in two tiers on the skyline and the upper slopes of the heights.

Attack of Scots Guards;

The Scots Guards, who were marching on the point marked c on map No. 10, were within about 150 yards of the foot of the kopje, and had hardly fixed bayonets, when the enemy opened upon them. Col. A. H. Paget ordered the charge to be sounded, and; with a ringing cheer, his men carried the hill with comparatively small loss, to find themselves exposed, not only to frontal but to cross fire from both flanks. The musketry from the right ceased as soon as the Grenadiers stormed the kopjes which they attacked, while, thanks to the initiative of Bt. Lt.-Col. W. P. Pulteney, that from the left was checked. This officer, whose company was on the left of the line of the Scots Guards, found himself under heavy fire from the kopje marked d. Advancing against it he dislodged its defenders, who, in their precipitate retreat to Table Mountain, left some thirty ponies behind them. Colonel Pulteney mounted as many of his men as possible upon them, galloped in pursuit across the valley, then dismounted and worked up the kopje at the south-western angle of Table Mountain (b on map No. 10), until he was stopped by the enemy concealed amongst its boulders.

of Grenadiers.

The front line of the Grenadiers was about 350 yards from the kopjes when they first came under fire. To close with their enemy, the men were ordered to double and then instinctively quickening their pace they arrived panting at the foot of the hills, which loomed black and threatening before them. Under a very heavy fusilade, which at times came from both flank and front, the Grenadiers carried the position, but not without considerable loss in officers and men. They were led by Col. E. M. S. Crabbe, who fell wounded within a few feet of the top of the kopje, and were reinforced as they reached the summit by the battalion reserve under Major D. A. Kinloch. The Boers fought gallantly on this part of the field; some indeed, as was also the case on Table Mountain, clung so tenaciously to their defences that they perished by the bayonet. As soon as the ground to the front of the Grenadiers and Scots Guards had been cleared of the enemy, both battalions were re-assembled by their commanding officers.

Thus on the right the battle so far had developed in substantial agreement with Lord Methuen's plans. On the left also matters were going well, but more slowly than the General had anticipated. At the time when fire was opened on the Guards, the leading battalions of the 9th brigade were crossing the railway line which lay between their rendezvous and their object, the western side of Table Mountain. They were guided by Lieut. F. L. Festing, Northumberland Fusiliers. The Northampton was on the right, the Northumberland Fusiliers on the left, both in column of double companies, with increased distances between the companies. In the same formation the Yorkshire Light Infantry followed as reserve to the brigade about 1,000 yards in rear. In rear of this battalion were two companies of the Royal Munster Fusiliers.* After passing through the railway fence both the leading battalions extended from their left, with the result that the Northumberland Fusiliers somewhat overlapped the Northampton. To correct this, the former battalion was ordered to take ground towards Belmont station, and in doing so was exposed to heavy, but ill-aimed, fire. The direction of the Northampton advance exposed the right of their leading line to the Boer musketry on Gun Hill, from which they suffered until the Guards captured that part of the position. The greater part of the Northumberland Fusiliers pushed forward against the south-west corner of Table Mountain, but were temporarily checked by heavy fire from outlying rocks and knolls. One or two misdirected British shells also contributed to delay the progress of the

The left attack.

---

* The half-battalion Loyal North Lancashire regiment had been left at Witteputs as baggage guard.

battalion, but the forward movement of the Northampton, some of whom charged with the bayonet, against the northern end of Gun Hill drove away the parties of Boers opposing the Northumberland Fusiliers, who were then able to continue their attack on Table Mountain. Two companies of the Northumberland Fusiliers, under Major the Hon. C. Lambton, had been left in reserve on the western side of the railway near Belmont station. When, about 5 a.m., the sun rose just behind Table Mountain, Major Lambton realised that, with the light shining straight in their faces, his men could not see to shoot. He therefore moved his two companies up the railway to the point marked **a**, and then across the open veld to ground from which, unbaffled by the morning sun, he was able to pour heavy volleys upon the burghers opposed to the main attack of his battalion. His flanking fire largely contributed to dislodge the Boers from Table Mountain, while the 75th battery, from the neighbourhood of the railway, played upon the north-west face of this portion of the western range. The positions occupied by the detachment of Northumberland Fusiliers and by this battery will be found on map No. 10 (**a**).

Left attack continued.

The stubborn resistance of the defenders of Table Mountain greatly delayed its complete occupation by the British troops; indeed, it required the united exertions of the Northumberland Fusiliers, of part of the Northampton, of several companies of the Guards, and of two companies of the Yorkshire Light Infantry to drive the Boers completely off the plateau. When the attack of the Northumberland Fusiliers upon the south-western corner of Table Mountain was checked, the Brigadier had brought up from his reserve half a battalion of the K.O.Y.L.I. under Col. C. St. L. Barter. It had entered the depression between Table Mountain and Gun Hill in the formation which the battalion had assiduously practised for several years—waves of double companies, in single rank, with an interval of 8 to 10 paces between the men. Being struck in the flank by musketry from Table Mountain, two companies turned and joined in the attack on that plateau. In the course of the fight on Table Mountain Major-General Fetherstonhaugh was severely wounded,

BELMONT.

and the command of the brigade devolved upon Lieut.-Col. C. G. C. Money, Northumberland Fusiliers.

The original orders for the battle had directed that, when the Grenadier and Scots Guards had carried Gun Hill, the two Coldstream battalions should reinforce them and support the 9th brigade in the attack on Mont Blanc. When, therefore, Gun Hill appeared to be occupied by his leading battalions, Major-General Colvile ordered the Coldstream to advance, the 1st battalion on the right, the 2nd on the left, but as they approached Gun Hill they came under a heavy fire from the Razor Back and the Sugar Loaf. To meet this attack they changed front half right, and gradually inclined still more to this direction until the Razor Back and Sugar Loaf Hills became the objects of their attack. General Colvile, desiring to arrest this movement, which threatened to become a purely frontal attack over most unfavourable ground, despatched his brigade-major, Captain H. G. Ruggles-Brise, to halt these two battalions. Ruggles-Brise succeeded in reaching the 2nd battalion, and led part of them back to Gun Hill, whence a portion of them, under command of Major H. Shute, were immediately despatched by Major-General Colvile to re-establish connection with the 9th brigade. This detachment gradually worked northwards towards Table Mountain, and joining hands with Brevet Lieut.-Col. Pulteney's company of Scots Guards, to which reference has already been made, took part in the capture of the northern extremity of the western range. But the remainder of the 2nd battalion of the Coldstream under Lieut.-Col. H. R. Stopford, and the 1st battalion, under Lieut.-Col. A. E. Codrington, were beyond recall; they pressed forward, and, materially aided by the fire of the 18th battery, assaulted and carried the Razor Back and Sugar Loaf kopjes. Captain J. T. Sterling, who commanded a company of the reserve of the 1st Coldstream, marching in rear of the remainder of the battalion, became aware that the hills to the south of the Sugar Loaf were occupied by Boers. Fearing that these burghers might attack Codrington in flank, Sterling, deviating from his proper line of advance, moved his men against them, in rushes of sections, at five paces

Coldstream are diverted from support of 9th brigade.

They carry Razor Back and Sugar Loaf.

interval, and using independent fire. That there were many of the enemy opposed to him is proved by the fact that he lost 20 men out of his company, 110 strong; but his prompt action prevented the counter-stroke which he had anticipated.

<small>Lord Methuen therefore changes his plan of attack.</small>

In consequence of this unexpected development in the battle, Lord Methuen, abandoning his intention of attacking Mont Blanc from the north, determined to support the Coldstream battalions, by launching every available man to reinforce their attack upon the main ridge. The Grenadiers and Scots Guards moved down into the valley which lies between the two ranges, and, to minimize the effect of the plunging cross fire from the heights of Mont Blanc and Table Mountain, passed it as rapidly as possible in three widely-extended lines. The valley once traversed, the Boer musketry ceased to be dangerous, but its passage cost the Grenadiers nearly as dear as their capture of the kopjes of Gun Hill. He also called up his last reserve, half a battalion of the Yorkshire Light Infantry, and the two companies of the Munster Fusiliers, and threw them into the fight, on the left of the 2nd battalion of the Coldstream Guards. Thus, on the right of the field of battle were long lines of skirmishers, either crossing the valley or actually ascending its northern heights, while on the left a fierce fight was raging between the 9th brigade and the stalwart defenders of the crags and works on the plateau of Table Mountain.

<small>Capture of Table Mountain and Mont Blanc.</small>

Gradually the Boers at these points weakened, and then retreated in all haste to the valley, where, pursued by long-range volleys, they mounted their ponies and disappeared among the kopjes of the main range. Then the 9th brigade, following them across the valley, scaled the steep slopes of Mont Blanc, and those of the enemy who were still holding this kopje, fell back before them, and galloped off to the east and north-east, under the heavy fire of the infantry.

<small>Boers escape untouched by shells or cavalry.</small>

Neither of the field batteries from their positions could see the Boers as they fled from Mont Blanc. The Naval guns, which had been successfully co-operating with the 18th battery*

---

* The 18th battery fired 141 rounds. For the greater part of the day it was in action at 1,375 yards.

BELMONT.

in shelling the Boers on the crest line of Mont Blanc, were the artillery nearest to Lord Methuen's hand as, from the summit, he watched the retreating Boers. He called upon the Naval brigade to bring one of their guns on to the top of Mont Blanc, by the deep gorge which cuts into the western face of the main range. But the ground was impossible; the heavy gun could not be dragged up the mountain side, and the Boers effected their retreat without molestation from artillery fire. The 18th battery indeed joined with Major Rimington in a pursuit of the Boers eastwards, from the extreme south of the hills, but with horses exhausted by thirst and fatigue, nothing could be effected. The detachment of cavalry and mounted infantry on the left of the British line pushed some distance to the north-east; its appearance scattered considerable parties of the enemy who otherwise might have harassed the left flank, but with this exception its influence on the fight was small. About midday its progress was arrested by a very well handled flank or rear-guard of the enemy in the neighbourhood of Swinkpan.*

By 10 a.m. the engagement was over, and by noon the greater part of the British force had returned to camp. After the action the outposts were furnished by the Northampton regiment, and half a battalion of the Scots Guards held Belmont station with a detached post on Table Mountain. The total loss of Lord Methuen's command was 3 officers and 51 N.C.O.s and men killed; 23 officers and 220 N.C.O.s and men wounded. The Grenadiers suffered more heavily than any of the other battalions. They lost 1 officer killed and 8 wounded, 2 mortally; 21 N.C.O.s and men killed and 107 wounded, 24 mortally. Of the Boers, it is known that more than 80 were killed, and 70 were taken prisoners. A large amount of cattle, a considerable number of ponies, and much ammunition were captured. *End of action. Casualties, Nov. 23rd.*

Though from the insufficient number of his mounted troops and from the want of horse artillery, Lord Methuen was unable to convert his successful engagement into a decisive victory, the action was satisfactory in many ways. The first advance *An indecisive but in some ways satisfactory engagement.*

---

* This water-hole is not shown on map No. 10; it appears on map No. 9.

was made in darkness, in a formation more extended than any practised at the same period in broad daylight by continental nations. Such men as became detached from their battalions promptly rallied upon the nearest officer of another corps. The leading of company officers when, in the stress of battle, they became separated from their battalions, and had thus to act entirely on their own initiative, was most satisfactory. As an instance of the manner in which troops become dispersed in modern engagements, it is well to record the movements of the companies of the 2nd battalion of the Coldstream Guards. One company joined or closely followed the Grenadiers in their attack on Gun Hill. Two companies worked with the Grenadiers in their attack on Mont Blanc. Three companies fought on Table Mountain. One company kept touch with the 1st battalion; another acted independently in clearing the eastern side of Gun Hill, and then fought on Table Mountain. The fire discipline proved distinctly good. Long range supporting fire, when the light permitted it, was freely employed. The arrangements by the R.A.M.C. for the removal of the wounded from the field of battle to the base hospitals were admirable.

CHAPTER XIV.

GRASPAN.*

ELEVEN miles north of Belmont station the road and railway leading to Kimberley enter a network of kopjes, which dominate the line until the plain through which the Modder river flows is reached. These rough outcrops of rock and boulders from the plains of the open veld have been arranged by nature in clusters of small hills, the most southern group being so shaped as to form a natural redoubt astride of the railway, midway between Graspan and Enslin, thus barring any advance from the south along the line. The larger portion of the Boer force, defeated at Belmont, had fallen back under Prinsloo, on the 23rd of November, across the Free State border to Ramdam, about 13 miles east of Enslin station. De la Rey, however, whose commando had taken but little part in that action, halted his men at Graspan, and occupied the excellent position which this redoubt offered for a further stand. That same evening the Transvaal General sent an urgent despatch to his Free State colleague, imploring him to return to the railway line, and in compliance with this request Prinsloo on the following day left Commandant T. van der Merwe with 800 men at Ramdam, and moved to Graspan with the rest of his men. On the arrival of the Free State commandos at Graspan, a Krijgsraad assembled, and decided to remain on the defensive for the next twenty-four hours, after which period, if no forward move were made by the British troops, the two republican leaders would themselves assume the offensive.

Boers gather at Graspan. Nov. 23rd/99.

* See maps Nos. 9 and 11.

Character of position.

The natural redoubt, which the Boer leaders had thus determined to hold, rises abruptly from the level, and commands the approaches across the veld on the south, east and west; the even surface of the plain, the sandy soil of which was barely concealed by dry tufts of coarse grass, presented not an inch of cover, save for a few ant-mounds dotted about here and there: their hard sun-baked walls afford good protection from bullets for a skirmisher lying close behind them. The kopjes are so grouped as to facilitate the reinforcement of either the front face or the flanks from a centrally placed body. They overlook, moreover, the only water available in the vicinity, a few muddy pans and wells within the hills to the rear. The southern face of the stronghold, tracing it from west to east, has a length of about a mile. The flanks of this face are very definitely marked by two razor-backed kopjes, the one on the east and the other on the west, rising some 150 feet above the surrounding ground; both these kopjes run approximately from the south to the north. In the centre of the southern face lies a third kopje, oval in shape, 200 yards in length and 30 feet higher than the flank hillocks with which it is connected by re-entrant ridges.

Its one weakness.

The left flank mentioned above consists mainly of that eastern razor-backed kopje already referred to, which runs northward for a distance of some 1,200 yards, its crest line broken by a series of small knolls. Further north on this flank are one or two smaller kopjes, then a mile of valley, on the far side of which, nestling under another cluster of hills, lie the Rooilaagte homestead and a Kaffir kraal. On the right flank in like manner the western razor-back is similarly continued in a northerly direction by two other small kopjes, the more northern of which is situated on the west side of the railway. A Nek of land connects this kopje with the apex of a triangular patch of broken ground, stretching several miles northward, with its eastern side at right angles to the railway. Yet further north, beyond the base or northern side of this third cluster of hills, a valley some two miles broad runs from the railway on the east to the open veld on the west, and thus completely separates the quadrilateral redoubt, the Rooilaagte, and the triangular clusters of hills

GRASPAN.

already described, from a fourth group termed Honey Nest Kloof Kopjes, which stretch northward to the Modder valley.* Strong, therefore, although this whole position, or rather series of positions, was on the front and flanks, it will be understood that if the valley in rear could be seized by a sufficient mounted force, while the front and flanks were threatened by infantry and guns, the defenders would be cut off from their line of retreat, and their safety seriously imperilled.

On the afternoon and night of 23rd of November Lord Methuen's division rested at Belmont. The forenoon of the 24th of November was spent in preparing for another march, supplies of ammunition being replenished by railway from Orange River station. Meanwhile an armoured train, escorted by the mounted company of the Loyal North Lancashire, had been despatched up the line to reconnoitre, and came under artillery fire from the Boers on Graspan. Its escort pushed on, the foremost scouts riding up to within fifty yards of the kopjes, and ascertaining, although with the loss of an officer (Lieutenant Owen-Lewis, I.S.C.) and two men, that these hills were held by a Boer force of about 400 to 500 men, with two guns. The mounted infantry, together with the train, then returned to Belmont. 23rd & 24th Nov. Preparation for advance.

On receipt of their report at 2.30 p.m. the General Officer commanding the division ordered the 9th Lancers and the whole of the mounted infantry to move forward, covering the front for three miles on each side of the railway, and further reconnoitring the enemy's position. Under cover of this reconnaissance, the rest of the division were directed to march at once to Swinkpan, so that they might be within easy striking distance of Graspan on the following morning. Intelligence, however, having reached the British commander that a party of Boers, stated to be 500 strong, were on his right flank, the Scots Guards and the two companies of Royal Munster Fusiliers, together with the Naval guns, remained at Belmont to protect the railway and the rear of the column, but were ordered to march to Enslin the next day. Forward to Swinkpan. Nov. 24th.

* Only the southern groups of kopjes are shown on map No. 11.

232   THE WAR IN SOUTH AFRICA.

Swinkpan lacks water.

This information as to the enemy and an unfounded rumour of a Boer movement to the westward somewhat delayed the start of the whole division; the troops, therefore, did not reach Swinkpan until after dark. On arrival barely sufficient water was found in the pan for the men, and none could be spared for the battery horses, a hardship which told against them severely in the fight of the morrow. The cavalry reconnaissance, which Lord Methuen personally accompanied, tended to confirm the original report that the strength of the Boer force holding the position did not exceed five hundred men. He considered, therefore, that on the following day he would be able to shell the enemy out of the kopjes, and hoped that by despatching his cavalry and mounted infantry well forward on both flanks he might have the good fortune to capture the entire detachment.

Methuen's intentions.

Advance on Graspan. Nov. 25/99. 3.30 a.m.

With this design the mounted troops, the Field artillery, and the 9th brigade under command of Lieut.-Col. Money, marched from Swinkpan bivouac on Graspan at 3.30 a.m. on the 25th of November, the Guards' brigade, under Major-General Sir H. Colvile, following in rear with the baggage train at an interval of more than an hour. The Naval guns at Belmont, mounted on goods trucks, simultaneously moved forward up the line with the armoured train, followed by the Railway Troops, viz., the 8th, 11th and 31st companies of the Royal engineers. The 1st Scots Guards and two companies Munster Fusiliers went by road as rear-guard.

To the 9th brigade had been attached this day a small Naval battalion, commanded by Captain Prothero, R.N., consisting of a company of bluejackets, one company of Royal Marine artillery, and two companies of Royal Marine Light Infantry, the total strength of the battalion being about 240 men. Besides this unit the brigade comprised the 1st Northumberland Fusiliers, 2nd Northamptonshire regiment, 2nd King's Own Yorkshire Light Infantry, and a half-battalion of the Loyal North Lancashire.

Methuen tries to

In conformity with his plan of action Lord Methuen directed Colonel B. Gough to pass beyond the enemy's position on the

GRASPAN.

east with two squadrons of the 9th Lancers, one company of mounted infantry, and Rimington's Guides; to pass beyond it on the west he likewise sent Major Milton with the third squadron of the 9th Lancers, the mounted company of the Northumberland Fusiliers, the mounted half company of the Yorkshire Light Infantry, and a detachment (thirty strong) of the New South Wales Lancers. The batteries (18th and 75th) moved at first with the main body of the 9th brigade, the Northumberland Fusiliers furnishing the advance guard, but, when the sun rose at 5 a.m. and the Boer position was approached, the guns were ordered forward and came into action about 6.15 a.m. against the kopjes held by the enemy east of the railway. The 75th on the left engaged in a duel with the Boer guns, but owing to the careful concealment of the latter was unable to produce much effect; the 18th on the right, at a range of 2,200 yards, searched carefully with shrapnel the sangars on the kopjes. The four companies of the Loyal North Lancashire were detailed as an escort to this battery, two of them lying down close to the guns, the other two being in support some distance in rear. The 75th battery at first lacked an escort, but later on a half-battalion of the Northamptonshire was sent to it, and remained near the railway until the end of the day.

intercept Boer retreat.

6.15 a.m. 18th and 75th batteries open fire.

Meanwhile the remainder of the 9th brigade halted out of the enemy's range midway between the two batteries, with a half-battalion of the Northumberland Fusiliers extended in front. The armoured train and the Naval guns, four 12-prs., commanded by Lieut. F. W. Dean, R.N., arrived in sight of the Boer position a little before 6 a.m., accompanied by the Royal engineer companies, who were in a repair train in rear. The leading train halted at Graspan station, from whence by means of field-glasses a large number of Boers could be seen standing on the crests of the kopjes commanding the line. Almost immediately a puff of smoke appeared on the ridge a little to the east of the railway, and a shell whistled over the train, bursting some 200 yards beyond. Lieutenant Dean at once detrained two guns (the strength of his party being insufficient to man-handle more than two in the soft ground),

Naval guns and field batteries shell the hills to drive out Boers.

and with them ranged on the crest line, finding the distance to be about 5,000 yards. The trains were then sent back about half a mile, leaving, however, a trolly with ammunition. The Naval guns, in conjunction with the field batteries, which had now come up, continued to shell the Boer guns, and by 6.30 a.m. these for a time ceased fire.

Boers, reinforced, are stronger than expected.

The estimate of the enemy's strength made by the reconnaissance of the 24th was not inaccurate, but the fact was that the situation had been entirely changed by the arrival of Prinsloo with large reinforcements later on that afternoon. The exact numbers of the Boers engaged in this fight are, as in other cases, difficult to state with any precision, but they were probably not less than about 2,300 men, with three Krupp guns and two pom-poms. This force was disposed as follows :—General De la Rey's commando of Transvaalers, consisting of 700 men and two Krupp guns, held the northern end of the kopjes on the western flank, and was therefore on the north-western side of the railway. Next on the western central kopje to the south-east of the railway came the Winburg commando, about 250 with a Krupp gun, under Commandant Jourdaan. These three Krupp guns were, however, controlled by Major Albrecht, the officer commanding the Free State artillery. The long kopje, at the southern end of which the western meets the southern face, was held by the Bloemfontein commando, 500 strong, under General J. Prinsloo. East of him, in the centre of the front face, was placed the Jacobsdal commando, 300 strong, under Commandant Lubbe. The eastern razor-backed kopje, which formed the left flank and part of the frontal defence, was assigned to detachments of the Bloemfontein, Hoopstad, and Fauresmith commandos under Commandants P. Fourie and H. van der Venter. Two pom-poms were mounted on this side of the defences. It will be seen from map 11 that the Graspan ground differed in a marked way from the majority of the positions selected by the Boers, being salient instead of re-entrant. It did not, therefore, lend itself readily to the adoption of those enveloping tactics which their forefathers learnt originally from the Zulus. Prinsloo sought to remedy this defect by ordering up from Ramdam a detachment to menace the eastern flank of the British advance.

It was now seen that the enemy available for the defence of the main position was too strong to be driven out therefrom by a brief artillery bombardment, and it soon became clear to the British Commander that an attack in due form had become necessary. Lord Methuen determined, therefore, to direct the 9th brigade to go forward and carry the kopjes. The artillery was to prepare the way for attack at closer range, while the Guards' brigade was ordered to come up in support and to hold the right flank, the presence of the Ramdam detachment to the south-east having already been discovered by the mounted troops. Boer strength involves attack instead of mere shelling.

These orders were issued at about 7 a.m. The 18th battery started off eastward, and a quarter of an hour later came into action under infantry fire at a range of 1,425 yards against the southern end of the long eastern kopje. Lord Methuen had already chosen that kopje as the main object of the infantry attack. A section of the battery was a little later moved round yet further east to search with shrapnel the eastern face. Although all the guns of the 18th battery were thus for a considerable period in action within long-range rifle fire of the enemy, it did not suffer a single casualty during the whole engagement. Two companies of the Loyal North Lancashire regiment followed the battery, and continued to act as escort; the other two companies of that half-battalion under Major Churchward were ordered personally by Lord Methuen to move forward, the right company against the eastern kopje, and the left against the central kopje of the southern face. But, soon after they had started to do this, they were instructed by a subsequent order to halt and await the arrival of the rest of the brigade. 7.15 a.m. 18th battery prepares for infantry attack on south-east. One section (two guns) against eastern face.

2 companies L.N.L., halted before eastern kopje, await 9th brigade.

Five companies of the Northumberland Fusiliers, which was still leading the 9th brigade, were ordered to protect the left of the attack and remained lying down 2,000 yards from the enemy, where the half-battalion as advance guard had been originally halted.* Two of the remaining companies were directed Northumberland Fusiliers leads 9th brigade.

* See p. 233, 2nd par.

to reinforce the escort of the guns (Naval and 75th battery) on the left flank, and the other one moved to the right to support the 18th battery.

<small>75th battery and Naval guns join in.</small>

The 75th battery advanced at the same time parallel to the line. It was accompanied by the two Naval 12-prs., and took up two successive positions 4,000 and 2,300 yards from the enemy's guns, which now re-opened fire. The Naval guns during these movements were dragged forward by the seamen, assisted by sappers lent from the Royal engineer companies. The fire of the enemy at the British as they came into action at the nearer range was accurate. The Naval guns, nevertheless, remained in action until the conclusion of the day. When, a little later, the 75th battery was moved to the eastward, Lieut. Dean held his ground. By making his men lie down as each flash at the enemy's battery was seen, he was able to save them from any heavy casualties. The effect of the British on the Boer artillery was also very slight, the enemy's casualties being limited to one gunner wounded and three horses killed.

<small>Advance of Guards.</small>

The Guards' brigade, in its march from Swinkpan, had been drawn to the north-west by the sound of the guns and had moved in extended lines in that direction, until the left company of its leading battalion, the 3rd Grenadier Guards, crossed the railway close to the spot where the Naval guns were stationed; but at this moment Lord Methuen's order to march to the south-east to protect the right rear of the main attack reached the Brigadier by heliograph. In compliance with this instruction Sir H. Colvile turned about the 3rd Grenadier Guards and 2nd Coldstream Guards, and moved them to the other flank; throughout this movement from left to right behind the 9th brigade, the two battalions were in extended order and beyond the range of the enemy. The 1st Coldstream Guards were still protecting the transport column; the 1st Scots Guards, which came up from Belmont, were also held back on the left, under the immediate orders of the Lieut.-General, and acted as a divisional reserve. Lord Methuen's preliminary dispositions, therefore, of the troops not actually employed in the assault, included the use of six field guns, two Naval guns, seven companies Northumberland Fusiliers, four companies Northampton-shire, and three companies Royal engineers, in facing the enemy's right and centre; two battalions of the Guards watched the right flank, in support of the main attack, and the other two battalions were available as a final reserve.

Meanwhile the units of the 9th brigade, intended to deliver the assault, had extended in front of the centre of the position. The Brigadier was, however, then instructed by Lord Methuen that he was to act against the eastern kopje, and a little later was further informed that the attack should also overlap its eastern face. Lieut.-Colonel Money accordingly moved his brigade to the right in extended order, and thus brought it to a point from whence a direct stroke could be made at the assigned object. There the brigade halted for a moment; the Naval battalion was immediately facing the eastern kopje and now slightly in advance of the other units. The latter had somewhat intermingled during the movement to the flank, with the result that two companies of the King's Own Yorkshire Light Infantry and one company of the Northampton were on the left of the Naval contingent, the remaining six companies of the King's Own Yorkshire Light Infantry and three of the Northampton being on its right. These preparations for the attack occupied nearly two hours, and were not completed until 9 a.m. The situation at this hour is shown on map No. 11. Meanwhile, an hour earlier, the 75th battery had by Lord Methuen's order been brought over from the western flank and co-operated with the 18th in shelling the eastern kopje. All being now ready for the attempt, the order to move was given by the Lieut.-General in person, and the Naval battalion pushed on to a level with the two companies of the Loyal North Lancashire regiment extended in their front.* Accompanied by these on the left flank, and supported by the three Yorkshire Light Infantry and Northamptonshire companies on that side, the Naval contingent steadily and rapidly pressed on against the eastern

marginal note: 9th Brigade prepare to attack eastern kopje.

---

* See p. 235, par. 2. The brigade, to the front of which the Naval battalion had passed during the flank movement, was now advancing to support these two companies in the attack.

kopje. The sailors and marines had originally been extended to four paces, but had somewhat closed in during the manœuvring which preceded the attack. The enemy remained silent until the assailants approached to within 1,000 yards, but then began to pour in a rapid and effective fire from the kopje attacked, and the ridge to the westward. At 600 yards the British line halted to return this, and then from that point onward advanced by rushes of from 50 to 100 yards at a time, the left company of the Loyal North Lancashire, supported by the companies of King's Own Yorkshire Light Infantry, moving on the centre kopje, and the Naval brigade with the other North Lancashire company, under the command of Lt. A. J. Carter, still leading towards the eastern kopje with the Northamptonshire company in support. The enemy's fire meanwhile increased in intensity, and both officers and men were falling fast on the British side. The last 200 yards to the foot of the hill were therefore traversed in a single rush. At the base of the kopjes a certain amount of dead ground allowed of a short breathing space, during which a consultation between the company officers left in command took place. They determined to scale the hill and ordered the men to fix bayonets.

Losses of attackers on south front.

The Naval contingent had already suffered heavily. Captain R. C. Prothero, R.N., was wounded; Commander A. P. Ethelston, R.N., Major J. H. Plumbe, R.M.L.I., and Captain Guy Senior, R.M.A., had been killed;* the command of the battalion thus devolving on Captain A. E. Marchant, R.M.L.I. The two companies of the North Lancashire, more fortunate, owing to their wide extension and their use of such cover as the ant-hills afforded, reached the base of the kopjes with considerably less loss than the Naval battalion.

Preparations for attack on east front.

While this advance against the southern face of the kopje was being executed, the six companies of the King's Own Yorkshire Light Infantry, and the three remaining companies of the Northamptonshire regiment, had gradually worked round the enemy's left flank. The two pom-poms posted on this side

---

* The officers of the Naval brigade wore the same headgear as their men, and, except Captain Prothero and Midshipman Wardle, all carried rifles.

proved troublesome, although endeavours were made to reach them by the two guns of the 18th battery* and by long-range rifle-fire. The Yorkshire Light Infantry were being carefully manœuvred in successive lines extended at ten paces interval, and having pivoted on the left flank, succeeded, notwithstanding the pom-poms and a heavy rifle-fire, in crossing the open plain to the foot of the eastern face of the kopje with only moderate losses.† The Northampton supported this attack on the right, the two companies of the Loyal North Lancashire, which formed the original escort of the 18th battery, joining in on the left.

The moment had now come for the assault. Under cover of a final artillery preparation the bluejackets, marines, and North Lancashire men began to climb the boulders which covered the front face of the kopjes. A third of the way up a momentary halt again became necessary, as the British shells were bursting just in front of the assaulting line. Then the Royal artillery ceased fire and the assailants, having been joined by their Brigadier, Lieut.-Col. Money, and the supporting Northamptonshire and Yorkshire companies, eagerly dashed on up to the crest. The eastern face of the position was carried at the same time. The enemy had no desire to await this final onslaught and had already retired to the broken ground further to the north. If the times were correctly recorded, the advance and capture of this kopje did not take more than half an hour, the final assault having been delivered at 9.30 a.m. *The assault, 9.30 a.m. Nov. 25th, carries the eastern kopje.*

The commando on the Boer right had had but little share in this fight, being held in check by the force on the British left detailed expressly for that purpose. The loss of the razor-backed kopje rendered the whole position untenable; De la Rey and Prinsloo therefore fell back with their men northwards, pursued by long-range volleys from the British infantry. As soon as he was informed that the infantry had made good the crest line, Lieut.-Col. Hall, commanding the Royal artillery, pushed on with both the field batteries to the ridge between the central *The Boers retreat.*

---

* See p. 235, par. 2.
† The K.O.Y.L.I. throughout the day lost only 7 men killed, 3 officers and 34 men wounded, and 4 men missing.

and eastern kopjes, but the enemy had by this time retreated too far for the fire of the British guns to be effective. The batteries then were taken to water, of which the animals were in dire need.

The attempt to cut off the fugitives.

Meantime the two bodies of mounted troops, which, according to Lord Methuen's scheme, were to seize ground in the path of the now retreating Boers, had set out on their mission.

The western march.

Major Milton, in the early morning, had led his small force of one squadron and one and a half companies of mounted infantry by a circuitous march well to the westward of the railway and thence northward until he reached that previously described valley which separates the three southern clusters of hills from Honey Nest Kloof Kopjes. On a sugar loaf hill at its entrance he left an observation piquet and, extending the Northumberland Fusiliers company very widely, with instructions to hold its southern side, he pushed up the valley eastward with the remainder (amounting now to less than two hundred men) and reached Honey Nest Kloof station. This small detachment had thus ridden completely across the Boer line of retreat, and was now six miles in rear of their captured position. Moving further to the east, Milton observed, in the plains beyond the distant end of the valley, the two squadrons under Colonel Gough, but failed in an attempt to attract their attention by heliograph. There were already signs of Boers coming to him, and, hoping to intercept fugitives, Milton moved back on the Fusilier company extended on the southern side. But the Boers swarmed out of the kopjes on this very side in greatly superior numbers, and opened a heavy fire upon the weak line of the Northumberland Fusiliers. The audacity of their position in the open with their horses some 1,000 yards in rear was apparent to the enemy. About 400 Boers, moreover, detached themselves from the main body and approached Milton's men. The situation thus became very critical, and the cavalry squadron fell back to the western entrance, covered by the mounted infantry, who succeeded in seizing a kopje on the northern side. The Boers continued their advance against the defending party to within three hundred yards of this kopje, but then swerved off to the east, thus enabling Major Milton to withdraw the whole of his detachment in safety. Any further attempt at pursuit would have ended in disaster, because of the great strength of the enemy, and the unbroken front they still presented.

Lieut.-Col. B. Gough's force on the east had similarly found itself to be insufficient in strength to reap the fruits of victory. During the earlier part of the fight it had done good service in holding back the Ramdam detachment of Boers which occupied a kopje about two and a quarter miles to the south-east of the battlefield. This detachment was reported at first to be about 500, but Major Rimington, who reconnoitred close up to it, saw other Boers advancing westwards to support it, and it is not improbable that the whole of van der Merwe's commando may have ridden out from Ramdam in the course of the morning. Fortunately, however, the Boers were not at this period of the war disposed to attack mounted troops in the open plain; the demonstration, therefore, of Rimington's Guides and the Lancers' squadrons sufficed to chain them to the kopje. *Lt.-Col. Gough on the east.*

As soon as the main attack had succeeded, Gough moved northward and sighted the Boer laager, which had been observed at Enslin the previous night, now retiring north-east along the road to Jacobsdal. The escort appeared, however, to be too strong to be charged. Urgent requests for guns were therefore sent back to Headquarters and ultimately the 18th battery, which had reached the bivouac at Enslin, was sent out to join Gough, but the horses were too exhausted for rapid movement and the guns only arrived in time to fire a dozen rounds at the last Boer wagons, which were now 5,000 yards away.* *Gough fails to stop Boers.*

Yet at Graspan, as at Belmont, the open plains across which the enemy was compelled to retire after his defeat were singularly favourable to cavalry action and, had a satisfactory mounted brigade with a horse artillery battery been available, the Boers could not have effected their escape without suffering very heavy losses. Not only were the mounted troops at Lord Methuen's disposal insufficient numerically, but their horses *Want of cavalry and horse artillery make Belmont and Graspan indecisive.*

* This battery fired in all 482 rounds during the action.

were already worn out by the heavy reconnaissance duty, which had of necessity been carried out by them day after day without relief, under the adverse conditions of a sandy soil, great heat, and a scarcity of water. The results of this deficiency in mounted men were far-reaching. Not only did the enemy avoid paying the material penalties of successive failures on the battlefield, but his *moral* was stiffened by these demonstrations of the immunity from disaster conferred by his superior mobility.

Losses at Graspan, Nov. 25th.

The casualties suffered by the 1st division on this day amounted to 3 officers and 15 men killed, 6 officers and 137 men wounded, and 7 missing.

Heavy Naval losses.

The proportion of these losses which fell on the Naval brigade was very high, their returns showing 3 officers and 6 men killed and 3 officers and 89 men wounded. The Marines, who took part in the actual attack, lost 47 per cent. of their strength. It is remarkable that the North Lancashire, two of whose companies shared in that assault, had only 1 man killed, 6 wounded, and 2 missing. The Guards' brigade did not suffer and did not fire a shot all day.

Boer losses.

The enemy's losses are not accurately known; the bodies of 23 Boers were found by the British troops, and buried after the fight; the total republican casualties probably, therefore, amounted to about 80 or 90. Forty prisoners and a few ponies were captured.

After the action. Night of Nov. 25th.

Lord Methuen's division bivouacked the night of the 25th November at or near Enslin station; the scarcity of water again caused much discomfort to men and animals. Under the supervision of Colonel E. Townsend, principal medical officer of the division, the wounded were collected and entrained during the afternoon, the less severe cases being sent off to Orange River, and the graver to Cape Town.

CHAPTER XV.

THE BATTLE OF THE MODDER RIVER.*

WHEN the Boers, after their defeat on the 25th November, retreated from the heights of Graspan,† the greater part of their force withdrew to Jacobsdal, little inclined to renew the combat. But General De la Rey induced the burghers to make another effort to arrest the British march on Kimberley, at a position of his own selection at the confluence of the Riet and the Modder rivers, where the terrain differed in character from that which had been occupied at Belmont and Graspan. In those engagements the Boers had entrenched themselves upon high and rugged kopjes, of which the apparent strength became a source of weakness. The hills afforded an excellent target for the British artillery. The riflemen who held the works had to aim downwards at the enemy as he advanced to the attack, and a "plunging" fire never yields satisfactory results. At their base was dead ground, inaccessible to the musketry of the defenders. Here the attacking infantry, after their rush across the open, could halt for breathing space before delivering the final assault. For these reasons De la Rey decided to adopt completely new tactics and to fight from the bed of a river, surrounded on every side by a level plain, destitute of cover

Boers learn to change their ideas of a "strong position."

---

* As a point of historical accuracy it should be noticed that, for the battle of the 28th November, the "Modder River" is a misnomer. The fighting, as will be seen in this chapter, took place on the banks of the Riet; but since the battle honours for the engagement have been given for "Modder River," the name has become officially recognised, and is therefore used here. See map No. 12.

† See map No. 9 and freehand sketch.

The ground chosen by De la Rey. Nov. 26th.

over the surface of which the burghers could pour a continuous and "grazing" fire upon the British from the time they first came within range, up to the very moment of their final charge. The plain, across which the railway from Orange River to Kimberley runs nearly due north and south, is intersected by the devious windings of two rivers, the Riet and the Modder. From Bosman's Drift (see map 12) the Riet, the more southerly of the two, runs north-west for about a mile and a half, and then for the same distance turns to the north-east. Its course next changes abruptly to the north-west for nearly two miles when, increased in volume by the waters of its affluent, the Modder, it gently curves to the westward for about a mile and a half. The meanderings of the Modder are even more remarkable. Its most southern elbow is half a mile north-east of the spot where the Riet turns for the second time north-west. Thence it runs for a mile to the north, then about the same distance to the west; it turns southward for a mile, and then flows westward for three-quarters of a mile, where, a few hundred yards above the railway bridge, it merges into the Riet. Both these streams have cut themselves channels so wide as to allow a thick growth of trees and scrub to line their sides, so deep that the vegetation which they contain hardly shows above the level of the surrounding plain. There are few practicable fords across the Riet. One exists at Bosman's Drift; there is a second near the railway bridge; among the group of islets at Rosmead there is a natural ford, while the retaining wall of the weir which dams the river at this village can be used, not without difficulty, by active men in single file. Elsewhere the depth of the water and the mud at the bottom of the Riet effectually combine to prevent the passage of troops. Thus the Riet and the Modder together formed not only a gigantic moat across the approaches to Kimberley from the south and south-east, but a covered way, by which its defenders could move unseen to any part of the position.

Two hamlets on the Riet. Other details.

On the right bank of the Riet there are two hamlets. One, known as Modder River village, is clustered round the station; the other, Rosmead, lies a mile further down the river. In

THE BATTLE OF THE MODDER RIVER. 245

both are farms and cottages with gardens, bounded by trees, strongly-built mud walls, and fences of wire and prickly cactus. On the left bank, close to the river, there are two or three farms, surrounded by gardens and substantial enclosures. About five miles to the north-east of the Modder River village the Magersfontein kopjes loom dark and frowning, a landmark for all the country round; while still further to the north the heights of Scholtz Nek and Spytfontein lie athwart the railway to Kimberley.* A glance at the reproduction of Captain Erskine's freehand sketch of the ground will help the reader to appreciate the strength of the Boer position.

On the 26th November, Lord Methuen halted in the neighbourhood of Enslin,† while supplies and ammunition were brought up by the railway. As far as the exhausted condition of his horses permitted, he reconnoitred in the direction of the Riet, and a strong patrol of mounted men, led by Lt.-Colonel Verner, ascertained that the Boers were in occupation of Honey Nest Kloof station (map No. 9), and saw considerable numbers of the enemy moving across the veld, trekking, as it seemed, from the river southwards towards Ramdam. But so tired were the artillery horses that, when the leader of the patrol sent back a request for guns with which to shell the Boers out of the railway station, Lord Methuen thought it better to give them absolute rest, and ordered the patrol to retire.‡

<small>Nov. 26th/99. Halt at Enslin.</small>

At 4 a.m. on the 27th the division marched to Wittekop, about six miles to the south of the Modder River bridge. Here the artillery and infantry bivouacked while the cavalry and mounted infantry reconnoitred on a front of six miles along the railway towards the river. In the distance, lines of wagons could be seen leaving Jacobsdal, apparently moving towards Modder River station, and at about 1 p.m. the advance patrols of the 9th Lancers reported that they had been forced to halt by the enemy's musketry from the direction of the railway

<small>1st Division marches, Nov. 27th, to Wittekop.</small>

---

* See map No. 13.

† See map No. 9.

‡ At the end of this reconnaissance Lt.-Col. Verner was so severely injured by his horse falling with him that he was invalided home.

bridge, which had been wrecked by the Boers at the beginning of the war. In the afternoon Lord Methuen joined Major Little, commanding the 9th Lancers, in a reconnaissance towards the Riet, but observed nothing to cause him to change the plan he had already formed. This was to mask the Modder River bridge by a reconnaissance in force, while he marched to Jacobsdal, and thence by Brown's Drift across the Modder river to Abon's Dam, lying about sixteen miles north-east of Jacobsdal, and thus turn the position of Spytfontein (see map No. 9), on which he was convinced the burghers intended to give him battle. The cavalry did not reconnoitre up the Riet river towards Jacobsdal, and therefore the existence of the ford at Bosman's Drift remained unknown to him. His only large scale sketch of the ground near the Modder bridge did not include the windings of this stream.* But in the course of the night much information came in. Major Little reported that he estimated the number of Boers near the Modder River village to be 4,000. Major Rimington ascertained that the Boers expected reinforcements, and that they were making entrenchments on the south bank near Modder River bridge. A loyal British subject, at great personal risk, succeeded in sending a message to the effect that the Boers were in force at the village, and were "digging themselves in like rabbits." On this evidence Lord Methuen concluded, and he continued to hold his opinion till the battle began, that Modder River village was merely used as an advanced post to cover the burghers' main position at Spytfontein. But as he did not wish to leave even a detachment of the enemy threatening his lines of communication, he decided to postpone his flanking movement on Abon's Dam until he had captured the entrenched village. Before dawn the orders were recast, and by 4.30 a.m. on the 28th, the division was on the

<small>Lord Methuen's first intention.</small>

<small>His purpose in moving on Modder River. 4.30 a.m. Nov. 28th the march begins.</small>

---

* This sketch had been made a few days before the outbreak of war by an officer who was ordered to report on the best method of defending the Modder River bridge with one or two companies of infantry. It was executed under circumstances which, even had his instructions been more comprehensive, would have prevented him from effecting any extensive reconnaissance of the Riet and Modder rivers.

THE BATTLE OF THE MODDER RIVER. 247

march,* but unfortunately the men were not all of them adequately prepared for the work which lay before them, for owing to the change of plan many started without their breakfasts.

The cavalry, who had moved off at 4 a.m., were brought to a standstill by the enemy's fire at about 5.30 a.m. Major Little then reported to Lord Methuen, who had accompanied the mounted troops, that all the information sent in by the officers of the advance squadrons showed that the river was strongly held from the railway bridge eastward to a clump of high poplars. Major Little's deduction, as far as it went, was perfectly correct; but he did not know, nor did anyone else in Lord Methuen's force suspect, that admirably concealed entrenchments had been thrown up along the left bank of the Riet, from Rosmead east, to the bend where the bed of the river turns sharply southwards. At many places on the northern bank shelter trenches had been constructed. The farms on the southern bank had been prepared for occupation by riflemen; the houses of Rosmead and Modder village had been placed in a state of defence. At various points behind the Riet, epaulments had been thrown up for the six field guns which the enemy had with them, while among the foliage on the bank three or four pom-poms were cunningly concealed. It is uncertain whether the whole of the long series of trenches was actually manned when the cavalry first appeared before the river, or whether the Boers only occupied the western works after it had become clear that Lord Methuen did not propose to force a crossing at Bosman's Drift, and that his line of attack was to be roughly parallel to the railway. But there is no doubt that the fear of being outflanked caused the burghers to take up a very wide front, and that the manœuvres of the mounted troops near Bosman's Drift, and of the 9th brigade at Rosmead, forced them still further to extend it on both flanks. When the whole position was taken up, Free Staters under Prinsloo were posted on the right; the centre, through which ran the railway line, was defended by De la Rey with part of the Transvaal commandos; to the left stood another

marginal notes: The cavalry stopped by concealed riflemen before division arrives. The real dispositions of defenders.

* The Northamptonshire was detailed to guard the baggage at Wittekop. The 1st battalion Argyll and Sutherland Highlanders joined Lord Methuen's column on the night of the 28th from the lines of communication.

contingent of Transvaalers, composed of some of the men who, two days earlier, had arrived at Edenburg, weary with the forced march and long railway journey by which P. Cronje had brought them from the siege of Mafeking to protect the Riet. In all, between three and four thousand burghers were in array.

Cronje fears for Bosman's Drift, which is unknown to British.

Noticing the direction of the British advance towards Modder River village, Cronje at first believed that Lord Methuen was about to cross the Riet at Bosman's Drift. He therefore hurriedly despatched a gun and a pom-pom from the delta formed by the junction of the two rivers, to support the outlying detachments of riflemen, already posted in the neighbourhood of the ford and of a farmhouse a mile further up the river. The 18th battery drove back the pom-pom and gun, and then, at about 7.15 a.m. supported the mounted infantry who had been despatched to capture the farm. Aided by the well-placed shells of the artillery, the mounted infantry carried it, and established themselves so solidly under cover of the mud walls of its kraal that a Boer gun, which later in the day played upon them for several hours, failed to dislodge them. The duty of watching the right rear was entrusted to the 9th Lancers. By their repeated attempts to cross the Riet they prevented the men who guarded it from reinforcing the main Boer positions; and they warded off the threatened attack of detachments of the enemy who, based on Jacobsdal, hovered on the right flank. Rimington's Guides at the beginning of the action were sent to the west, where they similarly covered the left flank. Among the first to cross the river was a party of the Guides, and these did good service during the subsequent fighting on the right bank.

Mounted infantry seize farm a mile above this drift, on Riet.

7 a.m. Guards attack east of railway bridge: 9th brigade towards bridge.

The infantry began to arrive on the battle-field at about 7 a.m., and Lord Methuen directed Major-General Colvile with the Guards' brigade to attack the left flank of the supposed frontage of the enemy, viz., the space from the railway bridge eastward to the clump of high poplars on the Riet. Major-General R. Pole-Carew* was meanwhile to lead the 9th brigade

* Major-General Pole-Carew had reached Lord Methuen's column on the 27th to assume command of the 9th brigade, of which Lieut.-Colonel Money, Northumberland Fusiliers, had been in temporary charge since the 23rd, when Major-General Fetherstonhaugh was wounded at Belmont.

THE BATTLE OF THE MODDER RIVER. 249

astride of the railway upon the broken bridge, conforming his advance to that of the Guards. A verbal message was at the same time sent by Lord Methuen to say that he thought that there were along the river bank no Boers except possibly some 400 men who might be covering the broken bridge itself.

It will be convenient to describe the operations of the Guards' brigade throughout the day, before touching upon those of the 9th brigade. On receipt of his instructions, Major-General Colvile formed his troops, then at some distance east of the railway, into two lines; the first consisted of the Scots Guards on the right, the Grenadiers in the centre, the 2nd battalion of the Coldstream on the left; the first battalion of the Coldstream was in reserve as second line. The clump of high poplars was selected as the point of direction. As the Guards deployed they were smitten by artillery, and later by rapid musketry. As soon as the deployment was completed, the Scots Guards were ordered to advance at once, swing round their right, and take the enemy in flank. Lieut.-Colonel Pulteney with two companies and a machine gun was pushing round to the right, to carry out the turning movement, when, at about 8.10 a.m. he came under a sudden and violent fire from the enemy concealed in the low bushes of the Riet or in the trenches on its left bank. The companies suffered considerably; and of the men forming the detachment with the Maxim all were killed or wounded by a well-concealed pom-pom. Colonel Paget, who commanded the Scots Guards, sent four companies to Colonel Pulteney's assistance, but even with this reinforcement it was impossible to make further progress across the plain.

Development of Guards' attack.

Scots Guards attempting outflanking attack are checked by concealed riflemen.

When Major-General Colvile saw that the Boers had thus arrested the march of the Scots Guards, he determined to employ his reserve, the 1st Coldstream, in prolonging the line of the brigade to the right so as to extend beyond the enemy's left. The 1st Coldstream was then on the right rear of the leading battalions and was formed in two lines, one behind the other, each in echelon of companies from the left. Lt.-Colonel Codrington, who commanded it, accordingly moved to the right, where he was unexpectedly stopped by the Riet, of the existence

1st Coldstream, thrown in on right, are stopped by Riet,

but move along it and entrench upon it.

of which he was unaware. Major Granville Smith's company, which was one of those that first reached the river, was ordered to line part of the left bank, to repel an expected attack in flank from burghers who had been seen on the plain beyond the further bank. In this part of its winding course the right of the Riet is higher than the left, so that Major Granville Smith's field of view was very limited. He therefore sought for a ford by which he could reach the dominant bank. Finding traces of a disused drift, he waded alone over a narrow spit of rock through water which reached to his chin, to the right side of the river, where he was soon joined by Lt.-Colonel Codrington with two other officers and 18 non-commissioned officers and men. After driving away some Boers by musketry, the little party reconnoitred up and down the stream in the vain hope of finding a more practicable ford, and was then ordered by a staff officer to recross and return. During the time employed in this unsuccessful quest the greater part of Colonel Codrington's battalion had pushed down the river, some companies in the bed, others along the bank. As they scrambled on, fording was attempted at many points, but in every case the deep water, and the almost equally deep mud at the bottom of the stream, proved impassable. The leading company reached the angle of the bend where the Riet breaks away to the westward, but there, shot down by invisible Boers, some hidden along the right bank, others holding a farm and garden on the left bank, they could get forward no further. A patrol worked down stream sufficiently far to the west of the bend to be able to see the railway bridge, but was driven back by musketry. The battalion took up a position along the left bank, entrenching itself with the Slade-Wallace tools, carried as part of the soldiers' equipment. Some companies faced to the west, the remainder to the north and east. Here they remained till nightfall. They were a target for the defenders of the banks of the Riet, for a detachment which lined the Modder near the northern reservoir, and for a pom-pom. This latter was, however, quickly driven away by a few well-aimed section volleys. Some time after 9 a.m. two companies of Scots

THE BATTLE OF THE MODDER RIVER.   251

Guards, by order of Major-General Colvile, fell back from where they were on the plain, and forming up along the river bank prolonged the line of the 1st Coldstream to the south-west. At dusk a handful of officers and men succeeded in making their way to the Scots Guards' machine gun which had been silenced in the morning, and brought it back, together with one or two wounded men of the detachment who lay around it. At intervals during the day the British right flank was annoyed by shots from Boers on the plain to the east of the Riet. These men several times appeared to be about to make a serious attack upon this part of the line, but their purpose always withered up under the fire of the Grenadiers' Maxim gun, of detachments of the Guards left to hold the southern reservoir, and of the mounted infantry and 9th Lancers on the extreme right rear.

When the Scots Guards commenced their turning movement, the Grenadiers and the 2nd battalion of the Coldstream began their frontal attack, and arrived within 1,000 or 1,100 yards of the enemy who lined the river bank.* At this range the hostile fire was so severe that it became impossible to get nearer and, as the day wore on, the difficulty of keeping the men supplied with ammunition grew more and more serious. When night put an end to the engagement, in many companies the soldiers had but ten cartridges left in their pouches with which to cover an attack, or repel a counter-stroke. So long as the men lay flat on the ground they were little molested, as a growth of thistles hid them from the enemy's view, but any attempt to move brought upon them a shower of bullets, to which they were unable to reply with any effect, as the Boers, perfectly protected by their trenches or concealed by the vegetation which lined the river bank, suffered little from the shrapnel of the supporting British guns, and could not be seen by the infantry. *(Grenadiers and 2nd Coldstream move at 7 a.m., Nov. 28th, straight for river east of bridge. They are stopped at 1,000 yards from it.)*

The 18th and 75th batteries came into action to the east of the railway, and after various short duels with Boer guns which appeared and disappeared on different parts of the field, they covered the movements of the brigade of Guards. The *(18th and 75th batteries support Guards.)*

---

* A few groups of officers and men were able to win their way three or four hundred yards nearer to the Boer defences, but with heavy loss.

75th battery was to the left rear of the 2nd Coldstream, first at 1,700, then at 1,200 yards, range. There it remained till 4 p.m. when, owing to casualties and want of ammunition, it was ordered to fall back a few hundred yards. The 18th battery, two hundred yards to the left rear of the 75th, opened fire at 1,400 yards range; the targets for both batteries were the buildings and enclosures stretching eastward for a mile from the railway bridge. The Naval brigade, about 250 strong, under the command of Major A. E. Marchant, R.M.L.I., had been brought up by rail from Enslin under the escort of an armoured train. At about 7 a.m. their four 12-pr. 12-cwt. guns began to engage the enemy's artillery from a knoll, a little to the west of the line, distant 4,800 yards from the broken bridge.

Naval guns engage Boer guns.

While the Guards, covered by the fire of the artillery, were preparing for the already described movements, Major-General Pole-Carew, as ordered by Lord Methuen, led the 9th brigade towards the broken railway bridge, the point assigned as his object. The Northumberland Fusiliers and the King's Own Yorkshire Light Infantry were ordered to advance along the railway, the former on its east, the latter on its west, each supported by half a battalion of the Argyll and Sutherland Highlanders, while the half-battalion of the Loyal North Lancashire was to prolong the line to the left, and if possible cross the river and threaten the enemy's right. But Pole-Carew speedily realised that by the time the first line of the Guards' brigade had fully extended, their left would almost reach the railway, and would therefore overlap his right. To obtain more room, and also in the hope of being able to turn the right flank of the enemy, he marched westward, and, thanks to a slight swell in the ground, was able to reach the railway, some 2,000 yards south of the broken bridge, without attracting much attention. But as soon as the Northumberland Fusiliers were in the act of crossing the line from east to west, the Boer guns opened upon them and a few minutes later, about 7.30 a.m., the whole river bed, west of the bridge, burst into one wide fusilade. In order to maintain touch with the Guards, and to protect the westward march of his brigade, the Major-General ordered the Northumberland

The 9th brigade advance.

THE BATTLE OF THE MODDER RIVER. 253

Fusiliers to change direction to their right, extend, and endeavour to beat down the enemy's enfilading musketry, which was pouring across the plain, here smooth as a glacis and as destitute of cover. Soon afterwards he found it necessary to leave half the battalion of the Argyll and Sutherland Highlanders to prolong the line of the Northumberland Fusiliers to the left; and, later, he was compelled to direct the King's Own Yorkshire Light Infantry yet further to prolong the covering force, behind whose protection he was making the westward march. The continual necessity thus to increase the numbers employed in this protective work now left him only the half-battalion of the Loyal North Lancashire and the half-battalion of the Argyll and Sutherland Highlanders available for carrying out the original design.

The left of the King's Own Yorkshire Light Infantry made their way to within a few hundred yards of a farmhouse and kraal, some 300 yards south of the river. These buildings and a patch of rocky ground to the west were strongly held as outworks by the Boers; and Major-General Pole-Carew, being convinced by a report from Captain E. S. Bulfin, his brigade-major, that they covered a ford across the Riet, endeavoured to take them, but without success. In the hope of bringing enfilade fire upon the defenders, he sent a small party of Argyll and Sutherland Highlanders into a donga, which runs into the river between the farmhouse and the nearest Boer trench on the left bank. Advancing with a rush, this detachment reached the river bed without loss, and was subsequently reinforced by another handful of the same battalion. *Attempt to take Boer outposts.*

About 11 a.m. an order reached Pole-Carew telling him that as the Guards were crossing the river, his battalion near the railway was to cease fire so as to avoid the possibility of injuring their comrades. This order was with the greatest difficulty conveyed to the right of the 9th brigade, but as soon as it was obeyed, the musketry of the Boers so redoubled in intensity that in self-defence the troops had to re-open fire. Almost immediately after the message had arrived, Lord Methuen came up and told Pole-Carew that the Guards had not succeeded in *After some delay they are captured.*

their attempt to cross. His purpose was to arrange for concerted action on the left flank. The Major-General explained to him the local situation, and said that he proposed to reinforce the little party of Argyll and Sutherland Highlanders in the river bank, and under cover of their fire on the farm, rush it, and then make every effort to cross the river by the islands at Rosmead. Lord Methuen approved, and some twenty or thirty more of the Argyll and Sutherland rushed down into the donga. A strong flanking patrol of the King's Own Yorkshire Light Infantry, under Lt. R. M. D. Fox, supported by a detachment of the Argyll and Sutherland, was now utilised for the attack on the house and kraal. The Boers did not make a vigorous resistance but retreated across the river as the British advanced, and at about 11.30 the farm and the rocky ground were in Major-General Pole-Carew's hands. The enemy on the north bank had been so greatly shaken by the fire of two guns of the 18th battery, under Capt. G. T. Forestier-Walker, that they were already in retreat from Rosmead when the King's Own Yorkshire Light Infantry attacked the farmhouse. This section, which at 10.15 a.m. was sent to assist the 9th brigade by Col. Hall, the officer commanding the artillery, had come into action on a small knoll south-west of the village of Rosmead, on the extreme left of the line, and its shells had dislodged a party of about 300 Boers, who were seen galloping away northwards from Rosmead and from the wood to the east of it.

Situation at 11.30 a.m. Nov. 28th.

At 11.30 a.m. the general situation was as follows:—the half battalion Loyal North Lancashire was close to the southern bank facing a ford, to which it had been sent by Capt. Bulfin. The farm covering the weir was in our hands; thence eastwards to the railway stretched the 9th brigade, immovable under the fire of the Boers entrenched along both banks. The small detachment of Argyll and Sutherland Highlanders held the donga between the farm and the nearest Boer trench on the south bank.

Lodgments on further bank.

A few minutes later Lieut.-Col. Barter, K.O.Y.L.I., followed by a few men of various corps, began to cross the river by the weir, while a quarter of a mile lower down the stream two companies of the Loyal North Lancashire under Major Coleridge

THE BATTLE OF THE MODDER RIVER. 255

commenced the passage of the drift. Major-General Pole-Carew now despatched a messenger to inform Lord Methuen, who had returned to the centre of the line, that he had made a lodgment on the right bank and required reinforcements. But there were no troops in hand. No battalions had been retained as final reserve, and the only troops not engaged were the baggage guard of six companies of the Northampton regiment and three companies of Royal engineers. All that could be done was to direct various officers to convey orders to the 9th brigade, and to the companies of the Guards in its immediate neighbourhood to move westward, in support of the movement on the extreme left. But their efforts served to prove once more the truth of the axiom that when once troops are heavily engaged in the fire-fight, they can only advance or retire; for it was found impossible to withdraw any large number of men from the right and centre of the 9th brigade. Without waiting for the reinforcements he had asked for, the Major-General, as soon as he had collected about 150 men of various corps, dashed into the river, and partly by wading through water up to the men's armpits, partly by scrambling along the wall of the weir, brought his party safely into Rosmead. *Rosmead is captured.*

After making preparations to repulse any attempt by the enemy to recapture the village, the Brigadier began to organise a force with which to push up the right bank towards Modder River village, and thus attack the heart of the defence. In about an hour he had collected some five hundred men of various corps, and leaving part of the Loyal North Lancashire to guard Rosmead, he advanced eastward to capture this important post. On his right, in the brushwood, were some of the Argyll and Sutherland Highlanders. On the left were parties of the King's Own Yorkshire Light Infantry under Colonel Barter, and some of the Loyal North Lancashire. A company of Northumberland Fusiliers, commanded by Major the Hon. C. Lambton, followed in support; and a patrol of Rimington's Guides scouted on the left flank. *Pole-Carew moves against Modder River village.*

At first his men were little exposed to fire, but when they reached the neighbourhood of Fraser's farm they found the *Vigorous resistance by Albrecht.*

enemy prepared for them. A storm of bullets, and of inverted shrapnel from Albrecht's guns* (at the spot where these guns are shown 500 yards north-west of the bridge), fell upon them as they endeavoured to cross long hedges of prickly pear, and to climb through strong wire fences. Nor were other Boer artillerymen, posted close to the railway station, unobservant of the British flanking movement. Their shells fell thick among the ranks of the detachment, while the burghers in the trenches on the south side of the river, turning their aim from the right and centre of the 9th brigade, poured their fire against those who were the more dangerous enemy, because threatening to cut off their retreat. The Brigadier had expected that the party of Argyll and Sutherland Highlanders, placed in the donga on the left bank of the river, would have kept these Boers in check by flanking fire; but owing to a mistake either in the delivery, or in the interpretation, of an order, the officers had brought their men across the Riet and had joined in the advance along the right bank.

Pole-Carew is obliged to fall back to Rosmead.

Captain Forestier-Walker, who was now in action with the section of the 18th battery near the farm which had been carried earlier in the day by the King's Own Yorkshire Light Infantry, vigorously shelled the trees and brushwood in front of our men as they advanced, but his efforts were much hampered by the fact that the undergrowth was so thick that it was impossible to see exactly how far forward they were. All attempts to establish communication by signal, between the officer commanding the 9th brigade and the troops on the south side of the river, failed. The attack broke down from want of strength to drive it home, and the baffled troops sullenly fell back to Rosmead. They were so closely pressed by the enemy's musketry that, in order to cover the retreat, two officers, Major H. F. Coleridge, North Lancashire, and Major T. Irvine, Argyll and Sutherland Highlanders, each with ten or eleven

---

* Major Albrecht fought his guns with great determination; his infantry escort, according to Boer accounts, retreated when they saw the advance of the British, and his ammunition was almost exhausted, but his gunners stood their ground.

THE BATTLE OF THE MODDER RIVER. 257

men of different battalions, threw themselves into farmhouses, which they stubbornly defended until, many hours later, after their detachments had suffered severe loss, they were ordered to evacuate their posts. On his return to the village Major-General Pole-Carew found that the British strength on the north bank had been increased by the arrival of 300 officers and men of the Royal engineers, and of part of a company of the 2nd battalion of the Coldstream Guards. After writing to Lord Methuen to report his failure to force his way up the right bank, and to ask for co-operation in the fresh attempt for which he was then rallying his troops, Pole-Carew heard a rumour that Lord Methuen had been wounded, and that Major-General Colvile was now in command of the division. The rumour was true. Lord Methuen had been wounded at about 4 p.m. near the centre of the line, and one of his staff officers, Colonel H. P. Northcott, had previously fallen mortally wounded, while conveying orders for the reinforcement of the troops on the north bank. Not long after this news came in, the officer commanding the two guns of the 18th battery, still in action near the farm to the south of Rosmead, reported that he heard through the officer commanding the artillery that Major-General Colvile had issued orders for a vigorous bombardment of the position by the artillery till dusk, when the Guards were to attack the left of the Boer line with the bayonet. Pole-Carew then considered whether, in view of the projected movement of the Guards' brigade, his local attack was still feasible. He decided that, owing to the configuration of the ground over which both bodies of troops would have to move in the darkness, the danger was so great lest his detachment should enfilade the Guards as to prohibit an advance from Rosmead. All, therefore, that could be done was to secure firmly that village.

While the little column had been striving in vain to force its way up the right bank of the river, the situation on the left bank had remained unchanged. The infantry lay prone on the ground, engaged in a desultory fire-fight with an unseen enemy, while the artillery continued to shell the buildings and

Nov. 28th/99.

Lord Methuen being wounded command devolves on Colvile.

62nd battery with four guns arrives after forced march.

the river-banks near the railway bridge. During the course of the afternoon Colonel Hall, commanding the artillery, had received a welcome reinforcement of four guns of the 62nd battery, under Major E. J. Granet. The 62nd, which had been left to guard the Orange River bridge, received orders late on the 26th to leave two guns at that camp, and proceed with all speed to rejoin Lord Methuen's division. Owing to a deficiency in rolling stock, no railway transport was available, and it became necessary for the battery to march the whole way. Starting at 10 a.m. on the 27th, Major Granet reached Belmont, thirty miles distant, at dusk. He halted there till 6 a.m. on the 28th, when, escorted by twenty-five of the Royal Munster Fusiliers mounted infantry, he marched to Honey Nest Kloof, where he decided to water and feed his horses. He had but just halted, when a message reached him that there was fighting on the Riet river and that guns and ammunition were urgently required there. He started immediately, and despite the heavy ground over which he had to pass, reached the battle-field a little after 2 p.m. In twenty-eight hours the 62nd battery had covered sixty-two miles, at the expense of six horses which fell dead in the traces, and of about forty more, which never recovered from the fatigue of this forced march. The battery was first sent to the left to support the advance up the north bank of the river, but before it had opened fire, Colonel Hall ordered Major Granet more to the eastward, as he was afraid that the shells might fall among the detachment during its progress through the trees and brushwood which concealed its movements. At 2.45 p.m., the 62nd came into action 1,200 yards from the south bank, behind a swell in the ground which covered the gunners from the waist downwards. Its fire, aimed first at the north bank, was distributed laterally, and then for depth, with good results, as the enemy's musketry slackened, and numbers of men were seen stealing away. About 5 p.m., to support the projected attack by the Guards, the battery was moved close to a sandpit on the west of the railway, where it was joined by the section of the 18th from the left of the line.

Colvile

After considerable delay, caused by the difficulty of sending

THE BATTLE OF THE MODDER RIVER. 259

messages across the shot-swept plain, Major-General Colvile was informed that Lord Methuen had been wounded, and that the command of the division had devolved upon him. He handed over the Guards' brigade to Colonel Paget, Scots Guards, with orders to collect his battalions for the attack upon the left of the Boer line, but soon afterwards decided that it was too late to risk the passage of the river at night with troops exhausted by hunger, thirst, and the burning heat of an exceptionally hot day. He therefore resolved to break off the fight till daybreak next morning, and directed Colonel Paget to form up his brigade for the night at the southern reservoir. *(breaks off the fight.)*

As soon as Major-General Pole-Carew reluctantly abandoned the idea of renewing his attack along the north bank of the Riet, he posted his troops for the defence of Rosmead. He realised the risks which he ran in holding so isolated a position throughout the night, but he and his staff considered that the importance of maintaining the lodgment, which had been effected on the enemy's side of the Riet, made it worth while to incur the danger. To the Royal engineers, under Major G. F. Leverson, was allotted the western face of the village; the Yorkshire Light Infantry held the north, and the Loyal North Lancashire the north-east; the Argyll and Sutherland guarded the east. The men lined the walls, banks, and houses at a yard and a half apart, in groups of six, of whom five rested while one stood sentry. In the centre of the village was the reserve, two companies of the Northumberland Fusiliers, and a company of the 2nd battalion Coldstream Guards. The remainder of the 9th brigade was ordered to cross the river. To guide them, two fires were lit at the drift; and by daybreak the whole command was concentrated on the north bank. It was reinforced by the 1st Highland Light Infantry, who had arrived during the night by rail from Orange River. In the grey of the morning, while the Guards were preparing to support the 9th brigade, the guns* re-opened *(Pole-Carew holds Rosmead, and concentrates 9th brigade on north bank.)*

---

* On the 28th, the field batteries expended ammunition as follows:—

    18th...................... 1,029 rounds.
    62nd...................... 247 ,,
    75th....................... 1,008 ,,
    The Naval guns............ 260 ,,

260   THE WAR IN SOUTH AFRICA.

Boers abandon position. Night, Nov. 28-29.

fire upon Modder River village, but it was soon discovered that during the night the enemy had abandoned his position, and had disappeared with all his guns and pom-poms. With horses utterly tired out, immediate pursuit was impossible, though by midday patrols of mounted men had regained touch with such of the Boers as had fallen back upon Magersfontein. By the afternoon, the whole division had crossed the Riet, and was concentrated on its northern bank.

Casualties of Nov. 28th.

The British casualties consisted of four officers killed (among whom was Lieut.-Colonel H. R. Stopford, commanding the 2nd battalion Coldstream Guards) and 19 wounded; among the other ranks 67 were killed, and 370 wounded.* The losses among the Boers are not accurately known, but 23 burghers were found dead in Rosmead and buried near the village, while 27 bodies were subsequently found in the river itself.

* For details as to casualties, see Appendix 6.

CHAPTER XVI.

THE RAID ON SOUTHERN NATAL.*

THROUGHOUT the operations in Natal during the opening phase of the war, Sir G. White had held that a mobile force, concentrated north of the Tugela, afforded better protection to the central and southern portions of the colony than any number of detachments stationed on the lines of communication. Face to face as he was with an enemy in superior strength, the retention with his field force of every available unit was essential to the British commander's plan of striking at his opponents whenever an opportunity offered. Sir W. Hely-Hutchinson, although anxious as to the security of Maritzburg and Natal from Boer raids, accepted Sir George's decision, telegraphing to the General on 26th October : " I shall do my best in consultation with General Wolfe Murray. . . . . I think we shall be able to deal with any small raid, but a raid in force, especially if supported by guns, will be a serious matter. We must take the risk, and hope for the best." On October 30th, the date of the battle of Lombards Kop,† the only regular unit on the Natal line of communication was the 1st Border regiment, which had arrived at Maritzburg that morning from East London. Detachments of colonial troops held Colenso bridge and Estcourt. To the eastward the Umvoti Rifles, a mounted corps rather more than one hundred strong, had been ordered to fall back from Helpmakaar and watch the ferry, by which the Dundee-Greytown road crosses the Tugela. A battalion of mounted infantry was being raised at Maritzburg by Lieut.-Colonel Thorneycroft,

margin: The relation of Ladysmith to the defence of Natal.

---

* See map No. 4.   † See Chapter X.

Royal Scots Fusiliers, and another at Durban by Lieut.-Colonel Bethune, 16th Lancers.

Threatened siege changes situation.
The result of the battle of 30th October made it probable that the field force at Ladysmith would be soon cut off from its communications. To keep the road open to the south, Sir George White that evening reinforced the garrison of Colenso by despatching thither by rail from Ladysmith the 2nd Royal Dublin Fusiliers, a company of mounted infantry, and the Natal Field battery, whose obsolete 7-pounder guns had been grievously outranged at Elandslaagte. On arrival at Colenso, the commanding officer of the Dublin, Colonel C. D. Cooper, assumed command of that post, finding there one squadron of the Natal Carbineers, one squadron Imperial Light Horse, a party of mounted Police, and the Durban Light Infantry (about 380 strong), and a detachment (fifty strong) of the Natal Naval Volunteers, with two 9-pounder guns. The total strength of the command, including the reinforcements from Ladysmith, was approximately 1,200 men. The Natal Royal Rifles (150 strong) were encamped at Estcourt, twenty-five miles in rear.

An anxious fortnight, Oct. 31st–Nov. 14th.
On the following day General White telegraphed to the Governor of the colony: "My intention is to hold Ladysmith, make attacks on the enemy's position whenever possible, and retain the greatest number of the enemy here." Sir W. Hely-Hutchinson and the officer commanding the Natal line of communication, Brigadier-General J. S. Wolfe Murray, were thus confronted with a difficult and anxious situation. It was obvious that, having regard to the numerical superiority and greater mobility of the enemy, the British force at Ladysmith would, in all probability, be unable to retain the whole of the Boer army. A raid on southern Natal was therefore to be expected immediately, and the strength of that raid might well be such as to overwhelm, or, at any rate, to ignore, the weak garrisons which so imperfectly covered Maritzburg and Durban. Moreover, General Murray was aware that even if Sir R. Buller should think fit to divert from Cape Colony any portion of the expeditionary force now on the high seas, a fortnight must elapse before a single man could be landed at Durban.

THE RAID ON SOUTHERN NATAL. 263

Maritzburg, from its topographical environment, is even less adapted by nature for defence than Ladysmith. Lying in a deep depression surrounded by high hills, the positions covering the capital of the colony are so extensive that a very large force would be needed for their effective occupation. Nevertheless, after consultation on the afternoon of 31st October with the Governor and the Prime Minister of the colony (Colonel Hime), the Brigadier-General decided that, although it was impossible to protect the town itself, it was advisable to prepare the cantonments, so-called "Fort Napier," for defence, and for that purpose to borrow Naval guns from the ships at Durban. As regards Durban, a telegram was received from Sir Alfred Milner stating that arrangements had been made by Sir Redvers Buller with the admiral for the immediate despatch to that port of H.M.S. *Terrible* and *Forte* as a reinforcement to the *Tartar* and *Philomel*, already in the harbour, and suggesting that in the case of a complete disaster to Sir G. White's force it would be wise to retire on the seaport and there make a stand. _{Provisional steps in case of Boer raid.}

But the responsible military authorities were by no means inclined to take a pessimistic view of the situation. The final instructions, dated 1st November, received from Sir G. White's Chief of the Staff, directed General Murray "to remain and defend Maritzburg to the last," and on the following day Sir R. Buller telegraphed from Capetown that a division would be despatched as soon as possible to Natal, adding: "Do all you can to hold on to Colenso till troops arrive." Meanwhile, a warning had been received from the Intelligence staff at Ladysmith, that a considerable body of Free Staters was moving on Colenso, and Brigadier-General Murray, realising that the situation of Colonel Cooper's force at the bridge, commanded by the heights on the northern bank of the Tugela, was becoming precarious, directed that officer to fall back on Estcourt, should he consider his position no longer tenable. On the afternoon of November 2nd, telegraphic communication between Colenso and Ladysmith was cut off by the enemy, and a large Boer commando, having occupied the high ground near Grobelaars Kloof (map No. 15), opened fire on the two little works, Forts _{Changes of stations, Nov. 2nd and 3rd, in expectation of raid.}

Wylie and Molyneux, which had been constructed by the Natal Volunteers on the left bank of the Tugela to cover the crossings of that river, and the approaches to Langewacht Spruit. The Natal Field battery and Natal Naval Volunteers' guns were again seriously outranged by the Boer artillery, and Colonel Cooper decided that, having regard to his instructions, he must fall back on Estcourt. The withdrawal to that town was effected on the night of November 2nd–3rd without molestation from the enemy, the infantry being conveyed in special trains, the mounted troops and field artillery moving by road. The 1st battalion Border regiment was simultaneously pushed forward by rail from Maritzburg to Estcourt, and Brigadier-General Murray proceeded, on 3rd November, to the latter station to take personal command of the force there concentrated, which now amounted in all to about 2,300 men. With this force, weak though it was in guns and mounted troops, he intended to dispute the Boer advance from the north, falling back, if necessary, on the prepared position at Maritzburg. A telegram, dated 4th November, conveyed General Buller's approval of these dispositions, but added: " Do not risk losing Durban by overprolonged defence of Maritzburg, but hold the latter so long as you safely can. I fear it will be at least ten days before I can send you substantial assistance."

After much delay, on Nov. 13th/99, 4,200 Boers under Joubert and Botha reach Colenso.

Fortunately, until the last but one of these ten days, the enemy held back on the north bank of the Tugela. A Krijgsraad, at which all the Boer generals and commandants attended, had assembled in front of Ladysmith on 1st November to decide whether the main effort of the Boer army should be concentrated on the attack of that town, or whether, leaving a detachment to hold Sir G. White's troops, they should at once advance on Maritzburg and Durban. Some of the younger leaders, including Louis Botha, as yet only plain commandant, were in favour of the latter course. The majority of the council decided that, so long as 12,000 effective British troops remained at Ladysmith, the commandos were not numerous enough to allow them to win the much-coveted prizes of the capital and seaport of Natal. It was believed that General White's troops would be

THE RAID ON SOUTHERN NATAL. 265

unable to withstand an assault. On the 9th November, therefore, an abortive and ill-arranged attack was made. It sufficed to show that the Ladysmith garrison was by no means disposed to yield, and that a formal and perhaps prolonged investment would be needed to weaken its powers of resistance. To this task, therefore, the main body of the Boer commandos was assigned; but, as an erroneous report had come in that 5,000 English troops had concentrated at Frere, it was decided that a strong reconnaissance, under the personal command of General Joubert, should cross the Tugela to ascertain the disposition and strength of the British column. On the evening, therefore, of the 13th November, a force about 4,200 strong was assembled at Colenso with orders to push to the south. As agreed, Joubert, although Transvaal Commandant-General, went with it. Louis Botha, promoted to the rank of "Fighting General," was second in command. There is reason to believe that the presence of the senior General was due to a desire to restrain the impetuosity of his subordinate.

The fifteen days' breathing space which the authorities in southern Natal had thus been given, after receipt of the disquieting intelligence of the battle of Lombards Kop, had been of great value. Captain Percy Scott, H.M.S. *Terrible*, had reached Durban on November 6th, and was appointed commandant of that town. A defence scheme was prepared and a battalion of "Imperial Light Infantry" was raised to assist the Naval contingent,* and guns (including two 4·7-in. guns and sixteen 12-pr. 12-cwt.) were landed for its protection. At Maritzburg a position in the vicinity of Fort Napier had, under the supervision of Col. C. C. Rawson, C.R.E., been prepared for defence, the work being executed by a hastily improvised Pioneer Corps of artisans, assisted by native labour. In selecting this position and planning its defence, it was assumed that if the force at Estcourt fell back on Maritzburg, 4,000 men in all would be available for its occupation. Meanwhile, in addi-

Defensive measures taken during the time of grace given by Boer delay.

---

* This contingent consisted of parties from the *Terrible, Forte, Thetis, Philomel* and *Tartar*, of a total strength of 35 officers and 423 men. Commander Limpus, R.N., was placed in command of the guns (see p. 120).

tion to Thorneycroft's corps, the recruiting and training of which were proceeding satisfactorily, a provisional garrison was arranged for Maritzburg by the despatch of two 12-pounders and a Naval detachment from the fleet at Durban, by the withdrawal of the detachment of the Naval Volunteers from Estcourt, and by the organisation into a Town Guard of all able-bodied citizens willing to carry a rifle. Moreover, some 150 loyal and zealous Natal colonists volunteered for scouting duties, and were formed into a corps under the command of the Hon. T. K. Murray, C.M.G., finding their own horses, saddlery, and rifles, and serving without pay. This body of patriotic men did useful work to the north of Maritzburg, in the neighbourhood of Mooi River, from the 4th to the 16th November, when on the arrival of reinforcements from the Cape they were released from further duty, and thanked in General Orders for their "excellent service."

Nov. 11th/99. Reinforcements begin to disembark. Sir F. Clery takes command, Nov. 15th.

On 11th November General Murray, with the approval of Sir R. Buller, handed over the command of the Estcourt garrison to Colonel Charles Long, R.H.A., and returned to Maritzburg to direct personally the heavy work falling on the line of communication staff in arranging for the disembarkation and equipment of the reinforcements, whose arrival at Durban was now hourly expected. He had been warned by Headquarters, on the 7th, that these reinforcements would be made up to three brigades and divisional troops, and that Lieut.-General Sir C. F. Clery would be sent in command. On the evening of the 11th the first battalion, the 2nd West Yorkshire, arrived at Durban with the Brigadier of the 2nd brigade, Major-General Hildyard, and was sent on the following day to Estcourt, accompanied by two naval 12-prs. and a 7-pr. manned by a detachment of bluejackets under the command of Lt. H. W. James, R.N.* These units reached Estcourt on the 13th. Lt.-General Clery reached Durban on November 15th, and assumed command of the troops south of the Tugela. By the 17th five more battalions and a brigade division of field artillery had landed at that port. The

---

* The 12-prs. were replaced at Maritzburg by two others sent up from Durban under command of Lieut. A. Halsey, R.N.

THE RAID ON SOUTHERN NATAL. 267

British troops in southern Natal were thus in numerical superiority to the Boer column, moving south of the Tugela. The dates of the disembarkation of the remaining units of the corps for the relief of Ladysmith, to which a fourth brigade was ultimately assigned by Sir R. Buller, are shown in Appendix 7.

On the morning of the 14th November, Joubert's men crossed the Tugela and off-saddled on the Colenso plain, pushing patrols forward to Frere and finding there only an observation post of eight of the Natal Mounted Police. These patrols, as well as the large number of horses grazing near Colenso, were observed and reported by the armoured train, which, according to the daily practice of the Estcourt garrison, was sent up the line to reconnoitre in the direction of the Tugela. No mounted troops accompanied these train reconnaissances, but doubtful ground was, as a rule, made good by flankers on foot, detailed when required from the infantry in the train.

Nov. 14th. The raid begins.

Early on the following morning, 15th November, the armoured train, carrying a 7-pounder M.L. gun, manned by five bluejackets, one company Royal Dublin Fusiliers, and one company Durban Light Infantry, was again despatched to reconnoitre northward from Estcourt. Captain J. A. L. Haldane, Gordon Highlanders, was placed in command. The train, after a brief halt at Frere to communicate with the police post, pushed on to Chieveley station. No flanking patrols appear to have been sent out; but as Chieveley station was reached a party of 50 Boers was seen cantering southward about a mile to the west of the railway. An order was now received by telephone from Estcourt: "Remain at Frere, watching your safe retreat." The train accordingly commenced to move back on Frere, but on rounding a spur of a hill which commands the line, was suddenly fired at by two field guns and a pom-pom. The driver put on full steam, and the train, running at high speed down a steep gradient, dashed into an obstruction which had been placed on a sharp curve of the rails. A detachment of about 300 men of the Krugersdorp commando had concealed themselves and their guns behind the hill during the train's outward journey, and blocked the line in its rear by filling the space between the

Nov. 15th. Disaster to the armoured train.

doubled rails at the curve with earth and small stones, thus forcing the wheels off the metals.

The reconnoitring party with train suffers severely.

An open truck and two armoured trucks were derailed, one of the trucks being left standing partly over the track. An engagement ensued, in which the British troops fought under great disadvantages. Mr. Winston Churchill, a retired cavalry officer, who had been allowed to accompany the train as a war correspondent, having offered his services, Captain Haldane requested him to endeavour, with the assistance of the Durban Light Infantry company, to clear the line. Haldane meanwhile with the naval gun and the Dublin kept back the enemy. The naval gun was almost at once put out of action. After an hour's work under a heavy shell and rifle fire, Mr. Churchill succeeded in his task, but the coupling between the engine and the rear trucks had been broken by a shell, the engine itself injured, and its cab was now filled with wounded. Captain Haldane accordingly ordered the engine to move back out of fire towards Frere, and, withdrawing his men from the trucks, directed them to make a dash for some houses 800 yards distant, where he hoped to effect a further stand. During this movement across the open veld two privates, without orders, held up white handkerchiefs; the Boers ceased fire, galloped in on the retreating soldiers, and called upon them to surrender. Thus Captain Haldane, a subaltern of the 2nd Dublin Fusiliers, Mr. Winston Churchill, and 53 men were captured. One officer and 69 men succeeded in making their way back to Estcourt, their retirement being covered by a detachment of mounted troops sent out to their assistance. The remainder of the 4 officers and 160 men, of whom the original party consisted, were killed or wounded. General Buller, in commenting subsequently on this unlucky affair, recorded his opinion that the officer in command " acted in trying circumstances with great judgment and coolness." A Boer account mentions that the British troops fought " with exceptional gallantry."

Joubert divides his column and pushes south.

Emboldened by this success, General Joubert determined to carry onwards his raid to the south. For this purpose he divided his force into two columns, 3,000 men being retained under his

THE RAID ON SOUTHERN NATAL.   269

personal orders to operate on the west side of the railway, and 1,200 detached to the eastward under the command of his son, David Joubert. The western column reached Tabanhlope, a hill thirteen miles west of Estcourt, on the 16th, and there remained for two days, reconnoitring Estcourt with patrols. The eastern column occupied Weenen on the 18th, and on the following day both columns continued their movement southward, inclining somewhat towards each other. On the 20th Piet Joubert arrived at Hlatikulu, and, having halted there a night, he further divided his command, sending forward a detachment with a field gun towards Mooi River, where they skirmished at long range on the 22nd and 23rd with the force which, under Major-General Barton, had recently been concentrated at that station. Some scouts of this detachment even pushed on as far as Nottingham Road. The remainder of the Commandant-General's column moved eastward, seized the railway between the Highlands and Willow Grange, and joined hands with David Joubert's commando, which since the 19th had remained halted at Warley Common, a farm three or four miles to the east of Highlands station.

The situation, therefore, on the night of the 22nd was remarkable. The British collected at Estcourt, whither General Hildyard had been sent on the 15th to take command, now amounted to 800 mounted troops (including Bethune's newly-raised battalion), one battery of R.F.A., the Natal Field battery, two naval 12-prs., and 4,400 infantry. Major-General Barton, who had reached Mooi River on the 18th, had, by the night of the 22nd, under his orders Thorneycroft's mounted infantry (490 strong), a battery and two sections of R.F.A., and about 4,000 infantry. Estcourt and Mooi River stations are 23 miles apart. Although, therefore, the Boers had cut the railway and telegraphic communication between the two stations, yet the situation of Gen. Joubert (halted between two British forces, each equal in strength to the two Boer commandos), was audacious, if not dangerous. Moreover, in rear of Mooi River, further British reinforcements were disembarking at Durban, and being pushed up to the front in a continuous

Situation. Night of Nov. 22nd.

stream. The composition and exact distribution of the troops actually in southern Natal on the 23rd November is given in Appendix 8. The pendulum had thus swung completely over. The armoured train incident was of no importance either tactically or strategically, and that momentary success was the only one achieved by Joubert. The slow and hesitating movements of the Boer columns had but hastened the disembarkation and concentration of the troops destined for the relief of Ladysmith. Finally, a tardy fit of rashness had induced the old Commandant-General to place his burghers in peril.

Exaggerated estimate of Boer strength causes hesitating British action. The danger of Joubert's situation was not fully realised by the British staff. The strength of the enemy's invading columns had been magnified by rumour to 7,000, and the number of their guns doubled. Moreover, the units at Mooi River, and in a lesser degree those at Estcourt, had for the most part only just arrived from a long sea voyage, and as yet lacked the organisation, transport, and physical fitness necessary for rapid movements in the field. At Mooi River, General Barton was without Intelligence staff, guides, or even a map. Under these circumstances, the instructions issued by General Clery from Maritzburg to his subordinate commanders were based on a policy of cautious defensive, although he hoped that in a few days an opportunity for striking at the enemy might arise. Thus, the six days, from the 17th to the 22nd, were marked on the British side by advances to, and withdrawals from, posts between Estcourt and Mooi River, which showed a strong desire to avoid all risks. A detachment of the West Yorkshire, with some mounted men, was despatched from Estcourt on the 17th to occupy Willow Grange, and on the following day a similar mixed garrison was sent up to the Highlands from Mooi River; but on the 20th, under instructions from Maritzburg, both these garrisons were withdrawn. The position of David Joubert's laager to the east of Willow Grange was ascertained by the mounted troops of both Barton's and Hildyard's forces, and on the night of the 20th the latter despatched to Willow Grange eight companies of infantry and 430 mounted men under the command of Colonel Hinde, 1st battalion Border regiment, intending an attack.

THE RAID ON SOUTHERN NATAL. 271

But the enemy was judged by General Hildyard to be too strongly posted, and the party was withdrawn to Estcourt on the following day.

On the morning of the 22nd, it was reported that the Boers had occupied Brynbella, a commanding hill to the south of Estcourt about 700 feet above the level of the surrounding plateau, as an advanced post. General Hildyard considered that this development offered a good opportunity for striking a blow at the enemy, and he determined to attempt the capture of the post, and of some guns it was reported to contain. That afternoon, therefore, he moved a Naval 12-pr., the 7th Field battery, a half-battalion 2nd West Surrey, 2nd battalion West Yorkshire, Durban Light Infantry, and seven companies of the 2nd battalion East Surrey regiment, to a height called Beacon Hill, which lay between Estcourt and the enemy's position, about 3,000 yards distant from the latter. Colonel W. Kitchener was entrusted with the command of this force and directed to seize Brynbella by a night attack. Beacon Hill was occupied without opposition, and the Naval gun, Field battery, and 2nd Queen's were detailed to hold it as a support to the attack; to these was subsequently added the 1st Border. A thunderstorm of great severity now delayed the advance upon Brynbella; the night was intensely dark; the rocky nature of the ground and the absence of beaten tracks made the task of assembling the troops and directing their movements extremely difficult. It was not, therefore, until after midnight that the column, led by Colonel Kitchener, moved forward under the guidance of a Natal colonist, Mr. Chapman, who was unfortunately killed in action after he had successfully accomplished his task. The march was made in column of double companies. Owing to the darkness of the night and the broken ground, the difficulty of keeping touch between the companies was great; firing had been forbidden, but when half the distance had been covered, a company reached a wall and rushed it, thinking that it was the enemy's position; the next company was thrown into confusion, and a third in rear and on higher ground opened fire and began cheering. Colonel Kitchener with great coolness suc-

[marginal note: Hildyard sends force against Brynbella, Nov. 22nd, under Col. W. Kitchener. Action of Willow Grange.]

ceeded in restoring order, but not before eight soldiers had been hit by bullets from their comrades' rifles. The advance was then continued and Brynbella Hill was occupied at 3.30 a.m. without further casualties. The Boer party, which consisted of eighty Johannesburg policemen, under Lieut. van Zyl, retired to a ridge about 1,500 yards further to the south. A Creusot field gun had been withdrawn the previous evening after a brief exchange of shots with the Naval gun on Beacon Hill.

<small>Kitchener seizes Brynbella.</small>

At daybreak next morning Kitchener's men came under the fire of the Boer commando holding the southern ridge, and after some two hours' skirmishing at long range the enemy began to creep forward, and the rifle and gun fire gradually became very effective. Kitchener, perceiving that no supports were being sent forward to him, decided to retire, and in this carried out the Major-General's intentions. A gradual withdrawal from the hill in groups of two or three was therefore commenced. Mounted troops, which had left Estcourt at daybreak under command of Lt.-Colonel C. G. Martyr, were now protecting Kitchener's right flank; the squadron of Imperial Light Horse, under Capt. H. Bottomley, dismounted and ascended Brynbella Hill, where with much coolness and gallantry they covered the retirement of the infantry. The Border was also moved forward from Beacon Hill to support the retreating troops. In this manner the whole was withdrawn and subsequently fell back on Estcourt, General Hildyard having decided that it was better to keep his brigade concentrated, ready to move in any direction that might be necessary. The total British loss in this action was eleven men killed, one officer and sixty-six men wounded, and one officer and seven men taken prisoners. A considerable portion of these losses was due to the attempts of combatants to assist the wounded to the rear during the retirement.*

<small>He falls back to Estcourt, Nov. 23rd.</small>

<small>Joubert, Nov. 25th, retreats.</small>

The action of Willow Grange brought home to Joubert the fact that his commandos were in a hazardous situation, and in that way, therefore, tended to clear south Natal of the

---

* This practice had grown up in the British service through the large number of wars with savages, who killed the wounded and mutilated the dead.

THE RAID ON SOUTHERN NATAL. 273

enemy. If the Estcourt and Mooi River forces could have closed on the Boer laager simultaneously, it is probable that more important results would have been achieved. To gain this object Major-General Hildyard despatched on the 22nd a written message to Major-General Barton, stating his plan of attack, and asking for his co-operation. Unfortunately this message was not sent in duplicate, and the native to whom it was entrusted did not deliver it until 10.30 a.m. on the following morning; by that time Hildyard's troops had withdrawn from Brynbella, and were retiring on Estcourt. The Boer Commandant-General was not disposed to run any more risks, and by the 25th the burghers were in full retreat back to the Tugela, taking with them much cattle and many valuable horses, which, in spite of the vehement remonstrances of Piet Joubert, had been looted from the rich grazing grounds of central Natal. The main body of the Boers moved eastward to gain the crossing of Bushman's river at Weenen. A small detachment passed round Estcourt about twelve miles to the westward.

A reconnoitring column, consisting of about 300 of Thorneycroft's regiment and four guns, with two infantry battalions left close to the camp, in support, was pushed out on the 24th November by General Barton from Mooi River to feel for the Boers. It came in touch with the enemy, but the force was not deemed sufficiently strong to press an attack. On the 26th General Hildyard, with the bulk of his troops, advanced to Frere, hoping to intercept the Boers' eastern column, and on the following day General Barton marched from Mooi River to Estcourt. But the burghers, now disorganised and alarmed, fell back too fast to be seriously molested, and on the 28th, when Lord Dundonald advanced with a field battery and all available mounted troops on Colenso, the Boer rearguard merely withdrew across the road bridge. The demolition that evening of the railway bridge was a proof that any lingering hope, which the Boers may up to that date have cherished of mastering southern Natal, was abandoned.

Boers escape over Tugela unscathed. Nov. 28th

On the eastern side of northern Natal,* a Boer force about

* See map No. 3.

Boers on east hold Helpmakaar and patrol from it.

800 strong, under Commandant Ferreira, consisting of the Piet Retief and Bethel commandos, and about 120 Natal rebels, was still in occupation of Helpmakaar, patrolling country on the left bank of the Tugela from below Colenso. They went as far as Rorke's Drift. One of these patrols attempted to cross the river at the Tugela Ferry on the 23rd November, but was repulsed by the Umvoti Rifles, commanded by Major Leuchars. Further east again small parties of Boers had raided into Zululand, but their movements were of no importance.

CHAPTER XVII.

OPERATIONS ROUND COLESBERG UP TO THE 16TH DECEMBER.*

A BOER force seized the passage of the Orange river at Norval's Pont on the 1st November.† It consisted of the Philippolis and Edenburg commandos, with a detachment from the Bethulie district and some burghers from the Transvaal, and was commanded by a Transvaaler named Schoeman. Schoeman's subsequent advance was extraordinarily cautious and hesitating, a caution probably more due to the existence amongst the Free State burghers of a strong party opposed on political grounds to the invasion of the colony than to strategical considerations. Although on the withdrawal of the British garrison from Naauwpoort on the 3rd, there was for the moment not a single British post between Port Elizabeth and the frontier, it was not until the 14th that the little town of Colesberg was occupied by the enemy. That this Boer force was not the advance guard of any large army had been shown by the destruction on the 5th of two railway bridges, at Van Zyl and Achtertang, between Colesberg junction and Norval's Pont; on the other hand, the aggressive intention of Schoeman's movement had been demonstrated by the issue on the 9th of a Boer proclamation, declaring the Colesberg district to be Free State territory. The main object of this proclamation, as well as of similar announcements made in the Aliwal, Albert, and Barkly East districts, was to apply the Free State commando laws to British subjects, and under that legal pretext force them to join the invading columns. Nor did this policy at first lack encouragement, for

<small>Schoeman at Norval's Pont Nov. 1st.</small>

<small>Colesberg Nov. 14th, is annexed.</small>

* See maps Nos. 9 and 16.   † See page 198.

VOL. I.   18*

a public meeting held at Colesberg on the day of its occupation passed a resolution in favour of throwing in its lot with the Orange Free State. These facts were duly reported to the Intelligence staff at Cape Town. The strength of Schoeman's column was variously assessed, one report placing it as high as 3,000, but the estimate considered most reliable stated that the Boer commandant had at this time under his orders 1,200 men, two field guns, and a Maxim. On the 17th the Intelligence department was informed that the column intended to occupy Naauwpoort, and there divide into two sections, one pushing across country to the south-west for the purpose of cutting the railway at Richmond Road, and the other moving south on a recruiting mission to Middleburg.

<small>Danger of the raid. French ordered to check it.</small>

A series of boldly-conducted raids on the long line of railway from Cape Town to De Aar might at this period have paralysed Lord Methuen's advance on Kimberley, while a Boer column in the central districts of the Colony would have formed a nucleus round which the disaffected and lawless might have rallied, before the loyal farmers could be armed and organised to defend their own homes. It was thus evident that immediate steps must be taken to check the commando at Colesberg, and it was for these reasons that the orders, already mentioned,* were issued by Sir R. Buller for the re-occupation of Naauwpoort by a half-battalion of the 2nd Berkshire, a half-battalion of the Black Watch, the New South Wales Lancers (40 all ranks), 25 Cape Police, and a party of Royal Garrison artillery manning two 9-pr. R.M.L. guns, and for the despatch of Lieut.-General French to organise as a combined force these and such further troops as Wauchope could spare, so as to oppose Schoeman's operations.

<small>French confers with Wauchope Nov. 19th.</small>

General French, accompanied by Major D. Haig as his Chief Staff Officer, and Captain the Hon. H. A. Lawrence as Intelligence Officer, left Cape Town by train on the evening of the 18th November, reaching on the following night De Aar, where he had been instructed to confer with Major-General Wauchope (at that time commanding the lines of communication from De

* See Chapter XI.

OPERATIONS ROUND COLESBERG.

Aar to Orange River) as regards the plan of campaign and as to the units that could be given him. In telegraphic orders sent to French on the 19th Sir R. Buller laid down his mission in the following terms:—

"I shall reinforce you as rapidly as possible; meanwhile do your best to prepare for a flying column, strength say, nearly 3,000 men, with which as soon as I get more troops, I mean you to attack the Boers about Colesberg. I think such an attack should be based on Hanover Road. Do all you can to reconnoitre the country, to obtain guides and information, and to be prepared to start; keep your men in condition, and exercise horses and mules." *French's instructions, Nov. 19th.*

As a result of his conference with Wauchope, General French reported to Headquarters on the 20th that Naauwpoort, which had already been re-occupied by the troops above-named, would be a better base than Hanover Road for a movement on Colesberg, considering both the flatness of the country, the fewer wire fences, and the railway and direct road. But for the moment Wauchope could spare no more troops except two companies of M.I. The telegram added that arrangements were being made for the formation at Naauwpoort of a depôt containing thirty days' supplies for 3,000 men, 600 horses, and 500 mules. After the despatch of this report General French, accompanied by his staff, proceeded by train to his destination, and immediately on his arrival issued orders for a reconnaissance on the following day. *French reports on situation, Nov. 20th.*

On the morning of the 21st, the General Officer commanding pushed forward up the railway with the N.S.W. Lancers, followed by a section of infantry in a train. The line was found to be broken one mile north of Tweedale siding, but the cavalry advanced to within eight miles of Colesberg without meeting the enemy (see map No. 10). On reporting by telegram the result of this reconnaissance, General French added that, on the arrival from De Aar of the two companies M.I., he proposed to occupy a strong position north of Arundel, and that he considered that, with a view to an attack on Colesberg, he should be reinforced by two and a half battalions and a few *Nov. 21st. French reconnoitres towards Colesberg. He asks for reinforcements.*

squadrons of cavalry, "most necessary for reaping fruits of victory in this country." The same afternoon R. battery R.H.A. and an ammunition column reached Naauwpoort by train from Cape Town. The two companies M.I., under Lieut.-Colonel R. J. Tudway, marched in from De Aar, but were found to be so insufficiently trained in their mounted duties that they were as yet unfit to take the field as complete units against the enemy.*

<small>Steps taken Nov. 22nd and 23rd. Reinforcements arrive.</small>

On the 22nd, culverts north of Tweedale siding were repaired, and an obstruction on the line was removed. A patrol of the N.S.W. Lancers was pushed on to a kopje north of Arundel, but no sign of the enemy was seen. On the 23rd the other half-battalion Black Watch came in from General Wauchope, and a reconnaissance of New South Wales Lancers and a picked detachment of the M.I., supported by a company of infantry in a train, was despatched up the line towards Arundel, with a view to observing by patrols the vicinity of Colesberg; the kopjes, however, north of Arundel station were found to be now occupied by the Boers in sufficient strength to check further progress. In reporting this to Cape Town by telegraph, General French stated that he did not think that the enemy intended to attack Naauwpoort, but considered that the Boers should be dislodged from Colesberg as soon as possible, as they were obtaining recruits there. Naauwpoort had meantime been placed in a thorough state of defence.

<small>French's command extended.</small>

Reconnaissances continued to be made almost daily towards Arundel. Meanwhile General French's sphere of command had been increased by the addition to it of the central line of communication down to Port Elizabeth, volunteer corps, including the Prince Alfred's Guards, of a strength of 900 all ranks, being placed at his disposal. Some difficulty, however, arising as to the movement of these colonial troops north of Cradock, detachments of regulars were sent temporarily from Naauwpoort to hold Rosmead Junction and the railway bridges near it against

---

* These two companies were part of the M.I. battalion of the cavalry division, and were composed of sections drawn from various infantry battalions, and trained in different districts in different ways.

OPERATIONS ROUND COLESBERG.

small rebel parties, which were reported to be under arms in that neighbourhood. The force at Naauwpoort was gradually augmented by the arrival of the 12th Lancers on the 25th, and O. battery R.H.A., and another ammunition column on the 27th. On the other hand, by the 1st December the whole battalion of the Black Watch had been, at the urgent request of Major-General Wauchope, returned to Orange River to replace infantry sent forward to Lord Methuen. The 1st Suffolk regiment arrived at Naauwpoort that afternoon, and on the 2nd December the New Zealand Mounted Rifles, a fine corps 400 strong, and the 26th company R.E., joined General French.

On the 26th November Sir R. Buller had telegraphed to Sir F. Forestier-Walker: "French should attack Arundel as soon as he feels strong enough, but not before, and he should be sure that he is strong enough. We can now afford to wait;" and on the following day he added: "Tell French to maintain an active defence, not running any risk." On the 30th another despatch from the General Commanding-in-Chief to General Forestier-Walker ran: "suggest to French that a policy of worry, without risking men, might have a good effect on the enemy at Colesberg and keep him occupied." Meanwhile the constant appearance of patrols from Naauwpoort had not only completely chained to the vicinity of Colesberg the main body of the enemy, but had made him nervous for the safety of his advance party on the kopjes north of Arundel station; and on the 29th November a squadron of the 12th Lancers discovered that those kopjes had been evacuated. On this, two days later, two squadrons of that regiment were sent forward to Arundel station to bivouac there that night with a view to a reconnaissance being pushed on to Colesberg on the following morning. But at 10 p.m. the Lieutenant-General received a telegram from the Chief of the Staff ordering the 12th Lancers to join Lord Methuen on the Modder river. The squadrons were, therefore, recalled from Arundel and the regiment entrained for the Modder on the following day, as soon as sufficient rolling-stock could be obtained. Its departure left French for the moment with insufficient mounted men to keep touch with the enemy, but the arrival of

Nov. 26th to Dec. 7th. The "policy of worry."

the New Zealanders on the 2nd December enabled active operations to be renewed, and on the 5th the Carabiniers, commanded by Colonel T. C. Porter, increased the Naauwpoort force sufficiently to warrant the adoption of the "policy of worry" suggested by Sir R. Buller. Moreover, arrangements had now been completed for the protection of the railway line from Cradock to Rosmead by part of the Port Elizabeth Volunteer Corps. The details of the Suffolk regiment and M.I., which had been guarding these localities, were thereupon recalled to Naauwpoort and rejoined on the afternoon of 5th December. On the 6th orders were issued for the occupation on the following day of a position near Arundel with mounted troops "with the object of pushing forward detachments to observe the enemy, and clear up the situation near Colesberg next day." In pursuance of these orders the New Zealand Mounted Rifles moved out to the ridge to the south of Arundel early on the morning of the 7th, and later in the day the Carabiniers, mounted infantry (less a detachment holding Hanover Road station), the N.S.W. Lancers, a detachment of the R.E. company, and Field Telegraph section were brought out by train from Naauwpoort under the command of Colonel Porter; and, having detrained at Hartebeestfontein farm, covered by the New Zealand Mounted Rifles, advanced with that regiment to Arundel without meeting any opposition. There the force bivouacked for the night, the enemy's piquets watching them from a ridge three miles north of the station.

Arundel occupied, Dec. 7th.

Dec. 8th to Dec. 11th, 1899. Schoeman's strength ascertained. French seizes hill north of Arundel.

At dawn on the 8th, Colonel Porter sent forward his mounted infantry, with some cavalry, and seized a hill three miles north of Arundel. General French, accompanied by his staff and two Berkshire companies, arrived at Arundel by train from Naauwpoort at 6 a.m., and by his orders the reconnaissance was then pushed home. The Boers were found to be now occupying a series of kopjes called Taaiboschlaagte which run in a south-easterly direction from Rensburg, and extend to the westward, across the line. The cavalry was sent round both flanks of the enemy, while the mounted infantry held him in front. This movement caused the Boers to fall back and disclose a second

OPERATIONS ROUND COLESBERG.

position athwart the railway, with a wide frontage both to the east and west. Artillery fire was opened on the British troops from three points of this new post, and a large gun was seen being dragged into action near Rensburg, which appeared to be the centre of the Boer line. It was estimated that the opposing commando was on this occasion about 2,000 strong. A prisoner was captured, who alleged that he was adjutant to the officer commanding a reinforcement just arrived from Pretoria. He stated that the total force under Schoeman's orders was now 3,000, exclusive of local rebels, that it included four field guns and three smaller pieces, and that Grobelaar's commando of 1,700 men at Burghersdorp would shortly receive a reinforcement of 600 men from the Free State and intended then to co-operate with Schoeman. A telegram, despatched by Major Haig in the evening to Cape Town, reported the above information and the day's operation, adding: "General French desires me to say that in face of attitude of enemy to-day he cannot do more than reconnoitre with forces here." The mounted troops, who had now been joined by R. battery R.H.A., continued in occupation of the kopjes north of Arundel, and on the 11th December, the railway having been repaired, three companies of the Royal Berkshire, under Major McCracken, were moved by train to that station, and a detachment of 50 M.I. was sent to Tweedale to patrol and guard the line; the remainder of the troops continued to garrison Naauwpoort under command of Lieut.-Colonel A. J. Watson, 1st Suffolk regiment.

Two squadrons of the Inniskilling Dragoons reached Naauwpoort on the 10th, and with two squadrons of the 10th Hussars, arriving on the 11th, were sent on to Arundel. Early on the morning of the 11th the British patrols reported that the Boers had seized Vaal Kop, an isolated hill some six miles west of Rensburg, with open ground all round it, and Kuilfontein farm, one and a half miles to the north-west of the kop. By the Lieut.-General's directions a squadron of the 10th Hussars and two Horse artillery guns were sent out against these detached posts, and having forced the enemy back remained in possession of Vaal Kop. Some anxiety was still felt as regards Schoeman's

French seizes Vaal Kop and repels Boer advance. Dec. 11th.

designs on his left side, as it was surmised that his continued occupation of a position so much in advance of Colesberg was probably due to an intention of holding out a hand to Grobelaar in the Burghersdorp district. Colonel Porter was, therefore, ordered to patrol widely to the east and north-east to discover whether any movements were taking place in those quarters. Early on the morning of the 13th his patrols reported that about 1,800 Boers were leaving their laagers in three detachments and pushing southward towards Naauwpoort. By 7 a.m. Colonel Porter had made the following disposition to meet this development—Vaal Kop on his extreme left was still occupied by a squadron and two guns, and the kopjes to the north of Arundel were held by the three companies of the Berkshire and two 9-pr. R.M.L. guns, supported by the M.I. on the right and the New Zealand Mounted Rifles on the left, with the N.S.W. Lancers at the Nek near the railway. The main body of the cavalry (six squadrons) with four guns of R. battery was concentrated on the threatened flank two to three miles to the east of the remainder. In a skirmish which ensued, the enemy brought up two guns, but these were quickly silenced and the Boer commandos were driven back by the cavalry. By 2 p.m. the bulk of the enemy's forces had returned to their old ground ; a party, which about that hour occupied Kuilfontein farm on the western flank, was driven away by the shell fire of the two British guns on Vaal Kop, suffering considerable loss. The British casualties during the day were limited to one officer and seven men wounded. A congratulatory telegram, received by General French from Sir R. Buller next day, commented : " You are following the right policy. Worry them." The tactics prescribed by General French at this period can be best realised from the following extract from the instructions issued by his Chief Staff Officer on the 14th to Major-General Brabazon, who, on his arrival on that date, was placed in command at Arundel :—

French's method.

" Your task is to prevent the enemy moving from his present positions closer to Naauwpoort, or reaching the railway connecting that place with Arundel. The Lieut.-

OPERATIONS ROUND COLESBERG. 283

General Commanding considers that the best method to pursue to attain this end is :

"(a) Hold Arundel as a pivot.

"(b) Using that as a pivot, act energetically with your mounted troops against any of the enemy's detachments which may leave his main position and cross open ground.

"(c) Select and hold certain points (such as Vaal Kop), to retain the enemy and make him fear an offensive movement against his line of retreat; (which is viâ Colesberg wagon bridge)."

On the 16th, however, notwithstanding these instructions, the officer commanding the detachment on Vaal Kop fell back from that post on its being threatened by distant artillery fire, and the whole of the troops at Arundel were turned out on a false alarm that the enemy was advancing. The defeats at Stormberg, Magersfontein, and Colenso, recorded in later chapters, had meantime darkened the prospect, so that manifestly the utmost care must be taken by all commanders to obviate mistakes which might lead to further misfortunes. General French, therefore, moved his Headquarters to the front, and assumed personal command of the troops at Arundel. He had telegraphed on the previous day offering to despatch all his cavalry to the Modder river, but this suggestion was negatived "on account of scarcity of water." He reorganised the Arundel command into a division as follows, appointing Major-General Brabazon second in command :— *French, because of effect of "Black Week," takes command at Arundel and reorganises. Dec. 16th.*

Dec. 17th.

1st Cavalry Brigade (under Colonel T. C. Porter).
The Carabiniers.
New South Wales Lancers (40 men).
1 company mounted infantry.

2nd Cavalry Brigade (under Lieut.-Colonel R. B. W. Fisher).
The Inniskilling Dragoons (2 squadrons).
10th Hussars (2 squadrons).
1 company mounted infantry.

Divisional Troops.

Brigade division R.H.A. (under Colonel F. J. W. Eustace).
New Zealand Mounted Rifles.
R.E. company.
Bearer company.
Half-battalion Royal Berkshire regiment.
2 guns R.G.A.
} under Major F. W. N. McCracken.

<small>French pivoting on certain strong points continues "policy of worry." Dec. 16th-17th, 1899</small>

Major McCracken was directed to fortify the kopjes north of Arundel, and to hold them " at all costs " as a pivot of manœuvre. The country, for purposes of reconnaissance, was divided into two zones, the railway being taken as the line of demarcation. The 1st brigade was assigned to the western zone, the 2nd to the eastern; the Brigadiers were instructed to occupy certain tactical points towards the front and flanks, and were made responsible that the enemy was not allowed to establish himself unmolested on any kopje south of the Arundel ridge. The Horse artillery and New Zealand Rifles were kept in reserve under the personal orders of the General Officer Commanding. With these arrangements the Lieut.-General felt assured that his position was secure, and hoped to be able to continue to pursue a bold and aggressive policy, a duty to which he was now able to devote his whole attention, as other arrangements had been made for the command of the lines of communication to Port Elizabeth.

CHAPTER XVIII.

STORMBERG.*

PRESIDENT STEYN early in November ordered an invasion of the north-eastern portion of Cape Colony. In doing so he acted against the advice of a Krijgsraad held at Bethulie to discuss the project. A considerable party of the Free State burghers was, in fact, opposed to an offensive plan of campaign, but the President held that success in the struggle against Great Britain could not be attained without enlisting in his favour all the external support he could obtain. The mission of the invaders was therefore to incite the discontented in the colony to open rebellion. Under these circumstances, although many communications passed between the disaffected amongst the local farmers and Olivier, the commandant of the Boer contingent which had crossed Bethulie bridge early in November, the movements of the burghers were at first slow and hesitating. Aliwal North was occupied on the 13th, and Burghersdorp—a town without any great reputation for loyalty—two days later. The districts of Aliwal North, Albert and Barkly East were at once proclaimed to be Free State territory. It was not until the 25th that the Boer commando seized the important railway junction of Stormberg, from which the British garrison had three weeks earlier been withdrawn by Sir R. Buller to Queenstown.† *The Boers occupy Stormberg, Nov. 25/99.*

Lieut.-General Sir W. Gatacre, with the staff of the 3rd division, the two brigades of which had been sent on to Natal, *Sir W. Gatacre reaches East London, Nov. 16th.*

---
* See maps Nos. 9 and 14. † Chapter XI.

disembarked at East London on 16th November. The tasks assigned to that General were to prevent British subjects from being persuaded or compelled to take up arms against their Sovereign, to encourage and protect the loyal, and, so far as possible, to stem the Boer invasion until the return of Lord Methuen's division from Kimberley enabled the country south of the Orange river to be swept clear of the enemy, preparatory to the general advance through the Free State.

Moves to Queenstown. His available strength.

Sir W. Gatacre moved immediately up to Queenstown, taking with him the 2nd Royal Irish Rifles (898 all ranks), who had landed the same day at East London. On arriving at Queenstown he found at that station the half-battalion and a mounted company of the 2nd Berkshire regiment (strength, 574 all ranks), a small detachment of Royal Garrison artillery, and a half company of Royal engineers, which, with the Naval contingent, had formed the original garrison of Stormberg. The *personnel* of the Naval contingent had been ordered to return to Cape Town, but had left with the Royal artillery their two 12-pr. guns. Besides these, the gunners had two obsolete field guns belonging to the armament of the naval base, but owing to the lack of mules and equipment none of the guns were mobile. In addition to these troops the local volunteers, consisting of the Kaffrarian Rifles, the Frontier Mounted Rifles (about 229 strong), and the Queenstown Rifle Volunteers (285), had been called out; a corps of mounted infantry was being raised locally from the farmers of the Eastern province by Colonel Brabant, and a contingent of the Cape Mounted Rifles and Cape Police had been placed at the Lieut.-General's disposal. The Kaffrarian Rifles, 285 all ranks, held the base at East London. The remainder of the local troops, except some posts of observation at Cathcart, Indwe and Molteno, were concentrated at Queenstown. An armoured train, commanded by Lieutenant F. J. Gosset, 2nd Berkshire, patrolled the railway.

Pushes on to Putterskraal, Sterkstroom.

For the moment it was obvious that no forward movement could take place; indeed, a telegram despatched by Sir R. Buller to General Gatacre, on 18th November, reminded him that "the great thing in this sort of warfare is to be perfectly certain that one position is safe before you advance to another, and that we are not yet strong enough in troops to play tricks." Yet patrols, furnished by the Cape Police, were sent out to Dordrecht, Stormberg and Tarkastad, and the employment of reliable native scouts was arranged. In a telegram, dated 21st November, Sir Redvers suggested that a portion of General Gatacre's force might be moved to Stormberg for the purpose of covering the coal mines at Indwe. Sir W. Gatacre replied on the same day that he had not sufficient men as yet to advance to Stormberg, but, as soon as more troops arrived, he intended to occupy that junction and clear the country round it. Meanwhile, as a result of a personal reconnaissance of the district, he proposed to occupy Putterskraal, a position which, with outposts at Bushman's Hoek and Penhoek, would "command Sterkstroom junction with the colliery line, reassure loyal farmers, and steady disloyal men." The arrival from England of two companies of mounted infantry (part of the mounted infantry of the cavalry division), under Capt. E. J. Dewar, King's Royal Rifles, on the 22nd, and of the 2nd Northumberland Fusiliers on the 27th November, enabled a concentration of all the mounted troops, the detachment of Royal Garrison artillery, the 2nd Northumberland Fusiliers, and the 2nd Royal Irish Rifles, to be effected at Putterskraal on the latter date. Sterkstroom was also occupied as an advanced post, and on the following day the Berkshire mounted infantry, four companies of the Irish Rifles, and the Kaffrarian Rifles, brought up from East London, were pushed on to Bushman's Hoek.

and Bushman's Hoek, Nov. 27th–28th.

The enemy was becoming bolder. A considerable number of disaffected farmers had joined the commando at Burghersdorp; more were known to be on their way up from Cradock, while at Barkly East a disloyal field cornet was issuing Government arms and ammunition to rebels. The Boer occupation of Stormberg on the 25th was followed immediately by the destruction of the railway and telegraph line to the westward. Thus French's force at Naauwpoort and Gatacre's troops at Putterskraal were cut off from each other, and the latter were left for the moment entirely dependent on their own resources. Sir Redvers,

Situation graver. Buller suggests closing with enemy.

who was kept daily informed of these developments, felt "anxious," and telegraphed orders from Maritzburg on 26th November to Sir F. Forestier-Walker : " Caution Gatacre to be careful. I think he is hardly strong enough to advance beyond Putterskraal, until Methuen's return ; " and on the following day he telegraphed instructions to reinforce General Gatacre by one, or, if possible, by two battalions, " and any mounted men that can be spared." Barkly East was reported to be in open rebellion, although Sir H. Elliott's action in defending the passes leading south to Griqualand East continued to be effective.* The "annexation" of Dordrecht to the Free State, proclaimed officially on its occupation by the enemy, further complicated the situation. General Gatacre accordingly telegraphed direct to the General Commanding-in-Chief :—

"Military situation here requires dealing with extreme carefulness. Boers have occupied Dordrecht and enemy is advancing in a southerly direction, evidently pointing for Queenstown. I have two British regiments only, and I am 33 miles to the north of Queenstown—I am holding Bushman's Hoek range to endeavour to prevent descent into Queenstown district, which would mean general state of rebellion of Dutch. Force will be strengthened at Queenstown by next British regiment which should arrive at Queenstown 5th December, but Queenstown is indefensible position. Are there any orders especially as regards my movements ? "

Sir Redvers replied the same day (2nd December) from Maritzburg :—

"Your No. A 514. We have to make the best of the situation, and if the enemy is advancing by Dordrecht, the importance of Bushman's Hoek is diminished. You have a force which altogether is considerably stronger than the enemy can now bring against you. Cannot you close with him, or else occupy a defensible position which will obstruct his advance ? You have an absolutely free hand to do what you think best."

Gatacre seizes Molteno and Penhoek, Nov. 29th.

Meanwhile, on the 29th November, a raid by train had been made from Putterskraal on Molteno, and a large amount of corn removed from a mill which it was feared might fall into the enemy's hands. An officer and 50 men of the Cape Police were left in observation at Molteno, and detachments of Cape Mounted Rifles and of the newly-raised corps, Brabant's Horse,

* Chapter XI.

STORMBERG.

of a total strength of 400 men, was pushed out to Penhoek, a pass through the hills ten miles east of Sterkstroom.

By the 6th December, Sir W. Gatacre had been reinforced by two batteries of his divisional artillery, the 74th and 77th, the divisional ammunition column, the 12th company R.E., the 1st Royal Scots, the 33rd company Army Service Corps, and 16th Field Hospital. The greater portion of his detachment was unfortunately only just free from the confinement of the voyage from England. Every effort had been made on board ship to keep the infantry in good condition by gymnastics and physical drill, but they were naturally not in the best trim for a long march. The horses of the artillery had suffered from a somewhat stormy passage of 31 days, during which 14 had died of influenza. They, too, therefore, were hardly yet ready for hard work. Nevertheless, the G.O.C. considered that, in the existing strategic situation, any further prolongation of the defensive attitude he had hitherto been obliged to maintain would be injurious.* He determined, therefore, to take advantage of the free hand left to him by Sir R. Buller, and to follow the further suggestion that he should close with the enemy. On the evening of the 7th he informed the commanding officers of units that he intended to make a night march on Stormberg and attack the Boer laager. It will be seen from map No. 14 that the buildings and sheds which mark the railway junction lie at the foot of a steep razor-back hill, called Rooi Kop, and on the eastern edge of a valley or vlei, about two miles in length from north to south, and one in breadth. This vlei, in which the enemy's main body was known to be, is shut in on the east by the Rooi Kop, which dominates all of the surrounding country. To the south and south-west, it is enclosed by a lower hill, named the Kissieberg, and on the north by a flat-topped kopje on which forts had been constructed by the British garrison when in occupation of the junction. Between this kopje and the northern point of the Kissieberg, there is a gap of a mile through which

Dec. 7th. Gatacre tells C.O.s of intended night march.

---

* The Intelligence reports of General Gatacre's staff show that they at this time believed that Olivier was expecting a large reinforcement from the Transvaal.

pass out the spruit, which drains the vlei, and the branch line to Naauwpoort. The railway from East London to Bloemfontein and the main road from Molteno to Burghersdorp, viâ Stormberg, cross a Nek between the Kissieberg and Rooi Kop, subsequently skirting the latter hill very closely. This Nek, on which the intelligence scouts reported the Boer guns to be posted, and the Rooi Kop, Sir W. Gatacre planned to seize before dawn on the morning of the 9th by a night march from Molteno. He proposed to employ on the enterprise the whole of the mounted infantry, one field battery, the R.E. company, the Northumberland Fusiliers, the Royal Irish Rifles, and a detachment of Cape Police. The mounted troops from Penhoek were also to co-operate on the right flank. Arrangements were also made with Sir H. Elliott for an advance of the Headquarters of the Cape Mounted Rifles in the direction of Dordrecht. By concentrating at Molteno late on the day previous to that chosen for the attack, General Gatacre hoped to surprise the enemy. Owing, however, to some difficulties in obtaining rolling stock, the movement was postponed till the 9th.

Move postponed to Dec. 9th.

Early on the morning of that day, camp was struck at Putterskraal, and the baggage packed, the wagons being ordered to travel by road to Molteno. The assembling of the troops at that village was effected during the afternoon in the following manner :—

Concentrates at Molteno, Dec. 9th.

By Train from Putterskraal.

Divisional Staff.
R.A. Staff, 74th and 77th batteries R.F.A.
R.E. Staff, 12th company R.E.
2nd Northumberland Fusiliers.
Headquarters and 4 companies Royal Irish Rifles.
Field Hospital and Bearer company.

By Train from Bushman's Hoek.

4 companies Royal Irish Rifles.

STORMBERG.

By Road from Putterskraal.

2 companies mounted infantry.
42 Cape Mounted Police.

By Road from Bushman's Hoek.

1 company Royal Berkshire mounted infantry.

Besides these, three companies Royal Scots were sent by rail from Putterskraal. One of them was dropped at Bushman's Hoek, the other two being taken on to Molteno. The units that went by train had with them their first line transport. Although the entraining of the troops began about 12 noon, it was not completed till after 5 p.m., owing to the lack of sufficient sidings. The movement to Molteno was covered by the armoured train, and was carried out without interruption. The detachments of Brabant's Horse and Cape Mounted Rifles ordered in from Penhoek to Molteno failed, however, to appear. A message to the officer commanding at Penhoek, conveying the order, had been handed in at the telegraph office at Putterskraal at midnight on the 8th, but owing to some carelessness had not been forwarded by the telegraph clerk. The precaution of demanding an acknowledgment of the receipt of this important order, or of sending a duplicate, does not appear to have been taken by the divisional staff.

The troops had dined before leaving Putterskraal, and took with them one and a half day's rations, the half ration to be eaten in the train on the way to Molteno, and the remainder to be carried by the men on the march. The preserved meat had been issued in 6lb. tins. These were very inconvenient. Therefore many of them were thrown away. Arrangements for feeding men.

On arriving at Molteno, Sir W. Gatacre assembled the commanding officers and issued personally to them his orders for the movement against Stormberg. His Intelligence staff had ascertained that the actual strength of the Boers in laager at that moment was about 1,700, and that the southern face of the Kissieberg and the Nek between that hill and Rooi Kop were entrenched. The General, on receipt of this information, deter- Dec. 9th, 1899. Orders for night march issued. Lack of maps.

mined to modify his original plan. Although Stormberg had been occupied for more than a month by British troops, no systematic sketching of the surrounding country had been undertaken. Except a plan made more than a year before of the ground in the immediate neighbourhood of the junction, and reproduced in one of the Intelligence hand-books, the only map at the disposal of the Staff was the Cape Survey, the scale of which, $12\frac{1}{2}$ miles to an inch, was too small for tactical purposes.

The method of march.

The local Cape Police, the Berkshire mounted infantry, and others were very well acquainted with the country; and, after a personal examination of Sergeant Morgan, Cape Police, and several native policemen, who had previously been selected as guides, Sir W. Gatacre determined to move his force out from Molteno by the Steynsburg road, and to diverge from that road by a cross track, leading northwards from a point near D. Foster's farm to Van Zyl's farm,* which was situated immediately in rear of the western face of the Kissieberg. Thus the position on the Nek would be turned. The distance to be covered during this flank march was said by his informants to be about nine miles. The actual distance was about ten miles. Allowing for intermediate rests for the men, the General anticipated that he would be able so to order the time as to place his men in a position to rush the Kissieberg with the bayonet before dawn, and then, as soon as daylight appeared, to plant the guns on that kopje, thus commanding the whole of the Stormberg valley. Sir W. Gatacre informed commanding officers verbally of these intentions, and arranged the following succession :

> Royal Irish Rifles.
> Northumberland Fusiliers.
> 74th and 77th batteries, escorted by
> Two companies M.I. and the Cape Police.
> Berkshire M.I. company.
> Machine guns, ammunition reserve, and
> Field Hospital, escorted by 12th company R.E.

* It will be observed that four houses marked Van Zyl's are shown in map 14, but, except when otherwise specified, the most northern of these is the one referred to throughout in the text.

STORMBERG. 293

The column was to move off in three echelons, the first consisting of the divisional staff and the infantry, the second the artillery and mounted infantry, and the third the field hospital, machine guns, etc. Guides were allotted to each unit. Complete reliance was placed on the efficiency of these guides, and the precaution of causing the road to be previously reconnoitred by a staff officer had not been taken. Both Sir W. Gatacre's intelligence officers, one of whom knew the ground intimately, had duties on the line of communication, and were thus unable to accompany the column. The General, with all the rest of his staff, took his place at the head of the leading battalion, which was preceded by eight infantry scouts under a subaltern. The remainder of the infantry marched in fours. The batteries were in column of route. The wheels of the 77th were covered with raw hide. The wheels of the 74th had not been so padded, as that battery was only added to the column at the last moment. The hide proved to be of but little value for the purpose of deadening the sound, and only made the draught heavier. *Dependance on guides.*

The head of the column moved off about 9 p.m., somewhat later than had been originally planned. The artillery and mounted infantry followed in due course along the Steynsburg road, but the machine guns, field hospital, and R.E., owing to a lack of staff supervision, took the one direct on Stormberg, and, finding that there were no troops in front of them, halted where they were until daylight, having first ascertained from the officer left in command at Molteno that he did not know the route by which the main column was advancing. *Mistake at starting.*

Meanwhile, the infantry of that column had pressed on with the keenness of soldiers eager for their first fight, and at 1 a.m. unexpectedly crossed a railway line, soon afterwards approaching a homestead, which proved to be that of Mr. J. Roberts. The guides had in fact passed the branch road leading to Van Zyl's farm, but on being interrogated, the head guide, Sergeant Morgan, assured Sir W. Gatacre that he and his assistants knew the way perfectly, and that they were leading the column by a road which, though slightly longer than that originally selected, avoided wire and a bad piece of track which the guns would have *The guides miss the road.*

found it difficult to cross at night. They added that they were within one and a half miles of the spot, to which the General desired to be guided. The map and freehand sketch show that the guides now proposed to lead the column to the rear of the Kissieberg by the wagon-track which leaves the Steynsburg road at Roberts' homestead, and after crossing the Bamboosberg Spruit and the colliery branch line, strikes, near Van Zyl's house, the track by which General Gatacre had intended to approach the enemy's position. The distance still to be traversed was, as will also be noticed, not one and a half, but about two and a half miles. Moreover, after crossing the spruit and the railway, the track traverses the northern slopes of a stony irregular underfeature which guards the approaches to the Kissieberg from the south and west. Progress over this ground was unlikely to be rapid. Roberts' homestead is $10\frac{1}{2}$ miles from Molteno. The troops had, therefore, already marched rather further than was originally anticipated; and, as they had halted for a short time every hour, their rate of marching had been fast for night-work over such country. The men were somewhat weary owing to the march. They were out of condition. They had been engaged on heavy fatigue work on the morning of the 9th. Whether, therefore, the guides had missed the true road in the dark, a supposition which is favoured by the fact that they had previously assured the General that the whole route was fit and easy for wheeled transport, or whether, not realising the importance in military operations of obedience to orders, they had, on their own judgment, diverted the column to the longer route in the belief that it would be easier, the effect on the General's plan of attack was serious. Sir W. Gatacre, nevertheless, decided that he would give his men an hour's rest, and then push on.

The march resumed. Column arrives at dawn at destined spot.

About 2 a.m. the march was resumed in the same order as before, except that the guns and mounted infantry had closed up to the infantry. But after crossing the railway the roughness of the ground added to the fatigue of the troops; moreover, doubt as to the manner in which the column was being guided had spread discouragement. The General, moving at the head of the leading battalion, constantly questioned the guide, but was as constantly assured by Sergeant Morgan that the right road was being followed, although the distance was greater than he had estimated. The column, therefore, trudged on until at length, as the first signs of dawn were beginning to appear, it reached the cross roads near Van Zyl's house, and thus was on the very ground from whence General Gatacre intended to make his assault on the Kissieberg. If the assault had been delivered at once, the ridge might have been carried and command over the Stormberg valley have been thus secured.

The Boers in and near Stormberg on the morning of the 10th December were under the command of Olivier: they consisted of about 1,700 burghers of the Bethulie, Rouxville and Smithfield commandos, with two guns and a Maxim. A detachment under Commandant Swanepoel, with one gun, held the Nek between the Kissieberg and Rooi Kop. A piquet of about fifty men was stationed on the western ridge of the former hill, and another piquet watched the north end of the vlei; the remainder of the burghers slept on the lower inner slopes of the two hills. The Boer accounts of the fight all agree in stating that Gatacre's night march was a complete surprise to them. So secure did Olivier feel in his position that on the 9th he had detached a commando of colonial rebels, amounting to some 500 or 600 men, under Grobelaar and Steinkamp, to Steynsburg to beat up more recruits in that direction. In consequence of a dispute about a gun, which was referred to President Steyn by telegram for settlement, Grobelaar had outspanned for the night some seven or eight miles away on the Stormberg-Steynsburg road, and his commando lay about a mile north-west of Roberts' farm. Sir W. Gatacre's information, therefore, as to the strength of the Boers in the Stormberg valley was accurate, their dispositions favoured the plan he had formed for a surprise, and the British assailants, notwithstanding the circuitous march, had now arrived in time, though only barely in time, at the spot for its execution. But either the chief guide did not fully comprehend the General's intentions, or he had lost his bearings, for he pointed to a kopje nearly two

<small>Boers quite unprepared for the surprise march. All circumstances favourable.</small>

296   THE WAR IN SOUTH AFRICA.

The column is taken away two miles further. En route it is surprised.

miles off, and said that that was the real place. The wearied men continued to trudge along the road, which, skirting the lower western slopes of the Kissieberg, leads to Stormberg junction. Day was breaking,* but no change was made in the formation of the troops. The infantry remained in fours, with no flankers out, and still only eight men were in front as an advance guard. The Boer piquet on the Kissieberg saw the grey thread as it wound its way slowly along the foot of the hill within effective range of the crest. A single shot echoed through the valley, and a corporal of the leading company of Irish Rifles fell dead. A rapid fire, although from but a few rifles, was then opened on the British troops at a range of about 400 yards. It was impossible to convey orders to a long column of route, thus taken at a disadvantage. Each company officer had to act on his own initiative, and as few, if any of them, knew where they were, or where was the enemy they were required to attack, confusion inevitably arose.

A confused attack on Kissieberg.

The three leading companies of the Irish Rifles, under their commanding officer, Lieut.-Colonel H. A. Eagar, front-formed, extended rapidly at right angles to the road, and dashed forward and seized the underfeature **a** (map No. 14), which faces the extreme northern spur of the Kissieberg. In pushing on towards this point, the men were much exposed to enfilade fire from their right, and a good many casualties occurred. The other five companies of the Irish Rifles and the Northumberland Fusiliers faced to the right, confronting the main ridge, against which they scrambled upwards by successive stages. The companies extended as they moved on, and gradually opened out into firing line and supports. The western face of the Kissieberg was found to be exceedingly steep and difficult to climb. A series of krantz, or perpendicular walls of rocks, barred the ascent, except at certain gaps, while between these krantz were interspersed bushes and large boulders. The company officers ordered their men to unfix bayonets, and to help each other up the rocks. The enemy's fire for the moment had ceased to be effective, as the British soldiers were more or less under cover of

---

* The sun rose at Stormberg on December 10th at 4.38 a.m. (Cape Government Railway time).

the krantz, but the clamber through the gaps in the first barrier, nearly twelve feet high, took a considerable time. On the top a halt was made to let men get their breath, and then began again the onward advance of small groups of twos and threes in the direction of the shoulder of the hill, where the burghers had managed to place a gun. The Boers' shooting from the crest now again became effective, whilst they themselves, carefully concealed, offered no target to the British rifles. The rocks and bushes made communication between the different parts of the line of the attack very difficult.

At the moment when the first shot killed the corporal, the batteries, under the command of Lieut.-Colonel H. B. Jeffreys, had rapidly moved off to the left by sub-divisions for about 1,000 yards, and then onward up the valley. There was no good position for the British guns, except the ridge 2,000 yards to the west of the Kissieberg. But the infantry's need of immediate support was too pressing to allow time for that ridge's occupation. Lieut.-Colonel Jeffreys therefore, by the direction of General Gatacre, caused the 77th battery to come into action near kopje **a**, the 74th unlimbering on the open veld to the westward. The mounted infantry continued to escort the batteries. In getting into place a gun of the 74th battery had stuck in a donga, owing to a horse being struck. It was smothered by a hail of bullets. The three drivers were almost immediately wounded, and all the rest of the team were shot down. The gun had therefore to be abandoned, part of its breech mechanism being first removed.   *Artillery come into action. A gun lost.*

Meanwhile the three companies of the Irish Rifles, which had seized kopje **a**, had made their way step by step up the northern extremity of the Kissieberg, and had struggled on to within close proximity of its crest line. The Boers from the main laager had now manned the hill, but the British artillery was bursting shells on the threatened crest, and a Boer gun which had come into action was for a time silenced. The attack had lasted about half an hour, and progress up the hill was being slowly made by the British infantry, when the five companies of the Northumberland on the right of the line were ordered to   *The course of the attack on Kissieberg.*

retire by their commanding officer. He considered that his battalion must leave the hill. The three foremost companies, who were nearly on to the summit, did not hear of this order, and, under the command of Capt. W. A. Wilmott, remained with the Irish Rifles, clinging on as they were. The fire of the enemy appeared to be slackening, and for the moment the groups of British officers and men were convinced that, if they were supported, they could gain the crest. But the withdrawal of a portion of the attacking line had made any further success impossible. Nor was that all. Seeing the five companies of the Northumberland Fusiliers falling back to the west, the batteries conceived that all the assailants were retreating, and exerted themselves to the utmost to cover the movement by their fire. The sun was now rising immediately behind the western face of the Kissieberg, so that all the upper part presented to the British guns a black target, on which neither friend nor foe could be distinguished. Thus a fatal mischance came about. A shell fused for explosion just short of the Boer defensive line burst over the foremost group of the Irish Rifles, and struck down Lieut.-Colonel Eagar, Major H. J. Seton, the second in command, Major H. L. Welman, Captain F. J. H. Bell, and three men. A conference had a few moments before been held between Lieut.-Colonel Eagar and Captain Wilmott as to the steps which should be taken to protect the men from the shells of their own gunners. The former officer had stated that as the situation of the infantry was evidently unknown to the batteries, and was masking their fire, it was necessary to fall back. Captain Wilmott, on the other hand, urged that if the men were once ordered to withdraw it would be very difficult to get them up the hill again. Colonel Eagar replied that there was no help for it. Therefore a general retirement now began from the main ridge of the Kissieberg downwards towards the rising ground a mile to the westward.

Retreat. The movement was made by rushes. The enemy had been reinforced by Swanepoel's detachment from the Nek, and coming down the slopes of the hill poured in a hot fire on the retiring infantry. The material effect of this was not great, because the Boers' shooting throughout the day was remarkably indifferent.

STORMBERG.

But under its influence a large proportion of the British troops took cover in the donga which drains the valley between the Kissieberg and the height to the westward. As an eye-witness describes it :—

> "This donga was too deep to be used as a line of defence, being six feet deep at least, with both banks washed away underneath, and with nothing for the men to stand upon to enable them to bring their rifles to bear. It was here that the trouble in the retirement commenced. The men retiring from the hill rushed to this donga for cover from the heavy rifle-fire, and on getting into it, and thinking they were safe from immediate danger, laid down and many went to sleep, and the greatest difficulty was experienced to get them on the move again and to leave the donga. Many men were by this time thoroughly done up and did not appear to care what happened to them. Many men still remained on the hill, some because they had not heard the order to retire, and some because, utterly weary, they had sunk down in sleep in the dead angle at the foot of the height."

Word-sketch of retreat.

On the extreme left the retreat to the western ridge was effected in good order, the three companies of the Irish Rifles moving back first, then the batteries in succession, the mounted infantry covering the first stage, and remaining in close touch with the enemy, until Colonel Jeffreys was able again to bring his guns into action on the spur marked **b** on the map. During this withdrawal, Major E. Perceval was severely wounded, but continued to command the 77th battery until the close of the day's operations. The artillery held this second position for over an hour, the infantry forming up in rear. The enemy now re-opened with a very long range gun, which made excellent practice, but fortunately the large majority of its shells only burst on impact, or not at all.

Stages of retreat.

At about 6 a.m. a further development began, one which might have proved fatal to the British force had the Boers then possessed the discipline and vigour in counter-attacks they acquired in the later stages of the war. Grobelaar and Steinkamp with the Burghersdorp commando had been roused by the sound of the guns from their bivouac on the Steynsburg road, and, riding back, lined the crest of the hill to the west of Bamboosberg Spruit, and thence opened a long-range fire threatening the line of retreat. Against this fresh enemy five guns of Major

New foes appear,

Perceval's battery were brought into action facing west, and with well-directed shrapnel at a range of 1,200 yards, drove back the dangerous force. The remaining gun of that battery and the 74th battery continued to check the Boers' pursuit from the eastward. Yet it was evident that the whole plan had failed, and that the troops were not in a physical condition to renew the attack on the Kissieberg. Sir W. Gatacre therefore decided to retire on Molteno, and directed the retreat on Van Zyl's farm, 1,200 yards to the north-west of D. Foster's homestead, the mounted infantry and artillery covering the retirement. The General, when he gave this order, had received no report that a considerable proportion of the infantry had failed to rejoin their proper units. He had remained with the mounted infantry throughout the action, and having seen numbers of men of both regiments crossing the valley, was under the impression that the battalions were now intact behind the western ridge. An extraordinary number of them were, in fact, still missing. The largest proportion of these had probably never left the Kissieberg. The equivalent of two companies of the Northumberland Fusiliers are known to have been taken prisoners there. Of those who had retired, some had remained in the donga. Besides all these, there was a considerable number of officers and men dispersed about the valley, and particularly in the enclosures near the northern Van Zyl's farm. It seems possible that, if the general retreat from the position at **b** could have been delayed even for a comparatively short time, some of the scattered parties of men, who were afterwards taken prisoners, might have rejoined their battalions.

The line of the retreat to Molteno was to the west of the ridge which rises between the colliery line and the Kissieberg, and so gave some shelter from the enemy's fire. The minished battalions struggled along, some of the companies being able at first to keep their formation, though, long before they arrived at Molteno, almost all had fallen into disarray. The fatigue of the men had reached its climax, and most of them could hardly keep on their feet. Whenever there was a necessary halt, not a few

STORMBERG. 301

fell down, asleep almost before they reached the ground, and it was with difficulty that they could be again roused. They suffered very much from thirst as there were no water-carts, and they had had no opportunity of drinking during many hours. The batteries of artillery remained in action at **b** for some time. They then retired alternately, and by their steadiness and the excellence of their practice held the enemy at bay.

The Boers followed in the rear sufficiently close to necessitate the abandonment of a second gun, which stuck in a water course, but there was no determined attempt at vigorous pursuit, and when once the kopjes had been passed, the mounted infantry were able to keep at a distance those of the enemy who did not linger in the valley to loot. *Boers gain a second gun, but do not seriously pursue.*

The various units of Sir W. Gatacre's force reached Molteno between 11 a.m. and 12.30 midday. In the evening they were moved as follows : *Distribution of troops after action.*

To Cypher Gat: Divisional staff and Royal artillery, by train; mounted infantry, by road.

To Sterkstroom : Northumberland Fusiliers and Royal Irish Rifles, by train.

To Bushman's Hoek : Royal engineers and two companies Royal Scots, by train.

The British casualties in the action at Stormberg were : *British losses, Dec. 10th/99.*

	Killed.	Wounded.	Missing.
Officers	—	8	13
Other Ranks	25	102	548
Total	25	110	561

Colonel Eagar, Royal Irish Rifles, died some months later of the wounds received in this action.

The casualties of the Boers were 8 killed and 26 wounded. Commandant Swanepoel afterwards died of his wounds. *Boer losses.*

Sir W. Gatacre's decision to advance on Stormberg was fully *Points to be noted.*

justified by the strategical situation. General Buller's telegram, although it left him a free hand as to time and opportunity, had suggested that operation. The plan, though bold, was sound in its design, and would have succeeded had not exceptional ill-fortune attended its execution. Several of the causes of failure stand out conspicuously in the narrative: the mistake of the guides in taking the longer route, which unduly fatigued the men; the failure to realise that the Kissieberg was within striking distance, when the cross roads near Van Zyl's farm were reached; the premature withdrawal of the five companies of one of the battalions from the attack, and the subsequent shelling of the British infantry who still clung to the hill. Without these accumulated mishaps a blow would in all probability have been struck at the enemy, such as would have had an important influence on the general situation in South Africa. Yet it cannot be held that chance was alone responsible for this miscarriage. A long night march to be followed by a night attack involves, under the most favourable circumstances, a considerable element of hazard, and it is therefore essential that every possible precaution should be taken to obviate mistakes and to ensure that the column should not, in its mission to surprise, be itself taken at a disadvantage. Careful reconnaissance by the staff of the route to be followed can, therefore, never be neglected with impunity. If a staff officer had examined beforehand the Steynsburg road, at least as far as the branch track which it was intended to follow, and if he had been made responsible for the supervision of the guides, the mistakes as to the route would in all probability have been avoided. This omission is the more remarkable in that one of the Intelligence staff, upon whom the duty of this reconnaissance would naturally have devolved, was well acquainted with the ground in the neighbourhood of Stormberg. It is perhaps doubtful whether in view of the fatigue shown by the troops on their arrival at Roberts' farm, and the uncertainty of the staff as to the situation, it was wise to persist in the enterprise. In any case, it is clear that the neglect to change the formation of the column, and to send out flank and advance guards when dawn appeared whilst the movement was being carried along a road surrounded by hills, was a dangerous and unnecessary risk. Finally, the abandonment of large detachments of infantry, when retreat was ordered, implies a serious lack of supervision both by the staff and by the officers then left in command of the battalions. Yet in weighing the responsibility for these errors, it must be borne in mind that the units composing the force had only just come together for the first time, that General, staff, and troops were all new to one another, and that the men engaged were not yet in hard condition.

CHAPTER XIX.

HALT ON THE MODDER BEFORE MAGERSFONTEIN.*

<small>Reasons for the halt on the Modder.</small>

THE Modder River battle (November 28th, Chap. XV.) had placed the 1st division within twenty miles of Kimberley. Signals were made to that town by a Naval searchlight fitted " with a flasher."† Lord Methuen ‡ halted for a short time on the banks of the Modder. Horses and men, worn out by the fighting and marching of the last six days, required rest. Reinforcements of troops and supplies were on their way to him along the lines of communication with the coast. Moreover, before he could attempt to carry out his orders to remove the non-combatant population of 8,000 Europeans and 25,000 natives from Kimberley, it was necessary to restore or replace the railway bridge which had been wrecked by the Boers. A message from Colonel Kekewich, who commanded at Kimberley, reached the General on the 4th December. It was to the effect that the town could hold out for forty days more. His fears for the immediate safety of the place thus allayed, Lord Methuen was able to concentrate his energies on the construction of the temporary (or " deviation ") bridge across the Riet. He also threw up a series of redoubts on both sides of the river to enable a small garrison to defend the bridge when the column should resume its march on Kimberley. By dint of great exertions on the part of the Royal

---

* Map No. 13 and freehand sketch.

† It was not until the 3rd December that the signals were clearly understood, and an exchange of messages properly established.

‡ Wounded at the action of the Modder on 28th, he left hospital on 29th, bu had to return there from 2nd to 6th December.

ON THE MODDER BEFORE MAGERSFONTEIN.

engineers and the infantry employed with them, the temporary bridge was completely finished by the 10th December.

After the engagement of the 28th November, Lord Methuen had reason to believe that the Boers would make their next stand at Spytfontein, twelve miles south of Kimberley. This was at first their intention, but on the 29th November a Boer council of war was held at Jacobsdal, at which two different plans of action were discussed. P. Cronje wished to take up a flank position at Jacobsdal, so as to compel the British troops to attack him, and thus diverge from their direct line for Kimberley. With the Boers so placed, if Lord Methuen had marched straight upon the town, he would have exposed himself to the danger of being cut off from his line of supply over the Modder bridge. De la Rey, on the other hand, desired to make one more effort to bar the direct road, and his scheme was eventually adopted. At first the heights of Spytfontein were chosen. Preparations for their defence were taken in hand on the afternoon of the 29th, when Cronje and the bulk of his force arrived from Jacobsdal. But De la Rey realised that if the heights of Magersfontein, which lay between Spytfontein and the river, were allowed to fall into the hands of the British, Lord Methuen could utilise them as artillery positions for a bombardment of the Spytfontein range. Under cover of this he would be able to deliver an infantry attack. De la Rey suggested that the Magersfontein heights should themselves be held as the cornerstone of the defence. His views prevailed, and the fortification of a position nearly nine miles in length was at once begun. The fight at Modder River had demonstrated the advantage of placing the main firing line so that it should just be able to graze the surface of the country over which the British had to advance. He therefore proposed to hold the ground, now to be occupied, in a similar manner. In the centre, Magersfontein Hill, a grim and rock-bound kopje, rises precipitously from the veld and dominates the plain, six miles in width, which stretches from its foot to the Modder River bridge. From this hill the Boer line extended five miles north-west to Langeberg farm along the foot of a series of kopjes, in some places sufficiently well

Boers select their position for stopping further advance.

Its nature.

defined to be marked on map No. 13, in others mere hillocks, but together forming a continuous and formidable line of defence across the railway. From the south-east of Magersfontein Hill a low scrub-covered spur, or ridge, three miles in length, runs southward to Moss Drift on the Modder. Though not of sufficient height to be fully shown upon the map, it exercised an important influence upon the course of the battle. From the river the ground rises gradually towards the heights of Magersfontein. There are two well-marked knolls upon its surface; one, equidistant between the kopjes and the railway bridge, was chosen by Lord Methuen to be his Headquarters for the coming battle; the other, about a mile to the southward of the main hill, was held by the Horse artillery battery during the engagement. The greater part of the plain was comparatively free from scrub, but in the neighbourhood of the low ridge the bush was thick enough to retard the movement of the troops, and in places it was so dense as to limit the range of vision to a few yards. Nor was the scrub the only obstacle for the assailants—two high wire fences crossed the plain; one, stretching away towards the north-east, marked the frontier of the Orange Free State; while the other ran across the trenches which guarded the centre of the Boer position. The reproduction of the freehand sketch of Magersfontein will show the strength of the ground taken up by the enemy.

Boers gather from all quarters. Their occupation of the ground.

During the twelve days which elapsed between the engagement at the Modder and the battle of Magersfontein large reinforcements reached General Cronje. These additions to his army were chiefly due to the energy of President Steyn, who ordered up every available burgher to oppose the British advance. Parties of men were summoned from the commandos watching the Basuto border; the Bloemhof and Wolmaranstad commandos, and detachments of Free Staters, were marched southward from the investment of Kimberley; and the Heilbron, Kroonstad, and Bethlehem commandos, detached from the Boer camps in Natal, increased Cronje's fighting power. Nor were the exertions of the President of the Orange Free State confined to hurrying fresh troops to the point of immediate danger, for realising that the *moral* of the Boers had been shaken by the losses they had already sustained, he went down to the laager on the 5th December, and by his fiery eloquence infused fresh life into the somewhat depressed burghers. By the 10th December the right and centre of the enemy were entrenched along the line of kopjes which runs south-east from Langeberg farm on the west to Magersfontein Hill on the east; their left held the low scrub-covered ridge which extends from Magersfontein Hill to Moss Drift on the Modder. Owing to the fact that many of the Boer field-works at Magersfontein were constructed after the battle of the 11th December, it is impossible to describe with accuracy the defences which they had thrown up before that date. On the right and centre these appear to have consisted of narrow trenches, dug about 150 yards in front of the hills. They were three or four feet in depth, and owing to the peculiar nature of the soil it was possible to make them with perpendicular sides—mere narrow slits in the ground which afforded complete protection from shrapnel fire. These trenches were not in one continuous line, but were dug along the waving foot-line of the hills, and so arranged that they flanked one another. The parapets, slightly raised above the ground, were well concealed by bushes and stones. On the Boers' left but little work had been done, and the men who held this section were largely dependent on natural cover. Cronje's dispositions were as follows: When the action of the 11th December began, the right was held by part of the Potchefstroom commando, who were soon afterwards ordered to reinforce the left wing. The works in the right centre were manned by another detachment of the Potchefstroom and part of the Fauresmith commandos; while further to the south-east the Ladybrand, Hoopstad, Kroonstad, Bloemhof, and Boshof commandos defended Magersfontein Hill. The Scandinavian corps, about sixty strong, connected the centre with the left wing, which was posted on the low ridge running southward to the river. The remainder of the Fauresmith and the Wolmaranstad commandos held the northern end of this low ridge, the centre of which was occupied by those of the Potchefstroomers who were transferred from the right wing. The south end was defended by the men of Lichtenburg, while across the Modder river near Brown's Drift was posted a detachment of 200 Jacobsdalers with a gun, under Albrecht. On the right the supervision was entrusted to A. Cronje, on the left to De la Rey, while the supreme command was vested in Piet Cronje. As regards the Boer numbers there is the usual conflict of evidence. A Boer general says that there were from 5,000 to 6,000 burghers present; an ambulance officer reckons them in all at 7,000; while two commandants estimate them at 4,000. The Boers had five field guns, distributed along their line; two pom-poms were posted on Magersfontein Hill; while three more pom-poms were allotted to the defence of the low ridge.

<small>Lord Methuen's reinforcements and detachments.</small>

By the 10th December all the reinforcements expected by Lord Methuen had gradually reached the Modder River camp. These consisted of the 2nd battalion Black Watch and the 2nd battalion Seaforth Highlanders, who, together with the 1st battalion Highland Light Infantry* and the 1st battalion Argyll and Sutherland Highlanders, composed the Highland brigade, commanded by Major-General Wauchope. The 12th Lancers, G. battery R.H.A., the 65th (Howitzer) battery R.F.A., and some details of mounted infantry, also joined the relieving column. Drafts of sailors and marines raised the strength of the Naval brigade, now under command of Captain Bearcroft, R.N., to 375 officers and men, with one 4·7-in. gun, and four 12-pr. 12-cwt. Naval guns. The latest arrival, that of the 1st battalion Gordon Highlanders, placed under Lord Methuen's command a total of about 15,000 officers and men. The lines of communication with Orange River were held by the 2nd battalion Duke of Cornwall's Light Infantry, the 2nd battalion Shropshire Light Infantry, and part of the 1st battalion Royal Munster Fusiliers, strengthened at various points by sections of P. battery R.H.A. The Royal Canadian regiment of infantry garrisoned Belmont, and a mixed force of Australians, consisting of a detachment of Victorian Mounted Rifles, and infantry com-

---

* This battalion reached the Modder battle-field on the evening of the 28th November.

ON THE MODDER BEFORE MAGERSFONTEIN. 309

panies from Victoria and South Australia, Tasmania and Western Australia, occupied Enslin.

During the halt on the Modder river small affairs had been of daily occurrence. The patrols had frequently come into collision with the enemy. On the 7th December, Prinsloo, the Free State Commandant-General, with about a thousand Boers and three guns had attacked Enslin station, which at that time (prior to the arrival of the Australians) was held by Captain H. C. Godley, with two companies of the Northamptonshire. Prinsloo did not press home the assault, and when the 12th Lancers and the 62nd battery arrived from the camp on the Modder, followed by an armoured train carrying the Seaforth Highlanders, he withdrew to Jacobsdal. Some damage was done by the enemy to the railway and telegraph lines, but this was quickly made good. *Minor engagements.*

When Lord Methuen, on the 10th December, issued orders for an advance, the information which he had been able to obtain from a reconnaissance by Major G. E. Benson, D.A.A.G., and from the reports of scouts, patrols, and strong reconnoitring parties, showed that the enemy's main line of defence ran along the foot of the hills stretching from Langeberg farm to Magersfontein Hill. It was known that the Boers had outposts on the low ridge, that they held Moss Drift, that they had detachments to the south of the river, and that near Langeberg farm and Brown's Drift were laagers of considerable extent. The General estimated the numbers opposed to him at 12,000 to 15,000 men, with six or eight guns. *Lord Methuen's information. Dec. 10th.*

Various projects for the further movement upon Kimberley had been weighed and found wanting. A purely frontal attack upon the kopjes between Langeberg and Magersfontein Hill involved the crossing of a wide extent of open and level ground, with the danger of a counter-attack by the enemy from the low ridge held by the left wing of Cronje's army. To the west of Langeberg farm the country was so waterless as to preclude any attempt in that direction. A flank march up the Modder river to Brown's Drift, and thence to Abon's Dam, about 16 miles N.E. of Jacobsdal, seemed feasible, for the British column *Plans proposed and rejected.*

would turn the works of Magersfontein and then fall upon the eastern flank of Spytfontein, the northern of the two lines of heights which lay athwart the railway between the Modder and Kimberley. But before the relieving column could thus swing clear of Magersfontein and strike off thirteen or fourteen miles to the eastward through a country cut up by wire fences, the consequent exposure of Modder River camp, with all its accumulation of stores and its newly-restored railway bridge, had to be taken into account. Lord Methuen considered its safety, and that of the line of communication along the railway to the nearest post at Honey Nest Kloof, essential to his enterprise. Now the adequate defence of the station and this section of the railway required a far larger detachment than he could spare from his division engaged in making a flank march and an attack on Spytfontein. The idea of assaulting the left flank of the Boers was discussed, but abandoned, because it was thought that the bush-covered ground would diminish the effect of the artillery and cause an undue loss of life among the infantry. Therefore, it was finally decided to carry the heights of Magersfontein, and after their occupation and entrenchment to make a turning movement against the left flank of the Spytfontein range. The tactics of Belmont were to be repeated. After a vigorous bombardment of the hill of Magersfontein in the late afternoon of the 10th, the Highland brigade was to march at night to its foot, and at dawn on the 11th attack this, the key of Cronje's position.

The plan finally chosen for Dec. 10th night attack.

Lord Methuen's orders, which are textually quoted at the end of the chapter, may be thus summarised. A preliminary bombardment of the main Boer position was fixed for the afternoon of the 10th; and to facilitate this a column, consisting of the 9th Lancers, mounted infantry, G. Battery R.H.A., the 18th, 62nd and 75th Field batteries, the 65th (Howitzer) battery, the Highland brigade, and the 2nd Yorkshire Light Infantry, was to move forward from the Modder river towards the southern end of Magersfontein Hill. The main body of infantry was to halt behind Headquarter Hill, while the 2nd Yorkshire Light Infantry was to proceed to Voetpads (or Bridle) Drift, and

ON THE MODDER BEFORE MAGERSFONTEIN.

entrench there against attack from all sides. The cavalry and mounted infantry were to cover the advance on a line from the railway to the river. After the reconnaissance they were to retire to the right of the Highland brigade, protect it, and leave a party to watch the outer flank of the artillery. Major-General Pole-Carew, with two battalions of the 9th brigade (1st battalion Northumberland Fusiliers and 2nd battalion Northampton), was to move with the 4·7-in. Naval gun, which from a position west of the railway was to co-operate with the artillery engaged in the bombardment. Major Rimington, with his Guides, was to guard the left of this column. On the following morning (the 11th December) fire was to be re-opened, care being taken that the guns were not directed against Magersfontein Hill, the point at which the Highland brigade was to break into the enemy's line. The camp on the Modder river was to be garrisoned by the half-battalion of the North Lancashire regiment, by details, and by the greater part of the Naval brigade, whose four 12-pr. guns were mounted in the works on the south side of the river. The supply column, with five days' rations, under the escort of half the Gordon Highlanders, was to move off at 4 a.m. on the 11th December, and to follow the route taken by the Highland brigade for two miles. Major-General Colvile, with the 12th Lancers, the 7th company Royal engineers, the Guards' brigade, with its Bearer company, the Field Hospitals of the Guards' and Highland brigades, and the ammunition column, by 3 a.m. on the 11th was to be 500 yards to the left rear of the ground to be occupied by the brigade division of Field artillery, *i.e.*, somewhat in rear of Headquarter Hill.

On Saturday afternoon, December 9th, Major-General Wauchope had a conversation with Lord Methuen in the hotel which was used for Headquarters. When he came out he said to Colonel Douglas, Lord Methuen's Chief Staff Officer: "I do not like the idea of this night march." Colonel Douglas urged him to see Lord Methuen again and frankly tell him so. He, however, did not go back again to Lord Methuen. The written orders for the march were received at General Wauchope's quarters at 7 a.m. on Sunday morning, December 10th. Later

Wauchope with Methuen, Dec. 9th.

Wauchope issues his orders.

in the day, Major-General Wauchope assembled the officers commanding the four battalions of his brigade, and explained to them the manner in which he proposed to carry out his mission. The brigade was to form a mass of quarter-columns, the battalions marching in the following order. The Black Watch was to lead, with the Seaforth and the Argyll and Sutherland Highlanders following in succession. The Highland Light Infantry was to close up the rear. The deployment from mass for attack was to be to the left. The Seaforth would thus be on the left of the Black Watch, the Argyll and Sutherland on the left of the Seaforth. The Highland Light Infantry was to remain in reserve.

Bombardment of Dec. 10th.

Late in the afternoon of the 10th December, the preliminary bombardment took place. The 4·7-in. gun came into action to the west of the railway, near the Ganger's Hut, two miles and a half north of Modder River bridge. The Howitzers went to a point near Headquarter Hill, the three field batteries took up a position somewhat more forward and to the east. As the artillery was brought into action the infantry was withdrawn, and the guns shelled Magersfontein Hill for two hours. At 6.30 p.m. Lord Methuen ordered the fire to cease.

Methuen sees Wauchope again.

Soon after the bombardment was over he visited General Wauchope at his quarters. Shortly afterwards he told Colonel Douglas that General Wauchope thoroughly understood his orders and appeared to be quite satisfied with the work he had to do. Though his guns had provoked no reply from the Boers, Lord Methuen felt confident that they had not only inflicted loss, but had produced considerable moral effect on the Boer commandos. This, however, was not the case. The fire had but one important result, that of warning the enemy that an attack was imminent.

ORDERS FOR ATTACK ON MAGERSFONTEIN RIDGE.

1. Enemy in occupation of kopjes to N. and N.E. of camp and also high ground between Modder and Riet rivers.

2. It is intention of G.O.C. to hold enemy on north, and to deliver an attack on southern end of Magersfontein ridge (see map). On the afternoon of 10th December the position will be

ON THE MODDER BEFORE MAGERSFONTEIN. 313

bombarded; it will be assaulted on the 11th. With this end in view three columns will be formed.

3. No. 1 Column will assemble on ground N.E. of 9th brigade camp at 3 p.m. on 10th December in following formation :— <small>No. 1 Column.</small>

> 9th Lancers.
> Mounted Infantry.
> G. Battery R.H.A.
> Brigade Division R.F.A. and Howitzer Battery.
> Highland Brigade (in mass).
> Bearer Company, Highland Brigade.
> 2nd Yorkshire Light Infantry.
> Sec. T.B., R.E.
> Balloon Sec. R.E.

The C.R.A. will arrange for a portion of the ammunition column to accompany this force.

4. The advance will be directed on the southern end of Magersfontein ridge.

5. At 3 p.m. the R.H.A., cavalry and mounted infantry will advance covering the front from railway to Modder river; the mounted infantry forming escort to R.H.A. After the reconnaissance the cavalry will withdraw to the right flank of Highland brigade and protect that flank, leaving a party to watch the left of artillery.

6. At 3.10 p.m. the remainder of the column will advance on the southern end of Magersfontein ridge, keeping well under shelter of Outpost ridge (concealed from view of enemy) in following order :

Advance Guard—half-battalion; followed at 2.30 p.m. by half-battalion, R.F.A., remainder of force (except 2nd Yorkshire L.I.) in the order of parade.

7. The R.F.A. will, when within range, open fire on the ridge, applying to G.O.C. Highland brigade for an escort.

8. The remainder of column will form up concealed to right rear of artillery in action.

9. The 2nd Yorkshire L.I. will proceed from place of assembly along the northern bank of Modder river (under guidance of

Rimington's Guides) to Bridle Drift* four miles up river, where they will entrench themselves against attack from all sides—especially from north-east to south.—Entrenching tools to be carried. Signal communication to be established (if possible) with Highland brigade, and with Modder River camp.

10. The Sec. T.B., R.E., will lay a field cable from 9th brigade camp to Highland brigade as they proceed.

11. G.O.C. will receive reports at head of main body of Highland brigade.

12. Half rations for 11th December will be carried in haversacks; and half forage for animals on them. These rations and forage not to be consumed before 11th.

13. One blanket per man will be carried (rolled by dismounted troops). Great coats will not be taken, but will be stored in tents or brigade stores, under charge of details left behind.

14. Tents will not be struck.

15. All horses will be watered immediately before starting.

No. 2 Column.

16. On the 10th December No. 2 Column, under the command of Major-General Pole-Carew, C.B., composed of 1 battalion, 9th brigade, Naval brigade (with 4.7-in. gun), and Rimington's Guides, will assemble at such hour and place as may be fixed by him, so that the column will be in position at 4 p.m. to co-operate with No. 1 Column, making a diversion against Magersfontein ridge (along the railway).

This force will remain in position on the night of 10th, and will recommence the bombardment on the morning of 11th; but the fire is *on no account to be directed on the southern end of the ridge which the infantry will be assaulting.*

No. 3 Column.

17. No. 3 Column, under command of Major-General Sir H. Colvile, K.C.M.G., C.B., composed as under, will assemble on the same ground as No. 1 Column at such hour as the commander will direct, so as to enable the column to reach 500 yards to the left rear of the R.F.A. brigade division position (of No. 1 Column) by 3 a.m. on the 11th December, where the commander will report to an officer of the Divisional Headquarter Staff sent to meet the column. A Staff Officer of No. 3 Column will accom-

* This was another name for Voetpads Drift; the latter name is used on map No. 13.

pany No. 1 Column to ascertain the position of artillery brigade division.

The orders regarding great coats, blankets, and tents (paragraphs 13 and 14) for No. 1 Column will apply to No. 3 Column.

No. 3 Column will consist of 12th Lancers, No. 7 Field Company R.E., Guards' brigade, Bearer Company Guards' brigade, Field Hospitals Guards' and Highland brigades and divisional troops, ammunition column.

18. The Supply Column (with five days' rations), escorted by half Gordon Highlanders, will assemble at the place of assembly of Nos. 1 and 3 Columns at 4 a.m. on the 11th December, and will follow the route taken by No. 1 Column for two miles, and await orders. Supply column.

19. The Divisional Signalling Officer will arrange for signalling communication being kept up between Nos. 1 and 2 Columns on the 10th December. General.

20. Outposts protecting Modder River camp will be taken over by 9th Brigade at 8 a.m. on 10th December.

21. No light is to be lit or smoking allowed from 7 p.m. on 10th to 4 a.m. on 11th.

22. During the absence of the Lieut.-General Commanding, the command at Modder River will, after departure of No. 3 Column, devolve on Major-General Pole-Carew, C.B., details of Nos. 1 and 3 Columns being attached to 9th brigade.

23. Arrangements will be made by G.O.C. Cavalry brigade for the care of all horses belonging to Nos. 1 and 3 Columns left at Modder River. Horses and men of Divisional Headquarter Staff left behind will be attached to 9th brigade.

24. If any of these orders are not understood, a Staff Officer should attend at Divisional Headquarters.

By Order,
C. W. DOUGLAS, Col., C.S.O.

Modder River, 10th December, 1899.

CHAPTER XX.

THE BATTLE OF MAGERSFONTEIN.*

<small>The 1st Division takes up assigned places, Dec. 10th, for night march.</small>

THE preliminary movements for the attack on Magersfontein Hill, the orders for which are given at the end of the last chapter, were duly executed. Major-General Wauchope's brigade spent the first part of the night of the 10th December bivouacked near the dam behind Headquarter Hill. Close to the Highlanders lay the artillery, the 9th Lancers, the detachment of New South Wales Lancers, the Balloon section, R.E., and the mounted infantry. The covering outposts were furnished by the mounted infantry and the Seaforth Highlanders. The brigade of Guards in the evening crossed the Modder and halted on its northern bank, while the 12th Lancers remained south of the river until midnight, when, though originally directed to accompany the brigade of Guards, they joined the 9th Lancers at their bivouac in accordance with a later order.

<small>Highland Brigade starts 12.30 a.m. Dec. 11th.</small>

The night was of a darkness such as might be felt. A drizzle in the afternoon had been succeeded by pouring rain, and a thunderstorm was imminent before the start was made. The ground between the bivouac and Magersfontein Hill was known to be obstructed by boulders, ant-heaps, and patches of bush. These various conditions strengthened Major-General Wauchope in his conviction that for the Highland brigade to advance in any but the most compact formation was impossible. At 12.30 a.m. he therefore marched from his bivouac in mass of quarter-columns—or in' other words in a column of thirty†

---

* See maps Nos. 13, 13(a), 13(b) and free hand sketch.

† The two companies of Seaforth Highlanders, who had been on outpost, did not accompany their battalion, but worked their way to the front later in the day.

THE BATTLE OF MAGERSFONTEIN. 317

companies, one behind the other. To minimise the chances of loss of connection during the night, the ranks were closed up as densely as possible, and each soldier was ordered to grasp the clothing of his neighbour. As an additional precaution, the left guides (*i.e.*, the non-commissioned officers on the left of each company) held ropes which ran from front to rear of the mass. At the head of the column was Major-General Wauchope with part of his staff, all afoot. The mounted officers' horses were led by grooms in rear. Major Benson, D.A.A.G., during his reconnaissances of the enemy's position, had taken the compass bearing of Magersfontein Hill, and to him was assigned the duty of guiding the troops to the foot of this kopje, towards which the march was made. On the directing flank, the brigade-major, Lt.-Colonel J. S. Ewart, continually passed up and down, having the names of the officers repeated to him in an undertone, so that he might identify the several companies, and see that they were not losing close touch.

To maintain regularity in the march occasional short halts were necessary; but at 2 a.m. there was a more serious check. The torrential rain had clogged Major Benson's compass, and he became uncertain whether the column had not trended away towards the left. Major-General Wauchope sent back for Lieutenant-Colonel Ewart. After a brief consultation, a slight change of direction to the right was made. In daylight and on a level parade ground this is a very simple matter; but in darkness and during a South African tempest, it was by no means easy. The inclination to the right was given to the column. The advance was resumed. Nothing else occurred seriously to retard progress until, just as the top of Magersfontein Hill was first made visible by the lightning, a growth of mimosa bush brought the brigade to a standstill. Major-General Wauchope, had already decided to deploy. To hasten this, he himself led the Black Watch in single file through the bush, and desired Lieutenant-Colonel Ewart to guide the remainder of the brigade round the obstruction. The three battalions in rear, easily avoiding the small patch of thorny shrubs, rejoined more quickly than had been expected, and soon fell into their proper places.

The Highland Brigade night march.

When the brigade-major reported their arrival, Major-General Wauchope issued instructions for deployment on the Black Watch, but not in the same order of battalions as he had laid down on the previous day.* The Seaforth Highlanders were now to come up on the left, the Argyll and Sutherland on the right, of the battalion of formation. Major-General Wauchope had originally intended that both the Seaforth and the Argyll and Sutherland should prolong the left of the Black Watch, each having two companies in the firing line, two in support and four in reserve. According to this design the twelve reserve companies were to have been formed in two ranks, and were to have occupied approximately the same space from flank to flank as that covered by the six companies in the firing line. The Highland Light Infantry was intended to act as the reserve to the brigade. The presumption is that he changed his plan at the last moment, in the hope of ensuring that his right should completely overlap the eastern flank of Magersfontein Hill.

4 a.m. the Boers smite the brigade in the act of deploying. The consequent rush forward.

At about 4 a.m., almost before the officers commanding battalions had issued executive orders for the deployment, a well-sustained fire from the Boer trenches a few hundred yards away, at the foot of Magersfontein Hill, was suddenly poured into the serried ranks of the Highlanders. The brigade was thus assailed at a most inopportune moment, when in the act of changing from mass of quarter-columns into fighting formation, a manœuvre which under the most favourable circumstances always requires time. To carry it out under the close range of magazine rifles was impossible. By a common impulse, such officers and men as were able to extricate themselves from the mass rushed towards the enemy. In the confusion caused by the unexpected bullets, and by the partial disintegration of the column, due to the onward dash, battalions became intermixed, and regular formation, though not discipline, was lost. Though the dull grey of early dawn nearly put a stop to all supervision, though the Major-General, while leading the two foremost companies of the Black Watch,† was almost

* See p. 312.
† These companies of this, the leading battalion of the brigade, had actually deployed when the Boers opened fire.

THE BATTLE OF MAGERSFONTEIN. 319

instantly shot dead, and no one knew who was present to assume the chief command—the crowd pushed forward. A mixed body of soldiers from various battalions succeeded in making their way to within 200 or 300 yards of the enemy. Then, unable to advance further, they flung themselves on the ground behind such scanty cover as there was, and opened fire. In the centre of the group were many of the Black Watch. Lieutenant-Colonel G. L. J. Goff, who commanded the Argyll and Sutherland, was killed, but his officers and men came up, some on the left, some on the right. Lieut.-Colonel J. W. Hughes-Hallett, in accordance with his instructions, brought the greater portion of the Seaforth towards the right. Such was, broadly speaking, the character of the movement, though all were greatly intermixed. The result was that Magersfontein Hill, originally assigned as the object to be assailed, had now an irregular line of Highlanders in the plain at its foot, lapping round its eastern extremity and spreading somewhat to the west of it. Those of the Highland Light Infantry who had not joined the men in front, extended as a reserve in rear.

The Scandinavians, posted on the level ground at the junction of the Boer left and centre, had, from the first, enfiladed the British troops. When some of the Highlanders came round the foot of the hill the opposing forces were at close quarters. The Scandinavian commando, resisting bravely, was destroyed by mixed detachments as they pressed onwards. Having thus succeeded in getting round the key of the whole position, Magersfontein Hill itself, these composite parties several times attempted to storm it. Some ninety or a hundred of the Black Watch, under Captain W. Macfarlan, made some progress up its steep slopes. A body composed of Seaforth and Black Watch, perhaps a hundred in all, under Lieut. R. S. Wilson, was also struggling upwards, as was Lieutenant E. Cox, with another party of the Seaforth. It was now daylight, and the British artillery, knowing that the Highland brigade had sustained a check, and unaware that their comrades were on the kopje, scourged the Boer position with shrapnel. Some of the

The course of the Highlanders' attempt on Magersfontein Hill.

shells burst over the assailants. Though, owing to this mischance, the rest of the stormers could not advance further, the men under Lieutenant Wilson, probably less exposed to the guns, pressed onwards till they were unfortunately taken in flank. Cronje, who had been sleeping at a farm six miles from the centre of his line, was aroused by the sound of battle, and galloping to the hill, chanced to arrive at this moment. The rifles of his escort suddenly smiting Wilson's men from an unexpected direction at short range, checked them and possibly changed the issue of the day. At the same time Boers from the northern end of their left wing, who had hurried up to fill the gap caused by the destruction of the Scandinavians, between the low ridge and the hill, opened upon Wilson's detachment from the rear. Thus assailed from two quarters at once, the attack withered away and all fell back. Some were captured; the remainder made good their retreat to the right of the brigade. The Boers, following up this success, pressed the right wing of the most advanced Highlanders in flank, and gradually drove it back.* The brigade came to a halt, and, although the greater part of the Highland Light Infantry was brought up on the right by Lt.-Colonel H. R. Kelham, no further progress could be made. The front line was now dissolved into groups of men, who lay grimly under the storm of bullets poured upon them by the well-concealed riflemen four or five hundred yards away. Then followed from time to time a series of gallant but spasmodic efforts by successive detachments, who attempted to storm as opportunity offered. Senior regimental officers led some of these; subalterns rushed forward with others, but all were equally unsuccessful. As soon as they moved they were fully exposed to a hail of lead, and after a short rush were arrested under close fire by the wire fence which ran across the central defences. Not a few as they attempted to struggle through it were caught by their clothes and accoutrements, and held there, targets for the defenders. The burghers who manned the trenches,

* An officer in the Highland brigade who took the time fixes the hour of this retirement at about 8 a.m.

THE BATTLE OF MAGERSFONTEIN.

though greatly harassed by the artillery, were therefore still able to hold their own against the troops who faced them, and the attack was brought to a complete standstill. For many hours this situation continued. The wearied soldiers remained, fasting and without water, exposed to the blazing sun of a South African midsummer's day and pinned to the ground by an unseen enemy.

The accurate and well sustained shooting of the artillery now saved the brigade from destruction. The resolute action of the cavalry and mounted infantry, of the brigade of Guards, and of the Yorkshire Light Infantry on the right, prevented the reverse from becoming a disaster for the whole division. The Naval 4·7-in. gun, under Captain Bearcroft, R.N., with two officers and 80 men, occupied the same ground as during the bombardment of the 10th, the ground, namely, on the west of the railway near the Ganger's Hut. To its right front was the Howitzer battery, while the three field batteries came into action to the north-east of Headquarter Hill, at a range of 2,000 yards. Their first target was Magersfontein Hill, on which they opened about 4.50 a.m., as soon as they could see to lay their guns, but the officers, soon realising that the Boers were holding, not the kopje itself, but trenches cut at its foot, reduced their range to 1,700 yards, with the result that the volume of the enemy's fire sensibly decreased. Half an hour later the officer commanding the artillery, Lieutenant-Colonel Hall, pushed the 18th battery to within 1,400 yards of the entrenchments, and shortly afterwards supported it with the 62nd battery. There these two batteries continued in action for the rest of the day and, thanks to a slight swell in the ground in front of the guns and to a favourable background, with exceedingly small loss. The 75th, which had been supporting the bombardment of the trenches by the other two batteries, was despatched between 9 and 10 a.m. to reinforce G. battery Royal Horse artillery, whose movements will now be recorded.

The artillery saves the brigade, and with other corps, the division.

Shortly before 4 a.m. Major-General J. M. Babington led the 12th Lancers, with G. battery and the greater part of the mounted infantry, to the eastward, hoping to turn the enemy's

Babington's mounted column on the east.

left flank. In a few minutes the sudden roar from the trenches warned him that fighting had begun, and soon afterwards his patrols were shot at from the low ridge which stretches from Magersfontein Hill to the Modder. He accordingly ordered G. battery to shell this ridge from the ground shown on the map, No. 13. In twenty minutes, the defenders had been at least temporarily silenced. About the time that G. battery opened Major-General Babington sent the 9th Lancers also eastwards, with instructions to force their way along the river to Brown's Drift and thus turn the enemy's left. Very early in the morning they reached Moss Drift, but their repeated efforts to advance further up the Modder were beaten back by musketry. While G. battery was employed against the low ridge, it became evident to Major-General Babington that the Highlanders not only had failed to carry the Magersfontein heights, but that they required instant reinforcement. He accordingly desired Major R. Bannatine-Allason, the battery commander, to move north-east over the scrubby ground, and not to come into action until he was stopped by the bullets or could get a clear view of what was going on at the front. The battery, with an escort of 12th Lancers and mounted infantry, advanced at a trot, and its commander, having obtained information from scattered Highlanders, pushed on towards the low knoll called on the map Horse Artillery Hill, the name by which it became known during the battle. Whilst the wire fence* which ran sixty or seventy yards to the south of Horse Artillery Hill was being cut to clear the way the battery came under infantry fire.† The commander, on reconnoitring the knoll in preparation for the battery, decided to run the guns up by hand and place them on the reverse slope.‡ Having taken up this situation he was able to continue in action there for twenty-four hours with the loss of only four men. The selected spot was 2,200 yards from the Boer trenches at the foot of Magersfontein Hill, and 1,400 yards from the low ridge, which was a few feet higher than Horse Artillery Hill. In consequence of the position

---

* The fence which runs north-west from Moss Drift.

† See map No. 13 (a).   ‡ See Footnote at the end of the chapter.

THE BATTLE OF MAGERSFONTEIN. 323

being on the reverse slope there was, between the hill on which the guns were, and the low ridge, "dead ground." That is to say, that no shells from the battery could reach the space which lay nearest in the valley below. Therefore, on the one hand, this could be safely occupied by protecting troops, and on the other, unless some were there, the Boers could almost without risk have assailed the battery and perhaps have carried it by surprise. Before Major Allason's arrival there were on this dead ground many of the Highland brigade. Very soon after G. battery opened fire these men were reinforced by part of two dismounted squadrons of the 12th Lancers under Lieut.-Colonel the Earl of Airlie, who passed between the guns, and by parties of mounted infantry who came up on the right under Major P. W. A. A. Milton. During the early hours of the morning, Major Allason distributed his shells over the trenches at the foot of Magersfontein Hill and along the low ridge down to the river; but on the arrival of the 75th battery R.F.A. on his left, the target was divided. From that time, the 75th ranged upon the Magersfontein trenches and the northern end of the low ridge, while the Horse artillery battery kept down the musketry from its centre and south.

At 1 a.m. the brigade of Guards fell in and moved towards its rendezvous, near the previous bivouac of the Highland brigade; the two battalions of the Coldstream were followed by the Grenadiers and the Scots Guards. Owing to the extreme darkness of the night, the storm, and difficulties similar to those experienced by Major-General Wauchope's brigade, connection was not maintained in the rear half of the column. The battalion of Scots Guards, in consequence of some confusion during the march, which they attribute to the fact that two companies of the regiment in front of them had lost connection, became detached from the column, and therefore halted till dawn. The two companies in question went on to the place ordered, but the Scots Guards marched to Headquarters, where they were detailed to act as escort to the Howitzers and Field artillery, and did not rejoin their brigade until the 12th. The three other battalions pushed on to the rendezvous which they reached

The night-march of the Guards, and their entry into the fight.

about half an hour before the Boers opened on the Highlanders. After Lord Methuen had realised that the attack had failed, he ordered Major-General Colvile to occupy the often mentioned low ridge, but to avoid committing himself to a decisive engagement. Keeping the Grenadiers as a general reserve, Major-General Colvile directed the two battalions of Coldstream, the 1st on the right, the 2nd on the left, towards Horse Artillery Hill. The 2nd battalion moved in echelon from the right with four half companies in the firing line, four half companies in support, and four companies in reserve. The 1st battalion was in much the same formation, but being on the immediately exposed flank, took the precaution of posting two companies in echelon on the right rear. As the brigade approached the low ridge it was seen that the 1st battalion was in danger of being enfiladed. The direction was accordingly changed to the right; and, as the new line of advance would necessarily carry the brigade to the south of Horse Artillery Hill and therefore connection with the Highland brigade would not be established, unless special provision for it were made, Major H. G. D. Shute was ordered to move half his company of the 2nd Coldstream to the left, to keep touch with Major-General Wauchope's right. This half-company reached Horse Artillery Hill, and passing the battery, pushed forward against the ridge about the same time as Major Milton with his mounted infantry and the dismounted 12th Lancers entered the dead ground in front of the guns. At about 6 a.m. Major-General Colvile was ordered to reinforce the right of the Highland brigade, and accordingly sent forward the 2nd battalion of the Coldstream. Several hours later he also sent two companies of the 1st battalion to strengthen this part of the line. Lt.-Colonel the Hon. A. H. Henniker-Major, who commanded the 2nd battalion of the Coldstream Guards, received urgent appeals for help from the dismounted Lancers and mounted infantry, then hotly engaged at very short range with the enemy, who were hidden behind the bush and boulders on the northern end of the low ridge. In order to enable them to retain this ground, so important because of the protection

THE BATTLE OF MAGERSFONTEIN.

its possession by infantry afforded to the two batteries on the hill behind it, he was compelled to send almost half of his battalion to their assistance. Later in the day the 12th Lancers and M.I. were withdrawn. From that time onwards, the portion of the 2nd Coldstream occupied the place hitherto held by these mounted troops, and remained there until the next morning; the rest of the 2nd Coldstream was more to the right, and like the 1st battalion, which prolonged the line towards the river, was engaged against the enemy's left wing until nightfall. During the course of the day two companies of the Grenadiers were sent up to reinforce the firing line, and to connect the 1st and 2nd battalions of the Coldstream.* Many of the Guards, the dismounted cavalry, and the mounted infantry, were fighting all day at exceedingly short range. In some cases barely 100 yards separated the skirmishers from the Boer riflemen, but Major-General Colvile had not sufficient strength to push home a decisive attack upon the ridge, even had his instructions not forbidden him to do so.

Lt.-Col. Barter and Major Little at Voetpads, Moss Drift and elsewhere.

The right bank of the Modder was guarded by the King's Own Yorkshire Light Infantry. Early in the morning their commanding officer, Lt.-Colonel C. St. L. Barter, whilst holding the works he had thrown up at Voetpads Drift, ascertained that a commando was passing along the left bank down stream towards Moss Drift, thereby threatening to turn the right of the Guards' brigade. Though the letter of his orders limited him to the defence of Voetpads Drift, he, on his own responsibility, marched up the river with five companies towards Moss Drift.† Owing to the severity of the Boer fire, the K.O.Y.L.I. failed to reach this ford; yet their presence not only frustrated the outflanking movement, but checked an intended demonstration on the left bank, and set free two of the three squadrons of the 9th Lancers, who, unable to make headway on horseback, had been fighting dismounted. Major M. O. Little, who was thus released for more suitable service, left one squadron to connect the K.O.Y.L.I. with the right of the 1st Coldstream, and led the remainder of his

* See map No. 13 (a).   † See map No. 13 (a).

regiment to the neighbourhood of Horse Artillery Hill, where they remained until ordered back to support the extreme right flank.

Fresh troops available up to 7 a.m. Dec. 11th.

Pole-Carew's dispositions.

Though the early failure of the attack had compelled Lord Methuen to throw the Guards, his reserve, into the fight almost from its beginning, a considerable number of his troops had not been engaged up to 7 a.m. Major-General R. Pole-Carew, to whom had been entrusted the double duty of guarding the camp and, without seriously committing himself, of demonstrating along the railway line, had disposed of his men in the following manner. The Headquarters of his brigade (the 9th), with the Northumberland Fusiliers and three companies of the 2nd Northamptonshire regiment, were near the railway. The other five companies of the Northampton remained in the camp, which was further protected to the north-west by outposts of the half-battalion of the Loyal North Lancashire regiment. Two companies of Royal Munster Fusiliers guarded the armoured train. Besides these, three companies of the Royal engineers and about 240 of the Naval brigade with four 12-pounder 12-cwt. Naval guns were available to man the works if necessity should arise. Close to Headquarter Hill six companies of the Scots Guards lay in rear of the field guns as their escort. A wing of the Gordon Highlanders, under Lt.-Colonel G. T. F. Downman, detached by Lord Methuen's orders from the original duty assigned to the battalion, that of convoying the transport of the division, was also at hand. On his arrival at Headquarter Hill, Lieutenant-Colonel Downman was ordered to march this half-battalion towards the extreme eastern point of Magersfontein Hill and to despatch a message to Lieutenant-Colonel F. Macbean, who was in charge of the rear wing, telling him to leave one company with the convoy and hasten with three companies to Headquarters.* When within 2,200 yards of the enemy Lieutenant-Colonel Downman extended, and in successive waves of skirmishers passed through various parties of the Highland brigade. In this formation he pressed forward until the leading line of the Gordon was within 290 paces of the Boers, when further advance became impossible, and a

Lt.-Col. Downman leads half of Gordons to support Highland brigade.

---

* This order was despatched to Lieutenant-Colonel Macbean at 7.40 a.m.

THE BATTLE OF MAGERSFONTEIN.

halt was ordered.* The supporting skirmishers also halted, and joined the groups which were nearest to them. The movement of these reinforcements across the plain attracted the enemy's attention and caused a recrudescence of his fire, which had been dying down. When the three companies of the rear half-battalion reached Headquarter Hill they were sent to report to Major-General Babington, then at Horse Artillery Hill. Finding that he was not required there, Lieutenant-Colonel Macbean rejoined the remainder of his corps. He is joined by Lt.-Col. Macbean and three more companies.

About 1 p.m. the Boers began to outflank the right and right rear of the Highland brigade. Colonel Hughes-Hallett, Seaforth Highlanders, who was on this side of the line, thereupon gave orders to the men near him, intending to throw back the flank so as to meet the threatened attack. Colonel Downman, Gordon Highlanders, who was in the centre, seeing what was Colonel Hughes-Hallett's intention, raised himself to give to those in his neighbourhood the necessary directions for its execution. He at once fell mortally wounded. The officers strove hard to effect an orderly change of front; but their signals were misconstrued by many of the rank and file, who began to retire. First the right gave way; then at about 1.30 p.m. the movement became general and, covered by a very rapid and well aimed hail of shells from the Field artillery against the works at the foot of Magersfontein Hill, nearly all the Highlanders who were immediately in front of the Boers, gradually and with considerable loss, ebbed away to the guns. The men were reformed at about 3.30 p.m. in rear of the 18th and 62nd batteries.† Some groups, however, perhaps altogether amounting to two or three hundred officers and men, held on A grave misunderstanding takes Highlanders to rear of guns.

---

* The distance is verified by Capt. W. E. Gordon, V.C., Gordon Highlanders, who, while in the leading line, fell wounded at a spot which many months later he was able to identify. Thence he paced to the Boer trench. Lt. H. E. M. Douglas, R.A.M.C., crept forward to inject morphia into various wounded officers and men at this very spot. He was awarded the V.C. for this act. This decoration was given to Capt. E. B. Towse, Gordon Highlanders, and Corporal J. Shaul, H.L.I., for gallantry during the action.

† During the battle the 18th battery fired 940 rounds, the 62nd about 1,000 rounds, the 75th, 721, G. battery R.H.A., 1,179, and the Naval 4·7-in. 73.

where they were till nightfall. As soon as Lord Methuen saw the situation, he sent forward the only formed unit that was near enough to the much dispersed troops to cover their retirement. This was that body of six companies of Scots Guards which had been detailed to act in support of the Field artillery. Passing through the broken ranks they halted about 1,500 yards from Magersfontein Hill.

Scots Guards protect dispersed Highlanders.

A lost battle.

The unfortunate incidents of the early morning had gravely compromised Lord Methuen's battle array. The attack on the key of the enemy's position, on the success of which his later combinations depended, had failed. The brigade employed in it had fallen back with heavy loss, and was for the moment not available for further employment. Of the three battalions of Guards left to Major-General Colvile, two were fully engaged in holding the right of the British line; the third, or reserve battalion, could not be withdrawn from their support. Major-General Pole-Carew's brigade was so weakened by the absence of the K.O.Y.L.I., who were keeping the enemy back at Moss Drift, and by the number of troops retained in the neighbourhood of the camp for its defence, that it could not be called upon for reinforcements. To oppose the centre of the Boer line Lord Methuen had to rely entirely upon his guns, and on the battalion of Scots Guards which formed their escort. The greater part of his cavalry was fighting dismounted in the bush on his right flank, and of other infantry immediately available he had none. Fortunately the Boers were unenterprising. After rapid shooting at the Highlanders, while they were retreating, the hostile musketry practically ceased, though against the right flank heavy bursts of spasmodic energy occasionally broke out, notably at 5.30, when for a short time it appeared as though an attack threatened Major-General Colvile's brigade. As the afternoon wore on, it became possible to withdraw the cavalry from their dismounted duties, and, although the enemy suddenly opened fire with their guns and pom-poms, these did but little damage before they were silenced by the British artillery. Yet some shells fell among the Highland brigade during its reorganisation behind the field batteries, and it was

THE BATTLE OF MAGERSFONTEIN.

found necessary to remove it to the original bivouac, which was well out of range.

At nightfall the 75th battery was transferred from Horse Artillery Hill to the left of the 18th battery. The guns of the brigade division, and of G. battery R.H.A., which was left on Horse Artillery Hill, were kept ready for instant action all night. The Scots Guards established outposts within 1,100 yards of Magersfontein Hill, and the 2nd Coldstream continued to hold the ground they had gained during the day's fighting. The mounted troops were withdrawn to the river, and such of the Guards' brigade as were not on outpost bivouacked on the field. *Arrangements for night of Dec. 11th.*

The 9th brigade were unable to play any important part in the battle. Major-General Pole-Carew, hampered by the necessity of leaving a considerable body of men to guard the camp, could only demonstrate along the railway in small force. This feint caused Cronje no anxiety, and did not prevent him from withdrawing many of the Potchefstroom commando from his right to strengthen his left during the action. The officer in charge of the balloon, despite a strong wind which impeded his operations, observed and reported this movement. He also informed Lord Methuen of the gradual trickling back of the Highlanders, and of the arrival of reinforcements for the enemy from Spytfontein and the north-east. Thanks also to the help of the balloon, the howitzer battery obtained the range of Boer ponies, concealed behind the low ridge, and accounted for more than 200 of them. *The part of 9th brigade and use of the balloon on Dec. 11th.*

The British casualties amounted in all to 22 officers and 188 other ranks killed, 46 officers and 629 other ranks wounded, and 1 officer and 62 other ranks missing. Of this total the Highland brigade lost 15 officers killed and 30 wounded, 173 other ranks killed, 529 wounded and missing. Among the battalions engaged the Black Watch suffered most severely: 7 officers were killed, and 11 wounded; 86 men were killed, and 199 wounded. The Boers are believed to have lost 87 killed and 188 wounded. *British and Boer losses.*

Soon after daylight on the 12th, Lord Methuen made a personal reconnaissance. He hoped to find that, as at Modder river, the Boers had withdrawn before dawn. His own *Dec. 12th. Lord Methuen decides to fall back to Modder.*

observations confirmed reports he had received during the night, showing that the ground was still strongly held. Major R. N. R. Reade, his intelligence officer, accompanied by a colonial scout named Harding, making his way across the battle-field, had investigated the Boer trenches, and found them occupied. A patrol from the Scots Guards had been received with many shots from the foot of Magersfontein Hill. The General then summoned his brigadiers and the Headquarter Staff to discuss the situation. Major-General Colvile suggested that the troops should continue to retain what had been gained; but Lord Methuen, agreeing with the remainder of his subordinates who took a different view, gave orders for a retirement to the Modder River camp at noon. He left the execution of the operation to Major-General Colvile.

The gathering in of the wounded.

While the dead and wounded were being gathered in, a messenger, bearing a flag of truce from the Boers, arrived at the outposts of the Scots Guards to say that the British might send ambulances for those who were lying near the foot of Magersfontein Hill. This was done, and the Royal Army Medical Corps worked side by side with the Boer doctors. For a moment this unofficial armistice was broken by the fire of a gun. The officer in charge of it had not been informed of the suspension of hostilities. A medical officer was sent with an apology, explaining the incident, and the labour of mercy proceeded unhindered.

The retreat carried out by 4 p.m. Dec. 12th/99.

When the truce was over, a rear-guard, composed of the cavalry brigade and mounted infantry, G. battery R.H.A., and the 62nd Field battery, the Guards' brigade and the Argyll and Sutherland Highlanders, was detailed to cover the retreat. The enemy's guns, which during the battle had been notably silent, sent a few shells after the column, but they were soon stopped by the batteries of the rear-guard, and by the 4·7-in. gun, which fired 50 rounds during the 12th. By 4 p.m. Lord Methuen's division, not otherwise molested, was once more collected round Modder River station.

THE BATTLE OF MAGERSFONTEIN. 331

The successful choice of the reverse slope at Horse Artillery Hill by Major Allason raises a point of considerable interest. During the war of 1870 the Germans habitually preferred the slope facing their enemy. Though as yet we have not had sufficient details as to the action of the Japanese to enable us to draw definite conclusions, it is practically certain that they will, at least at first, have followed their German instructors in this matter. Yet the two experiences, those of Magersfontein and of the greater wars, are not really in conflict. The reason of the selection of the forward slope during these was that when the battles began the two opposed artilleries were engaged against one another. The shell taking the curve of the hill was found to produce deadly effects both upon the guns, when placed on the reverse slopes, and on the limbers and wagons in rear. The target for the hostile layers against those placed on the slope nearest to them was much more difficult. Moreover, the Germans wished to be able to depend on the arm itself for the protection of its immediate front. For that purpose it was essential that the guns should be able to cover with their shells all the ground that lay before them: there must be no "dead ground." But at Magersfontein the Boer artillery was insignificant, the rifle fire exact and deadly. The circumstances therefore bore no analogy to one another, and Major Allason's judgment was unquestionably right. The infantry were not about to carry out any aggressive movement, and could without injury to the conduct of the whole operation occupy the "dead ground," and so render the position safe. Furthermore, the long array of the guns of a vast army affords very much more security for the artillery front than is given to a solitary battery which could be approached much more easily by skirmishers, so that some independent guardians were needed. It would, however, be a misfortune if this example were taken as one of general application under conditions different from those of this particular day.

CHAPTER XXI.

SIR REDVERS BULLER IN FACE OF COLENSO.*

<small>Sir Redvers, 25th Nov./99, to 6th Dec./99, in Natal.</small>

SIR REDVERS BULLER reached Durban on 25th November. He was greeted by the good news that the invaders were falling back from Mooi river, that Lord Methuen had driven the Boers from Belmont and Graspan, and that Generals French and Gatacre were holding their own at Naauwpoort and Queenstown. He spent a few days at Maritzburg in inspecting this advanced base of the Natal army, and in directing preparations for the reception of a large number of wounded. He then pushed on to Frere, reaching that place on 6th December. The enemy's raiding columns had now retired across the Tugela, and by the 9th a well-equipped British force of all three arms was concentrated at Frere.

<small>The force available for him at Frere.</small>

The mounted brigade, commanded by Colonel the Earl of Dundonald, consisted of the Royal Dragoons, 13th Hussars, Thorneycroft's and Bethune's newly-raised regiments of mounted infantry, the South African Light Horse, also only just enlisted and brought round from Cape Town, a squadron of the Imperial Light Horse, detachments of the Natal Carbineers and Natal Police, and one company of British mounted infantry. The Naval brigade, commanded by Capt. E. P. Jones, H.M.S. *Forte*, was composed of detachments (or landing parties) from H.M.S. *Terrible*, *Forte*, and *Tartar*; to it were attached the Natal Naval Volunteers; its armament consisted of two 4.7-in. and fourteen 12-pr. 12-cwt. guns. The Field artillery consisted of the 1st brigade division (7th, 14th, and 66th batteries) under Lt.-Col. H. V. Hunt, and the 2nd brigade division (64th and

* See maps Nos. 3, 4, 15, and freehand sketch.

SIR REDVERS BULLER IN FACE OF COLENSO. 333

73rd*) under Lt.-Col. L. W. Parsons. The infantry formed four brigades : the 2nd brigade, under Major-General H. J. T. Hildyard, consisting of the 2nd Royal West Surrey, 2nd Devonshire, 2nd West Yorkshire, and 2nd East Surrey ; the 4th brigade, under Major-General the Hon. N. G. Lyttelton, comprising 2nd Scottish Rifles, 3rd King's Royal Rifle Corps, 1st Durham Light Infantry, and 1st Rifle Brigade ; the 5th brigade, under Major-General A. FitzRoy Hart, composed of 1st Royal Inniskilling Fusiliers, 1st Border, 1st Connaught Rangers, and 2nd Royal Dublin Fusiliers ; the 6th brigade, under Major-General G. Barton, formed of the 2nd Royal Fusiliers, 2nd Royal Scots Fusiliers, 1st Royal Welsh Fusiliers, and 2nd Royal Irish Fusiliers. The 17th company R.E. and A. Pontoon troop were with the command.

The following table shows the approximate strength of the force :— *Tabular statement of strength.*

Arms.	Officers.	Other Ranks.	Horses, Riding & Draught.	Guns.			
				Naval. 4·7-in.	Naval 12-pr.	Field. 15-pr.	Machine.
Staff	34	137	123	—	—	—	—
Naval brigade	31	297	6	2	12	—	—
Mounted Troops	126	2,561	2,700	—	—	—	2
Royal Artillery	39	1,074	869	—	—	30	—
Royal Engineers	14	419	255	—	—	—	—
Infantry (4 brigades)	416	13,521	716	—	—	—	16
A. S. Corps	16	217	550	—	—	—	—
R. A. M. Corps	30	464	336	—	—	—	—
Total	706	18,672	5,555	2	12	30	18

Two battalions of regular infantry (the 1st Royal Dublin Fusiliers and the 2nd Somerset Light Infantry), and three Colonial corps (the Natal Royal Rifles, the Durban Light Infantry and the Imperial Light Infantry), with four Naval 12-pounders, manned by detachments from H.M.S. *Philomel* and *Forte*, and the Natal Field battery, held the line of communication with Durban. *On line of communication.*

* The 3rd battery of this brigade division had not yet arrived, having been shipwrecked on its voyage out.

Method of issuing orders.

Although Sir Redvers Buller had assumed personal command, it was arranged that, in the absence of the Headquarter staff, his orders should be issued by the divisional staff of Lieutenant-General Sir C. F. Clery, who had hitherto been the senior officer south of the Tugela.

Boers in the Natal region Dec. 6th-Dec. 14th.

In the chapter dealing with the constitution of the Boer army, it has been pointed out that any statement of the strength of a Boer force at a particular period is quite misleading, if regarded like a formal "daily state" of a European force in the field. Subject to this reservation, the aggregate strength of the original commandos, which invaded Natal on the outbreak of war, has already been assessed at 23,500, and it has been stated that Transvaal reinforcements, amounting to some 3,000 men, had subsequently been added; but this increase was reduced by the departure at the end of November of three Free State commandos to oppose Lord Methuen's advance on Kimberley. The commandos remaining in Natal were, moreover, much weakened by the practice of burghers returning to their farms to visit their families without leave, and, although some Natal Dutchmen had been commandeered to take up arms, the total Boer forces actually serving in Natal at this period did not probably much exceed 20,000 men. A detachment of 800 was at Helpmakaar,* watching the Tugela Ferry and the western frontier of Zululand, from which, throughout the middle of the month, the Boer Intelligence department expected an attack. Another detachment of 500 piqueted the river from the Tugela Ferry up to Colenso. To the west four commandos were stationed near Potgieters and Skiet's drifts, and detachments watched the intermediate crossings. The attacks of the Ladysmith garrison on Gun Hill and Surprise Hill and the destruction of the Waschbank bridge produced a considerable feeling of uneasiness at Boer Headquarters soon after Sir Redvers reached Frere. Their own official records show that there was a reluctance to detach any more burghers than were deemed absolutely necessary to the Tugela. Having regard to these facts, although no exact figures can be given, it is probable that an estimate made on 13th

* Map No. 3.

December by General Buller's Intelligence staff, that about 6,000 to 7,000 men had been concentrated under Louis Botha in the neighbourhood of Colenso, was not far from the mark. On the other hand, the Boer official telegrams of that date put the number as low as 5,000.

Botha's detachment and the Boer main army were, however, within an hour's ride of each other, and thus could readily render mutual assistance, unless an attack from the south should be combined with an exactly-timed sortie by the Ladysmith garrison. Yet the Boers had reason to fear this combination against them. The troops under Sir George White were still mobile, and the enterprises against Gun Hill and Surprise Hill, in the second week of December, had shown that both officers and men were keen to be again let slip at the enemy.* Moreover, the large number of mounted men, who, though shut up in Ladysmith, were in fact astride of the Boers' lines of communication, both with the Transvaal and with the Free State, would be likely to prove a serious danger in the event of Botha's defeat by Sir Redvers. *Close connection between Boer main army in Natal and Botha.*

Nevertheless, the task which the British commander-in-chief had decided to undertake was not an easy one. From Potgieters Drift on the west to the junction of the Tugela with Sunday's river, about 30 miles east of Colenso, a ridge of hills, broken only by narrow kloofs and dongas, line like a continuous parapet the northern bank of the former river. Westward the ridge is connected by the Brakfontein Nek with that spur of the Drakensberg which is entitled the Tabanyama Range. This was destined, a month later, to bar the advance of the relieving army on that side. The eastern flank was guarded by the lower slopes of the Biggarsberg, which run parallel to Sunday's river and fill the area lying between that stream and the Buffalo. The approaches to the beleaguered town from the south were thus covered by an immense natural redoubt. Opposite to the very centre of the front face of this redoubt lay Colenso. Behind this centre, and at right angles to the parapet, a cluster of hills was flung back to the ridge of Cæsar's Camp, *A formidable natural fortress.*

* See Volume II.

immediately to the south of Ladysmith. Through this confused mass of broken ground, so favourable to the methods of fighting of its defenders, ran the three roads which connect Colenso and Ladysmith. Of these roads the western passed over three very strong and presumably entrenched positions. The central had become by disuse impassable.* Much of the eastern was only fit for ox-wagons. Along the face of this strategic fort ran the Tugela, an admirable moat, as completely commanded by the heights on its left bank as is the ditch of a permanent work by its parapet. West of Colenso this moat was traversable by guns and wagons at only five places, *i.e.*, Robinson's, Munger's, Skiet's, Maritz, and Potgieters drifts. Of these the four first named were difficult for loaded wagons. Eastward of Colenso the only practicable drift was that by which the Weenen road crosses the river. Other fords, through which single horsemen or men on foot, breast-high, could wade, existed both to the east and to the west, but with the exception of a bridle drift near Colenso they were not marked on the maps in possession of the troops, and could only be discovered by enquiry and reconnaissance.

<small>Botha depends on mobility for holding his long line of defence.</small>

The commandos assigned to General Louis Botha for the defence of the line of the Tugela were obviously insufficient to man the whole of this immense position; yet he was able to rely on the mobility of his burghers; and on this, also, that he was so situated that his assailant would, in order to attack him anywhere, have to traverse distances greater than Botha need cover to reinforce from the centre either flank as soon as threatened. Moreover, not only did the heights he held afford a perfect view for miles over the country to the south, but the Tugela hills are precipitous and rocky as to their southern faces, while the approaches to them from the north present, as a rule, easy slopes and gentle gradients.

<small>Difficulty of finding out where the Boers were.</small>

In ascertaining the exact localities occupied by the enemy, Sir Redvers Buller was handicapped by many circumstances. A considerable space along the river could in the daytime only be approached by reconnoitrers under the close view and fire

---

* This central road, or old track, is not shown on maps 3 and 4, but is shown on map 15.

of the picked riflemen of the veld. The whole of the original Intelligence staff and the subordinate personnel of scouts and guides, organised for the Natal Field Force before the outbreak of the war, had been left locked up with the troops in Ladysmith. The nucleus of a fresh Intelligence staff had, however, been started by 2nd Lieut. A. N. Campbell, R.A., and was subsequently taken over by Mr. T. K. Murray, C.M.G., after the disbandment of his corps of scouts. The reports of Mr. Murray, who was subsequently created a K.C.M.G. for his services, as well as information sent out by runners, heliograph, and pigeon post from Ladysmith, agreed that the main body of Botha's force was concentrated immediately in front of Colenso. A reconnaissance, suggested by a Ladysmith message, dated 17th November, had been conducted by Captain H. De la P. Gough towards Potgieters drift on the 29th November, but had failed to get touch with the enemy. Intelligence scouts had, however, reported the Boer commandos at Potgieters and Skiet's drifts, and it was also known that Boer patrols were watching the intermediate crossings. It might therefore be assumed that the whole line of the river was kept under Boer observation.

It will be seen that the topographical conditions, though not at the time fully known, made it impossible to turn either flank of the great crescent of hills which barred an advance on Ladysmith. On the other hand, it seemed probable that a sudden march, eastward or westward, would find some passage of the river; and of the natural parapet beyond, unentrenched and but slightly guarded. An examination of the map, and a study of the country to the eastward, showed that a flank movement in that direction would be compelled to follow a circuitous route, and to traverse broken ground, covered with bush and exceedingly favourable to ambuscade and to surprise attacks. Sir Redvers judged that to commit troops, untrained to manœuvre over terrain of this description and hampered by many ox-wagons, to a rather long flank march in presence of a mobile enemy, would be too dangerous an enterprise. Moreover, the ground to the east was unfavourable for any sortie from Ladysmith, and in a telegram dated the 30th November, Sir George

White had definitely reported that he could give most help to the relieving force if it advanced viâ Onderbrook Spruit (*i.e.*, by the western of the two possible Colenso-Ladysmith roads) or viâ Springfield and Potgieters drift.

Sir Redvers' view of the choice open to him.

Sir Redvers thought that he must either assault the strongly entrenched position of Colenso or make a flank march to Potgieters. If that drift and the Brakfontein Nek were seized, the way would be opened to the rolling plain which lies westward of Ladysmith, between that town and the Tabanyama range. This course, though it presented difficulties of its own, was tactically by far the easier method of attempting the task before him. On the other hand, this flank movement would, for some days, expose the British line of communication with the coast.

He decides to march by Potgieters, 7th Dec./99.

A review of all these considerations led General Buller to decide in favour of the route viâ Potgieters drift, and on the 7th December he so informed Sir George White. He told him that he hoped to start on the 12th, and would probably take five days in bringing the operation to a successful conclusion. Sir George, in reply, reported by heliograph that he proposed to sally out from Ladysmith the night before the relieving force attempted its crossing of the Tugela at Potgieters, and to "work towards you as far as I can." He added: "As time is an all-important factor in co-operation, you will, I am sure, inform me of any change." On the 11th December, Sir Redvers answered that he could not be certain of his dates till his transport arrived, so that Sir George had better not try to help him until the relieving force had reached Lancer's Hill,* a point about six or seven miles west of Ladysmith, "unless you feel certain where I am." This limit was imposed by General Buller, as he was unwilling that Sir G. White's troops should be committed to a serious action against the enemy until his own army was within supporting distance. On the 12th December Sir Redvers moved the 6th brigade, accompanied by two 4·7-in. and six 12-pr. 12-cwt. Naval guns, to a camp two miles north of Chieveley, so as to cover the flank march to the west. He sent that day a despatch to the Secretary of State reporting

* See map No. 3.

SIR REDVERS BULLER IN FACE OF COLENSO.

that, after a careful reconnaissance by telescope, he had come to the conclusion that "a direct assault upon the enemy's position at Colenso would be too costly," and that he had therefore decided to "force the passage of Potgieters drift."

Only a few hours later telegrams, reporting the serious check suffered by Lord Methuen at Magersfontein, were placed in his hands. This disquieting intelligence, coupled with news of the reverse at Stormberg, in the opinion of Sir Redvers Buller, so entirely changed the situation that he no longer considered the movement by Potgieters advisable. "This operation," he told the Secretary of State, "involved the complete abandonment of my communications, and in the event of want of success, the risk that I might share the fate of Sir George White, and be cut off from Natal. I had considered that, with the enemy dispirited by the failure of their plans in the west, the risk was justifiable, but I cannot think that I ought now to take such a risk. From my point of view it will be better to lose Ladysmith altogether than to throw open Natal to the enemy."* News of Magersfontein and Stormberg changes his purpose, Dec. 13th.

Accordingly, on the 13th December he heliographed to Ladysmith: "Have been forced to change my plans; am coming through viâ Colenso and Onderbrook Spruit"; and later on the same day, in reply to an enquiry from Sir George White as to the probable date of his advance, he informed that officer: "Actual date of attack depends upon difficulties met with, probably 17th December." On receipt of these messages the commander of the Ladysmith garrison, after detailing some weak detachments to continue manning the defences, prepared the whole of the rest of his troops for fighting their way out southward under his personal command, at the moment of the attack on Colenso by the relieving army. No further notification of the date of that attack reached him until the 16th, when he was informed by the Commander-in-Chief that he had "tried Colenso yesterday and failed." The sound of very heavy artillery firing on the 15th was, it is true, heard in Ladysmith,

Informs Sir George that Dec. 17th is probable date of attack on Colenso. Sir George prepares to sally out.

* See despatch, Sir R. Buller to Secretary of State for War, dated 13th December, 1899.

but the Colenso position had been shelled by the Naval guns on the two previous days, and in face of Sir Redvers' message that the actual attack would probably be made on the 17th, there was doubt whether the firing heard on the 15th might not be merely a continuation of the preliminary bombardment. A premature sortie before the signal had been given might seriously hamper, or possibly entirely frustrate, concerted action between the two forces.

Features of Colenso position.

Map 15 and the hand sketch show that the hills facing Colenso from the north form a great amphitheatre, the western horn of which reaches down to the river near E. Robinson's farm about four miles due west of the village, the eastern horn being Hlangwhane. Immediately after completing the loop in front of the village, in which lie the road* and railway bridges, the Tugela turns sharply to the north for two miles, and then dashes north-eastward down a series of rapids through an abrupt gorge in the hills, ultimately resuming its course towards the east.

Hlangwhane.

Hlangwhane, the eastern horn of that amphitheatre, which, with its included area, formed the Boer position, lies on the southern bank of the river; and, as soon as the occupation of Chieveley by Barton's brigade denied the use of the Colenso bridges to the enemy, was for the time only accessible to the Boers by two bridle drifts near the rapids. It was not until after the Colenso fight that a bridge was thrown across the river near its junction with the Langewacht Spruit. The northern portion of the hollow of the amphitheatre is crossed from west to east by the Onderbrook Spruit. To the south of this spruit

The Colenso kopjes.

stand the Colenso kopjes, described by Sir Redvers as "four lozenge-shaped, steep-sided, hog-backed hills, each, as it is further from the river, being higher and longer than the next

Fort Wylie.

inner one."† The southernmost of these kopjes, Fort Wylie, had been used as a bridge-head by the British troops prior to their retirement from the Tugela. The Onderbrook road to Ladysmith runs north-west from the bridge across the arena of the amphitheatre and then ascends through the steep gorge of

---

* Shown on map No. 15 as the Bulwer bridge.
† Sir R. Buller's despatch, dated 17th December, 1899.

SIR REDVERS BULLER IN FACE OF COLENSO. 341

Grobelaar's Kloof, a defile of forbidding appearance. The other road and railway run north, following at first the general trend of the great bend of the Tugela, then penetrating the mass of hills and making their way eventually into the Klip valley.

In this section of the Tugela, the only crossings which seem to have been known to Sir Redvers Buller's staff, before the battle, were the two bridges, the drifts immediately above and below that over which the road passes, and the "Bridle Drift" four miles up stream to the south-east of E. Robinson's farm. There were other fords which will be mentioned later; but the river, in consequence of the difficulty of approaching it, had not been systematically reconnoitred, nor had the known drifts been tested, although, as elsewhere in South Africa, they are subject to sudden variations, here dependent on the rainfall in the Drakensberg. The Tugela is, as a rule, fordable at this season of the year at the regular passages, and has an average breadth of some 120 to 150 yards. The banks, fringed in places with low bushes, are near Colenso twenty feet above the summer level of water. Immediately to the south and to the south-west of the bridges the ground runs down to the bank in gentle glacis-like slopes, which, except where the Doornkop Spruit and a few dongas traverse them, afford no cover to troops advancing towards the river. East of the railway the terrain is more broken, and the fringe of bush country is soon reached. For this reason, but still more on account of its isolation on the south bank of the river, Hlangwhane Hill, which looked down on the Colenso kopjes, was tactically weak and has generally been regarded as the true key of the whole position. Nevertheless, even if Hlangwhane and the crossings close to Colenso had been captured, only one stage of the task would have been accomplished. Further severe fighting would have been necessary before the defiles and the very difficult country to the north-west or north could have been forced.

The river as known, and unknown to the staff.

The whole of the mountain redoubt had been elaborately fortified under the personal direction of General Louis Botha. A special commission, consisting of Generals Erasmus and Prinsloo, had been nominated by a Krijgsraad, held on 2nd December, to

The Boer defences.

supervise the defence arrangements on the Tugela, but the commission made but one inspection and Louis Botha was given practically a free hand. Three weeks of incessant labour had been spent on this task, the work being continued up to the very eve of the battle. The trenches had been constructed with remarkable ingenuity, so as to be almost invisible from the south bank. They ran for the most part along the lower slopes of the great hills on the west and across the flats round which circled the amphitheatre. The only part of these defences which caught the eye from the far side of the river were the tiers of entrenchments covering the Colenso kopjes, and especially Fort Wylie. Emplacements had been constructed in many more places than there were guns available to fill them, and, in order to ensure that the exact positions from which shells would be actually thrown should be unknown to the British commander, the guns were shifted from gun-pit to gun-pit the night before the battle.

Their occupation. The artillery at the disposal of General Botha was far less numerous than that of his opponent. On the day of the fight a 120 m/m howitzer was mounted on the crest of Vertnek (or Red Hill) on the right, a field gun being posted lower down on its south-eastern slope. Two field guns were placed in pits in proximity to the western Ladysmith road. This group of four guns was intended to command the crossings in, and near, the western salient loop of the river, including the Bridle Drift, a mile to the west of that loop. Four or five 75 m/m field guns and one or two pom-poms, posted on the Colenso kopjes, swept the bridges and drifts in front. The whole of these guns were under the command of Captain Pretorius, Transvaal Staats Artillerie. General Botha had placed his riflemen as follows:— on his right, which extended to the west of H. Robinson's farm, was stationed the Winburg commando of Free Staters under van der Merwe, supported by detachments of Ben Viljoen's Johannesburgers, and of the Middelburg commando; east of these, men of the Zoutpansberg, Swaziland, and Ermelo commandos, under the orders of Christian Botha, continued the line to the head of the western loop of the Tugela, where a donga enters the river on its left bank. The eastern face of this loop

SIR REDVERS BULLER IN FACE OF COLENSO. 343

was also manned by portions of the Ermelo, Standerton, and Middelburg corps. The ground intervening between the two re-entrants was considered to be sufficiently protected by the unfordable river in its front, save that a small detachment was posted in the building shown as "Barn" on map No. 15, thus acting as a connecting link. The centre, facing the Colenso crossings, was very strongly held. Here lay the Boksburg and Heidelberg commandos, the Johannesburg Police, and the burghers of Vryheid and Krugersdorp districts, the two last-named units being placed in the trenches along the flats immediately in front of Fort Wylie. Neither on the centre nor on the right were there any men posted to the south of the river. The story of the successive changes in the garrison of the eastern extremity of the crescent of hills, across the river on the left of the Boer position, is a curious one, and shows forcibly how much the element of chance at times influences the operations of war. From the 30th November to the 13th December, Hlangwhane, which was known to the Boers as "the Boschkop," had been occupied by part of the Wakkerstroom commando under a commandant named Dirksen. A Boer deserter informed Sir Redvers' Field Intelligence department on the 9th December that the strength of this detachment was then about 700; but the real numbers were not more than 400 to 500. The arrival of Barton's brigade at Chieveley intimidated the commando, and on the night of the 13th the burghers, against Dirksen's orders, withdrew across the river. Botha at first acquiesced in this abandonment, but Dirksen himself telegraphed to Kruger what had happened. "If we give this Kop over to the enemy," he added, "then will the battle expected at Colenso end in disaster." *The story of the Boers on Hlangwhane. 1st stage.*

The acting commandant-general, Schalk Burger, supported Dirksen's appeal,* and, as a result, a Krijgsraad was held the same evening, at which, with the concurrence of General Botha, it *2nd stage.*

* A telegram despatched by Schalk Burger to Botha on 14th December directed that "Under no circumstances must Dirksen's position be abandoned. . . . . . If this position be abandoned, all others are endangered." President Kruger telegraphed the same day to Botha, through Burger: "The Kop on the other side of the river must not be given up, for then all hope is over. . . . Fear not the enemy, but trust in God."

was unanimously resolved that Hlangwhane should be re-occupied. A fresh garrison about 800 strong, chosen by lot from the Middelburg, Ermelo, Standerton, Wakkerstroom and Zoutpansberg commandos, was therefore placed under the orders of Commandant J. J. Joubert, and moved to the hill during the night of the 14th. The burghers, on whom this duty fell, accepted it with much reluctance as they feared that they would be cut off from their main body. In a Boer official telegram dispatched during the battle of the 15th, Hlangwhane was referred to as "the dangerous position."

The Boers hide themselves and reserve their fire.

The details of the Boers' line of battle would have been difficult to discover even by the fullest reconnaissance and by the best trained Intelligence department. General Louis Botha was so sanguine of success that he had even proposed at a Krijgsraad, on 9th December, that a detachment of burghers should be sent again across the river to entice the British troops to advance against the prepared positions; but the Council held that this device was unnecessary, as the British commander was "bound to attack, and it was thought better to await the attack." The Boer commander so fully realised the advantage of reserved fire, that, giving effect to a telegram from General Piet Joubert,* he had issued stringent orders to ensure that

---

* 7.12.99. Telegram despatched by Commandant-General P. Joubert to Assistant-General Botha :—

"I cannot neglect to reiterate pointing out to you and begging you to insist sternly with the officers and men against wild firing at long and almost impossible distances. Our greatest good fortune in the Freedom war was the immediate nearness (of positions), so that the smoke from the two forces made one cloud through which our men were better enabled to defeat the enemy. It was always my endeavour as long as the enemy blustered with his guns to conceal my men as much as possible and to strengthen them in their positions till the enemy's guns were tired and they then advanced and attacked us; then and not before, when they were between their own guns and our men, the burghers sprang forwards and shot them away by batches. Now our burghers with their rapid-fire rifles begin to shoot at so great a distance, and it is much to be feared that in a fierce fight lasting a whole day, they fire away all their ammunition to no purpose without hurting the enemy, and the enemy is then able to make use of lance and sword after exhausting their ammunition. Warn your men thus and work against this error. You must also take good thought for your reserve ammunition, and its position and the way it can be brought up to firing

SIR REDVERS BULLER IN FACE OF COLENSO. 345

his men indulged in no casual shots. He made no reply whatever to a heavy bombardment maintained by the British Naval guns during the 13th and 14th December, intended to compel him to disclose his dispositions. The same system of silence was to be adopted when the real attack was delivered. Not a shot was to be fired against the British advance until he himself had given the signal by firing the great howitzer. He even hoped to be able to allow portions of the attacking columns to cross the river, and there to overwhelm them utterly by well-sustained fire at close range. The use of the Naval guns on the 13th and 14th and the accumulation at Chieveley, had convinced General Botha that a frontal attack was about to be made. Although his burghers were anxious, and even inclined to be despondent, Botha himself hoped not only to repulse the British troops, but also to envelop them with counter-attacks, from Hlangwhane on the east and the Wagon Drift on the west.

The advance of Barton's brigade on the 12th had been unopposed, and during the two following days the remainder of the Natal army was moved up to the north-west of Chieveley, and collected in a large camp on the western side of the railway, near Doornkop Spruit. It was, of course, impossible to conceal this movement from the Boer commander on the heights north of the river. *The army, in full view of the Boers, gathers for the fray.*

On the afternoon of the 14th Sir Redvers Buller, who had spent the earlier part of that day in examining the enemy's positions through a telescope, assembled his subordinate commanders and their staffs, to communicate, and personally explain to them his instructions for the operations of the following *Sir Redvers, Dec. 14th, issues his orders for attack.*

line. You know yourself how often we have already captured the English ammunition mules; do not let the same take place with ours. Now secondly, I am certain Buller will not operate against you with his whole force at once; he will place supports in his rear and again and again bring up fresh men. His cavalry will wait as far as possible, to make their attack from the rear, or to try to move round to our rear. So be on your guard. Place your supports so that at such times new forces can advance; let some one be just on some high and visible place so as to send support in time to the spot where it is required. It is bitter to lie here on my back and think and advise from such a distance, but God's Will be done, just in Heaven as on Earth. Best wishes."

day. His plan was to try to force the passage of the river by direct attack. The written orders signed by the Assistant Adjutant-General of the 2nd division were not issued until late in the evening, and did not reach the Brigadiers until about midnight. They will be found at the end of this chapter. The first paragraph of these orders appears to imply that the enemy's entrenchments were limited to the Colenso kopjes; at any rate, it is clear that the extent and strength of the Boer entrenchments westward were not then known. These kopjes were selected as the object of the main attack, and this duty was assigned to the 2nd brigade (Hildyard's). The crossing of this brigade "by the iron bridge," that is, the Bulwer bridge, was to be prepared by the fire of No. 1 brigade division Royal Field artillery, less one field battery which was replaced by six Naval guns. This artillery preparation was to be assisted by the fire of the remaining Naval guns, two 4·7-in. and four 12-pounders,* and by that of the 2nd brigade division, which was instructed to "take up a position whence it can enfilade the kopjes north of the iron bridge." This latter artillery unit was also to "act on any orders it receives from Major-General Hart."

Orders for Hart.

To Major-General Hart's brigade (the 5th) had been assigned a special rôle; it was ordered to cross the river at the "Bridle Drift, immediately west of the junction of Doornkop Spruit and the Tugela," and subsequently to move down the left bank of the river towards the Colenso kopjes. The Commander-in-Chief hoped that this supplementary crossing would be accomplished before the central attack was delivered, and that the 5th brigade would thus be able to render substantial assistance in the assault on the bridge; even if General Hart did not succeed in passing his battalions across the river, Sir Redvers anticipated that he would, in any case, be able at least to cover the left flank of the main attack by engaging the enemy on the western side.†

Orders for right flank

The right flank of the main attack was to be guarded by

* Two Naval 12-prs. had been left at Frere; the remaining two 12-prs. were placed on Shooter's Hill, at a distance of about 6,000 yards from the bridge.

† See despatch to the War Office, dated 17th December, 1899.

the 6th brigade (Barton's), less half a battalion on baggage guard duty, and the mounted brigade. Lord Dundonald, who was in command of the latter unit (the total effective strength of which was about 1,800), was instructed to detail 500 men to watch the right flank of the enemy, and 300 to cover Buller's right flank and protect the baggage. With the remainder of his brigade, and a battery detached from No. 1 brigade division, "he will," said the order, "cover the right flank of the general movement and will endeavour to take up a position on Hlangwhane Hill, whence he will enfilade the kopjes north of the iron bridge." and for watching left flank;

The 6th brigade was further charged with covering the advance of No. 1 brigade division. for 6th brigade;

The 4th brigade was directed to remain in reserve midway between the left and main attacks, ready to support either if required. for 4th brigade;

The ammunition columns and Pontoon troop were to be parked in the first line of the baggage in rear of Shooter's Hill, behind which the four Field Hospitals were also pitched. Two sections of the 17th company R.E. were attached to General Hart's brigade, the remainder of the company being allotted to General Hildyard's. The Bearer companies marched with their brigades. for ammunition columns, pontoons, hospitals, engineers, bearer companies.

Verbal instructions were given to general officers at the conference that if the Colenso kopjes were carried the force would bivouac among them on the night of the 15th.

ORDERS BY LIEUT.-GENERAL SIR FRANCIS CLERY, K.C.B.,
COMMANDING SOUTH NATAL FIELD FORCE.

Chieveley,

14th December, 1899. 10 p.m.

1. The enemy is entrenched in the kopjes north of Colenso bridge. One large camp is reported to be near the Ladysmith road, about five miles north-west of Colenso. Another large camp is reported in the hills which lie north of the Tugela in a northerly direction from Hlangwhane Hill.

2. It is the intention of the General Officer Commanding to force the passage of the Tugela to-morrow.

3. The 5th brigade will move from its present camping ground at 4.30 a.m., and march towards the Bridle Drift, immediately west of the junction of Doornkop Spruit and the Tugela. The brigade will cross at this point, and after crossing move along the left bank of the river towards the kopjes north of the iron bridge.

4. The 2nd brigade will move from its present camping ground at 4 a.m., and passing south of the present camping ground of No. 1 and No. 2 Divisional troops, will march in the direction of the iron bridge at Colenso. The brigade will cross at this point and gain possession of the kopjes north of the iron bridge.

5. The 4th brigade will advance at 4.30 a.m., to a point between Bridle Drift and the railway, so that it can support either the 5th or the 2nd brigade.

6. The 6th brigade (less a half-battalion escort to baggage) will move at 4 a.m., east of the railway in the direction of Hlangwhane Hill to a position where it can protect the right flank of the 2nd brigade, and, if necessary, support it or the mounted troops referred to later as moving towards Hlangwhane Hill.

7. The Officer Commanding mounted brigade will move at 4 a.m., with a force of 1,000 men and one battery of No. 1 brigade division in the direction of Hlangwhane Hill; he will cover the right flank of the general movement, and will endeavour to take up a position on Hlangwhane Hill, whence he will enfilade the kopjes north of the iron bridge.

The Officer Commanding mounted troops will also detail two forces of 300 and 500 men to cover the right and left flanks respectively and protect the baggage.

8. The 2nd brigade division, Royal Field artillery, will move at 4.30 a.m., following the 4th brigade, and will take up a position whence it can enfilade the kopjes north of the iron bridge. This brigade division will act on any orders it receives from Major-General Hart.

SIR REDVERS BULLER IN FACE OF COLENSO. 349

The six Naval guns (two 4·7-in. and four 12-pr.) now in position north of the 4th brigade, will advance on the right of the 2nd brigade division, Royal Field artillery.

No. 1 brigade division, Royal Field artillery (less one battery detached with mounted brigade), will move at 3.30 a.m., east of the railway and proceed under cover of the 6th brigade to a point from which it can prepare the crossing for the 2nd brigade.

The six Naval guns now encamped with No. 2 Divisional troops will accompany and act with this brigade division.

9. As soon as the troops mentioned in preceding paragraphs have moved to their positions, the remaining units and the baggage will be parked in deep formation, facing north, in five separate lines, in rear of to-day's artillery position, the right of each line resting on the railway, but leaving a space of 100 yards between the railway and the right flank of the line.

In first line (counting from the right) :—
  Ammunition column, No. 1 Divisional troops.
  6th brigade Field Hospital.
  4th brigade Field Hospital.
  Pontoon troop, Royal Engineers.
  5th brigade Field Hospital.
  2nd brigade Field Hospital.
  Ammunition column, No. 2 Divisional troops.

In second line (counting from the right) :—
  Baggage of 6th brigade.
  Baggage of 4th brigade.
  Baggage of 5th brigade.
  Baggage of 2nd brigade.

In third line (counting from the right) :—
  Baggage of mounted brigade.
  Baggage of No. 1 Divisional troops.
  Baggage of No. 2 Divisional troops.

In the fourth and fifth lines (counting from the right) :—
  Supply columns, in the same order as the Baggage columns in second and third lines.

Lieut.-Colonel J. Reeves, Royal Irish Fusiliers, will command the whole of the above details.

10. The position of the General Officer Commanding will be near the 4·7-in. guns.

The Commander Royal Engineers will send two sections 17th company, Royal Engineers, with the 5th brigade, and one section and Headquarters with the 2nd brigade.

11. Each infantry soldier will carry 150 rounds on his person, the ammunition now carried in the ox wagons of regimental transport being distributed. Infantry greatcoats will be carried in two ox wagons of regimental transport, if Brigadiers so wish; other stores will not be placed in these wagons.

12. The General Officer Commanding 6th brigade will detail a half-battalion as Baggage Guard. The two Naval guns now in position immediately south of Divisional Headquarter camp will move at 5 a.m., to the position now occupied by the 4·7-in. guns.

By Order,

B. Hamilton, Colonel,
Assistant Adjutant-General,
South Natal Field Force.

351

CHAPTER XXII.

COLENSO, DECEMBER 15TH, 1899.*

IN the cool of the early morning of December 15th, 1899, while it was yet dark,† the British troops were set in motion. The day was to prove intensely hot, a sign, at this period of the Natal summer, of the approaching rains. Captain E. P. Jones, R.N., commanding the Naval brigade, moved with two 4·7-in. and four 12-pounder guns to a site pointed out to him personally by Sir Redvers on the previous day, to the west of the railway and about 4,500 yards from Fort Wylie. From thence, at 5.20 a.m. he began to shell the kopjes on the far side of the river. For more than half an hour no reply was made and, even when the Boers opened fire, no guns appear to have been directed on Captain Jones' six pieces until about 7 a.m. These Naval guns with their escort, a company of the 2nd Scottish Rifles, remained on the same spot until the close of the action, suffering no loss. Their telescopes made it easy to see, their long range and powerful shells to silence, guns unseen by others. *The move begins. Power of the Naval guns.*

Meanwhile the larger units had begun to carry out their orders. The 14th and 66th Field batteries of No. 1 brigade division, under command of Lieut.-Colonel Hunt, and six Naval 12-pounders, under the command of Lieutenant F. C. A. Ogilvy, R.N., moved across the railway line at 3.30 a.m., accompanied by the officer commanding the whole of the Royal Artillery then in Natal, Colonel C. J. Long, who had been directed by General Buller personally to supervise the movements of these batteries. East of the railway these guns joined the 6th brigade and *The march of the 14th and 66th batteries and six Naval 12-pounders; and 6th brigade.*

---
* See maps Nos. 15 and 15(a), and freehand sketch.
† Sunrise at Colenso on 15th December is at 5 a.m.

352   THE WAR IN SOUTH AFRICA.

Dundonald and 7th battery.

advanced at 4 a.m. with that unit, northward. Lord Dundonald's brigade moved also at 4 a.m., accompanied by the 7th Field battery. The 2nd brigade, at the same hour, left camp and marched towards Colenso, followed at 4.30 a.m. by the 4th brigade.

2nd and 4th brigades.

5th brigade. 2nd brigade division.

The 5th brigade moved off at the same time. Lieut.-Colonel Parsons, commanding No. 2 brigade division, although directed by the written operation orders to follow the 4th brigade (Lyttelton) in order to enfilade the kopjes north of the iron bridge, had received verbal instructions from Sir R. Buller through Colonel Long that at least one of his batteries was to cross the river with Hart's brigade. He accordingly marched with his guns on the right rear of the 5th brigade.

Hart's instructions, guide, and map.

Major-General Hart had been provided with a tracing of a map, a Kaffir guide, and a colonist as interpreter to assist him in finding " the Bridle Drift immediately west of the junction of the Doornkop Spruit and the Tugela," by which he was to cross the river. This map was a plane-table sketch, prepared by an engineer officer shortly before the action. It was an attempt to fill into a farm survey, made for land registration, as many of the topographical features as could be seen from a distance. Unfortunately it had not been verified by any close reconnaissance of the river, and thus both the sketch and the orders were misleading. A Bridle Drift, used by natives in the dry season of the winter but uncertain in the summer, did indeed exist, although on that particular day it was unfordable. But the sketch, on which the order relied, showed the Doornkop Spruit as running into the Tugela at the western bend of the remarkable loop which that river makes to the north-west, about one mile east of E. Robinson's farm ; it showed, moreover, the Bridle Drift close to the junction of the spruit, and placed, also immediately to the west of the Drift, another loop of the river. On all three of these points the sketch was defective. Only a short but deep donga enters the river at this western end of the loop, near 2 on map No. 15. The Doornkop Spruit joins the river at the eastern, not the western bend of the loop. The Bridle Drift lies, not near to the western bend of the loop, but a mile to the westward. Finally, the Tugela makes no second loop for several miles to the westward. The effect of these topographical errors in the map, and in the written orders was further enhanced by another serious misapprehension. Major-General Hart had been informed on the previous evening that the Kaffir guide lived close to the drift where he was to cross, and could be relied on not to make any mistake about it. Unfortunately the native misunderstood his instructions, or had been given wrong instructions, for he conceived that he was intended to lead the column, not to the Bridle Drift, but to a point (marked 4 on map No. 15) close to his own kraal, at the head of and inside the loop, where, owing to the existence of rapids, the river was fordable, breast-high, by men on foot. The practicability of this drift had been personally verified by the native on the two previous nights, but no staff officer had accompanied him. Another similar foot-ford might have been found at point 6 immediately below the junction of the Doornkop Spruit with the Tugela, but the existence of neither of these fords was known to Major-General Hart or to the Headquarter staff.*

The march of Hart's (5th) brigade.

The 5th brigade marched from its parade ground in mass of quarter-columns, the battalions being arranged in the following order:—

    2nd Royal Dublin Fusiliers, commanded by Col. C. D. Cooper.
    1st Connaught Rangers, commanded by Col. L. G. Brooke.
    1st Border regiment, commanded by Col. J. H. E. Hinde.
    1st Royal Inniskilling Fusiliers, commanded by Lt.-Col. T. M. G. Thackeray.

Half of the 17th Company, R. E., under the command of Major H. H. Massy, followed in rear. A squadron of the Royal Dragoons acted as advance guard as far as Doornkop Spruit, where the cavalry moved off to the left.

Hart's intention.

The Brigadier had informed the commanding officers on the

---

* General Buller's telegram to the War Office, dated 15th December, 1899, states: "There are two fordable places in the Tugela . . . they are about two miles apart . . . . General Hart was to attack the left drift, General Hildyard the right."

previous evening that he intended the leading battalion to line the right bank of the Tugela, while the remainder crossed. After passing, the brigade was to move eastward, and attempt to close the enemy into the Colenso loop of the river.

Hart plunges into the loop.

Hart, following the directions of the Kaffir guide, led his brigade in a north-westerly direction to the first drift over the Doornkop Spruit,* and thence northward, the formation of the leading battalion being now changed to an advance in fours from the right of companies at deploying interval, the three rear battalions continuing in mass of quarter-columns. A few cavalry scouts preceded the brigade: the main body of the Royal Dragoons, under Lieut.-Colonel J. F. Burn-Murdoch, watched the left flank, his officers' patrols moving down to the river's bank, without provoking any fire. Colonel Burn-Murdoch despatched three successive gallopers to inform General Hart that these patrols reported the enemy in force on his front and left. General Hart replied that he intended to cross by the drift in front of him, and would ignore the enemy on his left, unless they attacked in strength. The column, therefore, continued to move steadily on the point, near to the western bend of the loop, where the sketch had placed the Bridle Drift. But, as the brigade was crossing a newly-ploughed mealie-field, within 300 yards of the entrance of the loop, the Brigadier riding at its head perceived that the map was misleading, and on enquiry, the Kaffir guide pointed up the loop, and stated, through the interpreter, that it was in that direction that the ford lay. Almost simultaneously

The Boer artillery opens fire, shortly after 6 a.m.

a Boer gun opened on the column from the underfeature below Grobelaar Mountain, and its shell, passing over the whole depth of the brigade, burst behind the rear battalion. A second shell, passing over the heads of the Dublin Fusiliers, fell in front of the Connaught Rangers. A third almost immediately followed and knocked over nine men of that battalion. These, the first shots from the Boer side, were fired by their artillery, in

* It is noteworthy that Major-General Hart is emphatic in asserting that "he did not cross the Doornkop Spruit." It will be understood from the explanation given in the text that he did not cross what was marked for him on the map as the spruit. The map was wrong. He crossed the spruit shown as "Doornkop Spruit" on map 15.

disobedience to the orders of Louis Botha, who had not given the signal, and hoped to entice the attack to closer range. The time was now a little after 6 a.m. The Dublin Fusiliers immediately front-formed and extended to the right; the battalions in rear were deployed to the left in single rank in quick time, and were subsequently opened out with from two to three paces interval, the enemy meanwhile continuing to shell them with shrapnel. The ground on the far side of the river presented a formidable appearance to these troops while deploying. It rose rapidly from the left bank to a line of hills, which, towards their crest, seemed steep, rugged, and inaccessible. After Hart had deployed, his brigade moved on the same point by rushes, the right half-battalions being directed on the gorge of the loop, while the left half-battalions overlapped this gorge, and were cramped by the bank on their western flank. As the brigade came near the river it was subjected to a very heavy fire from the long Boer trench to the north, occupied by the Standerton commando. The battalions were also enfiladed from trenches on the right and left. At the time it was only possible to guess from the course of the bullets where these shelter trenches were. The left half-battalions temporarily obtained a certain amount of cover from the bank of the river. The right half-battalions, when a little further on, gained for the moment some shelter from a long, narrow underfeature, towards the centre of the loop. With the exception of the 1st Border regiment, which was on the extreme left, the units rapidly intermingled. This mixture of commands was soon increased when the left half-battalions of the Dublin Fusiliers and Connaught Rangers, followed by two companies of the Border regiment, came up. They had been ordered to cross the donga, near 2 on map No. 15, and move eastward in succession in support of those in front. The passage to the flank in file of these half-battalions was carried out under a severe and accurate cross musketry fire, while the Boer guns continued to make excellent practice with shrapnel on the extended British lines. *Unseen riflemen enfilade the attack.*

As the Kaffir guide had disappeared, the actual position of the ford was unknown. Major C. R. R. McGrigor, King's Royal Rifle *The guide disappears.*

Corps, General Hart's brigade-major, had ridden up the river in search of the Bridle Drift, and, finding a spot where there appeared to be a ford, entered the river on foot, but was soon out of his depth, and was compelled to swim back to the right bank.

Hart's brigade struggles forward up the loop.

Meanwhile parties of the Connaught Rangers, the Dublin, and Inniskilling, Fusiliers, had worked their way up the loop by a series of rushes in extended order at about three to four paces interval, suffering heavy loss. Each group followed the nearest officer, irrespective of his corps, of its own volition, and worked forward, as it were, automatically, the rushes, however, varying in length, sometimes carrying the men through the group in front, sometimes not reaching it. There was very little shooting, as nothing could be seen to aim at. The enemy's fire was too heavy to allow of any combined command of the movement. Nevertheless, there was little or no confusion, and the advance continued with the steady progress of an incoming tide. Eventually a detachment of the Dublin Fusiliers, under Lieut. T. B. Ely, and Major M. G. Moore's company of the Connaught, mingled with men of other regiments, reached the kraal, about two hundred yards from the head of the loop; others of the Inniskilling, and Dublin, Fusiliers and of the Connaught Rangers pushed on to the river bank; there these handfuls of men remained for several hours, little more than one hundred yards from the Boer trenches on the far bank, but in face of the storm of bullets it was impossible to cross the river, nor were either officers or men aware that they were near a ford. The rest of the brigade, except the left half-battalion of the Inniskilling Fusiliers and one or two companies of the Border regiment who lined the river bank west of the loop, were on, or in rear of, the knoll, the cohesion of units being now almost entirely lost. The artillery and rifle fire, concentrated on the British troops from the far bank, was too continuous and accurate to permit of any further advance being attempted for the moment. The shrapnel of the two field guns, posted in emplacements on the lower ridge to the north-west, was particularly effective, and the Boer riflemen did not disclose whence their deadly shots came.

COLENSO, DECEMBER 15TH, 1899. 357

Volleys were fired from time to time by the British infantry, but comparatively little ammunition was expended. Yet, notwithstanding these trying conditions, the men clung on steadfastly, each group being well under the control of the officer nearest to them, whether of their own corps or of another.* Meantime, Parsons' batteries, the 64th and 73rd, had come into action on the right bank of the Doornkop Spruit, and were busily engaged in shelling a kraal immediately in front of the loop, and in endeavouring to silence the Boer guns. These somewhat outranged the Field artillery, and an attempt to cross over the spruit so as to come into closer action on its left bank was for the moment frustrated by a Boer shell bursting on the team of the leading gun, killing two horses, upsetting the gun, and thereby blocking the ford of this stream. On this the two batteries reopened fire from the right bank of the spruit.

Sir Redvers Buller had watched from Naval Gun Hill the original advance of the 5th brigade. As soon as he observed the movement into the loop, he despatched a galloper to order General Hart to halt; the messenger was caught in a bog and failed to reach his destination. A second officer was sent, but was unable to find the Brigadier. Finally, when the brigade had become heavily engaged, Colonel Stopford was instructed by Sir Redvers to direct Major-General Hart to retreat, and to inform him that his retirement would be covered by artillery fire. Major Cooper, A.D.C. to General Clery, conveyed orders to Lieut.-Colonel Parsons to move his guns across the spruit and divert the fire from Hart's brigade during the withdrawal. Subsequently, fearing a flank counter-attack on the left, General Buller directed Major-General Lyttelton to support the 5th brigade with two battalions of the 4th. *Sir Redvers recalls Hart.*

Major-General Barton at 4 a.m. had moved off with the 6th brigade on the east side of the railway in the following order: the 1st Royal Welsh Fusiliers, with six companies in line, each company having a sub-section in its front, and two companies *Barton's (6th) brigade marches.*

---

* In consequence of the heavy losses suffered by the commissioned ranks in previous actions all the infantry officers had been ordered to discard their swords, and for the most part carried a rifle and men's equipment.

in support; the half-battalion of the 2nd Royal Scots Fusiliers in echelon of companies on the left flank, the 2nd Royal Fusiliers in echelon of companies on the right flank, and the half-battalion 2nd Royal Irish Fusiliers in rear, at a distance of 1,500 yards from the leading battalion.* The direction of the brigade's advance was to the north-east, towards Hlangwhane Hill, in conformity with the operation orders of the previous evening.

<small>Col. Long's guns move off with Barton, then diverge.</small>
Colonel Long's guns accompanied the brigade for some distance, the field batteries leading, with the Naval guns, dragged by spans of oxen, in rear. After a time, however, the respective directions assigned by Sir R. Buller to the guns and the infantry brigade were found to diverge, and General Barton accordingly detailed two companies of the Royal Scots Fusiliers to continue with the guns as escort. At 5.30 a.m. the Brigadier halted his command, his leading battalion being then about two miles from the river.

<small>Col. Long's mission.</small>
The specific task assigned to No. 1 brigade division by the operation orders was, "to proceed to a point from which it can prepare the crossing for the 2nd brigade." Sir Redvers Buller, at the conference of the previous afternoon, had thought it desirable to supplement and anticipate this written order with verbal instructions as to the exact point at which the batteries should come into action. He had intended to convey to Colonel Long by these verbal instructions that the purposed preparation should be carried out at long range. But the impression left on the subordinate officer's mind, when he left the conference, was that medium range was meant. As he rode therefore with Lieut.-Colonel Hunt and Lieut. Ogilvy, R.N., at the head of the field artillery, now marching in battery column, Long was on the look out for a suitable position at a distance of not less than 2,000 yards and not more than 2,500 yards from Fort Wylie, the southernmost of the kopjes which had been pointed out as the brigade division's targets. Had a site between those limits been selected, the batteries would not have been seriously molested by the Boer riflemen entrenched on the far bank of

---

* The other half-battalion of the Royal Irish Fusiliers, under command of Lieut.-Col. J. Reeves, was on baggage guard. Headquarters and four companies of the 2nd Royal Scots Fusiliers were at Frere.

COLENSO, DECEMBER 15TH, 1899.

the river, and could, by superior strength, have crushed the enemy's gunners posted among the Colenso kopjes.

It was not until after 6 a.m. that Long arrived at the distance from the river at which he had intended to come into action. The batteries were still at a walk, with the Naval guns in rear, when suddenly heavy firing was heard on the left flank. It was evident that part of the British force was closely engaged. Anxious to afford immediate effective support, and deceived by the light as to his actual distance from Fort Wylie, Long ordered Hunt's brigade division to push on, and come into action at a point about eighty yards to the north of a broad and shallow donga, which runs at right angles to the railway and was just in front of his guns. Ogilvy's Naval guns were to follow with the infantry escort and to unlimber on the left of the field batteries. The ground scouts of the brigade division had by this time reached the bush, lining the south bank of the river, and had ascertained that this bank was clear of the enemy. A section of the infantry escort had also been sent forward to reconnoitre Colenso. Not a sign had been given by the Boer guns and riflemen concentrated in front of Hunt, on the far side, for the defence of the Colenso crossings. As soon as the batteries approached the spot selected by the artillery commander, it proved to be within 1,250 yards of Fort Wylie, and not much more than 1,000 yards from the Boer infantry entrenchments between that work and the river. Then Louis Botha, fearing that their further advance would intimidate his inexperienced burghers, gave the order to fire. Immediately a storm of bullets and shells burst on the British guns, both field and Naval. The Boers knew the exact range from whitewash marks on the railway fence and adjacent stones; their fire was therefore from the outset accurate.* The field batteries, led by Lieutenant-Colonel Hunt, continued to go forward at a steady trot and came into action at the chosen place in an excellent line. The limbers were taken to the rear and wagons were brought up in the ordinary manner.

_{Long brings his guns into action, after Boer guns open on Hart, *i.e.*, about 6.15 a.m.}

* In addition to the field guns on the Colenso kopjes, a heavy gun, north of them, was observed by the Naval officers of Capt. Jones', R.N., battery.

The Naval guns also come into action.

The two leading Naval guns, under Lieutenant James, R.N., had at this moment just crossed the drift of a deep donga, about 400 yards behind Hunt. The central section of the battery was still in the drift, and the rear section on the south side. The leading section, by direction of the battery commander, Lieutenant Ogilvy, moved a little to the left and opened fire against Fort Wylie. The native drivers of the ox-spans of the other four guns had bolted, and the central guns were, for the moment, jammed with their ammunition wagons in the drift, but eventually the oxen were cut loose, and the guns, together with those of the rear section, brought into action on the south side of the donga, whence they also fired on Fort Wylie. During all this delay the enemy's artillery, and in particular a pom-pom, had maintained a well-directed fire on the drift.

The batteries suffer severely.

Meanwhile, the personnel of the field batteries in the open, 400 yards in front of Ogilvy's guns, was beginning to suffer from the accurate shrapnel and rifle fire concentrated on them. The escort of " A." and " B." companies of the Royal Scots Fusiliers, under command of Captain D. H. A. Dick, extended on the immediate left of Long's guns up to the railway line; four companies of the Royal Irish Fusiliers, under Major C. R. Rogers, were sent in extended order by General Barton, two companies in advance and two in support, to aid this escort. Of these, one company halted in rear of the Royal Scots Fusiliers companies; one company remained in the donga near Ogilvy's guns, and the other two lay down about 300 yards to the right rear of the field guns. The Royal Scots Fusiliers companies* endeavoured to subdue the enemy's riflemen, but unsuccessfully. After a few minutes Colonel Long was very severely wounded. A little later Lieut.-Colonel Hunt was also wounded, and the command devolved on Major A. C. Bailward. Casualties amongst the men, especially in the centre gun detachments, were frequent. Nevertheless, the batteries continued to be served with great efficiency, the guns being worked steadily by sections with accurate eleva-

---

* The two companies of the Royal Scots Fusiliers subsequently ran short of ammunition, but a further supply was brought up to them under a heavy fire by Sergeant-Major J. Shannon, 2nd Royal Irish Fusiliers.

tion and fuse. Notwithstanding the heavy fire of the enemy, the second line ammunition wagons were brought up to the guns, and the empty wagons removed in strict conformity with regulations. The requisition, however, for further supplies for the batteries from the ammunition column three miles in rear was delayed by the death of Captain A. H. Goldie, 14th battery, and by the wounding of Captain F. A. Elton, 66th Battery. Officers and men the while, soldiers and sailors alike, fought their guns with the utmost determination, and with great effect. Fort Wylie became a mass of bursting shell and red dust, and for a time the Boer guns on the kopjes some 500 yards in rear of that work were silenced. The infantry fire of the enemy had been also greatly reduced,* but after being in action for an hour the ammunition of the British batteries began to run short, each gun having now fired from 80 to 100 rounds. Major Bailward therefore, after first obtaining Colonel Long's approval, decided to withdraw the gun detachments temporarily into the donga, and keep them under cover, pending the arrival of reinforcements of men and ammunition. *(The arrival of fresh ammunition being delayed, the gun teams are withdrawn to the donga.)*

The effective strength of the detachments was by this time reduced to an average of about four men per gun.† The remaining men were accordingly formed up and marched quietly to the donga at about 7.15 a.m. All the wounded were placed under cover in small dongas, close to the outer flanks of the batteries, but no attempt was made to disable the guns, as the officer in command only awaited fresh supplies of men and ammunition to open fire again. Captain G. F. Herbert, R.A., Colonel Long's staff officer, and an Australian officer attached to his staff, were instructed to ride at once to Sir Redvers Buller and report the situation and the needs of the batteries. *(Two messengers sent to Sir Redvers.)*

Sir Redvers had already felt some anxiety as to Long's guns, *(Sir Redvers)*

---

* Three burghers of the Krugersdorp commando, who were manning the trenches near the river, stated subsequently that it would have been impossible for them to have maintained "any sort of fire" on the infantry, if these had advanced while the guns were in action.

† Exclusive of prisoners, the 66th battery's losses throughout the day were 1 officer and 10 men killed, and 2 officers and 30 men wounded; these casualties include those incurred in the attempts to carry away the guns.

receives various reports and leaves Naval Gun Hill

as Colonel Stopford had already pointed out to him that they were not in the intended position. An aide-de-camp had been despatched to ascertain their exact situation, and, having observed the guns in action from a distance through field-glasses, that officer had reported that they were "all right and comfortable," but under a certain amount of fire. Sir Redvers' anxiety as to the guns was not relieved, and a little later he left Naval Gun Hill with the intention of seeing himself what was going on. On his way he met the Australian officer, who stated that the batteries, including the Naval guns, were all out of action, their ammunition exhausted, and every officer and man of the gun detachments killed or wounded. Shortly afterwards Captain Herbert rode up, and was understood by General Buller to confirm the previous report, with the exception that he estimated that six rounds per gun were still left. It was not until the following day that the General Commanding knew that men had been all along available to fight the guns. He had already ordered the retirement of Hart's brigade, but, until hearing of this fresh mishap, had still hoped to succeed with his main attack. The operation orders had contemplated that the fire of the whole of the Naval guns and of both brigade divisions of Royal artillery (amounting in all to 44 guns) should be concentrated on the Colenso kopjes, so as to pave the way for an attack upon them. The 2nd brigade division had been diverted to assist Hart's brigade and, conceiving from the reports now made that the 1st brigade division and six of the Naval guns were permanently out of action for the day, Sir Redvers immediately decided that the artillery left to him was insufficient and that "without guns it would be impossible to force the passage of the river." * He determined, before falling back, to make an effort to save Long's guns from what seemed to him their desperate position.

He decides to withdraw from the attack. 8 a.m.

The distribution of the troops at 8 a.m.

He came to this decision, which marks the crucial point of the action, a little before 8 a.m.† Hart's brigade was at that

* See despatch to Secretary of State, dated 17th December, 1899.

† The positions of the troops at this period of the action are given in detail on map No. 15.

moment slowly beginning to carry out the order to retire from the western loop of the river. Barton's brigade, save the two companies Royal Scots Fusiliers and the half-battalion Irish Fusiliers, which had been pushed forward to support Long's guns, had not been engaged, although, to meet any advance of the enemy from the bush near the river on the right front, the Brigadier had moved the Royal Welsh Fusiliers some 1,000 yards beyond the point where they had first halted. Neither the 2nd nor the 4th brigade had yet fired a shot. The former had been halted by Major-General Hildyard a little in front of Naval Gun Hill, with its right on the railway and its left near some kraals, awaiting the completion of the artillery preparation. Two battalions of the 4th brigade, the 2nd Scottish Rifles and the 3rd King's Royal Rifles, were lying close beside Hildyard's brigade, in rear of Captain Jones' Naval artillery. Two other battalions, 1st Rifle Brigade and 1st Durham Light Infantry, were moving in accordance with Sir R. Buller's orders to the left flank to cover the withdrawal of the 5th brigade; one company, however, of the latter battalion had been left with the Naval guns. The mounted brigade, whose proceedings will be narrated later, was advancing against Hlangwhane Hill, but no report of their progress had yet reached Sir Redvers Buller.

He himself now considered it advisable to go in person to the critical point, and ascertain by his own inspection the true facts about the guns. On his way to the front, he informed Major-General Hildyard that the attack, as originally planned, was to be given up, and instructed him to advance two of his battalions to cover the extrication of the guns, taking care not to get involved in any engagement with the enemy that could be avoided. The G.O.C., 2nd brigade, had already extended his two leading battalions, the 2nd Queen's and 2nd Devon, for the attack on the bridge, as first ordered. Both these battalions being to the west of the railway, Hildyard directed the 2nd Devon to pass through the Queen's and cross over to the east side of the line. The two battalions then advanced, the 2nd Queen's on Colenso and the Devon on

Hildyard moves 2nd brigade forward.

Long's guns, the formation adopted being columns of half companies at from fifty to eighty paces distance, the half companies being deployed in single rank, with six to eight paces interval. The 2nd East Surrey formed a second line in rear; the 2nd West Yorkshire was in third line. In this formation, the 2nd brigade moved forward across the open plain under a heavy fire, experiencing but slight loss. By 9.30 a.m. five companies of the Queen's, under the command of Major W. S. Burrell, had occupied the village of Colenso. About two sections of "C." and "G." companies of the Devon, accompanied by their battalion commander, Lieut.-Colonel G. M. Bullock, had reached the donga immediately in rear of Long's guns, the rest of that battalion being echeloned in the open, further back as a support. A little later "E." and "F." companies crossed the railway, and seized some farm buildings, close to the road near the village. Part of these were already occupied by the 2nd Queen's. Between Bullock's two foremost Devon sections and Burrell's five companies lay the companies of the Royal Scots Fusiliers, which formed the original escort to the guns, and behind them, in support, were those two other companies of R. S. Fusiliers which had been despatched by General Barton, when he observed that an attempt was being made to withdraw the field guns. To the right, and on the left rear of Bullock, four companies of Irish Fusiliers were still extended. At this time, therefore, nearly ten companies of infantry were in the firing line. Three companies of the Queen's, about seven of the Devon, two of the Irish, and two of the Scotch Fusiliers were in immediate support, and the remainder of the 2nd and 6th brigades and a battalion of the 4th brigade (the King's Royal Rifles) were near at hand in rear. During this period of the fight, Lieutenant R. E. Meyricke, Royal Engineers, of his own initiative, worked down the spruit above the Bulwer bridge to the river, and thence along its bank to the bridge, which he tested under heavy fire, and found not to be mined.

He occupies Colenso, and joins hands with Barton.

After giving his orders to General Hildyard's brigade, Sir Redvers rode forward with Lieut.-General Clery and his staff into the zone of fire, Captain M. E. Hughes, R.A.M.C., being

Sir Redvers, in zone of fire, orders Naval guns to retire.

killed, and Sir Redvers himself hit by a shrapnel bullet. On reaching that donga, where Lieutenant Ogilvy's Naval guns were still in action, General Buller ordered their retirement. Two of these guns, whose oxen had been kept at hand, went off to join the main Naval battery under Captain Jones. The remaining four were withdrawn out of range one by one with the help of artillery horses, and were eventually brought back to camp by fresh spans of oxen. This withdrawal was covered by " C." squadron of the 13th Hussars. The casualties among Ogilvy's party during the day only amounted to three men wounded, and twenty-eight oxen killed, wounded or lost.

The field guns were still in the open, beyond the further donga, under cover of which the surviving officers and men of the brigade division were lying, hoping for ammunition to enable them to resume the action. Major W. Babtie, R.A.M.C., who had volunteered to go forward to the gun line, was attending to the wounded. Captain Herbert, on his return, after his interview with the General Commanding-in-Chief, had again been despatched to the rear by Colonel Long to seek for ammunition. At his request Major W. Apsley Smith, commanding No. 1 ammunition column, ordered forward nine wagons, and to cover their advance Captain Jones, R.N., concentrated the fire of his Naval guns on Fort Wylie, but the wagons were stopped on their way by General Buller. He stops despatch of ammunition to Long's guns.

Sir Redvers, by the time he arrived at the Naval donga, had decided that it was impracticable to re-man the guns of the field batteries. Since the batteries ceased fire, Fort Wylie had been re-occupied by the enemy, and the fire therefrom, and from the neighbouring trenches, was so heavy that he considered that it was impossible that troops could live in the open by the guns. He sanctioned a series of gallant attempts being made by volunteers to withdraw them. Limber teams were collected for this purpose, in the rear donga. The first of these attempts was made by Captains Schofield and Congreve, both serving on Sir Redvers' staff, Lieut. the Hon. F. H. S. Roberts (who was acting as an extra A.D.C. to General Clery, until he could join Sir George White's staff), Corporal Nurse and others, gathered Gallant attempts to rescue guns.

from the drivers of the 66th battery. Two guns were limbered up and brought back to the rear donga under a very severe fire, but Lieutenant Roberts fell mortally wounded, and was carried into some shelter on the left flank by Major Babtie, R.A.M.C., Major W. G. Forster, R.F.A., and Captain Congreve. One of the limbers which had been brought for the guns had been reduced to a standstill by the enemy's fire. Lieutenants C. B. Schreiber and J. B. Grylls, both of the 66th battery, accompanied by Bombardier Knight and two gunners, thereupon made a valiant endeavour to assist the endangered drivers. Schreiber was shot dead, and Grylls severely wounded, but the bombardier and gunners succeeded in bringing back two wounded men.

The last effort. Later in the morning a final effort was made by Captain H. L. Reed, of the 7th Field battery, who, with three wagon-teams, came across from the eastern flank, but before the teams could reach the guns, Captain Reed was wounded and his horse killed. Of his thirteen men, one was killed and five wounded, while twelve of their horses were shot. After this failure Sir Redvers refused to allow any more volunteering to withdraw the guns.* Captain Reed, by General Buller's direction, and with the assistance of Major F. C. Cooper, A.D.C., withdrew from the rear donga the unwounded drivers and horses of No. 1 brigade division, and took them back to the wagons of the 7th Field battery. No order to retire appears to have been sent to the artillery officers and men in the front donga. A written message—"I am ordered to retire; fear that you cannot get away"—was sent by Lieut.-Col. E. O. F. Hamilton, commanding 2nd Queen's, to the donga, addressed to "O.C.R.A., or any other officer," but it did not reach an officer's hands.

The mounted brigade. Whilst the fortunes of the day had thus been proving unfavourable to the main attack, the mounted brigade had been

---

* For conspicuous gallantry displayed in the attempt to carry away the guns, the following were awarded the Victoria Cross: Captain W. N. Congreve, Rifle Brigade; Captain H. L. Reed, 7th battery R.F.A.; Captain H. N. Schofield, R.F.A.; Lieutenant the Hon. F. H. S. Roberts, King's Royal Rifle Corps (posthumous); Corporal G. E. Nurse, 66th battery R.F.A.; and Private C. Ravenhill, Royal Scots Fusiliers. For devotion to the wounded under very heavy fire, Major W. Babtie, C.M.G., Royal Army Medical Corps, also received the Victoria Cross.

endeavouring to carry out its part in the programme. The 7th battery R.F.A., according to orders, reported before daylight to Lord Dundonald. Lord Dundonald detached the Royal Dragoons to watch the left flank of the general advance, detailed Bethune's M.I. to act as baggage guard, and moved off from his rendezvous on the west side of the railway at 4 a.m. Crossing the line at the platelayer's cottage about 4.30 a.m., he advanced on Hlangwhane, employing the Composite regiment* to reconnoitre to the front and flanks.

The Commanding Officers were informed by the Brigadier that their mission was "to prevent the enemy working round on the right, to occupy Hlangwhane Mountain if possible, and to assist the main attack on Colenso by a flank fire." A little before 7 a.m., when the main body of the brigade was still about two miles from Hlangwhane, the scouts reported that the hill was held by the enemy. The 7th battery, commanded by Major C. G. Henshaw, had already come into action, at about 6 a.m., close to the right battalion of the 6th brigade, the Royal Fusiliers, on an underfeature to the north of Advance Hill, about 3,000 yards from Hlangwhane. The targets selected for the battery were at first Fort Wylie and the other Colenso kopjes, the range of the former being about 3,100 yards; but when Hlangwhane was found to be occupied by the enemy, the fire of the right section, and later on of another section, was directed on its south-western slopes at a range of from 2,400 to 2,600 yards. The mission of the mounted brigade.

Meanwhile, the Brigadier had despatched the South African Light Horse, under Lt.-Colonel the Hon. Julian Byng, to demonstrate against the southern slope of the hill, and had directed Thorneycroft's and the Composite regiment to work round by the Gomba Spruit, and to endeavour to push through the dense thorn-bush up the eastern face. The 13th Hussars were held in reserve close to Advance Hill. Deducting the horse-holders, It tries to capture Hlangwhane, but finds Boers in full possession.

---

* This regiment was made up of one squadron Natal Carbineers, a detachment of Natal Police, one squadron Imperial Light Horse, and one mounted company formed from 2nd King's Royal Rifles and Dublin Fusiliers; Major R. L. Walter, 7th Hussars, was on that day in command.

the force thus launched for the attack of Hlangwhane was somewhat less in strength than the commando defending it; the Boers were holding entrenched and well-concealed positions on the lower southern slopes of the hill, with their left flank prolonged for a considerable distance to the eastward. Lieut.-Colonel Thorneycroft's men gained ground to the north-east for about a mile, under cover of the spruit, and then moved through the bush northwards until they came in contact with the enemy at a distance of about 300 yards from the base of the hill. The two leading companies of Thorneycroft's corps still tried to push on, but they were stopped by finding that they were outflanked by Boers occupying the ridge to the eastward. The advance of the South African Light Horse against the southern spur of the hill was also checked. It was now about 7.40 a.m.

Dundonald asks for infantry support, but does not get it.

On receiving Lieut.-Colonel Thorneycroft's report that he could make no further progress, and that the enemy was outflanking him, Lord Dundonald sent "A." squadron of the 13th Hussars towards Green Hill to strengthen his right flank, and asked Major-General Barton to support his attack on Hlangwhane with some infantry. General Barton was unable to comply with this request. The Royal Fusiliers were at this moment his last reserve, and having regard to his instructions, the G.O.C., 6th brigade, did not feel justified, without the specific sanction of General Buller, in committing this battalion to what appeared to him a doubtful enterprise on intricate ground.

Sir Redvers decides that Hlangwhane would be useless without Colenso.

On receipt of this reply, Lord Dundonald directed his troops to hold on to the positions they were occupying, and reported the situation to the General Commanding-in-Chief, who now (about 10 a.m.) had left the donga and ridden over to the mission station at the cross roads between Advance Hill and Hussar Hill. There he received Lord Dundonald's and General Barton's reports; the former was of the opinion that, with the help of one or two battalions, he could carry Hlangwhane, while the latter considered that his whole brigade, including the eight companies now in the firing line by Long's guns, would be needed if the hill was to be taken. Sir Redvers decided that the

COLENSO, DECEMBER 15TH, 1899.

occupation of Hlangwhane would be useless unless he had first forced the passage of the Tugela at Colenso, and of this he had already relinquished all hope. He therefore ordered the Commander of the mounted brigade to keep his men well in hand, and not to allow them to become too closely engaged in the bush. As regards the 6th brigade, General Buller considered the Royal Fusiliers already too far forward on the right flank, and ordered that the battalion should be drawn in. Five companies of the battalion were accordingly moved to the south; the other three companies remained with the commanding officer, Lt.-Colonel C. G. Donald, in support of Thorneycroft, and were advanced to a point half a mile in front of the position of the 7th battery. General Buller now went back to the donga, and thence watched Captain Reed's effort to save Long's guns. After its failure, Sir Redvers, sending away his staff and escort, rode personally through part of the extended battalions of the 2nd brigade, and formed the opinion that the men were too exhausted with the extreme heat to be kept out all day, with the probability at nightfall of a severe fight at close quarters for the guns. He therefore decided to abandon the guns, and to withdraw the whole of his force forthwith to camp. The decision was given about 11 a.m. *(The decision 11 a.m. to abandon the guns and return to camp.)*

The retirement of the 5th brigade, which had been ordered more than three hours earlier, was now approaching completion. Lieut.-Colonel Parsons* had succeeded in moving the 64th and 73rd Field batteries across the Doornkop Spruit, somewhat higher up than the place of his first attempt; to afford the infantry better support, he advanced to a low ridge near a kraal, as close in rear of the left of the brigade as would permit of sufficient command to fire over them. Thence, at a range of 2,800 yards, the batteries searched with shell the kopjes on the north bank of the Tugela, and, assisted by the fire of Captain Jones' Naval guns, silenced the two Boer guns near the Ladysmith road, using for this purpose shrapnel with percussion fuse. Parsons' batteries were at this time only 1,200 yards from the river, and came under the rifle fire of the enemy. Their casualties were *(Parsons and Lyttelton successfully cover the retreat of Hart's brigade.)*

* See p. 357.

but slight. The 1st Rifle Brigade and the 1st Durham Light Infantry, which, under the personal command of Major-General Lyttelton, had gone to assist in covering Hart's retreat, had reached the Doornkop Spruit. The 1st Rifle Brigade and four companies of the Durham Light Infantry crossed it and opened out to six or eight paces interval on the far side, four companies of the Rifle Brigade and two of the Durham forming a firing line at a distance of about 500 yards from the river. The three remaining companies of the Durham Light Infantry lined the spruit.

The retreat down the loop.

The order to retire appears to have reached some of the units of the 5th brigade as early as 7.30 a.m., but under the heavy fire which still continued, the transmission of orders up the long salient of the loop was difficult, and the foremost detachments of the intermingled battalions did not begin to fall back until nearly 10.30 a.m. One or two small bodies of officers and men, who had reached the bank at the farthest end, never received the order, and were so absorbed in their duel across the Tugela that, failing to observe the withdrawal of their comrades until too late, they were eventually cut off and taken prisoners. The rest of the brigade retired slowly in small groups, the 1st Border regiment covering the movement. Thanks to the artillery fire of No. 2 brigade division and the presence of the two battalions of the 4th brigade, the Boers made no attempt at direct pursuit, and many of the British rank and file thought that they were engaged in a counter-march to bring them to another crossing, which their comrades had already found. Others, especially the Irish soldiers, were with difficulty induced to turn their backs on the enemy. Gradually the whole brigade, except the unlucky parties already mentioned, passed through the files of the Riflemen and Durham Light Infantry, and formed up out of range. The battalions were then marched back to camp. The men were in the best of spirits and eager for battle.

Botha orders right wing to cross river and attack Hart's brigade. They do not obey.

Louis Botha had directed that the Middelburg and Winburg commandos, who had been posted to the west of the salient loop, and had hardly fired a shot all day, should cross higher up and attack the flank of the Irish brigade as it fell back. The Free Staters, who at this period of the war were inclined to resent the control of a Transvaal Commandant, declined to take part in the enterprise. But as, irrespective of the Irish brigade, a cavalry regiment, two batteries, and two fresh battalions were available to repel any counter-attack, it was perhaps fortunate for the Boer Commandant-General that his orders were disregarded. A few Boers did actually pass the river, and were seen working round Parsons' left flank, just as Hart's rear companies came level with the guns. The work of the artillery as a covering force was then finished, and Colonel Parsons recrossed the spruit, moved somewhat to the eastward, and then again came into action for a short time. Colonel Parsons subsequently moved his brigade division further to the eastward, near Captain Jones' Naval guns and remained with them to the end of the day, till ordered by Sir Redvers Buller to return to camp. The gun of the 73rd battery, upset in Doornkop Spruit at the commencement of the attack, was retrieved by Captain H. S. White, of that battery, during the afternoon and brought back in safety.

The G.O.C. the 2nd brigade at 10 a.m. had sent written orders to his two leading battalions that they were to retreat on the Naval guns, as soon as the Field artillery had been withdrawn. Sir Redvers' order that the guns were to be abandoned, and that the force was to return to the camp of the previous night, was received by Major-General Hildyard at 11.10 a.m., and was immediately sent by him to Lieut.-Colonel Hamilton, commanding the 2nd Queen's, with instructions to pass it to Colonel Bullock, commanding the 2nd Devon on his right. Major Burrell had previously asked to be allowed to hold Colenso until nightfall, in the hope of bringing away the guns; but in face of this definite order to retire, the O.C. the 2nd Queen's felt unable to sanction his request. The same difficulty in sending such messages under modern quick-fire, which had made itself felt on the left flank, again arose. Colonel Hamilton passed the order to the officer commanding the rear half-battalion of the Devon, who received it about 12.30 p.m. and sent it on to the front companies, but it failed to reach Colonel Bullock, who, with two sections of his battalion, the remnant of the Royal

Burrell asks leave to hold Colenso and recover the guns, but the order to retire is general.

Scots Fusilier companies, and the survivors of No. 1 brigade division, was still in the donga, behind the ten guns remaining in the open.

The fate of those in the donga.

The remainder of the Devon conformed to the movement on their left. Of the infantry scattered in the donga, the curves of which hid one small party in it from another, some saw what was going on and also fell back. The retirement was carried out with coolness and precision under cover of the 2nd East Surrey, who were holding a shelter trench on the west and a donga on the east of the railway. The officers and men of the Queen's and Devon doubled back in small groups through their files.

Hildyard's (2nd) brigade, 3.30 p.m., reaches camp, except Major Pearse's half-battalion, which arrives 4 p.m.

By 2.30 p.m. the 2nd brigade, except a half-battalion of the East Surrey, was beyond the range of the enemy's guns, and by 3.30 p.m. had reached camp. This half-battalion of the East Surrey, under command of Major H. W. Pearse, remained for more than an hour in position near the platelayer's hut, hoping to cover the withdrawal of the detachments near the guns. Finally, finding that no more men fell back, and that his command was becoming isolated, Major Pearse also marched back to camp.

Gen. Lyttelton's (4th) brigade falls back, covering the rear.

Of General Lyttelton's battalions, the 1st Rifle Brigade and the Durham Light Infantry had already been drawn in from the left flank after the completion of the duty of covering Hart's brigade. The foremost of the two remaining battalions was the 3rd King's Royal Rifles. This unit, about 8.30 a.m., had advanced and extended some 800 yards in rear of Long's guns. When the general retreat was ordered, the senior officer with the battalion, Major R. C. A. B. Bewicke-Copley,* was told to furnish the outposts. He therefore held his ground. Each half company occupied a suitable knoll, with its supporting half company in rear ; the left of the battalion rested on the railway. At 2 p.m. he was directed to fall further back. On this Major Bewicke-Copley twice submitted a request to Lieut.-Colonel R. G. Buchanan-Riddell that he might be allowed to stay where he

---

* Lieut.-Colonel Buchanan-Riddell was the commanding officer of the 3rd K. R. R., but on the movement of General Lyttelton to the western flank he had assumed command of the battalions left in the centre (Scottish Rifles and King's Royal Rifles).

was, with a view to saving the guns, when dusk came. He was informed that Sir Francis Clery had issued definite instructions that the battalion must place all of the outposts further back and more to the west. The battalion accordingly retired by companies to a line in the immediate front of the camp. The Scottish Rifles on the left had covered the retirement of the 2nd brigade, and as soon as the last battalion had passed through its extended files, it also withdrew to camp.

The Naval guns under Captain Jones received the order to retire at 12.40 p.m., but as they had to send back to Shooter's Hill for their oxen, it was not until nearly 2.30 p.m. that the last gun limbered up and moved off. The central Naval battery had during the day fired 160 rounds of 4·7-in. and 600 rounds of 12-pounder ammunition. Lieutenant Ogilvy's six guns expended about 50 rounds per gun. *Captain Jones' guns withdraw from Naval Gun Hill, 2.30 p.m.*

The order to retreat reached the officer commanding the mounted troops about noon. The brigade was still hotly engaged with the enemy, and its gradual disentanglement took nearly three hours. Colonel Thorneycroft was told by Lord Dundonald to fall back slowly along the Gomba Spruit, protecting the flank of the South African Light Horse. His retreat, which was covered by the 13th Hussars and three companies of the Royal Fusiliers, was a good deal harassed by the enemy, who crept up through the bush on the east and on the north. The well-directed fire of the 7th battery checked this attempt at pursuit. Eventually, Lord Dundonald succeeded in extricating his whole force safely, except a small section of two officers and sixteen men of the South African Light Horse, who were taken prisoners. The Royal Dragoons had been recalled from the left flank by Sir Redvers Buller at noon, and were employed in conjunction with Bethune's mounted infantry in screening the retreat of the centre. *Mounted brigade retreats, fighting.*

Major-General Barton began to draw back his brigade about noon, and arrived with it in camp about 3.30 p.m. His order failed to reach the detachment of the Royal Scots Fusiliers, the survivors of which, some 38 men in all, had about noon been placed under cover in the donga behind Long's guns. After *Barton's brigade reaches camp, 3.30 p.m.*

five and a half hours fighting in the open, their ammunition, except the rounds in their magazines had been expended.

<small>Boers hesitate to take guns till Naval guns are withdrawn.</small>

But though the guns now stood unprotected on the open veld, save for the handful of gunners, Devon, and Scots Fusiliers left in the donga in rear, the Boers feared a trap, and could not at first realise their good fortune. A telegram despatched at 12.40 p.m., by Botha to Pretoria had reported that "we cannot go and fetch the guns, as the enemy command the bridge with their artillery." When the Naval battery had been withdrawn the burghers ventured across the river and made prisoners of the party in the donga, Colonel Bullock making a sturdy resistance to the last. Then the guns, with their ammunition wagons, were limbered up and taken leisurely over the river as the prizes of the fight. Lord Dundonald's brigade on its way back to camp had made a detour northward to help in stragglers, and, approaching to within 2,600 yards of Long's guns, had observed the Boers swarming round them. The 7th battery unlimbered and was about to open, when British ambulances approached the donga, and men in khaki were seen intermingled with the Boers. Under these circumstances it was judged impossible to fire, and the mounted brigade withdrew to camp, arriving there about 4.30 p.m. The 7th, Henshaw's, battery had expended 532 rounds in all.

<small>Mounted brigade sees capture, but cannot fire because of ambulances.</small>

<small>Mounted brigade reaches camp 4.30 p.m.</small>

<small>Casualties.</small>

The total casualties on the British side throughout were 74 officers and 1,065 men; of these seven officers and 136 men were killed; 47 officers and 709 men were wounded, and 20 officers and 220 men returned as prisoners or missing.* The Boer losses were six killed, one drowned, and 22 wounded, the relative smallness of these figures being largely due to their admirable system of entrenchment and to the invisibility of smokeless powder.

<small>Two views of the course of the day.</small>

The British Commander's plan for the passage of the Tugela was undoubtedly so hazardous that only the most exact sequence of the phases of its execution, as conceived by Sir R. Buller, could have brought it to a successful issue.† Imperfect know-

* For detailed casualties, see Appendix 6.

† This is Sir Redvers' own view. On the other hand Botha, after the war, said that the loss of the guns and the mistakes as to Hart's brigade deprived him of the opportunity of inflicting a ruinous defeat upon the British army. He had hoped to induce his assailants to cross the river without a shot being fired.

ledge of the topographical conditions of the problem, and of the dispositions of the enemy, combined with misapprehension of orders, sufficed to wreck it at the outset.

The gallant conduct and bearing of the regimental officers and men were conspicuous through this day of ill-fortune. The reservists, who formed from 40 to 50 per cent. of the men of the infantry battalions, displayed a battle-discipline which supported that of their younger comrades, while the newly-raised colonial corps gave a foretaste of the valuable services which such units were destined to render throughout the war. *Good points in a day of misfortune.*

The influence of the telescopes and long-ranging heavy guns of the navy has been noticed in the course of the narrative; but the subject is an important one and it was not only at Colenso that this influence was felt. It will be more convenient to deal with the general question when other instances of the same kind have been recorded. *The heavy Naval guns and telescopes.*

CHAPTER XXIII.

LORD ROBERTS' APPOINTMENT TO THE COMMAND IN SOUTH AFRICA.

<small>Realisation at home of the magnitude of the task before the country.</small>

AFTER three reverses at Stormberg, Magersfontein and Colenso, it was clear to all that forces far larger than had been estimated would be now required for the war. Much had already been done before the news of Colenso arrived. Another division—the 5th—prepared at home early in November for service in South Africa, was due in a few days' time at Cape Town. A sixth division had been mobilised at the end of November and was on the point of embarkation,* and the mobilisation of a seventh had been ordered as soon as the news of Stormberg and Magersfontein had reached England. Yet there was cause for anxiety. Until the 5th division actually landed, not a man was available to be sent forward to reinforce either Lord Methuen on the Modder, or the troops under Sir R. Buller's immediate command facing the Tugela. After Stormberg, Sir W. Gatacre had been strengthened with the 1st Derbyshire from the lines of communication. He had now a weak brigade to cover all the eastern province, from Queenstown northwards. Lt.-General French had, it is true, successfully checked the Boer advance into the Colesberg district, but his success had been due to skilful tactics and audacity, not to any superiority in strength.

---

* The despatch of a 6th division to South Africa had been offered to, and accepted by, Sir R. Buller. His telegram is dated 1st December, 1899. He wished this division to arrive in Cape Colony on 1st January, by which date he then hoped to begin his advance into the Free State by Bethulie.

The true strategy for the enemy would be to assume the offensive, and, using his superior mobility, attack the lines of communication with the coast of one or more of the three British columns in Cape Colony, each of which was in fact in a sense isolated. Bold raids executed for this purpose would have probably secured the active support of a large number of disaffected colonists, whose loyalty had been seriously impaired by the recent victories of their kinsmen. The attitude of many in the districts through which the Cape lines of communication passed was already very unsatisfactory.

Danger of possible Boer offence.

Nor was this all: for the moment Sir R. Buller thought that, by direct order of the Cabinet, the 5th division had been assigned to the task of relieving Kimberley,* and he judged that without reinforcements the relief of Ladysmith was impracticable. Late, therefore, in the evening of the 15th December, when the work of that exhausting and disheartening day was drawing to a close, he telegraphed in the following terms to the Secretary of State for War :—

Dec. 15th, after Colenso Buller sends message home, "I ought to let Ladysmith go."

"My failure to-day raises a serious question. I do not think I am now strong enough to relieve White. Colenso is a fortress, which I think, if not taken on a rush, could only be taken by a siege. There is no water within eight miles of the point of attack, and in this weather that exhausts infantry. The place is fully entrenched. I do not think either a Boer or a gun was seen by us all day, yet the fire brought to bear was very heavy. Our infantry were quite willing to fight, but were absolutely exhausted by the intense heat. My view is that I ought to let Ladysmith go, and occupy good positions for the defence of South Natal, and let time help us. But that is a step on which I ought to consult you. I consider we were in face of 20,000 men to-day. They had the advantage both in arms and in position. They admit they suffered severely, but my men have not seen a dead Boer, and that dispirits them. My losses have not been very heavy. I could have made them much heavier, but the result would have been the same. The moment I failed to get in with a rush, I was beat. I now feel that I cannot say I can relieve Ladysmith with my available force, and the best thing I can suggest is that I should occupy defensive positions, and fight it out in a country better suited to our tactics."

* On 14th December Lord Lansdowne had telegraphed to Sir F. Forestier-Walker : "On arrival, Warren is to be sent immediately to assume command of the forces under Methuen. Buller will be informed of this by telegraph." This telegram did not prescribe the disposal of the 5th division, but that of Lt.-General Sir C. Warren, its commander.

Sir R. Buller's arrangements for Natal;

In pursuance of this policy Sir R. Buller sent Sir G. White, next morning, a cipher message, which, with the reply, will be recorded in another chapter.* He also directed the Natal line of communication staff to select, on the route Eshowe-Greytown-Estcourt, positions for camps, which the Natal army could occupy "until the weather is cooler." As regards the western theatre of war, he was more sanguine. On receiving the news of the repulse at Magersfontein he had, it is true, at first considered that, if the British troops remained on the Riet, they might be enveloped by Cronje's force, with disastrous results. He sent instructions, therefore, to Forestier-Walker that Lord Methuen must be told either to attack Cronje again or to fall back at once on the Orange river. This order was received with dismay by Lord Methuen, for, after consultation with his brigadiers, he was convinced that, until reinforcements arrived, his force was not in a fit state to resume the offensive. He prepared to fall back. But in a telegram, dated 14th December, Sir F. Forestier-Walker urged Sir Redvers to support Methuen with the 5th division† and with a brigade of cavalry from Naauwpoort, so as to enable him promptly to relieve Kimberley. He added: "Methuen reports his force in safe position, and well supplied. His communications are held by detachments posted at no great distance apart, and can be further protected by mounted troops. The effect of retirement upon the spirit of Methuen's force after such hard fighting, and upon the general military and political situation, appears to me to justify my placing this alternative before you." Forestier-Walker's proposal was immediately accepted by Sir Redvers, with the exception that he forbad the reduction of French's strength at Naauwpoort. A telegram to that effect had been despatched from Headquarters at Chieveley to the General Officer Commanding Cape Colony the evening before the day of Colenso.

for the western theatre of war.

---

* See Vol. II. Siege of Ladysmith.

† Sir R. Buller had directed, on 9th December, that a brigade and a battery of this division should be sent to East London to reinforce General Gatacre, and that the remainder should disembark at Port Elizabeth and proceed to Rosmead junction.

LORD ROBERTS' APPOINTMENT. 379

Meantime the Cabinet had received and considered General Buller's suggestion that Ladysmith should be abandoned. They felt that to leave the invested troops to their fate would be equally injurious in its strategical, political, and moral effect on South Africa; a blow to British prestige throughout the world. Sir R. Buller was therefore informed by a cipher telegram, dated 16th December, that "Her Majesty's Government regard the abandonment of White's force and its consequent surrender as a national disaster of the greatest magnitude. We would urge you to devise another attempt to carry out its relief, not necessarily viâ Colenso, making use of the additional men now arriving, if you think fit." A War Office telegram of the same date advised Sir Redvers that the embarkation of the 6th division for South Africa had already begun, that the 7th division would begin to embark on the 4th January, that another cavalry brigade would be sent out as soon as ships could be provided, and that additional field artillery would replace the guns lost at Colenso. In reply to a request made by him that morning by telegram that 8,000 irregulars " able to ride decently, but shoot as well as possible," should be raised in England, the General Commanding-in-Chief was told that " a considerable force of militia and of picked yeomanry and volunteers will also be sent." *The Cabinet answers Sir Redvers' proposal to give up Ladysmith, Dec. 16th, 1896.*

These promises, and the assurance that the 5th division was at his free disposal, though that had always been the home view, greatly strengthened Sir Redvers Buller's hands. He decided to make another effort to break through the barriers round Ladysmith. He therefore ordered Warren's division to Natal. Warren himself, with two battalions of the 10th brigade, had disembarked at Cape Town, and been despatched by train up country. These battalions, the 1st Yorkshire and 2nd Warwick, were subsequently, at Forestier-Walker's request, left in Cape Colony for duty on the line of communication at De Aar. The rest of the 5th division, together with Sir C. Warren and his staff, went to Durban. *Sir Redvers, being promised reinforcements, prepares for new effort.*

The immediate response made by the Cabinet to Sir R. Buller's request for reinforcements, and their instant rejection of the proposal to abandon Ladysmith, expressed the spirit in *The nation roused.*

which the nation received the news of "the black week"* in South Africa. The experiences of such contests as had been waged by Great Britain since the great Indian mutiny had led public opinion to expect, in time of war, no strain on the national resources, no call for national effort. War was regarded as a matter for which the War Office and the army should make preparation, but not the nation. The despatch of the largest British Army ever sent across the seas had been regarded as ensuring rapid success. A decisive termination of the campaign before the end of the year was anticipated. The disappointment of these hopes at first caused dismay; but this was quickly replaced by a stern determination to carry through the South African undertaking, and, at all costs, not to shirk troublesome responsibilities in that sub-continent. It was realised that the task to be faced was serious, and that the time had come to devote to it the best resources of the Empire. The manhood of the country was eager to assist by any possible means, and therefore learnt with satisfaction that not only would the 6th and 7th divisions be sent out at once, but that nine militia battalions had been asked to volunteer for foreign service, and that yeomanry and select companies of volunteers had had their eager demands to be allowed to help gladly granted. With even greater pleasure was the announcement received, two days after the battle of Colenso, that the General in command in South Africa had been given *carte blanche* to raise mounted troops locally; that the self-governing Colonies, again with true patriotism rallying round the mother country, had proposed to send further military contingents, and that these also were to join in the struggle.

Lord Roberts is appointed to command, Dec. 16.

The action of the Cabinet in dealing with the difficult question of the command in South Africa was prompt. The size of the army which would in a few weeks be assembled at the seat of war, and the nature of the work which lay before it, made it necessary that an officer of the highest standing and experience should be selected for the supreme control. It was apparent that the direction of the operations for the relief of Ladysmith

* The popular name for the week in which occurred the defeats of Stormberg, Magersfontein and Colenso.

would absorb all the attention and energies of Sir R. Buller. Field-Marshal Lord Roberts, V.C., then commanding the forces in Ireland, was therefore asked to undertake the duty of Commander-in-Chief in South Africa, a responsibility which he instantly accepted. As Lord Roberts' Chief of the Staff the Cabinet, with the Field-Marshal's approval, recommended to the Queen the appointment of Major-General Lord Kitchener, who was still serving as Sirdar of that Egyptian army with which, stiffened by British troops, he had destroyed the power of the Mahdi little more than a twelvemonth earlier. The decision to make these appointments was notified to Sir R. Buller, in the telegram quoted below.* Sir Redvers, to use his own words, had "for some time been convinced that it is impossible for any one man to direct active military operations in two places distant 1,500 miles from each other." †

Within a few days Lord Roberts nominated the rest of his staff,‡ and, accompanied by the majority of them, embarked for South Africa on 23rd December, arrangements being made for Lord Kitchener to join him at Gibraltar. Lord Roberts embarks Dec. 23/99.

The fact that it had been decided to send the 5th division to Natal involved in Cape Colony the resumption of the policy of bluff which had proved so successful earlier in the war. It was now attended with greater risk, owing to the spread of disaffection amongst the sympathisers with the Boer Republics. Three distinct areas in the "old colony" were already in the actual Weakness of defence in Cape Colony.

---

* "In Natal and in Cape Colony distinct operations of very great importance are now in progress. The prosecution of the campaign in Natal is being carried on under quite unexpected difficulties, and in the opinion of Her Majesty's Government it will require your presence and whole attention. It has been decided by Her Majesty's Government, under these circumstances, to appoint Field-Marshal Lord Roberts as Commanding-in-Chief, South Africa, his Chief of Staff being Lord Kitchener."

† See letter from Sir Redvers Buller to Under-Secretary of State for War, dated 20th December, 1899.

‡ In a telegram dated 21st December, Sir R. Buller recommended that Lord Roberts should bring out a fresh Headquarter staff, reporting that there was already a lack of senior staff officers throughout the theatre of war. His own Headquarter staff left Cape Town to join him in Natal at the end of December.

occupation of the enemy, and had been annexed by Boer proclamations. The first of these areas included Griqualand West, Barkly West, Taungs, Vryburg, and Mafeking districts, in fact, with the exception of the besieged towns of Kimberley, Kuruman,* and Mafeking, the whole of the colony north of the Riet river and of the Orange river below its junction with the Riet. East of this came the Boer enclave round Colesberg, the extent of which was being much diminished by General French's operations. Further east again, the north-east angle of the colony, including the districts of Herschel, Aliwal North, Barkly East, Wodehouse, and Albert, had for the time being become *de facto* Free State territory. Kruger telegraphed to Steyn on the 20th of December: "I and the rest of the War Commission decide that every person in the districts proclaimed, so far as the annexed portions shall extend, shall be commandeered, and those who refuse be punished. So say to all the officials south of Orange river and in Griqualand West, that while we are already standing in the fire they cannot expect to sit at home in peace and safety." In all these areas, therefore, extraordinary pressure was placed on the colonists to renounce their allegiance and take up arms against their Sovereign. Indeed, but six weeks later the whole of the inhabitants of the Barkly West district who refused to be commandeered were, irrespective of nationality, removed from their homes by the Boers' Landrosts and thrust across the Orange river in a state of absolute destitution.† The number of recruits which had accrued to the enemy's commandos by these means was already, by the end of December, considerable; it was assessed at the time by the British authorities as high as ten thousand. But the danger for the moment was not so much the numerical strength of the

* A detachment of thirty-five Cape police and thirty-three civilians made a gallant defence of Kuruman, under Capt. A. Bates, against a Boer commando much superior in strength. The garrison held out from 12th November until their last redoubt was destroyed by artillery fire on 1st January (see General map of South Africa and map No. 17).

† For the details of this wholesale eviction see article in *Cape Times*, dated 16th February, 1900, enclosed in High Commissioner's despatch No. 85, dated 21st February, 1900 (p. 194-195 of C.O. White Book Africa 629).

LORD ROBERTS' APPOINTMENT. 383

actively disloyal as the attitude of the disaffected in the districts which the enemy had not reached. Here, again, the areas which caused special anxiety fell into three groups. In the eastern province certain of the farmers of the Stockenstroom and adjacent districts had gathered together in a laager on the Katberg Pass across the Winterberg Mountains, a strong position some forty miles in rear of General Gatacre at Queenstown. In the thinly-populated and backward regions bordered by the Orange river on the north, the Roggeveld and Nieuwveld Mountains on the south, and the main line from Cape Town to De Aar on the east, racial feeling was known to be greatly inflamed, and it was reported that, if a few recruiters crossed the Orange river from the districts occupied by the enemy to the north of the river, a rising would probably take place. Even nearer to Cape Town, in the fertile and wine-producing districts of Stellenbosch, Paarl, Ceres, Tulbagh, and Worcester, all most difficult to deal with, owing to the broken character of the ground and its intersection by rough mountain ranges, a portion of the inhabitants had shown signs of great restlessness. If even small bands of insurgents had taken up arms in these parts, the British lines of communication would have been imperilled. A very large force would be required for their protection.

On the other hand, although the loyalty of a portion of the population was shaken, there were large numbers not only steadfast in their allegiance, but anxious to fulfil the duty of good citizens. Considerable advantage had already been taken of this patriotic spirit. Practically the whole of the Volunteer forces of the colony had been called out in the first phase of the war and were still under arms. The good services of the South African Light Horse and of Brabant's Horse, raised respectively in the western and eastern province, showed that the time had now come to make fuller use of the admirable recruiting material that was available. [The enthusiasm of the loyal furnishes large numbers of Volunteers.]

On the 17th December Sir A. Milner telegraphed to Sir Redvers: " As rebellion in the colony is still spreading and our latest reinforcements are wanted elsewhere, I hope you will authorise G.O.C. here to raise all the men he can get in loyal [Full advantage taken of this by Sir A. Milner and Sir Redvers.]

districts. Mounted corps are being increased, and are no doubt what we most want. But for defence of ports, which we must hold at all costs, and of places like King William's Town and Grahamstown, even unmounted men, if otherwise fit, will be useful, and I think considerable numbers might be obtained. Where resistance is at all practicable I think it should be offered, if only to gain time." This suggestion that a large increase should be made in the forces raised locally was not a new one. Sir Redvers had already been in communication on the subject with the War Office, and had been informed by the Secretary of State, in a telegram, dated 16th December, that: "I hope that you understand that we are greatly in favour of the policy indicated in your telegram (10th December) of raising local mounted corps and that you are free to carry it out." On receipt of the High Commissioner's message General Buller gave Forestier-Walker a free hand to raise both mounted and dismounted men for the defence of Cape Colony, directing him to consult Sir A. Milner as to details. On the 27th of December the General Commanding-in-Chief was in a position to telegraph to Lord Lansdowne that, exclusive of the colonial troops belonging to Kimberley and Mafeking garrisons, 2,100 mounted and 4,300 dismounted irregulars were under arms in Cape Colony besides a Railway Pioneer regiment, 500 strong, in process of organisation.*

Large numbers of Volunteers. He hoped to increase still further these numbers by 2,000 mounted and 2,000 dismounted men. In Natal the Volunteers who had been called out, and the special service corps enrolled since the war, numbered in all 6,700 men, and efforts were being made to raise another 700. Including, therefore, the 4,000 colonial and local troops besieged in Kimberley, the 1,000 defending Mafeking, and 1,500 Southern Rhodesians, there were at this time 20,000 South African colonists employed in the defence of their country, and arrangements were being made to augment this total to about 25,000 men. The men who thus served their Sovereign were not all of British descent.

* The strength of the corps was soon afterwards raised to 1,000, and eventually expanded to four battalions.

Some were loyal Dutchmen. The figures no doubt include as "South Africans," because present in local units, Johannesburg Uitlanders,* as well as others who flocked to South Africa from various parts of the Empire to fight for the maintenance of equal rights for all white men. These large bodies might, had the Imperial Government thought fit, have been almost indefinitely reinforced by native levies; but such a course was impossible without danger to the future welfare of South Africa. It was deemed legitimate to sanction the organisation of the tribes of British Kaffraria, under Sir H. Elliott, for the defence of their own homes against the Boer commandos.

After withdrawing from the battlefield of Magersfontein, Lord Methuen had directed the whole of his energy to strengthening his hold on the Riet and establishing his troops firmly astride that river. General Buller had finally decided to retain Lord Methuen in that forward situation, for on reflection he perceived that a retirement would leave Cronje free to concentrate his whole force against Kimberley. Moreover, he foresaw that the so-called "Modder position" could be utilised later on as a pivot of manœuvre, or as a screen behind which a turning offensive movement might be made to the east into the Free State. With this end in view he proposed to begin constructing a railway from Honey Nest Kloof to Jacobsdal, to be extended eventually to Bloemfontein after the arrival of the 6th division. The occupation of Jacobsdal would, General Buller anticipated, "frighten" Cronje out of Magersfontein.† Lord Roberts, however, in telegraphing to Sir Redvers from Gibraltar on 26th December his concurrence in the retention of Methuen on the Modder, added: "As regards railway extension, I fear that construction of line will so seriously interfere with the utility of present working line that I should ask you to consult Girouard‡ on this subject before coming to any decision." The

_{Methuen since Magersfontein.}

---

* The term used by the Boers for all foreigners.

† Telegram to Secretary of State, dated 23rd December, 1899.

‡ Bt.-Maj. (local Lieut.-Col.) E. P. Girouard, R.E., who had at the outbreak of the war been appointed Director of Railways on the lines of communication staff. After Lord Roberts' arrival the Director of Railways worked under the immediate orders of the Chief of the Staff.

execution of this project was therefore suspended pending Lord Roberts' arrival.

<small>Cronje remains passive.</small>

Meanwhile, although with the mobile force at his disposal General Cronje might have struck at the British communications, the Boer commander remained passive, and devoted himself to the improvement and extension of his defences. He was indifferent to the fact that his line of supply to the eastward was exposed and almost entirely unguarded. Enterprises proposed by De Wet and others of his subordinates against the British connection with the sea he sternly forbad.

<small>Activity in the west.</small>

In the more western theatre of war, on the contrary, the Boers made some attempt to take advantage of the situation. Recruiting parties were sent across the Orange river, and visited Prieska. The village of Douglas, lying south of the Vaal, a little below its junction with the Riet, and commanding the road from Griqualand West to Belmont, was also occupied by a small commando. The section of Lord Methuen's line of supply from De Aar to Honey Nest Kloof was at this time held by some 11,000 men under the command of Major-General E. Wood.* The greater part of this force was distributed in strong posts at Honey Nest Kloof, Enslin, Belmont, Witteputs, Orange River bridge, and De Aar. The garrison of Belmont was under command of Lt.-Colonel T. D. Pilcher, and consisted of two guns of P. battery, R.H.A., a half company of the Munster Fusiliers mounted infantry, 250 Queensland M.I., two companies of the Duke of Cornwall's Light Infantry, and the Royal Canadian regiment, amounting in all to about 1,600 men. General Wood determined to use a portion of this garrison to brush away the hostile gathering on the left flank. With this object, Colonel Pilcher was directed to move out from Belmont on the afternoon of the 31st December with a flying column, composed of the two guns of P. battery, 42 officers and men of the Munster Fusiliers M.I., 12 officers and 187 men of the Queensland M.I. under command of Lt.-Colonel P. R. Ricardo, and a company of the Canadian regiment, the last-named unit being carried in ten buck

* Colonel H. S. G. Miles had been in command of this section up to 26th December, 1899.

LORD ROBERTS' APPOINTMENT.

wagons with mule transport. The two companies D.C.L.I. formed a supporting column and followed later. In order to deceive the enemy, Pilcher on the previous day had made a feint from Belmont towards the Free State, returning ostensibly on the ground that a mistake had been made as to supply arrangements; the real object of the column was Douglas, and it had been arranged to cover Pilcher's right flank, by moving Babington with his mounted brigade and G. battery westward from Modder camp. His left flank was protected by the despatch of the Scots Greys from Orange River station to Mark's Drift, a point close to the junction of the Vaal and Orange rivers. On the night of the 31st December, Colonel Pilcher halted at Thornhill farm, eighteen miles north-west of Belmont, and thence moved on the following morning to Sunnyside, where in a cluster of kopjes a small laager had been formed by an advance party of the enemy. This commando (about 180 strong), was surprised, and defeated, with a loss of fourteen killed and thirty-eight prisoners, after a brief engagement, in which the Canadian and Queensland troops proved their fitness to fight side by side with British regulars. On the 2nd January, the flying column pushing on to Douglas, found the village evacuated by the enemy. Meanwhile, a strong commando, detached by Cronje, had eluded the cavalry brigade and crossed the Riet river near Koodoesberg. Lt.-Colonel Pilcher had already fallen back on Thornhill on 3rd January, and evading the enemy by a night march, regained Belmont unmolested. Ninety loyalist refugees from Douglas accompanied him on his return. Simultaneously with this successful raid, a patrol of about a company of M.I. under Lieut.-Colonel Alderson had been sent to Prieska from De Aar, and on the 3rd January exchanged shots at that place with the enemy across the river, falling back subsequently on De Aar.

Pilcher's raid on Douglas.

Alderson threatens Prieska.

Lord Methuen now determined, in conjunction with Major-General E. Wood, to demonstrate to the eastward against the enemy's line of communication, which was known to run through Jacobsdal, Koffyfontein, and Fauresmith. On the 7th January Major-General Wood therefore, with a force of all three arms,

Wood seizes Zoutpans Drift.

seized Zoutpans Drift, a ford across the Orange river twenty miles above the railway bridge. The ford had been reconnoitred as early as 13th December. Here General Wood placed a permanent post on favourable ground on a hill, to protect the drift from the Free State side, and to command the road leading thence to Fauresmith. A Boer detachment remained in observation of this post on the adjacent farm of Wolvekraal, but did not attack. Further to the north, reconnaissances into the Free State, made by the cavalry brigade, and by Pilcher's troops at Belmont, ascertained that the enemy was not yet in great strength on the right flank, but that Jacobsdal was occupied. The Field Intelligence department at Cape Town had already (3rd January) received information from a trustworthy source that Cronje had at and near Magersfontein 8,000 to 9,000 men, and that he was relying on being attacked there. The report stated: "An advance on Bloemfontein up the right bank of Riet river by Kaalspruit would draw off the main Boer forces towards Bloemfontein. President O.F.S. is stated in district to have said that he 'could not cope with such a movement.' . . . . . Bloemfontein is undefended except by two forts, the guns of which have been moved to Kimberley."

CHAPTER XXIV.

OPERATIONS ROUND COLESBERG—DECEMBER 16TH, 1899, TO FEBRUARY 6TH, 1900.*

WHILST Lord Roberts was on his voyage to the seat of war, the three portions of the army which had sustained severe checks were chiefly employed in recuperating and receiving reinforcements. General French, on the other hand, was continuing his successful operations. These, therefore, with the exceptions mentioned in the last chapter, alone represent the active work in the field in South Africa between the time of the decision of the Cabinet appointing the new Commander-in-Chief and his arrival at Cape Town. The task of General French at Arundel was now as important as the strength of his command seemed inadequate to perform it. The enemy on his front formed one of four invading columns, three of which had already been victorious. Schoeman had, therefore, strong reasons for wishing to emulate the prowess of Cronje at Magersfontein, of Botha at Colenso, and of the fortunate trio at Stormberg. French had to deal with an opponent whose confidence must now be presumed to be at its height. Moreover, reinforcements might reach the Boer leader at any moment. It had become more than ever necessary to paralyse him before he could initiate even the semblance of an organised incursion into territory where disloyalty might largely increase his numbers in a night.

_{French's operations during Lord Roberts' voyage.}

* See maps Nos. 9 and 16.

Only by incessant activity could French hope to attain this object, and fortunately the force under his command, if small, was suitable both in composition and spirit to that most difficult of military operations, the surveillance and protection of a large area by mobility alone. His dispositions, detailed in Chapter XVII., whilst they denied a front of nearly forty miles to the enemy, effectually covered the Hanover Road–Naauwpoort–Rosmead line of railway. The area occupied by the Boers round Rensburg was, like that of the British, bisected by the railway. It was roughly as follows :—On the west of the line lay some 800 Transvaalers with a long-range gun ; on the east about 2,000 Free Staters, with two guns, were partly entrenched, whilst 600 burghers guarded the Boer Headquarters at Colesberg and their line of retreat. Against the enemy, thus distributed, French now began a series of reconnaissances and rapid movements in force, which, directed against Schoeman's flanks and rear, and often against his convoys, left him no peace. Some of these expeditions, notably an attack by the New Zealand Mounted Rifles and a battery R.H.A. on December 18th against the Boer left rear, led to brisk skirmishing ; but the British losses were always trifling, and Schoeman, continually forced to show his hand, eventually wearied of his insecurity. On the 29th he abandoned Rensburg, and fell back by night upon Colesberg. At daybreak on the 30th, French followed in pursuit with the Carabiniers, New Zealand Mounted Rifles, and two guns R.H.A. and, reaching Rensburg at 7 a.m., soon regained touch with the enemy upon the ridges south-west of Colesberg. A demonstration by the artillery disclosed a strong position, strongly held. Colesberg town lies in a hollow in the midst of a rough square of high, steep kopjes, many of them of that singular geometrical form described in Chapter III. Smaller kopjes project within rifle range from the angles of the square, whilst 2,000 yards west of its western face a tall peak, called Coles Kop, rises abruptly from the encircling plain, and dominates the entire terrain. The isolation of this hill was doubtless the reason why it was not occupied by the Boers. They were in strength everywhere along the hilly ramparts around Colesberg. French, therefore, per-

OPERATIONS ROUND COLESBERG. 391

ceiving the formidable nature of this "natural fortress," * contented himself with seizing a group of hills (Porter's Hill) 2,000 yards south-west of the south-western angle. Here he planted artillery, and, leaving Porter with the above mounted troops in observation, himself returned to Rensburg siding, which he made his Headquarters, calling up the main body from Arundel.

The rearward concentration of the enemy at Colesberg, in itself a partial triumph for the British Commander, had now cleared the situation, and opened to General French the final object defined by his instructions.† The arrival of reinforcements, moreover, seemed to warrant a serious attempt upon Colesberg. The third squadrons of the 6th (Inniskilling) Dragoons and 10th Hussars, which had been wrecked in the transport *Ismore*, had joined on the 18th and 21st December, the 1st Suffolk regiment from Naauwpoort on the 26th, and Rimington's Guides (173 strong) on the 28th, the 1st Essex regiment from De Aar relieving the Suffolk at Naauwpoort.

French decides to attempt Colesberg.

At daybreak on the 31st the General made in person a close reconnaissance of the enemy's position, and at noon he issued orders for an offensive movement. The most vulnerable, indeed, the only vulnerable portions of the bulwark of hills, seemed to be the kopjes previously described as projecting from the square, especially those upon the western face. These gained, it would be possible to push northward along the flank, threatening the Colesberg road bridge and the enemy's line of retreat, regarding the safety of which the Boers had shown themselves peculiarly sensitive. Seeking a base from which to attack these outlying kopjes, French settled upon Maeder's farm, lying five miles west-south-west of Colesberg, and at 4 p.m. a squadron 10th Hussars moved thither as a screen to the main body,‡ which

Dec. 31st/99 to Jan. 1st, 1900, makes night attack on McCracken's Hill and takes it.

---

* Despatch, February 2nd, 1900.

† "To seize and hold Naauwpoort, and whenever possible to push on and gain possession of Colesberg." Despatch, February 2nd, 1900.

‡ Composition :—Inniskilling Dragoons, 10th Hussars, ten guns R.H.A., one company M.I., with four companies, 2nd Royal Berkshire regiment, under Major F. W. N. McCracken, the whole under command of Lieut.-Col. R. B. W. Fisher, 10th Hussars. Two days' supplies went with the force and half the infantry were carried in wagons.

marched an hour later, and arrived at the farm between 8 p.m. and 9 p.m., the troops bivouacking there under arms. At midnight the men were roused, and at 12.30 a.m., January 1st, the column, led by the wing of the Royal Berkshire, set out in thick darkness towards the enemy.* The route taken ran for two and a half miles on Colesberg, and then north-east across the veld, past the east of Coles Kop. The infantry marched in profound silence; even the regimental carts were dropped behind, lest the noise of the wheels should betray the design. It was not until the leading companies at 3.30 a.m. were close to the base of the hill to be attacked, that a loud shout and a scattered fire of rifles from the right front broke the stillness, and showed that the enemy had detected the advance. Major McCracken, who had so organised the march of the Berkshire as to be ready for this, extended his ranks to two paces interval, and, without awaiting his supports, which had been delayed by the darkness, ordered the charge. Thereupon the enemy's piquet fled, and the Royal Berkshire, just as day dawned on January 1st, 1900, gained, without opposition, the crest of the hill, henceforward to be known as McCracken's Hill.

<small>Jan. 1st, 1900. Colesberg is shelled whilst Fisher works round the north towards the bridge road on Boer right, and Porter acts against their left.</small>

This point being won, General French immediately despatched Colonel Fisher on from the place, where he had halted with his cavalry, past Coles Kop towards the north-west corner of the heights encircling Colesberg, with orders to establish a squadron at the corner, and to work round the northern face against the Boer right. In this duty Fisher was only so far successful as to get his patrols astride the track to Colesberg road bridge, failing to secure the hills commanding the northern exits from the town. To distract attention from this movement, and to clear the kopjes on McCracken's front, ten guns had previously been placed opposite the western face of the Colesberg heights, and as soon as it became light enough, these opened a heavy bombardment. The enemy responded at once with field guns and a pom-pom from higher ground, and for three hours the batteries endured a galling fire of great accuracy, the Boer pom-pom

---

* Order of march :—Point of M.I., half battalion R. Berkshire, remainder M.I., 10th Hussars, R.H.A., Inniskilling Dragoons.

OPERATIONS ROUND COLESBERG.

especially bespattering the line of guns with a continuous stream of projectiles. Not until the Horse artillery had expended 1,043 rounds of shrapnel did the enemy's gunners desist. During this time Colonel Porter, based on Porter's Hill, was operating vigorously against the enemy's left. He had moved out overnight with two squadrons 6th Dragoon Guards (Carabiniers), one company New Zealand Mounted Rifles, and two guns, R.H.A. Reinforcing these mounted troops, Porter made a determined effort against the outworks of the Schietberg at the southwestern angle of the Colesberg heights. But the Boers were here in strength, and the New Zealanders, after a gallant attack up the stiff slopes, were compelled to fall back upon Porter's Hill, whence for the rest of the day Porter engaged, though he could not dislodge, large numbers of the enemy.

Meanwhile the wing of the Royal Berkshire regiment had not been left in peaceful possession of McCracken's Hill. To the east, and between this hill and Colesberg, another height of similar command was strongly held by the enemy, who not only opened a troublesome fire at daybreak, but a little later attempted first a counter-attack up the steep re-entrants to the north-east, or left, of the infantry, and next an enveloping movement around the right. *Boers try to retake McCracken's Hill, but fail.*

Both enterprises finally failed; but about 7 a.m., so insecure seemed the situation of the Berkshire, that the General sent orders to McCracken to evacuate. At that moment Fisher's appearance upon the heights to the north-west somewhat relieved the pressure, and McCracken, receiving to his satisfaction permission to retain what he had won, soon had his command so safely entrenched against musketry and shell fire, that, for the next forty-three days, during which it never ceased, his casualties numbered but eighteen. So passed the day without further incident until, late in the afternoon, Schoeman suddenly led a column, about 1,000 strong, out of the south-eastern corner of the Colesberg *enceinte*, making as if to envelop the British right. Fortunately, Rimington's Guides, who had been posted overnight at Jasfontein farm, six miles east of Rensburg, to watch this flank, detected the Boer advance. Simultaneously the *The first attempt stopped by Fisher's appearance, after evacuation of the hill had been ordered. Rimington's Guides and Porter's men stop the second.*

troops at Porter's Hill saw it also, and Schoeman, confronted by both detachments, retired to Colesberg. Thus by evening French, though disappointed with the results north of the town, where he had hoped to secure "Grassy" (later Suffolk) Hill, had cut off Colesberg from the rest of the colony on the south and west. His intercepting line ran north as far as Kloof camp.* As all the troops were thus fully occupied, French asked for reinforcements with which to "manœuvre the enemy out of his position." Schoeman himself, at the same time, was demanding assistance from the Boer Headquarters to enable him to hold his ground.†

<small>Jan. 4th, 1900. Schoeman attacks French's left, obtains a momentary advantage, but completely fails.</small>

Next day (January 2nd) General French delegated the command of the left attack to Major-General Brabazon, with Headquarters at Maeder's farm, and relieved the cavalry at Kloof camp by four companies of the 1st Suffolk regiment, one squadron alone remaining there to act as a screen to the northern flank. This day and the next passed uneventfully. Early in the morning of the 4th, Schoeman, baulked in his attempt of the 1st January against the British right, dashed suddenly from his lines with a thousand men against the left, and all but rolled it up. Eluding the cavalry piquets posted on the outer flank of the Suffolk, the burghers galloped for a line of kopjes which ran east and west across the left and left rear of Kloof camp, into which they therefore looked from the flank, and partially from the rear. The enemy's artillery at once opened fiercely from their main position upon the entrenchments of the Suffolk, who, assailed from three directions, were for some time seriously threatened. Much depended upon the action of the next few minutes. French's front line was for the moment truly outflanked, and, were the enemy to establish himself where he was, nothing would remain but a speedy and difficult evacuation of

---

* Casualties, January 1st :—Killed, one officer ; wounded, six officers, twenty-one N.C.O.s and men ; missing, one man.

† The former received the 1st Essex regiment, two companies 1st Yorkshire regiment, 4th battery R.F.A., and the Household cavalry composite regiment ; the latter the Johannesburg Police under Van Dam, and a commando under Commandant Grobelaar. The reinforcements reached the two opponents on January 4th, 5th and 6th.

the ground hitherto held, right back to Porter's Hill. The tables were quickly turned. General French, who was riding up from Rensburg, at this moment reached Porter's Hill, and immediately telegraphed to Maeder's farm for all the troops to turn out and move on Coles Kop. He also ordered two companies of the Royal Berkshire regiment from McCracken's Hill to reinforce the threatened point, and the 10th Hussars, a squadron 6th (Inniskilling) Dragoons, and two guns R.H.A. to advance upon the right of the Boer attack. Four guns had already opened against their centre from in front of Coles Kop. These movements chilled the Boers, who, especially alarmed at the approach of the cavalry from the direction of Windmill camp, abandoned the most advanced points they had reached, hotly pursued by the 10th Hussars on one flank and " B." squadron Inniskillings on the other. Yet some of them soon turned, and, standing on rocky hills, attempted to cover the flight of the rest, by checking the 10th Hussars. Colonel Fisher thereupon dismounted his men, and leading a charge on foot, brilliantly drove off the Boer rearguard and sent them after their comrades, whilst the Inniskillings continued the pursuit, getting amongst the fugitives with the lance. Still a part of the enemy, about 200 in number, clung stoutly to the broken hills in spite of the severe cross fire of the artillery. About 1 p.m., therefore, the General ordered Capt. H. de B. de Lisle to dislodge this remnant with 200 mounted infantry. De Lisle, using all the advantages of the ground, skilfully manœuvred his men, mounted, till he was within a distance convenient for attack. His dismounting was the signal for another break away of at least half of those fronting him, and the mounted infantry, in open order, scaled the hill with fixed bayonets against the remainder. There was a short encounter, but De Lisle's men were not to be denied, twenty-one prisoners falling into their hands as they cleared the summit. The rest of the Boers scattered in flight, and by 2 p.m. Schoeman's attempt was over. His failure had cost him ninety killed and wounded, and the loss of some forty prisoners.*

* Casualties, January 4th :—Killed, one officer, six N.C.O.s and men ; wounded, two officers and thirteen N.C.O.s and men.

During this (January 4th) and the two following days, the requested reinforcements, in number some 1,500 men of all arms, arrived. With this accretion of strength it was now possible to renew the offensive, and General French at once turned his attention to the capture of Grassy Hill (Suffolk Hill on map No. 16), which he had early marked as the key to the Boer stronghold. This height lay at the junction of the roads leading respectively to Colesberg road bridge and to Norval's Pont, both of which it commanded. Fisher's operations on the left flank on January 1st had been designed to seize this important point, and without it there was little hope of forcing the enemy from Colesberg. On the 5th, whilst all the artillery shelled the hill, French made a personal and careful reconnaissance,* and on his return to Headquarters issued orders for an attack next day. It was to be based on Kloof camp, whence a force of all arms† under the command of Lieutenant-Colonel F. J. W. Eustace, R.H.A., was to be in readiness to start at 5 a.m. As before, the 1st cavalry brigade and the post at Porter's Hill were to co-operate to the southward, both to divert attention from the true attack, and to prevent the enemy withdrawing his guns.

French, Jan. 5th, issues orders for attack on Grassy Hill next day.

Lt.-Colonel A. J. Watson, commanding the 1st Suffolk regiment at Kloof camp, who had frequently reconnoitred Grassy Hill in company with General French, had from the first expressed his belief that he could capture it with his battalion. On the previous day (5th January) his remaining half-battalion had joined him, and during an interview with Eustace in the evening regarding the arrangements for next day, he asked the latter to obtain from the General leave for him to rush the position in the night with four companies. Eustace, though he did not share the confidence of the infantry commander, neverthe-

Lt.-Col. Watson volunteers to take the hill, and is granted leave to try.

---

* During the reconnaissance, Lieutenant Sir J. P. Milbanke, Bart., 10th Hussars, the General's A.D.C., was severely wounded whilst rescuing a dismounted trooper under heavy fire, an act for which he subsequently received the Victoria Cross.

† Composition :—
  10th Hussars, 6th (Inniskilling) Dragoons, eight guns R.H.A.
  4th battery Royal Field artillery, three companies M.I.
  Detachments 1st Suffolk and 2nd Royal Berkshire regiments.

less carried the request to Headquarters. As a result, about 8 p.m., a message was sent to Watson authorising him to attack the hill if he saw a favourable chance. He was first, however, to inform the General and all troops in the vicinity of his intention. No more was heard of Watson and the Suffolk regiment until, about 3 a.m. on the 6th, a crash of rifle fire, breaking the silence from the direction of Grassy Hill, proclaimed that the attack had been delivered. The sound was clearly heard by General French and his staff who were riding up from Headquarters to witness the day's operations. Halting below Coles Kop, French immediately sent Eustace forward to get the guns into action, but soon afterwards received intelligence that the Suffolk were returning to camp, and that their colonel and 120 officers and men were missing. The attempt on Grassy Hill had failed, and the plan for the day was shattered before it had been properly set on foot.

Watson during night, 5th to 6th Jan. attacks and fails.

Having obtained the General's sanction, Watson, overlooking perhaps the attached conditions, had eagerly prepared to avail himself of it. The key of the whole situation seemed to be within his reach, and he determined not to lose the chance of seizing it. Not until 11.30 p.m., when they were roused from sleep to form up their companies, had even his own officers any inkling of the project on foot, and when, an hour later, under cover of profound darkness, four companies (305 officers and men) moved noiselessly out of camp, the soldiers for the most part marching in soft deck shoes, the least sanguine felt assured at least of secrecy. The formation was quarter-column in the following order of companies, " H." " D." " A." " B."; the men's bayonets were fixed. The Colonel, who was carrying a long white stick as a distinguishing mark, moved in front of his command and felt for the route. When about half way, a halt was called and Watson, sending for his officers, told them for the first time on what they were bent, and ordered, as the attack formation, column of companies at fifty paces distance. The advance was then resumed. The march seemed unduly long. The route to Grassy Hill from the British lines was more than twice the supposed length. In the darkness and over the

Watson's attempt.

difficult ground, it was impossible to maintain distances for any time at all, so that column had again contracted to quarter-column before the hill was reached. Arrived at the foot, there was a short halt in a donga. Then the ascent, which from the halting-place was at once very steep and covered with boulders, was essayed. Higher up, more gentle gradients led to the summit. Scarcely had the leading companies, somewhat disordered by the severe climb, emerged upon the easier ground near the top, when a single shot from a Boer sentry rang out close in front of the foremost files. It was instantly followed by a blaze of musketry which leaped from the whole crest. A volley so sudden and heavy could only come from men prepared for action; it was evident that the advance of the Suffolk was not only detected but awaited. Nevertheless, "H." company, supported by "D.," immediately dashed forward, at once losing both its officers and many men, the regimental adjutant and another officer being struck down at the same moment. Watson, recognising the preparations made to receive him, seeing from the confusion which had arisen the futility of so informal an attack, directed a retirement, intending, doubtless, no more than that his men should temporarily seek the cover of the dead ground from which they had just climbed. But such instructions, at such a time, were more easy to obey than to understand. Whilst some fell back but a short distance, many made their way to the foot of the hill, and so to the camp. Some again were unable to retreat under the tremendous fusilade, and together with those who had not heard the word of command, or did not credit it, held on in front, and suffered losses rapidly. In short, for a few moments, though the officers worked hard to restore regularity, confusion reigned in the column, whilst the Boer fire continued to rake it without cessation. Watson then desired the commander of the third company, ("A."), to support "H." company upon the crest. Captain C. A. H. Brett, having extricated about half his men from the press, pushed out to the right flank and advanced. A storm of fire, delivered at a few yards' range, met this attempt, and here, as before, all the officers (three) and many of the rank and file fell before they could close. Still Watson, whose gallantry

OPERATIONS ROUND COLESBERG. 399

compelled order wherever his influence could be felt, strove to retrieve the situation. Going back a little, he called up the rear company (" B.") and led it forward in person, making for the right front. Again a murderous fire shattered the effort, and no sooner had Watson disposed the remnants of " B." company on the crest, than he himself fell dead just as dawn appeared. Only about 100 officers and men were now scattered over the hill, many of them wounded, but opposing as hot a fire as they could deliver to the invisible enemy who was firing point blank into them. The pouches of the dead were rifled for cartridges with which to continue the struggle; but no hope remained; even the shrapnel of Eustace's artillery, which now opened from Kloof camp, became an added danger: while the Boers, aided by the increasing light, shot with ever-increasing accuracy. About 4.30 a.m. the survivors, ninety-nine in number, of whom twenty-nine were wounded, surrendered.*

In the evening the 1st Essex relieved the 1st Suffolk at Kloof camp, the latter battalion being sent first to Rensburg, and subsequently to the lines of communication to be re-officered. *Jan. 6th.*

It was now evident to General French that the Boer right was so strong and so watchful as to be proof against either stratagem or open attack. He therefore turned at once to the other flank for opportunities, seeking by a reconnaissance on the 7th January a suitable point to the eastward from whence to threaten the enemy's rear along the line of the Norval's Pont railway. The operation, which was carried out under long-range fire both of artillery and rifles,† disclosed the fact that owing to lack of water none of the kopjes that were near enough *Jan. 7th, 1900. French reconnoitres Boer left.*

---

* Casualties, January 6th :—
  Killed: Five Officers; thirty-two N.C.O.s and men.
  Wounded and taken prisoners: Three Officers; twenty-six N.C.O.s and men.
  Un-wounded and taken prisoners: Two Officers; sixty-eight N.C.O.s and men.
  Wounded and returned to camp: One Officer; twenty-two N.C.O.s and men.
  The Boers stated their losses as one officer and eight men killed, seventeen men wounded.
† Casualties, January 7th :—One officer and four men missing.

to the line were tenable as permanent posts. At Slingersfontein farm, however, eleven miles south-east of Colesberg, and seven miles from the nearest point of the Norval's Pont line, an excellent position was found. On January 9th it was occupied by two squadrons Household cavalry, three squadrons the 6th Dragoon Guards (Carabiniers), the N.S.W. Lancers and four guns, under command of Colonel Porter. To divert attention from this movement, the whole of the enemy's western flank was bombarded by twelve guns disposed from Kloof camp to Porter's Hill, whilst a section R.H.A. and a squadron 6th (Inniskilling) Dragoons made an attack on the southern front above Palmietfontein farm, drawing in reply the fire of two field guns and two pom-poms.*

Jan. 9th. Slingersfontein Farm on Boer left occupied.

During the 8th and 9th the 1st Yorkshire regiment arrived, and was posted at Rensburg. On the 10th Schoeman also received reinforcements from Norval's Pont, and these he placed so as to cover the railway south of Joubert siding, opposite to Porter, who turned out his men at Slingersfontein to stop further advance southward. French, on the 11th January, made a reconnaissance, employing the whole of Porter's force in an attempt to turn the left of this new development of the enemy. But the Boers, after a short retirement, received further strong reinforcements from Norval's Pont, and prolonging the threatened left, showed a bold front. French, therefore, who had no intention of becoming seriously engaged, ordered Porter to return to Slingersfontein. An attempt by Major A. G. Hunter-Weston, R.E., to reach the railway line round the enemy's left flank, and destroy the telegraph wire, was foiled at Achtertang when on the very point of success. A Boer laager was in fact close at hand. At the same time Captain de Lisle, pushing out from the extreme left towards Bastard's Nek, reconnoitred the country to the northward, and found the enemy in strength along the line Bastard's Nek—Wolve Kop—Spitz Kop—Plessis Poort.†

Feeling the enemy's left, Jan. 11th.

---

* Casualties, January 9th :—Two men wounded ; seventeen battery horses were struck by shells during this engagement.

† Casualties, January 11th :—Wounded, five men ; missing, one man.

OPERATIONS ROUND COLESBERG.

Whilst these affairs were in progress, a feat astonished both sides alike by its triumph over difficulty. Major E. E. A. Butcher, R.F.A., commanding the 4th Field battery, placed a 15-pr. gun upon the peak of Coles Kop, a kopje already described as standing by itself in the plain to the west of Colesberg. Rising to a height of 600 feet, its sides varying from the almost perpendicular to a slope of 30°, and covered with boulders, the hill presented a formidable climb even to an unhampered man, and its use for any purpose but that of a look-out post seemed impossible. Nevertheless, aided by detachments of the R.A., R.E., and Essex regiment, Butcher had his gun on the summit in three hours and a half. The supply of ammunition for it, and of rations for the gunners, were more serious problems even than the actual haulage of the piece itself. These were ingeniously solved by the installation of a lift composed of wires running over snatch-blocks affixed to standards, which were improvised from steel rails, and driven in, in pairs, five yards apart, both at the top and bottom of the kopje. Those at the top were wedged into natural fissures in the rocks, the bottom pair being driven twelve inches into the ground, and held upright by guy-ropes fixed to bollards or anchorages. To the top of each upright was lashed a snatch-block, over which, from summit to base of the hill, were stretched the carrying wires. Along these, suspended by blocks and tackle, loads up to thirty pounds in weight were hauled by means of a thin wire, which was wound upon a drum fixed between, and passed through, pulleys attached to the top of each of the two upper standards. The lift was so contrived as to be double-acting, the turning of the drum and a ratchet causing one wire bearing its load of supplies to ascend, whilst another descended, the hill.

Butcher places 15-pr. on precipitous height. Jan. 11th.

At 6 o'clock next morning this gun opened upon a laager in the very midst of the enemy's main position. The effect was instantaneous; the Boers, thunderstruck by the sudden visitation of shrapnel, which came they knew not whence, abandoned their camp and fled to the kopjes for shelter. Another laager, 2,000 yards more distant, then became the target with the same result, the enemy's doubt as to the situation of the gun being

It has immediate effect. Jan. 12th.

deepened by the simultaneous practice of two 15-prs. fired from the p ain below the kop. A few days later Butcher succeeded in getting a second gun up the hill, and by means of his great command, forced the Boers to shift every laager into sheltered kloofs, and caused them considerable losses.

Jan. 14th. A flying column under Allenby threatens Boer connection with the bridge.

On Jan. 14th, a flying column* under Major E. H. H. Allenby (Inniskilling), marched northward along the Seacow river. Turning to the east, he demonstrated against the enemy's communications at the Colesberg road bridge, at which about twenty shells were fired at 5,000 yards' range. The Boers thereupon appeared in three bodies in greatly superior numbers, and Allenby, having taken five prisoners, fell back, easily avoiding an attempt to cut him off. This reconnaissance had the effect of causing the enemy to cease to use the wagon road for transport purposes. Next day (15th) the Boers retaliated by a determined attack on the isolated post at Slingerfontein, held on that day by a half company 1st Yorkshire regiment,† commanded by Captain M. H. Orr and a company (58 men) New Zealand Mounted Rifles under Captain W. R. N. Madocks, R.A. (attached). These had their trenches above the farm, the New Zealanders upon the eastern and the Yorkshire upon the western sides of a steep and high hill, the lower slopes of which were largely dead ground to those in the defences. Other kopjes, accessible to the Boers, were within rifle range. The position was thus to the Boer rifleman an ideal one for the most exceptional of his fighting practices, the close offensive. In the subsequent attack, every detail was typical of his methods on such occasions. At 6.30 a.m. a long-range sniping fire began to tease the occupants of the hill. They vainly searched amongst the broken kopjes for sight of an enemy. Growing, certainly, but almost imperceptibly, in volume and accuracy, this fire was directed chiefly at the New Zealanders on the east, and by 10 a.m.

Jan. 15th. Boers attack Slingersfontein.

---

* Composition : One squadron 6th (Inniskilling) Dragoons, one squadron 10th Hussars, two companies M.I., and two guns R.H.A.

† This battalion had joined on January 8th and 9th. On January 12th, 1st half-battalion Welsh regiment and a squadron 10th Hussars had also arrived ; they were followed on the 14th by half a battalion, 2nd Worcestershire regiment.

OPERATIONS ROUND COLESBERG. 403

had become so intense that an attack in that direction seemed imminent. Meanwhile, a body of the enemy had been crawling from exactly the opposite quarter towards the western side, upon which they succeeded in effecting a lodgment unseen. They then began to climb, scattering under cover of the boulders. Not until they were close in front of the sangars of the Yorkshire regiment was their presence discovered by a patrol which Madocks had sent from his side of the hill. Thereupon the Boers opened a hot fire, striking down both the officer and the colour-sergeant of the Yorkshire, whose men, taken by surprise and suddenly deprived of their leaders, fell into some confusion. The Boers then occupied the two foremost sangars. The hill seemed lost. Then Madocks, hearing the outburst on the further side from him, took a few of his men and hurried round to assist, appearing amongst the Yorkshire just as the enemy were all but into them. Rallying the soldiers, and perceiving the Boers a few yards away behind the rocks, he immediately ordered a charge, and followed by a few, cleared the enemy out of the nearer of the two abandoned sangars. The Boers continued to shoot rapidly from the wall beyond, and Madocks, a few moments later, charged again. Accompanied this time by but three men, he closed to within a few feet of the more distant sangar. Two of the men with him were here killed, and Madocks, seeing the uselessness of remaining, made his way back again to the sangar in rear with his sole companion, called together the rest of the Yorkshire detachment, and began hurriedly to strengthen the wall under a searching fire. At this moment a party of his own New Zealanders, for whom he had sent back, doubled up to the spot, and led by himself, whilst a storm of bullets broke over them from the surrounding kopjes, charged down on the Boers with fixed bayonets. The enemy fled at once, rising from behind the stones upon the hillside. Pursued by volleys from the crest of the British position, they made their way back to their lines, leaving twenty-one dead upon the field.*

_{The Boers are repulsed.}

---

* Casualties, January 15th :—
  Killed, six N.C.O.s and men ; wounded, one officer, five N.C.O.s and men. Boer losses : twenty-one killed ; about forty wounded.

404   THE WAR IN SOUTH AFRICA.

Arrival, Jan. 15th, of Clements, and fresh troops then and later to Jan. 21st, causes changes in dispositions.

Whilst this affair was in progress, a welcome reinforcement arrived. Major-General R. A. P. Clements brought with him the 1st Royal Irish and the remainder of the 2nd Worcestershire of his brigade (12th), in all an addition of 18 officers and 874 men. Clements was immediately placed in command of the Slingersfontein area.* This increase of strength enabled French to extend his right still further by moving Porter's command† south-eastward to Potfontein farm, and that of Rimington,‡ hitherto stationed at Jasfontein farm, to Kleinfontein farm, five miles north of Porter. For a time Rimington was able to station some Household cavalry in close touch with the enemy at Rhenoster farm, on the Bethulie road, but it was thought prudent to withdraw them on January 21st, as a commando of 1,000 men had gathered opposite the post. A demonstration by Porter towards Hebron farm on the 19th disclosed, about Keerom, south of Achtertang, a large Boer laager, which was shelled with effect. A deserter reported the enemy in this direction to consist of 6,000 men. During the next two days the following reinforcements reached the camp:—2nd Bedfordshire regiment, 2nd Wiltshire regiment, detachments of the 1st Essex and 1st Yorkshire regiments and details of Royal engineers and Army Service Corps, a total accession of about 50 officers and 1,900 men. Two howitzers,§ which had come up on the 18th, shelled Grassy Hill on the 19th and following days with effect, their fire being directed by telegraph from Coles Kop.

Jan. 24th. French seizes Bastard's Nek.

Recognising that he was blocked to the eastward by the superior and apparently constantly increasing commandos, French now turned once more to the westward for a chance of gaining commanding positions, such as alone could enable him

* With the following:—1st Royal Irish and 2nd Worcestershire regiment, one squadron cavalry, one company New Zealand Mounted Rifles, and four guns.

† Three squadrons Carabiniers, two squadrons Household cavalry, N.S.W. Lancers, one company New Zealand Mounted Rifles and four guns.

‡ Rimington's Guides, one squadron Household cavalry, one company New Zealand Mounted Rifles.

§ A section of the 37th Howitzer battery, from Modder River.

OPERATIONS ROUND COLESBERG.

to manœuvre the enemy from Colesberg. An opening seemed to offer, because of the reported partial or entire abandonment of the important defile known as Plessis Poort, through which ran the road from Colesberg northward to the bridge and Botha's Drift. The possession of this pass would not only cut the Boers' line of retreat and northerly communications, but would seriously imperil those leading to Norval's Pont; for high ground, running south-eastward from the Poort, in parts parallel to the road and railway, in parts impinging on them, practically commanded both for a distance of some twenty miles from Colesberg. French, therefore, determined to lose no time in reconnoitring and, if possible, seizing on so valuable a point, and on the evening of January 24th, despatched de Lisle to occupy Bastard's Nek, a defile cutting the same range as Plessis Poort, and five miles to the westward of it. This being safely effected, early on the 25th a strong column* concentrated at the Nek. French's plan was as follows:—

Whilst the infantry, covered by a cross fire of artillery, pushed along the high ground towards Plessis Poort, the cavalry, diverging north-eastward, were to turn the Poort by the Boer right, and at the same time watch for any counter attack from the direction of the road bridge. To draw attention from these movements, demonstrations were to be made from every part of the British lines about Colesberg. As soon as it was light these operations began. Whilst McCracken, under cover of the howitzers and the two guns on Coles Kop, advanced from Kloof camp, whilst Clements, pushing out from Porter's Hill and Slingersfontein, shelled once more the laager at Keerom, and Porter from Kleinfontein, made as if to fall upon the railway towards Van Zyl siding, Brabazon's mounted force drew out to the northward, and Stephenson sent the infantry, the Essex leading, along the ridge towards the Poort. By 10 a.m. the four R.H.A. guns were in action against the Poort at

Jan. 25th. He strikes at Plessis Poort.

---

* Composition :—6th (Inniskilling) Dragoons, 10th Hussars, a battery R.H.A., under Major-General Brabazon; four companies 1st Yorkshire, four companies 1st Essex, the 2nd Wiltshire regiment, the M.I., and a field battery, under Colonel T. E. Stephenson, 1st Essex regiment.

a point 2,400 yards north-west of it. Brabazon's cavalry started late, owing to a delay on the part of the battalion told off to relieve the intermediate posts: the enemy, getting wind of his presence, advanced from the north with two guns, and from the east, and so delayed him that his turning movement was completed too late in the day to be utilised. Meanwhile the infantry, covered by the fire of the 4th battery, worked rapidly towards the Pass, driving scattered parties before them, and by 2 p.m. had reached favourable ground within 1,500 yards of it. Here Stephenson deployed the 2nd Wiltshire regiment, and sent it forward with orders to establish itself within 800 yards of the enemy, unless heavily fired upon whilst advancing. This the Wiltshire, moving in six lines 100 yards apart, did without loss, under a fire so trifling that the enemy seemed to be falling back, and Stephenson sent word to the General requesting permission to push the attack home. But French, who knew his opponents, had grown suspicious because of their silence. The hour was late, the cavalry turning movement had not been carried out, and finally instructions from the Commander-in-Chief had enjoined him to avoid serious fighting.* At 4 p.m., therefore, he gave the order to retire, and the Wiltshire firing lines rose to obey. Scarcely had they done so, before a burst of fire, both of rifles and guns, from the enemy's ridges, showed the nature of the trap that had been prepared. But in spite of the heavy fusilade which followed them back, the Wiltshire, retiring as steadily as they had advanced, rejoined the column with a loss of but ten men wounded. The whole force then returned to its bivouacs.

French avoids a trap, and returns to camp.

French, Jan. 29th, is summoned to Cape Town.

This reconnaissance, though it failed to give General French the Poort, succeeded in disclosing to him the nature of the enemy's dispositions in this neighbourhood, especially of those behind the hitherto impenetrable Grassy Hill. Such knowledge might have gone far towards a solution of the problem which had so long engaged his energies, the ousting of the Boers from their stronghold on British territory. The more vital portion of his task, the prevention of a further inroad into the colony, he

* See pages 434-5.

had already performed. He was now to be called away to a wider field. On January 29th he went down to Cape Town to receive instructions from the Commander-in-Chief. He returned to Rensburg on the 31st to break up his command. On February 6th he finally left Rensburg, after issuing an order in which he paid full tribute to the courage and energy of staff and troops, who had so long held in check "an enemy whose adroit skill in war demands the most untiring vigilance."* With French went all the Regular cavalry, except two squadrons, and also the 1st Essex and 1st Yorkshire regiments, the half-battalion 1st Welsh regiment, and O. and R. batteries, R.H.A. Major-General Clements was left at Rensburg with the remainder.†

* Despatch, February 2nd, 1900.
† General Clements' command was as follows :—
    Two squadrons 6th (Inniskilling) Dragoons.
    J. battery, R.H.A.
    4th battery, R.F.A.
    A section, 37th Howitzer battery, Royal Field Artillery.
    The Australian M.I. (490 men).
    The Victorian M.I. (175 men).
    Mounted infantry (450 men).
    2nd Bedfordshire regiment.
    1st Royal Irish regiment.
    2nd Worcester regiment.
    Half battalion 2nd Royal Berkshire regiment.
    2nd Wiltshire regiment.

CHAPTER XXV.

LORD ROBERTS AT CAPE TOWN; REORGANISES.*

10th Jan. 1900. Lord Roberts lands.

Situation at that date.

French before Colesberg.

Gatacre at Sterkstroom.

Boers in front of him.

FIELD-MARSHAL LORD ROBERTS landed at Cape Town on the 10th January, 1900, and assumed the supreme command.

The situation with which he was confronted will be more easily realised if a brief summary be here given of the facts as they now presented themselves at each of the several widely separated points of contact between the opposed forces.

As described in detail in the last chapter, the Boer commandos in front of General French having fallen back on Colesberg at the end of December, he had, on the 1st January, seized a group of hills on the south-western edge of the plain in which the town lies, and was continuing his tactics of active defence with constant success, save that a night attack made by the Suffolk regiment on 6th January had been repulsed with somewhat heavy loss. The Cavalry Lieut.-General's never-ceasing energy had not only foiled the enemy in his attempt to advance into the central districts of Cape Colony, but had appreciably diminished the pressure in other portions of the theatre of war. Gatacre was firmly established at Sterkstroom, with an advanced post at Cypher Gat, the main body of those fronting him remaining passively at Stormberg. A Boer commando had made a demonstration towards Molteno on 3rd January, and another party, about the same date, had driven out of Dordrecht a patrol of British mounted troops, which had occupied that place on the 23rd December. At Mafeking and Kimberley the garrisons

* See maps Nos. 9 and 17.

were still gallantly holding their own against the enemy, although in the latter town the hardships of the siege were telling much on the spirits of the civilian portion of the population. In Natal the 5th division had landed; and an attack, made by the Boers on Ladysmith on 6th January, had been repulsed after a severe struggle in which the fighting efficiency of the British troops was shown to be unimpaired. Yet disease, coupled with losses in action, was beginning seriously to reduce their effective strength and their capacity for active co-operation in the field with the relief force. {Mafeking and Kimberley. Natal. Ladysmith.}

The Boer scheme for the whole war still centred on the capture of Ladysmith. For the siege of that town, and for the repulse of the British relieving force, at least 21,000 burghers appear to have been still employed under the supreme command of Joubert. In the western theatre Grobelaar had probably 4,000 men under his control at Stormberg and in the adjacent areas: facing French at Colesberg were some 5,000 men, with Schoeman as leader; Boer reinforcements, gathered from various sources, amounting in all to some 2,000, were on their way, or would shortly be on their way, to that threatened point. The strength of Cronje's commando at Scholtz Nek may be estimated at 8,000, while 3,000 men, under Wessels and Ferreira, were investing Kimberley. Snyman had under his orders some 2,500, most of whom were encircling Mafeking, although a few detachments patrolled and dominated those western districts of Cape Colony which lie to the north of the Orange river. North of the frontier of the colony about 1,000 men, under Commandant Botha, opposed Plumer's efforts to relieve Baden-Powell's garrison from southern Rhodesia. Thus the total effective strength of the Boer forces actually in the field at this time may be approximately set down as nearly 46,500 men. Of these probably 1,000 were Natal rebels, and 5,000 British subjects belonging to Cape Colony, the latter being mainly distributed between the Stormberg, Colesberg, Kimberley, and Mafeking commandos. Of the Boer leaders, some, notably De Wet, had realised the folly of remaining on the defensive, but Joubert, whose appreciation of the conditions of the contest can be judged {Boers. In Natal. Cape Colony. 1. With Grobelaar at and near Stormberg. 2. With Schoeman at Colesberg. 3. Reinforcements on road. 4. With Cronje. 5. With Ferreira before Kimberley. 6. With Snyman before Mafeking, and in the west. 7. Under Botha fronting Plumer.}

from his circular letter printed at the close of this chapter, was opposed to any forward movement, and Joubert's views prevailed. Sir Redvers Buller personally, although the Field Intelligence staff in South Africa did not agree with his estimate, assessed the strength of the enemy in the field at far higher figures than those above given ;* and on 9th January he telegraphed to the Secretary of State that there was reason to believe that it was not less than 120,000 men, of whom 46,000 were in Natal.

<small>Buller's memorandum for Lord Roberts of Dec. 28th/99.</small>

Lord Roberts received on landing a memorandum, written by Sir R. Buller at Frere camp on 28th December, the following extracts from which will serve to explain the views of Sir Redvers :

"The whole Tugela river is a strong position ; there is no question of turning it ; the only open question is whether one part of it is easier to get through than another. I tried Colenso, because, though unaided I could not have forced the defile north of Colenso, it was the only place in the whole line in which Sir George White's force could aid me in my advance from the Tugela. I am now waiting for reinforcements, and am going to try and force a passage at Potgieters Drift. If I can find water to use in the subsequent advance, I think I ought to just pull through : but the difficulties are very great. If I succeed, it should be about the 12th January, and if then I join hands with Sir G. White, I think together we shall be able to force the enemy to retire and so free Sir G. White's force."

After stating that, in the event of success in the relief of Ladysmith, he hoped to be able to spare a division from the Natal army, and after referring Lord Roberts to instructions issued from time to time to Sir F. Forestier-Walker as regards the general plan of his operations in the western theatre, Sir R. Buller continued :

"You will see that my original idea was to bring Methuen back, but as his task has grown harder I have proposed a railway to Jacobsdal and thence to Bloemfontein. I think that for many reasons you would find such a line of advance easier and quicker than one up the main railway. Up that line the enemy will have a rail behind them, and will tear it up as you advance,

---

* The views of the Field Intelligence department as to the actual strength of the enemy may be gathered from Lord Roberts' report to the War Office on 12th January, that in his opinion the total strength against us had never been more than 80,000 men (telegram to Secretary of State for War).

and occupy positions that you must attack and from which they can escape. If I could have had my own way on arrival I should have pushed through Bethulie to Bloemfontein, but the fat was in the fire before I got out. Kimberley I believe will be saved. Ladysmith is a terrible nut to crack, but I hope it will (? be relieved). Then I would propose to attack Bloemfontein from Kimberley, and I think an army holding Bloemfontein based on Kimberley will be better off than one which holds Bloemfontein but has allowed Kimberley to be again invested. Time, after all, is in our favour. The Boers cannot reproduce their horses which are being used up, and if they lose their mobility, they lose their power. I believe that French and Gatacre are strong enough to prevent the spread of disaffection, and that when the 7th division arrives they will join hands, and the disaffected Dutch will go back to their homes."

This written memorandum was supplemented by a telegram, in which General Buller reported that he was leaving Chieveley the next day (11th January), and would operate towards Ladysmith from Potgieters Drift or Trickhardts Drift. From the larger point of view Lord Roberts would have preferred that the forward movement in Natal should have been delayed a little longer; but he felt that he was not in a position to judge how far Sir R. Buller was committed to an immediate stroke, or whether the situation before him or Ladysmith itself demanded prompt action. He decided, therefore, to give General Buller an absolutely free hand to carry out the operations he had planned.* Sir Redvers telegraphs, Jan. 10th. 1900, that he is about to try to reach Ladysmith by Potgieters or Trickhardts.

Before he left England Lord Roberts had determined on the line for the advance of the army which he had to command in person. Though in detail his scheme was somewhat modified afterwards, he began to prepare for the execution of it as soon as he had landed. For reasons which will be more fully recorded in his own words, he had decided to choose the route along the western line of railway, on which side alone a bridge over the Orange river was in his possession. In order to possess the freedom of movement essential to the execution of any sound schemes of war, he determined to make such arrangements as would enable him to cast himself loose from the railway and to march across the Free State eastward. His first idea was to strike the central railway as close as possible to Springfontein junction. He believed that the Boers would thus be compelled to evacuate Lord Roberts prepares to carry out his plan of campaign.

---

* See p. 461, Vol. I., Minutes of Evidence before War Commission.

their positions at Stormberg and Colesberg, and to abandon to him the Norval's Pont and Bethulie bridges over the river. The Commander-in-Chief was convinced, moreover, that this course, by menacing Bloemfontein, would oblige the enemy to relax his hold on the Modder river and Natal.* But, on the 27th January, increasing anxiety as to Kimberley led him to decide that the prompt relief of that town had become necessary. This involved, not a change of plan, but merely a modification of details. The initial march eastward was still to be carried out, but as soon as Cronje's flank had thus been effectively passed, a wheel northward would bring the British troops athwart the Boer line of communication, and, when the passage of the Modder was made, the way to Kimberley would be opened.† After relieving Kimberley the Field-Marshal's movements would depend on the situation, as it might then present itself, but should such a march appear possible, he determined to make straight for Bloemfontein.‡ The occupation of that capital would, he thought, make it easy to re-establish direct railway communication with Cape Colony through Norval's Pont and Bethulie. The considerations which guided Lord Roberts to the adoption of this plan, as finally formulated, were explained by him in detail nearly three years later to the War Commission in the following terms : ||

"Before leaving England I had practically determined that the advance must be through the Orange Free State, but by one, not by three lines through Cape Colony, as was originally intended ;§ and the western line commended itself to me for the following reasons :

"1. It was on that line only that we had possession of a railway bridge over the Orange river :

"2. It was by that line only that Kimberley could be relieved in time, and had Kimberley fallen, Mafeking must have fallen also :

"3. It was by that line only I could deal with the Boer forces in detail, and defeat Cronje before he could be reinforced.

* Telegram, Lord Roberts to Secretary of State, 26th January, 1900.
† Telegram, Lord Roberts to Secretary of State, 27th January, 1900.
‡ Telegram to Secretary of State, dated 30th January, 1900.
|| Minutes of Evidence of War Commission, Vol. I., pp. 460–1.
§ This would seem to be a misapprehension. Sir R. Buller's intention had been to advance by Bethulie (see page 411).

"Both the Norval's Pont and Bethulie bridges were in the hands of the enemy, and by the time I had forced them back into the Orange Free State, and had been able to repair either of these bridges (which I was certain would be destroyed, and which actually happened), and I had occupied Bloemfontein, I should have between me and Kimberley, not only Cronje, but the whole of the Boer force which was not engaged in Natal. I should have then been obliged either to march across the veld against this increased force, or to have transported the greater portion of my troops by rail to the Modder River camp (if the railway could have been kept intact, which was hardly likely, seeing how weakly it was necessarily guarded and the number of Boers who would have been available to destroy it), and then to turn the Magersfontein position. To carry out either of these operations, and for the onward advance on an extended front to Pretoria, at least the same amount of transport would have been required as was needed for the march from Modder River camp to Bloemfontein. But this would not have been forthcoming had I adopted the railway line to Bloemfontein and not organised the system of transport directly I arrived at the Cape.

*　　*　　*　　*　　*　　*　　*

"I felt convinced that an advance on Bloemfontein must draw the Free Staters back from Kimberley and Natal, and that the occupation of their capital would render the Boer positions to the south of the Orange river untenable. To carry out this scheme, as large a force as could be collected was necessary, as the enemy had through railway communication (about two days' journey) between Natal and Bloemfontein, and could transfer a considerable portion of their forces from one of the theatres of the war to the other in infinitely less time than we could. Moreover, rapidity was essential in concentrating this force and making an advance towards Bloemfontein, as Ladysmith and Kimberley were, so far as I know, only provisioned for a very limited time."

Lord Roberts' explanation why he chose the route he took.

It will be seen that Lord Roberts rejected Sir R. Buller's suggestion that a railway should be made through Jacobsdal to Bloemfontein. Colonel Girouard had estimated that this line could be constructed at the rate of a mile a day without interfering with the traffic for the supply of the troops, and, in an offer made to the Home Government by a private firm, hope had been held out that the work might be carried through at the rate of five or six miles a day, or in other words, that, assuming fighting conditions to be favourable, the whole would be finished in about a month. The latter estimate seemed altogether too sanguine. Moreover, the practical difficulty of guarding those employed on the required task from the raids of a mobile enemy would have been very great. Finally, the chance of surprise would have been lost, and, hard to secure as

His reason for deciding against the railway through Jacobsdal.

secrecy in military projects had been found in South Africa, Lord Roberts was certain that to obtain decisive results the complete concealment of his plan of operations was essential.

Great exertions had been made during the period of his voyage to South Africa, both by the Government and by private individuals, to provide the troops needed for the success of these schemes. He was informed of the result of these exertions by the following telegram from Lord Lansdowne of 9th January:

"Please let us know what you think about further reinforcements as soon as you have thoroughly examined the situation. We have arranged for the following reinforcements in addition to the 7th Division, viz.:

"1. Four brigade divisions Field Artillery, embarking as soon after the 20th January as possible.

"2. One volunteer company for each line battalion, amounting in all to about 7,000.

"3. The City of London regiment of Volunteers, and the battery of the Honourable Artillery Company.*

"4. One Field Artillery battery of Volunteers from Elswick.

"5. Colonial contingents, inclusive of four artillery batteries, mostly mounted, and amounting in all probably to about 3,000.

"6. Seven Militia battalions.

"Of these some have already started. As to the Imperial Yeomanry, it is not yet possible to say what number will be raised, but 4,000 at least will probably be the total, and the material, though raw, is good.† We have also mobilised a cavalry brigade which could embark at once. If, however, it is sent, only the remainder of the Household cavalry and five line regiments will

---

* The City of London Imperial Volunteers was formed as a special regiment under a Royal Warrant, dated 24th December, 1899, and organised under a Special Army Order, dated 6th January, 1900. The regiment was raised by the Lord Mayor and his committee under instructions informally given between the 16th December and the date of the Order of 6th January, which embodied these instructions.

The employment of the Service companies of the Volunteers was regulated by a Special Army Order, dated 2nd January, 1900.

† The original proposal to organise regiments of Yeomanry for service in South Africa was made by Lord Chesham and other Yeomanry officers in October, 1899. Sanction for the formation of the corps of "The Imperial Yeomanry" was given by Royal Warrant, dated 24th December, 1899. Under a Special Army Order of 4th January, 1900, a committee of Yeomanry officers was constituted to administer the force. This committee was dissolved in May, 1900, the administration being then taken over by the War Office. The first contingent, which went out early in 1900, numbered about 10,000. A second contingent went in the spring of 1901, numbering about 17,000; and a third contingent, of about 7,000, in the winter of 1901-1902.

LORD ROBERTS AT CAPE TOWN. 415

be left at home. Do you wish to have it? We are also mobilising the 8th division, which could begin to embark about the 20th February, but if it goes there will only be seven infantry battalions left, and unless the 8th division is urgently required this reduction of the home garrison does not appear desirable, in view of the general outlook. It might answer your purpose if we sent for the lines of communication eight or more Militia battalions instead."

To this telegram Lord Roberts replied on the 12th January:

"As to reinforcements that may be required, I am a little diffident about giving a definite opinion until matters still further develop and the result is known of Buller's operations to relieve Ladysmith. I trust that if White and Buller succeed, without very heavy losses, in joining hands, it will not be necessary to send the 8th division or another brigade of cavalry. For the lines of communication I shall require eight Militia battalions, in addition to the seven already detailed, but I should prefer thirteen Militia battalions, and if Lord Cromer agrees, the two Highland battalions which are now in Egypt, two of the Militia battalions to be sent there, taking the places of the latter. I hope, with the regular forces already under orders, the 4,000 Imperial Yeomanry, and the volunteer battalion, and the Colonial details referred to in your telegram, that the force in South Africa will be sufficient, and am most reluctant to request the despatch of more troops from home."

Immediately on his arrival the Field Marshal strove to systematise and support the efforts of the many South African colonists who were pressing to be allowed to take up arms in self-defence. Their embodiment had already been sanctioned by Sir R. Buller and approved by the Home Government. Colonel Brabant's corps was expanded into two regiments, and their leader appointed a brigadier-general to command a Colonial division, composed of his own two regiments (Brabant's Horse), the Cape Mounted Rifles, Kaffrarian Rifles, Border Horse, and Queenstown Rifle Volunteers. Two new mounted corps, entitled Roberts' Horse and Kitchener's Horse, were raised, besides numerous local defence corps, such as Nesbitt's and Bayley's from the eastern province, and Orpen's from the Hopetown district. The mounted troops at Lord Roberts' disposal were further substantially increased by the formation of mounted companies from all battalions of the line serving in Cape Colony.* By this means sufficient units were formed

Large numbers of mounted corps raised.

---

* It had for many years been the practice in South Africa to mount at least one company of each battalion in the command, but this had not been carried out at the commencement of the war in battalions as they arrived from England.

to make up eight additional mounted infantry battalions, but, owing to the difficulty in procuring remounts, the greater part of these did not receive their horses until the first week of February.

The transport arrangements.

The provision of sufficient and suitable transport for the new army now being organised was a question which naturally needed the consideration of Lord Roberts and his staff. From the first, even before war was generally regarded as inevitable, the subject had been found to be beset with difficulties. The nature of the country permitted little deviation from, or modification of, that form of transport which experience has taught the dwellers in the land to adopt. The roughness of the tracks across the veld, which were given the deceptive name of roads, necessitated a particular build of vehicle, while the draught animals which could be employed were almost exclusively oxen and mules. The pace at which oxen are able to move, and the fact that they must graze in the daytime, limit the length of a march and the hours of working. Nevertheless, oxen can draw far greater loads than mules, can work over heavy ground in wet weather, and for most of the year depend for their sustenance on grazing alone. On the other hand, mules travel more quickly, and can feed at any time of the day or night, but forage for them must be carried, since grazing alone is not sufficient to keep them in working condition—and their loads must be lighter; their use, therefore, increases the amount of transport and the length of the column. With mixed transport, drawn partly by mules and partly by oxen, the daily distance is regulated by the slower animal. In ordinary circumstances mules may do sixteen to eighteen miles a day, but oxen can hardly be counted on for more than twelve for many days in succession. It was because of such considerations that Sir R. Buller reported to Lord Roberts on his arrival that "there is no such thing as a rapid advance anywhere in South Africa, except by railway." *

Difficulties in providing both kinds

Ox-transport could only be obtained in South Africa itself. A system of contracts organised by Colonel Bridge and the

---
* Memorandum dated December 28th, 1899.

officers who accompanied him had hitherto enabled all troops to be fully supplied on their arrival with such ox-transport as was necessary for them.* The Bechuanaland district of Cape Colony was the best ox-wagon country, but as this was occupied by the enemy there remained only the eastern parts of the Colony upon which to draw. In default of a general application of Martial Law, "commandeering" was not possible. Prices consequently ruled high, and at one time some doubt existed whether all demands could be met. By the middle of November, the steady influx of imported mules dispelled this anxiety, and numbers in excess of the contracts were also assured. The local supply of mule-wagons could not, however, keep pace with the demand, and was supplemented by the despatch of vehicles from England. These began to arrive in December, and on the 11th January the General Officer Commanding the lines of communication was able to report to the Secretary of State that ". . . . . speaking in general terms, units of all sorts have been completed with authorised or extempore regimental transport and equipment on arrival." *of transport.*

The transference to Natal of a large part of the field force, originally destined to advance from Cape Colony, released the ox-transport prepared for those troops and left it available for the reinforcements which were on their way from England. The Transport staff had, therefore, no difficulty in providing a sufficient amount of ox-transport to meet Lord Roberts' needs. Of mules there was a large number in hand. These, for the sake of economy, had been collected in batches, at various places where they could be kept without heavy expenditure, pending the receipt of mule-wagons and harness. But although, as troops were placed under orders at home, every effort was made to provide both wagons and harness for them in advance, the supply reaching South Africa, especially of mule-harness, was necessarily intermittent. Transport and equipment for the 7th Division had been shipped from England in December, and was *Ox-transport, left by troops moved to Natal, available for reinforcements expected. Mule-wagons gradually received from England.*

* Col. C. H. Bridge, Army Service Corps, took up the duties of Director of Supplies and Transport on July 30th, 1899, and held this position until the arrival of Col. W. Richardson on October 3rd.

coming in daily. Sir F. Forestier-Walker reported on January 14th that, as far as could be foreseen, "the provision of wagons already made is much more than our known requirements," *i.e.*, on the scale which had hitherto been accepted.

<small>System existing. "The Regimental."</small>
The allotment of transport which had been made prior to the Field-Marshal's arrival was based on principles worked out by the Mobilisation branch of the War Office, and embodied in the regulations entitled, "War Establishments, 1898." Under these rules the distribution was as follows : *

(A.) Regimental transport, *i.e.*, transport allotted to regiments and battalions, and placed under charge of an officer and small staff furnished by the unit. This was available for the general service of the station where the unit was posted.† It was sub-divided into :

> 1. First Line Transport—for ammunition, entrenching tools, medical stores, signalling equipment, machine gun, and water-carts.
> 2. Second Line Transport—for regimental equipment, blankets, baggage, and rations and forage for one day or more.

(B.) The Supply Column.—An Army Service Corps organisation forming the first reserve, and carrying at least one day's ration, an emergency ration for every man, and one day's forage for every animal.

(C.) The Supply Park.—Under the supply and transport officers of the Army Service Corps. The park carried at least three days' rations and forage, but this amount could be increased as circumstances might dictate.

(D.) Auxiliary Transport.—To be composed of excess or reserve transport organised in companies under Army Service

---

* This system was commonly termed in South Africa the "Regimental System," although the regimental transport was in fact only about one-eighth of the whole.

† Para. 10A, "Instructions regarding Regimental Transport, South African Field Force," issued October, 1899.

LORD ROBERTS AT CAPE TOWN. 419

Corps officers. It was intended primarily for use on the lines of communication.*

(E.) Technical Transport.—To meet the requirements of ammunition columns, Royal engineers, technical equipment, medical units, and any special purpose, such as the Naval heavy guns.†

Arrangements had been made in South Africa that (A) the regimental transport and (B) the supply column should be entirely drawn by mules. The supply park (C) consisted solely of ox-wagons with spans of sixteen oxen. The remainder of the transport had partly ox and partly mule draught, although in Natal ox-transport was mainly used. Under the conditions of the local contracts all ox-wagons were grouped in sections of ten, with a conductor and sub-conductor for each section. These sections of ten were organised in sub-divisions of fifty and divisions of one hundred wagons, respectively under a sub-inspector and an inspector. *[marginal note: Proportion drawn by oxen and mules.]*

This system had the advantage that, being prescribed in the existing regulations, it was more or less familiar to staff and regimental officers; moreover, the organisation of the Army Service Corps for field service had been adapted to it. But against this had to be set the serious objection of its extravagance. Under the regulations, the transport allotted to units employed as garrisons or for other reasons remaining stationary, would be idle and wasted. Without the transport so lost the mobility needed to carry out the Commander-in-Chief's plan would be unattainable. Lord Roberts therefore decided that in order to equip his army, so as to enable it to operate with rapidity at a distance from the railway, the transport must be reorganised.‡ The regimental mule-transport from units was to be called in and formed into transport companies, which could *[marginal note: Lord Roberts recasts the transport system.]*

---

* A scheme for this existed and regulations had been issued, but prior to Lord Roberts' arrival there had been no excess transport to enable the scheme to be put into operation.

† Excepting for the last-named, transport for each of these units had been issued in Cape Town, October, 1899.

‡ The "regimental" system was, however, retained by the force under Sir R. Buller until the break up of the Natal army, in October, 1900.

be attached to brigades or columns in whatever manner the circumstances of the moment required. In short, decentralisation was to be replaced by concentration of the transport for redistribution in proportion to the wants of the service. The change of system was effected successfully under the supervision of Lord Kitchener and Major-General Sir William Nicholson whose experience of similar arrangements in Egyptian and Indian campaigns were of much assistance to the Commander-in-Chief.

<small>S. A. Army orders of Jan. 24th, 1900, and Jan. 29th determine details of change.</small>

Returns of the mule-transport in possession of units were called for, and on January 24th an Army order was published withdrawing mule-transport with certain exceptions. On the 29th January a further order was issued, giving the details of the vehicles which were to remain with units and stating how their draught was to be provided. The general transport obtained by this withdrawal was formed into companies of four sections each, each company consisting of forty-nine wagons, one Scotch cart, and a water-cart; it was calculated that one of these companies would suffice to carry the baggage and two days' supply of food and forage for an infantry brigade of four battalions or a cavalry brigade of three regiments. The ox-transport was organised in companies of one hundred wagons each, from which convoys could be formed, as required, to fulfil the functions of the supply columns of the previous system.* These transport companies were placed under Army Service Corps officers, and the administration of the whole was at first undertaken by the Deputy Adjutant-General for Supplies and Transport, Colonel Richardson, who had been transferred from the lines of communication to the Headquarter staff. The general principles now adopted were that complete transport, and transport animals for certain vehicles still left in charge of units, should be placed at the disposal of the commander of any force when it was ordered to move; such transport was to remain with that force during the move, but on its completion was to be returned to the transport department, so as to be again available for whatever duty was most urgent.

<small>Difficulties in practice.</small>

Some difficulties naturally arose. By the abolition of regi-

* Mule companies had 520 mules; ox companies, 1,600 oxen.

mental transport the services of the regimental officers and non-commissioned officers hitherto employed on that duty were regained by their corps, but were lost to the transport department. The personnel of the Army Service Corps was not equal to the demands thus made upon it, and it was found necessary to allot two transport companies to one company of Army Service Corps, and to attach to these so-formed companies officers of other branches as they happened to be available. Moreover, to ensure the requisite amount of mule-transport for the combatant portion of the troops that of bearer companies and of field hospitals was cut down. In the former the number of ambulances was reduced from ten to two, and for the latter only two wagons could be allowed in place of four. On the other hand, owing to fear of a scarcity of water on the intended march, the number of water-carts with the medical units was doubled. The mule-transport was speedily assembled at the places ordered. The concentration of the ox-transport for convoy purposes took a longer time, but partly by rail and partly by march route it was completed soon enough to enable the Field-Marshal to carry out his plan of operations.

Owing to the efforts of the Quartermaster-General's department of the War Office, a steady stream of supplies had, since the beginning of the war, been poured into the country, and had removed all anxiety as to the possibility of food or forage running short at the coast. The difficulty was the transmission of these up country simultaneously with the troops and their equipment. Arrangements were made by the railway staff which enabled sufficient quantities to be forwarded from the sea bases and to be accumulated at Orange River, De Aar, and at depôts between the Orange and Modder rivers. For the forward move into the Orange Free State two days' supplies were to be carried by the men and two days' in the mule-transport allotted to brigades; the brigade supplies were to be filled up from convoys moving in rear of the troops, and for this purpose some five hundred ox-wagons, carrying ten days' rations and forage, were assembled.* {Supplies on the coast ample. The difficulty of getting them forward and distributing them.}

* The cavalry division was accompanied by a supply park on the old system.

422   THE WAR IN SOUTH AFRICA.

Separation of supply and transport.

These changes foreshadowed the separation of supply and transport into two departments, a separation which, shortly after the advance into the Free State had begun, was carried out by the transfer of Major-General Sir W. G. Nicholson from the appointment of Military Secretary to that of Director of Transport. Colonel Richardson still continued to have charge of supplies.

Increase of heavy artillery.

Meantime, steps were taken to improve the artillery equipment of the army in South Africa. Prior to the war it had been ascertained by the Intelligence department that the Boers had in their possession several 150 m/m Creusots and a battery of 120 m/m howitzers, but the cumbersome carriages on which the former weapons were mounted had led to the belief that they were intended solely for use in the forts and positions near Pretoria and Johannesburg. The howitzers had been classified in the intelligence reports as field artillery armament, because in the year before the war the French, Austrian, and German armies had added howitzers to their field equipment. The enterprise of the Boers in bringing 150 m/m (6-in.) guns into the field at the outset of the campaign formed in a sense a new departure in modern warfare, although in 1870 fortress guns had been taken from Belfort and used in the fighting on the Lisaine. On the receipt of Sir George White's report that one of these guns had been employed against the troops at Dundee, telegraphic orders, at the suggestion of Major-General Sir John Ardagh, were sent out by the War Office to Cape Colony to insure the immediate despatch to Natal of two 6·3-in. R.M.L. howitzers, lying at King William's Town, the property of the Cape Government.* The arrangements made by the Naval Commander-in-Chief for the despatch to the front of Naval contingents, placed at the disposal of the military authorities, both in the western and eastern theatres of war, a number of long-range guns which, in the skilled hands of the officers and men of the Royal Navy and Marines who accompanied them, rendered valuable service. The War Office also took immediate action to

---

* As will be seen in the account of the siege of Ladysmith (Vol. II.), these howitzers arrived in time and proved most useful.

reinforce the arm. On the 9th of December a battery of four 4·7-in. Q.F. guns, manned by a company of R.G.A., was despatched from England to South Africa, together with eight 6-in. B.L. howitzers, which formed part of the approved siege train of the army. On the 22nd two companies with eight 5-in. B.L. followed. On the 22nd January two more companies with eight 4·7-in. Q.F., mounted on 6-in. howitzer carriages, were embarked for the Cape, and supplemented on the 28th by six additional guns of the same type, intended to replace any naval guns which might be showing signs of deterioration. On the 3rd of February another batch of eight 5-in. B.L. guns, accompanied by two companies R.G.A., left Southampton in order to relieve some of the naval contingents; on the previous day a battery of four 9·45-in. B.L. howitzers had been embarked with the necessary personnel. The only further additions made during the war to the heavy armament were four 6-in. howitzers sent out at Lord Roberts' request on 27th April, 1900, and two 5-in. B.L. guns despatched at the end of the same year to replace two which had become unserviceable. With the exception of the howitzers the whole of these guns were taken from forts. Carriages for them were improvised by the Ordnance department. The use by the Boers of the 37 m/m Vickers-Maxim Q.F. guns,* nick-named " pom-poms " by the men, was met by the despatch of forty-nine of these weapons from England. Another important change was the introduction of a longer time-fuse for use with field guns. The regulation time-fuse at the outbreak of the war burnt in flight for twelve seconds only, suited to a range of 4,100 yards for the 15-pr. B.L. guns and 3,700 yards for the 12-pr. B.L. Experiments had been already made by the Ordnance Committee to obtain a satisfactory time-fuse effective for longer ranges, and on receipt of reports of the extreme distance at which the Boers were using their field artillery, these were rapidly pushed on, with the result that by the middle of January

* It was known before the war that the Boers had purchased a considerable number of "pom-poms." The artillery authorities of the army did not at that time attach much importance to them, but, as their fire was found to produce great moral effect, guns of this type were sent out at Sir R. Buller's request.

Railway system.

fuses capable of burning twenty-one seconds, corresponding to a range of 6,400 yards, were sent to South Africa.

At no time was a heavier call made on the personnel and material of the Cape Government railways than during the concentration for Lord Roberts' advance into the Free State. At an early date an organisation for the control of the transport of troops and stores by rail had been instituted, and had gradually been perfected by experience. Lieutenant-Colonel Girouard, R.E., the Director of Railways, had arrived with a staff of fifteen officers at Cape Town towards the end of October, 1899, and had, under the orders of the General Officer Commanding the lines of communication, initiated a system based on the principle that it was the controlling staff's duty to keep in close touch with the permanent traffic officials of the railway and to act as intermediaries between them and the military commanders. Much to his satisfaction, the Director of Railways had found on his arrival that "all the British lines were in good working order and administered by a highly loyal, capable, and enthusiastic staff prepared for any emergency, including risks of war."* In conjunction with this permanent staff, of whom Mr. C. B. Elliott was the General Manager and Mr. T. R. Price the Traffic Manager, uniformity of military administration throughout the whole railway system of Cape Colony was speedily established.† The technical working of the railways was left entirely in the hands of the civil officials, supported and protected by the military controlling staff from interference by officers or men. Repairs to the line were undertaken by the railway troops of the R.E.,‡ with such of the British employés of the Orange Free State railway as had not, at the outbreak of the war,

---

* General Report on Military Railways, South Africa, by Lieut.-Col. Sir E. P. C. Girouard.

† The conditions in Natal differed considerably from those in Cape Colony, and the system of railway administration was modified accordingly, but here, too, the military staff received the most loyal assistance in every way from Sir David Hunter and the rest of the civil staff.

‡ The 8th and 10th Railway Companies, 20th, 31st and 42nd Fortress companies R.E.

been absorbed into the permanent staff of the Cape Government railways. The number of skilled artisans thus available was insufficient for the reconstruction of the Norval's Pont and Bethulie railway bridges and other extensive works which it was foreseen would be necessary in order to make good the damage done by the enemy in his retreat. The Director of Railways accordingly obtained leave to avail himself of the offer of Messrs. L. I. Seymour and C. A. Goodwin, leading mining engineers of Johannesburg, to form a corps of the miners and artisans, thrown out of employment by the war. With the title of the Railway Pioneer regiment, it was placed under the command of Lieutenant-Colonel J. E. Capper, R.E., Messrs. Seymour and Goodwin being appointed wing commanders, having the rank of major. The material needed for the construction of temporary bridges at Norval's Pont and Bethulie and for the rapid reconstruction of the permanent bridges at these points was, during the month of January, prepared.

Joubert's circular letter, referred to on p. 410 as having had great importance because it enjoined a passive defensive attitude on all Boer commanders at the very time when Lord Roberts was designing an active offence, ran as follows :—

29.12.99.

FROM COMDT.-GENERAL TO ACTG. GENERAL DU TOIT.

FELLOW OFFICERS,—

It is obvious that England is exasperated that her army is not able, against the will of our God, to annihilate us and to overwhelm us as easily as they had expected. While they were governed and inspired by this thought, the name of Sir Redvers Buller was on the lips of everybody and his praise and prowess were elevated to the clouds. Now that our God and Protector has revealed His will, and Buller has not succeeded in crushing the hated Boers, or, as Sir Alfred Milner has it, the Boerdom, and to subjugate them and to banish from the face of the earth the name which God, as it were, had given them—now they, instead of admitting and acknowledging their fault and looking for it in the right place, want to have a scapegoat, and for this purpose Sir Redvers Buller must serve; he is not brave enough, not wise enough; he is not strong and powerful enough to carry on the war for them against the will of the High God of Heaven and to annihilate the Africander in South Africa. Many a person now deems it well that Buller has been humiliated; but I have to say in regard to this that when I withstood General Colley in the same way in the War of Independence, he was urged to attempt a successful battle before his successor could arrive, as he would otherwise lose all military honour and fame. He was moved to such an extent that he acted on the suggestion, ascended Amajuba Hill, which is to-day still so intensely hated by the blinded Englishman and Jingo, where the Lord then said, "Thus far and no further." And now, my friends, you may suspect and expect that Mr. Buller will receive the same advice, and that he may attempt to do as the late Sir George Colley had done. Therefore, he will issue orders either here at Colenso, at Ladysmith, Scholtz Nek, or elsewhere where there is an English force in South Africa, to attempt a successful action, either by means of a sortie or attack, or in some other way, in order, if possible, to regain his good name and military fame. For this reason we must, in firm faith in the help of our faithful and beloved God, be on our guard against such action. I very much fear a night attack, when our men are not alert and on their guard. The fright in case of a false alarm, when so much ammunition is blindly wasted, makes me fear that a disaster may be in preparation, and demonstrates that the burghers are not organised properly on outpost duty. On dark nights the outposts should be strengthened to such an extent that they could almost independently hold their position. In all cases at least the half of the outpost guard, if not two-thirds, must remain awake, so that the men are not aroused from sleep with fright and confusion, but, being on the alert, can independently offer defence. Therefore, let the words of our Lord be impressed on the mind of everyone: "Watch and pray, lest ye enter into temptation."

Our enemy is not only powerful, but also artful, and treason is continually taking place, for it appears from the newspapers that the enemy is even cognisant of our most secret plans, and we cannot advance, but remain stationary, while the enemy is continually strengthening himself.

Your sincere friend,
P. J. JOUBERT,
Comdt.-General.

CHAPTER XXVI.

THE ARMY MOVES FORWARD.

<small>The intended stroke.</small>

THE first stage in the realisation of Lord Roberts' plan of campaign must necessarily be the transfer to the neighbourhood of Lord Methuen's camp of the army with which it was his purpose to manœuvre Cronje out of Magersfontein, to relieve Kimberley, and strike for Bloemfontein.

<small>The problem. How solved.</small>

The problem was to carry out this transfer without allowing the Boer General to suspect the design with which it was made, and, till this first movement was completed, in order to gain time for it, to keep him as long as possible uncertain whether the real advance would not be, as he had always hitherto supposed, along the railway which runs directly from Colesberg by Norval's Pont to Bloemfontein. Both purposes were accomplished with rare success. It becomes, therefore, in all ways interesting, as a study of the larger scope of the campaign, to realise by what means this result was secured. In all war, and in every campaign, so far as the two opposing commanders are concerned, it is the play of mind upon mind which is the ruling factor. To put himself in the place of the man whom he must outwit, if he is to give his soldiers the best chance of victory, is for each commander the essential preliminary. To take such steps as will tend to confirm that man in any false impressions he is known or reasonably suspected to have received, and to conceal as far as possible those measures which are preparing the way for the real stroke, are common characteristics of all triumphant achievement. The means by which the end is gained—reticence, the

THE ARMY MOVES FORWARD.

movement of troops in such a way as will suggest that they are placed with one object when, in fact, the posts chosen will make it easy to use them for another, the allowing of subordinate, even high, commanders, to misconceive, until it is necessary for them to know, why orders are given—all these are the well-tried methods. The fact that rumours spread almost automatically and quite invariably from camp to hostile camp, so that what is believed on one side largely affects belief on the other, is one of the fixed data on which much depends. The issue openly of fictitious orders, cancelled by cypher messages, is another available means of throwing a cloud over what is being done. The art lies in applying these well-known principles to the particular case to be dealt with. It will be found that in practice Lord Roberts took advantage of every one of them; but without a clear understanding of the methods which the long experience of war has taught those whose duty it is to study it, the underlying motive of much that has now to be described would not be clear.

Many things tended to convince Cronje that it was along the railway direct on Bloemfontein that the march into the Free State would be made. The capture at Dundee, in October, 1899, of certain Intelligence department papers by the Boers had shown them that this had been the first design. During the weeks which had immediately followed Lord Roberts' appointment to command, when, though he had not reached Cape Town, at least the wider scope of manœuvres might be supposed to be directed by him, or to be in accordance with his wishes, the only fierce fighting which had taken place was round Colesberg, and much of it suggested a wish to secure the passage of the Orange river at Norval's Pont, an obvious necessity if the great movement was to be made along the Colesberg—Norval's Pont—Bloemfontein route. Outside Natal this continued, after Lord Roberts arrived, to be even more the case, and so far as Cape Colony was concerned, the distribution of troops showed Norval's Pont as the central point of the front of attack. Lord Methuen's line of communications, supply and reinforcements through Orange River station marked the left, Gatacre's slowly gathering *[Causes tending to deceive Cronje,]* division the right, and French, now close to Norval's Pont, the centre. Without delaying the progress over Orange River bridge, it was possible to strengthen the conviction in Cronje's mind that it was at Norval's Pont that danger threatened.

<small>and means taken to hoodwink him.</small>

In the first place, the great number of wagons, horses and stores which had to be passed up under the protection of Lord Methuen's division, and of the troops immediately engaged in guarding the line, needed ample time, and, as it was not easy for the Boers to distinguish between what was required for Lord Methuen's army and the accumulations that were being made for a very different purpose, this necessary preparation for the decisive move was not likely to attract much notice. If, therefore, a freshly-arrived division were sent to French's neighbourhood, say from Port Elizabeth to Naauwpoort junction, since its coming there was sure to be reported to the Boers, it would not merely meet the need for having a reinforcement for French available in case of emergency, which, as will be seen further on, was the reason assigned at the time by Lord Roberts for sending it, but it would help to confirm the idea that it was towards Norval's Pont that the whole concentration was trending. The division and the whole of French's command could be kept in this district to the last moment, because of the cross railway which from Naauwpoort junction runs to connect the railway from Port Elizabeth with that from Cape Town to Kimberley. The troops moving up by this the most westerly line would draw the less attention as long as the force at and near Colesberg was formidable and active. When the right time was come—that is, as it worked out, when French handed over to Clements those who were to remain round Colesberg—all the rest, including the new division, could be carried from Naauwpoort junction and so on towards the Riet, being, during their passage, far in rear of the fighting line around Colesberg. It will be easily seen from the map how greatly the trace of the railways facilitated the removal of strong bodies from the Naauwpoort—Colesberg region to the Kimberley railway, the whole movement being screened by the fighting forces left round Colesberg.

Cronje himself was a Transvaaler, and his principal line of

THE ARMY MOVES FORWARD. 431

supply ran northwards through the ground held by the besiegers of Kimberley. Although, therefore, many of those under him were from the Orange Free State and likely to be disturbed by a movement against Bloemfontein, any such danger appeared to be remote as long as the Orange river, both at Norval's Pont and Bethulie, was in the hands of the Boers. His retreat northwards was at all events quite secure. The reports of the arrival of ever increasing numbers south of Lord Methuen's camp seemed to imply that, whatever might be done elsewhere, his entrenchments were to be again attacked, and as he wished for nothing better than this, he very naturally interpreted the information he received in accordance with his hopes. It was not difficult, therefore, to impose on him, in this respect also, by demonstrations against the opposite flank to that which Lord Roberts intended—not to attack but to pass by on his route northwards—so placing his army ultimately athwart Cronje's line of retreat. The execution of this scheme, the guiding principles of which have thus been sketched, will perhaps now be more easily followed in detail. It only remains to add here that the fictitious orders, cancelled by cypher telegrams, were actually sent, and were very useful in their effect of imposing on the Boers. *Further causes of success.*

The interest of the whole scheme for modern soldiers lies in the fact that it was an application of very ancient principles of war to the times of railways and telegraphs. Everything turned upon the facilities afforded by the railways on the one hand, upon the difficulties which the railway authorities had to surmount on the other, and, above all, upon this: that where accumulation of rolling stock, vast in proportion to the resources of the country, had to be collected from every direction upon a single line, it needed much tact and management to make the preparations required to enable the transport of troops, when once begun, to continue rapidly without interruption, and yet not to disclose the secret. Engines were more essential than anything else, and to obtain them in sufficient number the Port Elizabeth lines had to be swept almost bare, although the supply of the troops round Naauwpoort junction and Colesberg largely depended on that railway. It may, therefore, be imagined how *A railway scheme. Facilities and difficulties.*

hard it was to placate the zealous civil officials, who, without understanding why it was done, found themselves deprived of the very instruments needed for their work, and had as best they could to make bricks without straw. All the organisation of this fell upon Colonel Girouard, who had promised Lord Roberts to have the immense volume of stores necessary for the campaign, as well as the troops, delivered at the assigned stations by February 14th, on two conditions: one, that absolute secrecy as to all that was being done should be strictly observed, Girouard himself naming the men to whom he must disclose his plans; the other, that when he had received his instructions as to the places where delivery was to be made by the railway these should not be changed. Unfortunately this latter condition could not be kept. Honey Nest Kloof, which had been at first selected as the place for the great camp and depôt, was found to be inadequately supplied with water, so that Graspan and Belmont inevitably replaced it.

The nature of task.

The fact that, with the exception of the two Generals, Kelly-Kenny and French, who knew the scheme after French's visit to Cape Town, none of the officers in the trains had any idea where they were going or what was intended, and did not realise what was essential for the success of the undertaking, occasionally gave trouble to the railway authorities. For instance, water for the troops bivouacking at Graspan was some two miles from the station, but the water indispensable for the service of the railway was close to the spot where the disembarkation from the carriages had taken place. Colonel Girouard himself found to his horror that this, without which he could send no train forward, was being freely expended by men and officers for their own use. There was some delay before he secured an adequate guard to protect it. Despite many incidents, equally inconvenient to this, time was well kept and Lord Roberts' reliance on the silence and efficiency of the officials was fully justified.

Secrecy and orders adapted to case.

Throughout the month of January Lord Roberts so directed the conduct of operations and disposed of reinforcements arriving from England as to mislead the Boer General as to his designs.

THE ARMY MOVES FORWARD. 433

His real intentions were, in fact, known only to his Chief of the Staff (Lord Kitchener), his Military Secretary (Major-General Sir W. G. Nicholson), to the Director of Military Intelligence (Local Colonel G. F. R. Henderson), and to those who had to make the railway arrangements, Colonel Girouard, Major D. Murray, Assistant Director of Railways, Mr. T. R. Price, Chief Traffic Manager, Major H. Hamilton, who acted as intermediary for Lord Kitchener, and to Colonel C. P. Ridley, in charge of the western line of communications. To Lord Methuen the Commander-in-Chief wrote on the 11th January:—

> "I have come to the conclusion that I must ask you to act strictly on the defensive, and as it may be even necessary for me to withdraw a portion of your force, you should consider how your line of entrenchments could be sufficiently reduced to enable you to hold the position with two, instead of three, brigades, and possibly with one or two batteries and one regiment of cavalry less than you have at present. Your request for four of the siege 4·7-in. guns will be complied with, and when these reach you, you will doubtless be able to make your position practically impregnable. That the relief of Kimberley cannot be immediately effected I am as sorry for, as I am sure you must be, but I trust that it will still be possible for you to give the brave garrison at that place a helping hand before they run short of supplies and ammunition."

To the central line of operations where, owing to the activity of French, the strength of the enemy had increased, Lord Roberts despatched the 6th division and placed a portion of one of its brigades (the 12th, under Maj.-Gen. R. A. P. Clements) at French's disposal. It was decided to give Lieut.-General Kelly-Kenny a separate command from Naauwpoort southward, leaving French to continue his previous campaign against the enemy round Colesberg.* To General French, therefore, the Field-Marshal addressed the following instructions on the 12th January:—

> "As I see no chance of being able to leave Cape Town just at present, and cannot therefore offer you my congratulations in person, I write to let you know the satisfaction it has given me to hear of the good work you have been doing in the neighbourhood of Colesberg.

---

* Lt.-General Kelly-Kenny was very much senior in the army to Lt.-General French, but the latter's local commission as Lt.-General was of older date.

"You will have learnt by telegram that we have sent you three battalions of the 12th brigade under Clements. Kelly-Kenny, who commands the 6th division, sails to-morrow for Port Elizabeth, and the whole of his eight battalions will, I hope, be collected shortly at Naauwpoort junction. I gather that the Boers are increasing in strength between Colesberg and the river. It seems almost certain that their numbers will be still further augmented if Buller succeeds in relieving Ladysmith, for Joubert's force will then be free, and he is almost certain to hurry his men to the south-west in order to try and block our way into the Orange Free State.

"This may make the seizure of the Norval's Pont bridge out of the question; as it would, however, be of such supreme importance to get possession of this crossing of the Orange river, I shall be greatly obliged if you will inform me whether you think the operation in any way feasible. We could increase your force still more, or what would probably be of even greater assistance to you, we could threaten the enemy from the Orange River station direction. The greatest secrecy and caution would be required, and the seizure of the bridge could only be effected by a very carefully-thought-out and well-planned *coup de main*, for, if the Boers had the slightest inkling of our intention, they would assuredly blow it up. There would, moreover, be no object in our getting possession of the bridge, and thus risking a number of valuable lives, unless it could be made perfectly secure on its immediate northern bank, and this, from the nature of the ground, might be impossible.

"I hope that your men and horses are keeping thoroughly efficient. Please take every care of them and save the horses as much as possible, for, until we can get hold of some of the regiments now in Ladysmith, yours is almost the only cavalry we have to depend upon."

The seizure of the bridge* would have been useful both in deceiving Cronje and in facilitating later movements, but the intricate ground on the northern bank of the river at that point would have rendered further advance costly, and the defence of the bridge itself difficult, and as yet it was unnecessary. French, therefore, though he at the time knew nothing of the intended scheme, exactly carried out what was the purpose of Lord Roberts' instructions when, as recorded in Chapter XXIV., he, after the demonstration of January 25th, abandoned further efforts against Norval's Pont. It was not till January 30th, during his brief visit to Cape Town, that he was given two copies of the complete plan of operations, one for himself and one for General Kelly-Kenny. It was no doubt due to these careful precautions that the secret was so admirably kept as it was, and

* See map No. 9.

that the Boers were so completely deceived as they were as to what was going on.*

Kelly-Kenny, with his division, less Clements' brigade, was to cover the communications south of Naauwpoort, allay unrest and disaffection, and open up the railway line as far as possible from Rosmead in the direction of Stormberg, thus diverting attention from Gatacre. A proposal made on the 23rd by him that French should be instructed to seize Bethulie bridge by a forced march was refused by the Field-Marshal, who, not to disclose his real reasons, told him that the enterprise was a doubtful one; the country difficult, and strong opposition would be offered to the move. To Sir W. Gatacre the Commander-in-Chief issued orders on the 19th January that Dordrecht should be garrisoned, and that Brabant's newly-formed Colonial division should use that town as a base, and thence operate towards Jamestown so as to menace the line of retreat of the Boer force at Stormberg. Meanwhile Gatacre himself was to act strictly on the defensive. Brabant was placed under his orders, but was to be given a "perfectly free hand" and be allowed to report direct to Army Headquarters.

These various orders and instructions successfully effected Lord Roberts' purpose. The distribution of the British troops perplexed and confused the enemy, and the Boer leaders remained passive, making no substantial change in their dispositions save to increase the strength of the body covering *[margin: Enemy perplexed. Move begun.]*

---

* President Steyn telegraphed to C. De Wet as late as the end of January that the British advance would be made by Colesberg, and suggested the despatch of reinforcements to that point from Magersfontein. But De Wet, who was now in command of all Free State troops in the western theatre, having been transferred from Natal early in December, refused, on the ground that if Magersfontein were weakened, the British would make Kimberley their point of attack. The records of the O.F.S. railway at this period show how much anxiety was felt as to Colesberg. Between the 27th December and 13th January 2,700 burghers passed through Bloemfontein *en route* to Norval's Pont, and between the 25th January and 8th February (including a Heidelberg commando over 500 strong between 6th and 8th) another 1,442; not until the 9th was the stream of reinforcements for the south stopped at Bloemfontein. By that time Lord Roberts himself, and nearly all the army, including Kelly-Kenny's and French's divisions, had reached their destination south of the Riet.

the crossing to the north of Colesberg. By the end of January Lord Roberts' staff had nearly finished the work of preparation, and the Commander-in-Chief directed the concentration of all available troops between the Orange river and the Modder for the delivery of the stroke he had designed, leaving before Colesberg and Magersfontein sufficient forces under the respective commands of Major-General Clements and Lord Methuen to hold the enemy, at each of these points, in check. It was on January 29th that General French was summoned to Cape Town.* Immediately after his return the actual transfer northwards of an army corps, made up of a cavalry division, three infantry divisions, and some corps troops, was carried out. A few details had started as early as the 28th.

The cavalry division.

The commander of the cavalry division was Lieut.-General J. D. P. French. It consisted of three cavalry brigades and two M.I. brigades; of these the 1st cavalry brigade (Brig.-Gen. T. C. Porter) was formed of the 6th Dragoon Guards, 2nd Dragoons, one squadron of the Inniskilling Dragoons, one squadron of the 14th Hussars, New South Wales Lancers, and T., Q., and U. batteries R.H.A.; the 2nd cavalry brigade

---

* It is one of the sequels of any attempt to preserve in war that secrecy which is the very master-key of the house of success that the evidence of much that has been done during the period of reticence is conflicting. The actual motive which led Lord Roberts to desire General French's presence at Cape Town was anxiety as to the expenditure of horses and ammunition, which the brilliant operations around Colesberg had involved. He did not summon him in order to discuss with him the plan of campaign, which was only incidentally disclosed to him during his visit. The demonstration that in all essentials that plan had been definitely formed; and that Lord Kitchener and Sir W. Nicholson had been engaged in making the necessary changes in the distribution of transport in order to carry it out; and that they began this work about two or three days after Lord Roberts arrived, is complete. Moreover, there is not a trace in the records or in the memory of any of those at Cape Town of an idea of employing in command of the cavalry division anyone else but the man who had given so much cause to put trust in him. Nevertheless, there is no doubt that General French acquired the impression, from his conversations with Lord Roberts and Lord Kitchener, that he only with difficulty persuaded them on January 29th to send the cavalry division and himself in command of it. What, other things apart, makes it certain that this cannot have been so is that the cavalry division moved at once when General French returned to Colesberg. To make so sudden a change was a physical impossibility. The preparations had required weeks of strenuous work.

THE ARMY MOVES FORWARD. 437

(Brig.-Gen. R. G. Broadwood) was made up of the composite regiment of the Household cavalry, 10th Hussars, 12th Lancers, and G. and P. batteries R.H.A.; the 3rd cavalry brigade (Brig.-Gen. J. R. P. Gordon), of 9th and 16th Lancers, and O. and R. batteries R.H.A. To the 1st M.I. brigade (Colonel O. C. Hannay) were assigned the 1st, 3rd, 5th, and 7th regiments M.I., the New South Wales Mounted Rifles, Roberts' Horse, Kitchener's Horse, and the Grahamstown Volunteers M.I.; the 2nd M.I. brigade, commanded by Colonel C. P. Ridley, was made up by the 2nd, 4th, 6th, and 8th M.I. regiments, the City Imperial Volunteers, Queensland M.I., and Nesbitt's Horse.* Each cavalry brigade had an ammunition column, detachment of A.S.C., field hospital, and bearer company. The division was given a field troop R.E. and six transport companies.

The infantry divisions were the 6th (Kelly-Kenny), the 7th (Tucker†), which had landed from England during the fourth week of January, and a new division, the 9th, to be formed under command of Lt.-Gen. Sir H. Colvile. Of these divisions the 6th comprised the 76th and 81st Field batteries, an ammunition column, the 38th company R.E., the 13th infantry brigade, under Major-General C. E. Knox (composed of 2nd East Kent, 2nd Gloucester, 1st West Riding, and 1st Oxfordshire L.I.), and a new brigade, the 18th, made up of the 1st Yorkshire, 1st Welsh, and 1st Essex, under the command of Brigadier-General T. E. Stephenson. The 7th division retained its original constitution, viz.: the 14th brigade, under Major-General Sir H. Chermside (consisting of 2nd Norfolk, 2nd Lincolnshire, 1st King's Own Scottish Borderers, and 2nd Hampshire), the 15th brigade under Major-General A. G. Wavell (including 2nd Cheshire, 2nd South Wales Borderers, 1st East Lancashire, and 2nd North Staffordshire), and as divisional troops, the 18th, 62nd, and 75th Field batteries, an ammunition column, and 9th company R.E. The new 9th division, under Lieut.-General Colvile, had as its nucleus the 3rd, or Highland brigade, now under Major-General H. A. MacDonald (2nd Black Watch, 1st Highland Light Infantry,

The infantry divisions.

* The New Zealand Mounted Rifles joined the brigade on 14th February.
† Lt.-General C. Tucker.

2nd Seaforth, and 1st Argyll and Sutherland). The other brigade, to be termed the 19th, was assigned to Colonel H. L. Smith-Dorrien, and was to be organised from the 2nd Duke of Cornwall's L.I., 2nd Shropshire L.I., 1st Gordon Highlanders, and the Royal Canadian regiment. The 65th (howitzer) and 82nd Field batteries, an ammunition column, and 7th company R.E., formed Colvile's divisional troops. Each of the infantry brigades included a bearer company, a field hospital, and a detachment of the Army Service Corps. From each of these divisions the cavalry was withdrawn and included in the cavalry division. Two naval guns were attached to each of the 6th and 9th divisions, but the remainder of the naval brigade, under Captain J. Bearcroft, R.N., was at first ordered to remain with Lord Methuen. The only corps troops retained by the Commander-in-Chief were the 15th company Southern division R.G.A., the 1st Telegraph division, and the balloon section, Royal Engineers. Rimington's Guides were distributed amongst the various columns. The total effective strength of the force, including the Guards' and 9th brigades, which remained before Magersfontein to hold Cronje in check, was a little under 40,000 men and 108 guns. The battalions at this time much varied in strength, those of the 13th brigade averaged but 721, those of the Highland brigade 780, the battalions of the 15th brigade were as high as 900, and the Guards' battalions reached the figure of 938. The cavalry regiments had an average of about 473 all ranks. For details of units, see Appendix 10.

Reinforcements asked for. The intelligence of the failure of Sir R. Buller's operations against Spion Kop forced the Field-Marshal on 28th January to telegraph to the War Office that the despatch of the 8th division and another cavalry brigade from England had become advisable, but, in deference to reluctance felt by the Cabinet to denude further the home garrisons of regular infantry, Lord Roberts suspended his request for them at present until the result of later operations in Natal should be known.* The brigade of cavalry was at once promised.

* The 8th division was again definitely asked for on 28th February, and then granted.

THE ARMY MOVES FORWARD. 439

Lord Roberts did not wait for it, for his advance could no longer be delayed. As the troops were pushed forward successively, it was certain that the enemy must become aware of the assembly of so large a number very close to Magersfontein, even though the concentration was screened by Lord Methuen's and General Clements' forces. It was essential, therefore, to distract Cronje's attention from the flank, eastward of which the Field-Marshal meant to aim his blow. Nor were there lacking ample excuses for demonstrations to the westward. The very unsatisfactory condition of the districts south of Orange river west of the Kimberley railway was known to the Boer leaders. Cronje had already detached to Douglas 200 men and two guns, under Commandant Liebenberg, to support a Cape rebel, L. F. Steinkamp, in raising the standard of revolt in those regions. To counteract this effort, Prieska had been re-occupied on 27th January by Lieut.-Colonel Alderson with a battery and 600 M.I., but their immediate return to De Aar was necessary, as the mounted men were needed for the general advance. A diversion on a larger scale was now planned. By Lord Roberts' order Lord Methuen temporarily attached to the Highland brigade two squadrons of the 9th Lancers, the 62nd Field battery, and the 7th company R.E., and directed Major-General MacDonald to march at 5.30 on the morning of the 4th February to Koodoesberg Drift, where the road from Kimberley to Douglas crosses the Riet at about twenty miles below its junction with the Modder, and to begin the construction of a fort covering this passage of the river. The column halted at Fraser's Drift, seven miles out, and there bivouacked for the night. Koodoesberg Drift was reached the following day. The hot season was at its height. A reconnaissance was pushed to the north-west. The top of the Koodoesberg, a long, flat-topped kopje, about 1,200 yards from the river, was seized. It completely commanded the drift. A mounted patrol of fifteen Boers retired from this hill as the British cavalry approached. General MacDonald's force passed that night on the south bank, being covered by two companies of infantry on the far side of the river. At daylight, on the 6th of February, the construction of a redoubt

Demonstrations westward. MacDonald seizes Koodoesberg, Feb. 5th, 1900.

suitable for 200 men on a small knoll to the north of the drift was begun. Almost immediately a patrol of 9th Lancers reported that about 300 of the enemy* were creeping up the northern slope of the Koodoesberg. The Major-General accordingly ordered his brigade-major, Lieut.-Colonel Ewart, to advance rapidly with the working parties on the hill and try to anticipate the assailants at the summit. Ewart, supported by the Highland Light Infantry under Lt.-Colonel Kelham, succeeded in doing so. A Boer detachment which had already reached the top retired hastily. It was then found that the plateau was some two miles in length, and therefore too extensive for complete occupation. Kelham was accordingly ordered to hold its southern edge, and the R.E. began to build sangars across the narrow Nek which divided the south of the hill from the main plateau. The Black Watch was moved over the river to the right bank in support. In the afternoon arrived large reinforcements, which had been despatched by Cronje from Scholtz Nek to aid De Wet. These, estimated by the British troops to be about 2,000 strong,† enabled the enemy to push on again up the reverse slopes of the Berg and definitely establish themselves on the northern and western edges of the plateau. On this the British field-works were further strengthened. Visser's homestead, a farmhouse lying in the plain to the south-east of the kopje and to the north of the drift, was placed in a state of defence, and occupied by two companies of the Black Watch. The two squadrons of 9th Lancers during this time were manœuvred by Major Little near to the farm, with the object of inducing the Boers to come out into the open and attack, but they confined themselves all that afternoon to heavy sniping. At dusk the companies of the H.L.I. on the eastern extremity of the Berg were relieved by another company of that battalion and four companies of the Seaforth.

As soon as it was dark the Boers dragged a gun, which, with

* The actual strength of this force was 350. Its leader was C. De Wet.

† General De Wet officially reported that he only received a reinforcement of 200 men. Other Boer accounts give his total strength during the action as 800.

THE ARMY MOVES FORWARD. 441

a further reinforcement of 200 men, had been received from Cronje, up the north-western slopes of the hill, and at 9 a.m. (7th February) they opened with shrapnel on the breastworks at the eastern edge of the plateau. The troops holding that ground were now reinforced by two more companies of the H.L.I. and four of the Black Watch, Lieut.-Colonel Hughes-Hallett being placed in command. A little later the cavalry patrols reported that a party of Boers was passing across Painter's Drift, two miles down the river, to attack the left flank. The defence of the bank of the Riet had been entrusted to Lt.-Colonel A. Wilson, commanding the Argyll and Sutherland Highlanders, and that officer despatched two and a half companies of his battalion with two guns, under Major E. B. Urmston, to meet this movement. The rest of Major Granet's battery was in action on the left bank of the river against the enemy's artillery. On the Koodoesberg itself there was a sharp fight, and a few of the burghers crept within 300 yards of the British sangars. The heat of the day was intense, and considerable difficulty was experienced in conveying water and ammunition up the steep slopes of the kopje to the British fighting line. Unfortunately, this steepness at the same time rendered it almost impossible to withdraw the wounded. Meanwhile Major Urmston's detachment frustrated the attempt of the enemy, a Ladybrand commando under Commandant Froneman, to work down the bed of the river from Painter's Drift.
Course of struggle.

General MacDonald had early in the morning telegraphed to the Modder camp for reinforcements. In response to this request a cavalry brigade, with two batteries R.H.A. had been sent out under Major-General Babington,* and about 3.15 p.m. could be seen at a distance of about four or five miles to the north approaching the river. MacDonald now hoped to assume the offensive, and reinforced Hughes-Hallett with the remaining half-battalion of the Seaforth, preparatory to a direct attack upon the Boers on the plateau, but, owing to some misunder-
MacDonald receives reinforcements.

---

* O. and R. batteries R.H.A., composite regiment of Household cavalry, 16th Lancers, one squadron 10th Hussars, one squadron 12th Lancers, and two troops of the Scots Greys.

standing, concerted action with the cavalry brigade was not arranged until too late, and the general advance was accordingly postponed until the following morning. The enemy, meanwhile, fully realised that the arrival of the cavalry brigade rendered his isolated position on the plateau no longer tenable. The burghers, therefore, began slipping away from the hill, and by nightfall had practically evacuated it, leaving their gun for some time on the kopje unprotected save by a small escort. General Babington tried to follow them up, but the Household cavalry, which was in front, was checked by wire fences and came under heavy rifle fire. Their attempt to cut off the gun was also quite stopped by musketry from some thick bush and broken ground. The Boers subsequently succeeded in removing the piece during the night, although its descent from the kopje was a task of some serious labour and took two hours. The Commander-in-Chief's object in making this feint against the enemy's right had been gained. He had arrived that morning at the Modder camp, and now ordered the two brigades to return. General MacDonald therefore withdrew on the evening of the 8th of February, having first ascertained by a reconnaissance that the enemy had completely evacuated both the Berg and Painter's Drift.

MacDonald withdrawn.

The British losses during this action were two officers and four men killed, and five officers and forty-two men wounded. The Boers admitted a loss of five killed and six wounded. Locally the results of the engagement were hardly satisfactory, but nevertheless its effect was exactly what had been hoped for, as General Cronje at once began to reinforce his right and further strengthen his entrenchments on that side. A simultaneous demonstration, also made to the westward, by a body of 1,500 men under Brig.-Gen. Broadwood, helped to confirm the Boer leaders' assumption that the relief of Kimberley would be attempted by the west route. Broadwood reached Sunnyside on the 7th, hoping to strike a blow at Liebenberg's commando at Douglas; but it had already fallen back across the river, and the British, unable to spare the time to pursue, retired on the 8th to Richmond, a farm thirteen miles west of Graspan.

Results of demonstration.

The Commander-in-Chief had at first intended to leave Cape

THE ARMY MOVES FORWARD. 443

Town for the north on 30th January, but postponed his departure, as he found that a little more time was required to collect between the Modder and Orange rivers the troops he designed to employ. On the 4th February, "to correct any misapprehension which may exist at the War Office as to the total force at my disposal," the Field-Marshal informed the Secretary of State by telegram that the effective strength of fighting men in Cape Colony, exclusive of seven militia battalions and of the garrisons of Kimberley and Mafeking, was 51,900, and that the entire fighting strength of the force in Natal was estimated at 34,830, of whom 9,780 were invested in Ladysmith. Under these circumstances Lord Roberts recommended that the number of militia battalions in the country should be increased to thirty, and that, if possible, two more regular battalions should be sent, one from Malta and the other from Egypt. Four days later Lord Roberts informed the War Office that he would be glad if the whole of the 8,000 Imperial Yeomanry originally asked for by Sir R. Buller could be sent out, and more, if available. He suggested that additional mounted men should be raised in the colonies, and added,

Numbers in South Africa, 4th Feb. 1900.

"I trust you will make arrangements to supply us with horses from Australia, India, and America. Our wants will, I fear, be considerable."

On 6th February the Field-Marshal, accompanied by his Chief of the Staff, left Cape Town for Lord Methuen's camp. Meanwhile the concentration had gone on. The details of the moves by rail had been worked out by the Director of Railways and the General Traffic Manager; ten miles of additional sidings had been laid down between Orange River and the Modder, and at these sidings, between the 28th of January and the 12th of February, there were detrained some 30,000 troops, with horses, guns, equipment, and transport, besides an immense amount of supplies. Clements' brigade, with two squadrons Inniskilling Dragoons, 660 Australian infantry who were in process of being converted into mounted troops, 450 mounted infantry, two batteries (J., R.H.A. and 4th R.F.A.) and a section 37th Howitzer battery, lay round Rensburg to face General Schoeman's com-

Details of movement. 28th Jan. to 12th Feb. 1900.

mandos. The rest of Kelly-Kenny's division and French's original force were brought round by rail to Orange River, the former unit being there completed by the new brigade—the 18th—formed out of line of communication battalions, under the command of Brig.-Gen. T. E. Stephenson. Seven militia battalions, just disembarked from England, were hurried up country to replace these regular battalions, and protect the western and the central lines of rail. By the 8th of February the cavalry division, except detachments of the 6th Dragoon Guards and 14th Hussars and Hannay's M.I. brigade, had been assembled at the Modder River camp under Lieut.-General French. Hannay's brigade was at Orange River station; the 6th division at Modder River camp; the 7th at Enslin and Graspan. Of the 9th division, the Highland brigade was on the Riet, while the new 19th brigade was in process of formation under Smith-Dorrien at Graspan. The distribution of troops in South Africa on the 11th February, 1900, will be found in Appendix 10.

<small>Motives of Lord Roberts. Instructions given below.</small>

To Cronje it appeared that the English were about once more to hurl themselves against his carefully-prepared entrenchments. Lord Roberts had at last under his hand a force whose strength and mobility permitted of the execution of a great turning movement, and warranted the confident hope that the tide of fortune would turn in favour of the British flag. It was his desire that the troops, about to engage in this fresh enterprise, should reap to the full the benefit of the practical experiences of the earlier actions of the war, both as regards the special conditions of fighting in South Africa and the modifications in tactics necessitated by the introduction of smokeless powder and magazine small-bore rifles. He also recognised that the tasks he was about to assign to his mounted troops would tax their horses to the utmost, and was anxious to impress on all concerned the necessity for the most careful horsemastership. He therefore issued the following instructions :—

NOTES FOR GUIDANCE IN SOUTH AFRICAN WARFARE.

INFANTRY.

As it is desirable that full advantage should be taken of the experience gained during the past three months by our troops in South Africa, the following notes are issued for the guidance of all who may find themselves in command of a force (large or small) on service in the field.

We have to deal with an enemy possessing remarkable mobility, intimately acquainted with the country, thoroughly understanding how to take advantage of ground, adept in improvising cover, and most skilful in the use of their weapons.

Against such an enemy any attempt to take a position by direct attack will assuredly fail. The only hope of success lies in being able to turn one or both flanks, or what would, in many instances, be equally effective, to threaten to cut the enemy's line of communication. Before any plan of attack can be decided upon, the position must be carefully examined by reconnoitring parties, and every endeavour must be made to obtain all possible information about it from the people of the country. It must, however, be remembered that the position ostensibly occupied is not always the one the Boers intend to defend; it is often merely a decoy, a stronger position in the vicinity having previously been prepared upon which they move rapidly, and from which they can frequently bring a destructive fire to bear upon the attacking line. Their marvellous mobility enables them to do this without much risk to themselves, and also to be in strength at any point of the position that may be seriously threatened. It follows, therefore, that our object should be to cripple the mobility of the Boers, and to effect this, next to inflicting heavy losses on the men themselves, the surest means would be the capture or destruction of their horses.

When the extreme rifle range from the position is reached (1,500 to 1,800 yards) by the advance troops, or before, if they find themselves under artillery fire, all column formations must be given up, and, when advancing to the attack of the position, infantry must be freely extended, even on occasions, if necessary, to six or eight paces, the front and both flanks being well covered with scouts. This extended formation will throw increased responsibility on battalion and company commanders. The objective aimed at, therefore, should be carefully explained to them. They should be allowed to make use of any opportunity that may offer to further the scheme, on the distinct understanding that no isolated acts are attempted, such as might endanger the general plan. During the attack commanding officers must be careful not to lose touch with the troops on their right and left, and they should, as far as possible, ensure their co-operation. Every advantage should be taken of cover, and battalion and company commanders should look out for and occupy positions from which they would be able to bring an enfilading fire to bear upon the enemy. The capacity of these officers will be judged by the initiative displayed in seizing rapidly every opportunity to further the general scheme of attack.

An essential point, and one which must never be lost sight of, is the power of endurance of the infantry soldier. If infantry soldiers (carrying as they do a considerable weight on their backs) are called upon to march a longer distance than can reasonably be expected from men in a normal state of health, or if they are injudiciously pressed as regards the pace, they will necessarily commence to feel the strain before they reach a point where their best energies are required to surmount the difficulties which lie before them. If at such a period a man feels exhausted, moral deterioration and the consequences to our arms which such deterioration entails, must readily supervene.

ARTILLERY.

As a general rule the artillery appear to have adapted themselves to the situation, and to the special conditions which present themselves in a campaign in South Africa.

The following points, however, require to be noticed :—

1. At the commencement of an action artillery should

THE ARMY MOVES FORWARD. 447

not be ordered to take up a position until it has been ascertained by scouts to be clear of the enemy and out of range of infantry fire.

2. When it is intended to take a position with infantry the preparation by artillery should be thorough and not spasmodic. Unless a strong force of infantry is pushed within 900 yards of the position, the enemy will not occupy his trenches and the guns will have no target. It is a mere waste of ammunition also to bombard an entrenchment when the infantry attack is likely to be delayed, even for a short time. To be of real value the fire of the guns should be continuous until the assault is about to be delivered.

3. The expenditure of ammunition is a matter which can only be regulated by the circumstances of the moment, officers commanding should, however, always bear in mind that the supply of artillery ammunition in the field is necessarily limited.

4. It is of great importance that artillery horses should be kept fit for any special effort. They are not easily replaced, and it is the duty of artillery officers to represent to the commander of the column whenever they consider that their horses are being unduly worked, as regards either pace or distance.

CAVALRY AND MOUNTED TROOPS.

Similarly with cavalry horses. Every endeavour should be made to save them as much as possible, for unless this is done they cannot be expected to last through a lengthened campaign.

The men should dismount on every available opportunity, if for a few minutes only at a time, and, on the line of march, it will be advantageous for them to occasionally lead instead of riding their horses.

Horses should be fed at short intervals, and not allowed to be kept too long without water. A sufficiency of grain is necessary to enable horses to withstand hard work, but they will never keep in condition unless they have an ample supply of hay or some bulky equivalent.

On the line of march scouting must be carried out by the mounted troops in the most searching manner, in front and on both flanks. All high ground should be visited and, whenever practicable, horsemen should ride along ridges and hills. As soon as parties of the enemy are observed the mounted troops (after sending back word to the commander) should make a considerable detour round the position occupied by the Boers, endeavour to estimate their numbers, and to ascertain where their horses have been left. They should also see whether, by threatening the Boers' line of communication, they would not be forced to fight on ground unprepared for defence.

ROBERTS, Field-Marshal,
Commanding-in-Chief, South Africa.

Chief of Staff (Circular Memorandum).

Cape Town, 5th February, 1900.

The following notes by Field-Marshal Commander-in-Chief are communicated for the guidance of all concerned.

By Order,

KITCHENER OF KHARTOUM,
Chief of Staff.

NOTES FOR GUIDANCE IN SOUTH AFRICAN WARFARE.

CAVALRY.

1. On reconnaissances or patrols not likely to be prolonged beyond one day, the cavalry soldier's equipment should be lightened as much as possible, nothing being taken that can possibly be dispensed with.

2. It has been brought to my notice that our cavalry move too slowly when on reconnaissance duty, and that unnecessarily long halts are made, the result being that the enemy, although starting after the cavalry, are able to get ahead of it. I could understand this if the country were close and difficult, but between the Modder and the Orange rivers its general features are such as to admit of small parties of cavalry accompanied by field guns being employed with impunity.

ARTILLERY.

3. If the enemy's guns have, in some instances, the advantage of ours in range, we have the advantage of theirs in mobility, and we should make use of this by not remaining in positions, the precise distance of which from the enemy's batteries has evidently been fixed beforehand. Moreover, it has been proved that the Boers' fire is far less accurate at unknown distances. In taking up positions compact battery formations should be avoided. The guns should be opened out, or it may be desirable to advance by sections or batteries. Similarly, retirements should be carried out at considerably increased intervals, by alternate batteries or sections if necessary, and care should be taken to travel quickly through the danger zone of hostile artillery fire.

The following plan, frequently adopted by the Boers, has succeeded in deceiving our artillery on several occasions:—

Suppose A to be a gun emplacement, the gun firing smokeless powder; simultaneously with the discharge of the gun at A a powder flask of black powder will be exploded at B, a hill in the rear, leading us to direct our projectile on B. Careful calculation with a watch, however, will defeat this plan.

INFANTRY.

4. The present open formation renders it difficult for officers to exercise command over their men, except such as may be in their immediate vicinity. A remedy for this would appear to be a system of whistle calls by which a company lying in extended order could obey orders as readily as if in quarter column. I invite suggestions for such a system of whistle calls as would be useful.

5. It is difficult to recognise officers as equipped at present, and it seems desirable they should wear a distinguishing mark of some kind, either on the collar at the back of the neck, or on the back of the coat.

6. Soldiers, when under fire, do not take sufficient advantage

of the sandy nature of the soil to construct cover for themselves. If such soil is scraped even with a canteen lid, a certain amount of cover from rifle fire can be obtained in a short time.

7. The distribution of ammunition to the firing line is one of the most difficult problems of modern warfare. One solution, which has been suggested to me, is for a portion of the supports gradually to creep forward until a regular chain of men is established from the supports (where the ammunition carts should be) right up to the firing line. The ammunition could then be gradually worked up by hand till it reached the firing line, where it could be passed along as required. This would, no doubt, be a slow method of distributing ammunition, but it appears to be an improvement on the present method, which is almost impossible to carry out under fire.

8. Reports received suggest that the Boers are less likely to hold entrenchments *on the plain* with the same tenacity and courage as they display when defending kopjes, and it is stated that this applies especially to night time, if they know that British infantry are within easy striking distance from them. How far this is true time only can show.

ROBERTS, Field-Marshal,

Commanding-in-Chief, South Africa.

END OF VOL. I.

APPENDICES

APPENDIX I.

REINFORCEMENTS SANCTIONED ON THE 8TH SEPTEMBER, 1899.

(a) FROM INDIA.

Unit.	Officers.	Other Ranks.	Horses.	Guns.	Ship in which embarked.	Place of embarkation.	Date of embarkation.	Place of disembarkation.	Date of disembarkation.
General Staff	3	2	7	—	*City of London*	Bombay	21.9.99	Durban	5.10.99
Cavalry brigade Staff	9	15	23	—	*Pundua*	Bombay	22.9.99	Durban	5.10.99
5th Dragoon Guards	21	474	523	1	*Lindula*	Bombay	26.9.99	Durban	11.10.99
					Patiala		8.10.99		22.10.99
					Virawa		8.10.99		25.10.99
9th Lancers	15	476	515	1	*Wardha**				18.10.99
					Nowshera	Bombay	24.9.99	Cape Town	15.10.99
					Nairung		25.9.99		14.10.99
					Vadala		21.9.99		7.10.99
19th Hussars	23	474	533	1	*Pundua*	Bombay	22.9.99	Durban	5.10.99
					Warora		23.9.99		9.10.99
Brigade Division Staff	3	1	7	—	*Lalpoora*	Bombay	18.9.99	Durban	2.10.99
21st battery, R.F.A.	5	176	152	6	*Lalpoora*	Bombay	18.9.99	Durban	2.10.99
42nd battery, R.F.A.	5	169	153	6	*Secundra*	Bombay	17.9.99	Durban	4.10.99
53rd battery, R.F.A.	5	173	153	6	*Booldana*	Bombay	19.9.99	Durban	5.10.99
Ammunition column	3	90	149	—	*Nevassa*	Bombay	27.9.99	Durban	12.10.99
Infantry brigade Staff	9	20	14	—	*City of London*	Bombay	21.9.99	Durban	5.10.99
1st battn. Devonshire regt.	22	843	7	1	*Sutlej*	Bombay	21.9.99	Durban	5.10.99
					City of London				
1st battn. Gloucestershire regt.	29	846	5	1	*Nurani*	Calcutta	20.9.99	Durban	9.10.99
					India		24.9.99		13.10.99
2nd battn. King's Royal Rifle Corps	25	844	5	1	*Parnea*	Calcutta	18.9.99	Durban	5.10.99
					Nurani		20.9.99		9.10.99
2nd battn. Gordon Highlanders	29	843	6	1	*Palitana*	Bombay	23.9.99	Durban	9.10.99
					Sirsa				
Carried forward to (b)	206	5,446	2,252	25†					

* *Wardha* returned to Durban damaged and the squadron was transferred to *Nevassa*.   † Includes seven machine.

REINFORCEMENTS SANCTIONED ON THE 8TH SEPTEMBER, 1899—continued.

(b) FROM HOME AND THE MEDITERRANEAN.

Unit.	Officers.	Other Ranks.	Horses.	Guns.	Ship in which embarked.	Place of embarkation.	Date of embarkation.	Place of disembarkation.	Date of disembarkation.
Brought forward from (a)	206	5,446	2,252	25					
Brigade division Staff and 18th battery, R.F.A.	9	182	166	6	*Zibenghla*	Birkenhead	26.9.99	Cape Town	30.10.99
62nd battery, R.F.A.	4	169	151	6	*Zayathla*	Birkenhead	26.9.99	Cape Town	25.10.99
75th battery, R.F.A.	4	166	151	6	{ *Zayathla* *Zibenghla* }	Birkenhead	26.9.99	Cape Town	{ 25.10.99 30.10.99 }
Ammunition column	8	202	120	—	*Gaika*	Southampton	30.9.99	Durban	29.10.99
Headquarters and No. 1 Telegraph section, R.E.	3	55	—	—	*Jelunga*	Southampton	20.9.99	Durban	26.10.99
2nd Balloon section, R.E.	2	33	—	—	*Kinfauns Castle*	Southampton	30.9.99	Durban	26.10.99
1st battn. Northumberland Fusiliers	27	784	5	—	*Gaul*	Southampton	16.9.99	Cape Town	7.10.99
1st battn. Border regt.*	26	961	6	—	*Sumatra*	Malta	27.9.99	Cape Town	21.10.99
1st battn. Royal Irish Fusiliers	26	848	5	—	*Avoca*	Egypt	24.9.99	Durban	12.10.99
2nd battn. Rifle Brigade	26	835	5	—	*Jelunga*	Crete	2.10.99	Durban	26.10.99
Half 2nd battn. King's Own Yorkshire Light Infantry	12	438	3	—	H.M.S. *Powerful*	Mauritius	6.10.99	Cape Town	14.10.99
Army Service Corps	9	130	—	—	{ *Gaul* *Kinfauns Castle* }	Southampton	{ 16.9.99 30.9.99 }	Cape Town	{ 7.10.99 18.10.99 }
Army Ordnance Corps	1	50	—	—	*Gaul*	Southampton	16.9.99	Cape Town	7.10.99
TOTAL	363	10,299	2,864	43†					

* Subsequently went to Natal.   † Includes seven machine.

APPENDIX 2.

The distribution of British forces under arms in Cape Colony on 11th October, 1899.

CAPE PENINSULA
- Detachments 14th and 23rd cos., R.G.A.
- Headquarters 8th coy., R.E.
- Two cos., 1st battn. Royal Munster Fusiliers.
- 9th coy., Army Service Corps.

STELLENBOSCH
- Two cos., 1st battn. Royal Munster Fusiliers.
- 15th coy., Army Service Corps.

DE AAR
- One section, 7th coy., R.E.
- One section, 29th coy., R.E.
- 1st battn. Northumberland Fusiliers.
- Four cos., 2nd battn. King's Own Yorkshire Light Infantry.
- M.I. coy., 1st battn. Northumberland Fusiliers.

ORANGE RIVER STATION
- One section, R.G.A.
- One section, 7th coy., R.E.
- Four cos., 1st battn. Loyal North Lancashire regt.
- Four cos., 1st battn. Royal Munster Fusiliers.
- M.I. coy., 1st battn. Loyal North Lancashire regt., less detachment at Kimberley.
- M.I. coy., 1st battn. Royal Munster Fusiliers.

KIMBERLEY
- One section, 7th coy., R.E.
- 23rd coy., R.G.A.
- Diamond Fields artillery (six guns).
- Diamond Fields Horse.
- Four cos., 1st battn. Loyal North Lancashire regt.
- Kimberley regt.
- Town Guard.
- Detachment M.I. coy., 1st battn. Loyal North Lancashire regt.

FOURTEEN STREAMS
- Detachment Cape Police.

TAUNGS
- Detachment Cape Police.

VRYBURG
- Detachment Cape Police.
- Vryburg Mounted Rifles (one coy.)

MAFEKING
- Bechuanaland Rifles.
- Protectorate regiment.
- Detachment Cape Police.
- Detachment British South African Police.
- Town Guard.

TULI
- Rhodesian regiment (*en route* from Buluwayo).
- Detachment British South African Police.

NAAUWPOORT
- One section, (two guns) R.G.A.
- One section, 29th coy., R.E.
- Four cos., 2nd battn. Royal Berkshire regt.
- M.I. coy., 2nd battn. King's Own Yorkshire Light Infantry.

STORMBERG
- One section, (two guns) R.G.A.
- One section, 29th coy., R.E.
- Four cos., 2nd battn. Royal Berkshire regt.
- M.I. coy., 2nd battn. Royal Berkshire regt.

APPENDIX 3.

The distribution of British forces under arms in Natal on 11th October, 1899.

DUNDEE*
- 18th Hussars.
- One sqdn., Natal Carbineers.
- M.I. coy., 1st battn. Leicestershire regiment.
- M.I. coy., 1st battn. King's Royal Rifle Corps.
- M.I. coy., 2nd battn. Royal Dublin Fusiliers.
- Detachment Natal Police.
- 13th, 67th, and 69th batteries, R.F.A.
- 1st battn. Leicestershire regt.
- 1st battn. King's Royal Rifle Corps.
- 2nd battn. Royal Dublin Fusiliers.

LADYSMITH
- 5th Lancers.
- 19th Hussars.
- 21st, 42nd, and 53rd batteries, R.F.A.
- 10th mountain battery, R.G.A.
- 23rd coy., R.E.
- 1st battn. Liverpool regt. and M.I. coy.
- 1st battn. Devonshire regt.
- 1st battn. Manchester regt.
- 2nd battn. Gordon Highlanders.
- Natal Mounted Rifles.
- Natal Carbineers.
- Border Mounted Rifles.
- Natal Field artillery.
- Detachment Natal Police.
- Natal Naval Volunteers.
- Natal Corps of Guides.

COLENSO
- Durban Light Infantry.
- Detachment Natal Naval Volunteers.
- One sqdn., Natal Carbineers.

ESTCOURT — Natal Royal Rifles.

PIETERMARITZBURG
- 2nd battn. King's Royal Rifle Corps.
- Imperial Light Horse.

HELPMAKAAR — Umvoti Mounted Rifles.

ESHOWE — One mounted coy., 1st battn. King's Royal Rifle Corps.

DURBAN — One sqdn., 5th Dragoon Guards.

* The 1st battn. Royal Irish Fusiliers, and one section, 23rd coy., R.E., arrived at Dundee during 15th and 16th October.

APPENDIX 4.

STRENGTH OF BURGHER ARMY OF SOUTH AFRICAN REPUBLIC.

District.	Present on Mobilisation.	Subsequent Increase.
Bethel	700	
Bloemhof	800	
Carolina	506	
Ermelo	800	
Fordsburg	900	
Germiston and Boksburg	1,050	
Heidelberg	1,685	
Jeppestown	400	
Johannesburg*	1,000	
Krugersdorp	800	
Lichtenburg	850	
Lydenburg	1,230	
Marico	1,050	
Middelburg	1,317	14,779 ‡
Piet Retief	230	
Potchefstroom	3,000	
Pretoria	2,540	
Rustenburg	1,500	
Springs	60	
Standerton	1,100	
Swaziland*	290	
Utrecht	900	
Vryheid	944	
Waterberg	732	
Wakkerstroom	800	
Wolmaranstad	400	
Zoutpansberg	1,287	
	26,871†	14,779

Total Transvaal Burghers in the field ... 41,650

* Exclusive of police. † Boer evidence. ‡ Intelligence statistics on conclusion of peace.

STRENGTH OF BURGHER ARMY OF ORANGE FREE STATE.

District.	Present on Mobilisation.	Subsequent Increase.
Bethlehem	1,605	
Bethulie	385	
Bloemfontein	2,824	
Boshof	1,030	
Ficksburg	633	
Fauresmith	1,560	
Heilbron	1,671	
Harrismith	915	
Hoopstad	799	6,264 †
Jacobsdal	250	
Kroonstad	2,561	
Ladybrand	1,113	
Philippolis	402	
Rouxville	1,109	
Smithfield	797	
Vrede	1,006	
Winburg	2,114	
Wepener	571	
	21,345*	6,264

Total O. F. S. Burghers in the field ... 27,609

REGULAR FORCES OF BOTH REPUBLICS.

State Artillery S. A. R. ...	800
State Artillery O. F. S. ...	375
South African Republic Police (whites only) ...	1,209
Swaziland Police (whites only) ...	302
	2,686

FOREIGN CORPS.

Hollanders...	320
Italian	75
Scandinavian	100
Irish	500
German	200
French	50
Russian	25
American	50
Foreigners serving with Commandos	800
	2,120

* Boer evidence.   † Intelligence statistics on conclusion of peace.

APPENDIX 4.

ADDITIONS.

Rebels	13,000
Small bands*	300
	13,300

GRAND TOTAL.

Burghers of S. A. R.	41,650
Burghers of O. F. S.	27,609
Regular Forces	2,686
Foreign Corps	2,120
Rebels, etc.	13,300
	87,365

* *E.g.*, those under S. Eloff, W. Mears, J. Hindon, etc.

APPENDIX 5.

List of H.M. ships and vessels serving on the Cape station October 11th, 1899, to June 1st, 1902, showing the approximate dates when they were so engaged.

Those that were present on the station at the beginning of the war are shown with an asterisk.

Name of vessel.	Dates between which so serving.		Commanded by	Remarks.
	from	to		
BARRACOUTA*	10/99	6/02	Comder. R. H. Peirse Comder. H. Cotesworth Comder. S. H. B. Ash	
BARROSA*	10/99	3/01	Comder. W. F. Tunnard	
BEAGLE	7/01	6/02	Comder. H. V. W. Elliott	
BLANCHE	1/01	6/02	Comder. M. T. Parks	
DORIS*	10/99	4/01	Capt. R. C. Prothero, C.B.	Flagship of Rear Admrl. Sir R. H. Harris, K.C.B., K.C.M.G.
DWARF*	11/99	6/02	Lieut. H. F. Shakespear Lieut. W. N. England	
FEARLESS	12/99	8/00	Comder. H. R. P. Floyd	Detached from Mediterranean station.
FORTE*	10/99	6/02	Capt. E. P. Jones, C.B. Comder. C. H. Dundas Capt. R. C. Sparkes, C.M.G. Capt. P. Hoskyns, C.M.G., M.V.O.	
GIBRALTAR	4/01	6/02	Capt. A. H. Limpus	Flagship of Rear Admiral Arthur W. Moore, C.B., C.M.G.
MAGICIENNE*	10/99	11/00	Capt. W. B. Fisher, C.B.	
MAGPIE	11/00	5/02	Lieut. J. K. Laird	
MONARCH*	10/99	6/02	Capt. R. D. B Bruce Capt. C. H. Bayly Capt. W. L. Grant	

APPENDIX 5.

Name of vessel.	Dates between which so serving.		Commanded by	Remarks.
	from	to		
NAIAD	4/01	11/01	Capt. the Hon. A. E. Bethell	Detached from Mediterranean station.
NIOBE	11/99	8/00	Capt. A. L. Winsloe	Detached from Channel Squdrn.
PARTRIDGE*	10/99	6/02	Lieut. A. T. Hunt Lieut. E. La T. Leatham	
PEARL	4/02	6/02	Capt. E. P. Ashe	
PELORUS	12/99	6/00	Capt. H. C. B. Hulbert	Detached from Channel Squdrn.
PHILOMEL*	10/99	1/02	Capt. J. E. Bearcroft, C.B.	
POWERFUL	10/99	3/00	Capt. the Hon. Hedworth Lambton, C.B.	On way home from China.
RACOON	1/00	7/00	Comder. G. H. Hewett Comder. A. E. A. Grant	Detached from East Indies stn.
RAMBLER	11/99	6/00	Comder. H. E. P. Cust	Surveying Service.
RATTLER	9/01	6/02	Lieut. C. Tibbits	
REDBREAST	2/01	4/01	Lieut. M. R. Hill	Detached from East Indies.
SAPPHO	2/01	7/01	Capt. C. Burney	Dtchd. from S.E. Coast America.
SYBILLE	1/01	2/01	Capt. H. P. Williams	Wrecked near Lambert's Bay.
TARTAR*	10/99	7/01	Comder. F. R. W. Morgan Comder. R. H. Travers	
TERRIBLE	10/99	3/00	Capt. P. M. Scott, C.B.	On her way out to China station.
TERPSICHORE	3/01	3/02	Capt. C. H. Coke	Replaced the Sybille.
THETIS	11/99	4/01	Capt. W. Stokes Rees, C.B.	Detached from Mediterranean station
THRUSH*	10/99	6/02	Lieut. W. H. D'Oyly	
WIDGEON*	10/99	6/01	Lieut. A. F. Gurney Lieut W. Forbes	

APPENDIX 6.

SHOWING APPROXIMATE STRENGTH, CASUALTIES, &C., IN THE PRINCIPAL ENGAGEMENTS DESCRIBED IN VOLUME I.

TALANA HILL, OCTOBER 20TH, 1899.
CHAPTER VII.

APPROXIMATE STRENGTH OF TROOPS ENGAGED.

Arms.	Officers.	Warrant, N.C.O.s and men.	Horses (Riding and Draught).	Guns.	
				Field.	Machine.
Cavalry (includes detachment Natal Carbineers)	21	497	485	—	1
Royal Artillery	17	454	428	18	—
Infantry and details (includes mounted infantry companies)	89	3,285	655	—	4
Total	127	4,236	1,568	18	5

SUMMARY OF BRITISH CASUALTIES.

Ranks.	Killed.	Wounded.	Missing (Prisoners).	Total Casualties.
Officers	11	23	9	43
N.C.O.s and men	40	180	237	457
				500

APPROXIMATE BOER LOSSES :—Killed, 30; wounded, 100; prisoners, 12 = 142.

AMMUNITION EXPENDED.

	Description of Weapons.	
	15-pr. Field Guns.	·303 L.M. rifles.
Number of rounds	1,237	82,000

APPENDIX 6.

RIETFONTEIN, OCTOBER 24TH, 1899.

CHAPTER VIII.

APPROXIMATE STRENGTH OF TROOPS ENGAGED.

Arms.	Officers.	Warrant, N.C.O.s and men.	Horses (Riding and Draught).	Guns.	
				Field.	Machine.
Cavalry (includes Natal Mounted Volunteers)	110	1,842	2,024	—	6
Royal Artillery	16	479	553	18	—
Infantry	92	2,782	400	—	4
Total	218	5,103	2,977	18	10

SUMMARY OF BRITISH CASUALTIES.

Ranks.	Killed.	Wounded.	Missing (Prisoners).	Total Casualties.
Officers	1	6	—	7
N.C.O.s and men	13	92	2	107
				114

APPROXIMATE BOER LOSSES:—Killed, 13; wounded, 31 = 44.

AMMUNITION EXPENDED.

	Description of Weapons.		
	15-pr. Field Guns.	2·5-in. Mountain Guns.	·303 L.M. rifles.
Number of rounds	680	125	52,951

ELANDSLAAGTE, OCTOBER 21ST, 1899.

CHAPTER IX.

APPROXIMATE STRENGTH OF TROOPS ENGAGED.

Arms.	Officers.	Warrant, N.C.O.s and men.	Horses (Riding and Draught).	Guns.	
				Field.	Machine.
Cavalry (includes Imperial Light Horse and Natal Carbineers)	17	1,297	1,319	—	3
Royal Artillery (includes Natal Field Artillery)	20	532	481	18	—
Infantry	47	1,583	322	—	3
Total	84	3,412	2,122	18	6

SUMMARY OF BRITISH CASUALTIES.

Ranks.	Killed.	Wounded.	Missing (Prisoners).	Total Casualties.
Officers	4	31	—	35
N.C.O.s and men	46	182	—	228
				263

APPROXIMATE BOER LOSSES :—Killed, 67 ; wounded, 108 ; prisoners, 188 = 363.

AMMUNITION EXPENDED.

	Description of Weapons.			
	15-pr. Field Guns.	2·5-in. Natal F.A.	·303 L.M. rifles.	Pistol.
Number of rounds	423	74	61,212	241

APPENDIX 6.

LOMBARDS KOP, 30TH OCTOBER, 1899.
CHAPTER X.

APPROXIMATE STRENGTH OF TROOPS.

Arms.	Officers.	Warrant, N.C.O.s and men.	Horses (Riding and Draught).	Guns.				
				4·7-in.	12-pr. Naval.	15-pr.	2·5-in.	Machine.
Cavalry (includes Imperial Light Horse and Natal Mounted Volunteers)	160	2,946	3,121	—	—	—	—	7
Royal Artillery (includes Naval Brigade and Natal Volunteer Artillery)	74	1,677	1,230	2	4	50	6	6
Royal Engineers	10	224	95	—	—	—	—	—
Infantry	212	7,150	1,397	—	—	—	—	10
Total	456	11,997	5,843	2	4	50	6	23

SUMMARY OF BRITISH CASUALTIES.

Ranks.	Killed.	Wounded.	Missing (Prisoners).	Total Casualties.
Officers	6	10	37	53
N.C.O.s and men	63	239	917	1,219
				1,272

AMMUNITION EXPENDED.

	Description of Weapons.			
	15-pr. Field Guns.	2·5-in.	Naval 12-pr. 12-cwt.	·303 L.M. rifles.
Number of Rounds	2,359	330	25	433,247

BELMONT, 23RD NOVEMBER, 1899.

CHAPTER XIII.

APPROXIMATE STRENGTH OF TROOPS ENGAGED.

Arms.	Officers.	Warrant, N.C.O.s and men.	Horses (Riding and Draught).	Guns.		
				Naval 12-pr.	Field 15-pr.	Machine.
The Naval Brigade	18	384	10	4	—	—
1st Division Staff ...	12	55	46	—	—	—
Mounted troops ...	48	920	999	—	—	3
Royal Artillery ...	19	546	514	—	12	—
Royal Engineers ...	13	333	71	—	—	—
Infantry (2 brigades)	216	7,010	347	—	—	7
Army Service Corps and Royal Army Medical Corps ...	20	418	312	—	—	—
Total	346	9,666	2,299	4	12	10

BELMONT.

SUMMARY OF BRITISH CASUALTIES.

Ranks.	Killed.	Wounded.	Missing.	Total.
Officers	3	23	—	26
Other ranks	51	220	—	271
				297

Note.—The force engaged at Graspan was the same as at Belmont, less casualties, &c., of the 23rd November.

APPENDIX 6.

GRASPAN, 25TH NOVEMBER, 1899.
CHAPTER XIV.
SUMMARY OF BRITISH CASUALTIES.

Ranks.	Killed.	Wounded.	Missing.	Total.
Officers	3	6	—	9
Other ranks	15	137	7	159
				168

MODDER RIVER, 28TH NOVEMBER, 1899.
CHAPTER XV.
APPROXIMATE STRENGTH OF TROOPS ENGAGED.

Arms.	Officers.	Warrant, N.C.O.s and men.	Horses (Riding and Draught).	Guns.		
				Naval 12-pr.	Field 15-pr.	Machine.
The Naval Brigade	16	238	10	4	—	—
1st Division Staff ...	12	55	46	—	—	—
Mounted troops ...	47	866	895	—	—	3
Royal Artillery ...	23	656	704	—	16	—
Royal Engineers ...	13	333	71	—	—	—
Infantry	211	7,500	379	—	—	8
Army Service Corps and Royal Army Medical Corps ...	20	418	312	—	—	—
Total	342	10,066	2,417	4	16	11

SUMMARY OF BRITISH CASUALTIES, 28TH NOVEMBER, 1899.

Ranks.	Killed.	Wounded.	Missing.	Total.
Officers	4	19	—	23
Other ranks	67	370	18	455
				478

STORMBERG, 10TH DECEMBER, 1899.

CHAPTER XVIII.

APPROXIMATE STRENGTH OF TROOPS ENGAGED.

Arms.	Officers.	Warrant, N.C.O.s and men.	Horses (Riding and Draught).	Guns. Field.	Guns. Machine.
Divisional Staff	7	14	7	—	—
Mounted Troops (includes detachment Cape Police)	17	436	453	—	2
Royal Artillery	19	466	514	12	—
Royal Engineers	7	200	63	—	—
Infantry	50	1,710	84	—	2
Army Service Corps, Royal Army Medical Corps, &c.	8	101	88	—	—
Total	108	2,927	1,209	12	4

SUMMARY OF BRITISH CASUALTIES.

Ranks.	Killed.	Wounded.	Missing.	Total Casualties.
Officers	—	8	13	21
N.C.O.s and men	25	102	548	675
				696

SUMMARY OF AMMUNITION EXPENDED.

	Description of Guns, &c.		
	15-pr.	Machine.	Lee-Metford ·303.
Number of rounds	569*	1,146	137,382†

* Includes 67 rounds captured by the enemy.

† Includes 37,400 rounds lost in ammunition carts, and 86,560 rounds in the pouches of the killed and prisoners.

APPENDIX 6.

MAGERSFONTEIN, 11TH DECEMBER, 1899.
CHAPTER XX.
APPROXIMATE STRENGTH OF THE TROOPS ENGAGED.

Arms.	Officers.	Warrant, N.C.O.s and men.	Horses (Riding and Draught).	Guns.					
				Naval.		Field.			
				4.7-in.	12-pr.	Howitzer.	15-pr.	12-pr.	Machine.
The Naval Brigade	18	294	10	1	4	—	—	—	—
1st Division Staff ...	10	53	44	—	—	—	—	—	—
1st Cavalry Brigade	77	1,627	1,686	—	—	—	—	6	4
Royal Artillery ...	29	918	931	—	—	4	18	—	—
Royal Engineers ...	12	325	70	—	—	—	—	—	—
Infantry (3 brigades)	297	10,672	551	—	—	—	—	—	12
Army Service Corps and Royal Army Medical Corps ...	32	600	431	—	—	—	—	—	—
Total	475	14,489	3,723	1	4	4	18	6	16

SUMMARY OF BRITISH CASUALTIES.

Ranks.	Killed.	Wounded.	Missing.	Total.
Officers	22	46	1	69
Other ranks	188	629	62	879
				948

SUMMARY OF AMMUNITION EXPENDED.

	Description of Guns, &c.			
	Howitzers.	Field Guns.	Machine.	Lee-Metford .303.
Rounds	402	4,189	18,487	321,782

COLENSO, 15TH DECEMBER, 1899.

CHAPTER XXII.

APPROXIMATE STRENGTH OF THE TROOPS ENGAGED.

Arms.	Officers.	Other Ranks.	Horses (Riding and Draught).	Naval. 4·7-in.	Naval. 12-pr.	Guns. Field 15-pr.	Machine.
The Naval Brigade	31	279	6	2	12	—	—
Natal Army Staff	34	137	123	—	—	—	—
Mounted troops	126	2,561	2,700	—	—	—	2
Royal Artillery	39	1,074	869	—	—	30	—
Royal Engineers	14	419	255	—	—	—	—
Infantry (4 brigades)	416	13,521	716	—	—	—	16
Army Service Corps	16	217	550	—	—	—	—
Royal Army Medical Corps	30	464	336	—	—	—	—
Total	706	18,672	5,555	2	12	30	18

SUMMARY OF BRITISH CASUALTIES.

Ranks.	Killed.	Wounded.	Missing.	Total.
Officers	7	47	20	74
Other ranks	136	709	220	1,065
				1,139

NAVAL AMMUNITION EXPENDED.

	Rounds.
4·7-inch	160
12-pr. 12-cwt.	900

APPENDIX 7.

The Expeditionary Force as originally organised and sent to South Africa.

UNITS.	Officers.	Other Ranks.	Horses.	Guns.	Ship in which Embarked.	Date of Leaving England.	Date of Arrival at Cape Town.	Place of Disembarkation.	Date of Disembarkation.
Army Corps Staff	36	119	29	—	*Dunottar Castle*	14.10.99	31.10.99	Cape Town	31.10.99
13th Hussars	25	558	499	1	*Caspian*	17.10.99	18.11.99	Cape Town	18.11.99
					Carisbrook Castle	28.10.99	14.11.99	Cape Town	14.11.99
					Montfort	13.11.99	8.12.99	Durban	13.12.99
Corps artillery Staff	4	15	16	—	*Templemore*	10.11.99	2.12.99	Durban	5.12.99
G. battery, R.H.A.	5	178	196	6	*Pindari*	30.10.99	25.11.99	Cape Town	25.11.99
P. battery, R.H.A.	5	179	196	6	*Pindari*	30.10.99	25.11.99	Cape Town	25.11.99
7th brigade Division Staff, R.F.A.	4	13	14	—	*Pindari*	30.10.99	25.11.99	Cape Town	25.11.99
4th battery, R.F.A.	5	170	137	6	*Algeria*	7.11.99	4.12.99	Cape Town	5.12.99
38th battery, R.F.A.	5	173	137	6	*Sicilian*	15.11.99	10.12.99	Cape Town	10.12.99
78th battery, R.F.A.	5	171	137	6	*Algeria*	7.11.99	4.12.99	Cape Town	5.12.99
8th brigade Division Staff, R.F.A.	4	14	10	—	*Sicilian*	15.11.99	10.12.99	*East London	12.12.99
37th battery, R.F.A.	5	194	161	6	*Antillian*	17.11.99	9.12.99	Cape Town	10.12.99
61st battery, R.F.A.	5	194	152	6	*Antillian*	17.11.99	9.12.99	*East London	11.12.99
					British Princess	16.11.99	6.12.99	*East London	11.12.99
65th battery, R.F.A.	5	194	162	6	*Montfort*	13.11.99	8.12.99	Cape Town	4.12.99
					Canning	12.11.99	4.12.99	Cape Town	6.12.99
Ammunition Park	17	269	260	—	*British Princess*	16.11.99	6.12.99	Cape Town	4.12.99
					Canning	12.11.99	4.12.99	Cape Town	10.12.99
					Sicilian	15.11.99	10.12.99	Durban	27.11.99
Royal Engineers	10	245	—	—	*Kildonan Castle*	4.11.99	22.11.99	Cape Town	22.11.99
1st battn. the Royal Scots	27	1,014	2	1	*Dictator*	6.11.99	1.12.99	East London	4.12.99
Army Service Corps	19	326	—	—	*Braemar Castle*	6.10.99	27.10.99	Cape Town	27.10.99
					Moor	21.10.99	9.11.99	Cape Town	9.11.99
					Pindari	30.10.99	25.11.99	Cape Town	26.11.99
Royal Army Medical Corps	4	35	—	—	*Englishman*	6.11.99	30.11.99	East London	4.12.99
					Dictator	6.11.99	1.12.99	East London	4.12.99
					Ranee	5.12.99	5.12.99	Cape Town	5.12.99
					Arawa	7.11.99	1.12.99	Cape Town	2.12.99
Army Service Corps	21	482	—	—	*Braemar Castle*	6.10.99	27.10.99	Cape Town	27.10.99

*Battery subsequently went to Natal.

472 THE WAR IN SOUTH AFRICA.

APPENDIX 7—continued.

Units	Officers	Other Ranks	Horses	Guns	Ship in which Embarked	Date of Leaving England	Date of Arrival at Cape Town	Place of Dis-embarkation	Date of Disem-barkation
Cavalry Division									
Cavalry Division Staff	4	16	17	—	*City of Vienna*	22.10.99	16.11.99	Cape Town	16.11.99
Field troop, R.E.	4	116	88	—	*Rapidan*	13.11.99	9.12.99	Cape Town	9.12.99
1st cavalry brigade Staff	3	13	4	—	*City of Vienna*	22.10.99	16.11.99	Cape Town	16.11.99
1st cavalry brigade									
6th Dragoon Guards	25	563	499	1	{ *Chicago*	8.11.99	1.12.99	Cape Town	2.12.99
					Wakool	4.11.99	27.11.99	Cape Town	28.11.99
10th Hussars	26	565	502	1	{ *Ismore*	4.11.99	Wrecked.	*Columbine Pnt.	3.12.99
					Columbian	6.11.99	2.12.99	Cape Town	3.12.99
12th Lancers	26	559	500	1	{ *Mohawk*	22.10.99	16.11.99	Cape Town	16.11.99
					City of Vienna	22.10.99	16.11.99	Cape Town	16.11.99
Southern, Aldershot, South-Eastern and Cork M.I.	25	575	—	4	*Malta*	22.10.99	16.11.99	Cape Town	16.11.99
R. battery, R.H.A.	6	180	198	6	*Aurania*	23.10.99	11.11.99	Cape Town	11.11.99
Ammunition column	3	83	75	—	*America*	24.10.99	18.11.99	Cape Town	19.11.99
No. 11 Bearer company	4	57	—	—	*America*	24.10.99	18.11.99	Cape Town	19.11.99
No. 11 Field Hospital	5	35	—	—	*Ismore*	4.11.99	Wrecked.	*Columbine Pnt.	3.12.99
2nd cavalry brigade Staff	3	13	4	—	*Mohawk*	22.10.99	16.11.99	Cape Town	16.11.99
2nd cavalry brigade									
1st Royal Dragoons	27	562	520	1	*Carisbrook Castle*	28.10.99	14.11.99	Cape Town	14.11.99
2nd Dragoons	25	548	498	1	{ *Manchester Port.*	30.10.99	22.11.99	Durban	27.11.99
					Antillian	17.11.99	9.12.99	Cape Town	10.12.99
					British Princess	16.11.99	6.12.99	Cape Town	7.12.99
					Ranee	9.11.99	5.12.99	Cape Town	5.12.99
6th Dragoons	25	557	498	1	{ *Jamaican*	23.10.99	18.11.99	Cape Town	18.11.99
					†*Persia*	28.10.99	11.12.99	Cape Town	11.12.99
O. battery, R.H.A.	6	180	198	6	*Siberian*	24.10.99	19.11.99	Cape Town	20.11.99
Ammunition column	3	86	61	—	*Glengyle*	27.10.99	20.11.99	Cape Town	21.11.99
Northern, Western, Eastern and Dublin M.I.	24	581	—	4	*Glengyle*	27.10.99	20.11.99	Cape Town	21.11.99
2nd cavalry brigade Bearer company	2	55	—	—	{ *Orient*	22.10.99	12.11.99	Cape Town	13.11.99
					Cephalonia	24.10.99	18.11.99	Cape Town	18.11.99
					Idaho	3.11.99	26.11.99	Cape Town	26.11.99
No. 6 Field Hospital	5	35	—	—	*Cephalonia*	24.10.99	18.11.99	Cape Town	18.11.99

* Arrived Cape Town, 6.12.99.   † *Persia* broke down at St. Vincent.

APPENDIX 7—continued.

APPENDIX 7.   473

	Units.	Officers.	Other Ranks.	Horses.	Guns.	Ship in which Embarked.	Date of Leaving England.	Date of Arrival at Cape Town.	Place of Disembarkation.	Date of Disembarkation.
1st Infantry Division										
Divisional Troops	1st Division Staff	10	4	—	—	*Moor*	21.10.99	9.11.99	Cape Town	9.11.99
	"A" squadron, 1st Life Guards	8	186	191	—	*Maplemore*	29.11.99	25.12.99	Cape Town	25.12.99
	Brigade Division Staff and 7th battery, R.F.A.	9	183	152	6	*Armenian*	24.10.99	13.11.99	Durban	17.11.99
	14th battery, R.F.A.	5	172	137	6	*Armenian*	24.10.99	13.11.99	Durban	17.11.99
	66th battery, R.F.A.	5	170	136	6	*Armenian*	24.10.99	13.11.99	Durban	17.11.99
	Ammunition column	5	129	94	—	*Armenian*	24.10.99	13.11.99	Durban	17.11.99
	Royal Engineers	8	208	—	—	*Goorkha*	21.10.99	15.11.99	Durban / Cape Town	21.11.99 / 15.11.99
	No. 7 Field Hospital	5	35	—	—	*Gascon*	21.10.99	12.11.99	Cape Town	12.11.99
	1st brigade Staff	2	16	3	—	*Goorkha*	21.10.99	15.11.99	*Cape Town	15.11.99
1st Infantry brigade	3rd battn. Grenadier Guards	32	1,083	6	1	*Goorkha*	21.10.99	15.11.99	*Cape Town	15.11.99
	1st battn. Coldstream Guards	31	1,090	5	1	*Malta*	22.10.99	16.11.99	*Cape Town	16.11.99
	2nd battn. Coldstream Guards	31	1,082	3	1	*Gascon*	21.10.99	12.11.99	Cape Town	12.11.99
	1st battn. Scots Guards	30	1,089	3	1	*Nubia*	21.10.99	13.11.99	Cape Town	14.11.99
	No. 1 bearer company	3	58	—	—	*Gascon*	21.10.99	12.11.99	Cape Town	12.11.99
	No. 1 Field Hospital	4	35	—	—	*Nubia*	21.10.99	13.11.99	Cape Town	13.11.99
	2nd brigade staff	3	18	3	—	*Roslin Castle*	20.10.99	8.11.99	Durban	12.11.99
2nd Infantry brigade	2nd battn. Royal West Surrey regiment	26	1,064	3	1	*Yorkshire*	20.10.99	11.11.99	Durban	14.11.99
	2nd battn. Devonshire regiment	24	1,041	3	1	*Manila*	20.10.99	15.11.99	Durban	19.11.99
	2nd battn. West Yorkshire regiment	27	936	3	1	*Roslin Castle*	20.10.99	9.11.99	Durban	12.11.99
	2nd battn. East Surrey regiment	26	1,082	3	1	{ *Harlech Castle* / *Lismore Castle* }	20.10.99 / 20.10.99	15.11.99 / 11.11.99	Durban / Durban	20.11.99 / 14.11.99
	No. 4 bearer company	3	58	—	—	*Roslin Castle*	20.10.99	9.11.99	Durban	15.11.99
	No. 3 Field Hospital	4	35	—	—	*Roslin Castle*	20.10.99	9.11.99	Durban	15.11.99

* Started from Gibraltar.

APPENDIX 7—continued.

474   THE WAR IN SOUTH AFRICA.

	Units.	Strength.				Ship in which Embarked.	Date of leaving England.	Date of arrival at Cape Town.	Place of disembarkation.	Date of disembarkation.
		Officers.	Other Ranks.	Horses.	Guns.					
2nd Infantry Division										
Divisional Troops	2nd infantry division Staff	11	8	4	—	*Moor*	21.10.99	9.11.99	Durban	14.11.99
	"B." squadron, Royal Horse Guards	9	191	199	—	*Maplemore* / *Pinemore*	29.11.99 / 4.12.99	24.12.99 / 29.12.99	Cape Town / Cape Town	25.12.99 / 29.12.99
	5th brigade division, R.F.A.	4	12	16	—	*Urmston Grange*	1.11.99	27.11.99	Durban	2.12.99
	63rd battery, R.F.A.	5	170	137	6	*Ismore*	4.11.99	Wrecked *	Durban	27.12.99
	64th battery, R.F.A.	5	170	137	6	*Urmston Grange*	1.11.99	27.11.99	Durban	2.12.99
	73rd battery, R.F.A.	5	170	139	6	*Idaho*	3.11.99	26.11.99	Durban	1.12.99
	Ammunition column	5	123	93	—	*Idaho*	3.11.99	26.11.99	Durban	1.12.99
	Royal Engineers	9	208	—	—	*Aurania*	23.10.99	11.11.99	Cape Town	11.11.99
	2nd divisional Field Hospital	5	35	—	—	*Cephalonia*	24.10.99	18.11.99	Durban	23.11.99
3rd infantry brigade	3rd infantry brigade Staff	2	18	1	—	*Aurania*	23.10.99	11.11.99	Cape Town	11.11.99
	2nd battn. Royal Highlanders	29	1,014	3	1	*Orient*	24.10.99	14.11.99	Cape Town	14.11.99
	1st battn. Highland Light Infantry	26	1,087	—	1	*Aurania*	23.10.99	11.11.99	Cape Town	11.11.99
	2nd battn. Seaforth Highlanders	27	927	3	1	*Mongolian*	21.10.99	18.11.99	Cape Town	18.11.99
	1st battn. Argyll and Sutherland Highlanders	30	1,081	3	1	*Servia* / *Orcana*	4.11.99 / 27.10.99	24.11.99 / 17.11.99	Cape Town / Cape Town	24.11.99 / 17.11.99
	No. 3 Bearer company	3	58	—	—	*Aurania*	23.10.99	11.11.99	Cape Town	11.11.99
	No. 10 Field Hospital	5	35	—	—	*Mongolian*	21.10.99	18.11.99	Cape Town	18.11.99
4th infantry brigade	4th infantry brigade Staff	3	22	3	—	*Cephalonia*	24.10.99	18.11.99	Durban	23.11.99
	2nd battn. Scottish Rifles	26	939	3	1	*City of Cambridge*	23.10.99	16.11.99	Durban	22.11.99
	3rd battn. King's Royal Rifle corps	29	1,074	3	1	*Servia*	4.11.99	24.11.99	Durban	28.11.99
	1st battn. Durham Light Infantry	28	921	3	1	*Cephalonia*	24.10.99	18.11.99	Durban	23.11.99
	1st battn. Rifle brigade	29	1,082	3	1	*German*	28.10.99	21.11.99	Durban	25.11.99
	No. 9 Bearer company	2	54	—	—	*Servia*	4.11.99	24.11.99	Durban	29.11.99
	No. 9 Field Hospital	6	38	—	—	*Servia*	4.11.99	24.11.99	Durban	29.11.99

APPENDIX 7—continued.

APPENDIX 7.

	Units.	Strength.				Ship in which Embarked.	Date of leaving England.	Date of arrival at Cape Town.	Place of Disembarkation.	Date of Disembarkation.
		Officers.	Other Ranks.	Horses.	Guns.					
3rd Infantry Division	3rd infantry division Staff	11	8	4	—	*Moor*	21.10.99	9.11.99	East London	16.11.99
Divisional Troops	"C" squadron, 2nd Life Guards	9	186	193	—	*Pinemore*	4.12.99	29.12.99	Cape Town	29.12.99
	6th brigade division, R.F.A.	4	13	5	—	*Englishman*	6.11.99	30.11.99	East London	4.12.99
	74th battery, R.F.A.	5	170	138	6	*Englishman*	6.11.99	30.11.99	East London	4.12.99
	77th battery, R.F.A.	5	170	137	6	*Englishman*	6.11.99	30.11.99	East London	4.12.99
	79th battery, R.F.A.	5	173	141	6	*Montfort*	13.11.99	8.12.99	East London	11.12.99
	Ammunition column	5	128	94	—	*Englishman*	6.11.99	30.11.99	East London	4.12.99
	Royal Engineers	9	220	—	—	*Bavarian*	10.11.99	28.11.99	Cape Town	28.11.99
	No. 16 Field Hospital	4	35	—	—	*Cheshire*	9.11.99	29.11.99	East London	5.12.99
5th infantry brigade	5th infantry brigade Staff	3	21	3	—	*Catalonia*	5.11.99	30.11.99	Durban	5.12.99
	1st battn. Royal Inniskilling Fusiliers	29	969	3	1	*Catalonia*	5.11.99	30.11.99	Durban	5.12.99
	2nd battn. Royal Irish Rifles	25	875	3	1	*Britannic*	26.10.99	14.11.99	East London	16.11.99
	1st battn. Connaught Rangers	28	855	3	1	*Bavarian*	10.11.99	28.11.99	Durban	1.12.99
	1st battn. Royal Dublin Fusiliers	28	923	—	1	*Bavarian*	10.11.99	28.11.99	Durban	1.12.99
	No. 8 Bearer company	3	57	—	—	*Bavarian*	10.11.99	28.11.99	Durban	1.12.99
	No. 15 Field Hospital	5	35	—	—	*Bavarian*	10.11.99	28.11.99	Durban	1.12.99
6th infantry brigade	6th infantry brigade Staff	3	21	3	—	*Oriental*	23.10.99	13.11.99	Durban	17.11.99
	2nd battn. Royal Fusiliers	25	769	3	1	*Pavonia*	22.10.99	18.11.99	Durban	23.11.99
	2nd battn. Royal Scots Fusiliers	29	870	2	1	*Oriental* / *Pavonia*	23.10.99 / 22.10.99	13.11.99 / 18.11.99	Durban / Durban	17.11.99 / 23.11.99
	1st battn. Royal Welsh Fusiliers	27	1,074	3	1	*Oriental*	23.10.99	13.11.99	Durban	17.11.99
	2nd battn. Royal Irish Fusiliers	29	946	3	1	*Hawarden Castle*	23.10.99	12.11.99	Durban	16.11.99
	No. 12 Bearer company	3	58	—	—	*Catalonia*	5.11.99	30.11.99	Durban	5.12.99
	No. 17 Field Hospital	5	35	—	—	*Oriental*	23.10.99	13.11.99	Durban	17.11.99

APPENDIX 7—continued.

Units	Strength.				Ship in which embarked.	Date of leaving England.	Date of arrival at Cape Town.	Place of dis-embarkation.	Date of Disem-barkation.
	Officers	Other Ranks	Horses	Machine Guns					
Lines of Communication { 2nd Northumberland Fusiliers	29	977	3	1	*Kildonan Castle*	4.11.99	22.11.99	East London	26.11.99
2nd Somerset Light Infantry	29	875	3	1	*Briton*	4.11.99	20.11.99	Durban	24.11.99*
2nd Duke of Cornwall's Light Infantry	29	920	3	1	*Formosa*	5.11.99	29.11.99	Cape Town	29.11.99
1st Welsh regiment	28	823	3	1	*Kildonan Castle*	4.11.99	22.11.99	Port Elizabeth	26.11.99
2nd Northamptonshire regiment	28	990	3	1	{ *Harlech Castle* *Nubia* }	20.10.99 21.10.99	14.11.99 13.11.99	Cape Town Cape Town	14.11.99 13.11.99
2nd Shropshire Light Infantry	29	905	3	1	*Arawa*	8.11.99	1.12.99	Cape Town	1.12.99
1st Gordon Highlanders	29	855	4	1	*Cheshire*	9.11.99	29.11.99	Cape Town	29.11.99

* The battalion transhipped to S.S. *Oreana*, which arrived at Durban 24.11.99.

APPENDIX 8.

The composition and distribution of British troops in southern Natal, 23rd November, 1899, the morning of the fight at Willow Grange.

ESTCOURT.

MAJOR-GENERAL H. J. T. HILDYARD.

- 2nd brigade Staff.
- Naval detachment with two 12-pr. 12-cwt. guns.
- 7th battery, R.F.A.
- Natal Field artillery.
- 2nd battn. The Queen's (Royal West Surrey regiment), five companies.
- 2nd battn. West Yorkshire regiment.
- 2nd ,, East Surrey regiment.
- 1st ,, The Border regiment.
- 2nd ,, Royal Dublin Fusiliers.
- Mounted infantry company of 2nd battn. King's Royal Rifle Corps.
- 16th company, Army Service Corps.
- Natal Royal Rifles.
- Durban Light Infantry.
- Natal Carbineers (one squadron).
- Imperial Light Horse (one squadron).
- Bethune's mounted infantry.
- Natal Police.

MOOI RIVER.

MAJOR-GENERAL G. BARTON.

- 6th brigade Staff.
- 14th battery, R.F.A.
- 2nd battn. The Queen's (Royal West Surrey regiment), three companies.
- 2nd battn. Devonshire regiment.
- 2nd ,, Royal Scots Fusiliers (one company).
- 1st ,, Royal Welsh Fusiliers.
- 2nd ,, Royal Irish Fusiliers.
- 24th company, Army Service Corps.
- Thorneycroft's mounted infantry.

NOTTINGHAM ROAD.

- 66th battery, R.F.A. (two guns).
- 2nd battn. Scottish Rifles.

PIETERMARITZBURG.

LT.-GENERAL SIR C. F. CLERY.

- Divisional Staff of 2nd division.
- Headquarters line of communication.
- Naval contingent with four 12-pr. 12-cwt. Naval guns.*
- 66th battery, R.F.A. (four guns).
- Divisional ammunition column.
- General depôt.
- Natal Naval Volunteers.
- Imperial Light Infantry.
- Pietermaritzburg Rifle association.
- Home Guard.
- Reserve Rifle association.
- Railway Rifle association.

GREYTOWN.
MAJOR G. LEUCHARS.

- Umvoti Mounted Rifles.

DURBAN.

CAPT. PERCY SCOTT, R.N.

- Naval contingent, two 6-in. guns, two 4·7-in. guns, 12 Naval 12-pr. 12-cwt. and two Naval 12-pr. 8-cwt. guns.
- † 2nd battn. Royal Fusiliers.
- † 2nd ,, Royal Scots Fusiliers (seven companies).
- † 1st ,, Durham Light Infantry.

* Two of these guns were *en route* to Mooi River.   † *En route* to Pietermaritzburg.

APPENDIX 9.

REINFORCEMENTS LANDED IN SOUTH AFRICA UP TO THE 13TH OF FEBRUARY, 1900, OTHER THAN THOSE GIVEN IN APPENDICES 1. AND 7.

(A) REINFORCEMENTS SENT TO SOUTH AFRICA AFTER "LOMBARDS KOP."

Units.	Strength.				Ship in which Embarked.	Place of Embarkation.	Date of Embarkation.	Place of Disembarkation.	Date of Disembarkation.
	Officers.	Other Ranks.	Horses.	Guns.					
No. 4. Mountain battery, R.G.A.	6	276	18	6	*Narrung*	Royal Albert Dock	16.11.99	Durban	12.12.99
1st battn. Suffolk regiment	22	1,081	3	1	*Scott*	Southampton	11.11.99	Cape Town	28.11.99
1st battn. Essex regiment	23	912	3	1	*Greek*	Southampton	11.11.99	Cape Town	3.12.99
1st battn. Derbyshire regiment	29	1,091	5	1	*Dunera*	Malta	21.11.99	East London	15.12.99

(B) FIFTH INFANTRY DIVISION.

Units.	Officers.	Other Ranks.	Horses.	Guns.	Ship in which Embarked.	Place of Embarkation.	Date of Embarkation.	Place of Disembarkation.	Date of Disembarkation.
Divisional Staff	11	29	7	—	*Norham Castle*	Southampton	25.11.99	Cape Town	13.12.99
14th Hussars	25	559	497	1	*Victorian* / *Cestrian*	Southampton	13.12.99	Durban	6.1.00
Brigade division Staff	4	13	13	—	*Atlantian*	Southampton	21.12.99	Cape Town	10.1.00
19th battery, R.F.A.	5	170	133	6	*Atlantian*	Queenstown	5.12.99	Durban	1.1.00
20th battery, R.F.A.	5	170	137	6	*Victorian*	Liverpool	3.12.99	Durban	1.1.00
28th battery, R.F.A.	5	170	137	6	*Atlantian*	Southampton	13.12.99	Cape Town	1.1.00
Ammunition column	5	128	93	—	*Canada*	Queenstown	5.12.99	Durban	1.1.00
37th Field company, R.E.	7	207	—	—	*Gaul*	Liverpool	30.11.99	Durban	1.1.00
10th infantry brigade Staff	*1	17	2	—	*Gaul*	Southampton	24.11.99	Cape Town	23.12.99
2nd battn. Royal Warwickshire regiment	25	1,078	3	1	*Gaul*	Southampton	24.11.99	Cape Town	16.12.99
1st battn. Yorkshire regiment	22	956	4	1	*Doune Castle*	Southampton	24.11.99	Cape Town	15.12.99

* Maj.-Gen. Talbot Coke embarked at Mauritius, 1.12.99.

APPENDIX 9—continued.

(B) FIFTH INFANTRY DIVISION—continued.

Units.	Strength.				Ship in which Embarked.	Place of Embarkation.	Date of Embarkation.	Place of Disembarkation.	Date of Disembarkation.
	Officers	Other Ranks	Horses	Guns					
2nd battn. Dorset regiment	22	944	3	1	*Simla*	Southampton	24.11.99	Durban	21.12.99
2nd battn. Middlesex regiment	25	1,023	4	1	*Avondale Castle*	Southampton	2.12.99	Cape Town *	26.12.99
11th infantry brigade Staff	3	12	3	—	*Canada*	Liverpool	30.11.99	Durban	23.12.99
2nd battn. Royal Lancaster regiment	25	1,049	3	1	*Dilwara*	Southampton	2.12.99	Durban	30.12.99
2nd battn. Lancashire Fusiliers	21	1,082	3	1	*Norman*	Southampton	2.12.99	Cape Town †	19.12.99
1st battn. South Lancashire regiment	22	1,049	3	1	*Canada*	Liverpool	30.11.99	Durban	23.12.99
1st battn. York and Lancaster regiment	24	838	4	1	*Majestic*	Liverpool	13.12.99	Durban	2.1.00
Army Service Corps, No. 27 coy.	2	47	—	—	*Canada*	Liverpool	30.11.99	Durban	23.12.99
,, ,, No. 32 coy.	2	60	—	—	*Gaul*	Southampton	24.11.99	Cape Town	16.12.99
,, ,, No. 25 coy.	2	60	1	—	*Canada*	Liverpool	30.11.99	Durban	23.12.99
Royal Army Medical Corps	15	153	—	—	{ *Simla* / *Dilwara* }	{ Southampton / Southampton }	{ 24.11.99 / 2.12.99 }	{ Durban / Durban }	{ 21.12.99 / 30.12.99 }

(C) ADDITIONAL UNITS MOBILIZED WITH FIFTH INFANTRY DIVISION.

Units.	Officers	Other Ranks	Horses	Guns	Ship in which Embarked.	Place of Embarkation.	Date of Embarkation.	Place of Disembarkation.	Date of Disembarkation.
Brigade division Staff, R.H.A.	4	16	18	—	*Cestrian*	Southampton	21.12.99	Cape Town	10.1.00
Q. battery, R.H.A.	4	174	194	6	{ *Manchester Corporation* }	Southampton	19.12.99	Cape Town	25.1.00 ‡
T. battery, R.H.A.	5	170	196	6	{ *Manchester Corporation* }	Southampton	19.12.99	Cape Town	25.1.00
U. battery, R.H.A.	3	178	196	6	*Cestrian*	Southampton	21.12.99	Cape Town	10.1.00
Ammunition column	5	107	93	—	*Cestrian*	Southampton	21.12.99	Cape Town	10.1.00
Army Ordnance Corps	2	80	—	—	*Guelph*	Southampton	18.11.99	Cape Town	10.12.99

* The battalion was transhipped to *Mongolian*, which arrived at Durban on 1.1.00.
† The battalion was transhipped to *Roslin Castle*, which arrived at Durban on 23.12.99.
‡ Accident to propeller twice during voyage.

APPENDIX 9—*continued*.

(D) SIXTH INFANTRY DIVISION.

Units.	Strength.				Ship in which Embarked.	Place of Embarkation.	Date of Embarkation.	Place of Disembarkation.	Date of Disembarkation.
	Officers.	Other Ranks.	Horses.	Guns.					
Divisional Staff ...	10	40	8	—	*Dunottar Castle*	Southampton	23.12.99	Port Elizabeth	15.1.00
Brigade division Staff	4	13	16	—	*Cymric* ...	Liverpool	1.1.00	Cape Town	21.1.00
76th battery, R.F.A.	5	170	137	6	*Cymric* ...	Liverpool	1.1.00	Cape Town	21.1.00
81st battery, R.F.A.	5	170	137	6	*Cymric* ...	Liverpool	1.1.00	Cape Town	21.1.00
82nd battery, R.F.A.	5	170	138	6	*Cymric* ...	Liverpool	1.1.00	Cape Town	21.1.00
Ammunition column	4	123	96	—	*America*	Royal Albert Dock	5.1.00	Cape Town	31.1.00
Royal Engineers ...	10	208	10	—	*Tintagel Castle*	Southampton	17.12.99	Cape Town	8.1.00
12th infantry brigade Staff	3	21	—	—	*Gascon* ...	Southampton	16.12.99	Port Elizabeth	12.1.00
2nd battn. Bedfordshire regt.	22	903	2	1	*Sumatra*	Royal Albert Dock	16.12.99	Port Elizabeth	13.1.00
1st battn. Royal Irish regt.	18	843*	185	1	*Gascon* ...	Southampton	16.12.99	Port Elizabeth	12.1.00
2nd battn. Worcestershire regt.	27	1,055†	117	1	*Tintagel Castle*	Southampton	17.12.99	Cape Town	8.1.00
2nd battn. Wiltshire regt.	8	823	3	1	*Gascon* ...	Southampton	16.12.99	Port Elizabeth	12.1.00
13th infantry brigade Staff	3	21	3	—	*Gaika* ...	Southampton	22.12.99	Cape Town	14.1.00
2nd battn. East Kent regt.	21	934‡	120	1	*Gaika* ...	Southampton	22.12.99	Cape Town	14.1.00
2nd battn. Gloucestershire regt.	26	930§	119	1	*Cymric* ...	Liverpool	1.1.00	Cape Town	21.1.00
1st battn. West Riding regt.	27	981‖	109	1	*Orient* ...	Southampton	29.12.99	Cape Town	19.1.00
1st battn. Oxfordshire Light Infantry	26	768¶	87	1	*Gaika* ...	Southampton	22.12.99	Cape Town	14.1.00
Army Service Corps, No. 10 company	2	60	—	—	*Tintagel Castle*	Southampton	17.12.99	Cape Town	8.1.00
Army Service Corps, No. 7 company	2	60	—	—	*Sumatra*	Royal Albert Dock	16.12.99	Port Elizabeth	13.1.00
Army Service Corps, No. 23 company	3	46	—	—	*Tintagel Castle*	Southampton	17.12.99	Cape Town	8.1.00
Royal Army Medical Corps ...	20	221	—	—	*Gaika* ... *America* *Cymric* ...	Southampton Royal Albert Dock Liverpool	22.12.99 5.1.00 1.1.00	Cape Town Cape Town Cape Town	14.1.00 31.1.00 21.1.00

* Strength includes mounted infantry company in *America*.
† Strength includes mounted infantry company in *British Prince*.
‡ Strength includes mounted infantry company in *British Prince*.
§ Strength includes mounted infantry company in *British Prince*.
‖ Strength includes mounted infantry company in *Pindari*.
¶ Strength ...

APPENDIX 9.

(E) SEVENTH DIVISION.

Units.	Strength.				Ship in which Embarked.	Place of Embarkation.	Date of Embarkation.	Place of Disembarkation.	Date of Disembarkation.
	Officers.	Other Ranks.	Horses.	Guns.					
Divisional Staff...	18	48	31	—	Kildonan Castle.	Southampton	3.1.00	Cape Town	20.1.00
Brigade division Staff, R.F.A.	4	12	14	—	Dwarka	Bombay	4.1.00	Cape Town	18.1.00
83rd battery, R.F.A.	5	170	134	6	Manchester Port	Tilbury	18.1.00	Cape Town	11.2.00
84th battery, R.F.A.	5	170	135	6	Manchester Port	Tilbury	18.1.00	Cape Town	11.2.00
85th battery, R.F.A.	5	170	137	6	Manchester Port	Tilbury	18.1.00	Cape Town	11.2.00
Ammunition column	3	126	93	—	Glengyle	S. W. India Dock	10.1.00	Cape Town	4.2.00
Royal Engineers...	7	213	—	—	Goorkha	Southampton	4.1.00	Cape Town	25.1.00
14th infantry brigade Staff	2	20	3	—	Goorkha	Southampton	4.1.00	Cape Town	25.1.00
2nd battn. Norfolk regt.	26	984	5	1	Assaye	Southampton	4.1.00	Cape Town	23.1.00
2nd battn. Lincolnshire regt.	25	971	5	1	Goorkha	Southampton	4.1.00	Cape Town	25.1.00
1st battn. King's Own Scottish Borderers	28	1,067	3	1	Braemar Castle.	Southampton	4.1.00	Cape Town	26.1.00
2nd battn. Hampshire regt.	22	838	3	1	Assaye	Southampton	4.1.00	Cape Town	23.1.00
15th infantry brigade Staff	3	21	1	1	Briton	Southampton	13.1.00	Cape Town	29.1.00
2nd battn. Cheshire regt.	27	963	3	1	Britannic	Southampton	7.1.00	Cape Town	27.1.00
1st battn. East Lancashire regt.	27	948	3	1	Bavarian	Southampton	13.1.00	Cape Town	3.2.00
2nd battn. South Wales Borderers	29	1,064	3	1	Bavarian	Southampton	13.1.00	Cape Town	3.2.00
2nd battn. North Staffordshire regt.	27	998	3	1	Aurania	Southampton	15.1.00	Cape Town	3.2.00
Army Service Corps, No. 12 company	2	41	—	—	Braemar Castle.	Southampton	4.1.00	Cape Town	26.1.00
Army Service Corps, No. 17 company	2	37	—	—	Braemar Castle.	Southampton	4.1.00	Cape Town	26.1.00
Army Service Corps, No. 34 company	2	42	—	—	Braemar Castle.	Southampton	4.1.00	Cape Town	26.1.00
Royal Army Medical Corps	16	164	—	—	Braemar Castle.	Southampton	4.1.00	Cape Town	27.1.00
					Britannic	Southampton	7.1.00	Cape Town	27.1.00
					Goorkha	Southampton	4.1.00	Cape Town	25.1.00
					Bavarian	Southampton	13.1.00	Cape Town	3.2.00

VOL. I.

APPENDIX 9—*continued*.

(F) (*a*) ARTILLERY UNITS UNALLOTTED TO BRIGADES AND DIVISIONS AT THE TIME OF LORD ROBERTS' ADVANCE.

Company.	Date of Embarkation.	Date of Arrival at Cape Town.
No. 15 company, Southern Division, R.G.A.	9th December, 1899.	26th December, 1899.
No. 15 company, Western Division, R.G.A.		
No. 16 company, Southern Division, R.G.A.	22nd December, 1899.	18th January, 1900.
No. 36 company, Southern Division, R.G.A.		
No. 2 company, Southern Division, R.G.A.	22nd January, 1900.	13th February, 1900.
No. 5 company, Eastern Division, R.G.A.		
No. 14 company, Southern Division, R.G.A.		
No. 17 company, Southern Division, R.G.A.		
No. 10 company, Eastern Division, R.G.A.	2nd & 3rd Feb. 1900.	24th to 27th Feb. 1900.
No. 2 company, Western Division, R.G.A.		
No. 6 company, Western Division, R.G.A.		
No. 10 company, Western Division, R.G.A.		

These companies arrived in various ships.

APPENDIX 9. 483

APPENDIX 9—continued.
(F) (b) UNITS UNALLOTTED TO BRIGADES AND DIVISIONS LANDED IN SOUTH AFRICA UP TO 13TH FEBRUARY, 1900.

Units	Strength.				Ship in which Embarked.	Place of Embarkation.	Date of Embarkation.	Place of Disembarkation.	Date of Disembarkation.
	Officers.	Other Ranks.	Horses.	Guns.					
Militia. { 4th battn. Royal Lancaster regiment	25	658	2	—	*Nile*	Southampton	13.1.00	Cape Town	1.2.00
6th battn. Royal Warwick regiment	25	687	4	—	*Umbria*	Southampton	11.1.00	Cape Town	29.1.00
3rd battn. S. Lancashire regiment	24	735	4	—	*City of Rome*	Liverpool	16.1.00	Cape Town	13.2.00
4th battn. Derbyshire regiment	31	651	4	—	*Umbria*	Southampton	11.1.00	Pt. Elizabeth	2.2.00
3rd battn. Durham Light Infantry	29	703	4	—	*Umbria*	Southampton	11.1.00	East London	3.2.00
4th battn. Argyll & Sutherland Highlanders	28	772	5	—	*City of Rome*	Queenstown	18.1.00	Cape Town	13.2.00
9th battn. King's Royal Rifle Corps	24	672	2	—	*Nile*	Queenstown	13.1.00	Cape Town	1.2.00
Imperial Yeomanry Staff	4	5	—	—	*Kinfauns Castle*	Southampton	20.1.00	Cape Town	5.2.00
City of London Imperial Volunteers	28	812	—	—	{ *Garth Castle*	Southampton	13.1.00	Cape Town	4.2.00
					Briton	Southampton	13.1.00	Cape Town	29.1.00
					Gaul	Southampton	20.1.00	Cape Town	12.2.00
					Kinfauns Castle	Southampton	20.1.00	Cape Town	5.2.00

(G) REINFORCEMENTS FROM INDIA.

16th Lancers	23	551	540	1	{ *Lindula*	Bombay	6.1.00	Pt. Elizabeth	23.1.00
					Fazilka	Bombay	6.1.00	Pt. Elizabeth	21.1.00
					Nairung	Bombay	6.1.00	Pt. Elizabeth	23.1.00
A. battery, R.H.A.	3	174	206	6	*Urlana*	Bombay	8.1.00	Durban	22.1.00
J. battery, R.H.A.	5	179	208	6	*Ujina*	Bombay	11.1.00	Pt. Elizabeth	28.1.00
Burma mounted infantry	18	308	340	—	*Palamcotta*	Rangoon	24.1.00	Cape Town	13.2.00

VOL. I. 31*

484 THE WAR IN SOUTH AFRICA.

APPENDIX 9—continued.

(H) OVERSEA COLONIAL CONTINGENTS LANDED IN SOUTH AFRICA UP TO 13TH FEBRUARY, 1900.

Units.	Strength.				Ship in which Embarked.	Place of Embarkation.	Date of Embarkation.	Place of Disembarkation.	Date of Disembarkation.
	Officers.	Other Ranks.	Horses.	Guns.					
New South Wales Lancers	2	68	—	—	*Nineveh*	London	10.10.99	Cape Town	2.11.99
New Zealand mounted rifles	15	205	251	—	*Waiwera*	Wellington	20.10.99	Cape Town	23.11.99
Victorian Rifles	5	120	9	—	*Medic*	Melbourne	28.10.99	Cape Town	27.11.99
Tasmanian infantry	4	76	4	—	*Medic*	Melbourne	28.10.99	Cape Town	26.11.99
Victorian mounted rifles	8	118	157	—	*Medic*	Melbourne	27.10.99	Cape Town	27.11.99
South Australian infantry	6	121	3	—	*Medic*	Adelaide	31.10.99	Cape Town	26.11.99
West Australian infantry	5	125	17	2	*Medic*	Albany	5.11.99	Cape Town	26.11.99
New South Wales Lancers	5	33	130	—	} *Kent*	Sydney	28.10.99	Cape Town	1.12.99
New South Wales Army Medical Corps	6	85	50	—					
2nd batth. Royal Canadian regiment	43	997	6	2	*Sardinian*	Quebec	30.10.99	Cape Town	30.11.99
Queensland mounted infantry	14	248	285	1	*Cornwall*	Brisbane	1.11.99	Cape Town	14.12.99
New South Wales mounted rifles	3	73	35	—	*Aberdeen*	Sydney	3.11.99	Cape Town	7.12.99
New South Wales infantry	4	121	9	—	*Aberdeen*	Sydney	3.11.99	Cape Town	6.12.99
1st Australian Horse	2	32	37	—	} *Langton Grange*	Newcastle, N.S.W.	14.11.99	Cape Town	19.12.99
New South Wales mounted rifles	1	26	69	—					
A. battery, New South Wales Artillery	6	170	140	6	*Warrigal*	Sydney	30.12.99	Cape Town	7.2.00
2nd contingent Victorian mounted rifles	14	249	305	—	*Euryalus*	Melbourne	13.1.00	Cape Town	7.2.00

APPENDIX 10.

Distribution of troops in South Africa on 11th February, 1900, when the march from Ramdam began.

FIELD-MARSHAL LORD ROBERTS.

Commander-in-Chief's Bodyguard.

Cavalry division. Lt.-Genl. J. D. P. French.

- 1st Cavalry brigade (Brig.-Genl. T. C. Porter).
    - 6th Dragoon guards (Carabiniers).
    - 2nd Dragoons (Royal Scots Greys).
    - 6th (Inniskilling) Dragoons (one squadron).
    - 14th Hussars (one squadron).
    - New South Wales Lancers.
    - Q. T. and U. batteries, Royal Horse Artillery.
- 2nd Cavalry brigade (Brig.-Genl. R. G. Broadwood).
    - Composite regiment of Household cavalry.
    - 10th Hussars.
    - 12th Lancers.
    - G. and P. batteries, Royal Horse artillery.
- 3rd Cavalry brigade (Brig.-Genl. J. R. P. Gordon).
    - 9th Lancers.
    - 16th Lancers.
    - O. and R. batteries, Royal Horse artillery.
- Divisional troops.
    - 1st, 2nd, 3rd, 4th, 5th, 6th, 7th and 8th regiments of mounted infantry.
    - Roberts' Horse.
    - Kitchener's Horse.
    - Rimington's Guides.
    - New Zealand mounted rifles.
    - Queensland mounted infantry.
    - New South Wales mounted rifles.
    - Nesbitt's Horse.
    - Ammunition Column.
    - Field Troop, R.E.
    - Det. A.S.C.
    - Bearer Companies.
    - Field Hospitals.

6th infantry division.
Lieut.-General T. Kelly-Kenny.

- 13th brigade (Maj.-Genl. C. E. Knox).
  - 2nd battn. East Kent regiment.
  - 2nd ,, Gloucestershire regiment.
  - 1st ,, West Riding regiment.
  - 1st ,, Oxfordshire Light Infantry.
  - Det. A.S.C.
  - Bearer coy.
  - Field Hospital.
- 18th brigade (Brig.-Genl. T. E. Stephenson).
  - 1st battn. Yorkshire regiment.
  - 1st ,, Welsh regiment.
  - 1st ,, Essex regiment.
  - Det. A.S.C.
  - Bearer coy.
  - Field Hospital.
- Divisional troops.
  - Two 12-pr. 12-cwt. Naval guns.
  - 76th battery, R.F.A.
  - 81st battery, R.F.A.
  - Ammunition column.
  - 38th Field company, R.E.
  - Det. A.S.C.
  - Field Hospital.

7th infantry division.
Lieut.-General C. Tucker.

- 14th brigade (Maj.-Genl. H. Chermside).
  - 2nd battn. Norfolk regiment.
  - 2nd ,, Lincoln regiment.
  - 1st ,, King's Own Scottish Borderers.
  - 2nd ,, Hampshire regiment.
  - Det. A.S.C.
  - Bearer Coy.
  - Field Hospital.
- 15th brigade (Maj.-Genl. A. G. Wavell).
  - 2nd battn. Cheshire regiment.
  - 2nd ,, South Wales Borderers.
  - 1st ,, East Lancashire regiment.
  - 2nd ,, North Staffordshire regiment.
  - Det. A.S.C.
  - Bearer Coy.
  - Field Hospital.
- Divisional Troops.
  - 18th battery, R.F.A.
  - 62nd battery, R.F.A.
  - 75th battery, R.F.A.
  - Ammunition Column.
  - 9th Field company, R.E.
  - Det. A.S.C.
  - Field Hospital.

APPENDIX 10.

**9th infantry division.
Lieut.-Genl.
Sir H. Colvile.**

3rd brigade (Maj.-Genl. H. A. MacDonald).
  2nd battn. Black Watch.
  1st ,, Highland Light Infantry.
  2nd ,, Seaforth Highlanders.
  1st ,, Argyll and Sutherland Highlanders.
  Det. A.S.C.
  Bearer Coy.
  Field Hospital.

19th brigade (Maj.-Genl. H. L. Smith-Dorrien).
  2nd battn. Duke of Cornwall's Light Infantry.
  2nd ,, Shropshire Light Infantry.
  1st ,, Gordon Highlanders.
  2nd ,, Royal Canadian regiment.
  Det. A.S.C.
  Bearer Coy.
  Field Hospital.

Divisional Troops.
  Two 4·7-in. Naval guns.
  65th (Howitzer) battery, R.F.A.
  82nd battery, R.F.A.
  Ammunition column.
  7th Field company, R.E.
  Det. A.S.C.
  Field Hospital.
  City of London Imperial Volunteers mounted infantry.
  Grahamstown Volunteers mounted infantry.

LIEUT.-GENERAL LORD METHUEN, MODDER RIVER.

1st brigade (Maj.-Genl. R. Pole-Carew).
  3rd battn. Grenadier Guards.
  1st ,, Coldstream Guards.
  2nd ,, Coldstream Guards.
  1st ,, Scots Guards.
  Det. A.S.C.
  Bearer Coy.
  Field Hospital.

9th brigade (Maj.-Genl. C. W. H. Douglas).
  1st battn. Northumberland Fusiliers.
  1st ,, Loyal North Lancashire regiment (four companies).
  2nd ,, Northamptonshire regiment.
  2nd ,, King's Own Yorkshire Light Infantry.
  Det. A.S.C.
  Bearer Coy.
  Field Hospital.

Divisional Troops.
  Two 4·7-in. and two 12-pr. 12-cwt. Naval guns.
  20th battery, R.F.A.
  37th (Howitzer) battery, R.F.A. (four Howitzers).
  38th battery, R.F.A.
  Detachment 14th company, Southern Division, R.G.A.
  Ammunition Column.
  Field company, R.E.
  Balloon section, R.E.
  Det. A.S.C.
  Field Hospital.

488 THE WAR IN SOUTH AFRICA.

LIEUT.-GENERAL SIR F. FORESTIER-WALKER.

83rd battery, R.F.A.
84th battery, R.F.A.
85th battery, R.F.A.
A. battery, New South Wales artillery.
Detachment 14th coy., Southern Division, R.G.A.
15th coy., Southern Division, R.G.A.
15th coy., Western Division, R.G.A.
Two 5-in. guns 16th coy., Southern Division, R.G.A.
2nd battn. Royal Warwickshire regiment.
1st ,, Suffolk regiment.
1st ,, Royal Munster Fusiliers.
4th ,, Royal Lancaster regiment.
6th ,, Royal Warwickshire regiment.
3rd ,, South Lancashire regiment.
9th ,, King's Royal Rifle Corps.
4th ,, Argyll and Sutherland Highlanders.
City of London Imperial Volunteers.
Railway Pioneer regiment.

MAJOR-GENERAL R. A. P. CLEMENTS, NAAUWPOORT AND COLESBERG.

6th (Inniskilling) Dragoons (two squadrons).
J. battery, R.H.A.
37th (Howitzer) battery, R.F.A. (two Howitzers).
4th battery, R.F.A.
2nd battn. Bedfordshire regiment.
1st ,, Royal Irish regiment.
2nd ,, Worcestershire regiment.
2nd ,, Royal Berkshire regiment (four companies).
2nd ,, Wiltshire regiment.
4th ,, Derbyshire regiment.
Detachment 14th coy., Southern Division, R.G.A.

LIEUT.-GENERAL SIR W. GATACRE, STERKSTROOM.

Two 12-pr. 12-cwt. Naval guns.
74th battery, R.F.A.
77th battery, R.F.A.
79th battery, R.F.A.
Detachment, R.G.A. (two 9-pr. guns).
1st battn. The Royal Scots.
2nd ,, Northumberland Fusiliers.
1st ,, Derbyshire regiment.
2nd ,, Berkshire regiment (four companies).
2nd ,, Royal Irish Rifles.
3rd ,, Durham Light Infantry.
Two companies of mounted infantry.
Cape Mounted Rifles.
Brabant's Horse.
Kaffrarian Rifles.
De Montmorency's Scouts.
Queenstown Mounted Volunteers.

COLONEL R. G. KEKEWICH, KIMBERLEY.

23rd company, Western Division, R.G.A.
7th Field company, R.E. (one section).
1st battn. Loyal North Lancashire regiment (four companies).
Diamond Fields artillery.
Kimberley regiment.
Diamond Fields Horse.
Kimberley Light Horse.
Cape Police.
Town Guard.

APPENDIX 10.

Colonel R. S. S. Baden-Powell, Mafeking.

Protectorate regiment.
Bechuanaland Rifles.
British South Africa Police.
Cape Police.
Town Guard.

South Rhodesia and Bechuanaland Protectorate.

Rhodesia regiment.
British South Africa Police.
Buluwayo Volunteers.
Buluwayo Town Guard.

General Sir G. White, Ladysmith.

Naval brigade, with two 4·7-in. and four 12-pr. 12-cwt. Naval guns.
Natal Naval Volunteers.

Cavalry brigade (Maj.-Genl. J. F. Brocklehurst).
    5th Dragoon Guards.
    5th Lancers.
    18th Hussars.
    19th Hussars.
    Imperial Light Horse.

Mounted brigade (Colonel W. Royston).
    Natal Carbineers.
    Natal Mounted Rifles.
    Border Mounted Rifles.
    Natal Police.

    13th battery, R.F.A.
    67th battery, R.F.A.
    69th battery, R.F.A.
    21st battery, R.F.A.
    42nd battery, R.F.A.
    53rd battery, R.F.A.
    No. 10, Mountain battery, R.G.A. (two guns).
    Two 6·3-in. Howitzers.

7th brigade (Colonel I. S. M. Hamilton).
    1st battn. Manchester regiment.
    2nd ,, Gordon Highlanders.
    1st ,, Royal Irish Fusiliers (two companies).
    2nd ,, Rifle Brigade (seven companies).

8th brigade (Colonel F. Howard).
    1st battn. Leicestershire regiment.
    2nd ,, King's Royal Rifle Corps.
    1st ,, Liverpool regiment (four companies).
    2nd ,, Rifle Brigade (one company).

Divisional Troops (Colonel W. G. Knox).
    23rd Field coy., R.E.
    Telegraph section, R.E.
    Balloon section, R.E.
    1st battn. Liverpool regiment (four companies).
    1st ,, Devonshire regiment.
    1st ,, King's Royal Rifle Corps.
    1st ,, Gloucestershire regiment.
    Town Guard.

GENERAL SIR R. BULLER, CHIEVELEY.

Naval Brigade (Captain E. P. Jones, R.N.).
    One 6-in. gun.
    Five 4·7-in. guns.
    Eight 12-pr. 12-cwt. guns.

Corps Troops.
    19th battery, R.F.A.
    61st (Howitzer) battery, R.F.A.
    Two 5-in. guns, 16th company, Southern Division, R.G.A.
    No. 4, Mountain battery, R.G.A.
    Ammunition Column.
    Telegraph Detachment, R.E.
    "A." Pontoon Troop, R.E.
    Balloon section, R.E.

2nd Mounted brigade (Colonel the Earl of Dundonald).
    Composite regiment of mounted infantry.
    South African Light Horse.
    Thorneycroft's mounted infantry.

2nd infantry division. Major-Genl. the Hon. N. G. Lyttelton.

    2nd brigade (Maj.-Genl. H. J. T. Hildyard).
        2nd battn. Queen's regiment.
        2nd ,, Devon regiment.
        2nd ,, West Yorkshire regiment.
        2nd ,, East Surrey regiment.
    4th brigade (Colonel C. H. B. Norcott).
        2nd battn. Scottish Rifles.
        3rd ,, King's Royal Rifle Corps.
        1st ,, Durham Light Infantry.
        1st ,, Rifle brigade.
    Divisional Troops.
        One troop, 13th Hussars.
        7th battery, R.F.A.
        63rd battery, R.F.A.
        64th battery, R.F.A.
        17th Field company, R.E.

5th infantry division. Lieut.-Genl. Sir C. Warren.

    10th brigade (Maj.-Genl. J. Talbot Coke).
        2nd battn. Somerset Light Infantry.
        2nd ,, Dorset regiment.
        2nd ,, Middlesex regiment.
    11th brigade (Maj.-Genl. A. S. Wynne).
        1st battn. Royal Lancaster regiment.
        1st ,, South Lancashire regiment.
        Rifle Reserve battalion.
    Divisional Troops.
        One troop Royal Dragoons.
        Colonial Scouts.
        28th battery, R.F.A.
        73rd battery, R.F.A.
        78th battery, R.F.A.
        Ammunition Column.
        37th company, R.E.

APPENDIX 10.

6th brigade (temporarily attached to 5th division). (Major-Genl. G. Barton).
   2nd battn. Royal Fusiliers.
   2nd ,, Royal Scots Fusiliers.
   1st ,, Royal Welsh Fusiliers.
   2nd ,, Royal Irish Fusiliers.

5th brigade (unattached). (Major-Genl. A. F. Hart).
   1st battn. Royal Inniskilling Fusiliers.
   1st ,, Border regiment.
   1st ,, Connaught Rangers.
   2nd ,, Royal Dublin Fusiliers.

AT SPRINGFIELD.

1st Cavalry brigade (Colonel J. F. Burn-Murdoch).
   1st Royal Dragoons.
   13th Hussars.
   14th Hussars (two squadrons).
   A. battery, R.H.A.
   Two Naval 12-prs.
   1st battn. York and Lancaster regiment.
   Imperial Light Infantry.

AT GREYTOWN.

Colonel E. C. Bethune, 16th Lancers.
   Bethune's mounted infantry.
   Natal Police.
   Umvoti Mounted Rifles.
   Two 7-pr. Field guns, Natal Field artillery.
   Two Naval 12-pr. 8-cwt. guns.
   Detachment mounted infantry.

LINES OF COMMUNICATION.

   2nd battn. Lancashire Fusiliers.
   1st ,, Royal Dublin Fusiliers.
   Natal Royal Rifles.
   Colonial Scouts.
   Durban Light Infantry
   Natal Field artillery.

GLOSSARY.

BAD	A spring, bath.
BERG	A mountain.
BILTONG	Dried meat.
BOER	Literally farmer; often used as generic term for a Dutchman of South Africa.
BRANDWACHT	An outpost, or picket; literally beacon or camp fire.
BULT	A ridge in a rolling down country; literally a hump.
BURG	A town; literally a borough.
BURGHER	A male inhabitant of one of the Boer Republics who possessed full political rights.
BUSH	Country covered in a varying degree with trees and undergrowth.
BUSHVELD	Generally used in the Transvaal in reference to the low veld, in contrast to the high veld of the south and east and the bushveld of the north-east and north.
COMMANDANT	Senior officer of a commando; a commander.
COMMANDEER	To requisition for military service.
COMMANDO	A Boer military force of any size, usually the fighting force of one district.
CORPORAL	Assistant to a Veld-Cornet (q.v.).
DONGA	A cutting made on the surface of the ground by the action of water—sometimes filled with water, often dry.
DOPPER	A sect, religious, and to some extent political, among the Boers.

GLOSSARY.

DORP	A village.
DRIFT	A ford.
FONTEIN	A spring; literally a fountain.
HOEK	A re-entrant in a range of hills; literally corner; also used for pass and ravine.
HOOFD	An adjective signifying head or chief.
HOUT	Wood.
IMPI	A Zulu army.
INDABA	Native council.
INDUNA	Zulu, or Kaffir, chief.
INSPAN	To attach transport animals of any kind to their vehicles—to get ready to march—to harness-up.
KLOOF	Ravine, a gorge; literally a cleft.
KOP	A hill; literally head.
KOPJE	A small hill.
KRAAL	Native village, or collection of huts; an enclosure for cattle.
KRANZ, KRANTZ or KRANS	Cliff.
KRIJGSRAAD	War council.
LAAGER	Camp, bivouac.
LANDDROST	Boer magistrate.
MORGEN	A land measurement, roughly equal to two acres.
NEK	A pass between two hills of any height.
PAN	A pond, full or empty; a saucer-like depression, usually dry in winter.
PLAATS	House or farm. The term is equivalent to "an estate," large or small.
PONT	A ferry-boat or pontoon, worked by ropes or chains.
POORT	A gap, breaking a range of hills; literally gate.
RAND	Ridge or edge—*i.e.*, the edge of a plateau.
ROER	An old-fashioned gun or rifle.
SANGAR	Anglo-Indian term for a stone breastwork.
SCHANZ	Stone entrenchment or breastwork.

SLOOT or SLUIT	Open watercourse; an artificial ditch or gutter.
SPAN	A team of animals.
SPRUIT	A watercourse, sometimes dry.
STAD	Town.
STOEP	A masonry platform in front of a house; a verandah.
TREK	To travel—march.
UITSPAN	To detach transport of any kind from their vehicles—to halt—to unharness. Used as a substantive to denote the public places on main roads set aside for watering cattle and encamping.
VALLEI	Valley.
VECHT-GENERAL	Fighting General as opposed to the Administrative General.
VELD	The country as opposed to the town; the open country.
VELD-CORNET	The senior officer of a ward or sub-district.
VLEI	A small lake, usually formed by the widening of a stream.
VOLKSRAAD	Parliament; People's Council.
WAPENSCHOUW	Rifle meeting.
WARD	Sub-district.
WIJK	Ward, constituency.
WINKEL	Shop or store.
ZARP	A member of the Transvaal Police (Zuid-Afrikaansche-Republiek-Politie).
ZWART or SWART	Black.

INDEX

INDEX TO VOLUME I.

ABDY, MAJOR A. J., 184.
Abon's Dam, 246, 309.
Achtertang, 275, 400, 404.
Acton Homes, 157, 158.
Adelaide Farm, 140, 181.
Aden, 91.
Adjutant-General's Department, 8, 10, 16.
Admiralty, 6, 16, 97–122; acts as agent for War Office for shipping army, 98, 107; assistance on shore ordered by, 117; conference between War Office and, 110; contracts, 105; control of transport service, 99; conveyance of mules by, 23; early measures taken by the, 100; embarkation arrangements between War Office and, 111; Messrs. Hogg & Robinson, shipping agents of the, 98; office accommodation, additions to, 101; Royal Commission, as to the success of the, 110; statement that stock of horse-fittings and water-tanks was inadequate, 110; Transport Department, 98; transports engaged by the, 109; transport work carried out by the, 97, 98. *See also* NAVY.
Advance Hill, 367, 368.
Adye, Major W., 186, 188, 194, 195.
Afrikanders, the, 68.
Airlie, Lieut.-Col. the Earl of, 323.
Albert (district), 275, 285, 382.
Albrecht, Major, 234, 256, 308.
Aldershot, brigades direct from, 204.
Alderson, Lieut.-Col. E. A. H., 387, 439.

Aliwal (district), 275.
Aliwal North, 48, 50, 208, 285, 382.
Allenby, Major E. H. H., 402.
Aller Park, 183.
Amajuba, or Majuba, 72, 426.
America, 443.
Ammunition (British):—rifle, 31; gun, 31; reserves of, 32.
Ammunition columns, 437, 438.
Anderton, Lieut. T., 121.
Animals purchased abroad, 20.
Annexed districts, 382.
Ardagh, Sir J. C., K.C.I.E., C.B., 14, 422. *See also* INTELLIGENCE DEPARTMENT (BRITISH, HOME).
Argyll and Sutherland Highlanders (1st). *See* REGULAR UNITS.
Armed forces of the British Empire, 92–95.
Army, British. *See* BRITISH ARMY.
Army Board, 26.
Army Corps, 26, 110.
Army Medical Department, 26, 30. *See also* ROYAL ARMY MEDICAL CORPS.
Army Orders, 12, 414, 420.
Army remounts. *See* REMOUNT DEPARTMENT.
Army reserves. *See* RESERVES.
Army Service Corps. *See* REGULAR UNITS.
Army Veterinary Department, 27.
Artillery. *See* REGULAR *and* COLONIAL UNITS.
Artillery equipment, 422.
Arundel, 277–284, 389, 391.
Atlantic Transport Co., 103.

Australia, 34, 443. *See also the various Australian Colonies.*
Australian Mounted Infantry. *See* COLONIAL UNITS.
Auxiliary troops of the United Kingdom, 93.

BABINGTON, MAJ.-GEN. J. M., 321, 322, 327, 387, 441, 442.
Babtie, Major W., C.M.G., M.B., 365; awarded the V.C., 366.
Baden-Powell, Colonel R. S. S., 2, 39, 42, 44, 48-49, 197, 207, 409; influence of, on the Boer dispositions, 50.
Bailward, Major A. C., 360, 361.
Bamboosberg Spruit, 294, 299.
Bannatine-Allason, Major R., 322, 323, 330, 331.
Barbados, 89, 91.
Barkly East, 53, 208, 275, 285, 287, 288, 382.
Barkly West, 214, 382.
Barrett, Lieut. N., 121.
Barter, Lieut.-Col. C. St. L., 224, 254, 255, 325.
Barton, Major.-Gen. G., C.B., 203, 269, 273, 333, 345, 347, 357-373.
Bastard's Nek, 400, 405.
Basutoland, 36, 37, 48, 56-59, 61, 64, 94, 197, 306.
Basutos, 40.
Batteries. *See* ROYAL ARTILLERY *and* NAVAL BATTERIES.
Bates, Captain A., 382.
Battalions, average strength of, in February, 1900, 438.
Bayley's Corps. *See* COLONIAL UNITS.
Beacon Hill, 271, 272.
Bearcroft, Captain J. E., R.N., 120, 308, 321, 438.
Bearer companies. *See* ROYAL ARMY MEDICAL CORPS.
Beaufort West, 53, 210.
Bechuanaland, 52, 65, 95, 207, 417.
Bedfordshire regiment (2nd). *See* REGULAR UNITS.
Beith, 147, 148.
Belfort, 422.

Bell, Captain F. J. H., 298.
Bell Spruit, 173, 177, 183, 186, 188-191.
Belmont, 52, 63, 212, 213, 215-217, 218-228, 229, 231, 232, 241, 258, 308, 310, 332, 386, 432.
Benson, Major G. E., 309, 317.
Berkshire regiment, Royal (2nd). *See* REGULAR UNITS.
Bermuda, 89, 91.
Besters station, 158, 171.
Bethel commando. *See* COMMANDOS.
Bethlehem commando. *See* COMMANDOS.
Bethulie commando. *See* COMMANDOS.
Bethulie, 40, 50, 275, 411-413, 431.
Bethulie bridge, 39, 48, 50, 198, 202, 210, 413, 425, 435.
Bethulie road, 404.
Bethune, Lieut.-Col. E. C., 206, 262.
Bethune's Mounted Infantry. *See* COLONIAL UNITS.
Bevan, Lieut. F., 213.
Bewicke-Copley, Major R. C. A. B., 372.
Bezuidenhout's Pass, 49, 58, 157.
Biggarsberg Range, 37, 38, 58, 59, 125, 147, 159, 335.
Black Watch (2nd). *See* REGULAR UNITS.
"Black week," the, 380.
Blesboklaagte, 147.
Bloemfontein, 5, 48, 85, 197, 202, 210, 290, 385, 388, 410-413, 428, 429, 431, 435.
Bloemfontein commando. *See* COMMANDOS.
Bloemhof commando. *See* COMMANDOS.
Blue Mountains, 81.
Board of Trade, 101, 105.
Boers: advance on Colesberg, 275; advance on Kimberley, 50, 52; advance on Mafeking, 49, 50, 52; advance into Northern Natal, 124; advance into Southern Natal, 265; advance on Stormberg, 285; annexations by, 382; armament of, 79-85; enterprise of, in use of heavy guns, 422; initial numerical superiority of,

INDEX.   499

2, 35, 49, 50; leaders of, deceived by Lord Roberts' movements and secrecy, 435; methods of warfare of, 69–75, 402; military system of, 75–79; proclamations by, 52, 275; strength of, 1, 49, 334, 335, 409, 410.

Boer commandos: assembly of, behind the Drakensberg, 47; preliminary distribution of, at beginning of war, 49, 50; waiting in July, 1899, till grass fit to invade Colonies, 116. *See also* COMMANDOS.

Boer Intelligence Department. *See* INTELLIGENCE DEPARTMENT.

Boksburg commando. *See* COMMANDOS.

Boomplaats, 70.

Border Horse. *See* COLONIAL UNITS.

Border Mounted Rifles. *See* COLONIAL UNITS.

Border regiment (1st). *See* REGULAR UNITS.

Boshof commando. *See* COMMANDOS.

Bosman's Drift, 244, 247.

Botha, Commandant Christian, 342.

Botha, General Louis, 264, 265, 332–375, 389.

Botha, Commandant (Mafeking), 409.

Botha's Drift, 405.

Botha's Pass, 49, 58, 124.

Bottomley, Captain H., 272.

Brabant, Brig.-General E. Y., C.M.G., 415, 435; raises mounted corps, 206, 286.

Brabant's Horse. *See* COLONIAL UNITS.

Brabazon, Major-General J. P., C.B., 282, 394, 405, 406.

Brackenbury, Lieut.-General Sir H., K.C.B., K.C.S.I., 7, 16, 18, 19, 26, 28, 29, 32, 33.

Brakfontein Nek, 335.

Brett, Captain C. A. H., 398.

Bridge, Colonel C. H., C.B., 416, 417.

Bridle Drift (Colenso), 310, 314, 341, 342, 346, 348, 352–354, 356.

Bridle Drift (Magersfontein). *See* VOETPAD'S DRIFT.

Brigades. *See* CAVALRY *and* INFANTRY BRIGADES.

British Agent at Pretoria, 1; leaves, 123.

British Army, 87–95; distribution of the, previous to the war, 89; composition of the, 91; effective strength of the armed land forces of the Empire, 92–95; number of troops in South Africa when war began, 1, 2, 89; regiments of the, *see* REGULAR UNITS; short service system in the, *see* SHORT SERVICE SYSTEM *and* RESERVES; organisation of, as affected by conditions of shipping, 115.

British Government. *See* CABINET.

British Intelligence Department. *See* INTELLIGENCE DEPARTMENT.

British Kaffraria, 385.

British Navy, duties of the, 96. *See also* ADMIRALTY *and* NAVY.

British Regular Army (European), effective strength of the, 92; (Colonial), 92; (India), 92.

British Regular Units. *See* REGULAR UNITS.

British South Africa Police. *See* COLONIAL UNITS.

Broadwood, Brig.-General R. G., 437, 442.

Brocklehurst, Major-General J. F., M.V.O., 181.

Brooke, Colonel L. G., 353.

Brown's Drift, 246, 308, 309, 322.

Brynbella Hill, 271–273.

Buchanan-Riddell, Lieut.-Col. R. G., 372.

Buffalo River (Cape Colony), 57.

Buffalo River (Natal), 38, 59, 124, 137, 140, 335.

Bulfin, Captain E. S., 253, 254.

Buller, The Right Hon. Sir Redvers H., V.C., G.C.B., G.C.M.G., 17, 18, 42, 43, 120, 262, 415, 416, 419, 425, 426, 434, 438; appointed to command army for South Africa, 2; arrival at Cape Town, 196; arrival at Durban, 332; arrival at Maritzburg, 332; arrival at Frere, 332; Colenso, battle of, 351–375; decision to go to Natal, 200, 209; decision to relieve Ladysmith viâ Pot-

VOL. I.   32*

Buller, Sir Redvers H.—*continued.*
gieters Drift, 338 ; decision to make direct attack on Colenso, 339 ; informs General White of his intention to attack Colenso, 339 ; informed that Lord Roberts is appointed Commander-in-Chief in South Africa, 381 ; Lord Roberts gives him " free hand " to try Potgieters or Trickhardts Drifts, 411 ; measures on arrival at Cape Town, 200–207 ; memorandum of his views awaits Lord Roberts at Cape Town, 410 ; message after Colenso, to Secretary of State for War, 377 ; message after Colenso to General White, 378 ; orders to generals in Cape Colony, 207–210, 277, 288 ; orders for battle of Colenso, 345–350 ; receives news of Stormberg and Magersfontein, 339 ; reports he is about to renew attempt to relieve Ladysmith, viâ Potgieters or Trickhardts Drifts, 411 ; Secretary of State for War replies to telegram announcing result of Colenso, 379 ; situation in South Africa on arrival of, 197–200 ; Spion Kop, failure at, 438.
Bullock, Lieut.-Col. G. M., 364, 371, 374.
Buluwayo, 36.
Bulwana, or Umbulwana, 150, 176, 181, 182.
Bulwer bridge, 340, 346.
Burger, General Schalk, 50, 343.
Burghers, mobilisation of, 49 ; number of, under arms at outbreak of war, 50.
Burghersdorp, 39, 208–210, 281, 282, 285, 287.
Burghersdorp commando. *See* COMMANDOS.
Burma, 87.
Burnett, Captain C. K., 142.
Burn-Murdoch, Lieut.-Col. J. F., 354.
Burrell, Major W. S., 364, 371.
Bushman Land, 66.
Bushman's Hoek, 287, 288, 290, 291, 301.
Bushman's river, 273.

Bush veld, 62.
Butcher, Major E. E. A., mounts two 15-prs. on Coles Kop, 401, 402.
Butler, Lieut.-Gen. Sir W. F., K.C.B., 35, 37–39, 42, 45, 46.
Byng, Lieut.-Col. the Hon. J. H. G., 367.

CABINET : date of choice of plan of campaign by, 5 ; dates of successive sanctions of expenditure and of mobilisation by, 6 ; date of decision by, appointing Lord Roberts, 380, 389 ; decision by, as to this history, 1 ; decision by, not to employ coloured troops, 89 ; effect of wish of, not to provoke war, in delaying preparation, 3, 6, 16–19, 207 ; effect of wish of, in postponing plan of campaign, 4 ; misunderstanding of decision of, in *re* 5th division, 377 ; reply by, to Sir R. Buller in *re* Ladysmith, 379 ; selects Sir R. Buller as Commander-in-Chief, 2.
Cæsar's camp (Ladysmith), 335.
Caledon commando. *See* COMMANDOS.
Campbell, 2nd Lieut. A. N., 337.
Campbell (Town, Cape Colony), 214.
Canada, 31, 88, 89, 91, 93 ; offers assistance, 34.
Canadian regiment, Royal. *See* COLONIAL UNITS.
Cape Colony, 2, 14, 22, 36, 94, 197, 199, 206, 262, and appendices ; distribution of British troops in, at the outbreak of war, 44 ; President Steyn orders invasion of N. E. of, 285.
Cape Garrison artillery. *See* COLONIAL UNITS.
Cape Government, 14 ; howitzers of, 422 ; railways of, 424, 425.
Cape Medical Staff Corps. *See* COLONIAL UNITS.
Cape Police. *See* COLONIAL UNITS.
Cape Mounted Rifles. *See* COLONIAL UNITS.
Cape Town, 43, 52, 53, 57, 106, 111, 113, 197, 206, 211, 276, 406, 408, 436, 442, 443.

INDEX. 501

Cape Town Highlanders. *See* COLONIAL UNITS.
Cape Volunteer forces. *See* COLONIAL UNITS.
Capper, Lieut.-Col. J. E., 425.
Carbineers, *See* REGULAR UNITS.
Carbineers, Natal. *See* COLONIAL UNITS.
Carinthea (freight ship), loss of the, 107.
Carleton, Lieut.-Col. F. R. C., 132, 149, 174–177, 183, 186–195.
Carolina commando. *See* COMMANDOS.
Carter, Lieut. A. J., 238.
Cathcart, 53, 286.
Cathkin Castle, 58, 59.
Cattle ships, 111.
Cavalry Brigades :—
   1st Cavalry brigade (Porter), 283, 396–398, 436.
   2nd Cavalry brigade (Fisher, later Broadwood), composition of, at Arundel, 283 ; composition of, at Modder river, 437.
   3rd Cavalry brigade (Gordon), formation of, 437.
   4th Cavalry brigade, despatch of, advisable owing to failure at Spion Kop, 438 ; embarkation of, 9 ; orders for mobilisation of, 9 ; to be sent out as soon as ships ready, 379.
Cavalry Division :—
   Assembly of, at Orange river, 444 ; bearer companies and Field hospitals of, 25 ; composition of, at Arundel, 283–284 ; composition of, at Modder river, 436–437 ; to form part of expeditionary force, 6, 90 ; to go to South Africa, 43 ; to take the field by middle of December, 51 ; war equipment complete for, 29.
Cavalry in Ladysmith. *See* APPENDIX 10, page 489.
Ceres, 383.
Ceylon, 91 ; offers assistance, 34.
Champagne Castle, 58, 59.
Channel Isles militia, 93.

Chapman Mr. (guide at Willow Grange), 271.
Charlestown, 36.
Chermside, Major-Gen. Sir H. C., G.C.M.G., C.B., 437.
Chesham, Lieut.-Col. Lord, 414.
Cheshire regiment (2nd). *See* REGULAR UNITS.
Chiazzari, Lieut. N., 121.
Chichester, Captain Sir E., Bart., R.N., C.M.G., 106.
Chieveley, 267, 338, 340, 343, 345, 347, 378, 411.
China, 89, 91.
Chisholme, Colonel J. J. Scott, 163, 164.
Churchill, Mr. W. L. S., 268.
Churchward, Major P. R. S., 235.
City of London Imperial Volunteers, 414, 437.
Clark, Rear-Admiral Bouverie F., R.N., 106.
Clarke, Lieut.-Gen. Sir Charles M., Bart., K.C.B., 111. *See also* QUARTER-MASTER-GENERAL'S DEPARTMENT.
Clements, Major-Gen. R. A. P., D.S.O., 404, 405, 407, 430, 433–436, 439, 443.
Clements' brigade. *See* INFANTRY BRIGADES.
Clery, Lieut.-General Sir C. F., K.C.B., 197, 199, 200, 202, 205, 208, 266, 270, 334, 347, 357, 364, 365, 373.
Climate of South Africa, 61.
Clothing, changes made in, for South African campaign, 30.
Coal, consumption of, by high speed vessels, 105.
Coaling of transports, etc., 105.
Codrington, Lieut.-Col. A. E., 225, 249, 250.
Coldstream Guards (1st and 2nd). *See* REGULAR UNITS.
Colenso, 44, 122, 159, 197, 200, 216–263, 265, 267, 273, 332–375, 389, 410.
Colenso bridge, 200 ; Colonial troops hold, 261.

Coleridge, Major H. F., 254, 256.
Colesberg, 39, 48, 209, 275-284, 376, 382, 389-409, 412, 429, 430, 431-436.
Colesberg road bridge, 48, 283, 391, 392, 396, 402.
Colesberg Junction, 275.
Coles Kop, 390, 392, 395, 397, 401, 404, 405.
Colley, Major-General Sir George P., K.C.B., 426.
Colonial corps, work of, 375.
Colonial forces, 414.
Colonial troops in previous campaigns, 33.
Colonial Units :—
 Australian Mounted Infantry, 407.
 Baden-Powell's contingent, 50.
 Bayley's Corps, 415.
 Bethune's M.I., 206, 269, 332, 367, 373.
 Border Horse, 415.
 Border Mounted Rifles, 34.
 Brabant's Horse, 206, 286, 288, 291, 383, 415.
 British South Africa Police, 94.
 Cape Garrison artillery, 53.
 Cape Medical Staff Corps, 53, 215.
 Cape Police, 42, 94, 276, 286-288, 290-292, 382.
 Cape Mounted Rifles, 208, 286, 288, 290, 291, 415.
 Cape Town Highlanders, 53.
 Colonial division, 435.
 Colonial Scouts, 491.
 Duke of Edinburgh's Volunteer Rifles, 53.
 Durban Light Infantry, 34, 262, 267, 268, 271, 333.
 Frontier Mounted Rifles, 53, 286.
 Grahamstown Volunteer M.I., 437.
 Hore's regiment, 51.
 Imperial Light Horse, 155, 158-160, 163, 165, 167, 169, 170, 175, 183, 184, 262, 272, 332, 367.
 Imperial Light Infantry, 159, 175, 183, 265, 333.
 Kaffrarian Mounted Rifles, 53, 286, 287, 415.
 Kimberley Corps, 53.
 Kitchener's Horse, 415, 437.
 Komgha Mounted Rifles, 53.
 Mafeking Corps, 53.
 Murray's Scouts, 266, 337.
 Natal Carbineers, 34, 157-159, 180, 262, 332, 367.
 Natal Field Artillery, 34, 160, 171, 175, 262, 264, 269, 333.
 Natal Mounted Rifles, 34, 124, 153, 155, 159, 164, 171.
 Natal Naval Volunteers, 34, 121, 262, 264, 266, 332.
 Natal Police, 44, 45, 94, 124, 262, 267, 332, 367.
 Natal Royal Rifles, 34, 262, 333.
 Nesbitt's Horse, 415, 437.
 New South Wales Lancers, 34, 214, 233, 276-283, 316, 400, 404, 436.
 New South Wales Mounted Rifles, 437.
 New Zealand Mounted Rifles, 279, 280, 282, 284, 390, 393, 402-404, 437.
 Orpen's Corps, 415.
 Pioneer Corps of Artisans, 265.
 Plumer's regiment, 51.
 Port Elizabeth Volunteers, 278, 280.
 Prince Alfred's Own Cape Field Artillery, 52, 53.
 Prince Alfred's Volunteer Guard, 53, 278.
 Protectorate regiment, 94.
 Queensland Mounted Infantry, 386, 387, 437.
 Queenstown Rifle Volunteers, 286, 415.
 Railway Pioneer regiment, 384, 425.
 Rhodesian regiment, 94.
 Rimington's Guides, 200, 212-214, 220, 227, 233, 241, 246, 248, 255, 311, 314, 391, 393, 404, 438.
 Roberts' Horse, 415, 437.
 Royal Canadian Regiment, 308, 386, 387, 438.
 South African Light Horse, 206, 332, 367, 368, 373, 383.
 South Australian Infantry, 309.

INDEX.

Tasmanian Infantry, 309.
Thorneycroft's M.I., 206, 261, 269, 273, 332, 367-369, 373.
Town Guards, 51, 266.
Uitenhage Rifles, 53.
Umvoti Mounted Rifles, 34, 261, 274.
Victorian Infantry, 309.
Victorian Mounted Infantry, 407.
Victorian Mounted Rifles, 308.
West Australian Infantry, 309.
Colonies, offers of assistance from the, also in previous campaigns, 33, 34; strength of armed forces in the, 93-95.
Colvile, Major-General Sir H. E., K.C.M.G., C.B., 211, 215, 218-225, 232, 236, 248-257, 259, 311-330, 437.
Commandeering, impossible in Cape Colony, 417.
Commander-in-Chief. *See under respective heads:* BULLER, HARRIS, ROBERTS, WOLSELEY.
Commandos :—
  Bethel, 49, 126, 128, 274.
  Bethlehem, 49, 152, 156, 158, 306, 344.
  Bethulie, 50, 275, 295.
  Bloemfontein, 50, 220, 234.
  Bloemhof, 50, 306, 307.
  Boksburg, 49, 124, 343.
  Boshof, 50, 220, 307.
  Burghersdorp, 299.
  Caledon, 50.
  Carolina, 49, 50.
  De la Rey's, 216, 234.
  Edenburg, 275.
  Ermelo, 49, 124, 128, 172-3, 342-344.
  Fauresmith, 50, 220, 234, 307.
  Fordsburg, 50.
  German Corps, 49, 125, 159, 162, 167.
  Germiston, 49.
  Grobelaar's, 281, 394.
  Harrismith, 49, 152, 155, 158.
  Heidelberg, 49, 124, 343, 435.
  Heilbron, 49, 152, 156, 158, 306, 334.
  Hollander Corps, 49, 125, 166.
  Hoopstad, 50, 220, 234, 307.
  Irish Corps, 49, 370, 371.
  Jacobsdal, 50, 220, 234, 308, 325.
  Johannesburg, 49, 125, 162, 191, 342.
  Joubert's, 269.
  Jourdaan's, 214.
  Kock's, 124.
  Kroonstad, 49, 152-155, 158, 220, 306, 307, 334.
  Krugersdorp, 49, 126, 128, 343, 361.
  Ladybrand, 50, 307, 441.
  Lichtenburg, 49, 308.
  Liebenberg's, 442.
  Lydenburg, 49, 50.
  Marico, 49.
  Middelburg, 49, 124, 128, 342-344, 370.
  Orange Free Staters, 158-159, 161, 171, 173, 191-192, 207, 229, 247, 306, 370, 390, 413.
  Philippolis, 50, 275.
  Piet Retief, 49, 128, 274.
  Potchefstroom, 49, 307, 329.
  Pretoria, 49, 124, 191.
  Rouxville, 50, 295.
  Rustenburg, 49, 50.
  Scandinavian Corps, 50, 307, 319, 320.
  Smithfield, 295.
  Standerton, 49, 124, 343, 344, 355.
  Swaziland, 49, 342.
  Transvaalers, 174, 234, 247-248, 390.
  Trüter's, 125.
  Utrecht, 49, 128.
  Van der Merwe's, 241.
  Vrede, 49, 152, 155, 156, 158, 162.
  Vryheid, 49, 128, 343.
  Wakkerstroom, 49, 124, 128, 343, 344.
  Waterberg, 50.
  Winburg, 49, 152, 155, 158, 214, 220, 234, 342, 370.
  Wolmaranstad, 49, 306-307.
  Zoutpansberg, 50, 342, 344.
Compass Peak, 56.
Composite regiment, 332, 367.
Composite regiment (Household Cavalry). *See* REGULAR UNITS.

Concentration stations for animals, 22, 25.
Congreve, Captain W. N., 365; awarded the V.C., 366.
Connaught Rangers (1st). See REGULAR UNITS.
Conner, Captain R., 194.
Cookhouse, 53.
Cooper, Colonel C. D., 262-264, 353.
Cooper, Major F. C., 357, 366.
Cove Redoubt, 177.
Cox, Lieut. E., 319.
Cox, Major-General G., 44-45.
Coxhead, Lieut.-Colonel J. A., 149-151, 161, 166, 172, 177-178, 184.
Crabbe, Lieut.-Colonel E. M. S., 222.
Cradock, 206, 278, 280, 287-380.
Crete, 2, 91.
Creusot guns, 49, 82-83, 128, 146, 177, 179, 185, 272, 422.
Crimea, 380.
Crocodile river (Limpopo), 60.
Cromer, Major the Right Hon. Viscount, G.C.B., G.C.M.G., K.C.S.I., C.I.E., 415.
Cronje, General A. P., 153, 172, 308.
Cronje, General P., 50, 248, 305-310, 320, 378, 385-389, 409-412, 429-431, 434, 438-442, 444.
Cundycleugh Pass, 58.
Cypher Gat, 301, 408.
Cyprus, 91, 93.

DANNHAUSER ROAD, 142, 143.
Dartnell, Colonel J. G., C.M.G., 146.
De Aar, 22, 39, 42, 43, 52, 207, 209-211, 276, 379, 386-387, 391, 421, 439.
Dean, Lieut. F. W., R.N., 233, 236.
De Beers Co., 44.
De Beers Pass, 58, 158.
De Jager, Field-Cornet, 162.
De Jager's Drift, 123-127.
Delagoa Bay, 50, 60, 116.
De la Rey, General J. H., 50, 216, 220, 229, 234, 239, 243-244, 247, 305, 308.
de Lisle, Captain H. de B., D.S.O., 395, 400, 405.
Denton Grange, loss of the, 107.
Depôts, 421.

Derbyshire regiment (1st). See REGULAR UNITS.
De Villiers, General C. J., 153.
Devonshire regiment (1st and 2nd). See REGULAR UNITS.
Dewaas, 147.
Dewar, Captain E. J., 287, 292.
Dewdrop, 157.
De Wet, General Christian R., 151, 192, 386, 409, 435, 440.
Dick, Captain D. H. A., 360.
Dick-Cunyngham, Lieut.-Col. W. H., V.C., 167.
Director-General of Ordnance. See BRACKENBURY.
Dirksen, Commandant, 343.
Divisions. See CAVALRY *and* INFANTRY DIVISIONS.
Donald, Lieut.-Col. C. G., 369.
Donegan, Major J. F., 147.
Donkerpoort, 50.
Doornberg, 123-124, 126-127, 137.
Doornkop Spruit, 341, 345, 346, 348, 352-354, 357, 369-371.
Doris, H.M.S., 117.
Dordrecht, 287-288, 290, 408, 435.
Douglas (Town, Cape Colony), 214, 386, 387, 439, 442.
Douglas, Colonel C. W. H., 311, 312, 315.
Douglas, Lieut. H. E. M., awarded the V.C., 327.
Downing, Colonel C. M. H., 177-178, 180-181.
Downman, Lieut.-Col. G. T. F., 326, 327.
Dragoon Guards, 5th. See REGULAR UNITS.
Dragoon Guards, 6th. See REGULAR UNITS.
Dragoons, 1st (Royal). See REGULAR UNITS.
Dragoons, 2nd (*Royal Scots Greys*). See REGULAR UNITS.
Dragoons, 6th (Inniskilling). See REGULAR UNITS.
Drakensberg Mountains, 37, 38, 40, 47, 54-67, 125, 157, 174, 335.
Dublin Fusiliers, Royal (1st and 2nd). See REGULAR UNITS.

INDEX. 505

Duck, Vety.-Colonel F., C.B., 27.
Duke of Cornwall's Light Infantry (2nd). See REGULAR UNITS.
Duke of Edinburgh's Volunteer Rifles. See COLONIAL UNITS.
Duncan, Captain S., 193–194.
Dundee, 35, 44, 47, 49, 58, 125–141, 429; retreat from, 142–151. See also GLENCOE.
Dundonald, Colonel the Earl of, C.B., M.V.O., 273, 332, 347, 352, 366–368, 373–374.
Durban, 48, 57, 113, 117–121, 200, 209, 262; Boer raid contemplated on, 158, 206; locomotive works assist mounting Naval guns at, 119; protection at, from land attack, 197; scanty means of defence at, 117.
Durban Light Infantry. See COLONIAL UNITS.
Durham Light Infantry (1st). See REGULAR UNITS.
Du Toit, Acting-General, 425.

EAGAR, LIEUT.-COL. H. A., 296, 298, 301.
East and Central Africa, 95.
Eastern Cape Colony, 62.
East Kent regiment (The Buffs) (2nd). See REGULAR UNITS.
East Lancashire regiment (1st). See REGULAR UNITS.
East London, 43, 52, 53, 57, 106, 113, 119, 120, 197, 200, 261, 286, 290, 378.
East Surrey regiment (2nd). See REGULAR UNITS.
Edenburg, 248.
Edenburg commando. See COMMANDOS.
Egypt, 2, 88–89, 92, 415, 443.
Elandslaagte, 127, 144–145, 148, 151–152, 157–172, 182–183, 192.
Elandslaagte road, 179, 182.
Elliott, Major Sir H. G., K.C.M.G., 208, 288, 290, 385.
Elliott, Mr. C. B., General Manager, Cape Government Railways, 424.
Elswick battery, 414.

Elton, Captain F. A., 361.
Ely, Lieut. T. B., 356.
Embarkation, dates of, for South Africa, 9, 101, 107; importance of Army being practised in, 112; numbers embarked from South Africa, 107; not delayed by mobilisation, 115; political situation greatly delays, 115; ports of, 100.
Empire, British, 1, 13, 32, 87, 89, 380.
Engineers, Royal. See REGULAR UNITS.
Englebrecht, Commandant, 128.
Enslin, 229–242, 247, 309, 386, 444. See also GRASPAN.
Enteric fever, 64.
Equipment and clothing, 30, 417; boots, 30; camp, 31; hospital, 26; in previous campaigns, 17; khaki drill, 30; serge clothing, 30.
Erasmus, General, 124–127, 131, 148, 151, 170, 172, 341.
Ermelo, 124.
Ermelo commando. See COMMANDOS.
Erskine, Captain W. C. C., 245.
Escombe, The Right Hon. H., 14–15.
Eshowe, 378.
Essex regiment (1st). See REGULAR UNITS.
Estcourt, 44, 59, 197, 208, 261, 262, 268, 273, 378.
Ethelston, Commander A. P., R.N., 120, 205, 238.
Eustace, Lieut.-Col. F. J. W., 284, 390, 396, 397, 399.
Ewart, Lieut.-Col. J. S., 317, 440.

FALKLAND ISLES, 95.
Fauresmith, 387, 388.
Fauresmith commando. See COMMANDOS.
Ferreira, Commandant, 274.
Ferreira, General J. S., 409.
Festing, Lieut. F. L., 223.
Fetherstonhaugh, Maj.-Gen. R. S. R., 200, 203, 211, 215, 224, 248.
Field artillery, Royal, 52, 332, 414, 417. See also REGULAR UNITS.
Field Cornets, 75–76.

Field hospitals, 25, 26, 31, 289, 290, 292, 421, 437, 438. *See also* ROYAL ARMY MEDICAL CORPS.
Fiji, 94.
Financial Secretary, 28–29.
Fincham's farm, 216.
Fingo tribe, 208.
Fisher, Captain W. B., R.N., 116.
Fisher, Lieut.-Col. R. B. W., 283, 391–396.
Flag Hill, 176.
Food supplies, 17, 209, 421. *See also* SUPPLIES.
Forage: and horse-gear, 106; in freight ships, and in transports, 106; supplied from Government stores, 106, 421.
Fordsburg commando. *See* COMMANDOS.
Forestier-Walker, Lieut.-General Sir F. W. E. F., K.C.B., C.M.G., 2, 42, 43, 45, 53, 204, 207, 209, 279, 288, 377–379, 383, 409–411, 413, 417, 418, 424.
Forestier-Walker, Capt. G. T., 254, 256.
Forster, Major W. G., 366.
Forte, H.M.S., 116, 120, 121, 263–265, 332, 333.
Fort Molyneux, 264.
Fort Napier, 263, 265.
Fort Wylie, 264, 340, 342, 343, 351, 358–361, 365, 367.
Foster's Farm, 292, 300.
Fourie, Commandant P., 234.
Fourteen Streams, 39, 50.
Fourteen Streams Bridge, 36.
Fox, Lieut. R. M. D., 254.
Fraserburg Road, 53.
Fraser's Drift, 439.
Fraser's Farm, 255.
Free State. *See* ORANGE FREE STATE.
Freight ships: contracts for, nature of, 98; engaged by Colonial governments, 97; forage supplied by owners of, 106; for mules, 109; for troops, 109; full cargoes of, 109; hired by Remount Department, 98; stores from England carried in, 104.

French, Lieut.-Gen. J. D. P., 159–171 (Elandslaagte), 172–174, 176, 181, 182, 183, 186, 200–203, 208–210, 215, 275–284 (Colesberg), 287, 332, 376, 378, 382, 389–407 (Colesberg), 408, 409, 411, 430, 432–436, 444.
Frere, 121, 265, 267, 268, 273, 332, 333, 358, 410.
Froneman, Commandant, 441.
Frontiers of British South Africa, 36–41.
Frontier Mounted Rifles. *See* COLONIAL UNITS.
Fuse, time, 423.
Fyffe, Captain B. O., 186, 193.

GATACRE, LIEUT.-GEN. SIR W., K.C.B., D.S.O., 197, 199, 202, 203, 208–210, 285–303 (Stormberg), 332, 376, 378, 383, 408, 411, 429, 435.
German Corps. *See* COMMANDOS.
Germiston commando. *See* COMMANDOS.
Giants Castle, 58, 59.
Gibraltar, 89, 92.
Girouard, Lieut.-Col. E. P. C., D.S.O., 385, 413, 424, 432, 433, 443.
Glencoe, 38, 44, 46, 47, 58, 145, 159, 172. *See also* DUNDEE.
Gloucestershire regiment (1st and 2nd). *See* REGULAR UNITS.
Godley, Captain H. C., 309.
Goff, Lieut.-Colonel G. L. J., 319.
Goldie, Captain A. H., 361.
Gomba Spruit, 367, 373.
Goodenough, Lieut.-Gen. Sir W. H., K.C.B., 35, 44.
Goodwin, Mr. (later Major) C. A., 425.
Gordon, Brig.-General J. R. P., 437.
Gordon, Captain W. E., V.C., 327.
Gordon Highlanders (1st and 2nd). *See* REGULAR UNITS.
Gore, Lieut.-Col. St. J. C., 163, 167–169, 171.
Gosset, Lieut. F. J., 286.
Gough, Col. B., 220, 221, 232, 240, 241.
Gough, Captain H. de la P., 337.

INDEX.   507

Graaf Reinet, 56.
Graff, Mr. S. J., 106, 110.
Grahamstown, 384.
Grahamstown Volunteer Mounted Infantry. *See* COLONIAL UNITS.
Granet, Major E. J., 258, 441.
Grant Committee, 32.
Grant, Major S. C. N., 14.
Graspan, 63, 120, 216, 229-242, 243, 332, 432, 442, 444. *See also* ENSLIN.
Grassy (later "Suffolk") Hill, 394, 396-399, 404, 406.
Great Fish River, 56.
Great Karroo, 55.
Great Kei River, 56.
Great Winterberg, 56.
Green Hill, 368.
Grenadier Guards (3rd). *See* REGULAR UNITS.
Greytown, 147, 159, 261, 378.
Grimshaw, Lieut. C. T. W., 128-131.
Grimwood, Col. G. G., 174-176, 178-182, 184.
Griqualand East, 36, 208, 288.
Griqualand West, 52, 62, 207, 382.
Griquatown, 214.
Grobelaar, Commandant E. R., 50, 281, 282, 295, 299, 394, 409.
Grobelaars Kloof, 59, 263, 340, 354.
Grylls, Lieut. J. B., 366.
Guards' Brigade. *See* INFANTRY BRIGADES.
Guns, 6-in. Boer, 422 ; British, 422, 423 ; heavy, 433.
Gun Hill (Belmont), 219-221, 223-238.
Gun Hill (Ladysmith), 172, 174, 176, 180, 334.
Gunning, Colonel R. H., 132, 136.

HAGUE CONVENTION, 31.
Haig, Major D., 276, 281.
Haldane, Capt. J. A. L., D.S.O., 267, 268.
Halifax, 139, 140.
Hall, Lieut.-Col. F. H., 203, 211, 214, 217, 239, 258, 321.
Hall, Lieut. H. C., 213.
Halsey, Lieut. A., R.N., 121, 266.
Hamilton, Colonel B. M., 346, 350.

Hamilton, Lieut.-Col. E. O. F., 366, 371.
Hamilton, Col. Ian S. M., C.B., D.S.O. 159, 163, 168-170, 172, 175-177, 183, 185.
Hamilton, Major H. I. W., D.S.O., 433.
Hammersley, Major F., 133.
Hampshire regiment (2nd). *See* REGULAR UNITS.
Hannah, Lieut. W. M. J., 143.
Hannay, Colonel O. C., 437, 444.
Hanover Road, 212, 277, 280, 390.
Harding, Mr., 330.
Harness, 19, 31 ; mule, 417.
Harris, Rear-Admiral Sir R. H., K.C.M.G., Commander-in-Chief of Cape of Good Hope and West Coast of Africa Station, 53, 116-119, 121, 185, 205, 263, 422 ; in July, 1899, sees that Boers are only waiting for the grass to invade Natal, 116.
Harrismith, 44, 58, 157.
Harrismith commando. *See* COMMANDOS.
Hart, Major-Gen. A. FitzRoy, C.B., 203, 204, 210, 333, 346, 348, 352-357, 362, 369-372.
Hart's brigade. *See* INFANTRY BRIGADES.
Hartley, Lieut.-Col. E. B., V.C., 215.
Hartebeestfontein Farm, 280.
Hatting, Commandant, 128.
Hatting Spruit, 126-127.
Hartzogsrand (mountain), 56.
Headquarter Hill, 306, 310-312, 316, 321, 323, 326, 327.
Hebron Farm, 404.
Heidelberg commando. *See* COMMANDOS.
Heilbron commando. *See* COMMANDOS.
Helpmakaar, 261, 274, 334.
Helpmakaar Road, 146-147, 150, 181.
Hely-Hutchinson, The Honourable Sir W. F., G.C.M.G., 45, 123, 207, 261-262.
Henderson, Colonel G. F. R., 15, 433.
Henniker-Major Lieut.-Col, the Hon. A. H., 324.

Henshaw, Major C. G., 367, 374.
Herbert, Captain G. F., 361, 362, 365.
Herschel, 382.
Her Majesty's Government. *See* CABINET.
Higgins, Lieut. J. F. A., 184.
High Commissioner. *See* MILNER, SIR ALFRED.
Highland Brigade. *See* INFANTRY BRIGADES.
Highland Light Infantry (1st). *See* REGULAR UNITS.
Highlands, 59, 269–270.
High Veld, 62, 63, 66, 67.
Hildyard, Maj.-Gen. H. J. T., C.B., 202, 204, 266, 269–273, 333, 346, 347, 363, 364, 371, 372.
Hime, Lieut.-Col. the Hon. Sir Albert H., K.C.M.G., 144, 263.
Hinde, Colonel J. H. E., 270, 353.
His Majesty's Commissioners. *See* ROYAL COMMISSION ON SOUTH AFRICAN WAR.
His Majesty's Government. *See* CABINET.
Hlangwhane (mountain), 340, 341, 343–345, 347, 348, 358, 363, 367–369.
Hlatikulu, 269.
Hogg & Robinson, Messrs., 98.
Hollander Corps. *See* COMMANDOS.
Home, Colonel, 7.
Honey Nest Kloof, 213, 231, 240, 245, 258, 310, 385, 386, 432; railway proposed from, to Jacobsdal, 385.
Hong Kong, 89, 91; offers assistance, 34.
Honourable Artillery Company of London, 93.
Hoopstad commando. *See* COMMANDOS.
Hopetown Road bridge, 52. *See also* ORANGE RIVER BRIDGE.
Hore, Bt. Lieut.-Colonel C. O., 51.
Horse Artillery Hill (Magersfontein), 306, 322, 324, 326, 327, 329, 331.
Horses, 16, 434, 443, 444, 447; Argentina, 20; Australian, 21; embarking, 113; for infantry regiments, grant in 1897, 17; in South Africa, 21;

Royal Commission's report on system of supply of, 23; supply of, in excess of demands, 23.
Horse-shoes, deficiency of, 31.
Hospitals, equipment of, 26, 31; general, 31; stationary, 31; stores for, 31; veterinary, 27.
Hospital ships, 103.
Household Cavalry. *See* REGULAR UNITS.
Howard, Colonel F., C.B., C.M.G., 174.
Howitzers, 9; 6·3-in. Cape Government, 422, 423; Boer, 422.
Hughes, Captain M. L., 364.
Hughes-Hallett, Lieut.-Col. J. W., 319, 327, 441.
Humphery, Major S., 192.
Hunt, Lieut.-Col. H. V., 203, 332, 351, 358–360.
Hunter, Major-General Sir A., K.C.B., D.S.O., 123, 144, 171, 184, 197, 198.
Hunter, Sir D., K.C.M.G., 424.
Hunter-Weston, Major A. G., 400.
Hussar Hill (Colenso), 368.
Hussars (10th). *See* REGULAR UNITS.
Hussars (13th). *See* REGULAR UNITS.
Hussars (14th). *See* REGULAR UNITS.
Hussars (18th). *See* REGULAR UNITS.
Hussars (19th). *See* REGULAR UNITS.
Hutchinson. *See* HELY-HUTCHINSON.
Hyderabad contingent, 92.

IMPATI, 124, 126, 131, 137, 138, 140, 142–147.
Imperial Commonwealth, 33.
Imperial Light Horse. *See* COLONIAL UNITS.
Imperial Light Infantry. *See* COLONIAL UNITS.
Imperial Service troops, 92.
Imperial Yeomanry, 10, 414, 415, 443.
India, 31, 34, 41, 54, 89, 92, 443.
Indian Government, 20.
Indian Marine, Director of, 97.
Indian Military Police, 93.
Indian Volunteers, 93.
Indumeni, 142–146.
Indwe, 286, 287.

INDEX. 509

Infantry Brigades :—
  1st brigade (Guards) (Colvile), 200, 211, 212, 215, 219-228, 232, 235, 236, 242, 248-260, 311-315, 316-330, 438.
  2nd brigade (Hildyard), 202, 204, 266, 272, 333, 346, 348, 357-373.
  3rd brigade (Highland) (Wauchope, later MacDonald), 203, 207, 211, 215, 308, 310-315, 316-330, 415, 437, 439-442, 444.
  4th brigade (Lyttelton), 202, 204, 333, 347, 348, 351-373.
  5th brigade (Hart), 203, 204, 210, 333, 346, 348, 351-373.
  6th brigade (Barton), 203, 269, 273, 333, 345, 347, 348, 351-373.
  7th brigade (Ian Hamilton), 163-171, 172-195.
  3th brigade (Yule, later Howard), 123-141, 142-151, 172-195.
  9th brigade (Fetherstonhaugh, later Pole-Carew), 203, 211, 212, 215, 219-228, 229-242, 248-260, 311-315, 316-330, 438.
  12th brigade (Clements), 404, 407, 430, 433, 435, 443.
  13th brigade (C. E. Knox), 437.
  14th brigade (Chermside), 437.
  15th brigade (Wavell), 437.
  18th brigade (Stephenson), 437, 444.
  19th brigade (Smith-Dorrien), 438, 444.

Infantry Divisions :—
  1st division (Methuen), at Belmont, 218-228 ; at Graspan, 229-242 ; at Magersfontein, 316-331 ; at Modder river, 243-260 ; change in composition of, 202-203 ; detailed fresh composition of, 214-215 ; equipped with drill clothing, 30 ; final decision as to employment of, 200 ; Lord Roberts' instructions to G.O.C., 433 ; march of, from Orange river, 216 ; Naval brigade joins, 120 ; on Modder before Magersfontein, 304-315 ; retained on Modder as a screen, 385 ; Sir R. Buller's instructions to G.O.C., 201 ; Sir R. Buller's instructions, before leaving for Natal, to G.O.C., 209-213; to be employed in relief of Kimberley, 199 ; to disembark at Cape Town, 197.
  2nd division (Clery), arrives in Natal, 266-267 ; at Colenso, 351-375 ; change in composition of, 203 ; equipped with drill clothing, 30 ; final decision as to employment of, 200 ; Sir R. Buller issues orders through Divisional staff of, 205 ; to be employed in relief of Kimberley, 199 ; to disembark at Port Elizabeth, 197.
  3rd division (Gatacre), change in composition of, 203-204 ; destination changed to Natal, 199 ; equipped with drill clothing, 30 ; final decision as to employment of, 200 ; G.O.C. and staff arrive at East London, 285 ; instructions to G.O.C., 202 ; portion of, at Stormberg, 285-303 ; Sir R. Buller's instructions, before leaving for Natal, to G.O.C., 209-210 ; to disembark at East London, 197 ; to operate towards Jamestown, 435.
  4th division, Naval brigade joins, 120, 185 ; troops under Sir G. White considered as, 9.
  5th division (Warren), Buller informed that it is to be sent to South Africa, 201 ; Buller thinks division assigned to relief of Kimberley, 377 ; departure of, involves policy of bluff in Cape Colony, 381 ; due at Cape Town, 376 ; embarkation of, 9 ; lands in Natal, 409 ; ordered to Natal, 379 ; orders for mobilisation of, 9 ; proposal to support 1st division with, 378.
  6th division (Kelly-Kenny), brought to Modder river, 444 ; Buller advised of embarkation of, 379,

Infantry Divisions—*continued*.
380; composition of, 437; despatched to Naauwpoort, 433–435; embarkation of, 9; on point of embarkation 376; orders for mobilisation of, 9.

7th division (Tucker) at Graspan and Enslin, 444; composition of, 437; embarkation of, 9; embarkation of, to begin on 4th January, 1900, 379, 380, 414, 417; mobilisation of, ordered, 376; orders for mobilisation of, 9.

8th division (Rundle), despatch of, advisable owing to failure at Spion Kop, 438; embarkation of, 10; embarkation of, if required, about 20th February, 1900, 415; Lord Roberts hopes division not necessary, 415; orders for mobilisation of, 9.

9th division (Colvile), assembled on the Riet and at Graspan, 444; composition of, 437, 438.

Infantry, Mounted :—
Mounted Brigades and Mounted Infantry Brigades :—
Mounted brigade (Dundonald), 332, 351–375.
1st Mounted Infantry brigade (Hannay), 437, 444.
2nd Mounted Infantry brigade (Ridley), 437.
Mounted infantry in Ladysmith. See APPENDIX 10, page 489.

Ingagane, 38, 125.
Ingogo, 58.
Inniskilling Dragoons. See REGULAR UNITS.
Inniskilling Fusiliers, Royal (1st). See REGULAR UNITS.
Inspector-General of Fortifications, 27, 28, 32.
Inspector-General of Remounts, 20–23.
Intelligence Department (British, Home), 7, 8, 13, 17, 40, 276, 292, 422, 429; (British, Field), 15, 47, 48, 157, 198, 213, 231, 263, 270, 276,
289, 291, 302, 330, 335, 337, 343, 388, 410; (Boer), 73, 216, 334.
International law, 96.
Intintanyoni, 152–156, 172, 173, 190.
Intonganeni or Emtonjaneni, 36.
Irish Corps. See COMMANDOS.
Irish Fusiliers, Royal (1st and 2nd). See REGULAR UNITS.
Irish regiment, Royal (1st). See REGULAR UNITS.
Irish Rifles, Royal (2nd). See REGULAR UNITS.
Irvine, Captain T., 256.
Ismailia, 113.
Ismore (transport), 107, 111, 119, 391.

JACOBSDAL, 50, 63, 216, 241, 243, 245, 246, 248, 305, 309, 385, 387, 388.
Jacobsdal commando. See COMMANDOS.
Jacobsdal to Bloemfontein railway project, 410, 413.
Jagersfontein, 63.
Jamaica, 89, 92.
James, Lieut. H. W., R.N., 120, 266, 360.
Jameson raid, 3, 81.
Jameson, Surg.-Gen. J., M.D., C.B., Q.H.S., 26.
Jamestown, 435.
Japanese disembarkations, 114.
Jasfontein farm, 393, 404.
Jeffreys, Lieut.-Col. H. B., 297, 299.
Jeppe, Mr. C., 15.
Johannesburg commando. See COMMANDOS.
Johannesburg police, 394.
Johannesburg, Uitlanders in, 38, 385.
Johnstone, Capt. R., awarded the V.C., 170.
Jones, Capt. E. P., R.N., 120, 121, 122, 332, 351, 359, 363, 365, 369, 371, 373.
Jonono's Kop, 152, 161–163.
Joubert, Commandant D., 269, 270.
Joubert, Commandant J. J., 128, 344.
Joubert, Field Cornet, 162.
Joubert, Comt.-Gen. Piet, 49, 117, 124, 125, 148, 151–2, 185, 191, 202, 265,

INDEX. 511

267-270, 272, 273, 344, 409, 410, 425, 427, 434; circular memorandum of, 425-427.
Joubert siding, 400.
Jourdaan, Commandant, 214, 234.
Junction Hill, 176.

KAALSPRUIT, 388.
Kaffrarian Mounted Rifles. *See* COLONIAL UNITS.
Kainguba height, 186-189, 191.
Kankana mountain, 149.
Karree Bergen, 56.
Karroos, 55.
Katberg Pass, 383.
Keerom, 404, 405.
Keith-Falconer, Lieut.-Col. C. E., 213.
Kekewich, Colonel R. G., 44, 304.
Kelham, Lieut.-Col. H. R., 320, 440.
Kelly-Kenny, Lieut.-Gen. T., C.B., 432-435, 437, 444.
Kenrick, Lieut. G. E. R., 142.
Khama's country, 60.
Kimberley, 5, 36-40, 42, 43, 44, 48, 50, 52, 53, 120, 197, 198-207, 209, 211, 212-216, 218, 229, 243, 244, 276, 304-5, 310, 334, 377-8, 382, 384, 388, 408, 409, 411-413, 428, 430, 431, 433, 435, 439, 442, 443.
Kimberley Corps. *See* COLONIAL UNITS.
Kincaid, Major C. S., 186.
King's African Rifles, 95.
King's (Liverpool regiment) (1st). *See* REGULAR UNITS.
King's Own Scottish Borderers (1st). *See* REGULAR UNITS.
King's Own Yorkshire Light Infantry (2nd). *See* REGULAR UNITS.
King's Royal Rifle Corps (1st, 2nd, and 3rd). *See* REGULAR UNITS.
King William's Town, 53, 384, 422.
Kinloch, Major D. A., 223.
Kissieberg, 289-292, 294-300, 302.
Kitchener, Colonel F. W., 271-272.
Kitchener of Khartoum, Major-Gen. The Lord, G.C.B., K.C.M.G., 420, 433, 436, 443, 448; (Sirdar of the Egyptian Army), appointed Chief of Staff, 381.

Kitchener's Horse. *See* COLONIAL UNITS.
Kleinfontein (near Ladysmith), 173.
Kleinfontein farm (near Colesberg), 404, 405.
Klip Valley, 341.
Kloof camp, 394, 396, 399, 400, 405.
Knight, Bombardier W., 366.
Knox, Major-General C. E., 437.
Knox, Lieut. C. S., 193.
Knox, Major E. C., 138-141.
Knox, Colonel W. G., C.B., 183, 185.
Kock, General, 124-127, 159, 170.
Koffyfontein, 63, 216, 387.
Komati Poort, 50.
Komgha Mounted Rifles. *See* COLONIAL UNITS.
Koodoesberg, 387, 439-442.
Koodoesberg Drift, 439.
Kopjes, description of, 63, 64.
Koranaberg, 59.
Krijgsraad (council of war), 77, 229, 264, 285, 341, 343-344.
Kroonstad commando. *See* COMMANDOS.
Kruger, President S. J. P., ultimatum of, 1; commandeers his burghers, 34; designs of, 48; telegraphs to Botha to hold on to Hlangwhane, 343; to President Steyn to commandeer everyone in annexed districts, 382.
Krugersdorp, 60.
Krugersdorp commando. *See* COMMANDOS.
Kuilfontein farm, 281, 282.
Kuruman, 207, 382.

LADYBRAND COMMANDO. *See* COMMANDOS.
Lady Grey, 208.
Ladysmith, 9, 38, 44-47, 58, 118, 120, 123, 144, 146-147, 150-153, 157-202, 205-210, 262-265, 334-340, 377, 379, 380, 411, 415, 434, 443; arrival of Sir G. White at, 157; attack on, of 6th January, 1900, repulsed, 409; communication with Dundee cut, 127; invested, 197, 198, 262; Naval reinforcements for, 120.

512 THE WAR IN SOUTH AFRICA.

Ladysmith Naval Brigade. *See* NAVAL BRIGADES.
Lagos, 33.
Laing's Nek, 37, 44-46, 58, 124-125; action of, 1881, Australia offers help after, 33.
Lake St. Lucia, 59.
Lambton, Captain The Hon. H., R.N., 120, 185-186, 205.
Lambton, Major The Hon. C., 224, 255.
Lancers (5th). *See* REGULAR UNITS.
Lancers (9th). *See* REGULAR UNITS.
Lancers (12th). *See* REGULAR UNITS.
Lancers (16th). *See* REGULAR UNITS.
Lancer's Hill, 338.
Landman's Drift road, 128, 139.
Landrosts, 382.
Langeberg farm, 305, 307, 309.
Langewacht Spruit, 264, 340.
Lansdowne, The Most Hon. the Marquis of, K.G., G.C.S.I., G.C.M.G., G.C.I.E., 4, 5, 11, 29, 32-34, 98, 110, 197, 199-201, 338, 377, 384, 414, 443.
Lawrence, Captain the Hon. H. A., 276.
Leckie, Lieut. H. S., R.N., 116.
Leicestershire regiment (1st). *See* REGULAR UNITS.
Lennox Hill, 129-140.
Leuchars, Major G., 274.
Leverson, Major G. F., 259.
Lichtenburg commando. *See* COMMANDOS.
Liebenberg, Commandant, 439, 442.
Limit Hill, 176, 177, 183-184, 186.
Limpopo (river), 50, 56, 57, 59, 60.
Limpus, Commander A. H., R.N., 111, 115, 120, 265.
Lincolnshire regiment (2nd). *See* REGULAR UNITS.
Lisaine, 422.
Little, Major M. O., 246-247, 325, 440.
Little Karroo, 55.
Little Namaqualand, 62, 66.
Liverpool regiment (1st). *See* REGULAR UNITS.
Lobombo Mountains, 59.

Lombards Kop, 120, 150, 172-195, 196, 261.
Long, Colonel C. J., 266, 351, 352, 358-365, 369, 372-374.
Long Hill, 173-177, 180, 183-184.
Lord Mayor of London, 414.
Lourenço Marques, 116.
Low Veld, 62-63.
Loyal North Lancashire regiment (1st). *See* REGULAR UNITS.
Lubbe, Commandant, 234.
Lydenburg, 59.
Lydenburg commando. *See* COMMANDOS.
Lyttelton, Major-Gen. the Hon. N. G. C.B., 202, 204, 333, 352, 357-373.

MACBEAN, LIEUT.-COLONEL F., 326, 327.
McCracken, Major F. W. N., 281, 284, 391-393, 405.
McCracken's Hill, 392, 393, 395.
MacDonald, Major-General H. A., C.B., D.S.O., 437, at Koodoesberg, 439-442.
Macfarlan, Captain W., 319.
McGrigor, Major C. R. R., 355.
Madocks, Captain W. R. N., 402, 403.
Madura, loss of the, 107.
Maeder's farm, 391, 394, 395.
Mafeking, 38, 39, 42, 44, 48-53, 197, 207, 248, 382, 384, 408, 409, 412, 443.
Mafeking Corps. *See* COLONIAL UNITS.
Magaliesberg, 60.
Magersfontein, 63, 245, 260, 283, 304-331, 339, 376, 385, 389, 413, 428.
Magersfontein position, 304-331, 428, 436, 438, 439.
Magicienne, H.M.S., 116.
Malaboch, 81.
Malay States, 33, 95.
Malta, 2, 89, 92, 93, 443.
Malungeni, 141.
Maluti Mountains, 57.
Manchester regiment (1st). *See* REGULAR UNITS.
Maps. *See* MILITARY MAPS.
Marchant, Major A. E., 238, 252.
Marico commando. *See* COMMANDOS.

INDEX.

Marico valley, 60.
Marine Artillery, Royal. *See* REGULAR UNITS.
Marine Light Infantry, Royal. *See* REGULAR UNITS.
Maritzburg, 46, 47, 120, 158, 175, 197, 199–200, 208, 261–266, 270, 288, 332; conference at, 123; scanty means of defence of, 117; threatened by Boer raid, 206; topographical environment of, 263.
Maritz Drift, 336.
Mark's Drift, 387.
Martial law, 417.
Martyr, Lieut.-Col. C. G., D.S.O., 272.
Mashonaland, 60.
Massy, Major H. H., 353.
Massy-Dawson, Lieut. F. E., R.N., 116.
Matabele, 70.
Matoppo Hills, 60.
Mauch Berg, 59.
Mauritius, 2, 52, 59, 89, 92.
Maybole farm, 128.
Medical Staff Corps, Royal. *See* REGULAR UNITS.
Meiklejohn, Captain M. F. M., awarded the V.C., 170.
Memorandum, Mr. Stanhope's, of 1st June, 1888, 5, 12, 13, 89.
Merwe, Commandant T. van der, 229, 241.
Merwe, Commandant van der, 342.
Methuen, Lt.-Gen. The Lord, K.C.V.O., C.B., C.M.G., 120, 197, 199–203, 205, 207, 209–220, 223, 231, 232, 235–237, 240–242, 252–255, 257–260, 276, 279, 286, 288, 332, 334–339, 376, 386–387, 410, 428–431; advance from Orange river, Belmont, Graspan, and Modder river, 211–260; at Magersfontein, 304–331; camp of, Lord Roberts arrives at, 443; division (1st), strength of, 214, 215, 308; ordered to throw reinforcements into Kimberley, 211–213; to attack Cronje again or fall back (order cancelled), 378, 385; ordered by Lord Roberts to remain on defensive, 433, 436, 438, 439.
Meyer, General Lukas, 49, 124, 126–128, 134, 137, 148, 172–173.
Meyricke, Lieut. R. E., 364.
Middelburg commando. *See* COMMANDOS.
Middleburg, 206, 210, 276.
Milbanke, Lieut. Sir J. P., Bart., awarded the V.C., 396.
Miles, Colonel H. S. G., M.V.O., 386.
Military maps, 13–15.
Military Secretary's department, 16.
Militia (home), 10, 12, 93–95, 379–380, 414–415, 443, 444. For names of Militia units which landed up to 13th February, 1900, *see* Appendix 9, page 483.
Milner, Captain A. E., 148.
Milner, Sir A., G.C.M.G., K.C.B., High Commissioner for South Africa and Governor of Cape Colony, 17, 117, 196, 198, 200, 207, 263, 383, 384, 425.
Milton, Major P. W. A. A., 233, 240, 241, 323, 324.
Mobilisation, complete success of, 8; danger lest political considerations shall postpone, 115; date of, 6; development of scheme, 7, 8; details of later stages of, 9; extent of, limited by Mr. Stanhope's Memorandum, 5, 6; must be based on shipping available, 115; war establishments for, 418; section and sub-division, 8, 10. *See also* SHORT SERVICE *and* RESERVES.
Mobilisation of burghers, 49.
Mobility of Boers, 66, 336.
"Modder position" (also called "Modder River camp" and "Lord Methuen's camp"), 229, 279, 304, 313, 385, 413, 428, 441, 443, 444.
Modder river, 63, 211–214, 231, 243–260, 304–316, 325, 412, 421, 436, 439, 443, 444.

VOL. I.

Modder Spruit, 148, 151-153, 161-162, 172-173, 178-180.
Mohawk, S.S., 209.
Möller, Lieut.-Col. B. D., 131, 138-140.
Molteno, 39, 53, 210, 286, 288, 290-294, 300-301, 408.
Money, Lieut.-Col. C. G. C., 52, 225, 232, 237, 239, 248.
Monarch, H.M.S., 117.
Mont Aux Sources, 36, 57.
Mont Blanc, 218-228.
Mooi river, 200, 208, 266, 269, 270, 273, 332.
Moore, Major M. G., 356.
Morgan, Sergeant, 292-293, 295.
Mossamedes, 55.
Moss Drift, 306, 307, 309, 322, 325, 328.
Mounted infantry, 131, 138-140, 148, 157, 203, 214, 233, 240-241, 278, 280-283, 287, 291, 292, 310, 313, 316, 332, 391-392, 402, 405, 407, 415, 416, 437, 439, 444. See *also* INFANTRY, MOUNTED.
Mount Hamilton, 58.
Mount Hampden, 60.
Mount Tintwa, 58.
Mowatt Committee, 32.
Mozambique current, 61.
Mules, 18, 21-23, 150, 176, 416-422.
Mule wagons and harness, 417, 418.
Müller's Pass, 58, 125, 158.
Mullins, Captain C. H., awarded the V.C., 170.
Munger's Drift, 336.
Munster Fusiliers, Royal (1st). See REGULAR UNITS.
Murchison Range, 59.
Murray, Major A. J., 142.
Murray, Major D., 433.
Murray, Lieut. F. D., 142.
Murray, Brig.-Gen. J. Wolfe, 261-264, 266.
Murray, the Hon. T. K., C.M.G., 266, 337.

NAAUWPOORT, 22, 39, 42, 43, 57, 198, 199, 201, 203, 207, 209, 210, 275, 276, 282, 287, 290, 332, 378, 390, 391, 430, 431, 433-435.
Namaqualand, 55.
Natal, 4-34, 36-94, 196-210, 261-274, 334, 351, 381, 384, 409, 411, 413, 417, 422, 429, 438, 443; strength of local forces in, 94; Natal Government Railway staff, 424.
Natal Carbineers. See COLONIAL UNITS.
Natal Field Artillery. See COLONIAL UNITS.
Natal (South) Field Force, 350.
Natal Mounted Rifles. See COLONIAL UNITS.
Natal Naval Brigade. See NAVAL BRIGADES.
Natal Naval Volunteers. See COLONIAL UNITS *and* NAVY.
Natal Police. See COLONIAL UNITS.
Natal Royal Rifles. See COLONIAL UNITS.
Navy, Royal: assistance of, required, 116, 117; delay in preparation due to Cabinet's unwillingness to cause war throws exceptional responsibility on, 97; guns and improvised carriages, 116-121; Natal Naval Volunteers' connection with the, 121, 122; mutual aid between Army and, 97; necessity of special practice together of Army and, 114; number of troops, etc., carried by, 108; ready for landing, 116; Royal Commission, report on success of, 115; statistics of transport work of the, 106-109; stoppage of contraband by the, 115, 116; triumph of the Admiralty administration of sea transport, 111; votes, cost of sea transport not charged to the, 99; conditions of, and use of mercantile marine, by fixed Army organisation, 115.
Naval brigades, 116-122, 185-186, 205, 214, 218-260, 266, 267, 304-375, 438.
Naval Commander-in-Chief. See HARRIS.

INDEX. 515

Naval Gun Hill, 357, 362, 363.
Naval staffs, 106.
Nel, Commandant, 154.
Nesbitt's Corps. See COLONIAL UNITS.
Newcastle, 44, 58, 123-126, 160, 170, 175.
New South Wales, 93; offers help, 33, 34.
New South Wales Lancers and Mounted Rifles. See COLONIAL UNITS.
New Zealand, 94; offers help, 34.
New Zealand Mounted Rifles. See COLONIAL UNITS.
Nicholson's Nek, 9, 174, 186-195. See also LOMBARDS KOP.
Nicholson, Major-General Sir W. G., K.C.B., 13, 420, 422, 433, 436.
Nieuwveld Mountains, 55, 383.
Nodashwana, 152-153, 155.
Norfolk regiment (2nd). See REGULAR UNITS.
Northamptonshire regiment (2nd). See REGULAR UNITS.
Northcott, Lieut.-Col. H. P., C.B., 257.
North Staffordshire regiment (2nd). See REGULAR UNITS.
Northumberland Fusiliers (1st and 2nd). See REGULAR UNITS.
Nottingham Road, 208, 269.
Norval's Pont, 50, 198, 202, 210, 275, 396, 399, 400, 405, 412, 413, 425, 428-431, 434, 435.
Norwood, 2nd Lieut. J., awarded the V.C., 177.
Nurse, Corporal G. E., 365; awarded the V.C., 366.

OBSERVATION HILL, 183.
Ogilvy, Lieut. F. C. A., R.N., 351, 358-360, 365, 373.
Oliphant river, 59.
Olivier, Commandant, 50, 208, 285, 289, 295.
Olivier's Hoek Pass, 49, 58, 157.
Onderbrook, 159, 340.
Onderbrook Spruit, 338-340.
Orange Free State, 3-85, 157, 196, 229, 275, 276, 306, 335, 382, 388, 411-413, 421, 431-435; advance

VOL. I.

through, 196; armament of, 79, 85; frontier of, 36; railway staff of, 424; regular forces of, 85.
Orange river, 37-40, 56, 60, 61, 197-198, 201, 203, 207, 211-218, 258, 259, 382, 383, 386-388, 409, 411-413, 421, 430, 431, 434, 436, 439, 443.
Orange River station, 39, 42, 43, 50, 52, 203, 207, 211, 213, 231, 258, 387, 429, 434, 444.
Ordnance department, 28-33; committee, 423. See also BRACKENBURY.
Ordnance factories, administration of, 28, 29.
Orr, Captain M. H., 402.
Orpen's Corps. See COLONIAL UNITS.
Outbreak of war, 35-53.
Owen-Lewis, Lieut. F., 231.
Oxfordshire Light Infantry (1st). See REGULAR UNITS.
Ox transport, 22, 416-422.

PAARL, DISTRICT OF, 383.
Paget, Colonel A. H., 222, 249, 259.
Painter's Drift, 441, 442.
Palmietfontein farm, 400.
Park, Major C. W., 165.
Parsons, Lieut.-Col. L. W., 202, 333, 352, 357, 369, 371.
Pearse, Major H. W., 372.
Penhoek, 287, 289-291.
Pepworth Hill, 161, 172-175, 177, 178, 182, 184-186, 191.
Perceval, Major E., 299-300.
Philippolis commando. See COMMANDOS.
Philipstown, 39.
Philomel, H.M.S., 120, 121, 263, 333.
Pickwoad, Colonel E. H., 135, 177, 178.
Pienaar, Field Cornet, 159, 162.
Pietermaritzburg. See MARITZBURG.
Pieters, 58, 173.
Piet Retief commando. See COMMANDOS.
Pilcher, Lieut.-Col. T. D., 386-388.
Pitt, Captain F. J., R.N., 106, 110, 111.
Plessis Poort, 400, 405, 406.

33*

Plumbe, Major J. H., 238.
Plumer, Bt.-Lieut.-Col. H. C. O., C.B., 51, 409.
Pohlmann, Lieut., 192.
Pole-Carew, Major-General R., C.B., 248, 252–259, 311, 314–315, 326, 328, 329.
Pom-poms (37-m/m Vickers-Maxim Q.F. guns), sent out from England, 267, 423.
Pondo tribe, 208.
Pongola river, 59.
Pontoons, 27.
Port Elizabeth, 43, 53, 57, 58, 106, 113, 119, 197, 278, 284, 378, 434.
Port Elizabeth Volunteers. *See* COLONIAL UNITS.
Porter, Colonel T. C., 280, 282, 283, 391, 393, 400, 404, 405, 436.
Porter's Hill, 391, 393–396, 400, 405.
Portuguese East Africa, 65.
Potchefstroom commando. *See* COMMANDOS.
Potfontein farm, 404.
Potgieter, Field Cornet, 128, 159.
Potgieters Drift, 334–339, 411.
Potong (Mont Aux Sources), 57.
Powerful, H.M.S., 52, 117, 118, 120, 121, 185.
Preparation for war, 1–34.
Pretoria, 1, 38, 40, 48, 60, 123, 413.
Pretoria commando. *See* COMMANDOS.
Pretorius, Captain, 342.
Price, Mr. T. R., traffic manager, Cape Government railways, 424, 443.
Prieska, 213, 386, 387, 439.
Prince Alfred's Own Cape Field Artillery. *See* COLONIAL UNITS.
Prince Alfred's Volunteer Guard. *See* COLONIAL UNITS.
Princess of Wales. *See* HOSPITAL SHIPS.
Prinsloo, Commandant-General J., 216, 220, 229, 234, 239, 247, 309.
Prinsloo, General, 341.
Protectorate regiment. *See* COLONIAL UNITS.
Prothero, Captain R. C., R.N., 120, 205, 214, 232, 238.

Pulteney, Bt.-Lieut.-Col. W. P., 222, 225, 249.
Putterskraal, 287, 288, 290, 291.

QUARTERMASTER-GENERAL, 16, 17, 19, 20, 24, 27, 99, 100, 111, 421.
Quathlamba (mountain range), 56.
Queen Alexandra, H.M., 103.
Queen's (Royal West Surrey regiment) (The) (2nd). *See* REGULAR UNITS.
Queensland, 93; offers assistance, 33; renews offer, 34.
Queensland Mounted Infantry. *See* COLONIAL UNITS.
Queenstown (Cape Colony), 22, 53, 120, 202, 210, 285–287, 332, 383.
Queenstown Rifle Volunteers. *See* COLONIAL UNITS.

RAILWAY PIONEER REGIMENT. *See* COLONIAL UNITS.
Railways, 36, 37, 39, 56, 57, 61, 63, 390, 413, 428–436; Bloemfontein, 428, 429; cross from Naauwpoort, 430; essential condition of Lord Roberts' scheme, 430, 431; proposed to Jacobsdal, 385; railway troops (R.E.), 424; staff of, 421, 424; system of, 421, 424.
Ramah, 61.
Ramdam, 229, 235, 241, 245.
Rands, 59.
Ravenhill, Private C., awarded the V.C., 366.
Rawson, Colonel C. C., 265.
Razor Back Hill, 218, 225.
Reade, Major R. N. R., 213, 330.
Red Hill ("Vertnek"), 342.
Reed, Captain H. L., 366, 369; awarded the V.C., 366.
Reeves, Colonel H. S. E. (Army Service Corps), 18.
Reeves, Lieut.-Col. J. (Royal Irish Fusiliers), 350, 358.

REGULAR UNITS.
Cavalry :—
Household Cavalry, Composite regiment of, 394, 400, 404, 437, 441, 442.

INDEX. 517

5th (Princess Charlotte of Wales's) Dragoon Guards, 2, 161, 163, 164, 169, 171, 175, 177, 181, 186.
6th Dragoon Guards (Carabiniers), 210, 280, 283, 390, 393, 400, 404, 436, 444.
1st (Royal) Dragoons. 203, 332, 353, 354, 367, 373.
2nd Dragoons (*Royal Scots Greys*), 387, 436, 441.
5th (Royal Irish) Lancers, 46, 124, 149, 150, 153, 157, 159, 161, 163, 165, 167, 169, 171, 174, 180, 181.
6th (Inniskilling) Dragoons, 281, 283, 391, 392, 395, 396, 400, 402, 405, 407, 436, 443.
9th (Queen's Royal) Lancers, 2, 52, 203, 211, 213, 214, 216, 220, 231, 233, 245, 246, 248, 251, 310, 313, 316, 322, 325, 437, 439, 440.
10th (Prince of Wales's Own Royal) Hussars, 210, 281, 283, 391, 392, 395, 396, 402, 405, 437, 441.
12th (Prince of Wales's Royal) Lancers, 203, 279, 308, 309, 311, 315, 316, 321-325, 437, 441.
13th Hussars, 203, 332, 365, 367, 368, 373.
14th (King's) Hussars, 436, 444.
16th (Queen's) Lancers, 437, 441.
18th Hussars, 46, 124, 126, 131, 138, 140, 143, 145, 148, 149, 175, 181.
19th (Princess of Wales's Own) Hussars, 124, 153, 157, 158, 174, 180, 181.
Artillery :—
 Royal Horse Artillery, 9, 91, 210, 284, 390-393, 395, 396, 399, 400, 402, 405.
 G. battery, 308, 310, 313, 321-323, 327, 329, 330, 387, 437.
 J. battery, 407, 443.
 O. battery, 279, 407, 437, 441.
 P. battery, 308, 386, 437.
 Q. battery, 436.
 R. battery, 278, 281, 282, 407, 437, 441.
 T. battery, 436.
 U. battery, 436.

Royal Field Artillery :—
 4th battery, 394, 396, 401, 406, 407, 443.
 7th battery, 203, 271, 332, 352, 366, 367, 369, 373, 374.
 13th battery, 131, 133, 182-184.
 14th battery, 203, 332, 351, 361.
 18th battery, 203, 214, 217, 220, 225-227, 233, 235-239, 248, 251, 252, 254, 256-259, 310, 321, 327, 329, 437.
 21st battery, 150, 163, 164, 173, 178, 182, 186.
 37th (Howitzer) battery, 404, 407, 443.
 42nd battery, 153-155, 161, 163, 164, 173, 178, 182.
 53rd battery, 153, 154, 173, 177, 178, 182, 184.
 62nd battery, 52, 203, 214, 258, 259, 309, 310, 321, 327, 330, 437, 439, 441.
 63rd battery, 202, 210.
 64th battery, 202, 210, 332, 357, 369.
 65th (Howitzer) battery, 308, 310, 321, 329, 438.
 66th battery, 203, 332, 351, 361, 366.
 67th battery, 130, 131, 145, 148, 182.
 69th battery, 130, 131, 133, 145, 148, 181, 182, 186.
 73rd battery, 202, 210, 333, 357, 369, 371.
 74th battery, 204, 289, 290, 292, 293, 297, 300.
 75th battery, 52, 203, 214, 217, 220, 224, 233, 235-237, 251, 252, 259, 310, 321, 323, 327, 329, 437.
 76th battery, 437.
 77th battery, 204, 289, 290, 292, 293, 297, 299.
 79th battery, 204.
 81st battery, 437.
 82nd battery, 438.
Royal Garrison Artillery, 42, 91, 276, 284, 286, 287, 423, 433, 438 ; 10th Mountain battery, 153, 154, 174-177, 183, 186, 188.

518   THE WAR IN SOUTH AFRICA.

Regular Units—*continued.*
  Ammunition columns, 315, 349, 361, 437, 438.
  Royal Marine Artillery, 214, 232, 238.
  Royal Malta Artillery, 91, 92.
Engineers :—
  Royal Engineers, 42, 91, 183, 202, 211, 214, 215, 217, 232, 236, 237, 255, 257, 259, 279, 280, 284, 286, 289, 290, 292, 293, 301, 305, 311, 313, 314, 316, 326, 333, 336, 347, 349, 350, 353, 364, 373, 385, 400, 401, 404, 424, 425, 437–439, 440.
Foot Guards :—
  Grenadier Guards (3rd), 215, 221–223, 225–228, 236, 249, 251, 323–325.
  Coldstream Guards (1st), 215, 221, 225, 226, 228, 236, 249–251, 323–325.
  Coldstream Guards (2nd), 215, 221, 225, 226, 228, 236, 249–252, 257, 259, 260, 323–325, 329.
  Scots Guards (1st), 215, 221–223, 225–227, 231, 232, 236, 249–251, 323, 326, 328–330.
Infantry :—
  Royal Scots, Lothian (1st) [formerly 1st Foot], 203, 289, 291.
  The Queen's (Royal West Surrey) (2nd) [formerly 2nd Foot], 271, 333, 363, 364, 366, 371, 372.
  The Buffs (East Kent regiment) (2nd) [formerly 3rd], 437.
  Northumberland Fusiliers (1st) [formerly 5th], 2, 43, 52, 203, 214, 215, 223, 224, 225, 232, 233, 235, 237, 240, 252, 253, 255, 259, 311, 326.
  Northumberland Fusiliers (2nd) [formerly 5th], 203, 287, 290, 292, 296–298, 300, 301.
  Royal Warwickshire (2nd) [formerly 6th], 379.
  Royal Fusiliers (City of London regiment) (2nd) [formerly 7th], 333, 358, 367–369.
  The King's (Liverpool) (1st) [formerly 8th], 124, 153, 154, 157, 158, 173–175.
  Norfolk (2nd) [formerly 9th], 437.
  Lincolnshire (2nd) [formerly 10th], 437.
  Devonshire (1st) [formerly 11th], 124, 153, 154, 161, 163–168, 172, 175, 186.
  Devonshire (2nd) [formerly 11th], 333, 363, 364, 371, 372, 374.
  Suffolk (1st) [formerly 12th], 279, 281, 391, 394, 396–399, 408.
  The Prince Albert's (Somersetshire Light Infantry) (2nd) [formerly 13th], 333.
  Prince of Wales's Own (West Yorkshire) (2nd) [formerly 14th], 266, 270, 271, 333, 364.
  Bedfordshire (2nd) [formerly 16th], 404, 407.
  Leicestershire (1st) [formerly 17th], 46, 131, 143, 144, 146, 151, 174–180, 185.
  Royal Irish (1st) [formerly 18th], 404, 407.
  Princess of Wales's Own Yorkshire (1st) [formerly 19th], 379, 394, 400, 402–405, 407, 437.
  Royal Scots Fusiliers (2nd) [formerly 21st], 333, 358, 360, 363, 364, 366, 372–374.
  Cheshire (2nd) [formerly 22nd], 437.
  Royal Welsh Fusiliers (1st) [formerly 23rd], 333, 357, 363.
  South Wales Borderers (2nd) [formerly 24th], 437.
  King's Own Scottish Borderers (1st) [formerly 25th], 437.
  The Cameronians (Scottish Rifles) (2nd) [formerly 90th], 333, 351, 363, 372, 373.
  Royal Inniskilling Fusiliers (1st) [formerly 27th], 333, 353, 356.
  Gloucestershire (1st) [formerly 28th], 153–155, 174–176, 186–194.
  Gloucestershire (2nd) [formerly 61st], 437.
  Worcestershire (2nd) [formerly 36th], 402, 404, 407.

INDEX. 519

East Lancashire (1st) [formerly 30th], 437.
East Surrey (2nd) [formerly 70th], 271, 333, 364, 372.
Duke of Cornwall's Light Infantry (2nd) [formerly 46th], 308, 386, 387, 438.
Duke of Wellington's (West Riding) (1st) [formerly 33rd], 437.
Border (1st) [formerly 34th], 2, 52, 204, 261, 264, 270, 271, 333, 353, 355, 356, 370.
Hampshire (2nd) [formerly 67th], 437.
Welsh (1st) [formerly 41st], 402, 407, 437.
Black Watch (Royal Highlanders) (2nd) [formerly 73rd), 203, 276, 279, 308, 312, 317-319, 329, 437, 440, 441.
Oxfordshire Light Infantry (1st) [formerly 43rd], 437.
Essex (1st) [formerly 44th], 391, 394, 399, 401, 404, 405, 407, 437.
Sherwood Foresters (Derbyshire) (1st) [formerly 45th], 376.
Loyal North Lancashire (1st) [formerly 47th], 44, 203, 212, 214, 215, 223, 231-233, 235, 237-239, 242, 252-256, 259, 311, 326.
Northamptonshire (2nd) [formerly 58th], 203, 215, 223, 224, 232, 233, 236-239, 247, 255, 309, 311, 326.
Princess Charlotte of Wales's (Royal Berkshire) (2nd) [formerly 66th], 276, 281, 282, 284, 286, 291, 292, 391-393, 395, 396, 407.
Royal Marine Light Infantry, 52, 99, 205, 214, 232, 238, 239, 242, 422.
King's Own (Yorkshire Light Infantry) (2nd) [formerly 105th], 2, 52, 203, 214, 215, 223, 224, 226, 232, 233, 237-239, 252-256, 259, 310, 313, 321, 325, 328.
King's (Shropshire Light Infantry) (2nd) [formerly 85th], 308, 438.
King's Royal Rifle Corps (1st) [formerly 60th], 46, 127, 131-136, 138, 140, 143, 144, 147, 151, 174-176, 178, 179.
King's Royal Rifle Corps (2nd) [formerly 60th], 153, 154, 158, 174-176, 179, 185, 367.
King's Royal Rifle Corps (3rd) [formerly 60th], 333, 363, 364, 372.
Duke of Edinburgh's (Wiltshire) (2nd) [formerly 99th], 404-407.
Manchester (1st) [formerly 63rd], 46, 150, 160, 163-167, 171, 173, 175, 183, 186.
Prince of Wales's (North Staffordshire) (2nd) [formerly 98th], 437.
Durham Light Infantry (1st) [formerly 68th], 333, 363, 370, 372.
Highland Light Infantry (1st) [formerly 71st], 215, 308, 312, 318-320, 327, 437, 440.
Seaforth Highlanders (Ross-shire Buffs, The Duke of Albany's) (2nd) [formerly 78th], 308, 312, 316, 318, 319, 327, 438, 440, 441.
Gordon Highlanders (1st) [formerly 75th], 308, 311, 315, 326, 327, 438.
Gordon Highlanders (2nd) [formerly 92nd], 124, 150, 163-167, 169, 170, 173, 175, 176.
Royal Irish Rifles (2nd) [formerly 86th], 10, 204, 286, 287, 290, 292, 296-298, 301.
Princess Victoria's (Royal Irish Fusiliers) (1st) [formerly 87th], 2, 131-136, 142-144, 147, 149, 173, 174, 186-192, 195.
Princess Victoria's (Royal Irish Fusiliers) (2nd) [formerly 89th], 333, 358, 360, 363, 364.
Connaught Rangers (1st) [formerly 88th], 333, 353-356.
Princess Louise's (Argyll and Sutherland Highlanders) (1st) [formerly 91st], 247, 252-256, 259, 308, 318, 319, 330, 438, 441.
Royal Munster Fusiliers (1st) [formerly 101st], 43, 212, 215, 223, 226, 231, 232, 258, 308, 326, 386.

Regular Units—*continued*.
  Royal Dublin Fusiliers (1st) [formerly 102nd], 333.
  Royal Dublin Fusiliers (2nd) [formerly 103rd], 46, 123, 124, 127-129, 131, 132, 135, 139, 140, 143-145, 148, 149, 174, 175, 180, 262, 267, 268, 333, 353-356, 367.
  Rifle Brigade (The Prince Consort's Own) (1st), 333, 363, 370, 372.
  Rifle Brigade (The Prince Consort's Own) (2nd), 2, 175, 177.

Army Service Corps:—8, 23-25, 91, 211, 289, 404, 417-421, 437, 438.
Royal Army Medical Corps (includes Bearer companies, Field hospitals, etc.):—25, 91, 134, 147, 148, 211, 215, 228, 242, 284, 289, 290, 292, 313-315, 327, 330, 333, 347, 349, 364-366, 374, 421, 437, 438.

Remount department, 19-23, 24, 27.
Rensburg, 280, 390, 391, 395, 399, 400, 407, 443.
Reserves : necessity of announcement in Parliament before summoning, 6; date of proclamation calling out, 6; numbers who obeyed the call and were fit, 8; value in the field of, 375; supply of, furnished during war, 10; inconvenience of Act requiring all classes A. B. C. to be exhausted before D. was summoned, 12; not numerous enough, 11; number in 1899, in British Islands, 90; great assistance rendered to army in field, 67, 11; a real reserve for war, not a mere substitution, 90; no delay caused by necessity for filling up ranks by, 115.
Retreat from Dundee. *See* DUNDEE.
Rhenoster farm, 404.
Rhodes, The Right Hon. Cecil J., 17, 44.
Rhodesia, 16, 36, 39, 94, 409.
Rhodesian regiment. *See* COLONIAL UNITS.
Ricardo, Lieut.-Col. P. R., 386.
Richardson, Colonel W. D., C.B., 417, 420, 422.
Richmond farm, 442.
Richmond road, 276.
Ridley, Colonel C. P., 433, 437.
Rietfontein, 142, 151-156, 172.
Riet River, 63, 243, 244, 246-248, 250, 251, 253, 256, 259, 260, 304, 378, 385, 387, 388, 430, 439, 441, 444.
Rifle Brigade (1st and 2nd). *See* REGULAR UNITS.
Rimington, Major M. F., 220, 227, 246.
Rimington's Guides. *See* COLONIAL UNITS.
Roberts, Field Marshal the Right Hon. F. S. Lord, V.C., K.P., G.C.B., G.C.S.I., G.C.I.E., Army Corps re-constituted, 436-438; appointed to command in South Africa, 376, 381, 386, 389; appoints his staff, 381; arrives at Cape Town, 408; Buller reports fresh attempt to relieve Ladysmith, 411; plan of campaign, 411-413, 428-436, 439; railways in Cape Colony, 425, 426; railways in Cape Colony, strategic value of, 430, 431; raises more local corps, 415, 416; reinforcements promised of troops, 414, 415; reinforcements promised of guns, 422-424; situation on his arrival, 408-411; transport reorganised, 416-421; telegram from Gibraltar, 385.
Roberts, Lieut. the Hon. F. H. S., 365; awarded the V.C. (posthumous), 366.
Roberts' Horse. *See* COLONIAL UNITS.
Roberts', Mr. J., farm, 293-295.
Robertson, Sergt.-Major W., awarded the V.C., 170.
Robinson's Drift, 336.
Robinson's farm, 340, 341, 352.
Rogers, Major C. R., 360.
Roggeveld mountains, 383.
Rooi Kop, 289, 290, 291, 295.
Rooilaagte, 216, 230.
Rorke's Drift, 274.

INDEX.

Rosmead, 244, 247-260.
Rosmead Junction, 278, 378, 435.
Rouxville commando. See COMMANDOS.
Royal Army Medical Corps. See REGULAR UNITS.
Royal Berkshire regiment (2nd). See REGULAR UNITS.
Royal Canadian regiment. See COLONIAL UNITS.
Royal Commissions, on South African hospitals, 26; on South African war, 13, 110, 411, 412.
Royal Dragoons. See REGULAR UNITS.
Royal Dublin Fusiliers (1st and 2nd). See REGULAR UNITS.
Royal Engineers. See REGULAR UNITS.
Royal Field Artillery. See REGULAR UNITS.
Royal Fusiliers (2nd). See REGULAR UNITS.
Royal Garrison Artillery. See REGULAR UNITS.
Royal Horse Artillery. See REGULAR UNITS.
Royal Inniskilling Fusiliers (1st). See REGULAR UNITS.
Royal Irish Fusiliers (1st). See REGULAR UNITS.
Royal Irish regiment (1st). See REGULAR UNITS.
Royal Irish Rifles (2nd). See REGULAR UNITS.
Royal Malta Artillery. See REGULAR UNITS.
Royal Marine Artillery. See REGULAR UNITS.
Royal Marine Light Infantry. See REGULAR UNITS.
Royal Munster Fusiliers (1st). See REGULAR UNITS.
Royal Scots Fusiliers (2nd). See REGULAR UNITS.
Royal Scots regiment (1st). See REGULAR UNITS.
Royal Warwickshire regiment (2nd). See REGULAR UNITS.
Royal Welsh Fusiliers (1st). See REGULAR UNITS.
Royal West Surrey regiment (2nd). See REGULAR UNITS.
Royston, Colonel W., 174.
Ruggles-Brise, Captain H. G., 225.
Rustenburg, 59, 60.
Rustenburg commando. See COMMANDOS.

ST. HELENA, 92, 95.
St. Vincent, 105.
Salisbury (Rhodesia), 60.
Salisbury plain, 2.
Sand river, 140.
Sand Spruit, 128, 129, 131, 133, 135, 138, 140.
Sangars, 73.
Scandinavian commando. See COMMANDOS.
Schanzes, 71.
Scheme, Lord Roberts', 428.
Schietberg, 393.
Schiel, Colonel, 125, 167.
Schoeman, Commandant, 275, 276, 280, 281, 389, 390, 393-395, 400, 409, 443.
Schofield, Captain H. N., 365; awarded the V.C., 366.
Scholtz Nek, 245, 409, 426, 440.
Schreiber, Lieut. C. B., 366.
Schreiner, The Hon. Mr. W. P., C.M.G., Q.C. (Premier of Cape Colony), 206.
Schultz' farm, 139, 140.
Scots Greys, Royal. See REGULAR UNITS.
Scots Guards (1st). See REGULAR UNITS.
Scott, Captain P., R.N., 117-121, 205, 265.
Scottish Rifles (2nd). See REGULAR UNITS.
Seacow river, 402.
Seaforth Highlanders (2nd). See REGULAR UNITS.
Secrecy, 414; essential to Lord Roberts' scheme, 431.
Secretary of State for War. See respectively, LANSDOWNE, SMITH, STANHOPE.
Senior, Captain G., R.M.A., 238.

Seton, Major H. J., 298.
Seymour, Mr. (later Major) L.I., 425.
Shannon, Sergeant-Major J., 360.
Sharpe, Lieut.-Col. J. B., 215, 217.
Shaul, Corporal J., awarded the V.C., 327.
Sheridan, General, 75.
Shipping, necessary dependence of nature of effective British army organisation on, 115; patriotic conduct of owners of, 107; success of Admiralty administration of, 110, 111; small quantity of, available at given moment, 103, 104, 105; statistics of, 108, 109; time required for getting ready, 100, 101, 102, 104. *See also* ADMIRALTY *and* NAVY.
Shooter's Hill, 347, 373.
Short Service, the system as worked in the Boer War, 90; how it supplied fresh drafts during war, 90; comparison with other wars, 91; effect of, on strength in the field, 11; caused no delay, 115; *See also* RESERVES *and* MOBILISATION.
Shropshire Light Infantry (2nd). *See* REGULAR UNITS.
Shute, Major H. G. D., 225, 324.
Sierra Leone, 91.
Simon's Bay, 117, 119, 120.
Simon's Town, 52, 118.
Slade-Wallace tools, 250.
Slingersfontein, 400, 402, 404, 405.
Sluits, 61.
Skiet's Drift, 334, 336, 337.
Smith, Major Granville, R. F., 250.
Smith, The Right Hon. W. H., 7.
Smith, Major W. Apsley, 365.
Smith-Dorrien, Colonel H. L., D.S.O., 438, 444.
Smithfield commando. *See* COMMANDOS.
Smith's farm, 129, 132, 135.
Smith's Nek, 129, 133, 137.
Sneeuw Bergen (mountain), 56.
Snyman, General, 50, 409.
Somaliland, 95.
Somerset East, 206.

Somersetshire Light Infantry (2nd). *See* REGULAR UNITS.
South Africa: absence of roads in, 18, 65; agriculture in, 62; as a theatre of war, 64; climatic influences on, 61; cool nights in, 65; dearth of bridges in, 61, 65; drifts of, 61; eminently healthy, 64; harbours of, 57, 65, 113; hill systems of, 55; nature of the country in, 18; physiological features of, 61; rainfall in, 66; rivers of, 60, 61, 65; scarcity of well-built towns in, 65; special clothing prescribed for, 30; tableland of, 54.
South African Light Horse. *See* COLONIAL UNITS.
South African Republic Police (Zarps), 49, 81, 84.
South African War. *See* WAR IN SOUTH AFRICA.
South Australia, 93; offers assistance, 34.
South Australian Infantry. *See* COLONIAL UNITS.
South Natal raid, 261–274.
Southern Rhodesia. *See* RHODESIA.
South Wales Borderers (2nd). *See* REGULAR UNITS.
Spartan. *See* HOSPITAL SHIPS.
Spion Kop (mountain), 58, 438.
Spitz Kop, 400.
Springfield, 338.
Springfontein Junction, 411.
Springs, 60.
Spruits, 60.
Spytfontein, 63, 245, 305, 310, 329.
Standerton commando. *See* COMMANDOS.
Stanhope, The Right Hon. E. (Secretary of State for War in 1888), his memorandum of June 1st, 1888, 5, 12, 13, 20, 89.
Steenkamp, Commandant, 192, 195.
Steinkamp, Commandant L. F., 439.
Steinkamp, Commandant, 295, 299.
Stellenbosch, 22, 43, 383.
Stephenson, Brig.-General T. E., 405, 406, 437, 444.

INDEX. 523

Sterkstroom, 53, 301, 408.
Sterkstroom Junction, 287.
Sterling, Captain J. T., 225.
Steyn, President M. T., 48, 285, 295, 306, 382, 388; outwitted by Lord Roberts, 435.
Steynsburg, 295.
Steynsburg road, 292, 293, 299, 302.
Stockenstroom, 383.
Stopford, Colonel the Hon. F., C.B., 209, 357, 362.
Stopford, Lieut.-Col. H. R., 225, 260.
Stores, deficiency of, 31, 32; in freight ships, 104; tonnage of, 108, 109; those wanted first placed at bottom of ships, 113.
Stormberg, 39, 42, 43, 52, 57, 66, 120, 198, 199, 205, 210, 283, 285–303, 339, 376, 389, 408, 409, 412, 435.
Stormbergen, 56, 57.
Straits Settlements, 89, 92.
Strength of army in South Africa, at various dates, 1, 2, 443, and Appendices.
Strength of Boers, estimated, 1, 2, 38, 265, 377, 409, 410, 459.
Strength of regular army and armed forces of the British Empire, 89–95.
Strength of various arms, average, 438.
Suffolk Hill. *See* GRASSY HILL.
Suffolk regiment (1st). *See* REGULAR UNITS.
Sugar Loaf Hill, 218, 225.
Sunday's river, 59, 127, 149, 335.
Sunday's River Passes, 58.
Sunnyside, 387, 442.
Supplies, 19, 43, 44, 67, 106, 108, 200, 206, 209, 210, 216, 310, 315, 418, 421, 443; supply department, 422.
Surprise Hill, 188, 190, 334, 335.
Survey department of Cape Colony, 14.
Swaatbouys Kop (or Nodashwana), 152.
Swanepoel, Commandant, 50, 295, 298, 301.
Swaziland, 50, 65.

Swaziland commando. *See* COMMANDOS.
Swaziland Police, 49, 81, 84.
Swinkpan, 227, 231, 232.
Symons, Major-General Sir W. Penn, K.C.B., 45–47, 123–137, 160.

TAAIBOSCHLAAGTE, 280.
Taal language, 121.
Tabanyama (mountain), 58, 335, 338.
Tabanhlope, 269.
Table Bay, 119, 206.
Table Mountain (Cape Town), 48.
Table Mountain (Belmont), 218–228.
Tactics, Lord Roberts' instructions for, 445–450.
Talana, 123–142.
Tarkastad, 287.
Tartar, H.M.S., 120, 263, 265, 332.
Tasmania, 309; offers assistance, 34.
Tasmanian Infantry. *See* COLONIAL UNITS.
Taungs, 382.
Telegraph, essential to Lord Roberts' scheme, 431.
Tembu tribe, 208.
Teneriffe, 105.
Terrible, H.M.S., 117, 120, 205, 263, 265, 332.
Thaba Bosigo, 72.
Thackeray, Lieut.-Col. T. M. G., 353.
Theatre of war, 54–67.
Thetis, H.M.S., 120, 265.
Thomas' farm, 216, 217.
Thompson, Sir Ralph, K.C.B., 7.
Thorneycroft, Major A. W., 206, 261, 368, 369, 373.
Thorneycroft's Mounted Infantry. *See* COLONIAL UNITS.
Thornhill farm, 387.
Thwaites, Captain W., 184.
Tintwa Pass, 49, 58, 123, 157.
Touw's river, 53.
Town Guards. *See* COLONIAL UNITS.
Townsend, Colonel E., M.D., C.B., 242
Towse, Captain E. B., awarded the V.C., 327.
Transport (land), 413, 416–421; delay imposed by peace wishes, during time

524 THE WAR IN SOUTH AFRICA.

Transport (land)—*continued*.
  needed for getting, 19; difficulty because of, in having British army ready for war, 18; early attempts made by Sir Evelyn Wood, Lord Wolseley, and Sir A. Milner to provide, 16, 17; harness for, 19; impossibility of keeping British ready for war, 17; in previous campaigns, 17; mules for, purchased abroad, 20; mules in South Africa, 22; native drivers needed for, 24; necessary change of vehicles for South Africa for, 18; necessity for, 18; peculiarities of South African, 416, 417; reorganised by Lord Roberts, 416-421; respective advantages of ox and mule, 416, 417; successive demands for, 18; transport by rail, 424; transport companies, 421, 437; transport department, 422; transport, regimental, 418, 419; transport staff, 417; transport (sea). *See* Navy; varied character of British, 17; vehicles for, 19.
Transvaal, 3-85, 335.
Transvaalers. *See* COMMANDOS.
Transvaal Police. *See* SOUTH AFRICAN REPUBLIC POLICE.
Transvaal Staats Artillerie, 49, 81-84.
Trichardt, Commandant, 128, 140.
Trichardt's Drift, 411.
Trojan. *See* HOSPITAL SHIPS.
Trüter's commando. *See* COMMANDOS.
Tucker, Lieut.-Gen. C., C.B., 437.
Tudway, Lieut.-Col. R. J., 278.
Tugela Ferry, 274, 334.
Tugela river, 14, 58, 208, 261, 263-265, 267, 273, 332-376, 410.
Tulbagh district, 383.
Tuli, 42.
Tunnel Hill, 176.
Tweedale siding (or station), 277, 281.

UGANDA, 95.
Uitenhage Rifles. *See* COLONIAL UNITS.
Uitlanders, 38, 385.

Ultimatum of October 9th, 1899, 1, 86.
Umbulwana (or Bulwana), 150, 172, 176, 181, 182.
Umvoti Mounted Rifles. *See* COLONIAL UNITS.
Union Castle, S.S. Co., 100, 107.
Urmston, Major E. B., 441.
Utrecht, 124.
Utrecht commando. *See* COMMANDOS.

Vaal Kop, 281, 282.
Vaal river, 36, 37, 61, 387.
Van Dam, 191, 192, 394.
Van der Merwe's commando. *See* COMMANDOS.
Van der Merwe, Commandant. *See* MERWE.
Van Reenen's Pass, 37, 38, 44, 45, 49, 58, 125, 157, 158, 171, 173.
Van Staaden, Commandant, 128.
Van Tonders Pass, 147, 148.
Vant's Drift, 128.
Van Zyl, Lieut. *See* ZYL.
Van Zyl's farm, 292-295, 300.
Van Zyl Siding, 405.
Venter, Comdt. H. van der, 234.
Verner, Lieut.-Colonel W. W. C., 216, 245.
Versamelberg (mountain), 59.
Vertnek (Red Hill), 342.
Veterinary Department. *See* ARMY VETERINARY DEPARTMENT.
Viceroy of India, 1.
Vickers-Maxim, 37 m/m Q.F. guns. *See* POM-POMS.
Victoria, 94; offers assistance, 33, 34.
Victorian Infantry, Mounted Infantry, and Mounted Rifles. *See* COLONIAL UNITS.
Victualling of troops at sea, 99, 105.
Vierkleur, 48.
Viljoen, General Ben, 125, 127, 159, 342.
Visser's homestead, 440.
Voetpads Drift, 310, 314, 325.
Volksrust, 124.
Volunteers: Home, 10, 12, 93-95, 380, 414. *See also* COLONIAL UNITS.
Vrede commando. *See* COMMANDOS.

INDEX. 525

Vryburg, 382.
Vryheid, 124.
Vryheid commando. *See* COMMANDOS.

WAKKERSTROOM COMMANDO. *See* COMMANDOS.
Wakkerstroom Nek, 49.
Walker, Lieut.-Gen. Sir F. Forestier-. *See* FORESTIER-WALKER.
Walter, Major R. L., 367.
Wapenschouws, 80.
War Department of Pretoria, 38.
"War Establishments," 418.
War in South Africa: British preparations for, 1-34; outbreak of, 35-53; theatre of, 54-67.
War Office, 6, 15, 22, 28, 35, 38, 44, 89, 100, 110, 111, 117, 199-201, 353, 379-381, 384, 410, 412-415, 418, 421, 422, 438, 443.
Wardle, Midshipman T. F. J. L., R.N., 238.
Warley Common, 269.
Warren Lieut.-Gen. Sir C., G.C.M.G., K.C.B., 201, 377, 379.
Warrenton, 39.
Warwickshire regiment, Royal (2nd). *See* REGULAR UNITS.
Waschbank, 58, 127.
Waschbank bridge, 334.
Waschbank river, 147-151.
Water, story of, at Graspan, 432; carts, 421.
Waterberg commando. *See* COMMANDOS.
Watson, Lieut.-Colonel A. J., 281, 396-399.
Wauchope, Major-Gen. A. G., C.B., C.M.G., 203, 207, 211, 212, 215, 276-279, 308, 311, 312, 316-319, 323, 324.
Wavell, Major-General A. G., 437.
Weenen, 269, 273.
Weenen road, 336.
Weil, Messrs., 16.
Welman, Major H. L., 298.
Welsh regiment (1st). *See* REGULAR UNITS.
Wessels, Commandant, 409.

West Africa and various African protectorates, 91, 95.
West Australia, 94; offers assistance, 34.
West Australian Infantry. *See* COLONIAL UNITS.
West Indies, 95.
West Riding regiment (1st). *See* REGULAR UNITS.
West Yorkshire (2nd). *See* REGULAR UNITS.
White, Lieut.-General Sir George S., V.C., G.C.B., G.C.S.I., G.C.I.E., 9, 46-48, 51, 52, 123, 126, 127, 143, 144, 148, 149, 205, 208, 210, 261-264, 335, 377, 378, 410, 415, 422; arrives in Natal, 46; at Elandslaagte, 157-171; at Lombards Kop, 172-184; at Rietfontein, 151-156; his knowledge of Buller's plans, 338, 339; isolated, 200; suggests that Navy should be consulted, 117, 118, 120; unable to protect southern Natal, 196-198.
White, Captain H. S., 371.
Wickham, Major W. J. R., 146.
Widgeon, H.M.S., 116.
Wilford, Colonel E. P., 154, 155.
Willcock, Captain S., 193.
Willow Grange, 269, 270, 272.
Willmott, Captain W. A., 298.
Wilson, Lieutenant R. S., 319, 320.
Wilson, Lieut.-Colonel A., 441.
Wiltshire regiment (2nd). *See* REGULAR UNITS.
Winburg commando. *See* COMMANDOS.
Windmill camp, 395.
Wing, Major F. D. V., 181.
Winterberg mountains, 383.
Wire fences, 71, 155, 166, 167, 221, 256, 320, 442.
Witfontein Berg (mountain), 59.
Witmoss, 53.
Witteberg (mountain), 59.
Wittekop, 245.
Witteputs, 213, 216, 223, 386.
Witwaters Rand, 60.
Wodehouse district, 382.

Wolmaranstad commando. *See* COMMANDOS.
Wolseley, Field Marshal the Right Honourable G. J. Viscount, K.P., G.C.B., G.C.M.G., 7, 17, 39, 101, 197, 207.
Wolseley-Jenkins, Brig.-Gen. C. B. H., 158, 159.
Wolve Kop, 400.
Wolvekraal farm, 388.
Wood, Lieutenant C. C., 213.
Wood, General Sir H. Evelyn, V.C., G.C.B., G.C.M.G., 16, 17.
Wood, Major-General E., C.B., 386-388.
Woodcote farm, 160, 161, 167.
Wools Drift, 124.
Worcester district, 383.
Worcestershire regiment (2nd). *See* REGULAR UNITS.
Wyk, 75.

YEOMANRY, 12, 93, 379, 380. *See also* IMPERIAL YEOMANRY.
Yorkshire Light Infantry (2nd). *See* REGULAR UNITS.
Yorkshire regiment (1st). *See* REGULAR UNITS.
Yule, Major-Gen. J. H., 123, 131, 133, 137, 138, 142–156, 161, 172.

ZAMBESI, 48, 60.
Zandspruit, 49, 124.
Zarps. *See* SOUTH AFRICAN REPUBLIC POLICE.
Zibenghla (transport), 203.
Zoutpansberg commando. *See* COMMANDOS.
Zoutpansberg Range, 59.
Zoutpan's Drift, 387, 388.
Zululand, 36, 65, 94, 158, 274.
Zulus, 70.
Zuurbergen (mountain), 56.
Zwarte Bergen (mountain), 55.
Zyl, Lieutenant Van, 272.

www.ingramcontent.com/pod-product-compliance
Lightning Source LLC
Chambersburg PA
CBHW052009290426
44112CB00014B/2169